Roberto Rossellini

Roberto Rossellini

PETER BRUNETTE

UNIVERSITY OF CALIFORNIA PRESS
Berkeley   Los Angeles   London

Parts of chapters 6 through 11 have previously been published as "Rossellini and Cinematic Realism," in *Cinema Journal,* 25, no. 1 (Fall 1985). An earlier version of chapter 7 appeared as "Unity and Difference in *Paisan,*" in *Studies in the Literary Imagination,* 16, no. 2 (Fall 1983).

Acknowledgment is hereby made to The Museum of Modern Art/Film Stills Archive and to The British Film Institute/National Film Archive for the stills reproduced in this book. Acknowledgment is also made to the distributors of the films illustrated.

University of California Press
Berkeley and Los Angeles, California

University of California Press
London, England

Library of Congress Cataloging-in-Publication Data

Brunette, Peter.
    Roberto Rossellini / Peter Brunette.
       p.   cm.
    Originally published: New York: Oxford University Press, 1987.
    Includes bibliographical references and index.
    ISBN 0-520-20053-5
    1. Rossellini, Roberto, 1906-   —Criticism and interpretation.
I. Title.
PN1998.3.R67B78 1996   95-10239
791.43'023'092—dc20   CIP

Printed in the United States of America

1 2 3 4 5 6 7 8 9

The paper used in this publication meets the minimum requirements of American National Standard for Information Sciences—Permanence of Paper for Printed Library Materials, ANSI Z39.48-1984 ∞

To My Mother and Father

Preface

Roberto Rossellini is perhaps the greatest unknown director who ever lived. Andrew Sarris has stated flatly that Rossellini "must be accorded the top position in the Italian cinema."[1] Vincent Canby has claimed that "when the history of cinema's first hundred years is recollected in tranquillity—say in about 150 years—Rossellini's films will be seen as among the seminal works of what, for lack of any more definite term, can be called the New Movie."[2] But as Robin Wood has rightly pointed out, though Rossellini "belongs, with Eisenstein, Murnau, Welles, Godard, among the key figures of film history," curiously "with no other director is there such a discrepancy between the estimate of his achievement by a handful of experts and the apathy or scorn of non-specialist critics and the public at large."[3]

Certainly, the sheer variety of Rossellini's achievement is astounding. Such films as *Open City* and *Paisan* make him a central, founding figure of neorealism, the startling return to reality in postwar Italian filmmaking that has drastically influenced all subsequent cinema practice. In his imaginative, purposeful use of what might be called "antinarrative" devices such as dead time and dedramatization, he is also an obvious forerunner of Antonioni and other filmmakers who began to be noticed in the early sixties. Unfortunately for Rossellini, the intellectual world was unable to accept these techniques in 1950. Thus, while many have thought Antonioni demanding, he has always been considered "artistic"; Rossellini was simply thought to be amateurish and incapable of making a competent film. His grand television project—to provide information to a mass audience about its collective history—was a courageous feat that, if theoretically inconsistent, will never be equaled in scope and audacity. Despite these formidable accomplishments, however, Rossellini is primarily known to the average educated filmgoer over forty as the man who seduced Ingrid Bergman. To those under forty, he seems hardly to be known at all.

In most cases this lack of familiarity is simply a logistical matter, as, for example, in the United States, where the great bulk of Rossellini's work is still unavailable. His brilliant innovations in narrative technique have always challenged the viewer's attention and patience in ways that usually spell disaster at the box office; thus, few of his films since *Open City* have been successes in any country. And it must be said that he somehow rubs audiences the wrong way; even his greatest films contain intellectual, emotional, or technical rough (but exciting) edges that put us off at first. Other films, such as *The Miracle*, have so upset conventional religious views that they have been banned and picketed. The result is that many of his more or less minor films have never been shown in the United States, or have been unavailable since their original release. Even several of his major films—such truly great works as *Viva l'Italia!*, *India*, and *The Messiah*—have yet to be released in this country. This lack has not, however, prevented a great number of American critics from making vast generalizations about Rossellini's career based on the handful of films currently in circulation. It is for this reason that I have devoted much of this book to films that, for the moment at any rate, cannot be seen.

But the problem goes beyond one of mere availability. All his life Rossellini affected a complete indifference to the fate of his films, claiming, with only one or two exceptions, never to have seen them once they were finished. Some films, like most of the early shorts and *Giovanna d'Arco al rogo* (Joan of Arc at the Stake), made with Ingrid Bergman in 1954, have not been seen for decades. Another film, *Un pilota ritorna* (A Pilot Returns, 1942), recently surfaced in Italy after having been thought lost for thirty-five years. There is also the problem of sheer numbers: the television series *La lotta dell'uomo per la sua sopravvivenza* (Man's Struggle for Survival) runs for twelve hours, *Acts of the Apostles* for six, *L'età del ferro* (The Age of Iron) for five. Merely *seeing* Rossellini's films is an immense task, and there are one or two films that I, too, in the course of eight years of research, have been unable to locate; they are duly noted in the text. Still another problem is the familiar one of versions. Thus, for example, a great deal of negative criticism has been directed at Rossellini's first film with Bergman, *Stromboli* (1949), but most critics do not realize that the version seen in the United States has been disowned by Rossellini and that the Italian version is some twenty minutes longer and lacks the offensive voice-over at the end that has rightly bothered so many viewers.

Another gap in our knowledge of Rossellini arises from the unfortunate Anglo-American tendency to avoid Continental criticism, except when it is theoretical. Unsurprisingly, an enormous body of first-rate writing, in French and Italian especially, already exists on Rossellini. In attempting to take it into account, this book has also become a minisurvey of the history of European postwar film criticism, its ebb and flow, its violent attacks on Rossellini, as well as its equally intense espousal of him. He has provided a battleground for phenomenologists and Marxists (the former always approving, the latter generally opposed); others have stressed his modernist, Brechtian, formal side to the exclusion of his spiritual themes; and liberal Catholic critics have applauded Rossellini's religious subjects, conveniently forgetting that he considered himself an atheist. American critics in general need to understand better that the making of European film has histori-cally taken place within an intellectual, as well as a social, environment, within the terms of specific ideological debates. We forget that many European film-makers, for example, actually read and even write for what would be dismissed as esoteric academic film journals in the United States. I have tried to incorporate this grand debate, without letting it overwhelm my readings of the films them-selves, because the history of the reception of a work of art, of course, is always part of its meaning.

If I have sought to pay attention to film and intellectual history, however, my Marxist friends will surely feel that I have unduly neglected Italian political and social history itself, and that I am therefore committing the same kind of essen-tialist "error" I often describe in Rossellini. The problem is that, while I believe film is always deeply marked by the dominant ideology of the culture in which it is produced, this particular fact is true of all mainstream commercial cinema and thus does not need to be repeated in a specific discussion of Rossellini. On the other hand, what generally passes for historically oriented film criticism is the vulgar and reductive matching of specific historical events with contemporaneous films (for example, Rossellini made *Paisan* to flatter the newly arrived Ameri-cans), and this I want to avoid as well. As will be seen, however, the question of history itself, and the possibility of representing it, are very much at the heart of my book.

This study in no way purports to be a biography. I have included biographi-cal information where I thought it illuminated Rossellini's films or his thinking, but I have sought primarily to develop critical readings of the films themselves. I should say right away, however, that I have no desire to provide untainted, origi-nal, formalist readings that pretend to spring from an unmediated encounter be-tween text and critic. It just does not work like that, and along the way I try to show why. The readings I offer seek to explore Rossellini's films rather than pro-vide organic, unified interpretations of them. To my mind, traditional criticism all too often achieves consistency by repressing textual evidence that does not fit preformed interpretive paradigms. I want to open up these texts in order to hear their multiple voices, and thus I apply poststructuralist techniques when they seem to "work," when they seem to "illuminate" the specific characteristics of a film. I can provide no final justification for such terms, of course; it is simply where I must construct my imaginary ground, posit my assumptions, in order to proceed. I sometimes also use what has come to be known as deconstruction to approach Rossellini's inveterate humanism and his accompanying need to essen-tialize. What he wanted, finally, was a formless content, an essential image, and it is this ancient urge, as we shall see, that can be more easily understood from a deconstructive point of view.

A related problem concerns the status of the auteur. Critics increasingly have come to doubt the proposition that directors stand in the same relation to their films as novelists do to their novels. However, if *any* body of films can be said to be marked principally by the consciousness of their director, it is Rossellini's. But, given what semiotics has taught us about the "death of the author" in favor of a "birth of reading," should one be speaking about Roberto Rossellini at all? This is a difficult question, for a book "about" Rossellini inevitably seems to assume that he possessed a unified consciousness that worked in more or less consistent, linear, and clearly chartable ways through a nearly forty-year career. There is no room in this schema for the discontinuous work of the unconscious, nor for a theory of the subject as constituted by discourse.

The crux of the auteur problem is the thorny, probably unresolvable question of intentionality. Traditional notions of works of art as more or less transparent containers in which artists have enclosed their fully present, self-identical thought, their intentions, to be pulled out by audience or reader no longer seem workable. Nevertheless, I do depend heavily in this book on Rossellini's many interviews in several languages—this garrulous and articulate man, who loved to talk about his films and his ideas, surely holds the record for interviews given by a film director—because I think we need to consider his sophisticated ideas to better understand his films. At the same time, I try to avoid any special privileging of his stated intentions over the evidence of the films themselves. I also realize, however, that at some level intentionality (even if we impute it to the text itself) is what we all must surreptitiously employ to anchor textual meaning. "Freeing" oneself completely from this interpretive anchor would lead quickly to meaninglessness, to triviality.

Thus, centering one's discussion around the films made by a given director seems to me equally distorting and equally true. The solution is perhaps not to seek the *real* Rossellini, the *essence* of Rossellini—for in this way one always represses whatever does not fit—but rather to content oneself with an exploration of themes, techniques, and concerns. Strictly speaking, it is impossible to get around essentializing, and this book is no exception, but at least if the critic is self-aware in this matter, the worst excesses can be avoided. For example, many critics spend time establishing an "essence" of neorealism, usually by means of repressing all internal differences. Then a figure like Rossellini, who is often considered one of the founders of neorealism, is castigated for not being, in this film or that, truly neorealistic. In fact, the reader will hear little of neorealism itself in this book, for the label often obfuscates more than it clarifies. When Rossellini's films are considered on their own terms, rather than as part of a putative movement, what immediately results is a reevaluation of his so-called failures, which are usually quite interesting films.

I have also chosen to treat the films chronologically, on an individual basis, though I am aware of the pitfalls of this sort of organization. Nevertheless, the benefits seem to outweigh the disadvantages. In practical terms, such an organization allows a reader to find, in one place, a specific discussion of a single film (which is, after all, still the way we experience films). Second, theoretically speaking, any other organizing principle (for example, by theme or period) invariably seems to find overriding themes and techniques, once again, at the expense of the often disparate particulars of each film. My use of chronology, however, is in no way meant to imply a linear, historical, or forward-moving progression in Rossellini's career, and I have tried to avoid falling into a narrative that provides unity and meaning at any cost. In fact, Rossellini sometimes seems to take one step forward and two steps back, and I draw comfort from the knowledge that even a more traditional-minded critic would be hard pressed to find a unified development in these films.

Finally, I want to apologize in advance for what may seem to be significant shifts of tone and terminology at various points in the book. Since I have taken up very different questions, depending on the specific group of films under consideration, these shifts were to a large extent unavoidable. Thus, while the questions I raise in regard to the films made before *Open City* are primarily formal and historical (Out of what aesthetic context did *Open City* and *Paisan* come? What was the extent of Rossellini's allegiance to fascism?), in the great neorealist period I turn to theoretical questions and offer an extensive analysis of what we mean when we say that these films are more "realistic." Next, I try to show how Rossellini consciously or unconsciously subverted the prevailing neorealist aesthetics in what might be called the expressionist films that follow. In my consideration of the Bergman-era films, I concentrate again on describing just what is distinctive about these films in terms of theme and technique. Finally, in the section on Rossellini's grand didactic project, the history films made for television, I return to theoretical questions concerning the representation of history and Rossellini's claim to be objectively presenting the past.

In any case, critical reservations must now be put aside in order to consider the films themselves.

N.B.: Where a printed source is not given, all quoted dialogue is taken directly from the sound track. Except where an English translation is cited in the notes, all translations are my own. The English titles of Rossellini's films are generally used if they have been released in Great Britain or the United States; they appear in Italian if they have not.

Acknowledgments

One of the most rewarding things about writing on film is that the author must invariably depend upon others. This book, in particular, would not have gotten very far without the generosity of the Rossellini family, who assisted me in countless ways. First thanks must therefore go to Renzo, Ingrid, and especially Isabella Rossellini, the director's children, and to Marcella Rossellini Mariani, his sister. Both Rossellini's legendary charm and his intelligence live on in this talented family. Daniel Toscan du Plantier, formerly head of Gaumont and a close friend of the director in the last years of his life, was also helpful.

Innumerable archivists and librarians aided me in locating prints of films. Signor Alfredo Baldi and his staff at the Centro sperimentale di cinematografica in Rome, Charles Silver at the Museum of Modern Art in New York, and Patrick Sheehan and Barbara Humphries at the Library of Congress in Washington, D.C., cheerfully arranged screenings. Thanks also to Intercinematografica and Stemax in Rome for allowing me to see the long-lost film *Un pilota ritorna*. Michael Calder, here in Virginia, provided timely assistance with word processing.

Financial support for this project came at crucial moments in the form of travel grants from George Mason University's Office of International Programs and a National Endowment for the Humanities fellowship for 1981–82, which allowed me to begin a first draft of the manuscript. That task was immeasurably advanced by an associate fellowship awarded for the same period by the Center for Advanced Study in the Visual Arts of the National Gallery of Art in Washington, D.C. Henry Millon, its dean, and Shreve Simpson, its associate dean, along with their friendly and helpful staff, tirelessly fostered a fertile and humane environment for serious work. Daily conversations over lunch and at colloquia throughout the year with other fellows at the center—especially Donald Preziosi, Irene Bierman, and Barbara Stafford—provided a warm and intellectually challenging atmosphere for refining my ideas about important theoretical questions.

Thanks also are due to Dudley Andrew and to my colleagues Terry Comito and Cóilín Owens for reading and commenting upon individual chapters of the book, and especially to Robert Kolker, who read the entire manuscript and whose astute remarks proved essential in rethinking many complicated areas. This is perhaps also the place to acknowledge, with gratitude, the support and encouragement for this project and others given me over the years by J. Hillis Miller and Leo Braudy. To all many thanks.

As always, my most profound debt, in myriad ways I could not begin to specify here, is to Lynne Johnson, my wife.

Arlington, Va.   P.B.
September 1986

Contents

I. Before *Open City*

II. The War Trilogy and After

III. The Bergman Era

IV. *India* and the "Commercial" Period

V. The Grand Historical Project

Roberto Rossellini

I

Before *Open City*

1

Early Film Projects

Born on May 8, 1906, in Rome, the city that was to figure so importantly in his films, Roberto Rossellini was the first child of wealthy parents. Twenty months later, Roberto's birth was followed by that of his brother Renzo, who was to compose most of the music for Roberto's films and become a highly regarded composer in his own right. A year or so later came Marcella and then, apparently as an accident, Micaela twelve years after that.

According to Marcella, their childhood was "simply marvelous."[1] She readily admits that they were all thoroughly spoiled, the beautiful Roberto, as the oldest, perhaps even more than the others. The Rossellinis were among the first in Rome to own an automobile, and the various palazzi in which they lived always included enough room for a chauffeur, cook, butler, maid, and their mother's personal servant. Roberto ruled the game room, which their indulgent father had filled with an immense wooden battlefield complete with Italian and Turkish lead soldiers (this was the time, just prior to World War I, when Italy was contending with Turkey for control of Libya). Roberto, the aggressive, dominant figure, always claimed the Italian soldiers, while Renzo, frailer, more introspective, and—even by his own later account—unhealthily dependent on his brother, would be stuck with the Turks. Marcella willingly served as Roberto's "little slave."

There is no doubt that growing up rich had a great impact on the future director's life and films. Some reproached Rossellini later on, especially when it became fashionable to speak of his abandonment of neorealist principles, for not having had the proper background to understand the poor people who were the orthodox subjects of neorealist films. Others have suggested, with equal plausibility, that his privileged childhood and consequent disdain for money account for his lifelong battle with the compromises of commercial cinema. In any case, it is clear that Rossellini made few artistic decisions based on money.

From a young age enormously attracted to mechanical things, Roberto established a small workshop in the attic of their building, where he busied himself inventing things, readily receiving financial assistance from his father, who was clearly the most important influence on his childhood. A successful builder, like his father before him, he had been mortally infected by the germ of culture and for years harbored the dream of becoming a novelist. In his autobiography, Renzo Rossellini describes how his father would sometimes get up in the middle of the night to write, or try to write, until it was time to go to work in the morning. Years later, in fact, Renzo was still upset by his father's torment over writing and remained convinced that it contributed to his premature death at age forty-nine. His novel was published just before he died but, unfortunately, went unnoticed.[2] Roberto himself would later think of becoming a novelist, but more out of the desperation caused by his initial inability to raise funds for another film after *Open City* than in imitation of his father. It is clear that the cinema—that unique hybrid of the artistic and the mechanical—would be a more appropriate place for this lover of culture and the intellectual life who was no less enamored of science and technology.

But if Roberto's father could not fulfill his dream of becoming a writer, he "felt like a poet and lived like one" on Sunday afternoons, when all of his intellectual friends dropped in to discuss each other's work and debate the great aesthetic matters of the day. The children would be allowed to listen, and all of them remember it as the most exceptional schooling imaginable. According to Renzo, the men were much influenced by the Croceans in the group, whose aesthetic exalted the romantic notion of art as self-expression, an aesthetic that Rossellini, as an adult, would utterly reject. It is clear that this sort of learning by discussion, in bits and pieces over a wide range of topics, set the pattern for Rossellini's lifelong intellectual habits. Never having completed a unified educational program of any sort—again, perhaps, because his family's wealth made preparation for a career seem superfluous—Rossellini's immensely varied learning nevertheless astounded everyone he met throughout his life.

Roberto's halcyon childhood was marked by only one blemish. When the influenza epidemic stalked the world immediately after the end of World War I, everyone in the family contracted it. Roberto was afflicted most seriously and hovered between life and death for some months. Marcella recounts how her elegant, refined mother, overwhelmed by the apparently imminent death of her firstborn, made a vow that if he came out of it alive she would wear only black the rest of her life. When Roberto recovered, she kept the vow.

From his sickbed, Roberto was for perhaps the first time in his life dependent on Marcella, who would bring him anxiously awaited reports each week on the latest exploits of whatever movie serial hero was their current favorite. The children had become enamored of the movies because of a marvelously fortuitous circumstance: their father had built two of the most elaborate theaters in Rome, the Corso and the Barberini. This entitled them to free access, and Roberto quickly became the scourge of both managements because he would insist on bringing along twenty or thirty of his and Renzo's sailor-suited, spirited classmates from the Collegio Nazareno.

It is not clear how Rossellini became seriously interested in the cinema, at least beyond these paradisal teenage days of free viewing. In later years he was to confess to having been struck by Vidor's films *The Crowd* and *Hallelujah,* and the early version of *The Four Horsemen of the Apocalypse.* He told the Italian film critic Pio Baldelli and his students in 1969 that he went to the movies constantly as a youth and was especially impressed by the work of Griffith and Murnau. He also recounted a scene from *The Crowd* in which a character, nervous about meeting his bride's family, forgets to wipe a bit of soap from his earlobe after shaving: "These things struck me and perhaps put me on the road of truth, of reality, no?"[3]

It is clear that Rossellini never made a conscious, specific decision to become a director, but instead drifted into it the way rich, idle young men are apt to drift into things. His sister Marcella thinks it was because he was in love with the well-known actress Assia Noris. Already a notorious playboy, Rossellini hung around the studio and ended up doing sound effects and some editing, and writing parts of screenplays.[4] He began making short documentaries with his own money, perhaps simply to master a new territory. Next to nothing is known about most of these short films, unfortunately, since all but one have long since disappeared. Massimo Mida, who wrote the first full-length treatment of Rossellini's films in 1953, says that the director began experimenting with his new toy as early as 1934. By the mid-thirties he had produced two short films on nature subjects: *Daphne,* about which nothing seems to be known, and *Prélude à l'après-midi d'un faune.* The latter, Rossellini was to point out in later years, was *not* a filmed ballet, as the title might suggest. Rather, the film was inspired by his closeness to nature and by Debussy's music. According to Mida, it was never projected in Italy because the censors had decided that a few of the shots were indecent. Mida feels that even in these slight documentaries Rossellini was demonstrating his "revolutionary" new vision of life, simply by refusing to make the standard tourist landscape documentaries and instead turning directly to nature.[5] Rossellini told Mario Verdone in 1952 that, in one of these early shorts, he "was struck by the water with the serpent slithering about in it and the dragonfly overhead. It's the kind of sensitivity you see in the puppies on the main deck in *La nave bianca,* or the flower caught by the sailor as he disembarks."[6]

Refusing to be discouraged by the Fascist censorship of *Prélude,* Rossellini went ahead with plans to set up a complete studio in his family's summer villa outside Rome. It was here that he made his next short, *Fantasia sottomarina* (1939), which Mida calls his best, and which, in any case, is the only one still extant. The story, if one may call it that, concerns the vicissitudes of some fish and other underwater denizens that Rossellini staged in a large aquarium. He admitted to two Spanish interviewers in 1970 that the fish were sometimes moved by strings (Mida says by long hairs) "because we were filming in an aquarium and some fish died very quickly, so that for some scenes we had to manipulate them like puppets."[7] This apparently throwaway answer indicates, I think, that Rossellini, at least at this time, was not moved by any special sensitivity to nature, which presumably would have made him upset about the fish he was killing, but rather by a simple and absolutely implacable desire to understand how things worked. The film took a great deal of time and effort to put together, was sold to Esperia Films, and, given the modesty of its means, was quite successful.

If an absolute veracity is demanded, this little film will disappoint: since Rossellini's camera pans but is unable to dolly or move in depth, given the limitations of the tank, alert viewers will quickly become aware that they are not really on location in the briny deep. Immediately noticeable as well is Rossellini's heavy reliance on montage, given the later fame of his long take. Here he unreservedly uses crosscutting to provoke a sense of conflict and suspense—in this case between an octopus and the fish it is about to strike, and later, when some larger fish, in turn, attack the ink-squirting octopus. And he has somewhere learned about film's basic potential to deceive, for his cuts often suggest a particular action that we never quite see. Further on, the cutting becomes feverish when the wounded octopus is attacked by hundreds of smaller fish who sense its vulnerability.

The music, by Edoardo Micucci, is also tightly keyed to the editing to allow for the maximum in "thrills," an aim that Rossellini's later aesthetic will denounce. When the various creatures are introduced to us, the music is the sort of impressionist composition that convinces us of the idyllic, easy harmony of nature. Later, when open struggle has broken out, the music matches the frenzy of the editing and at one point even sounds like a kind of Morse code that warns away the smaller fish. The principal struggle between the octopus and what appears to be a moray eel serves, interestingly enough, more as a focusing device than as the real subject of the film. Though the reliance on close-ups is extensive, Rossellini generally takes pains to stress the overall ambience and the complex interrelations among the various species. Hence, the *coralità* so often stressed by his early admirers—Rossellini's choice of portraying the collective group rather than concentrating solely on the main figures—perhaps can be seen here in embryo.

One other aspect of Rossellini's later films in evidence here is an interest in lighting and shot composition for their own sake—an interest that, in spite of his continual denials, persists in a subdued fashion throughout his career. Rossellini's focus, of course, is on presenting the reality of these fish as best he can (even if it means, paradoxically, a bit of *trucage* here and there in his watery studio), but the creatures also clearly function as abstract elements of a formal composition.

At the end, the octopus escapes the fish, lobsters, and crabs that have been tearing at it, and the music reverts to the sweet melodies heard in the film's beginning. Strong light comes from the right, beautifully modeling the fish and perhaps suggesting the end of day, and then becomes a dramatic, but peaceful, backlighting. Near the end, several fish come together, and harmony is restored. The final shot, beautifully composed, is of two fish of the same species who slowly swim toward each other. One is above the other, and their heads point toward the center of the frame, perfectly perpendicular to the camera. The composition suggests an aesthetic stasis that symbolizes the reigning natural stasis; once this is achieved, we fade to "The End."

After the small, but encouraging, success of *Fantasia sottomarina,* Rossellini went on to make three other short nature films, *Il tacchino prepotente* (1939), *La vispa Teresa* (1939), and *Il ruscello di Ripasottile* (1941), none of which survive. (Two of their titles signal their subjects, an overbearing turkey and a babbling brook; *La vispa Teresa* means simply "The Lively Teresa.") What is perhaps finally most significant about this early period—at least as far as one can judge by *Fantasia sottomarina,* whose very title points to the fact that Rossellini's reality is always informed by the imagination—is the tentative emergence of a dialectic between the facts of the real and a personal interpretation of these facts. We shall have to address these concepts more closely later on, but it is clear that Rossellini understood from the first that neither could exist without the other. Mario Verdone has said of these films: "They don't go only in the direction of a simple photographic recording, but also allow for a personal and poetic creative interpretation. These are the same qualities which will emerge even more clearly in Rossellini's later films, where creation, lyricism, and personal interpretation almost always arise from the document, from the world that we know, from man, from the epoch itself."[8]

It was about halfway through this period of making documentary shorts that Rossellini got his first real opportunity in the world of cinema, when he was asked to collaborate on the screenplay of *Luciano Serra, pilota,* a film ostensibly directed by Goffredo Alessandrini and released in 1938. One of the most popular films of the entire decade, it shared the prestigious Mussolini Cup with Leni Riefenstahl's *Olympia* at the 1938 Venice film festival. It concerns the exploits of a young pilot, Luciano Serra, who, disillusioned at the end of World War I, abandons his family and goes off to South America for nearly fifteen years. There he becomes a kind of flying adventurer, but when Italy gets involved in the war with Ethiopia, he returns, at age forty, to help his country. His son, whom he has never known, has also become a pilot; the younger Serra is killed attempting to protect the train on which his father is traveling, unknown to him, from an Ethiopian attack. Sergio Amidei, Rossellini's great collaborator on *Open City,* whose relations with the director were later to be marked by some bitterness, has insisted in a discussion of Rossellini's "sins" that *"Luciano Serra, pilota* was a film produced by Vittorio Mussolini, supported by his father; it was a Fascist film."[9]

Actually, the situation was more complicated than Amidei would have us believe. It is true that Mussolini's son Vittorio, an avid flier, came up with the idea for the film, and it is also true that he and Rossellini were friends. But even most anti-Fascists who knew him felt that Vittorio was really a "good guy"—progressive-minded and actually rather embarrassed by his father. He had become greatly attracted during this period to the filmmaking industry, had worked as a producer and screenwriter behind the anagrammatic pseudonym Tito Silvio Mursino, and had been set up as editor of the avant-garde journal *Cinema.* This government-sponsored journal, published in Rome, was later to prove of enormous importance to the beginnings of neorealism. It was in the pages of *Cinema,* in fact, that the first calls for a return to the scenes and concerns of "real life" were heard, and within its editorial board that Visconti's revolutionary project *Ossessione* was born.

Luciano Serra, pilota did indeed have the Duce's support as well. Both Vittorio Mussolini and Ivo Perilli (a popular screenwriter and director who was to work on the script of Rossellini's *Europa '51*) have agreed in interviews that the treatment for the film was approved by the elder Mussolini after his son read it to him while he was shaving, and that it was the Duce, surprisingly, who came up with the rather simple, straightforward title that replaced other more rhetorical suggestions.[10] Rossellini is traditionally listed as coscreenwriter, but recent interviews with many of those involved present a rather more confusing picture, and the nature of Rossellini's participation in the making of this film is unclear. Alessandrini, as might be expected, tended to play down Rossellini's role, claiming that he put Rossellini to work on the script with Vittorio Mussolini because he felt sorry for him. On the other hand, he insisted that if the film had a political message, it came from the screenwriters and not from him.[11] Amidei maintained, on the contrary, that "Rossellini was making *Luciano Serra, pilota* with a sort of second team, grabbing the film from Alessandrini, who was in Africa; Rossellini, in Rome, was doing things his way."[12] Rossellini spoke vaguely of his part in the film, as he did of all his pre–*Open City* work: "You must remember what the cinema was in those days. Its ritual was complicated: if you didn't wear the tiara on your head, have the staff in your hand, the ring, the cross, then you didn't make films. . . . Film was a rite which was continually celebrated, and so you could watch the rite, but not enter it and do it yourself."[13] In the more detailed interview with Baldelli, however, he stated flatly and unconvincingly, "It's a film by Alessandrini, and I did absolutely nothing on it."[14]

One of the reasons for this indirection and faulty memory, of course, is the desire to disclaim any closer connection than he needs to with yet another Fascist-era film, especially one conceived by the Duce's son and titled by the Duce himself. Yet like Rossellini's other films of this period, as we shall see, this film is not openly propagandistic in favor of the regime. Fascist ideology in Italy was never as well formed as its counterpart in Nazi Germany; instead, leftists and rightists, priests and atheists, futurists who decried Italy's obsessive regard for its past and imperialists who dreamed of reestablishing that past on a scale that would rival ancient Rome all found something they could associate with in that mess of porridge known as fascism. Hence, Italian films seldom vaunted the Fascist party itself, or its hodgepodge "ideology," which was really little more than belligerent attitudes and rhetorical posturing. Instead, the accent was on nationalism, patriotism, loyalty, bravery, and, above all, efficiency, especially in terms of Italy's preparedness for war. Certainly, some of these films had an offensively martial air—but again, unlike Nazi films, the accent was on the excellence of the Italian fighting units and the durable values that motivated them, rather than on the denigration of enemies like the blacks conquered in Ethiopia. Edward Tannenbaum reports in his *Fascism in Italy* that even the Istituto LUCE, which had been established by the government precisely to make propaganda films, restrained itself in this area.[15] For instance, he gives this account of *Il cammino degli eroi* (The Heroes' Road), an hourlong view of the war with Ethiopia, which he considers the most effective documentary LUCE ever produced:

> At no point are Ethiopians ever shown, even in the few war scenes. The whole tone is that of a well-planned civilizing expedition. Technically, the film is excellent and, for this type of documentary, very convincing. There are happy, busy soldiers, to be sure, but the film is not sentimental or moralizing. The predominating images are of efficiency and modernity, rather than heroism.[16]

It could also be argued, however, that in many ways this sort of sanitized view of war and imperial conquest is even more harmful because it substitutes a fascination with technology and process for the human reality of pain and suffering, but at least the enemies' absence guarantees that they will not be portrayed as subhuman.

Clearly, this and other war "documentaries," and especially *Luciano Serra, pilota* and Rossellini's three fictional war films made prior to *Open City,* are important forerunners of neorealism, primarily for their accent on the sheer facticity of men and machines. As Adriano Aprà and Patrizia Pistagnesi say in an overview of Rossellini's pre–*Open City* films: "It is not surprising that he relied on the cinema of propaganda, in the 'soft' version (as compared with Nazi cinema) propounded by Luigi Freddi and realized through Vittorio Mussolini, since this is the most explicit manner in which the Fascist cinema dealt with contemporary life."[17] This is simply true: the only other possibilities for making films at this time would be the highly formalized "calligraphic" literary adaptations of Castellani and Soldati, historical costume dramas, melodramas, or the infamous "white telephone" pieces of fluff, those popular bedroom farces (named after one of their ubiquitous props) that crowded Italian screens. One clear purpose of all these films, like so much Italian popular culture during the Fascist era, was to cover over reality, to hide any unpleasantness, to propagate the simple message that under fascism everything was getting better. Stories about crime, for example, were much more heavily censored than critiques of the regime in the daily newspaper, all to protect the great lie. Thus, it could be argued that the war films—both documentary and fictional—provided at least some access to the "real" that filmmakers and writers were hungering for, and which is usually given as the reason behind the tremendous push toward realism that was to make postwar Italian film famous throughout the world.[18]

Nevertheless, it is also clear that these war films served the same function as the other genre films, finally, and did so even more convincingly because of the appearance and trappings of reality that they displayed. Thus, by concentrating on the efficiency and modernity of the troops, the message was being sent that in yet one more area of life the Duce had been good for Italy; at the same time, the absence of any actual fighting kept the audience anesthetized to its real costs. For one thing, this portrayal of the Italian armed forces was far from the truth. Italy's armies were woefully unprepared for war and were in fact overcome on all fronts only a short time after entering the conflict on Germany's side in June 1940. But even more important than this factual, technical lie is the message that war is simply a neutral, technological area—like clearing the Pontine marshes or making the trains run on time—a message that offered more fantasy, disguised this time in clean and pressed uniforms, shining guns, and impressive tanks. As Georges Sadoul has concluded in his *Le Cinéma pendant la guerre:* "The formula *real* locations, *real* details, *real* characters arrived at infinitely graver lies than the obvious mistakes of crazy sets in the studio."[19]

This much can be said of all these films, including Rossellini's trilogy. But perhaps the indictment should be even stronger in the case of *Luciano Serra, pilota,* especially if the film is read symbolically, beyond the specificity of its factual and object-laden "reality." Vittorio Mussolini himself considered it a parable of Italy's defiance of the League of Nations: "The film vividly symbolizes today's Italian, who was beaten and then won out over fifty-two nations."[20] Director Alessandrini has spoken of Luciano Serra as a product of the discontent that flourished after World War I, that feeling of being lost, of never finding again what one had experienced as a man at the front. But now, "Italy had found its road, right or wrong," and Luciano returns from exile to find his son in Ethiopia.[21] Tannenbaum neatly sums up the film's thematic implications:

> A good case can be made for the argument that *Luciano Serra, pilota* had a more specifically Fascist message than conventional patriotism. As one critic has put it: "The confusion, the perplexity of the character who is transformed from a negative to a positive being is really the confusion and perplexity of the country, which Fascism [allegedly] banished, salvaging all the national energies—including those that had deviated or gone astray—for a destiny of greatness achieved by a heroic act in which the objective and the subjective are reunited." It was all very well for the ideal Fascist hero to have a bronzed skin, a body of granite, a will of iron, but most Italians could not identify themselves with such an ideal. A much more insidious and effective technique of propaganda was to encourage them to identify themselves with an ordinary and even confused man who finally does the right thing. *Luciano Serra, pilota* was the best made and most popular film of this type.[22]

This film, therefore, while perhaps not blatantly pro-Fascist, was clearly inscribed in a certain Fascist discourse, marked by an "official," if unstated, view of Italian history and fascism's beneficial role in that history. Nevertheless, as we have seen, it is finally impossible to fix the extent of Rossellini's participation in the film. In order to determine just how politically compromised Rossellini's early career actually was, we will now have to turn to those films in which he played a more overtly active part: *La nave bianca* (The White Ship, 1941), *Un pilota ritorna* (A Pilot Returns, 1942), and *L'uomo dalla croce* (The Man of the Cross, 1943).

2

La Nave Bianca
(1941)

In early 1941 Rossellini was approached by Francesco De Robertis, head of the film section of the Italian Naval Ministry, to direct a film, under De Robertis' supervision, about the efficiency and modernity of the Italian navy. De Robertis had had an enormous impact on Italian film earlier that year with his innovative *Uomini sul fondo* (Men on the Bottom), a fictionalized documentary of the lives of men on a submarine. His aim had been to make a didactic film on the Italian navy's superiority in rescue work, and since the film was meant to give information, yet was cast in a fictional form, it was something of a novelty. Obviously, it made a great impression on Rossellini and would prove to be a significant influence on his work. Yet Mario Bava, who worked with Rossellini as cameraman on some of the earliest nature shorts, is clearly exaggerating when he says that "Commander De Robertis, who for me was a real genius, was the inventor of neo-realism, not Rossellini, who stole everything from him. De Robertis was a genius, a strange man, who felt sympathy for Rossellini and had him do *La nave bianca,* and then did everything over but allowed Rossellini to get credit for it."[1]

Polemic and score settling run high in the always politically charged arena of Italian cinema, and one despairs of ever attaining the truth. Certain matters are clear, however. For one thing, while *Uomini sul fondo* is usually praised, De Robertis was unable to repeat its success, and his later films like *Alfa Tau* and *Uomini sul cielo* (Men in the Sky) are distinctly inferior. Nevertheless, De Robertis must be given credit for the innovations of *Uomini sul fondo,* which, while hardly new to Italian film, he managed to put together in a fresh way. The film uses nonprofessional actors and real locations; furthermore, it is generally antispectacular and antiliterary, and even contains some narrative ellipses that allow the action to be conveyed with maximum efficiency. In addition, the film uses no voice-over and little dialogue, preferring to let the visuals carry most of the meaning. Soon enough, in fact, we realize that the real stars of the film are not the men but the gadgets and gauges we see in profusion before us.

Though it is often said that this film, as opposed to *La nave bianca,* is solely documentary, purely factual, De Robertis was not above using the conventional techniques of sentimental melodrama. So, for example, shots of the men working in the submarines are often intercut, especially after one of the submarines crashes, with shots of girlfriends waiting for their brave men. The return of one submarine is greeted with joyous shouts from the women, but another melodramatic shot singles out two young women, disappointed in their wait for the submarine that has crashed, as the gates are closed on them. At one point De Robertis even irises out on a cute little dog who also awaits the men's return and irises back in on a matched shot of a dog aboard the submarine. Later one of the two submarines thought lost returns, and the two waiting women—one smiling and the other frowning—are contrasted in an obvious, overstated shot. Even more insistent is the crosscutting that occurs near the end of the film, when all of Italy, through the radio, is involved in the rescue attempt. Cute children pop their heads into familial tableaux around the radio sets, and during one sequence the camera comes to rest on a sleeping baby, perhaps implying his or her unconscious involvement as well. By the end of this sequence, the listeners are shown only as shadows, presumably to heighten the sense of grim foreboding.

Most important is the fact that in spite of the hyperbolic editing that assails us throughout the film, *Uomini sul fondo* is finally rather uninteresting. The problem is that the shots themselves are often exasperatingly similar, and the final effect is an artificially induced, unconvincing excitement imposed on the editing table rather than arising from the images themselves. The exterior shots, which contain little visual tension and less movement, are especially dull (and sometimes even overexposed and out of focus, giving the impression of incompetence rather than newsreel veracity) and relate poorly to the rest of the film. Thus, if Rossellini did in fact borrow his style and approach directly from De Robertis (and this is debatable), he made great improvements in the process.

What De Robertis originally wanted from Rossellini on *La nave bianca,* as the title shows, was a short, reassuring film on the efficient and humane care received by wounded sailors on hospital ships before they were sent home. It is unclear why Rossellini was asked to do this, though perhaps De Robertis knew his short nature films or Vittorio Mussolini had put in a good word for him. Apparently, Rossellini had bigger ideas, however, as he related years later: "I began with the idea of making a ten-minute documentary on a hospital ship, but ended up doing something completely different. . . . The film that I tried to make was simply a didactic film on a naval battle. There was no heroism involved because the men were closed up in so many sardine cans and had absolutely no idea what was going on around them."[2] After completing the initial shooting, Rossellini returned with some 50,000 feet of exposed footage, and it was decided, not without some bitterness in various quarters, to pad the film out to feature length by adding a love story, which would also make it more appealing to a mass audience. (Both Rossellini and De Robertis have denounced this addition, but ironically, it is the love story, though seriously flawed, mawkish, and clearly supportive of Fascist values, that humanizes the film and makes it more appealing.) De Robertis has admitted, "I, not without having asked for forgiveness from my conscience, inflated the short film by cramming into the primitive linearity of the narrative an utterly banal love story between the sailor and the Red Cross girl." Nevertheless, he went on to hint darkly that Rossellini did not really deserve the credit for the film: "The authorship [of this film] conceals a question so delicate as to force on me the duty of leaving the clarification of the case to the correctness and professional loyalty of Signor Roberto Rossellini."[3] Rossellini told interviewers, "Half of the copy of *La nave Bianca* now in circulation isn't mine. . . . The whole of the naval battle is mine, but the sentimental part was done by De Robertis."[4] What is unclear, yet important, here is whether De Robertis merely wrote the sentimental part of the film or actually filmed it himself. In yet another interview given near the end of his life, Rossellini said, "I was supposed to do a ten-minute documentary on rescue operations in the navy. Once they saw what I had done, a whole operation began: they took the film out of my hands, redubbed it, recut it, changed it, and then took my name off. They then put it back when I became known, after the war. They even had others shoot some of the scenes."[5] The only conclusion to draw out of this welter of claims and counterclaims is that one is on very shaky grounds approaching this film from a purely auteurist point of view. We will probably never know exactly what Rossellini was responsible for, and what was contributed by De Robertis and others, still unnamed.

La nave bianca opens with bold titles that explicitly ratify the realist aesthetic of *Uomini sul fondo,* while at the same time going beyond it in certainty of purpose, if not clarity of rhetoric:

IN THIS NAVAL STORY, AS IN "UOMINI SUL FONDO," ALL THE CHARACTERS ARE TAKEN FROM REAL LIFE AND FROM TRUE LOCATIONS

AND ARE FOLLOWED THROUGH THE SPONTANEOUS REALISM OF THE EXPRESSIONS AND THE SIMPLE HUMANITY OF THOSE FEELINGS WHICH CONSTITUTE THE IDEOLOGICAL WORLD OF EACH OF US

PARTICIPANTS: THE NURSES OF THE VOLUNTARY CORPS, THE OFFICIALS, THE SUBOFFICIALS, THE TEAMS

THE STORY WAS FILMED ON THE HOSPITAL SHIP "ARNO" AND ON ONE OF OUR BATTLESHIPS.

From the very beginning the urge is to specify, to name, to assure that all this is *real*—in other words, not what one is used to seeing on the screen. The first shots are focused on the large guns of the battleship, appropriately enough in a film that, like *Uomini sul fondo,* will be obsessed with the weight and presence of objects. We see the guns from many different angles, all of them dramatic, and all of them reminiscent of the guns in *Battleship Potemkin;* in fact, Eisenstein, against whom Rossellini has usually been ranged by Bazinian realist theory, is clearly the predominant influence in this film. The effect of this beautifully composed initial sequence is cold and machinelike, but it also signals an interest in formal composition and mise-en-scène that is enhanced by superb

The influence of Eisenstein: *Potemkin*-like guns fire from the battleship in *La nave bianca* (1941).

lighting and rich blacks and whites. The shots seem spontaneous and carefully chosen at the same time. Rossellini, of course, claimed that he never strove to make a shot beautiful but only "true." (In 1947 he even went so far as to say, "I don't like and I have never liked 'beautiful shots.' If I mistakenly make a beautiful shot, I cut it."[6]) Happily, this false and naive dichotomy, considering the illusionistic basis of all realism, was seldom adhered to by Rossellini in his actual practice. In the first scene, when the individual sailors are presented to us in all their regional and idiosyncratic specificity, Rossellini organizes space by putting the men behind a table, a technique he will employ for the next thirty-five years. The effect of the tables here and elsewhere is to give spatial coherence and visual density to a specific scene. In the opening few minutes, we also see a very Eisenstein-like shot of sailors sleeping in their rhythmically sway-ing hammocks and an excellent group shot in which the closest men, in shadow, have their backs turned toward the camera, which thus ends up shooting through dark to light, giving a dramatic impression of depth. Other borrowings from Eisenstein's mise-en-scène are the sailors sweeping the deck in rhythmic unison, and perhaps the decision to intercut shots of the cat and dog playing, rather than bringing them into the frame with the men. In spite of such attention to the composition of the frame, however, this film's shots seem infinitely more spontaneous—and certainly more interesting—than the rigidly planned shots of *Uomini sul fondo,* whose director expressly avoided any form of improvisation.

Rossellini is obviously fascinated by the sheer presence and authenticity of the many gauges, pieces of equipment, and even doctor's instruments that his camera lingers over. We feel a sharp sense that no studio ever could have invented these things that we are seeing, that we have been transported back to the early days of the cinema, when the Lumières were astounding audiences simply by showing them the real. An excellent sequence occurs in the boiler room, in the bowels of the ship, where the restless camera finally slows down a bit and plays over the multitude of dials and knobs and buttons, and on the real sweat of these convincingly real ethnic faces. What comes to the fore is Rossellini's lifelong interest in capturing a specific time and place—think of all the titles that are so utterly localized in both dimensions, like *Europa '51, India '58,* and *Germany, Year Zero.* Here, Rossellini's formidable powers of observation are especially focused on place: the battleship becomes the star of the film, the center of the universe. The white ship of the title, in fact, is actually a misnomer, since it does not even appear until part 2, when the film has lost most of its energy and much of its interest.

In his later remarks Rossellini has, not surprisingly, stressed what might be called the humanistic themes he sees in the work. He told François Truffaut and Eric Rohmer in 1954 that the same moral position evident in *Open City* was already present in *La nave bianca:*

> Do you know what it's like on a battleship? It's horrible: the ship must be saved at all costs. There are these little guys there who don't know anything, guys recruited out in the country, trained to run machines they don't understand: they only know that a red light means to press a button and a green light means to push a lever. That's all. They're locked up this way, nailed into their sections . . . sometimes even the ventilation is cut off so that the gas from explosions won't spread through the ship. . . . They don't know anything; they just have to watch the red and green lights. From time to time a loudspeaker says something about the Fatherland and then everything falls back into silence.[7]

One cannot doubt Rossellini's sincerity here, but it must also be admitted that the film itself only partially supports his view of its theme. Rather, the overriding impression is not of the brutish oppression of these men—no matter what was intended—but of Rossellini's terrific fascination with the workings of things. One is in fact more likely to be struck by the appositeness of one of the Duce's slogans that happens to be caught by the camera eye: "Men and machines: a single heartbeat." What emerges in the film is the Hawksian thrill of men working together, supremely competent, in a dangerous collective enterprise; their frenzied activity ultimately becomes that of a machine, an effect heightened by the crisp precision of the editing and camera movement.

The *coralità* theme of Rossellini's early career also emerges in the men's collective activity. As he told Mario Verdone in 1952, *"La nave bianca* is an example of a 'choral' film: from the first scene, in which the sailors write to their pen pals, to the battle and the wounded who attend Mass or who sing and play music."[8] There are no stars in this film other than the ship itself, no individuals whose fate seems to be privileged. The needs of the collectivity are favored over the individual ego, yet the men are not reduced to heroic automatons, empty symbols for the masses, as they sometimes are in Soviet films, nor faceless cogs, as they are in *Uomini sul fondo*. Instead, Rossellini humanizes them with small details that give us a glimpse of their individual personalities, without, of course, actually making them fully rounded characters. For example, in perhaps the most powerful sequence of the film—the loading and firing of the big guns—we see how frightened the sailors are, though, characteristically, Rossellini understates. The greatest humanization of the film's material by far, however, is effected later through the much-maligned love story, in which one sailor's pen pal turns up as a nurse on the hospital ship. The lovers have earlier exchanged halves of a heart locket, and when she sees his half hanging from a chain around his neck, she recognizes the sailor but he does not recognize her. Duty, however, forbids her from favoring him over the others, or from even revealing her identity. Though mired in the mindless sentimentality that the rest of the film tries to transcend, the love story at least serves to make the men flesh and blood, and acts as a saving, if somewhat labored, counterpoint to the cold efficiency of the machines.

By the end of part 1, the sharp blacks and whites have been replaced by mist and smoke, as the ship, like the men, has been gravely wounded; disorder and human vulnerability have spread to the lifeless world of the machine. A peaceful calm reigns over all, as though, the battle over, some primal order has been reestablished, as at the end of *Fantasia sottomarina*. The overall rhythm of part 1—stasis, chaos, stasis (another nod to Eisenstein)—is marked and satisfying; the images themselves finally resolve into a complex, circular whole with the reappearance of the guns with which the film began.

It is true, as most critics have felt, that part 2 of the film is much less vibrant than part 1. Whereas in part 1 the love story lightened the material and humanized the characters, here its ubiquity is a serious drag on the film's innovative energy.[9] But it is also true that the slowness of the second part of the film is a function of the attempt to document life aboard the hospital ship this time, where the action will, naturally, be radically slowed down. The aim is to build carefully, to create a mood and a fuller sense of a specific reality through the accretion of small details, purposefully avoiding high drama and fast cutting. Here we can see the first inconsistent glimmerings of what will soon become Rossellini's celebrated—and, to many, alienating—techniques of dedramatization and an undirected narrative that allows for the inclusion of the aleatory and the irrelevant.

The ending of the film is cinematically interesting and thematically problematic. In the final scene Rossellini treats us to a complex montage taken directly from Eisenstein: the camera cuts quickly from one wounded sailor to another as they hear a passing ship (they are anxiously awaiting news of their mother ship), and the effect is repetitive and yet cumulative at the same time. In other words, the cuts are matched (each sailor is seen from the same angle and distance, making the same head-turning gesture), but since the action is slightly advanced with each shot, the result is to stress their camaraderie and *coralità* and to lengthen the moment artifically, in Eisenstein's manner, in order to underline the event and its attendant emotion.

Again, as in part 1, the newly returned ship occupies our attention: the men who can walk hobble out onto the deck to see the ship passing. They stand at attention, though with none of the Fascist salutes seen earlier in the film, and the general feeling is strongly patriotic. Basso, the closest the film has to a protagonist, watches with his Red Cross girlfriend through the porthole, and though she has yet to reveal her true identity, we sense that she will do so soon. At the very end, the love story is revealed for the vehicle it is, for the emphasis is clearly on the ship and the feeling the men have toward it, a relationship perhaps more emotionally complex, one senses, than they could ever have with a woman.

Critics have disagreed about the Fascist elements of the film. The ending is certainly patriotic, but it is difficult to put a more specifically "Fascist" interpretation on it (Mussolini's government was hardly the first to extol the virtue of duty to one's country and the comradeship of men at war). At one point during the middle of the film, we are shown a meeting room adorned with portraits of the king and Mussolini, but again, this seems to serve a documentary, rather than rhetorical, purpose. Some anti-Rossellini critics have even spoken of a nonexistent shot near the end that focuses approvingly on the Fascist insignia, but this is clearly a mistake, or worse.[10] On the other hand, critics like Massimo Mida, who has said that this film and *Un pilota ritorna* represent "the first break at the very heart of official Fascist cinema," are surely exaggerating.

More interesting are the charges brought by the Italian feminist Maria-Antonietta Macciocchi who, in her important study *Les Femmes et leurs maîtres,* refers in passing to *La nave bianca* as a "film-text of pure-mystical-repressive fascism, which confirms that mysticism favors sexual repression, and consumes sexual energy."[11] Actually, her critique here applies rather more forcefully to the films Rossellini made ten years later with Ingrid Bergman, as we shall see, which often do end in a kind of mystical haze not unrelated to sexuality. Macciocchi more closely describes the particular sexual dynamics of *La nave bianca* in her excellent little book on the role of women during the Fascist period entitled *La donna "nera."* Though I think she oversimplifies Rossellini's relation to technology in this film, and his reasons for not showing the enemy, she is right that the film manifests the quintessential Fascist view of woman as producer of heroes, or failing that, a nurse or a schoolteacher. (The woman in *La nave bianca* is a nurse and formerly was a schoolteacher.) Women are only meant to take care of men and, as Macciocchi points out, the *madrina* (godmother) of the film, as she is called, gives constant encouragement to her sailor boy and, in her last letter, writes: "In war, there is only one feeling: duty." Further, says Macciocchi, "The man-woman relationship is presented in a light that is purely protective and maternal." When the *madrina* helps the wounded sailor sign a letter, she has a flashback (the only one in the film) to the students' hands she held while teaching them to write. Since she never played favorites among her students, she cannot now give special treatment to one of the wounded, even if she is in love with him. "Here we find the equation man = son, and woman = mother = teacher, key to the Fascist ideology of the woman." It is particularly appropriate, Macciocchi believes, that the *madrina* does not reveal herself to the sailor even after he has seen her half of the heart locket, nor does she respond when he calls her name. At the very end they lean toward each other, but do not kiss: "Chaste love, purity, the abnegation of the woman for the wounded, exhortation to patriotism, all these clichés of Fascist ideology find their consecration in the film's ending."[12] Macciocchi's analysis is provocative, but it remains unclear whether the depiction she accurately describes is really Fascist or merely an extension of already prevailing attitudes toward women in Italian culture.

When the film first appeared, critics were sensitive to the fact that something a bit different, at least in its mode if not in its ideology, was going on here; in many cases, in fact, they seemed more aware of the film's possibilities than did its makers. Pietro Bianchi, for example, writing under the nom de plume Volpone, in *Bertoldo*, a leading intellectual journal of the time, complained, "It seems they were afraid of the masterpiece that was about to be born, far from the sentimental equivocations of the petty bourgeois mentality, and unfortunately, they stopped just in time." (He concludes, however, with the more typical Fascist notion that "recently, we have rarely been treated to such a high vision of military duty and of the manly confrontation of the combatants of the sea with dark destiny and unlovely death".)[13] More palatable is the view of Adolfo Franci, writing in October 1941, the first to speak of Rossellini's characteristic search for the "essence" of reality, rather than simply presenting what happened to be in front of his camera. This notion, as we shall see, will reappear in many different contexts through the ensuing forty years of Rossellini criticism. Here, Franci does not belabor the point, but merely mentions the battle scene in which the director "shows an extraordinary capacity for getting to the essence of such a description, which he conveys successfully with an urgent and precise rhythm, to a very beautiful cinematic effect."[14]

3

Un Pilota Ritorna
(1942)

Un pilota ritorna (A Pilot Returns) represents Rossellini's look at the second branch of the Italian armed forces, the air force; the army will provide the background for his next film, *L'uomo dalla croce*. Never mind inclined to discuss this film with interviewers, the director often grew quite testy with those who pursued the subject. Perhaps this is because the film was thought lost for nearly forty years, and since none of his interviewers had seen it, he may have thought that the less information he provided about another compromising film, the better. *Un pilota retorna* resurfaced, finally, in 1978.

One major reason Rossellini would not be proud of the film is that the subject came from Vittorio Mussolini (again under the anagrammatic pseudonym Tito Silvio Mursino), who acted as the film's supervisor, and who claims that he got Rossellini the job of directing. According to Mussolini, the film was quite baldly meant to "make known the heroism of our air force."[1] Massimo Girotti, who played the lead, later said that he considered it a patriotic film, though not propagandistic, even if the son of Mussolini was involved: "It was a dramatic film like any other, though with a heroic-patriotic background, of course."[2] The film's opening titles, however, are more direct. The first one states that "this film is dedicated with a fraternal heart to the pilots who did not return from the skies of Greece"; the second informs us that the film was made under the auspices of the "General Command of Fascist Italian Youth [Gioventù italiana del Littorio]." Like *La nave bianca*, in other words, it is not exactly propaganda, but it clearly propounds the official values of the regime. In one of his rare comments on the film, Rossellini told Francesco Savio in 1974 that he did not want to talk about it:

Men at war: Lieutenant Rossati (Massimo Girotti, left) and fellow pilot in *Un pilota ritorna* (1942). Courtesy of Intercinematografica.

Today it's becoming extremely disagreeable to talk about these things because it has become so much a way to proclaim yourself a victim of political pressure, which is also boring. I can say that certainly all the dialogue of *Un pilota ritorna* was changed. All of it.

Q: With regard to the original subject?

A: Yes.

Q: Which was by Vittorio Mussolini.

A: Well, it was just an idea. I always maintained complete freedom, and never started with little scraps of writing.[3]

At the beginning of this exchange, Rossellini hints at some form of political struggle over the film that he is too large-minded to excuse himself with. By the end, however, he seems merely to be referring to his lifelong practice of refusing to write out completed scripts before beginning production.[4] Though it is difficult to give credence to Rossellini's claim that all the dialogue has been changed, responsibility for the film remains uncertain.

The plot of *Un pilota ritorna* is slight and undistinguished, allowing the director to concentrate his attention elsewhere. (Interestingly, the young Antonioni also worked on the screenplay.) The action takes place in Italy and Greece in the early spring of 1941. The first part shows the Italian air force to great advantage, as it relentlessly attacks the Greek enemy. A young pilot arrives in camp and becomes part of a squadron of older, more experienced men, and we are shown scenes of camaraderie that do little to advance the narrative. During an air battle, the young pilot's plane is hit, and he and his comrades must parachute to save themselves. They are captured, and the rest of the film shows them as prisoners of war, first of the British and later of the Greeks. In one of the camps, an Italian officer, gravely wounded in the leg, is operated on by an Italian doctor who just happens to be there along with his seventeen-year-old daughter. The young pilot, as might be expected, falls in love with the daughter. During an aerial bombardment, he manages to steal a plane and fly back to his home camp in Italy; from the air he sees the various landscapes of his country in a highly lyrical passage and, though under fire from his compatriots, manages to land safely, just in time to hear the news of Greece's surrender.

One major difference between this film and *La nave bianca* is that, while the documentary element is still very much in evidence, the fictional human interest aspect is stronger as well and more closely integrated into the whole. The attempt at a psychological portrait, however tentative, is obviously the most important change here, and one suspects that the inclusion of a talented star (Massimo Girotti, who played the lead in Visconti's *Ossessione* the same year) had something to do with this. Yet in spite of the increased psychological realism, Rossellini shows his willingness to oppose conventional filmmaking practice by refusing, at least in the first part of the film, to focus unduly on Girotti. *Coralità* is more important to the director at this stage of his career and thus we see the pilot as part of a group; only when the love interest becomes dominant is he emphasized as an individual.

Thematically noteworthy are the scene in which the pilots scoff at accounts of "heroism" in the newspapers and the overwhelming images of forlorn refugees that dominate the last half of the film. Little glory is associated with combat, and Rossellini's later, more fully developed theme of war as destructive of all human relationships is more than hinted at here. The pilot at times seems pleased about the Italian advance and at other times displeased. The final shot of the film is a close-up of his face after he has safely landed; all around him his fellow aviators are celebrating his return, but his expression is more enigmatic, a combination of relief and unease about the girl he left behind. In spite of its glorification of military life, in other words, the film also raises doubts about Fascist rhetoric. Furthermore, the pilot's captors are generally seen to be civilized and decent, ready to break the rules of the camp for a humanitarian reason. (With the sole exception of the Germans in *Open City* and *Paisan,* Rossellini will continue throughout his career to insist upon the humanity of the enemy.) Yet, later in the film, the British leaders seem completely undismayed about the prospect of making "a desert in front of the enemy." This, by the way, is said in English (and the Greeks speak Greek, sometimes at length), thus initiating an ongoing, rigorous allegiance to authenticity of language that will baffle many an Italian audience and even be complexly thematized in *Paisan.*

Un pilota ritorna is perhaps most interesting in terms of technique, which tends to mitigate its conventional melodramatic elements (such as the leg amputation scene with cognac as the only anesthetic). The controlled studio lighting makes it seem much more polished than Rossellini's later films, but the director seems to be striving for visual unconventionality as well. The editing, for example, looks forward to later experiments, for much of it is elliptical to the point of incomprehensibility. Similarly, a remarkable shot early in the film shows the pilots emerging from a theater; for an exceptionally long time all we see is a small bit of light through the curtain leading to the auditorium. A lengthy bit of dialogue goes on in almost complete darkness, and then finally several characters light cigarettes, illuminating themselves in the process. Even more daring is the 360-degree pan around the interior of the farm building in which the pilot, the girl, and the wounded prisoners have taken refuge. The pan begins with the girl reading aloud to solace the prisoner whose leg has been amputated, but by the time the pan comes back to her, we understand it as a kind of dissolve, and she is asleep. A world-weary sense of the destructiveness of war is the result.

Equally innovative, and characteristically Rossellinian, is the relative lack of interest in a strong narrative thrust. Thus, when the pilots take off on a bombing raid, a remarkably long time is devoted to the minutiae of their occupation and environment (altimeters, oxygen masks, and so on) before the battle begins. Later, they ride bicycles around the camp for no apparent narrative purpose; clearly, Rossellini is intent on giving us a picture of the pilots' everyday lives that refuses to be subsumed into the merely dramatic. Furthermore, emotion is drastically understated, as when a crew member indicates to the protagonist, by the slightest nod of his head, that the pilot of the airplane has been killed. The real drama, we come to understand early on, concerns the overall war effort, the large movements of armies, rather than the plight of specific individuals.

By far the most important, and most symptomatic, contemporary review of the film was written by Giuseppe De Santis for *Cinema* when the film first appeared in April 1942. Despite De Santis' obvious desire for something new, something "real," his model is still the illusionistic, dramatic, and psychologizing Hollywood style of filmmaking that, above all, follows a conventional narrative pattern. At the close of his review, he complains:

> Each sequence of *Pilota* overlaps the next, neither one of them properly expressed because neither is concluded. What is the meaning of the pilots' visit, at the beginning of the film, to the girls of the city, if in the story the courage isn't there to get into its motives? What is the poetic necessity of that descriptive pan of the prisoners' shelter, when the girl reads something aloud after the operation? . . . What environmental coloring did Rossellini want to add when he has the aviators ride around the camp on bicycles during a break? If he meant to show us a documentary episode on military life, the episode itself should have told us something we didn't already know, in a narrative and psychological progression.[5]

Evident here is the demand for authenticity, the longing for the real thing—but a reality artfully arranged in a coherent, conventional narrative form—that was beginning to stir in Italian cinematic culture. Naturally, it was never asked whether this narrative form itself was "true" and "real." For De Santis, each scene must have a meaning or point, an express purpose that furthers the plot line or the psychological portrait of the characters. No latitude is allowed for the aleatory or the "irrelevant," elements whose significance might transcend that of conventional narrative. To ask what is the "poetic necessity" behind this shot or that shot is to assume that every shot must contribute to an overall organic project, where every element works not for itself, but is subsumed into the whole.

But Rossellini was already thinking of alternatives to this model. Less than a year later, in fact, after having been forced to abandon his next project, Rossellini was discouraged about his prospects as a filmmaker and went to see the novelist R. M. DeAngelis. Out of work, he confessed to DeAngelis that, even though he did not know much about narrative technique, he wanted to become a novelist because he despaired of ever finding the wherewithal to make another film. But Rossellini was not satisfied with DeAngelis' definition of the novel and its possibilities, and realized that for him it would have to be the cinema or nothing. His reply to DeAngelis is important for understanding what he was trying to do at this early stage of his career:

> I need a depth of field which perhaps only the cinema can give, and to see people and things from every side, and to be able to use the "cut" and the ellipsis, the dissolve and the interior monologue. Not, of course, that of Joyce, but rather that of Dos Passos. To take and to leave, inserting that which is around the fact or event and which is perhaps its remote origin. I can adapt the camera to my talents and the character will be pursued and haunted by it: contemporary anxiety derives precisely from this inability to escape the implacable eye of the lens.[6]

For the next forty years, in fact, Rossellini was to be faulted for not meeting the demands of a conventional narrative form whose own validity and "naturalness" would seldom be questioned. Though they overstate their case, especially for these early films, Aprà and Pistagnesi are right to insist:

> What is so striking in the first three films, beyond their quality, which is actually quite modest, is that Rossellini has left behind the "strong" models of the classic cinema, that is, the propaganda films and the two examples of *Luciano Serra, pilota* and *Uomini sul fondo. . . .* In respect to these two models he makes a work of deconstruction, of *disassembly,* taking out of them the elements which make them "classic" films. For example, [Rossellini's] films, even though they tend toward narrative, are told "badly," with ellipses which often make the events obscure, or better, "incomplete." . . . Rossellini will often be accused of not knowing how to tell a story, but what is not noticed is that Rossellini *wants* to tell the story badly, because he is not interested in the plots but in the pauses, the moments of rest, the waiting, or certain contrasts between characters or between characters and the background, which manifest themselves only on the screen, not in the plot.[7]

This point of view is one I most emphatically share concerning the later films, including perhaps *Paisan,* but especially those made during the Ingrid Bergman era. For one thing, this penchant for narrating "badly" helps us to under-stand why Rossellini's films have always fared so poorly at the box office. The antinarrative elements of films like *Un pilota ritorna,* however, are only barely in evidence; Rossellini himself can hardly be said to be fully aware of them, or actively seeking to alter conventional techniques of cinematic narration. But they are there, seeds barely sprouted, of a new way of making films.

4

L'Uomo dalla Croce
(1943)

Rossellini's next film, *L'uomo dalla croce* (The Man of the Cross, 1943), completes his trilogy on the armed forces. The integrity of this film has not been tarnished, for once, by an association with Vittorio Mussolini; unfortunately, however, his place as screenwriter has been taken by the Fascist ideologue Asvero Gravelli, a journalist well known for his nightly radio commentaries supporting the government and for his work as editorial chief of *Fascist Youth* and *Antieuropa*. It is also true that this film is even more overtly ideological than the two earlier films of the trilogy, but again, its ideology is more complicated than some have made it out to be. Not coincidentally, it is also more heavily weighted toward the fictional and away from the documentary, and actually is the most melodramatic of all the pre–*Open City* films.

The man of the cross referred to in the title was based on a real army chaplain, Father Reginaldo Giuliani, who had been recently killed on the Russian front. In this, the film resembles *Open City*, whose main character was also to be based on a real-life priest. The plot, which centers around a small Russian village, is surprisingly simple. In the beginning Rossellini presents his Italian soldiers with all the "reality" he can muster as they wait for their friends to return from a tank attack. When they do return, one of the men is found to be so seriously wounded that he cannot be moved; the chaplain, who is also a doctor, resolves to stay with the man even though the Russian troops are advancing. (The chaplain, despite the heavily "acted," rhetorical nature of his role, is played by a nonprofessional who was an architect friend of Rossellini's.) The next day the village is captured by the Communist forces, the priest is interrogated, and a young Italian soldier is executed because a Fascist party membership card has been found on his person. The Italians counterattack, and the village finds itself caught between the opposing armies. During the course of the night, a motley assortment of Italian soldiers, Russian peasants, children and dogs, committed Communist commissars, and the priest ends up seeking shelter in the same small farm building, or *izba*. The priest teaches the children to make the sign of the cross, delivers and baptizes a baby, and brings the word of God to a young Communist woman whose lover, Sergei the commisar, is killed during the night by another Russian. The next morning the priest himself is mortally wounded while attempting to save the life of the man who killed Sergei, having first taught this man to say the Our Father. Just as the chaplain dies, the Italian forces recapture the village.

Like the two previous films, *L'uomo dalla croce* is divided between a real documentary interest in the daily activities of the Italian soldier and a thoroughly conventional melodramatic intensification of danger, suffering, and psychological drama. Even the hoary stage device of having all sorts of different characters seek refuge in the same location was, at least in American films, a cliché by 1943. The music, by Renzo Rossellini, is equally melodramatic and is in fact strikingly similar to that of *Open City*, Rossellini's next completed film. In spite of all this, however, as a war picture, *L'uomo dalla croce* is impressive. It was singled out by critics at the time for its realistic battle scenes, which of course are altogether different from the documentary realism of the soldiers' everyday lives, the subject perhaps most interesting to Rossellini. The battle scenes are "realistic" mostly because they are what an audience raised on American films would expect and demand, but this is not the same kind of reality Rossellini is after when he lovingly and lengthily concentrates on the details of the tanks in close-ups, or later, on the horrifying, but visually magnificent, flamethrowers to which we are treated to relieve the boredom of the plodding tanks. This distinction between realism and reality is in fact a crucial one, and will be examined in greater detail in a later chapter.

The same kind of critical misunderstanding that we saw earlier in regard to *Un pilota ritorna* reappears, and again it centers on a review by Giuseppe De Santis in *Cinema*. De Santis speaks glowingly of the battle scenes, whose "authenticity is worthy of the best shots of LUCE [the government agency responsible for informational films]," but he complains that the rest of the drama is conducted slowly and "inflated with empty places and unfillable pauses." He is right, of course, to critique the film's clichéd content and most of the dramatic scenes in the *izba* for their employment of "terminology already used by cheap novels." But he is less sensitive to Rossellini's hesitant steps to go beyond what might be considered clichéd narrative form. De Santis' key word, which stands in for "conventional narrative and dramatic form," is *rhythm*. Thus, Rossellini's attempt to reflect the minor events of a given reality is regarded as an error because it is not rhythmic, that is, it does not contribute to the onward rush of the narrative. Hence, De Santis is in favor of the "drama of waiting" not for the sake of the waiting itself, and the creative *temps mort* that Rossellini is just beginning to explore in these films, but for the suspense of the drama, the end point, the product rather than the process: will our comrades return or not? He is clearly bothered by Rossellini's dilatoriness ("The camera carries out its movements lingering slowly, describing: a bird perched on the branches of a tree, a shirtless soldier stretched on the ground, others who tell each other their life stories, remembering their studies or their homes") because nothing seems to be happening. He also finds the little scenes with the peasants, which do not clearly advance the narrative, banal and extraneous because they offer "psychological reactions which don't fit with the drama of waiting."[1]

A more modern and more appreciative view of Rossellini's particular gifts (which benefits, of course, from a hindsight unavailable to De Santis in 1943) is offered instead by Gianni Rondolino. He feels that, in spite of the banality of the story, "once again, Rossellini reveals himself in the little things, not in the cut of the narrative or in the psychological penetration of the characters or in spectacular high points, but in the moments of quiet, of waiting, of simple observation of men's behavior in a given situation."[2]

Similarly, Pio Baldelli, one of the director's harshest but most intelligent critics, points out that, in spite of all its faults,

> within this opaque material twists a nonrhetorical vein which is a prelude to Rossellini's expressive growth. An antiheroic, antimonumental manner of cutting across certain facts emerges (the reverse of a bourgeois populism), which is uninvolved in military glory and pomp: in other words, the inclination of the camera for the little guy, for the fate of the humble, the victims, the wounded and dead of war. It's the documentary immediacy, when the frame gathers up real objects, discovering the men amid the factual reality; here the long take discovers the surroundings, without emphasis.[3]

Despite the above, however, it must not be forgotten that what might be called the antinarrative elements of *L'uomo dalla croce* remain thoroughly dominated by the conventional story, filled as it is with clichés of the action genre: the wounded man who cannot be moved, faced with the advance of the enemy; the selfless hero who decides to stay with him; the children and dogs who are nearly killed when they wander out of the *izba;* the pregnant woman who gives birth just *then,* in the middle of the night, stuck between rival armies; the grieving woman who draws renewed hope from the birth of another's child; the wounded soldier who asks to be propped up to look at the stars; the hero who gives up his life, ironically, at the very moment of his countrymen's victory. And so on.[4]

In terms of its visual style, the film is somewhat more complex than its predecessors. In general the camera is fluidly mobile, and, appropriately perhaps for a war movie, its intense activity matches the film's frenetic editing. Nor does Rossellini avoid the self-conscious, artfully composed shot now and then, though such shots are much less evident than in *La nave bianca.*[5] Under the prodding of a student interviewer, Rossellini much later spoke cryptically of the "rhetoric of the long take" of this film,[6] but his memory of past practice seems to have been colored by what he was doing at the time of the interview. *L'uomo dalla croce* does contain some relatively long takes—especially, of course, in the "documentary" sequences of the passing tanks and the flamethrowers—but not more than in any American action film of the time, and they are a great

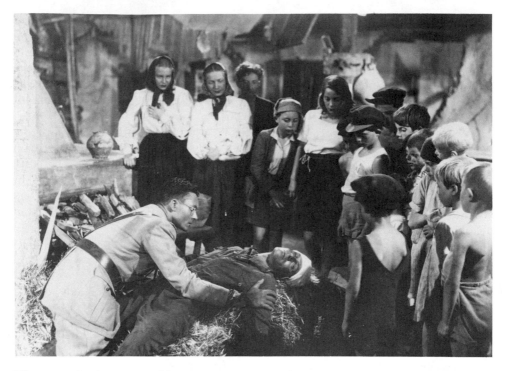

The group, in the protected inner space: the man of the cross (Alberto Tavazzi) ministers to the wounded in *L'uomo dalla croce* (1943).

deal shorter than those of Rossellini's later films (for example, the eleven-minute shot in *Blaise Pascal*).

The film's visual images also have a clear, if subtle, thematic resonance. For example, the men in the opening sequences are striking in their very ordinariness and their evident, if unspoken, sense of helplessness. They are all so incredibly small and unimpressive—some without shirts, some in shorts—a far cry from both the Nazi superman and the Fascist bringer of civilization to the expanding Italian empire. Rather, they seem frail and worried, and no Sergeant John Wayne arrives to buck up their spirits and make men of them. In fact, the priest's heroism in this film is clearly not meant to inspire the others to feats of courage; it is, finally, a lonely act, simply an accomplishment of what he sees as his duty. Despite the priest's solitary act of courage, the thematic center of the film seems to reside in the collective, communal spirit of *coralità*. Hence the importance of the idea of return in all these early efforts: the wounded sailors of *La nave bianca* anxiously await the return of their battleship from its dangerous mission; the pilot's struggle in the next film is aimed at the fulfillment of its title, his return to Italy; and finally, in *L'uomo dalla croce,* whose entire first part is devoted to the common soldiers' longing for the return of the tanks, and thus their friends, to the group. Though the film's intense cutting, as in *La nave bianca,* forces us to see the men as separate individuals, each one caught in his own frame, the men are anonymous, and thus blend more easily; the additive or cumulative nature of montage also results ultimately in a collective effect. Additionally, in at least one sequence the cutting from soldier to soldier is the same as the Eisensteinian progressive sequence we saw at the end of *La nave bianca*. Because each soldier the film cuts to is matched with all the other shots in this sequence, the effect is paradoxically one of togetherness arising from separateness, collective identity transcending individual identity. Totally absent is the Hollywood technique of humanizing war movies by following the course of a battle in the specific terms of a small group we have come to know, in order to allow for the maximum psychologization of the characters. In *L'uomo dalla croce*, when we do follow troop movements or witness battle scenes, we see men acting together, unheroically and anonymously.

Coralità is even more evident during the agonizing night spent in the *izba*. There, a Renoirean theme of the artificiality of national boundaries develops, and in this coveted inner space of protective warmth, in spite of occasional conflicts, a structural opposition to the war outside is established. Thus, at one point, a baby wanders out into the night and immediately machine guns begin to chatter; the line between the outside and the inside is exceedingly thin and in fact will break, if not then, the morning after. The inner space is also sacred for Rossellini because it is here that one's personal salvation must be worked out—in the context of the group, certainly, for it is there that we realize our common humanity and find the aid and comfort that we seek, but in the final account, one is alone, face-to-face with God. This theme is embodied most directly in the encounter between the chaplain and the disillusioned Communist woman he comforts. She is utterly bereft in the wake of her lover's death, and the priest tells her that she cannot be reborn because she has no hope. God is waiting to save us all, and instead of thinking about the dead Sergei, she should think of Jesus Christ, who gave his life so that everyone, including she and Sergei, might live. The priest finally asks the woman to consider the baby who has been born during the same night her lover was killed (and whose crying we hear on the sound track). As the woman thinks of this new life, a smile comes over her face, and, having become hopeful once again, she presumably is saved.

The point here is heavy-handed, to be sure, and even rather embarrassing to a secular audience, but it is significant in terms of Rossellini's later development. Most critics, who have begun to study Rossellini's career with *Open City*, rarely considering the earlier trilogy, have lavishly praised the dominant "choral" elements of that film and *Paisan*, films in which the individual's search for salvation is lost amid the epic sweep of history at its most eventful. Then, with *Germany, Year Zero, The Miracle*, and especially the Bergman-era films, Rossellini was accused of betraying neorealism and *coralità* in favor of the petty concerns of the individual. The truth, seen clearly in *L'uomo dalla croce*, is that for Rossellini there has always been something more important than politics and mere physical survival, and that without the spiritual, a human being is nothing. Furthermore, this spiritual salvation cannot be reached by the group, for it is achievable only in the private realm of the self. Thus, the character who outraged so many critics in 1950—Karin, the seeker of God and spiritual awakening in *Stromboli*—finds her precursor in the lonely and desperate Russian woman of *L'uomo dalla croce*. For Rossellini, both women are lost souls because they have been following either the false god of communism or the materialist, confused ethos of the postwar world that has made Karin so cynical and manipulative. Both turn to a priest for aid, and the Communist woman, obviously a less sophisticated artistic creation, is easily solaced (after all, Rossellini still has an action war story to tell—even if "badly"), while Karin cynically tries to manipulate her priest, even sexually, for she has not yet understood what she is looking for. Both obtain their salvation by first achieving hope through the intermediary of a baby (the sexist nature of this male vision of what fulfills a woman is clear)—the Russian when she contemplates the newborn of another, and Karin when she finally realizes the meaning of the new life within her. As Rossellini told Eric Rohmer and François Truffaut in 1954, *L'uomo dalla croce* "poses the same problem [as *La nave bianca*]: men with hope, men without hope. It's pretty naive, but that was the problem."[7]

Cast in these terms, of course, Rossellini's project can seem utterly innocent. Yet an enormous charge of ideology is apparent in the film as well, for while the priest's message appears to be solely religious and spiritual, in no way promoting fascism, this message occurs in the context of a rabid anticommunism. There is simply no way around it: in this film, Rossellini treats communism in exactly the same terms he will treat nazism in *Open City,* and in both cases, his more usual insistence on fairness disappears. Since, despite his characteristic emphasis on facticity, what really interests him as much as anything else in his films is the clash of ideas, communism, like the nazism of *Open City* and *Germany, Year Zero,* is presented as a bad *idea*—poisonous, viciously destructive of human values and human freedom. Thus, when the young woman finally gives in to the priest's religious blandishments and tells him the story of her life, we learn that communism has taught her that her mother, the timid, impressionable daughter of a businessman, was unable to bear the enormous physical hardship of the postrevolutionary period because, as a member of the middle class, she was too weak. The priest, however, insists that her mother was not weak, but humble, and had the strength of the truth. The philosophy not very covertly attributed to communism here—that the weak must give way to the strong—is the same warped worldview under whose baleful influence the young Edmund of *Germany, Year Zero* will poison his sick, "useless" father. Against both of these options Rossellini poses the promise of Christianity, which for him is simply a better idea, the greatest idea humanity has ever found, and the only one through which freedom can be realized.[8] What is interesting in all this is that Rossellini himself was a lifelong nonbeliever, a partisan of no church; he seems rather to have been taken with the Christian idea, apart from its actual institutional manifestations. For Rossellini, being Christian is simply the best way to be human; this is its true value, far beyond the narrowly sectarian. Hence, for much of the time in the *izba,* the priest is seen without his uniform, ostensibly to disguise him from rabid Communist anticlerics, but also perhaps making the point that one's humanity is prior to both one's country and one's specific religious affiliation.

The problem comes in relating a third term, fascism, to this duality of communism and Christianity. Probably the most important scene in this regard is the interrogation of the chaplain and some other Italian soldiers after the Russians have regained the village. The interrogator, an Italian, is portrayed as a vicious turncoat, similar in morality and physical unpleasantness to the spoiled priest informer of *Era notte a Roma* (1961). The Communist cynically accuses the priest of necromancy because he wears the image of a dead man around his neck. The point here seems to be that the fault of communism is its overliteralization, its abusively restrictive dependence on reason and matter at the expense of the spiritual and the symbolic. (Interestingly, Rossellini's filmmaking trajectory can be described, *grosso modo,* as moving in the opposite direction, from a preoccupation with the spiritual toward the rational.) The interrogator mocks the priest's refusal to give information concerning the Italian troops and his appeal to international law, which Rossellini has the corrupt Communist scoff at. In another display of perverted reasoning, the Communist accuses the priest of propagandizing—not permitted, according to him, by international law—and threatens to shoot him. When the priest replies that he does not propagandize, but, as a man of the cloth, speaks the truth, his interrogator spits back that in war the only truth lies with the strongest.

The Communist then begins harassing a young Italian soldier on whom a Fascist party membership card has been found. He is told that because he is a Fascist, he is not considered a regular soldier, but a subversive or spy, and that "we can exterminate you as an enemy of the *idea of communism* unless you renounce your beliefs by signing this paper" [my emphasis]. The soldier, obviously a nonprofessional actor, says in an unpolished, absolutely convincing fashion, "I won't sign anything," and to the accompaniment of a quick crescendo in the musical score, is taken out and shot. The priest makes the sign of the cross. (Significantly the same situation, in mirror image, of course, will occur at the end of *Open City*—the priest refusing to answer questions, being offered by the decadent Nazi Bergmann, and witnessing the death by torture of the partisan Manfredi, who also dies for his beliefs, this time Communist ones. Here, as well, the priest makes the sign of the cross, and both films end with the heroic death of their priest protagonists.) Yet in spite of the image of the noble Fascist youth dying for his beliefs, this episode seems aimed more at demonstrating the inhumanity and intolerance of communism than the legitimacy of fascism. The boy is being lauded more for his adherence to principle than for any loyalty to the Duce.

A further complication, however, arises at the end of the film. As the priest is dying, after having taught the wounded Communist soldier the Lord's Prayer just prior to *his* death, we can hear the shouts of the victorious Italian troops growing in strength. The camera indulges in long pans on the troops and their horses, trying somehow to put the priest's impending death in a larger context—perhaps of ideology, perhaps simply attempting to locate it in a specific nonnarrative reality. As the priest dies, the camera pans down from his face to the cross he is wearing, neatly recalling the identity of the two parts of the title's equation (and the final shot of *La nave bianca* as well). But then a final intertitle is flashed on the screen, just before "The End": "This film is dedicated to the memory of the military chaplains who fell in the crusade against the 'godless ones' in defense of the fatherland and to bring the light of truth and justice also to the land of the barbaric enemy."

It is difficult to know exactly how to take this, but linking barbarism and "the godless ones," on one side, and the fatherland, truth, and justice, on the other, is hardly neutral or benign. Clearly, the inclusion of this title at the very end is an attempt to bring into line and master any lingering political ambiguities the film has raised. In this context Mino Argentieri has usefully linked the conjunction of religion and politics in this film with the same operation in *L'assedio dell'Alcazar* (The Siege of the Alcazar, directed by Augusto Genina), an openly pro-Fascist work favoring Franco's side in the Spanish Civil War:

> The prevalence of the Catholic accent . . . if it attested to a collusion which was simply in the nature of things, served also to spread with greater ease sermons which were useful to the Fascist cause. In the conquest of a vast consensus which would defeat every prejudice concerning fascism, [these two films], diluting the explicit references to Fascist political practice and ideology, were useful for a second-level recuperation which was quite successful since it was directed at social strata and feelings which were not instantly at home with the regime.
>
> Films like these operated a mediation and their perniciousness was contained in the wish to mobilize also those who were not convinced Fascists in Fascism's crusades.[9]

Yet, as Argentieri has also insisted, "It is necessary to make distinctions. In *L'uomo dalla croce* [unlike *L'assedio*], Rossellini did not put on the frock of the propagandist who disguises the sermon to subjugate the audience." It must also be said that, despite the open propagandizing of the final intertitle, the final images and sounds of the film speak as well, offering their own counterrhetoric. Thus we are struck by the complete absence of patriotic flourish when the Italian troops finally win the battle. Rather, the forlorn music and the sad, sweeping movement of the camera over the smoking remains of the village signal an obvious world-weariness at the horror and destruction of war and look forward to the desolate endings of *Open City* and *Paisan*.

Whatever its ultimate political implications, *L'uomo dalla croce* had the shortest possible life on Italian screens and has rarely been seen since, in Italy or elsewhere. Released in Rome in June 1943, the film was, according to Georges Sadoul, "taken off the screen a few days later because of the catastrophic situation of the Eastern front."[10] More likely, the film ran for a few weeks, but was doomed by the king's removal of Mussolini from power on July 25, 1943, and the subsequent declaration in September of the armistice with the Allies. It is not one of the great films of cinema history, so its loss has not been especially important—except to Rossellini studies, which, fashioning generalizations beginning with *Open City* and *Paisan,* will never understand how it all came about and that great works of art are never created ex nihilo.

5

Desiderio—A Special Case (1943–46)

One more film must be discussed before we arrive at *Open City* and the beginning of Rossellini's fame. This is a project he began working on in 1943 as *Scalo merci* (Freight Yard); completed by his old schoolboy friend Marcello Pagliero (who became more famous for his role as the partisan chief Manfredi in *Open City*), it was released in 1946 as *Desiderio* (Desire). (More accurately, the film was originally released in 1946 as *Rinuncia* [Renunciation], ran into problems with the censor, then, with some scenes cut, was rereleased as *Desiderio*.) As finally made, it concerns a young call girl named Paola, sick of the corrupt sophistication of the city, who returns to her native village only to find the same destructive passions rampant there. Pursued by her brother-in-law (Massimo Girotti) and a blackmailing former lover, the pressure finally becomes too great and she commits suicide. Rossellini has essentially disclaimed any responsibility for the film (insisting that only about ten or fifteen minutes of what remains are his). But though he did little of the actual filming,[1] he was involved from the very beginning in planning its locale, characters, and themes. Hence, a brief discussion seems warranted.

The spring and summer of 1943, just before *L'uomo dalla croce* was released, were difficult times. The tide of the war had finally begun to turn against the Axis powers, with their defeat in North Africa and the Allied landing in Sicily on July 10, 1943, and a general malaise pervaded the civilian population. It was in this climate that Rossellini was trying to find an appropriate subject for his next film. In an interview with Francesco Savio in 1974, he said that he and another director had been refused permission to make films by the newly organized Consortium of Filmmakers, but he could not remember why. He went to see his friend Vittorio Mussolini, president of the consortium, and argued that since his father's antistrike law also forbade lockouts, the consortium had actually violated the law because he was not being allowed to work. Convinced, Mussolini *fils* obtained permission for Rossellini to begin filming again. "Thus I jumped on an idea of Peppe [Giuseppe] De Santis' which was called *Scalo merci*, and we got this thing together in about a month's time. . . . I started shooting on July 19. . . . A bad day to start a film."[2] A bad day because, after spending a month in planning specifically in terms of the San Lorenzo quarter of Rome, where the freight yard was located, on this day that entire area of Rome was destroyed in an Allied bombing attack. Since the actual physical environment, which was becoming increasingly important to the director, no longer existed, the treatment had to be drastically changed.[3]

At this point the story was shifted to the mountains, an especially convenient location given the confusion of the moment (Mussolini had just been arrested) and the general fear that the Germans were about to descend en masse on Rome. According to De Santis' version of the events:

> [After the bombing of San Lorenzo], Rossellini thought that in order to finish the film it would be more prudent to get away, and so he took off for the Abruzzi, inviting me to follow, but I declined the invitation because I had some work that was a little more important, and not in films, work at the heart of the [Communist] party and with the clandestine group, and so I didn't budge. Actually, I don't think that Roberto shot a single meter of film in the Abruzzi; more than anything else, it was an excuse to get away from the bombs.[4]

According to Giuseppe Ferrara, however, who has given the most complete accounting of the background of *Desiderio*, Rossellini did continue filming in the mountains, right through a roundup of draft dodgers and the confusion of the armistice signed with the Allies on September 8.[5] Finally, however, in spite of already legendary skills in the financial area, Rossellini ran out of money and had to put away the film for good.

De Santis' involvement in the film was significant, for a year earlier he had been working with Visconti on *Ossessione*, clearly the most aesthetically progressive Italian film to be made during the war. *Desiderio*, like *Ossessione*, is concerned with the arousal of "illicit" passions among people living in close proximity, and De Santis seems the obvious link between these two films (his own *Bitter Rice* [1949] is both socially aware and sexually melodramatic). Carlo Lizzani, another Communist member of the staff of *Cinema*, has said in an interview that, while Rossellini was not as close to the journal as Visconti, De Sica, or Zavattini, they felt he was one of them, especially because they liked some of the documentary scenes of *Un pilota ritorna*. Lizzani is convinced that their long discussions with the director during the planning of *Scalo merci* influenced the choices he made.[6]

The film also shows Rossellini moving closer to making human beings, within their environment, the central focus of his documentary impulse. Before this, one always feels that his loyalties are divided between a depiction of human realities and a fascination with the sheer facticity of objects, especially the mechanical.

The intent in *Desiderio* is to examine place as a locus of motivation for a character's actions, and we see the powerful influence the village has over Paola, far from the glamorous call-girl's life she leads in Rome. In the mountains she is trapped by atavistic passions and a rigorous, uncompromising system of values that rob her of her freedom and prevent her from being welcomed into the unity of her family. Probably the most significant thematic connection between this film and Rossellini's later work, however, is the obsession with death and, more particularly, suicide. In fact, the picture opens with a suicide that foreshadows and is repeated by Paola's suicide at the end. Both *Open City* and *Paisan* will close on the sad, sour notes of executions, and both the third film in the postwar trilogy, *Germany, Year Zero,* and the later *Europa '51* contain child suicides. The deaths in these films are clearly linked, but there are differences as well, and it should be remembered that *Desiderio,* like *Ossessione,* remains principally a tale of sexual passion. Edmund's suicide in *Germany, Year Zero,* on the contrary, implies the rejection of an entire world.

In purely formal, and especially visual, terms, it must be admitted that one finds little of Rossellini in the final product, though some critics have seen more than others. The editing, supervised by Pagliero, is so superfluously fast that annoying jump cuts often result. At times the camera even moves slightly after cutting, simply to get a better angle or tighter shot—an awkward, amateur's mistake—instead of dollying, a standard technique Rossellini had mastered by the time of *L'uomo dalla croce.* Similarly, the camera is obsessively taken by the face of Elli Parvo, who plays Paola, even when someone else is talking, in a total indulgence of the male gaze that is uncharacteristic of Rossellini. Throughout the film, in fact, the camera resolutely stresses reaction shots, something equally inconsistent with the rest of Rossellini's work, including the early films.

But it would be incorrect to suggest that the film does not have occasional brilliant visual moments. Chief among these is the powerful shot of Paola's sister Anna, in bed with her husband Nando (Massimo Girotti), who is becoming ever more obsessed by Paola. Anna is talking to him, but remains in the background of the shot while her husband, his back to her, is close to the camera so that we can detect his slightest reaction to everything she says. The lighting is also excellently suggestive in this scene, as well as at the end, when Paola has made up her mind to kill herself. It is strongly reminiscent of French thirties film and the American *film noir* yet to come.

As Gianni Rondolino has pointed out, "on one side the upsetting of the dramatic conventions, with the sudden suicide of the heroine, and on the other, the deep analysis of a split society particularized in its contradictions, misery, selfishness and cruelty, confer on *Desiderio* an unusual dimension in Italian cinema of those years."[7] This much is clearly true. The problem, with *Desiderio,* as with most of Rossellini's early films, concerns the precise locus of the auteur. The original subject and at least part of the treatment came from De Santis; the vast majority of the images and all of the editing seem to have come from Pagliero. Again we must ask: where is Rossellini in all of this?

How can these early films be summarized? What conclusions can be drawn? In thematic terms, we have seen the importance of *coralità,* which will become further emphasized in *Open City* and *Paisan,* yet also the first stirrings of interest in the lone individual trying to work out his or her—usually her—salvation amidst the world's hostility. Perhaps even more important, we have seen that the startling realism that was to take the film world by such surprise in 1945 had been prepared for in the earlier trilogy; it is all there—the use of actual languages, real locations, and real props, as well as nonprofessional actors for all the secondary roles and many of the principal roles as well. Furthermore, Rossellini's documentary impulse also jostles with standard narrative patterns in the most basic formal ways; thus, an aesthetic of montage, used primarily to heighten excitement, exists alongside the tentative use of the long take to convey *temps mort* and a sense of lived experience.

At this stage, I think two points of tension or opposition can be sketched out, one perhaps more consciously apparent to Rossellini than the other. In a sense, these are enabling or dialectical oppositions, for they establish the disturbance, the disharmony, that in turn provide the energy that motivates the films. The first is a tension between Rossellini's desire to document the material world, the sheer "thereness" of the natural and the built, on the one hand, and his belief in the imaginative capability of human beings, the spiritual nature that makes them strive for something beyond the material, on the other. The second, related tension—of which Rossellini was probably less aware and which is only slightly in evidence in the early trilogy—is that between depicting human beings as fully historical, always marked by the particular social forces acting upon them at any given time, and the opposite desire to reveal an eternal human essence. Thus, specific places and times will become supremely important—*India '58, Europa '51, Era notte a Roma*—and Rossellini is intent on being as precise as possible about the exact historical realities into which he places his characters. Yet, as we shall see more fully in subsequent chapters, his ultimate project is finally transhistorical or ahistorical, for the careful specificity is *always* meant to reveal the permanent or general, that which manifests itself as an unchanging human nature throughout the whole of history. Difference, in Rossellini, always ends up as sameness.

But the more particular historical question we must summarize at this point, before embarking upon a study of the superb accomplishment of the postwar trilogy and the problematics of realism, is the nature and extent of Rossellini's putative fascism. Most of his earlier critics, for various polemical reasons, have had very specific views on the subject. The Marxist critics Raymond Borde and André Bouissy, for example, apropos of *La nave bianca, s*ay that "in selling his soul to the regime, Rossellini was learning his trade," and admit freely that "we scarcely like the character," but patronizingly give him credit for "the pioneering role he had on the financial and technical level."[8] Nino Frank, on the other hand, in his study of Italian film entitled *Cinema dell'arte,* lets Rossellini off too easily—or perhaps unwittingly condemns him even more grievously by his defense.

> If there were anti-Fascist politicians who emigrated, writers even, or artists, there were never any anti-Fascist Italian filmmakers. And if a Camerini or a Soldati didn't make anything which could be taken, from near or far, as ap-

proval of the acts of Mussolini, or those close to him, both probably hoisted the insignia of the party, as everybody who wanted to work in Italy was obliged to do. So, one more uniform [that is, of those making military propaganda films], over the black shirt, scarcely counts.[9]

To be a member of the Fascist party merely in order to work, however, is hardly tantamount to wearing the black shirt. For one thing, as the Communist De Santis has pointed out, the Communist party recommended that its sympathizers join the Fascists to work against them from within.[10] It is also clear that for a filmmaker, who depends upon collaboration, a large mass audience, and great sums of money, political exile is much more disabling than for the writer, say, who presumably can take his work with him.

Another "apology" for Rossellini that does more harm than good is that offered by Giuseppe Ferrara. Like many other young men of the time, he says, Rossellini was "intrigued by fascism but not corrupted by it." Ferrara compares Rossellini with the confessional Renzo Renzi, who, in *Rapporto di un ex-ballila*, describes how he was taken in by the promise of fascism, its hope for the future, its declared openness to all solutions, its synthesis of ideologies, and, above all, its professed interest in change. Specifically, Ferrara points out, the opportunity for renewal that fascism seemed to offer was the war, which also lent new possibilities to the cinema and a renewal of "seen facts."[11] The problem with Ferrara's theory is that it implies a greater consciousness, on Rossellini's part, about Fascist ideology and its future "promise" than is warranted by the facts. It seems much more likely that Rossellini never really thought in specifically political terms and thus tended to see the situation statically, as a simple given. The Fascist march on Rome had occurred when Rossellini was sixteen, and thus he had grown into adulthood knowing no other form of government. In the manner of most self-professed "apolitical" artists, it was probably easier to accept the apparent stability of a more or less fixed system, right or wrong, in order to pursue one's own private goals in peace.[12] De Santis says of the Rossellini of this period that he was like those "big Mississippi gamblers who have such great talent for getting things together, for setting themselves up. . . . But I want to insist that Rossellini always did this with a great respect for others and always with enormous generosity. . . . The number of people he helped is infinite."[13]

Perhaps the simplest and best explanation for Rossellini's "collaboration" with the regime can be found in the fact that he was a Roman through and through. Italian intellectuals from other cities have never considered Rome a very serious place and are fond of pointing out that no major publishing house is located there. Roman culture so easily became the seat of Fascist culture because it was the home of the demimonde and hundreds of idle, penniless minor aristocrats. On the other hand, rich families with an intellectual tradition—the Agnellis, Olivettis, and Pirellis—are closely associated with modern, urban industrial life and have all been from northern Italy. The key concept, perhaps, is what Italians call *trasformismo*—that particularly Roman talent, honed through centuries of constantly changing power relationships, for knowing which way the wind is blowing, for being able to shift loyalties quickly in order to survive.

And fascism is simply what Rossellini and most of his fellow Romans had adapted to, but with no greater loyalty attached to it than to any other "external" force that had ever impinged on Roman life.

But all of this changed when Mussolini was forced from power, the armistice with the Allies was signed (effectively unleashing a civil war), and, above all, the Germans occupied Rome. It was declared an "open city," of course—Rossellini's title is meant to be grimly ironic—but the German presence was ubiquitous and violent. It was during this nine-month period of occupation, from September 1943 until the city was liberated in June 1944, that, through the medium of its infinitely more brutal twin from Germany, the citizens of Rome finally came to understand the true nature of their government. Accounts of the period speak movingly of the horrible tortures in the S.S. headquarters on Via Tasso, the roundups of able-bodied men in the middle of the night to keep the German munitions factories going, and the utter lack of electricity, clothing, and, at times, even food and water. And through it all ran the continuous terror of the ongoing skirmishes between the Nazi occupiers and the Resistance. This desperate urban warfare reached its zenith in the spring of 1944, when, after an especially severe partisan bomb attack that killed thirty-two German soldiers, Hitler, beside himself with anger, ordered the execution of ten Italians for every German killed. Not enough Jews or partisans could be found in the jails at the time to accommodate the order, so hundreds of men were simply grabbed off the street. Over three hundred were then led into the bowels of caves known as the Fosse Ardeatine, just outside Rome, sadistically murdered a few at a time, and piled on top of one another. The Nazis then dynamited shut the entrance to the caves, but the extent of the heinous reprisal became known a few days later.

As countless interviews and personal testimonies have shown, it was in this climate of fear and violence that Rossellini and other lukewarm "Fascists," overwhelmed by the brutality of events, became instantly and genuinely politicized. There is absolutely no reason to doubt Rossellini's sincerity in this change, though it is possible, of course, to see in the movement from courageous Fascist priest of *L'uomo dalla croce* to courageous partisan priest of *Open City* merely another example of Roman *trasformismo*. But the conviction of the great postwar trilogy, to which we now turn, burns too brightly for this explanation to be acceptable.

II

The War Trilogy and After

6

Open City
(1945)

Roma, città aperta (Open City) is widely regarded as the most important film in Italian cinema history. Hence, a great deal of commentary has arisen concerning it, including a whole mythology of originality and difference. It seems an inherent human need to look continually for the *truly* new that will challenge and break through the rigid determinism of the forms of expression available to us. At the time it was first shown, the film must have seemed utterly different from anything that had gone before. When it is looked at more closely, however, what is most striking is its overwhelming similarity to previous cinema.

It is well known, of course, that the making of the film was carried out in the worst possible conditions, when the occupying German troops had barely left Rome; the producers were all gone, the studios at Cinecittà had been bombed to smithereens, and in a country that was on the verge of social and economic collapse, there was little money available for something as frivolous and nonessential as a film. It is also known that the very hardships borne by Rossellini and his colleagues are precisely what gave the film its unique look and what made it appear, at first, to be so startlingly new. Thus, for example, the fact that Rosselini had to buy his raw film stock from street photographers, splicing together unmatched bits and pieces of thirty-five-millimeter film, also gave to the film its documentary, newsreel "feel" that has been so remarked on over the years. Similarly, Rossellini was forced to film in the streets because the large studios were all gone. Ambient sound and the actors' voices were dubbed in later, after the film was edited, simply because it was cheaper; most of the filming was done blindly, in fact, because daily rushes would have been a luxury. The problem with most accounts of these creative hardships, however, is that they can easily lead one to believe that the bracing felicities of *Open City* all came about by accident, as it were, and that Rossellini and the others were only *bricoleurs* who didn't have the slightest idea what they were doing. In later years Rossellini sought to counter this impression by insisting that, while the exigencies of the wartime situation posed certain problems that had to be dealt with creatively, they knew exactly what they were after and knew that they were getting it, rushes or no rushes.

The difficulties encountered making *Open City*, of course, were nothing compared with those of the German occupation itself, to which many attribute the film's power. Rossellini has many times indicated how profoundly upset he was during this period. The police wore armbands that proclaimed Rome an open city—and thus not to be considered a military target, according to the international rules of war. The film's title is bitterly ironic, however, for the city was, according to "Jane Scrivener," the pseudonym of an American woman who later published her diary chronicling those days in Rome, totally controlled by German martial law. The penalty for harboring Allied escapees, for example, or for desertion of work, or even for owning a radio transmitter was death. Taking photographs outside was punishable by life imprisonment. At one point it was even forbidden to ride a bicycle because so many Nazi soldiers were being killed from them.

Details in the accounts of the various screenwriters, actors, and others associated with *Open City* differ widely, but the basic outlines of the story of how the film came to be made are fairly clear. It seems that the original intention was to make a brief documentary on the life of Don Morosini, the partisan priest who had been executed by the Nazis only a short time earlier. A certain countess had become interested in the project, and, according to Fellini, had herself written a short treatment, though the principal treatment had been done by Alberto Consiglio. In order to make the documentary a success, Aldo Fabrizi, a popular Roman dialect comedian with relatively little film experience, was wanted to play the part of the priest. Since Fellini and Fabrizi were friends, Rossellini came around to meet Fellini so that he, in turn, could be introduced to Fabrizi. The countess was willing to offer Fabrizi 200,000 lire ($350) to play the part, but when Fellini approached him, he shouted, "Eh! What do I give a damn about Don Morosini; they'll have to give me a million (about $1,750)."[1]

The other actors came by diverse, largely unconventional paths to the film. Anna Magnani, who was to achieve worldwide fame in the part of Pina, actually was the director's second choice. He had originally wanted Clara Calamai—the steamy protagonist of *Ossessione*, a role Visconti had first offered to Magnani—but Calamai was under contract and in the middle of working on another film. Magnani wanted to be paid as much as Fabrizi, however, and she later admitted that it was only a matter of 100,000 lire, a point of principle, that almost caused her to lose "the most important film of my career. I realize now that I was wrong."[2] Magnani was hardly a newcomer to the screen—she had already some sixteen films to her credit since her first role in 1935—but while she was well known to Italian audiences, it was mostly in the guise of broad comedy and revues. The third principal was Marcello Pagliero, in the role of the partisan Manfredi, who was later to finish Rossellini's aborted *Desiderio;* he had never before acted in a film. Harry Feist, who plays the Nazi, Bergmann, was a dancer, and Maria Michi, Manfredi's debauched girlfriend Marina, had been a theater usherette who seems largely to have been chosen on the strength of her amorous ties to scriptwriter Sergio Amidei.

Meanwhile, Rossellini had had the idea of making another short film on the subject of the partisan children who had been active against the Germans, and in a brilliant stroke, apparently the idea of Fellini and Amidei, it was decided to put the two films together, making a full-length fictional film. "And so," according to Fellini, "in one week, working at my house, in the kitchen because there wasn't any heat, we wrote the script which became *Roma, città aperta,* but frankly, without much conviction."[3] Considering that it was now a matter of a full-length film, a million lire for Fabrizi seemed less outrageous.[4]

The plot that the team of screenwriters came up with is relatively simple in outline, but at the same time delicately interwoven with many diverse strands. Giorgio Manfredi (Pagliero), one of the heads of the Italian Resistance, enlists the aid of the anti-Fascist priest Don Pietro (Fabrizi) and a partisan printer named Francesco (Francesco Grandjacquet) in keeping him hidden from the Germans. The next morning, Francesco's wedding day, he is captured by the Nazis and his pregnant fiancée, Pina (Magnani), is shot down by the Germans when she attempts to interfere. Manfredi is betrayed by his girlfriend Marina (Michi), a dancer and prostitute who has been corrupted by drugs by the Nazi lesbian, Ingrid, and he, Don Pietro, and an Australian deserter the priest has been sheltering, are arrested. The deserter hangs himself, and when Manfredi refuses to talk, he is tortured to death in the presence of Don Pietro; the next morning the priest himself is executed while the young boys of his parish, who have been waging their own war against the Germans, look on.[5]

Open City is not easy to write about. While probably Rossellini's best-known film, and the film that brought him international fame, it is in many ways his least typical. This film that was quickly to be seen as a direct challenge to the conventional cinema of the time—read, Hollywood cinema—is, in fact, one of Rossellini's most conventional films, at least in terms of its narrative and dramatic structures. Thus, the many documentary moments of the earlier trilogy that work against the main narrative flow are no longer to be found in *Open City.* Here, unlike in his previous films, all elements of the mise-en-scène, lighting, dialogue, and everything else, however "realistic," are rigorously enlisted in the service of the linear narrative. It is difficult to find a reason behind this shift, but it is important to realize that it is *Open City,* rather than *Paisan* as most critics have thought, that is the enigma. In other words, if Rossellini's *other* films are kept in mind, it becomes clear that the supposedly radical change his filmmaking undergoes between *Open City* and *Paisan* is in many ways actually a return to something more characteristic, if more radical vis-à-vis the conventional Hollywood film. True, the antinarrative devices of *La nave bianca, Un pilota ritorna,* and *L'uomo dalla croce* are barely more than nods in that direction. Yet, the presence of such devices is unmistakable, as is their absolute absence from *Open City.* It is this absence that demands explanation, rather than the dedramatization and "deviant" narrative devices of *Paisan* and later films.

The most probable explanation for the change represented by *Open City* is that, for the first time, Rossellini's story was so powerful, and so demanded to be told that a driving narrative impulse pushed aside his subtler, perhaps more typical, concerns. Reality itself had become conventionally "dramatic," in a sense, by means of a specific series of *events*—in other words, narratively— and a strong story line may have seemed the best way to capture it. Similarly, he must have realized that simply showing wartime Rome—its visual presence before us continuously—would have an enormous impact. In other words, Rossellini's characteristic antinarrative interest in documenting a given reality manifests itself here in the ongoing, unspoken statement of the devastated background—Rome itself.

Thus, conventional narrative elements abound, such as the rather obvious slapstick involved when the Austrian deserter frightens us and Don Pietro by pulling out his gun, when he means only to deliver a message rolled up in an ammunition cartridge. Or when Romoletto's bomb is nearly knocked over in a masterfully choreographed vaudeville gesture. The partisan attack on the truck full of prisoners is clearly in the action-film category, though it is accomplished with a paucity of means that paradoxically causes it to be more convincing than a well-bankrolled Hollywood version would have been. Sergio Amidei, who is generally credited with (or cursed for) these elements of popular narrative, has himself clearly pointed out their utter conventionality:

> *Open City* was made, unfortunately, in an old-fashioned way. From real-life, sure, but old-fashioned, both in its techniques and its script. Certain effects, like Fabrizi's hitting the old man with the skillet, and the characters played by Michi and Galletti, are the most traditional. Also the technique: we filmed using classic lighting. . . . *Open City*, which seems the founding film in the renewal of filmmaking is, at base, the continuation of previous films.[6]

Similarly, the script also manages to stay on the easy level of heroism and cowardice, and these simple notions, the staple of Hollwood Westerns, are never for a moment seriously interrogated. Thus, near the end of the film, when Manfredi the partisan, Don Pietro the priest, and the Austrian deserter find themselves in the same cell, the deserter acts cowardly, later even killing himself, and his cowardice is seen as a moral failure on his part. Manfredi claims that "we're not heroes," but every other element of this film conspires to contradict his assertion. (Though Rossellini does perhaps display a bit of self-awareness when he has the Nazi Bergmann say a bit later, "You Italians, whatever party you belong to, are all addicted to rhetoric.")[7]

But however we might want to chastise Rossellini for his embrace of conventional narrative in this film—if we do—it is clear that he does it very well indeed. There is no slack, no narrative fat. All of the characters are tightly intertwined for maximum efficiency, and the result is a complex and thickly populated fresco. Exposition is accomplished instantly, in bold, swift strokes, and we are plunged into the narrative at a gallop from the first minute of the film. As many critics have noticed, comic and tragic moods alternate throughout the film in an invigorating and emotionally involving way, each providing a counterpoint to the other. Individual scenes are also exquisitely accomplished. Thus, the sequence in which Pina is shot down as she runs after the truck carrying her fiancé Francesco is one of the most brilliantly affecting moments in all film. Pushed up against the wall with the other women, she seems out of harm's way, so her suicidal outburst is even more shocking when it comes. On one hand, the power of this moment seems to come from the placement of the camera inside the truck as it moves away. Pina runs after it, and when she is cut down, her movement forward in tandem with the camera's movement forward is abruptly halted and the distance between the camera in the truck and her dead body, lying in the middle of the street in a lump, multiplies at a dizzying rate. But the effect of this sequence is also achieved by an awareness of dramatic balance, for it immediately follows one of the most humorous moments in the film, mentioned earlier by Amidei, when the priest has to knock the grandfather over the head with a frying pan in order to keep him from attracting the attention of the Fascists. We instantly move, then, to Pina's death sequence, all of which lasts no more than a few seconds, and the emotional and dramatic buildup of which is astounding to watch.[8] Leo Braudy, in the introduction to his anthology *Focus on Shoot the Piano Player,* insightfully links this purposeful alternation of tone with later examples in Truffaut's film and Joseph Heller's tragicomic novel *Catch 22.* An early French reviewer, Jean Desternes, likened the use of comic counterpoint to enhance the film's horror to earlier uses in Shakespeare.[9]

Matching this turn toward a more conventional narrative stance is a kind of "relapse" in the technical area as well. Thus, the two ends of the stylistic spectrum that Rossellini had previously used—the long take and the quick cutting of Eisensteinian montage—are both absent here. The editing is, instead, "classic," that is, illusionist, meant to be as invisible as the traditional Hollywood variety because primarily in the service of the narrative line and increased emotional involvement. Hence, the editing is rarely elliptical, as it was in earlier films. Close-ups, likewise, though not common, are almost always uncharacteristically used to increase the emotional charge of a scene. On the other hand, the long take we had begun to see in the earlier films is also missing, except for a few tracking shots that follow characters who are walking while they talk. Rossellini has maintained in the Baldelli interview that the long take is absent in this film because he couldn't obtain long enough pieces of film. This argument is less than convincing, however, since the normal-length shots in fact mesh very well with each other and with the other elements of the film's style.[10]

But let us now turn to a consideration of the ideas and themes of the film. Most important, of course, is the exploration—thoroughly metaphorized in various ways throughout the film—of nazism as corruption. The evil Major Bergmann tortures and murders in the name of the destiny of the Third Reich. His cohort, Ingrid, is a lesbian; for Rossellini, sexual inversion is the signifier par excellence for decadence, as we shall see again in the homosexual Nazi teacher of *Germany, Year Zero.* (In a similar vein, later in *Open City* a Nazi corporal leeringly asks Pina if the priest has been making eyes at her.) Likewise, Rossellini obviously worries that all the young women are being corrupted by the overturning of normal life; this is usually represented as the perversion of the

Nazism as corruption: Ingrid (Giovanna Galletti) "comforts" the drugged informer
Marina (Maria Michi) in *Open City* (1945).

normal (for Rossellini) goal of marrying and having a family. Rossellini attributes this problem to the war in general, however, and is not content to assign it only to the Germans: the young women are corrupted by the Germans
in this film, by the Americans in *Paisan* (Maria Michi plays a somewhat similar role in both films, further enhancing the connection), and by the French
and English occupying troops in the Berlin of *Germany, Year Zero*. Marina's
corruption by promiscuity and drugs in *Open City* leads her into a kind of
lascivious exhaustion, an exhaustion that will become generalized onto the
whole German people in *Germany, Year Zero;* here, however, the impetus of
the corrupters' forward movement keeps the disease projected outward onto
the Italians they cynically use.

The vehemence of Rossellini's outrage against the Nazis in this film is genuine, and it causes him to portray the struggle between good and evil in clear,
uncomplicated black-and-white terms—for the last time. But this vehemence
also serves to underline the fact that he is taking it very easy indeed on the
Italian Fascists. One of the difficulties for a non-Italian audience in watching
this film is visually distinguishing the Fascists from the Nazis, and thus Rossellini's subtle exculpation may be missed. Throughout the film, in fact, the Nazis
are seen as the evil ones, the actively malevolent force; the Fascists and other

Italian collaborators are portrayed in the humiliating, but decidedly less culpable, role of lackey. The Nazis' obvious hatred of the Italians is itself thematized, and conveniently serves as one more example of Nazi evil. The occupation of Rome by the Germans has given Rossellini, the quintessential outraged Roman, a clear-cut, one-to-one replacement for the Communist villains of *L'uomo dalla croce,* and Italian guilt never has to be addressed. At the end of *Open City,* when Don Pietro is to be executed, the Italian firing squad, respecting the cloth—unlike the barbarian Nazis—wavers and ends up shooting harmlessly into the ground. By a curious reversal, cowardice and bumbling inefficiency become moral values, and it is the Nazi officer who finally has to kill the priest. Throughout the film the Italian collaborators, portrayed as having managed to retain their deepest human values in spite of everything, themselves come to be seen as much the Nazis' victims as any other group, and therefore have our sympathy. (Even the camera underlines this point, usually shooting down on the humiliated Italian police commissioner and up on the dominant Bergmann in their scenes together.)

Clearly, the most important—and most complicated—theme of *Open City* concerns the nature of the partnership formed (if not in historical actuality, at least in Rossellini's mind) to combat Nazi corruption, that between the communists and the Catholic church. This was no mean trick for Rossellini, considering that his previous picture had posed them as natural, bitter enemies. But he does manage, in a remarkable balancing act, to portray them both favorably, primarily because of the handy presence of a common enemy whose horribleness everyone could agree on. For one thing, the director is acknowledging the historical fact that no matter what one personally felt concerning its politics, in effect, the Communist party *was* the Resistance. The flavor of Rossellini's accommodation can be gathered in the initial meeting between atheist Manfredi and believer Pina:

> MANFREDI: So you're having a church wedding. . . .
> PINA: Yes. Actually, Francesco didn't want to, but I told him: better for Don Pietro to marry us, at least he's on the right side, rather than go to City Hall and be married by a Fascist. Don't you think so?
> MANFREDI: In a way, you're right.
> PINA: Yes; the truth is that I . . . really believe in God (p. 32).

Bergmann's obsessive questioning of the priest at the end of the film provides the chance to offer a new rationale for accepting the Communists. Bergmann shouts that Manfredi is "a subversive, an atheist, an enemy of yours!" and Don Pietro calmly, if rather vaguely, replies: "I am a Catholic priest and I believe that a man who fights for justice and liberty walks in the pathways of the Lord—and the pathways of the Lord are infinite" (p. 130). Hardly a ringing endorsement, as not a few Marxist critics have pointed out, but in terms of the emotion projected at that moment on the screen, certainly convincing. Later, Bergmann plays his trump card in his psychological game with Manfredi when he points out that, while various political and social groups are now allied against the Germans, surely the Communist party will be forsaken when the common enemy is gone. This, of course, is a clear articulation of precisely the

The Christlike Communist Manfredi (Marcello Pagliero) being tortured by the Nazis in *Open City*.

fear felt by many progressives at the time that the coalition of Resistance groups was really only a matter of convenience, opposed to any lasting change in Italian political or social life. Further connections between the Communists and Catholics are given a visual palpability. For example, many of the shots of Manfredi while he is being tortured strongly suggest the bruised and battered Savior of Christian iconography. In one shot his arms are even pinned up to the wall. At the end of the torture sequence, an apparatus of some sort subtly casts a crosslike shadow.

Nevertheless, while the Catholic and Communist are, ostensibly, on the same footing, at least in terms of their moral rectitude, the entire film is seen in Catholic, or Christian, terms. Don Pietro is the moral lens through which we are meant to regard the various forms of iniquity on display. Manfredi, in other words, is not really given any thematically important dialogue, and the heavily dramatic form of the story insists that his encounter with the Nazi, Bergmann, take place not on the level of ideas, but rather on the level of action-film machismo—not is he right, but can he withstand torture? The only character who does get to express the presumably Communist version of things is Francesco, in his wistful and captivating talk about the future as he sits with Pina on the stairs in front of his apartment. Here again, however, his desire for freedom and hope in the future are expressed in lovely, but vague and utterly unrealizable terms.

Early Marxist views, like that of the important film theoretician Umberto Barbaro, held that the film had "such a wise and balanced political evaluation that it undoubtedly merits the applause of all honest men."[11] Most early critics, both leftists and nonleftists, agreed primarily in seeing the film as above all "historical" in a way that no other Italian film had ever been. But more recent Marxist critics like Pio Baldelli have complained, with some justice, that Rossellini's film actually forgets history. For one thing, the blame for Nazi occupation is seen clearly in Christian—that is, ahistorical—terms. This is evident in the scene between Pina and Don Pietro, when, overloaded by misery, she plaintively asks him, "Doesn't Christ see us?" The priest replies:

> A lot of people ask me that, Pina. . . . Doesn't Christ see us? But are we sure we didn't deserve this plague? Are we sure we've always lived according to the Lord's laws? And nobody thinks of changing their lives, of examining their lives. Then, when the piper has to be paid . . . everybody despairs, everybody asks: Doesn't the Lord see us? Doesn't the Lord pity us? . . . **Yes,** the Lord will take pity on us. But we have so much to be forgiven, and so we must pray, and forgive much (p. 53).

This particular passage is only one among many, but it is emphasized both visually and narratively, and nothing else in the film ever really says anything to the contrary. The victim, conveniently, is being blamed for being victimized.

Similarly, Armando Borrelli complains that in this film Rossellini is only interested in stressing the tragic destiny of his characters, and makes no attempt to see the Resistance as a critique of the past. Nor do we ever learn what they are fighting *for,* beyond getting rid of the Nazis.[12] Yet, as Mario Cannella has pointed out in an important essay translated some years ago in *Screen,* it is now clear that the Italian Communist party had *itself* given up all class analysis during this period in favor of a Stalin-inspired anti-fascist "unity" that was thoroughly uncritical and un-Marxist. Interest, in other words, had shifted imperceptibly from protecting the workers to protecting the "fatherland," and any party member who disagreed was disciplined. In Cannella's view, it was this that led to the reestablishment of bourgeois democracy and the defeat of the party.[13] Thus it seems beside the point to blame Rossellini for not portraying the revolutionary potential of the Resistance. But the Marxists are right when they say that despite appearances, Rossellini is not really interested in history in *Open City.* As the non-Marxist Mino Argentieri has pointed out, the "historic conjunction" of the Church and the Communist party leads, in Rossellini, to an "ahistorical meaning, a spiritual propensity, the nth degree of the tragedy of existence and life together."[14] Rossellini is not, strictly speaking, historical precisely because he is looking for what, in human beings, transcends history.

Another of Baldelli's complaints, related to the forgetting of history, is that the common people are only shown, even in terms of the Resistance, as pawns, as sufferers, as executors of the will of others: "The masses . . . belong to the important moments, they even die; but always impulsively, following their instincts and 'nature.' "[15] (But Baldelli is forgetting the admittedly brief but anonymous and successful partisan attack on the Nazi convoy.) The chief sufferers, of course, are the women. Rossellini's men are often larger-than-life figures who fight for causes that are vaguely defined but nevertheless transcend their own meager individual selves. They are the initiators of all the action; the women, on the other hand, both good and bad, are seen as acted upon, rather than as actors in their own right. Pina is killed when she takes action, to be sure, but, again, her action is motivated by natural "womanly instinct" in the defense of her man. The only woman who is depicted as an active force is Ingrid, and she is seen significantly as a lesbian, and thus thoroughly masculinized. The short colloquy between the young boy Marcello and a young girl about his age, Andreina, who sleeps in the same room with him, is symptomatic in this instance, and hints at the greater complexities of sexual role that are to come in *Fear* and other films made during the Bergman era:

> MARCELLO: We sure fixed them good, eh?
> ANDREINA: You never take me with you!
> MARCELLO: You? You're a woman!
> ANDREINA: So what? Women can't be heroes?
> MARCELLO: Sure they can, but Romoletto says that women always mean trouble (p. 65).

The sexist implications of this colloquy are perhaps "innocent," but clear.[16]

The positive side of the film's depiction of the masses concerns Rossellini's much-praised (by Marxist and non-Marxist alike) sense of *coralità*, that concern for the group above the individual, which we saw in operation in the earlier films. Thus, the warm-hearted working-class jokes and the good-natured kidding begin almost immediately. Pina gives some of the bread she has obtained by staging a riot on the baker's to the policeman whose family is just as hungry as everyone else's. A delightful Renoirean forgiveness pervades the film; human error and petty wrongdoing, seen in the context of the massive brutality of the Nazis, is treated indulgently and largely regarded as an unavoidable product of the times. Thus, the sexton crosses himself before he, too, plunges into the crowd assaulting the bakery, and the embarrassing fact of Pina's prewedding pregnancy is tacitly forgiven by all, including the priest. Again, however, despite Marxist approval, it is clear that this *coralità* is not motivated in Rossellini's mind by any class solidarity; instead, he sees it in terms of Christian love for one's neighbor.

Most conflicting interpretations of the film's basic theme center visually around its final images. As Don Pietro is about to be executed, he hears the young boys whistling as a signal of their support. He is shot, and the last image of the film shows the boys, weary, but supporting each other, trudging down a hill back toward the center of town. The Roman skyline, dominated by the dome of Saint Peter's, forms the background of the shot as the film ends. The sequence is clearly symbolic, but of what? Some have chosen to emphasize the dome, insisting that only in the Church is there hope for the future of Italy. But the dome is seen firmly in its context of the entire city of Rome, just as the Church is an important part of Italian society, but hardly everything. Some have chosen to see the ending as utterly pessimistic, full of death and destruction,[17] while others have emphasized the fact that the boys, symbols of Italy's future even though crippled and depressed, are at least supporting one another down the hill.

In any case, the film appropriately ends with this evocative long shot of Rome, for in many ways, Rome is its chief protagonist, standing synecdochically for the rest of Italy. It is the first word of the film's Italian title, and is before us at all times throughout the film, either directly, as visual background, or indirectly suggested through its particular social relations reenacted in the interiors. The film opens, as well, with vibrant location shots that set us firmly in the midst of the ancient city, and we recognize the antlike Germans we see running about from our bird's-eye perspective as the interlopers they are. We first meet the German officer Bergmann after the camera pulls back from a map of Rome in his office, suggesting that his contact with the city, and by extension that of the other Germans as well, can only be of an abstract, second-order level. The point is further underlined when we learn that all of Bergmann's dealings with the city are through photographs of its inhabitants. When the Italian police commissioner asks how Manfredi was tracked down, Bergmann replies: "I met him right here, on this desk. Every afternoon I take a long walk through the streets of Rome, but without stepping out of my office" (p. 13). Again, the Germans are associated with all that is artificial, second-hand, cut off from the organic life of the people. Rome is eternal, the Nazis are temporary.

When the film was first screened for prospective distributors and other film people about town, the reception was intensely disappointing. They were appalled at how "badly" the film was made and were shocked by the rawness of many of its scenes. Rossellini and his coworkers were crushed. Yet out of their disappointment arose a legend of utter rejection that is simply not borne out by the facts. In many interviews Rossellini complained that the condemnation was universal, and his brother, Renzo, speaks bitterly in his autobiography of carrying negative press clippings around in his wallet for years. According to the legend, all of Rossellini's friends hated the film and every distributor refused to take it, but for lack of anything better it was presented as the Italian selection at Cannes in 1946, where it enjoyed a similar lack of success. The big breakthrough occurred when the film opened two months later in Paris to rave reviews and an equally strong response at the box office. Soon after, the same thing happened in the United States; Italian critics and distributors finally saw the error of their ways, the film was rereleased in Italy, and thus the film's makers were vindicated when it became successful in its birthplace as well.

But as with most legends of total failure or total success, the truth lies somewhere in between. Obviously, Rossellini's friends and potential distributors were put off by a film that so thoroughly repudiated the canons of accepted good taste, in terms of both its content and its "unprofessional" form. When *Open City* came along, it represented the first full-fledged look at those unpalatable aspects of life that had been kept off the screen for so long—the reality of torture, sexuality, and dirty streets. Visconti's *Ossessione* had explored similar territory, but had been suppressed a mere week after its release in 1942 and thus had little effect on the public's (and the critics') cinematic expectations. The condemnation of *Open City* was far from universal, however. For example, Carlo Lizzani, writing in *Film d'oggi* in November 1945, shortly after the film's first appearance, exclaimed in the opening line of his review: "Finally I've seen an Italian film! By this I mean a film which tells a story about us, about the experiences of our country, about facts that concern us." Lizzani also grasped the immense historical importance of the film as well:

> An Italian director can offer our cinema those gifts of communication and a wide and popular persuasiveness which it has been lacking up to this time, even in the works of the best directors, and which alone can guarantee it a national and especially international success. The people today don't want an empty and sloppy cinema, but neither do they want a cinema for aesthetes. Rossellini's essential merit is to have found the rhythm and the movement best suited to make accessible to the vast public the new contents of which the film is messenger, to relate them to the most diverse sensibilities. . . . I would say that this film could be just the thing to start off our new rebirth.[18]

The novelist Alberto Moravia, writing his film column in the September 30, 1945, issue of the anti-Fascist journal *La nuova Europa,* praised the film's intense realism.[19] Alessandro Blasetti, by that time a kind of elder statesman of Italian cinema and one of its most respected practitioners, says that after the first press screening of *Open City,* "I felt the need to go meet Rossellini who was waiting outside with 'indifferent' trepidation and I hugged him for all of us; the gesture was really emotional and grateful."[20] Rossellini later complained that the film was barely noticed when it came out, but Mario Gromo, the veteran reviewer for the powerful Turin newspaper *La Stampa,* wrote of it very favorably and suggested later that it was little mentioned (and thus little seen) because of a simple lack of space in the newspapers, pointing out that in 1945, newspapers came out in only two pages. In the introduction to his collected reviews written some years later, Gromo remembers with frustration "the breath I had to spend one evening in November 1945 to be able to devote thirty-six lines to *Open City* instead of just twenty."[21]

The film was an even greater success with the public, earning over 61 million lire in its first four months and going on to become the largest-grossing film of the year. (Ironically, no other neorealist film, nor any other film of Rossellini's, was ever to be as successful at the box office again.) Reactions in France and America were even more favorable. One reason was that *Open City* and *Paisan* were released in these countries within a few months of each other, and thus the effect of witnessing something new was reinforced. Jean Desternes spoke of them as "overwhelming," and offered a sophisticated analysis of the films that placed them firmly in European literary, philosophical, and cinematic traditions of realism. He also sounded the first stirrings of a theme that was later to be taken up and amplified by the French phenomenologists, when Rossellini's countrymen had thoroughly given up on him. According to Desternes, Pina and Marcello "really are that woman and that child, giving proof to their existence: they are there and that's how it is."[22] An even more important review was that by the widely known film historian Georges Sadoul, who discussed *Open City* and *Paisan* in *Les Lettres françaises,* mistakenly referring throughout to the director as Alberto Rossellini. He compared them to two French films of the Resistance, Lindtberg's *La Dernière Chance* and Clement's *La Bataille du rail* (both now largely forgotten), especially in terms of their similar use of real locations and nonprofessional acting.[23] Sadoul also struck a note that was especially to preoccupy American reviewers when he said that *Open City* was clearly more important to cinema history than the last two hundred films made in Hollywood. Thus, John McCarten, in the *New Yorker,* called it "the best that has ever come from Italy," and wondered why the characters were all so fresh, especially the children, compared with the "saccharine and inept" children offered us by Hollywood.[24] *Life* magazine, in a picture spread, approvingly pointed to the film's "earthy verisimilitude" and noted that its violence and "plain sexiness" went far beyond anything Hollywood could do in projecting "a feeling of desperate and dangerous struggle."[25]

The most dramatic American reaction to the film was surely that of James Agee, at that time the film critic for the *Nation.* His March 23, 1946, review opened with this remarkable statement: "Recently I saw a moving picture so much worth talking about that I am still unable to review it. . . . I will probably be unable to report on the film in detail for the next three or four weeks."[26] When Agee did finally feel up to writing about the film for the April 13 issue, he praised its immediacy and its avoidance of the phony populist sentimentality of Works Progress Administration murals. But what struck Agee above all, and critics of all nationalities ever since, was the film's startling realism. This is a notoriously difficult concept to deal with, of course, but our thinking about Rossellini, especially during this period, is so tied up with it that we must now consider it more abstractly and in some depth.

Because most of the filming was done in the midst of actual exteriors, and not those recreated in a studio or on the back lot, the film quite naturally has a look that makes it utterly different from the conventional film of the time; in this sense, then, "realistic" means "different from Hollywood." The anti-Hollywood bias is also evident in the choice of individual actors for their similarity to the mix of people one finds on the street, rather than for their good looks. Thus, makeup, favorable lighting and soft focus are eschewed in favor of something closer to the way we encounter people in real life. But something happens to "real life" when it is translated to the screen, and what we call realism actually consists of a set of expectations that is related to reality, of course, but in conventional rather than natural ways. Thus, for example, it would obviously be more "real," more like real life, for people being photographed to look at the camera, but then, paradoxically, the film would no longer seem realistic to us at all.

Furthermore, as the Soviet semiotician Jurij Lotman has pointed out, the "poetics of 'refusals'" associated with Italian neorealism "can only be effective against a remembered background of cinema art of the opposite type."[27] The meaning and emotional effect of neorealism, in other words, resides not in itself, but precisely in how it *differs* from what preceded it. Neorealism's vaunted window on reality thus depends at the most basic level, paradoxically, on practices of *artifice* to be understood. As Lotman says concerning Visconti's *La terra trema,* "The art of naked truth, trying to rid itself of all existing kinds of artistic conventionality, requires an immense culture in order to be perceived as such."[28]

Naturally, Rossellini and the other directors associated with neorealism did not consider their practice in these analytic terms, nor did their earliest supporters such as the French critic André Bazin. They did not think of themselves as operating within the confines of preexistent codes, but rather—and this is what makes them almost unique in cinematic history—as moving ever closer to *reality itself.* In Rossellini's most limpid and direct formulation of this tendency, "Things are there. Why manipulate them?"[29] The underlying assumption, of course, is that when these "things" have been transferred to the screen, they will somehow still be "there." At one point, Bazin even makes the translation process almost quantifiable: "We shall call *realist* any system of expression, any narrative procedure which tends to make more reality appear on the screen."[30] His most gnomic statement specifically concerning Rossellini is that he "directs facts"[31]—not, of course, cinematic facts, but the facts that are seen as inhering in external reality (and available to us), rather than as constituted in a system of signification. For Bazin, reality signifies, at its deepest level, *directly:* "The world of Rossellini is a world of pure acts, unimportant in themselves but preparing the way (as if unbeknownst to God himself) for the sudden dazzling revelation of their meaning."[32] By logical extension, then, the greatest film will, paradoxically, do away with itself (as representation) in its direct minfestation of being. Thus, Bazin is led to speak of De Sica's *Bicycle Thieves* as "one of the first examples of pure cinema. There are no more actors, no more story, no more mise-en-scène, that is to say finally in the aesthetic illusion of reality—no more cinema."[33]

Bazin was, of course, always aware that screen reality was only an "aesthetic illusion." What else could it be? Furthermore, the most epistemologically sophisticated of these directors and critics knew and freely admitted that this raw reality must be "filtered" through the consciousness of the director, because otherwise what one ended up with was an arbitrary surface depiction that barely pierced the skin of the real. But the purpose and result of this authorial intervention, this mediation, in effect, was always to get to a cinematic representation of reality that was somehow more "real" than reality itself. The appeal is made to a truth that exists beyond, though not so far beyond as to be uncapturable, of course. Associated with this cinematic pursuit of truth is a concomitant theory of essences, of a "truer," "higher" reality, that has always been linked with the notion of aesthetic realism since the advent of the mimetic theory of art. Thus we find Hegel, for example, maintaining, "Far from being simple appearances and illustrations of ordinary reality, the manifestations of art possess a higher reality and a truer existence."[34] The long shadow of Plato is everywhere here.

In order to question and perhaps begin to account for the fierce energy invested in this neorealist, phenomenological compulsion toward the essence of reality, we will first have to consider more closely the nature of the film's relation to that preexistent reality that may be called its "raw material." To do this, we will have to take yet another step backwards and examine what we mean by reality itself. My basic assumption is that there is a given reality that preexists our intentions and desires and that forms a ceaseless copresence for all our activity, whether we are aware of it or not. I am thinking of the entity, "the world," that Maurice Merleau-Ponty speaks of in "What Is Phenomenology?" as "not what I think, but what I live through. I am open to the world, I have no doubt that I am in communication with it, but I do not possess it; it is inexhaustible."[35] In contrast to Merleau-Ponty, however, I would hold that, whenever we regard this preexistent reality as in any way meaningful, these meanings are being imposed by our own consciousness (collectively speaking, of course). Reality, in other words, is not constituted by an uncomplicated "out there" to which we can have direct, unmediated access. We cannot help but process everything through our own particular culture, which exists beyond our individual control and not only filters what we experience, but actually produces it. Harold Brown, a philosopher of science, has argued in his book *Perception, Theory, and Commitment* that, far from perception providing us with pure facts, "the knowledge, beliefs and theories we already hold play a fundamental role in determining what we perceive." In his felicitous, and disarmingly simple phrase, we actually "perceive meanings."[36] We continuously make representations to ourselves, mostly as metaphors, as Nietzsche saw, that mediate reality for us. Prior artistic practice is also implicated here, for, as Roman Jakobson has maintained, the traditions and conventions of visual representation largely determine the very act of visual perception itself. In other words, before we can talk about how a film represents reality, we must be aware that we already represent and thus construct this reality, continually, in our normal daily mental activity.

Film, in its turn, then, represents what is in fact an already "represented" reality. Compared with other systems of representation, of course, film seems to enjoy a privileged status in terms of its relations to its referent. Jean-Paul Fargier has suggested some of the ideological implications of this fact:

> People used to say about statues and portraits, "He looks as though he might open his mouth any minute and say something." or "He looks as though he might burst into movement." But the "as though" gives the game away; despite the appearance, something was *lacking,* and everybody knew it. Whereas in the cinema, there is no "as though." People say "The leaves are moving." But there are no leaves. The first thing people do is deny the existence of the screen: it opens like a *window,* it is *"transparent."* This illusion is the very substance of the specific ideology secreted by the cinema.[37]

What we must remember, in other words, is that this privileged link to reality does not in any way lessen the fact that cinema is as dependent upon preexistent, "nonnatural" codes and systems to be understood as any other medium. The point is that the inherently greater superficial proximity to reality of film can lead easily into essentialist assumptions about the cinema as a place of direct, unmediated experience that avoids the problems that beset other, more obviously artificial, systems of representation.

In cinema we are lulled by the fact that aspects of film can seem to be "like" aspects of reality. But, according to Lotman, "The very concept of 'likeness' which seems so immediate and axiomatic to the audience is, in actuality, a fact of culture derived from previous artistic experience and from certain types of artistic codes employed at a particular time in history."[38] Lotman's example is that of the black-and-white film that, until very recently at any rate, has always been taken as somehow inherently more "realistic" even though we know, of course, that reality is in color.

Seeing a film, then, presupposes first an ongoing, unconscious daily operation that consists of systematizing an inchoate reality and "reading" it in terms of the codes that we both put and find there. This already represented reality is then represented again in film by means of a certain labor on the part of the filmmaker. It does not simply happen "naturally." Much avant-garde cinema in fact deliberately foregrounds the notion of production, thus helping us to see that the reality depicted, as well as the film, is a made, constructed, and thus historical reality. Most classic cinema, however, is interested in depicting an emotionally and psychologically complicated world, perhaps, but not one that is ontologically complicated or open to question. The very power of the image to show "real" objects, "real" people, and "real" behavior thus seems to grant it a privileged point of view. Even the correspondence between the seen and the heard, between the images on the screen and the sound track, reinforces the comforting notion of wholeness and coherence, the idea that the world is a place where things make sense. This very obviousness of film's depiction of reality has its political aspect as well, and can be seen as implicated, despite its apparent "innocence," in the maintenance of the political and social status quo. As the Marxist paradigm has it, the dominant ideology of the ruling class always poses itself as natural, as *not* constructed, precisely because if the working classes could ever realize that the social reality in which they lived less well than others was *made*— in other words, the product of historical forces and not "the way things were meant to be"—they might begin to take steps to *unmake* that reality.

This very sense of wholeness I have been outlining above, which seems to be produced by most films, is seen by Bazin as the distinguishing characteristic of neorealism. In his remarkable essay entitled "In Defense of Rossellini," he approvingly maintains that neorealism's main feature is "its claim that there is a certain 'wholeness' to reality. . . . To put it still another way, neorealism by definition rejects analysis, whether political, moral, psychological, logical, or social, of the characters and their actions. It looks on reality as a whole, not incomprehensible, certainly, but inseparably one."[39] Bazin praises Rossellini's *Europa '51* because in it he "strips the appearances of all that is not essential, in order to get at the totality in its simplicity."[40]

One immediate effect of this privileging of the *essence* of reality over mere appearance and the accompanying insistence on film's ability to re-present this essence on the screen is to place the practice of neorealist filmmaking firmly within the Western metaphysical tradition of *presence,* most recently and powerfully critiqued by the French philosopher Jacques Derrida. In this ubiquitous, inescapable system, being is defined as that which is present, or is capable of being present, in time or space, or self-present to the mind. No provision is made for the enabling absent, which, if meaning is always constituted differentially (as day, for example, "creates" night, and vice-versa), must also be paradoxically "present" in the form of a "trace" that is both there and not there. It is thus necessary for neorealism and its theorists to employ what Derrida calls the "logic of the supplement" (the completion of the supposedly already "full" term through its "incomplete" opposite), for this *essence* of reality can, of course, only be made manifest through the specific and the particular, which are, by definition, non-essential. As Derrida points out in *Of Grammatology*, imitation (mimesis), it is believed, adds nothing; it is, in other words, merely a kind of "supplement." But if mimesis really adds nothing, why bother? In terms of our inquiry, what arises in cinema is the paradoxical situation in which the neorealist representation of reality somehow *adds,* as a supplement, the essence of that reality it represents. Hence, the essence comes from the outside, from elsewhere. But, as Derrida rhetorically asks, "Is that imitative supplement not dangerous to the integrity of what is represented and to the original purity of nature?"[41] In fact, this very danger shows up in Bazin's complaint that the "necessary illusion of film . . . quickly induces a loss of awareness of the reality itself, which becomes identified in the mind of the spectator with its cinematographic representation.[42]

For Bazin and the other phenomenological critics, the project is at base a religious one, and the finding of fullness in a cinema that embodies the fullness of reality itself is a way to find (or to constitute) what Derrida has called the transcendental signified, or, in a more familiar formulation, God. This is not a project to be taken lightly, of course, for with this end point firmly in place all of the difference, discontinuity, and incompleteness that characterize the world can be made meaningful or at least disguised, and the yawning abyss of absence covered over by this ground of last resort. If reality is whole, and if the cinema can convey this wholeness, then everything that we experience in life that is contingent or in some way compromised (in other words, everything) can be naturalized and made to seem ultimately explicable and thus less threatening. The fixity of the end point (God, the totality, or the essence of reality) can then be seen as grounding the play of difference and the endlessly receding chain of signification.

This neorealist and phenomenological goal of reproducing the seamless web of reality directly on the screen, however, is foredoomed by the difference that makes it always dependent for its meaning on something outside itself. Even what is called neorealism, as we saw earlier, is constituted at least as much by differences both external and internal as by its own identity. This is why endless polemical pages have been wasted in trying to fix its defining characteristics (in other words, its essence), its beginning and end, and so on. Similarly, each filmmaker's body of work—and each individual film—will be marked by gaps and discontinuities, rough edges, details that do not fit, all of which must be forgotten or repressed if we are to make general statements about the "essence" of a filmmaker's career or even the meaning of a specific film. But because these films, like all works of art, are in fact the site of an endless, finally irrepressible, play of difference, if allowed to speak freely, they will tell a jumbled, but perhaps exciting, tale that points to their own internal discrepancies and in so doing will then deconstruct themselves.

This play of difference can be seen clearly at work in Rossellini's films in a problematic area where the *represented real* (that is, what we think of as part of ordinary experience) and the *realistic* come into conflict. Conventional cinema demands a basic level of plausibility, enough to allow us to put ourselves emotionally into the created world of the film. It accomplishes this through the use of real surface detail (this is why most films are shot on location nowadays, and is closely related to Roland Barthes' description of *l'effet de réel* in literature), but even more importantly through "realistic" acting, which is actually only tangentially, though complexly, related to our sense of the way people act in real life. Another way of achieving this believability is through the overt naturalizing devices of narrative technique and structure, with their well-defined beginnings, middles, and ends, clear plot lines, and well-constructed dramatic and emotional building, none of which, of course, could be further from our daily experience of life. We perceive something as realistic, in short, when it corresponds to a set of conventionalized expectations (largely derived from previous film or novelistic practice) about what people in movies do, not when it corresponds to actual empirical experience. All of this provides the comforting envelope of believability of the conventional film that enables us to be inserted into the complex dual process of what we loosely call audience identification. We are not actually meant to take what we see as *reality*, of course, or we would try to jump into the screen to help out of their predicaments the characters to whom we have become emotionally tied.[43] But when we experience, with excitement, a film as *more* realistic than usual—that is, more like "real life" than previous films we have seen—I would argue it is because it is pushing against the currently accepted boundaries of the realistic, closer toward the dangerous unpredictability of the (represented) *real*.

This "reality effect" seems to stem from the ironic fact that we think an event or image is more real precisely because we have not seen it before on the screen. In the theater we assume unconsciously that we are in the midst of coded behavior and rule-governed spectacle whose purpose is to represent that which it is not, and that if we see merely what we have already seen in other movies it will only be comfortably believable rather than truly real. I would say, therefore, that the very thing we quite properly bewail—movies are getting ever more gruesome and violent—may be part of their inexorable logic. The thrill of a "more realistic" film always comes when we sense, at some level, that an already accepted (and thus tamed) realism is being pushed beyond, toward *the real itself*, and thus, as in life, screen events are "out of control" and we cannot predict what will happen. What is especially interesting is that when the event or image does push through this barrier of the realistic, we can experience it as more "real" (in other words, closer to our perceptions of life outside the theater) and at the same time as somehow *fake* because the illusion of an independently existing, uncontingent world, laboriously created on the screen, has been broken. It is this partially controlled infusion of the real that keeps us on the edge of our seats; when it overcomes the fiction, however, it can rudely threaten to reveal that it is all only make-believe.

Thus, *Open City* was seen as more realistic because it was, in effect, expanding the boundaries of the prevailing code of realism by incorporating the real in the form of location shooting, authentic languages, unglamorous actors, and so on. Forty years later we can easily see how many of its novelties have become standard filmmaking practice, in the process losing much of their power. What is more interesting is that, in the films following *Open City*, Rossellini will use this tension between the realistic and the real, along with other elements we

Marcello (Vito Annichiarico) tries to revive his murdered mother Pina (Anna Magnani) in *Open City.*

might provisionally call expressionist, to question his own filmmaking practice and the easy assumptions of the neorealist aesthetic. In *Open City,* however, Rossellini contents himself with a few stylized touches that have upset critics bent on seeing him as the quintessential realist. Their complaints usually take the form of finding fault with certain elements of the film that are "unrealistic," and thus said to clash with its prevailing texture. Some, for example, have objected that the layout of the gestapo headquarters—an office flanked on one side by a torture chamber and on the other by an officers' lounge where Beethoven is heard and champagne is drunk—is utterly impossible. These critics object that the inauthenticity of the Nazi interiors clashes continually with the realism of the exteriors, without ever realizing that this is surely the point, for it is in perfect keeping with the association, insisted upon throughout the film, between the Germans and a decadent, sterile artificiality.[44] (It also allows for some brilliant sound editing when, at various points, Manfredi's screams merge with the light strains of classical music coming from the other room.) Defenders of Rossellini like Giuseppe Ferrara take the wrong tack, I think, when they offer elaborate arguments that these are not really violations of realism because that is the way it really was.

It seems far more productive to posit an expressionist side to Rossellini— barely visible here, of course—even if it destroys the comforting, symmetrical certainty of the director's standard realist label. The arrangement of the gestapo headquarters then becomes clearly symbolic, a stylized landscape and almost mathematical demonstration of the corruption of Nazi culture. The lack of a total commitment to realism, in other words, enables the director to get at things that lie beyond realism. Looking at Rossellini provisionally as an expressionist, as we shall see, also helps us to recover many of his films that have been written off as failures because they are not realistic enough. It is tempting to say that this very tension between realism, expressionism, and the real is "at the heart" of the Resistance trilogy, but this would only serve to ground my reading of Rossellini in my own, no less culpable, version of essentialism.

In *Open City* the stylized, self-reflexive touches that point to the film as artifice are light. The gestapo Bergmann can operate in Rome only through the second-level order of representation found in his photographs, as we saw earlier, and the partisan Francesco reminds Pina, his wife-to-be, of their long-gone innocence when they imagined an early end to the war: "And everybody thought it'd be over soon, and that we'd only get to see it in the movies. But . . ." (p. 69). It *is* over now, and we *are* seeing it in the movies, and what we see in the movies is not what happened, exactly, nor can it ever be. What Francesco is hinting at, perhaps, is that film reality and lived experience are, truly, worlds apart.

7

Paisan
(1946)

With the artistic, if not the financial, success of *Open City* guaranteed, Rossellini, Amidei, Fellini, and the others began to think of bigger things. Rod Geiger, the fast-talking, self-styled American entrepreneur, had returned from the United States with money he had received from a distributor for the rights to *Open City;* soon an Italian coproducer, Mario Conti, was found, and according to Fellini, it was he who provided the bulk of the money to begin work on the film already known as *Paisa (Paisan).*[1] The idea in 1946 was to make a film that would somehow encompass the whole of Italy and reflect honestly, in the vein of *Open City,* on what the filmmakers found in their travels. They had a general idea of what the film would be about before shooting began, but the script was never really fixed, in accordance with an already emerging neorealist aesthetic orthodoxy. Likewise, characters, plots, and locations were continuously and sometimes drastically changed—a procedure soon to become standard neorealist practice—to correspond more closely with the people and the places they found in the course of their six months spent traveling from one end of the country to the other.[2]

For the filmmakers, it was as though they were seeing the world for the first time, at least that part of the world that was Italy. Fellini relates with obvious joy:

> We were surrounded by a whole new race of people, who seemed to be drawing hope from the very hopelessness of their situation. There were ruins, trees, scenes of disaster and loss, and everywhere a wild spirit of reconstruction. In the midst of which, we did our tour. The troupe of people working on *Paisà* traveled through an Italy they scarcely knew, because for twenty years, we'd been in the grip of a political regime which had literally blindfolded us.[3]

61

Allied troops were everywhere, complicating the Italians' efforts to learn how to live with one another again after the mortal divisiveness of the war years. Italy's always intense regionalism exacerbated the problem, and the struggle for geographical and cultural unity is itself thematized, in a minor way, in the film. On the one hand, the constant linking presence of the map of the Italian peninsula, which appears between the film's six separate episodes, and the relentless chronological movement forward (there is only one flashback in this obsessively present tense movie), a temporal movement that meshes with the equally relentless linear, spatial movement upward on the map, insist upon a sameness, a unity to the Italian experience. The film wants to be, in other words, a history of *Italy* during this period. Yet the chronological movement, which seems to describe merely different temporal points in a homogeneous space (Italy), or different "aspects" of a homogeneous, single national experience, cannot disguise the fact that the spaces, the regions of Italy, insist on their heterogeneity in each episode just as strongly as ever. The clearly proclaimed regionality of the map thus defeats in advance its simultaneous proclamation of unity.

This regionality is more sharply depicted in some parts of the film than in others, primarily because of the contribution of landscape—the last episode, shot in the Po region, is the prime example—and the visual "thereness" of the built environment, seem most clearly in the Florence episode. In that segment, the Duomo, the Uffizi Gallery, and the entire tourist panoply of "sights" that the British officers so intensely discuss from their vantage point in the Boboli gardens of the Pitti Palace cause the city to become an active "character" every bit as present as any human. In Naples, it is the very fact of "cityness" and slum life—but meant to be taken in a generalized, abstract way, unlike the specificity of Florence—that marks the episode; Sicily, on the contrary, is the atavistic place of brute rock, stodgy towers, and primitive emotions. The Roman episode is one of the least specially marked—the ironic story of missed opportunity that unfolds there, it might be argued, could have taken place anywhere—a fact that could easily be attributed to the exhaustion of Rome's signifying capability in *Open City*. To dwell on the city's visual specificity, in other words, as in the Florence episode, would have constituted an unwelcome and static repetition. Nevertheless, this episode's story is linked explicitly to the *history* of Rome, albeit the most recent installment of it, the liberation; it is this historical event, seen by those who participated in it as profound as any other previous event in the city's history, that marks this particular story, finally, as possible only in that city.

Curiously enough, the only episode that seems relatively abstracted from its location is the one that takes place in the monastery, and it was in filming this sequence, and this sequence alone, that Rossellini "cheated," by fictionally placing southern monks in the north-central part of Italy. This episode is principally concerned with an abstract idea of serenity and innocence made flesh in the monks' faces. One point elaborately developed in the episode is that outside reality has had no effect on their lives, and thus we quite properly see nothing that is exterior to their own interrelationships and their relationship with God. Rossellini deliberately draws a frame, the outer walls of their monastery, around them, thus highlighting what goes on inside the frame and at the same time pointing to the absolute artificiality (and impossibility), however desirable it may seem to a war-weary world, of this exile from the rest of reality outside.

Perhaps it would be useful at this point to rehearse the plot details of the six episodes. The first episode, as I have mentioned, takes place in Sicily just after the Allies have landed. The sense of the confusion of war is nicely captured by showing the local residents initially convinced that the American soldiers are Germans, and then, realizing their mistake, welcoming them, though somewhat ambivalently. As the local Fascist bewails the loss of "freedom" for his country that their presence represents, the soldiers take along a young woman of the village to lead them through a minefield. Finding an ancient, abandoned tower, they leave "Joe from Jersey" there with Carmela while they search the area. Most of the episode centers on the efforts of these two in the tower to communicate with one another, since each is innocent of the other's language. Things progress so well on this preverbal, gestural level, however, that Carmela is already displaying signs of jealousy when Joe shows her a wallet-sized photo of his sister and her child, who she mistakenly takes for his wife and his own child. To demonstrate the facial resemblance between him and the woman in the picture, he holds a lighter up to his face. Suddenly, the film cuts to a German outpost—in a truly startling intrusion of otherness that destroys the fragile unity the couple seem to have achieved—and the Nazi soldier who, because he has seen a light, fires a single shot that instantly kills Joe. Carmela hides, and the Germans take over the tower; deeply upset by Joe's death, Carmela kills one of them with his rifle. The Americans return, find Joe dead, and assume that Carmela, "the dirty Eye-Tie," was responsible. The next shot shows the Germans looking down from the cliff off of which they have thrown Carmela, and the last thing we see, as the irony rushes over us like the sea, is Carmela's body lying smashed on the rocks.

The next episode takes place amid the rubble of bombed-out Naples, as children and adults display an endlessly fertile imagination, usually in illegal ways, in order to survive. Here a shoeshine boy (less saccharine than the boys of De Sica's *Sciuscià*), in an incredible scene, "buys" a black American soldier who is drunk.[4] The boy hides his prize from the police by taking him into a puppet show, where a white Crusader puppet is beating up a black Moor; the black soldier drunkenly enters the fray on the side of his race and gets thrown out of the theater. Sitting on a pile of rubble, the soldier and the boy try to make themselves understood through the confusion of language and alcohol. When the soldier seems about to fall asleep, the boy warns him that he will have to rob him if he does. A few days later, the soldier, who turns out to be an M.P., finds the boy again and demands that he return his boots. Intent on taking the boy home to his parents for a scolding, he discovers that the boy's parents have been killed in the bombing and that he has no home at all.

The film next moves to Rome, where another drunken G.I. encounters a prostitute who takes him to her room. Through a mixture of Italian and English, Fred bitterly tells her, in flashback, the story of his first entry into the city, on the day of Liberation, and the lovely, innocent girl Francesca he met but has been unable to find ever since.[5] The prostitute realizes that she is the one he has been looking for, but since she is ashamed to reveal herself, she asks the landlady

Harriet, the English nurse (Harriet White), drags a dying partisan to shelter in the Florence episode of *Paisan* (1946).

to give Fred her old address when he awakes the next morning. The last shots in the episode are again in an ironic vein: Francesca desperately waits for Fred in front of the building in which they had first met, once again looking like the girl next door, while he is seen at the very end throwing away a slip of paper, because, as he tells his friend, it is only "the address of a whore."

The fourth tale takes place in Florence, a city dangerously divided between the Nazis and the partisans, who are fighting street by street while the British wait outside for reinforcements. Harriet, an American nurse, and her Italian friend Massimo desperately want to get over to the other, still-occupied side of the Arno, she to find her lover Lupo, a capo in the Resistance, and he to rejoin his wife and child. The story consists solely of their dangerous journey across the city. When they finally arrive, Harriet learns accidentally, even casually, from a partisan who is dying in her arms that Lupo was killed earlier that morning.

A monastery, ostensibly in the Emilia-Romagna area, is the setting for the fifth story. There, monks who have spent the entire war in an otherworldly peace, take in three American chaplains for the night. When they discover that one of the chaplains is a Protestant and the other, even worse, a Jew, they decide to fast to try to save these "lost souls." The American priest is deeply touched by the serenity of the monks' religious feeling, a quality he has lost in the horror of war.

The last episode, and the one most consistently touted ever since, takes place in the marshland of the Po River. The opening shots show a dead partisan floating down the river on a white lifesaver to which the Germans have attached a sign labeled "partisan." Dale, an American O.S.S. man there to give technical assistance to the underground, and his friend Cigolani bury the dead man; they stick the accusing sign into the freshly dug earth and it instantly takes on dignity and worth. The Germans have completely cut off the small group of partisans, but, nevertheless, British orders are to cease all activity. They all know that this means that, while the Americans will only be made prisoners, the partisans will be executed as common criminals. When the partisans are inevitably caught, the Germans tie them up and push them one by one off a boat to drown; Dale and another American rush to protest, and are shot down. As the last two bodies splash into the water, the voice-over matter-of-factly tells us, "This happened in the winter of 1944. At the beginning of spring, the war was over." On this ambivalent note, the film ends.

Superficially, the various episodes seem to have little to do with one another, as some critics initially objected, but in fact the connections are many and subtle. On the most mechanical level, as we have seen, they are linked by the chronological and spatial chain created by the map. More important, however, is the link of emotion, or rather the lack of emotion caused by so much deprivation and exhaustion (a theme that will be brought to its zenith in Rossellini's next film, *Germany, Year Zero*), a relation formed by mood and tone—mostly negative—that serves, on one level at least, to unite the film. The principal linkage, of course, is in terms of subject and theme, in that all the episodes in one way or another depict the aftermath of war and "victory," and most importantly, the impossibility of communication.[6] We see people struggling to understand one another in nearly every episode, through the false but troublesome divisions of language, and not always being very successful at it.[7] War creates obvious horror everywhere it goes, but its subtler and more insidious manifestation is, for Rossellini, the way it prevents or distorts the normal, everyday sources of pleasure, like simple communication, which are no less important for being mundane. What emerges in the first episode in Sicily, in which Carmela and Joe from Jersey try so hard to make themselves understood to one another, is a Renoirean theme that through the *attempt* to communicate, at any rate, one can work one's way back to the basic, primitive level of cooperation that both Renoir and Rossellini obviously feel underlies the surface chaos and distrust of human relationships. This can, I think, be seen most clearly in Renoir's case in the episode near the end of *La Grande Illusion* when the escaped prisoner of war played by Jean Gabin has his own private rapprochement with the German woman, as they stumble through pidgin French and German to some kind of human community and warmth. In *Paisan,* the elementary nature of the struggle to communicate is further underlined by the fact that most of the Sicilian episode is shot in an unobtrusive long take, at night and in an ancient tower, whose rough texture is strongly suggestive of a cave. It is almost as though some primitive ritual of connection were here being rehearsed, as though human history were beginning all over again. (The image of the primitive cave will reappear at the final climactic moments of the next episode, where it seems to stand for a symbolic descent into hell.)[8]

Closely connected with this preoccupation with communication is what might be called the humanity theme, for the horrors of war, Rossellini shows, also lead people to treat each other as objects. That is clearly the case in the first two episodes of this film. Carmela is little more than a detection device, employed for the purpose of avoiding German land mines, and as far as she is concerned Joe and his friends are no better than the Germans, as she clearly says at one point. Yet once they have communicated, their humanity is revealed to one another and they can no longer treat each other as objects. By shooting at him, the German effectively turns Joe back into an object—literally so, of course, when he dies. It is this that Carmela is reacting against when she later shoots the German soldier in order to revenge, suicidally, this American soldier she hardly knows. In the Naples episode, the shoeshine boy is thoroughly taken in by the black soldier's singing and his incomprehensible stories; responding to his humanity, the boy can no longer consider him an object to sell. This is why he warns him that if he falls asleep, he will rob him. Once sleep cuts off the flow of humanizing language, the soldier returns to object status, and the boy, with little choice given the exigencies of war, does what he must.

Rossellini wants to find a latent humanity, and thus a basic sameness or essence, deep down in all of his characters, but one division that seems irreconcilable is that of gender. As in *Open City,* the women of *Paisan* are seen as passive creatures, those upon whom history acts, and those, therefore, who history makes to suffer. Francesca, in the Roman episode, can only be sexually used by men or wait for a man who will never come. Those women who *do* act have no political opinions and act solely from whatever their "nature" calls them to do. Thus, in the Sicilian episode, Carmela tells Joe, "You're all alike, you, the Germans, the Fascists! All you people with guns! You're all the same!" But a short while later, she shoots a German soldier because "her" Joe has been killed, even though she knows it will mean her own death. Her act is totally selfless, almost primevally ritualistic. Similarly, Harriet of the Florence episode will brave the most dangerous fighting in order to reach her man. Thus, when she and Massimo are told that they cannot use the Galleria passage (which runs above the Ponte Vecchio, from the Pitti Palace to the Palazzo Vecchio), for fear that the Germans might discover it and thus endanger them all, Massimo hesitates. He is just as desperate to get to his family as Harriet is to get to Lupo, but he seems on the point of giving up because of the possible danger to the others. In spite of his aroused emotions, in other words, as a man he will listen to reason. Precisely at this point, however, Harriet impetuously plunges headlong into the Galleria, and Massimo has no choice but to join her. Rossellini clearly admires these gestures, which he sees as manifestations of a kind of direct, intuitive naturalness, in spite of the fact that Carmela's causes her death and Harriet's should actually be condemned. It must also be said in his defense that Rossellini sees women, for all their political ignorance, or perhaps *because* of it, as the inveterate enemies of war. Again, they seem to have a natural inclination against war that most men stupidly repress. In any case, the nurse figure Harriet enacts is quite a step beyond an earlier Rossellini nurse in *La nave bianca,* a passive, pure little charmer spouting nationalist slogans about duty and honor. When Rossellini begins making films with Ingrid Bergman in 1949 (and when, due partially to the exigencies of the star system, the female figure moves to center stage), she becomes a richly complex, full human being, motivated by more than the intuitively "feminine."

Another aspect of this question raised by Rossellini's women resides on the symbolic level. Armes believes that Harriet is meant symbolically to stand for the Allies who are powerless to help the Italians sort out their internal differences,[9] but this is rather too mechanically literal a view and seems unwarranted. Carmela, on the other hand, clearly seems to stand for Italy. At the end of the Sicilian sequence we realize that she has been the victim of both the Americans and the Germans, for neither understands what she has done or why. The irony is especially bitter, of course, in terms of the Americans' lack of comprehension. In representing the fate of her country, Carmela continues, in effect, Rossellini's exculpation of Italy and Italian guilt that he began in *Open City*. Like the women in these two films, Italy is the powerless, dependent victim who, despite occasional outbursts of primordial passion, is acted upon and brutalized by others—the men of Germany, the United States, and England. Not a very flattering role, perhaps, but certainly better than that assigned to Italy's ally, Germany. Thus, most Italians depicted in the film seem more than anything else to be bystanders, perhaps with the exception of the partisans in Florence and on the Po (though the latter, significantly, are led by an American); for the most part they are seen favorably or at worst neutrally. We do see some bad Italians—the Fascist sympathizer in Sicily and the Fascists killed in Florence—but they are marginal figures, either buffoons or empty faces, who disappear from the screen in a matter of moments. The Germans, on the other hand, largely absent through most of the film (though decidedly present in terms of the havoc and misery they have wreaked), are portrayed in the final episode on the Po in the same brutally negative way that they were in *Open City*.

There are those who have accused Rossellini of overtly playing up to the new regime, the Americans. Robert Warshow, in particular, has mounted a distorted but provocative list:

> The six episodes can be plausibly interpreted as representing the fantasies of the eternally defeated as he tries anxiously to read his fate in the countenance of a new master. In Sicily, the Italian girl is rejected: the American does not know that she was really his friend, and the one who could testify for her is dead. In Naples, the American finds his heart overflowing with pity: he *understands;* he, too, has suffered. In Rome, the Italian girl is rejected again: she is a whore; she has not waited. But in Florence the American nurse presses the dying partisan's head to her breast; and in the monastery, the arrogant victor is humbled before the simple goodness and wisdom of those who have chosen to exempt themselves from history. . . . Finally, on the Po, the American is at last both loved and loving, directing the Italians in their struggle and then losing his life in a protest against their murder.[10]

The British critic M. T. McGregor, however, felt at the time that the film was actually *anti*-American: "These strange new barbarians are taken apart gently,

like a mechanical toy, to see how they tick. And here they are: indifferent, obtuse, kindly savages."[11]

More important to the great majority of European critics has been Rossellini's overall depiction of history and human possibility. The terms of the debate,
as might be expected, are similar to those of *Open City*, with Armando Borrelli,
for example, bewailing Rossellini's apparent "need to express the fundamental
tragicness of things, their lack of logical order, the impossibility of understanding the why of events." He even reads the ending of the Po episode as a mockery
of the ideals of the Resistance when the voice-over, announcing the final victory,
clashes ironically with the shot of the partisans being pushed into the water by
the Germans.[12] Similarly, Freddy Buache complains that, in spite of the film's
brilliance, the facts of the case are not presented in their political, social, and
economic contexts; nor does Rossellini choose to depict the class struggle. Echoing a common theme, Buache accuses Rossellini of forgetting that the Resistance
was also a *social* revolt that was braked by the bourgeoisie.[13] But since Rossellini
was rather unabashedly bourgeois, Buache is obviously asking for the impossible. There would have been no reason for the filmmaker to choose to highlight
the class struggle, since he never considered it, as would Marxist orthodoxy, the
primary motive force of history. In some ways Rossellini is the archetype of the
man depicted by Roland Barthes in "Myth Today," the brilliant essay that
serves as coda to his *Mythologies*. This bourgeois has so thoroughly naturalized
his contingent status that he speaks in essences; he takes himself, his opinions,
and his worldview as natural, and thus not particularly susceptible to being
individuated. He is involved in an "ex-nomination" process that serves to cloak
history and arbitrary conventionality in the guise of the natural.[14] In all this, of
course, Rossellini was merely acting like everyone else he knew.

Thus, these critics are right when they accuse Rossellini of forgetting history.
As in *Open City*, it is the very specificity of event in *Paisan* that can mislead the
casual spectator into thinking this film is historical in any analytic sense. For,
though Rossellini always deeply enmeshes his characters in a precise environment, both temporally and spatially, what he wants to portray, for better or
worse, is that which transcends this specificity, what is eternal, what is essential
in man. It must also be pointed out, however, that Rossellini's Marxist detractors—in spite of their own (correct, to my mind) view of man as conditioned by
history—are not attacking essentialism per se, but rather Rossellini's view of
what man's essence is. Many of them would simply put another essence in its
place. Robert Warshow provides a better way into the film, I think, when he
frankly describes its fascination with defeat and death, contrasting it favorably
with American films rather than wishing that Rossellini had been more optimistic:

> American culture demands victory; every situation must somehow be made an
> occasion for constructive activity. The characters and events in serious Ameri-
> can films are given a specifically "universal" or "representative" meaning in
> order to conceal the fact that there are situations in which victory is not pos-
> sible. The idea survives—that is a victory; the man dies—that is a defeat; the
> "GI" is created to conceal the man's death.
>
> Rossellini neither requires nor dreams of victory; indeed, it is only defeat

that has meaning for him—defeat is his "universal." . . . From this hopeless-
ness—too inactive to be called despair—Rossellini gains his greatest virtue as
an artist: the feeling for particularity. In the best parts of *Paisan,* it is always
the man who dies, and no idea survives him unless it is the idea of death itself.[15]

Another way of describing this feeling for particularity is to see it as part of
the ongoing dialectic between Rossellini's avowed search for unity and the
necessarily discontinuous particulars through which this unity must always
finally manifest itself, and which thus always negate it at the same time. The
film's famous realism might also be considered in these terms. The paradoxical
dynamic of the Hollywood movie is that we are meant to believe it and take it
as "real" while watching it, at least on one level, but that when we consider it
abstractly as part of a generic whole, it becomes, due to its basis in conventions
of representation, the very definition of unreality and artificiality. "That only
happens in the movies," we tell ourselves (except in the theater). On the other
hand, any film that is perceived as being unconventional in its narrative, as
violating accepted codes of realism, is often seen, again paradoxically, to be
more "real." Because its disjunctures continually reveal its constructed, fictional
status to us, thus preventing the Coleridgean "willing suspension of disbelief" or
an easy identification with the characters, sophisticated spectators, at least, can
come to see the unconventional representation as somehow more like "real life,"

Partisans bury a dead comrade in the Po episode of *Paisan.*

that is, disjointed, confused, unable to penetrate the exterior of the other, undirected, multiple, and incomplete. As I indicated briefly in the previous chapter, the realism of *Paisan* is startling precisely because it pushes outward from commonly accepted notions of realism (which in fact are constituted by highly stylized conventions) toward the inclusion of what I called the "represented real." The self-reflexivity that is an important by-product of this operation also points inevitably toward a critique of the conventions of realism (and, thus, a critique of neorealism itself) that Rossellini will fully develop in subsequent films.

In *Paisan* this tension between the codes of realism and the real is present everywhere. Perhaps its most obvious manifestation is the fact that the film is composed of six episodes that are linked in various ways, as we have seen, primarily in their presentation of themselves as a unity under the guise of a revealed essence of humanity, but that also stubbornly retain their status as diverse fragments. Similarly, as Bazin pointed out, the film resembles a collection of modern short stories, and was indeed the first film to do so. (A short story collection is by definition a unity of differences.) What Bazin neglects to add, however, is that precisely what makes the episodes so narratively unconventional—their quick, unexpected climaxes that come at the end of each story, thus omitting the traditional denouement of both conventional film and fiction—is what links them most closely to the specifically modern form of the short story, with its accent on the sudden, climactic end, with or without the character (or the reader) coming to any moral realization or Joycean epiphany. Adding to this connection is Rossellini's strong use of irony, that staple of twentieth-century fiction. This is the pattern:

FIRST EPISODE: Climax comes at very end, but epiphany is denied to characters; irony reigns.

SECOND EPISODE: Climax at end, epiphany achieved through irony at level of character.

THIRD EPISODE: Repeats the first.

FOURTH EPISODE: Realization of fact of death is climax, but no real epiphany, because the knowledge is empty.

FIFTH EPISODE: Climax and epiphany (in lighter key) at end.

SIXTH EPISODE: Climax at end; unclear whether characters experience epiphany, or only the audience, as in first and third; closure comes from outside the story, through overview and voice of history.

The effect of this narrative schema is once again to dedramatize the episodes and thus to cause them to be perceived as more real and less conventionally realistic at the same time, primarily by holding off the "drama"—or at least the more blatant moments of emotion—until the very end. The audience barely has time to experience an emotion even momentarily before the map of Italy and the officious newsreel voice are thrust back at them. Nevertheless, it would be a mistake to think of this film as totally dedramatized and unemotional, for the endings, brief as they may sometimes be, are often quite moving. A key factor at work here is music, though its effects are, as usual, relatively unnoticed. On several occasions, in fact, the music indicates to us precisely what we are supposed to feel (in other words, just like any other film). In the Naples episode, for example, everything looks so completely miserable and ruined throughout the entire episode that an American audience, at any rate, would not initially know that the cavelike dwellings that the soldier enters at the end are to be taken as any more deprived than anything else that has been seen. But when he does enter, the tragic musical theme prepares us to read and react properly to the visual images we will soon be shown. There are, of course, many long passages in which all music has been suspended and where we must make our own way, emotionally and intellectually. But to hold, as Gian Luigi Rondi does in *Cinema italiano oggi,* that this film is a "dry documentary," "without tears," in which Rossellini trusts the emotion of pure facts, is to miss how subtly—and conventionally—music and other elements work to produce and guide emotion.[16]

The film's primary mode, however, especially compared with the standard Hollywood product, is certainly dedramatized—even if "impurely" so—and its workings are complex. On one level, the brevity of each episode effectively prevents a traditional viewer identification with the characters. Yet, at the same time, a paradoxical increase in what might be called empathy or, better, sympathy, arises. As in Hitchcock's *The Wrong Man,* the avoidance of "normal" emotional moments (in other words, moments normally heightened in the classic Hollywood film) actually allows the spectator a greater sense of sympathetic involvement, but in a way that is somehow more liberating than the usual emotional identification that is fostered. Thus, while the spectator is not subjected to the roller-coaster ride of predictable emotion because the narrative material has been distanced, at the same time the realization of the character's plight (seen as other, not as self) is all the more powerful. In the Hitchcock film, for example, the low-key style of the acting, the apparently simple mise-en-scène, and the editing somehow combine to make the spectator feel even more strongly what it must be like to be wrongfully locked up; in *Paisan,* these same factors add up, say, in the Florence episode, to the overwhelming realization of how a war can turn even the simplest of tasks, like getting across town, into a monumental effort. This may have something to do with the lowering of each episode's emotional pitch to the point that the spectator *sees* (rather than gets "inside the skin of") a common man or woman—like him or her—in a difficulty that is not emphasized in a movielike fashion, nor put into the kind of emotional shorthand that eliminates everyday, lifelike, even distracting details in favor of nonlifelike realistic drama.

Another site of the confrontation between the represented real and the realistic in this film is in the documentary footage that Rossellini has incorporated into the fictional text, especially at the beginning of episodes. The contrast between the two is not as great as in American war films of the period, and sometimes only a sharp eye can tell where one leaves off and the other begins. Though the intention seems to have been to enhance the believability of the ensuing fiction, as in the Hollywood film, the documentary footage also continues to present itself *as such,* partly at least because it is so directly presenting itself *as past:* it is accompanied by an explanatory map and a businesslike voice-over that explains everything in past historical rather than present, individually dramatic terms. This tension reaches its zenith at the very end of the film when the voice-over says *"This happened* in the winter of 1944. A few weeks later, spring came to Italy and the war in Europe was declared over," thus further insisting, retrospectively, on the fictionality and "constructedness" of all that has just been offered to us in the present tense.[17]

The "acting" and speech of the American soldiers, which often seem to bother American audiences especially, are also relevant here. It is obviously true that the soldiers do not sound right; but in my view this is because they sound like *real* soldiers (or as we might imagine real soldiers sound). Their voices and their barely functional "acting," in fact, stand starkly opposed to the slickness of the code of what is thought of as realistic in the conventional cinema. The paradigmatic case is the voice of "Joe from Jersey" in the first episode. His voice is thin, reedy, and thoroughly "unconvincing," precisely, I would argue, because it is real. It does not sound like the voice of an actor—smooth, deep, and above all, clear—in other words, that which we ironically take to be realistic once we have put ourselves under the operation of the code. Nor does his awkward dialogue sound "believable." In real life, of course, words and sentences are unheard or misunderstood, people mumble and repeat themselves, and communication turns out to be a surprisingly inefficient process. What we take to be realistic on the screen, however, shows few of these imperfections.[18]

Another version of this dynamic is manifested in the sexual tension generated by Carmela. As Robert Warshow has noticed, Carmela's body is "to an American eye almost repellent in its lack of physical charm, and at the same time disturbing in its persistent suggestion that charm is irrelevant."[19] When we are involved in a conventional Hollywood-style picture, we unconsciously know (at least we did in 1946) that no matter how sexy its star might seem, there is a limit beyond which she will not go. We know, in other words, that her sexuality will necessarily be something faked. However, when the spectator (I am necessarily going to have to limit myself to what I take to be a male perspective here) is confronted with what seems to be a real woman on the screen, an unglamorous nonprofessional, a subliminal sense of risk is at some level reestablished. Though one knows, of course, that the director, the distributors, the theater owners, and a hundred others have all intervened to insure, finally, that the rough edges of experience that may have been captured in the film are mostly rubbed smooth, nevertheless it seems to me that the very presence of the girl—slovenly and directly sensual in a way no real actress would ever chance—gives an edge to her encounter with Joe that makes the film seem bracingly out of control.

Formal elements such as camera movement, lighting, and the mise-en-scène also work here in the direction of reality and away from Hollywood realism. In the last episode, for example, the faces of the partisans are often so thoroughly obscured that we become consciously aware that we cannot see them, and thus we momentarily escape the grip of the film's narrative. In a shot near the end of this episode, Rossellini breaks the rules of conventional cinematography when he "shows" us the captured partisans virtually in the dark; the entire sense of the sequence comes about through the anguished conjunction of their mumbled despair and the utter blackness that surrounds and engulfs them. Even more important in this regard is the editing. In the first episode, for example, as soon as Joe shows his face by his lighter, the film cuts abruptly to a group of German

The sensuality of the real: Carmela (Carmela Sazio), the Sicilian girl of the first episode of *Paisan*.

soldiers; the effect is startling, for this is the first time we have seen them in the film. Without the least hesitation or dramatic buildup, the German shoots, and the film cuts back with equal abruptness to a shot of Joe being hit by the bullet. (The effect of this very brief shot of Joe is heightened by being in slow motion.) In the Florence episode, the famous sequence of the killing of the Fascists seems so powerfully real precisely because it happens so fast: they are dragged into and out of the frame and summarily shot without the slightest fanfare, all in a matter of a few seconds. The same thing happens when Harriet is suddenly told of Lupo's death. Not a moment is spent on preparations for or reactions to either event, and we take this as somehow more lifelike because it is not what we see in conventionally "realistic films," where the maximum emotional effect is usually wrung from each image and event.[20]

On one level, then, the film seems to be striving for a unity of theme and effect, as we saw earlier, while at the same time recalcitrant elements push toward the "real" and toward fragmentation and dispersal, ineluctably revealing unreconcilable differences that obviate any kind of final, univocal reading of the film. The most problematic episode, which might serve as a paradigm of how difference works here, is in fact, the one that seems the tamest—the episode in the monastery. Critics have had great difficulty reconciling this segment with the overall structure and themes that seem to be operating in the film, and have tried in vain to naturalize its perplexing sentiment. The problem is that its themes clash in "impermissible" ways, for the reading that the episode seems to demand does not correspond with traditional views of brotherhood, kindness, or even good sense. The innocent, unworldly *fraticelli*, stunned by the presence of two lost souls in their midst—a Protestant minister and a Jewish rabbi—offer up their painful fast to God for the conversion of the heathens' souls. On the one hand, this gesture of concern for one's fellow man, to the point of denying oneself, is obviously praiseworthy, and Rossellini has his American Catholic priest spokesman end the sequence by praising it. But is he not also thereby praising intolerance? Some critics have thought that, in spite of the American's kind words for the selfless idealism of the "innocent" brothers at the end of the episode, the moral is precisely what the other American chaplains marvel at earlier, in the briefest of comments, lightly passed over: how can these monks judge real men and worldly right and wrong if they are so utterly isolated from it all? If this reading is to be accepted, however, we would have to see the episode in quite radical narrative terms. For the thematically privileged position we normally assign to the main character's speech at the end of a narrative sequence, when all attention is solemnly focused on him or her and the rhetoric of language, image, and music continues to underline the moment's importance, would have to be completely overturned. A casual remark dropped halfway through the sequence would have to be privileged over the highly foregrounded, final dramatic scene toward which everything has been moving, and I do not think that what is hermeneutically at stake here has been truly understood. Pio Baldelli and other critics, on the other hand, have struggled to decide exactly what the director "means" in this episode, but in so doing, they have revealed that any approach that grounds itself on a presumably self-present and consistent artistic intentionality will ultimately prove fruitless. When the attempt finally breaks down, as it inevitably must, these critics find the whole episode absurd or confused because, in effect, it is not unified. A better reading might be to admit that the irreconcilable interpretations cannot, in fact, be reconciled, despite the uncomfortable lack of closure that results.[21]

Final editing chores unfortunately had to be left to Renzo, according to his later account, because of the sudden tragic death of Rossellini's firstborn, eight-year-old son while on a visit to his grandmother, who was living in Spain. The crew rushed to finish the film in time for the Venice film festival, where, again according to Renzo, it went virtually unnoticed. In his version of the story, the reception of the film in Italy was subdued until its great success in France and the United States made local critics sit up and take notice. As we saw with *Open City*, however, one wonders if the neglect of the film could not also have come about through various material reasons unconnected with the proverbial inability of whatever locals to perceive the genius residing in their midst until that genius is certified by an outside world.

The phenomenal effect of the film on a subsequent generation of film directors is much easier to determine. Fellini, who became quite close to Rossellini during the filming (and who, with the help of cameraman Otello Martelli, shot some scenes himself, such as the one of the Germans walking near the Baptistery in Florence, as well as the passage of the carboy of water under gunfire in the same episode—two very strong images, in fact) said later that in *Paisan* "Rossellini taught me humility in living. . . . By looking at things with the love and communion that are established from one moment to another between a person and myself, between an object and myself, I understood that the cinema could fill my life, helping me to find a meaning in existence."[22]

The Taviani brothers, Paolo and Vittorio, whose *Padre padrone* Rossellini would vociferously champion at Cannes in the last few days of his life, had this reaction when they wandered into a theater one day after school:

> They were showing *Paisan*. Everybody in the half-empty room was protesting the film. The public was rejecting what for us two was a shock: to find on the screen that which we had just left on the street. We finally ended up getting in a fight with some of the spectators. Our decision was made: we had understood what we wanted to do with our lives. The cinema.[23]

Ermanno Olmi speaks of having a similar reaction, and when Gillo Pontecorvo saw *Paisan* in Paris, he was so excited that he gave up everything else, went out and bought a sixteen-millimeter Paillard camera, and began shooting his own documentaries. But perhaps the most fateful reaction was that of a beautiful young actress, then at the pinnacle of success in Hollywood. Ingrid Bergman had already been overwhelmed by *Open City* when she first saw it in 1948, but imagined that the film had been merely a flash in the pan. Then, later that year, while in New York to do a radio show, she watched *Paisan,* all alone:

> So he *had* made another great movie! And nobody had ever heard of him! I looked down the theater. It was almost empty. What was going on? This man had made two great films and he was playing to empty houses. I think it was at that moment the idea came to me. Maybe if this man had somebody who was a *name* playing for him, then maybe people would come and see his pictures. . . . And this immense feeling grew inside me that movies like this simply *must* be seen by millions, not only by the Italians but by millions all over the world. So, I thought, I am going to write him a letter.[24]

This letter, to which Rossellini responded instantly, was to change both their lives drastically. But before we can consider the brilliant, if troubled, "Bergman-era" of Rossellini's career, we must first attend to the complex films that immediately followed *Paisan*.

8

Germany, Year Zero
(1947)

Buoyed by the delayed, but substantial, acclaim accorded to *Open City* and *Paisan*, Rossellini next decided to internationalize his subject by shifting its focus from Italy to Germany. As with his previous films, an urge to document a particular reality and to bear witness to a given state of affairs is evident in *Germania, anno zero* (*Germany, Year Zero*), but now Rossellini also wants to pose a particular question: "The Germans were human beings like everybody else. What could have led them to this disaster?"[1] The answer, as in *L'uomo dalla croce*, is a corrupt *idea*—though now the idea is of the Right rather than the Left—an idea that, exactly like the communism of *L'uomo dalla croce*, encourages "the abandoning of humility for the cult of heroism, the exaltation of strength rather than weakness, pride against simplicity."[2] In the earlier film, Christianity was explicitly offered as an antidote to the poisonous idea of communism, but in *Germany, Year Zero*, there seems to be no counterforce available to match the despair caused by nazism, the war it made necessary, and, on a personal level, the death of Rossellini's son. The hope of the earlier films, as well as their benevolent priests and monks, through whom this hope was articulated, is now completely missing. In the films to come, like *The Miracle, Stromboli*, and *Francesco*, Christianity will be reinstated, but only partially, and certainly not in its institutional forms.

After getting clearance in Paris from the French occupying authorities to film in Berlin, Rossellini drove alone to the city, without any particular story in mind, some time in March 1947 to join Carlo Lizzani, one of the screenwriters on the project. He spoke of his initial impressions of the city in "Dix ans de cinéma," written in 1955 for *Cahiers du cinéma:*

The city was deserted, the gray of the sky seemed to run in the streets and, from the height of a man, you could look out over all the roofs; in order to find the streets under the ruins, they had cleared away and piled up the debris; in the cracks of the asphalt, grass had started to grow. Silence reigned, and each noise, in counterpoint to it, underlined it even more; the bittersweet odor of rotting organic material constituted a solid wall through which one had to pass; you floated over Berlin. I went up a wide avenue; at the horizon, there was a single sign of life, a large yellow sign. Slowly I got closer to this immense sign placed on a stone cube in front of a store with a minuscule facade, and I read "Bazaar Israel." The first Jews had returned to Germany, and that was really the symbol of the end of Nazism.[3]

In the meantime, Lizzani had been gathering information from the Communist party in Berlin on the condition of German youth, since the idea of having a young boy as protagonist had already been settled on.[4] Rossellini was already a celebrity by that time, according to Lizzani, and so their work was undertaken in an atmosphere of constant receptions given them by the Americans, the French, and the Russians.

Finally, we ended up with about fifteen pages in hand which, however, were fifteen very precise pages. Each sheet contained one sequence, and each sequence was extremely clear. For example: "A horse falls, people gather around the dead horse, quarter it, each one takes a piece of meat, the child sees the scene, passes by and goes away." So, this great scene was actually written in three lines, but they were three very precise lines. Rossellini had this ability to concentrate and to synthesize his story in a few lines and in very clear scenes.[5]

During their stay in Germany, all of the exteriors were shot, but to save money the company was soon moved to Rome, where the Berlin interiors were recreated in the studio. The result was a clash of realism and artificiality, much more obvious than in *Open City* that has bothered many critics over the years but also provides for a resonant self-reflexivity. In any case, the fifteen principal members of the cast were moved to Rome, despite enormous bureaucratic difficulties. But a two-month delay in shooting because of financial problems and, according to Lizzani, "an emotional storm with Magnani," who had become Rossellini's mistress, led to unforeseen problems. During the month that they were in Rome, the starving German cast had begun to eat so much pasta that they grew immense: "The pieces didn't go together on the editing table, because the tall and thin gentleman walking the streets in Berlin, and approaching a door, when the door was opened, was another person, well fed, and with the face of well-being." Filming was suspended for two weeks while the Germans went on a diet.[6]

The opening montagelike sequences of the film, when we first meet Edmund, its twelve-year-old protagonist, make very clear, with a minimum of dialogue, just how deep the city's misery really was. At home, the situation is equally grim: Edmund's father is sickly and unable to work; his older brother Karlheinz, a Nazi who fought the Allied troops until the very end, is afraid of being sent to a concentration camp if he turns himself in, and thus is ineligible for a ration card; and Eva, Edmund's older sister, a "nice" girl who tries to keep the family together, is perilously close to losing her honor in her nightly encounters with the Allied troops, like the young *romana* of *Paisan*. They manage to stay alive only because the father has an attack and is taken to a hospital to recover, thus becoming one less mouth to feed, and for the first time getting some proper food for himself. Edmund goes to his former schoolteacher, an unreconstructed Nazi and homosexual, for advice on how to keep his father in the hospital; in a moment of impatience the teacher tells Edmund that he must accept his father's condition because the strong are meant to survive and the weak to perish. This remnant of a corrupt Nazi philosophy, coupled with the father's complaints that it would have been better for the family if he had died, lead Edmund to poison him, thinking that he is doing the right thing. When the enormity of his deed sinks in, after a superb and justly famous final sequence of his long, nearly wordless wanderings around Berlin, he throws himself out of a window and dies.

At a certain level the film obviously revolves around the archetypal theme of its young protagonist's passage from childhood to adulthood. But in the Berlin of 1947, the familiar rites de passage have become speeded up and horribly distorted, and Edmund is simply too young to shoulder the adult burdens, both physical and psychological, that are placed upon him. Though this twelve-year-old finds himself the sole support of a family of adults, his natural inclinations toward hopscotch and other aimless play continue to pull him back to a childlike state that is irrevocably disappearing. His sister at one point calls him her "baby,"[7] and his father insists that "he's still a child" and that his brief stint as a gravedigger (which we learn of in a lugubrious early scene) "wasn't any kind of work for a boy your age" (pp. 362–63). At the end of the picture, when its sad work is nearly accomplished, Karlheinz, finally assuming his proper authority, says, "Who do you think you are anyway? You're still a child." By this point, considering all that Edmund has been through, the statement strikes us as ridiculous, and the youth bitterly replies on his way permanently out the door, "How come you didn't think of that before, when I had to go out and get food for everybody here?" (p. 448)

Besides bearing the responsibility for feeding his family, Edmund is exposed to multiple corruptions that Rossellini clearly finds upsetting. He overhears his landlord's hints that his sister is whoring for the Allied soldiers she meets in a dance hall each night. She is not, in fact, but finds it necessary to be friendly at least, in order to cadge the scarce cigarettes that have become Berlin's new currency. The somewhat older teenagers with whom Edmund increasingly becomes involved—little better than rootless thieves—are cynically casual about sex and jeeringly force their young "moll" on him in a powerful, degrading scene.

The most grievous assailant against Edmund's innocence, of course, is the homosexual former schoolteacher, Herr Enning, who openly paws Edmund in a sequence whose effect may vary according to the spectator's own sexual attitudes, but which Rossellini obviously means to horrify. Enning has become a procurer of young boys for the former Nazi general with whom he lives, and his apartment reeks of moral corruption. For Rossellini this individual sexual depravity is emblematic of the wider philosophical and moral depravity known as nazism, and thus looks forward to the ugly sexual allegory of Pasolini's *Salò*. Ingrid, the lesbian Nazi of *Open City* functions in the same way, as we have seen, and even

Enning's apartment recalls the Nazi headquarters of that earlier film. Again, it is the *idea* of nazism that so obsesses Rossellini, for it is this corrupt idea that has led to all the specific individual corruption that fills this film from beginning to end. Here, the situation is even worse because Enning is a *teacher,* and as such is in a privileged, and for the later Rossellini, nearly sacred, position, from which he is able to inflict his poisonous notions on the most vulnerable.[8] He never actually tells Edmund to kill his father, of course, but this result is the logical conclusion of Enning's "philosophy," that same philosophy of the strong over the weak that Rossellini attacked in the Communists of *L'uomo dalla croce:*

> ENNING: That's how life is. We were molded in other times. You're afraid Papa'll die? Learn from Nature: the weak are always eliminated by the strong. We must have the courage to sacrifice the weak. This is a law that not even Man can escape. What counts in a defeat like ours is to survive. (*He distractedly fondles Edmund's neck.*) Come, Edmund, don't be a goose! You must recognize your responsibilities. Goodbye (p. 428).

Enning seems to be a man caught up, like Shakespeare's Brutus, with his own metaphors and does not really mean, in a specific sense, what Edmund thinks he means. As Edmund is still only a child, however, he is unable to distinguish rhetorical from literal language, and later, when his father moans that he is a burden on the family, Edmund takes him at his word.

Nor is the teacher the only Nazi influence on Edmund, for these pernicious ideas have penetrated the entire society. Thus, the landlord Rademaker early in the film calls Edmund's father a "useless old man" and an "old mummy," who he threatens to "put . . . away if he doesn't kick the bucket soon" (pp. 361, 360). Later he asks Edmund "When's [your father] going to drop dead and give us a little peace?" (p. 415). Similarly Edmund's cowardly brother Karlheinz keeps insisting that life is hopeless and that he should commit suicide. Nazi philosophy has also been responsible for the corruption of the natural bonds found within the family as we learn in a passing comment of Enning's: "Remember, Edmund, your father once handed in a forged certificate so you wouldn't have to join the Hitler Jugend, but you told me right away it was forged, because you knew what your duty was. (*He touches Edmund's cheek.*) And I ought to have reported him to the Party . . . and the reason I didn't was because I'm fond of you" (p. 386). This contrast between natural affection and artificial Nazi values, already supercharged in the context of sexual perversion, is reinforced gesturally when Edmund visits his father in the hospital after seeing Enning. There, the father caresses Edmund's arms in the same way that Enning has, and kisses him, as if to stress that the greatest evil is the warping of that which is most natural and innocent. We are also meant to see Edmund's situation universalized. Thus, at one point while they are waiting in line, one woman tells another of a boy who is "only ten, and he makes more money on the black market than the whole family put together" (p. 377).

In the deprivation caused by the war, Rossellini implies, humankind's natural inclination toward *coralità* is threatened. When the situation is further complicated by the infection of nazism, it becomes even less likely, and in this

Nazism as corruption, again: Edmund (Edmund Moeschke) watches as his father (Ernst Pittschau) drinks the poisoned milk he has prepared for him in *Germany, Year Zero* (1947).

film any possibility of group solidarity is utterly destroyed. Eva at one point tries to convince her depressed brother Karlheinz to have hope—as we have seen, a key commodity for Rossellini—but later, and more convincingly, she asserts, "I don't believe in being helped by other people. Everybody has to help themselves these days" (p. 370). Edmund is continually rebuffed, for no apparent reason, by the other children he comes in contact with, and when he turns for community to a roving band of young thieves, their leader tricks him by selling him a fake bar of soap made from a block of wood. What surfaces is an existentialist vision of individual alienation, an emphasis Rossellini will maintain through the desolate period of the Bergman films, with the exception of the luminous *coralità* of the microcosmic society of *Francesco*.

Rossellini's attack on the Nazi idea continues in the fantasmagoric scene that follows Edmund's first visit to Herr Enning. Afraid of being caught himself, Enning gives Edmund a phonographic recording of one of Hitler's speeches to sell to the occupying Allied troops who now have the leisure to sightsee. The scene is especially striking because it takes place amid the rubble of the Reichs Chancellory and when Edmund plays the record on a portable phonograph for the benefit of two British soldiers, the effect of Hitler's voice is uncanny. Throughout the whole of the untranslated speech, the camera swings widely over the ruins, giving the lie to the puffed-up militancy of the Führer's words. His voice resounds through the debris-filled hallways as we cut to an old man walking hand-in-hand with a young boy (clearly symbolizing Germany's past and future). They marvel, though quietly, at the sudden reappearance of the familiar voice, and because it is both disembodied and incomprehensible to us, we understand it more abstractly as representing, again, a pernicious idea. The scene is especially effective because Rossellini foregoes any conventional attempt to explain to these two characters where the voice is coming from. They are just as baffled concerning its specific provenance when we last see them, and thus a symbolic point about the invisible pervasiveness of this corrupt philosophy (and its causal relationship to the ubiquitous ruins) is clearly made.

Despite the insistence by some phenomenologists that the film's themes are absolutely "unpremeditated," and by Marxist critics that the film contains no analysis, it is obvious, in other words, that *Germany, Year Zero* is a *film-à-thèse*. This can even be seen in its opening legend, which for some reason does not exist in the American release print, but which is reprinted in the English translation of the script. The legend further solidifies the link with Rossellini's earlier films and his partiality for the Christian idea:

> When an ideology strays from the eternal laws of morality and of Christian charity, which form the basis of men's lives, it must end as criminal madness.
> It contaminates even the natural prudence of a child, who is swept along from one horrendous crime to another, equally grave, in which, with the ingenuousness of innocence, he thinks to find release from guilt (p. 353).

Since the camera has been panning the ruins of Berlin from the opening moment, even before the appearance of the legend, as well as after, an obvious cause-and-effect relationship is again visually implied. In a sense, then, Rossellini's original question concerning German motivation has already been answered, and the rest of the film is simply its illustration. Just after the legend comes a voice-over, which is contained in the American version of the film:

> This film was shot in Berlin in the summer of 1947. It is intended to be simply an objective, true-to-life picture of this enormous, half-destroyed city, in which three and a half million people are carrying on a frightful, desperate existence almost without realizing it. They live in tragedy as if it were their natural element, but out of exhaustion, not through strength of mind or faith. This film is not an act of accusation against the German people, nor yet a defense of them. It is simply a presentation of the facts. But if anyone who has seen the story of Edmund Koeler comes to realize that something must be done, that German children must be taught to love life again, then the efforts of those who made this film will have been amply rewarded (pp. 353–54).

The first thing we notice in this voice-over editorial is the concern with fixing an exactly specific time and an exactly specific place, common Rossellinian interests. Also, the naive insistence on the objectivity of the film—"simply a presentation of the facts," as though it is ever possible not to have some point of view on these "facts," which helps *create* them—manifests a particular blindness with which, as we shall see, Rossellini was to have recurring bouts all his life. Even here, however, Rossellini blatantly contradicts himself with the obvious partisan-ship of the last sentence.

The poignancy of the intertitle also indicates how depressed Rossellini had become at this point in his life, his sensibilities rubbed raw by personal and public tragedy. The effect, unsurprisingly, is to accentuate the film's dark ex-pressionism, the evidence for which has been repressed by most realist critics (who also begin to speak at this time of Rossellini's "crisis"). Expressionism is a notoriously problematical term, of course; here it means something like styli-zation of acting, lighting, or narrative, overt symbolization—in short, anything that calls attention to the film as artifice and tends to work against the easy illusionism of the traditional codes of realism discussed in earlier chapters. In the larger scheme of Rossellini's work, the term is related to his continual in-sistence on the importance of fantasy and the imagination, especially evident in films like *La macchina ammazzacattivi,* despite all efforts to make him out as a realist *tout court.*

The expressionist elements of *Germany, Year Zero*—which will also predomi-nate in Rossellini's next film, *Una voce umana,* and will reappear even more strongly in *Fear*—can first of all be seen in the obvious clash between the ex-teriors and the interiors that was spoken of earlier. In addition, there is the film's often overt symbolism. The emblematic old man and young child, as we have seen, are thematically functional, being placed before us without any special concern for what would be most believable. The film is also populated with baroquely decorated yet dried-up fountains that obviously stand for the sterility of nazism and the present state of German culture. Trams operate the same way: the film opens and closes with the noise of their passing, and Edmund is forever jumping on and off them—well beyond the needs of the narrative—suggesting the absolute aimlessness of his life, in constant motion but never get-ting anywhere. Furthermore, the first place we see Edmund is at work in a ceme-tery digging graves, which suggests his personal end, and even the ubiquitous ruined cityscape carries a consistent symbolic charge that goes well beyond *l'effet de réel.* At many points in his long walks in the city, Edmund is overwhelmed by barely standing buildings that emphasize his vulnerability and isolation and strongly foreshadow Antonioni's equally masterful symbolic use of a threatening urban environment.

The film's sound track often functions expressionistically as well. The bizarre music (composed by Renzo Rossellini) continuously calls attention to itself, rather than blending in unnoticed, especially the loudly pounding bass drums that force themselves into the spectator's consciousness at key moments of ten-sion. The sterility of the ruined landscapes seems almost to become audible through the resulting noise. Just before Edmund jumps to his death, in fact, in a kind of final insult to his mind and body (and ours), a tram roars by with an obviously heightened, physically painful clatter. Even more important is the film's enormously stylized lighting; throughout, light and dark areas are overtly used both symbolically and for their expressive, emotional potential. We often see Edmund pacing between light and dark areas of an interior, for ex-ample, when he is feeling psychological pressure. The dark subway where he is initiated into crime, and the forlorn rocks where the gang leader, Joe, abandons him at one point, both suggest the sinister and the unnatural. When the gang strips the train in the railroad yard of its cargo of potatoes, the scene's finale is accomplished around a fire whose violent patterns of light and dark suggest a Walpurgisnacht or some hellish interior of the soul. When Edmund's former schoolteacher first takes him to his apartment, the two characters move from intensely bright light to the dark shadows in front of his building; the camera lingers, but we see nothing, suggesting perhaps the moral darkness that is about to engulf the boy. When the electricity in Edmund's apartment building is cut off because the landlord has been tampering with the meter, most of the interiors of the second half of the film, including the scene of Edmund murdering his father, are shot in a fantastic candlelight. Near the end, when the boy returns to his old apartment house after he has poisoned his father, and broodingly plants himself on the outer steps, the light of the hallway timer suddenly goes out, plunging him into darkness. The symbolic overtones are obvious—to Edmund as well, it seems—and he quickly leaves to begin the famous walk that will end in his death.

The expressiveness of the already highly artificial interiors is further heightened by camera placement and movement. Thus, while many of the interior scenes are in medium shot, they are somewhat tighter than conventional interiors—certainly tighter than in *Open City*—and the effect is claustrophobic. This is especially true because characters are often seen in normal two-shots that are drastically altered when first one, then the other, walks into a close-up directly in front of the camera, one head suddenly looming over the other, provoking a heightened tension in the spectator. In these interiors, and even more obviously in the exteriors, the camera relentlessly, suffocatingly stalks the vulnerable Edmund. Most critics have understandably focused on the obvious lateral tracking and dollying involved here, but even from the very beginning (in the cemetery scene when Edmund is being roughed up by the adults afraid of losing work to him), this tracking movement is often accompanied by an unique circular gesture that tightly pens him in. In the graveyard the camera becomes one more antagonist in the threatening circle that encloses him. As Enzo Ungari has pointed out: "Rossellini has no shame in *Germany, Year Zero.* . . . This is his profound lesson for modern film: the implacable camera."[9] As mentioned earlier, the director himself told the novelist DeAngelis at this time that he preferred making films to writing fiction because "I can adapt the camera to my talents and the character will be pursued and haunted: contemporary anxiety derives precisely from this inability to escape the implacable eye of the lens."[10]

The editing figures here as well. During one interior scene in the kitchen near the end of the film, for example, the camera disconcertingly reverses itself three times. Elsewhere, the editing is awkward, causing scenes to begin and end abruptly, further contributing to the viewer's disorientation and thus making palpable the forces that buffet Edmund. Many early reviewers in fact complained about the film's rough editing, but, intentional or not, it contributes to the overall expressionistic effect. The framing and composition are also important in this regard. Early in the film, for example, Edmund moves, in an out-of-focus extreme close-up, into the frame that had been occupied solely by his father in medium shot. The effect, again, is threatening and foreshadows the more literally physical displacement that is to come. At another point, when Edmund has been cheated out of the scales he was supposed to sell, he escapes the scene—but not really—by running further and further into the center of the image, trying unsuccessfully to make himself disappear into the shot's vanishing lines. The most suggestive use of framing occurs during the scene in which Herr Enning belittles the weakness of Edmund's father. At this moment, meant to represent the height of Nazi corruption, the framing is completely off, the composition is unbalanced and asymmetrical (but not in a way that would suggest reality caught *sur le vif*), the heads are partially cut out of the frame, a threatening black spike fence holds them in from behind, and Enning continually distracts the viewer by looking out of the frame, to the latest young boy found for the general.

The heightened expressionism of *Germany, Year Zero* is accompanied by the continuing tension between elements of the "real" and the prevailing code of realism, which was discussed in the previous chapter. For example, the British soldiers we see as tourists and to whom Edmund tries to sell the Hitler record are *real* British soldiers. In other words, they "play" themselves, they *are* what they play, and because of their inexperience as actors, they, like "Joe from Jersey" in the first episode of *Paisan*, have not cultivated the mannerisms and the delivery associated with realistic acting. Because they sound so false (precisely because they are so utterly "true"), they tend to disturb and even challenge the very illusionism and dynamics of identification that the film, at another level, is at pains to establish. We suddenly become aware, yet once more, that all is artifice before us.

The general strategy of the film, similarly, is toward an emotional distancing between Rossellini and the characters, which counters the "warmth" of his relationship with the characters of *Open City* but continues the bold experiments of *Paisan*. One *is* emotionally involved in this film, but the relation seems to occur not so much between the spectator and the characters as between the spectator and the film's formal elements, thus enhancing the sense of stylization. Edmund, who in a more conventional film would be the focus of audience identification, here seems rather a kind of null set, an empty integer, a focal point of effects. Rossellini's increasingly typical dedramatization is also at work in several scenes, and the lack of conventional emotional underlining makes us aware, again, of the film's status as constructed representation. The hospital scene of Edmund's initial theft of the bottle of poison, for example, is, like the killings in *Paisan*, thoroughly unstressed. After an intercut close-up on the bottle for identification purposes (and what could be less conventionally believable than a bottle of poison left on a patient's hospital tray?), the theft is carried out quickly, without benefit of cuts, camera movement, or emotional buildup. The scene of the poisoning itself is equally underplayed, but even more thematically suggestive: while Edmund prepares the poison in a workmanlike fashion, we hear his father's voice offscreen droning on about the history of Germany. His words fill the space created by Edmund's silence, dedramatizing Edmund's activities (by distracting us) and yet suggesting at the same time a causal link between the history of nazism that he recounts and what Edmund is about to do.[11]

The film's climax—emotional, thematic, and formal—comes during the stunning final sequence, which traces Edmund's aimless wandering through the Berlin ruins and culminates in his suicide. Even Rossellini's detractors have found this sequence brilliant; in a way, it has been overvalued, especially by the phenomenologists,[12] for too many critics have taken too seriously Rossellini's own words belittling the rest of the film in favor of its ending:

> Every film I make interests me for a particular scene, perhaps for a finale I already have in mind. In every film I see on the one hand the narrative episodes—such as the first part of *Germania, anno zero* . . . —and on the other the *event*. My sole concern is to reach that *event*. In the other narrative episodes I feel myself hesitating, alienated, absent.
>
> I don't deny that this is a weakness on my part, but I must confess that scenes which are not of key importance weary me, and make me feel quite helpless. I only feel sure of myself at the decisive moment. *Germania, anno zero*, to tell the truth, was conceived specifically for the scene with the child wandering on his own through the ruins. The whole of the preceding part held no interest at all for me.[13]

This is, of course, one way to account for the film's hesitations and rough spots, and many critics have been all too ready to agree with Rossellini that he was not really interested in what he was doing. It must be remembered, however, that the last sequence, no matter how striking, is mute, and that the development of the film's themes (as well as the power of the last scene), depends completely on everything that comes before.

Yet it is clearly the ending that makes the film unique. Here the "artificial" verbosity of the other scenes (exacerbated by having Germans improbably speak Italian—a complete, if practical, departure from Rossellini's standard practice) is reduced to nothing, and the plethora of words and theories and posturing is replaced by a deep, brooding silence of remarkable resonance. As at the end of Bresson's *Mouchette* (1967), the camera shadows Edmund even more relentlessly than before. At one point he passes a bombed-out church, and the sound of its organ fills the empty sound track; people stand about on the street in stylized, spiritually empty groups, reminiscent of a De Chirico cityscape. After pausing a moment or two, Edmund strides away from the ineffectual solace of institutional religion—ineffectual, at least, at this point in his life and in the life of an exhausted Europe. Other children inexplicably, but somehow appropriately, refuse to let him join their game; he is the pariah, cut off from all human community. He awkwardly plays hopscotch for a few moments in a last attempt to regress to a vanished childhood. Entering a building under construction, located just across the street from his own half-destroyed apartment building, he climbs the slippery, stairless ramps (repeatedly and suggestively disappearing from the frame), plays with a hammerhead that he puts to his temple like a gun, and watches absently as a coffin-laden truck comes to pick up the one containing his father.

The new, unfinished building is the only future-oriented thing in the whole film, and perhaps can be seen as standing metaleptically for the prosperous Germany we know is to come. But Edmund cannot participate in this future and must cast himself down from it. His sister, Eva, calls to him, offering the consolation of language and its promise of human community in the midst of this overwhelming cosmic silence, but having sinned too grievously, he cannot accept her solace. He hides from her instead. A few moments later he closes his eyes, and simply and suddenly jumps. One of the women who has been sharing the crowded apartment, known only in the film and the script as "the expatriate," runs to his side, but in this film marked by entropy and exhaustion—both physical and spiritual—she is not even able to cry out. She sits in a heap, next to Edmund's crushed body; where a Pietà might be expected in this thoroughly symbolic film, there is no contact between the bodies, and Rossellini's symbolic point is further underlined by the refusal to symbolize, the refusal to refer to an extratextual religious and artistic iconographic tradition that could signal some semblance of human love and possibility, as it does in Bergman's *Cries and Whispers* and later in Rossellini's own *Messiah*. The camera tilts up, and our last image is of the ruined apartment house that has been the site of so much physical and psychological destruction.

A great deal of diversity has marked interpretations of Edmund's suicide. The egregious Marcel Oms condemns the scene (and the entire film) because it proclaims "the necessity of the great pardon. In 1948–49, it was necessary to stick all the dead in a common grave, all of them: hangmen and victims."[14] Borde and Bouissy, who in general think that *Germany, Year Zero* is Rossellini's best film because of its "documentary quality," reject the suicide as "a concession to the traditional rules of punishing the guilty," and fear the possibility of interpreting the film as "condemnation of the Allied victory," with Edmund symbolizing a Germany brought down by coalitions. "Across this Christian sympathy for the victims/hangmen [note the similarity to Oms' language], you can see the profile of a pardon of fascism."[15] To find a pardon for fascism in this rabidly anti-Fascist film requires, it seems to me, a very determined effort. Rossellini's own view is idiosyncratic, but revealing in its insistence, once again, on a moral idea and its corruption:

> The finale of *Germany, Year Zero* seemed clear: it was a true light of hope.
> . . . And the gesture of the child in killing himself is a gesture of abandonment, a gesture of exhaustion with which he puts behind him all the horror he has lived and believed because he acted exactly according to a precise set of morals. He feels the vanity of all this and the light goes on inside him and he has this moment of abandonment. . . . But it's the kind of abandonment to rest that has to come before any new action; and he abandons himself to the great sleep of death, and from there is born a new way of living and of seeing, the accent of hope and faith in the future and in men.[16]

Given Edmund's death, one might ask in whom this vision and new mode of life is born, and in whom this new hope for the future arises. Apparently, Rossellini is positing a kind of symbolic reality to the humane, Christian ideas that have been raised, even if only implicitly, by their absence, and that have a real, if abstract, life of their own beyond that of any single individual like Edmund. In any case, it is clear how crucial the transcendental and, in stylistic terms, the expressionistic are to this "realist" film that seems finally to revel in its own multivalence.

9

Una Voce Umana
(1947–48)

Rossellini's next film, of an awkward thirty-five minute length that forced him later to pair it with *The Miracle* in order to make it commercially feasible—they were released together as *L'amore* in 1948—is based on *La Voix humaine*, a one-act play by Jean Cocteau. Disparaged or avoided by most critics, the film is actually thematically and philosophically complex, even if its subject—the rejected woman—may not be particularly palatable, especially thirty-five years later. The realist-expressionist tension of *Germany, Year Zero* continues, but now the focus is so obsessively on the individual that nothing else remains. As we have seen, in *Germany, Year Zero* Rossellini appears to have lost faith in the *coralità* that animated the first two films of the postwar trilogy, turning back instead to the lone individual, as in *L'uomo dalla croce,* who tries unsuccessfully to make his or her way through a hostile world to personal salvation. If the group had lost its moral force in *Germany, Year Zero,* however, the environment still reigned supreme, a clear determinant of behavior. In *Una voce umana* (A Human Voice), not only does the group disappear—for no one other than the main character (played by Anna Magnani) is even seen or heard, except by inference—but the environment disappears as well. (Curiously, the presence of a dog serves to heighten the woman's isolation even more, rather than relieve it.) In this film, transcendence is no longer even a theoretical possibility. We are locked in a woman's tiny apartment (actually, the bedroom and bathroom) while she has her last telephone conversation with the lover who is rejecting her for another woman. That is the whole of the plot.

Coralità is now reduced to a single other voice, the lover's, of which we can just faintly hear the hum. Also barely noticeable are the sound effects of starting cars, a party, a crying baby (the last two clearly symbolic), which arise between calls. But the woman rejects all others, for they are just "people," who do not understand them and their love. The lovers have alienated themselves from human community because they have lost their reason, as Rossellini might have put it twenty years later, just like Edmund in the horrible act of murdering his father. In the earlier film, however, language is still a sign of human community, and when Edmund is ostracized (or ostracizes himself), language disappears. Here, however, we see language's other side: a means of falsifying feelings, the site of the struggle for mastery of one human over another, the place where narcissistic self-absorption can make the whole communal enterprise meaningless. We hear a slight buzzing at the other end of the line, signifying for us the presence of another human being, but that "presence" is actually constituted only differentially by Magnani, as a kind of sick projection of her own ego. (It is symbolically fitting that we hear only the lover's mumbles and murmurs, absent of human meaning.) In fact, we are only able to infer what he says through her responses. In the play version the audience hers *nothing* of the man, not even the murmurs, and in his preface Cocteau maintains that the actress is really playing two roles: one when she speaks, and the other when she listens and thus "delimits" the other.[1]

In *Una voce umana* the authenticity of words is no longer guaranteed: when Magnani is apparently asked what she is wearing at that moment, she constructs for her lover a portrait that is completely false. She also lies by saying that she has been taking the whole thing very well, when she is in fact on the verge of a breakdown. He, too, is lying, for though he is obviously calling from his new lover's apartment, he insists (we infer) that this is not the case. Lying is, in fact, directly thematized, or rather, the incommensurability between language and the external world. As such, the rhythm of the film proceeds in exactly the opposite direction of that of *Germany, Year Zero,* which moves from language toward its absence. Here the beginning is played out in almost dead silence: there is only isolation and the naked self, and we wait for this silence to be filled by the community of language. When it does come, in an annoying barrage, it is entirely rhetorical and overemotionalized—pure artifice, barely referential. In the largest sense, Rossellini is probing the nature of linguistic and, by extension, cinematic representation and its adequacy to the real world. He seems to have become more consciously aware that one cannot get to nature through culture (language, film) without that "nature" being profoundly altered. *Una voce umana* thus becomes a meditation on this very notion; if artifice cannot be avoided in one's pursuit of "reality," then perhaps one had best embrace it openly. Rossellini always spoke of this film as an "experiment," but he seems to have regarded the experiment as inconclusive or worse, and perhaps better forgotten. *The Miracle,* as we shall see, is precisely this forgetting, for in it both the environment and the group are reinstated and, in the best tradition of realism, the problems of representation are once again elided.

In his 1955 article in *Cahiers du cinéma* entitled "Dix ans de cinéma," Rossellini gives us a sense of the complexities of this film:

> The cinema is also doubtless a microscope. The cinema can take us by the
> hand and lead us to discover things that the eye couldn't even perceive (for

example in close-ups and detail shots). . . . More than any other subject, *La Voix humaine* gave me the chance to use the camera as a microscope, *especially since the phenomenon to examine was called Anna Magnani.* Only the novel, poetry, and the cinema allow us to riffle around in the characters to discover their reactions and the motives which make them act [my emphasis].[2]

A dual perspective seems to be operating here. On the one hand, the film is an intensely emotional story portraying a woman's psychological state at being spurned by her lover, while on the other, it is a thoroughly self-aware, simultaneous dismantling of that story.

On the first level, Rossellini, following Cocteau, has tried to present a believable, but universalized, portrayal of a woman of "this sort." The film thus continues the grand project, begun in earnest in *Germany, Year Zero* but hinted at earlier, of the discovery of the individual self, and the claustrophobia and implacable camera of the previous film haunt *Una voce umana* as well. Here the portrait is not very flattering: the woman is seen as utterly emotional, unable to get her feelings under control, suicidal, totally dependent on the man's will. Clearly the product of an earlier day—Cocteau's play was first performed on February 17, 1930—it is, perhaps not surprisingly, still being revived, most recently by Liv Ullman. Ironically, when he made the film, Rossellini said he wanted to show the truth—that women were so often the victims of men—but the film also serves to reinforce the stereotype of woman as eternal victim.[3] Here he seems largely to have followed his source, for the misogyny of victimization is adopted directly from Cocteau's play, as is the tale of attempted suicide recounted by the woman. The image near the end of the film when the actress wraps the telephone cord around her neck in symbolic self-destruction, after making much of the fact that her lover's voice is in the wire, is also an explicit stage direction in the play. Cocteau's misogynistic violence is at times even more blatant than that, especially, for example, when the "author" suggests to the actress in the play's preface that "she give the impression of bleeding, of losing her blood, just like an animal which is limping, of finishing the act in a room full of blood." Earlier in the preface, Cocteau has spoken of the room as a scene of murder.

There is another level to Rossellini's film, however, and what redeems it, at least on an aesthetic plane, is its brilliant self-awareness. The director's insistence, quoted above, that "the phenomenon to examine was called Anna Magnani," is manifested everywhere in the film and virtually ensures that it will be intensely aware of its own artifice. So, for example, the film is expressly dedicated in its opening credits to Magnani and her "great artistry," immediately underlining her own presence and her function as representation, and thus helping to delay the spectator's belief in the fiction of her screen character. Once the film begins, intensely long takes from a seemingly immobile camera predominate, foregrounding Magnani's tour-de-force performance with the help of dialogue that calls attention to itself because it is so obviously overheated. Some of her lines are even repeated six or seven times in a row, calling upon the actress's utmost skill to sustain the high level of emotion and to offer sufficient variation in expression and intonation to keep the audience interested. (In the film version, in fact, the emotion has been purposely heightened beyond Cocteau's original, which lacks the final breakdown scene.) At other times, the

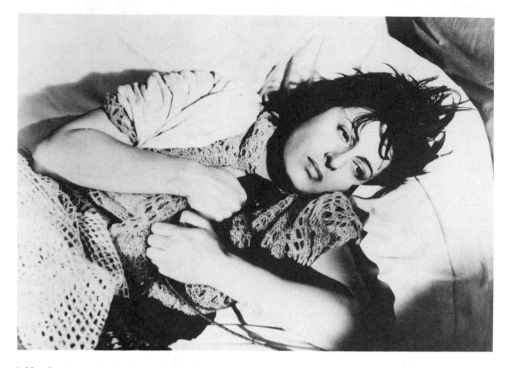

Self-reflexive tour de force: Anna Magnani and telephone in *Una voce umana* (1948).

scene is even played with Magnani's back to the camera, so that her voice and sheer presence must carry the whole. In this latter instance, it seems as though a technically "bad" shot is deliberately retained to raise the stakes and the level of challenge for the actress. The stolid immobility of the furniture serves further to push her to the fore.

Thus, while the worst proclivities of "rhetoric" (as Italian critics call it) are being yielded to, the paradoxical effect is that the film betrays and reveals its artifice by keeping us always aware of the real woman's presence. On one level, in other words, it attempts to create an illusionism that would make us psycholocigally substitute the person of the actress for her character, while on another level it blocks this attempt. *Una voce umana* thus sets up an ontological identity between the actress and the character she is playing, intermittently collapsing the two categories while it deconstructs its own surface realism by means of the preexisting reality of Magnani herself. (Appropriately, the dog in the film was Magnani's dog and is called by its real name). Like the British soldiers of *Germany, Year Zero,* whose very reality as British soldiers created a "stylized" element that could not be successfully assimilated into the film's coded realism, Magnani's acting in *Una voce umana* stands the process of realistic representation on its head.

Nor is this project peculiar to Rossellini's version, for it is obvious from Cocteau's preface that he also conceived of his play as a kind of challenge or experiment, of theater stripped to its essentials (and thus inevitably self-aware).

He makes it very clear that he is not interested in psychological problems, but wants to "resolve problems of a theatrical order." He would have called it "pure theater," he says, if that phrase were not a pleonasm. Even more important, he says he wrote the play as "a pretext for an actress," since he had been previously reproached for always putting himself over his actors.

Other elements in the film increase its self-awareness as well. For one thing, we are regularly subjected to jump cuts that are almost as jarring—and as purposeful—as those of Godard's *Breathless*. The director also often leaves his signature within a shot as, for example, when we see a microphone dangling into the frame. This is an amateur's mistake, of course, the mistake of a director who was, according to Adriano Aprà, shooting with live sound for the first time in his career. Yet it is tempting to see this exposed microphone as one more sign of the director's presence, unconsciously signaling the artifice that he is creating. Mirrors also constantly function in this film in a self-reflexive way: in fact, the very first shot is a close-up of Magnani's mirror image, from which the camera then pulls back to reveal it for what it is, a reflection of a reflection (which it can only do differentially, by showing something external, that is, what it is *not*). At other points, there are three or four mirrors in evidence in a single shot, all reflecting one another, further heightening the claustrophobic, abyssal mise-en-scène and further underlining the presence of the artist and the refusal of realistic illusionism.

What results from this strange mixture of misogynism and self-reflexivity is a complex sexual dynamic. For if "the phenomenon to examine was called Anna Magnani," the rather ruthless examiner is Roberto Rossellini. He is the lover at the other end of the line, of course, just as he is, in some ways, the various complex husbands that Ingrid Bergman will do battle with in *Stromboli, Voyage to Italy, Europa '51*, and *Fear*. What complicates things is that he is also their creator.

10

The Miracle
(1948)

When Rossellini realized that *Una voce umana* was too short to be released separately, he immediately began casting about for another subject to accompany it that might be treated at roughly the same length. One night, Fellini, a close collaborator at the time, came up with an idea about a confused and somewhat disturbed goatherd, Nanni, who imagines that a passing wanderer she meets one day is Saint Joseph. The wanderer plies her with wine in order to take advantage of her, and some months later Nanni realizes she is pregnant. Rather than becoming remorseful, she takes her pregnancy to mean that she is "in God's grace" and because this baby will be no ordinary one, she refuses to work out of respect for her divine mission, or to put anything aside, because she knows the Lord will take care of his own. A nun, one of the few representatives of organized religion who appear in the finished film, tells her that she should confess her sin, but Nanni rejects this advice because she is favored by God. The townspeople begin to make fun of what they take to be her spiritual pretensions and cruelly mock her. When her time finally comes, she turns her back on the village and climbs high up the mountain toward a desolate church where she gives birth alone.[1]

Convinced that Rossellini would find the story ridiculous, Fellini at first tried to pass it off as the work of a Russian short story writer. But when the director, who had become completely enamored with the idea, was becoming more and more frustrated at not being able to find the story so that he could buy the rights to it, Fellini finally admitted that he had made the whole thing up, basing it loosely on a story he had heard many times during his childhood.[2] According to Angelo Solmi, Fellini's biographer, the story's particular combination of mysticism and hallucination comes from Tullio Pinelli, who is credited in the film as coscreenwriter and who was a powerful emotional influence on Fellini at the time.

The Miracle continues the questioning of the prevailing neorealist aesthetic that we have noted at work in the films made subsequent to *Open City,* though in somewhat different terms. Unlike the claustrophobic interior of *Una voce umana,* the primary locus of the action is now outdoors, and hence this film is reinscribed in the kind of gritty surface realism of real locations and nonprofessional acting (in the secondary roles) that brought the director such fame in his earlier films. Nevertheless, these are not the exteriors of *Open City,* and the documentary element (which will reappear in *La macchina ammazzacattivi*) is once again minimized in favor of an intense concentration on Magnani's performance, which in fact remains as highly foregrounded as it was in *Una voce umana.* In the seduction scene, for example, "Saint Joseph" (played by Fellini), has not a single word of dialogue, thus further emphasizing Magnani's bravura performance. Quentin Reynolds, who visited Rossellini during the filming, reports being "overwhelmed" by Magnani's acting even before her voice and the rest of the sound track had been dubbed in, and he quotes Rossellini to the effect that "she is a genius, the greatest since Duse."[3] In *The Miracle,* therefore, the ground against which the figure is seen has been expanded over *Una voce umana,* but the figure has for all that been scarcely reduced. Thus Giuseppe Ferrara complains with some justice (at least if one insists on seeing the earlier films as normative) that here southern Italy and the Amalfi coast become merely "a scenic background (never before had the landscape been simply a backdrop) utilized aesthetically."[4]

This foregrounding of Magnani's performance also accords well with Rossellini's increasing insistence on individual salvation, and camera angles and cutting consistently reinforce this movement away from the group toward the self. Nanni is held, or rather pinned, in the tight grip of Rossellini's close-ups, which track backward but never give her any breathing space. In fact, in one interesting shot the camera stays on her even though she is being called by someone outside the shot, contrary to normal practice, which would identify the source of the voice. Only when Nanni has moved close enough to the woman calling her is the woman included in the shot.

The *coralità* absent from *Una voce umana* is partially reintroduced in *The Miracle,* however, as befits its centrifugal movement. But Nanni's community fails her utterly, yet in a complex way that Rossellini means to study. Thus, though the continual close-ups stress the individual, the film also has its share of deep-focus medium and long shots that attempt to situate her in relation to her physical and social environment. In one particularly effective shot, we see Nanni huddled in a corner made by the fence on the church porch, while part of the village becomes a kind of backdrop behind her. (What can also be seen in this same shot is the enormous presence of the mountain—stolid, yet transcendent—that will function in a similar iconographic way in *Stromboli* and *Voyage to Italy.*) At other moments, extreme long shots, with the camera shooting straight down on her, complement the tracking tight shots mentioned earlier by implying that the cause of the claustrophobic pressure being applied to her lies in the uncharitable attitude of the villagers. Her difference from them is continually stressed both verbally and visually, as will be Karin's in *Stromboli*.

The film's most memorable scenes are the most vicious, as for example when Nanni comes down into the village, leaving the protection offered her by the church porch only to be cruelly made fun of (in a mock religious procession whose *Open City* iconography—particularly the bowl on her head that first suggests a halo, then, in close-up, a crown of thorns—is clearly meant to recall the sufferings of Christ). Yet other details point in a kinder direction. The woman who called out to Nanni in the shot mentioned earlier, for example, tries to convince the students not to make fun of Nanni. Earlier, when Nanni steals an apple from a woman's basket while at mass, it is significant that the woman moves the basket out of further harm's way, but makes no attempt to recover the lost apple that in some way seems to be Nanni's due. Also, she and the other indigents are fed by the nuns, and the church porch seems to be universally respected as their legitimate home.

One of the more interesting aspects of the film concerns its complex visual and narrative structuring of the dynamic between Nanni's spiritual faith and the cynicism of the majority of the villagers. The opposition between the spiritual and everyday, ordinary life is cast throughout the film in remarkably consistent, if predictable, spatial terms (just as it will be in *Stromboli*), the transcendent always being associated with what is higher, and the everyday and terrestrial, naturally, with what is lower. It is thus fitting that the village is at the bottom and the monastery, which symbolizes for us and for Nanni (at least until she finds it is locked) the summit of spirituality, at the top. In the very first scene, we see Nanni completely alone, far above the village, and it is here that she has her "spiritual" encounter with "Saint Joseph." When she comes back down from the mountain with her firewood and goats, precisely halfway down she appropriately meets two monks, one whimsical, who believes completely in her miraculous vision, and the other, characterized by the first as a "materialist," who says he has never seen a vision in his life. Occupying a similar halfway position between the two realms is the church whose porch is her home, toward which she runs when she finds out she is pregnant. When she does come down into the village later on, she says that she had not come down from God's house any sooner because she was afraid. After a brutal encounter with the villagers, who throw vegetables at her and otherwise violently mistreat her, she seeks refuge further up, away from their dangerous unbelief. When it is time for her to deliver, she at first begins making her way back down the mountain, in a natural movement toward human community, but when she spots a religious procession from afar, she remembers her cruel treatment and abruptly turns around to begin her ascent. Her physical climb heavenward thus becomes a literalization of her spiritual struggle, as earthly words melt away into the complete silence of the otherworldly.

There is another dynamic at work here, beyond the spatialization of spirituality, and that is the one between the "realistic" and the "real" that we have seen in operation in previous films. It is in fullest operation in the scene—which, like the sequence of Edmund's final peregrinations around Berlin in *Germany, Year Zero*, Rossellini misleadingly claimed to be the only sequence he was really interested in—where Cosimino, Nanni's erstwhile suitor and companion "village idiot," kicks all her worldly possessions off the church porch. By sending her tattered blankets and empty cans flying, he, too, like the rest of the village, is rejecting her for putting on spiritual airs. To play this role, Rossellini found a local character who apparently had few inhibitions. His retarded-looking physiognomy itself is more "real" than anything normally seen on the screen at that time, even the neorealist screen, thus stretching the bounds of realism, but during the filming of this particular scene, he went slightly berserk and could not be calmed down. Rossellini wisely kept shooting, and the exciting result makes us feel that we have been treated to a glimpse of "real life," again, something out of control. The hand-held camera follows the decidedly upset (and perhaps inspired) Nanni around in a tight 360-degree movement, which is visually different from anything else in the film and clearly disturbs its "realistic" texture. The effect is all the greater because it contrasts so strongly with the prevailing sense of this film, which, even more than *Open City,* is one of a thoroughly worked-out scenario in which the aleatory is kept to a minimum. The very "reality" of the scene, again, as well as the unorthodox hand-held camera movement, breaks the film's illusionistic spell, at least momentarily.

In addition, neorealism's unspoken claim to represent reality fully is also problematized from a new direction, a direction that will be followed through the next five years of Rossellini's career. What happens, in effect, is that the director now begins to redefine "realism"—or, perhaps better, to go beyond it—to include a new, more insistent awareness of something beyond the merely material, a feeling that was always present by implication in the earlier films but that now becomes overt. As Rossellini told Mario Verdone in 1952:

> I constantly come back, even in the strictest documentary forms, to *imagination,* because one part of man tends towards the concrete, and the other to the use of the imagination, and the first must not be allowed to suffocate the second. This is why you find fantasy at work in *Il Miracolo, La Macchina ammazzacattivi,* and *Paisà,* as well as in *[Francesco].*[5]

Rossellini seems to be positing fantasy and the imagination as values in their own right in these remarks, but most Italian critics of the period (and since)—both his detractors and his defenders—could think of fantasy only in terms of realist rhetoric. The critics who defend these films do so by claiming that Rossellini is still just as much a realist as ever, but that now he is enlarging the *scope* of his realism to include interior spiritual states as well. This claim has some merit, of course, but it also serves to dilute further the already nearly useless term realism. For socially minded critics, on the other hand, especially the Marxists, the films of this period were utter failures because in them Rossellini began indulging in an unforgivable mysticism and other equally unprogressive attitudes. Talk of a "crisis" became widespread. For Borde and Bouissy, writing somewhat later, *The Miracle* is the beginning of all of Rossellini's future problems. For them the film is a "naive Golgotha" that "marks a great turning point for him: he has just tasted the drug of Christian lyricism."[6] Those who know the earlier films, like *L'uomo dalla croce,* however, will recognize these spiritual concerns as nothing new.

Rossellini told another interviewer that, immediately after the war, it was proper to try to help man see the world, but

> Today I have other things on my mind. Today I believe that we must find a new and solid base on which to construct and represent man as he is, in the union which exists inside him between poetry and reality, between desire and action, between dream and life. For this reason, I made *L'amore* and *La macchina ammazzacattivi.*[7]

But what is this world of poetry, desire, and dream? For the purposes of this film, at any rate, it is the world of religious faith, but a religious faith unattached to any specific religion. What obviously interests Rossellini much more than dogma is accounting for man's spiritual longing, that "oceanic feeling" that Freud belittled in *Civilization and Its Discontents.* Rossellini said in a 1954 *Cahiers du cinéma* interview that Nanni "has a kind of religious mania, but, in addition to this mania, a deep and true faith. She is able to believe whatever she wants."[8] It is this same expression of faith that will precipitate the sudden, transcendent ending of *Stromboli.* In both cases, of course, the object of faith is God, but for Rossellini the mere existence of faith is finally more important than its object. In Rossellini's view, postwar Europe was rapidly losing the spiritual values that had brought it through the terrors of the war, and it is his urge to resuscitate this lost faith that accounts for the strong religious strain of the films of this period. And, as Adriano Aprà has mentioned, *The Miracle* is the first postwar film of Rossellini's to end with a birth, a hopeful note that inevitably looks outward, beyond itself, beyond tragedy, beyond the suicides, executions, and murders that occupy the earlier films.

Yet the religious faith of *The Miracle* is hardly an endorsement of conventional religion. In fact, the film continues and develops the implied critique of organized religion that began in the final sequence of *Germany, Year Zero* when Edmund stares blankly at the ruined church that no longer has any meaning for him nor promises any hope of salvation. When the nun in *The Miracle* suggests to Nanni that she go to confession, she rejects her advice. Nanni's long struggle to climb to the top of the mountain, intercut with promising long shots of the monastery as a haven toward which she is moving, ends in her discovery that the church is empty and locked. She pulls on the bars in a frustrating, futile effort to gain entry. (A subtle hint of this failure has come in an earlier sequence in the village church when she first discovers she is pregnant. She prostrates herself before the altar, as if offering her obeisance to the Lord, but of course nothing happens: the overwhelming impression is one of cold, sterile emptiness.) At the top of the mountain, the religion of men fails her, as it has in the villagers' mockery, and she must go back to the primal source of Christianity itself. Entering the church by an open side door, she moves down into a rocky, rough cellar, which is reminiscent of the primitiveness of the caves in the Sicilian episode of *Paisan,* and even more importantly, recalls the standard iconography of Christ's Nativity.

Many of those who first saw the film readily recognized this latter reference, but unfortunately they were able to see the possibilities of such a representation only in a reductive, binary way as either "properly" respectful, or, failing that, a blasphemous parody. The latter view predominated, of course, and as soon as the film was released, it was violently attacked in Europe, Latin America, and the United States, and instantly banned in Argentina and Australia. In the United States, Joseph Burstyn had packaged *The Miracle* with two other films of inconvenient length (Jean Renoir's *A Day in the Country* and Marcel Pagnol's *Joffroi*), into a triptych called *Ways of Love*. It opened, to mixed reviews, on December 12, 1950, at the Paris theater in Manhattan. The next day Edward T. McCaffrey, the comissioner of licenses in New York City and a former commander of the New York State branch of the Catholic War Veterans, found *The Miracle* "personally and officially blasphemous," and took it upon himself to overrule the censorship board of the New York State Regents, which had already passed it. This government official, whose previous activity had mostly concerned the granting of liquor and restaurant licenses, ordered the theater to stop showing the film or risk losing its license. When Burstyn and the Paris decided to fight back, fire inspectors began appearing to check for safety infractions in the nearly new theater.

Since McCaffrey had no legal grounds to support his censorship, the ban was immediately lifted by the courts. This was the signal for the Catholic church to enter the fray through its Legion of Decency, which had been pressuring Hollywood for some time with its film rating system. While Burstyn was holding press conferences insisting that Rossellini was a good Catholic, the national head of the Catholic War Veterans was saying that the script "reflected the writings of Moscow, even though the picture was reputed to be a piece of art from Italy."[9] A statement, signed by 167 American Legion posts across the country, maintained that the film "ridicules the American principles for which we fought in both wars,"[10] and over one thousand pickets showed up at the Paris to protest the film's "Communist blasphemy." Several bomb threats were received, conveniently allowing the authorities to disrupt the screenings. The New York Film Critics had chosen *Ways of Love* as best foreign film of 1950, but intense lobbying forced them to move the award ceremonies from Radio City Music Hall. Pressure was also applied to the New York Board of Regents, which had never before reversed a decision by its censorship committee to *pass* a film, and the film's license was revoked on February 16, 1951. Catholics like Allen Tate fought hard against the boycott, with the *New York Times*' Bosley Crowther emerging as the film's principal spokesman, defending it in an article in the April 1951 issue of the *Atlantic Monthly*. He suggested that Catholic fury directed against *The Miracle* was part of a larger strategy to extend the Church's control over the content of foreign films as well as those produced in Hollywood. Burstyn decided to push the issue as far as he could, and the Supreme Court ultimately decided in favor of the film on May 26, 1952. In what became a landmark decision for the film industry, the Court held, for the first time, that films were not merely a business, and that they should therefore enjoy the same First Amendment rights of freedom of expression applied to other media. In addition, it ruled that it was not the business of the state to protect specific religions from attacks on their views, and therefore sacrilege could no longer serve as a basis for censorship.

Of course much of the animus directed against this film was a result of the

Rossellini–Bergman scandal that had so recently been filling the newspapers. Rossellini attempted to mitigate in some way the adverse reaction to the film by sending Cardinal Spellman the following telegram:

> Men are still without pity because they have not gone back to God. But God is already present in the faith, however confused, of that poor persecuted woman, and since God is wherever a human being suffers and is misunderstood, the miracle occurs when at the birth of the child the poor demented woman regains sanity in her maternal love."[11]

At first glance this seems, to anyone who has seen the film, to be little more than a kind of pitiful stab at public relations; Rossellini's view that the title refers to Nanni's sudden regaining of her sanity through the birth of the child is hardly convincing. In terms of his other films, however, the explanation makes more sense. For one thing, of course, it is characteristic for Rossellini to put the epiphanic moment of character realization and change at the very end of the film. As we saw earlier, this was the consistent pattern of the individual episodes of *Paisan*. But it is also the pattern of the films he was to make after *The Miracle: Stromboli* and *Voyage to Italy* in fact, have always bothered viewers with what seem to be unconvincing "miracles" that occur at the very end, changes of heart that appear unmotivated in the context of the films' narratives. Thus, the ending of *The Miracle* can also be seen to be miraculous; it simply does not insist on its status as such, as the other films do, and thus might ironically be more palatable to modern, secularized, audiences because it is, in effect, misunderstood. In a similar vein, Rossellini has said elsewhere that it is precisely Nanni's immense faith that leads this otherwise disturbed women to a "gesture which is absolutely human and normal: giving her breast to her baby."[12]

It is also useful in this context to concentrate more intensely on just what Nanni says at the end. This film, so full of talk at the beginning (and in this way replicating and extending Magnani's loquaciousness in *Una voce umana*), becomes in its final third, like *Germany, Year Zero*, utterly speechless. Thus, when Nanni does speak to her child at the very end, her words are highlighted. During the labor itself, she cries *"Dio"* over and over, but the word is now articulated in a decidedly human context of pain, and is clearly not meant to be an appellation for the child. Once the baby is born, she covers him with words that insist upon his humanness rather than the divinity she had earlier been concerned with. She calls him "my son, my flesh, my blood"—and part of this, at least, is translated in the English subtitles. What is not translated at all, however (and this seems to be an instance of a completely innocent choice of the subtitler), are her final words, where she says *"bambino mio"* (my baby) three times before settling into maternal bliss. In other words, the ending can be read Rossellini's way, as the site of the miracle where Nanni regains her sanity through human childbirth, and not as a parody of Christ's Nativity.

One final area that must be examined, since it is crucial for the films to come, is the portrayal of women and sexuality in *The Miracle*. Cardinal Spellman, interestingly enough for a churchman of the early fifties, claimed to have been scandalized as much by the film's negative portrayal of Italian womanhood as

An aroused Magnani and the silent "Saint Joseph" (Federico Fellini) in *The Miracle* (1948).

by its putative sacrilege. He complained strenuously that "it presents the Italian woman as moronic and neurotic and in matters of religion fanatical. Only a perverted mind could so misrepresent so noble a race of women."[13] His stubborn insistence on seeing Nanni exclusively in universal terms makes his comment hardly worth considering, yet there is something about the portrayal of woman in this film that bears scrutiny. Like the woman in *Una voce umana*, Nanni is again related to a man, "Saint Joseph," as victim. In addition, both men are silent—strongly present, but paradoxically absent at the same time—while the women fill the sound track with the driven babbling that seems at least psychologically suicidal. Nanni is also surrounded by animals, as Ingrid Bergman's several characters will be as well. This is not because Rossellini necessarily sees women as "earth mothers" or somehow more closely related to nature,[14] but because they share with animals the role of victim in a man's world.

Yet what mitigates Nanni's status as victim is her own ripe sexuality. Despite one early English reviewer's complaint about Rossellini's "loathing of sex" in this film (a misreading that perhaps says more about the beholder than the beheld), the film's sexuality seems healthy and ebullient. This fact is somewhat obscured, unfortunately, by the English subtitles, which do not give an accurate picture of just how sexually motivated is Nanni's attraction to "Saint Joseph."

Her *"quanto sei bello!"* (you are so handsome) is translated once or twice, perhaps, but in fact she repeats it over and over, obsessively, during the course of
her monologue. Thus, while it might be said that Nanni is the man's victim
here, since she is presumably not intelligent enough to know what she is getting
into, it is also clear that she consents because she has been sexually aroused
herself. As she drinks more and more wine, she begins to perspire and says at
one point, "I have a fire burning inside me!" Various bizarre camera angles—
as well as her more obvious tearing at blouse and undershirt—also suggest her
increasing sexual openness. Finally, she is writhing so continuously at one point
that the viewer assumes momentarily that she is actually having sexual inter-
course—which must have been an exciting moment in 1948—but a cut away from
this shot of the upper half of her body reveals "Saint Joseph" standing over her.
At the very end of the film, the camera again focuses on the upper half of
Nanni's body, when she puts her arms up on the walls for support in a gesture
that directly recalls both Christ on the cross and Manfredi in *Open City*'s torture chamber. She begins writhing with the pain of labor, and the entire event
is portrayed so "earthily" that its sexual suggestivity is obvious. (What is also
problematic here—and worrisome—is the positioning of Rossellini's "male"
camera, which possesses her no less than does "Saint Joseph.")

The end result of this ambivalence—Nanni as victim of males (including the
director), Nanni as fully sexual being—is to suggest that she, like all women, like
all human beings, is not one-dimensional. This complexity is also reflected on
the religious level, as Nanni is recalled to her "senses" through—or in spite of—
her intense spiritual faith. The film's final scene, in fact, looks forward to the
reconciliation of body, mind, and spirit that will take place at the end of
Voyage to Italy. In this light, in spite of her isolation from her society and her
victimization by its men, we must imagine Nanni happy.

11

La Macchina Ammazzacattivi
(1948–52)

La macchina ammazzacattivi (The Machine to Kill Bad People) was begun just after *L'amore* was completed in 1948, and thus manifests much of the same questioning found in the two parts of this earlier film. Due to various production problems, however, it was not completed and released until the beginning of 1952. In its wry probing of social relationships and its comic vision of man's fallen state, it must clearly resembles another "atypical" Rossellini film, *Dov'è la libertà?*, the bulk of which was filmed in 1952, but not released until 1954. The social investigation of the later film, however, occurs in the context of a conventional commercial product in which the mediation of the film itself is not foregrounded, as it is in *La macchina ammazzacattivi*.

Massimo Mida, who worked as Rossellini's assistant on *La macchina ammazzacattivi*, insists that the director was not really very interested in the film. While this may indeed have been the case, this denial, as we have seen, is a common gesture that allows critics bent on seeing Rossellini as a realist to dismiss films or parts of films that do not fit the realist paradigm. The film is spotty, according to Mida, because it was done in fits and starts, without inspiration or enthusiasm.[1] Jose Guarner adds the further details that shooting was finished by Mida and Renzo Cesana and taken over and edited by another company, Fincine, but does not cite any source for his information. In any case, it seems incorrect to claim, as Guarner does, that the film "occupies a similar position to *Desiderio* on the list of unfinished films, written off by their director,"[2] given the fact that all critics agree that Rossellini did the majority of the shooting, at the very least, and the fact that he never publicly disclaimed responsibility for this film, as he did with *Desiderio*.

Celestino the photographer (Gennaro Pisano) talks to the devil in *La macchina ammazza-cattivi* (1948–52).

The plot, after the spareness of *La voce umana* and *The Miracle*, is quite complicated, but that, of course, is in the nature of comedies.[3] It concerns a small-town photographer, Celestino, who is visited by an old man who turns Celestino's camera into a killing device to mete out justice to "bad people." All that Celestino need do is take a picture of a previously taken picture, and its subject will freeze dead in whatever position he or she had assumed for the first picture. Along the way, comic subplots (concerning municipal fraud, young love, and American entrepreneurs with sexy nieces) bloom and wither, as Celestino is more and more outraged by the evil he finds everywhere. Celestino is convinced that the old man is actually Sant'Andrea, the town's patron saint, and soon enough "miracles"—like a gigantic catch of fish and an unexpected check for town improvements from the government in Rome—occur, which appear to benefit the village but succeed only in bringing out everyone's latent selfishness. Celestino's vengeance grows greater and greater and becomes utterly self-righteous, to the point that he even turns against the wise doctor who has tried to convince him that it is finally impossible to separate good and evil in such absolute terms. Desperate, he decides to take his own picture, thus killing himself, but first wants to take a picture of the *old man's* picture, the one who had originally started all the trouble. At the moment he snaps the shutter, the old man magically appears before him and is revealed to be a minor devil looking to curry favor with the powers below. Celestino has him make the sign of the cross, and in so doing, all those Celestino thought he had photographically killed are brought back to life, and everything returns to normal. The film ends with the moral:

> Coltiva il bene senza esagerrare
> Rifiuti il male, se ti vuoi salvare,
> Non affrettare troppo a giudicare
> E pensaci tre volte prima di punire.

> [Cultivate good without exaggerating
> Reject evil if you want to be saved,
> Don't be too quick to judge
> And think about it three times before punishing.]

One of the most interesting things about the film is that it is cast in the form of the Italian commedia dell'arte (a form that was also to interest Renoir), and thus largely concerned with broad character types rather than sharply individual psychological portraits. Even more than *Una voce umana,* the film is thoroughly stylized, delightfully and purposely artificial. (The comic lovers are even called Romeo and Juliet!) Enormously self-aware, much to the dismay of realist critics, it continuously and exuberantly foregrounds its own status as artificial construct rather than real life. At the same time, however, Rossellini's typical documentary impulse is also greatly in evidence, and the disruptive combination of stylization and documentary, not unlike De Sica's *Miracle in Milan* (1950) has bothered many. From another point of view, however, it is precisely this unstable, contradictory blend of ingredients that, in posing the problem of realism, makes the film so interesting.

Though critics have been reluctant to come to grips with this side of Rossellini, preferring to see in him alternatively the great realist or the failed realist, the director himself has been very clear, as we saw in the previous chapter, about the importance of imagination and fantasy in his work. In a specific discussion of *La macchina ammazzacattivi,* he has said that it "shows . . . places where I'd been happy, places I love, where some poor devils are convinced they have seen Satan. One of them told me one day, 'I've met the werewolf, I ran over him on my bicycle last night.' They are mad, crazed by the sun. But they have a power few of us possess—the power of the imagination."[4] From this perspective, Rossellini's interest in fantasy can itself be seen as a form of documentation of the people of this area.

From the very beginning of the film, the fantasy elements are stressed, probably more intensely than in any film Rossellini ever made. The first thing we see is a large hand and arm, in choreographed, flowing movements, self-consciously placing all the elements of the story before us in the form of paper cutouts (a nice literalization of the phrase mise-en-scène). Like any good neorealist, even an expressionist one, the locale, or what the voice-over, stressing the commedia dell'arte features calls the *"scena"* (stage), is put in place first, followed by the *"personaggi"* (characters) who are not named but called by generic types, such as "rich men" and "thieves." The theatrical elements foreground the artificiality of the narrative, of course, and the status of *La macchina ammazza-*

cattivi as *filmed* artifact is appropriately underlined by carrying out this stylized presentation by means of continuous dissolves, a uniquely cinematic device. The hand also plays a game of alternating revelation and concealment with the variout elements. Most important of all, when the stage setting—complete with pictures of the characters as they will be later frozen by Celestino's camera—dissolves to the first "real" scene, a car going downhill around a bend, the hand and arm of the "creator" are seen to linger for some seconds as a superimposition, thus making overt the carryover of the artifice to the realistic part of the film itself.

After we are introduced to the bumbling American entrepreneurs in the car (the man is played by Bill Tubbs, the same American actor who played the Catholic chaplain in the monastery sequence of *Paisan*), the film's self-aware elements continue. When the American's shapely, if mindless, niece sees *"Viva Sant'Andrea!"* written on a rock and asks who he is, the director provides a blatantly artificial partial wipe that moves from the middle simultaneously to the left and right (suggesting the parting of a stage curtain), revealing the old man we will later follow through town and who will make Celestino's camera the magical arbiter of justice. The curtain wipe then closes, and the scene on the winding road returns. In thus using montage to imply, visually, an equivalence that is in fact untrue, the film suggests that the medium cannot ever be fully trusted.

The major feature of the self-reflexive questioning, of course, is Celestino's role as photographer. (A more correctly literal, if more cumbersome, translation of the title would be "The Apparatus to Kill Bad People"; it is also important to know that *macchina* is the common Italian word for "camera"). Celestino's shop is called *La Foto Chiara,* but his photographs are less clear in sorting out good and evil than he would like. More and more obsessed with punishing evildoers—who turn out to be everybody in town, including himself—he exclaims that he is more powerful than the atomic bomb. It seems possible to read in this a specific warning to Rossellini's fellow neorealists, men for the most part more politically committed, as to the limits of their moral judgment, especially through the medium of film. In some ways, this pointed message and the insistence on fantasy can even be seen as an overt separation by Rossellini from what neorealism had become. The self-reflexivity of *La macchina ammazzacattivi* is further insisted upon by the very fact that the "deaths" caused by the camera are portrayed on the screen precisely by the use of uniquely cinematic devices such as stop motion, montage, and reverse action, tricks as old as Méliès. And, of course, they are just that, *tricks,* and thus to be shunned by all proper realists; what Rossellini seems to be coming to understand at some level, however, is that *all* cinema, including the realist variety, is, and can only be, trickery.

The precise nature of the self-reference is ambiguous. Interestingly, Celestino's camera can be effective only when it takes a picture of another previously existing picture. On a purely functional level, of course, this is understandable because it is much more visually humorous—the bullying policeman stiffens into the Fascist salute (Rossellini feels secure enough for parody by this point), the mayor assumes the pose of his baby picture, and so on. But it seems to go further than this. The American Peter Bondanella, who has attempted what is certainly the most detailed examination of this motif, has this to say:

> In good neorealist fashion and reminiscent of statements made by such important figures as Cesare Zavattini, Celestino views the camera as a means of separating reality from illusion, good from evil, substance from appearance. Photography is, for him, a metaphor for a way of knowing, for a means of apprehending essential moral and ethical facts; it enables him, so he believes, to penetrate the surface of events to the bedrock of reality and to fulfill a god-like role in his small village (not unlike that of a film director on the set).[5]

Elsewhere in his essay, Bondanella points out, "The camera, viewed as a means of acquiring knowledge of social reality by overly optimistic neorealist theorists, has been reduced to a fallible instrument which reflects not reality but human subjectivity and error."[6] The trouble is that Celestino's camera is never really considered by either him or Rossellini as a "way of knowing," as a device by which one might separate good from evil. Rather, the camera is merely a tool by which Celestino metes out punishment to those who have already been judged guilty by the independent moral consciousness, before the photographic or film-making process enters in. Rossellini's point thus seems to be that the photographic or cinematic "capturing" of reality is morally neutral (or impossible or irrelevant), and thus significant only as the actualization of a prior *idea* or moral stance that the filmmaker takes toward a particular reality. This idea or stance preexists any taking up of the camera, though the idea is, of course, only actualizable through it. This, in turn, helps to explain Rossellini's cryptic, if famous, 1954 definition of neorealism as "above all a moral position from which one looks at the world. It then becomes an aesthetic position, but it begins as a moral one."[7]

Thus far we have been stressing the film's fantasy elements. But it would be a mistake to focus upon them to the exclusion of all else, for the film's simultaneous insistence on a documentary realism is what constitutes its rough, unconventional appeal. Many of the scenes of the Amalfi coast seem to have been taken from stock documentary footage, or else Rossellini shot new footage himself; in any case, the particularization of locale is remarkable. The blessing of the boats and the procession for Sant'Andrea are also obviously real rather than staged, and, as the film opens Rossellini adds, in the self-congratulatory manner of *La nave bianca,* "and others taken from real life" to the list of screen credits. This continued concern for the "real," in the face of doubts about the possibility of achieving it, is what distinguishes *La macchina ammazzacattivi* from De Sica's better-known *Miracle in Milan,* made on a similar subject around the same time. As Jose Guarner has rightly pointed out, for De Sica the Duomo in Milan is little more than "an element in the decor."[8] In *La macchina ammazzacattivi,* on the other hand, the fantasy combines uneasily with the documentary footage to call into question what is after all the predominantly realistic mode of the individual dramatic scenes. A brilliantly *staged* religious procession, in other words, achieved at great expense of time and money, would insert itself seamlessly into the fabric of the film, and we would take it as happening before our eyes, and thus give ourselves to it. Here, however, it is precisely the rough reality of the actual procession's documentary images (rather than a smooth realism) that makes us aware that we are watching a film, and that, in this film, nearly everything else we see is fake.

Many other motifs from Rossellini's earlier (and later) films make an appearance as well, though now transmuted into comic form. Thus, the theme of language is restated (we see how language is often little more than puffery and rhetoric, used to deceive rather than enlighten, as in *Una voce umana,* and how, as in *Paisan,* it keeps cultures, and therefore, people, apart) but here it is all played for laughs. Similarly, the motif of the miracle, so significant for *Stromboli* and *Voyage to Italy* and such an important, if ambivalent, part of *The Miracle,* is parodied. In addition, Celestino teaches the sign of the cross, as the priest did in *L'uomo dalla croce,* but now the pupil is a minor devil; the Americans "land" and corrupt the eager natives as they did in *Paisan;* God is present in the sky at the end, as at the end of *Stromboli, Francesco,* and, twenty-five years later, *The Messiah;* the deadly serious fishing and price haggling of *Stromboli* and Visconti's *La terra trema,* are here treated humorously. The steps and incessant climbing of *The Miracle,* struggling against all odds, is here comically cursed; the doctor says that he prefers the poor to the rich because he does not have to climb stairs to care for them, and the Americans, continually moving from one unsatisfactory guest house to another, complain about the ubiquitous steps. (The oppositional motif of high and low camera shots, as well, continues from *The Miracle.*) Even suicide has become funny. Most importantly, the failure of *coralità,* so bitterly remarked in *Germany, Year Zero* and the films immediately following, now seems attributable to the comic selfishness of all humanity.

It is on this last point that the film has been most seriously attacked. Rossellini refuses to assign blame solely to the rich, and his "condemnation" assumes the global, exculpatory dimensions of "that's the way people are." The director's thoroughly bourgeois attitude thus allows him to criticize the poor for being just as "selfish" about money as the rich are. The doctor, as the man of reason and science, and thus a typical Rossellini stand-in, as we shall see, gives the thematic summation that in real life good and evil exist side by side; he claims that he has never been able to tell them apart. A moral position, in other words, once again substitutes for a political one. It is this that annoys Pio Baldelli about the film, and though his rhetoric may be a bit harsh, it is hard to disagree, finally, with his position: "The photographer claims to be doing justice, to punish evil-doers, but things gradually go from bad to worse, and the poor are even worse than the well-to-do: so let's just keep things as they are, and be patient: there's still the sun, happiness, and Sant'Andrea.[9]

III

The Bergman Era

12

Stromboli
(1949)

At about the same time *La macchina ammazzacattivi* was being shot, Ingrid Bergman, then at the height of her popularity, wandered into a small "art house" in Los Angeles with her husband, Petter Lindstrom, to see the film that all serious film people had been talking about—*Open City*. The film was already three years old, but the effect was staggering. After the screening, Bergman turned to her husband and said: "Petter, we must get this director's name straight. If there is such a man who can put *this* on the screen, he must be an absolutely heavenly being!"[1]

It is revealing that even at the moment of this initial contact, Bergman should translate her emotional experience of the film into a fascination with its director. Later in her autobiography, in fact, she admits that "deep down I was in love with Roberto from the moment I saw *Open City*, for I could never get over the fact that he was always there in my thoughts. . . . Probably, subconsciously, he offered a way out from both my problems: my marriage and my life in Hollywood" (pp. 210–11).

A few months later Bergman saw *Paisan* alone, in an empty theater, and decided that if this wonderful director only had a "big name" actress to work with, "then maybe people would come and see his pictures." She wrote him the following letter:

> Dear Mr. Rossellini:
> I saw your films *Open City* and *Paisan*, and enjoyed them very much. If you need a Swedish actress who speaks English very well, who has not forgotten her German, who is not very understandable in French, and who, in Italian knows only "ti amo" I am ready to come and make a film with you (pp. 4–5).[2]

In his excited response, Rossellini outlined at great length the film that was to become *Stromboli*. It concerned an East European refugee who marries a poor, uneducated fisherman from the volcanic island of Stromboli (pronounced with the accent on the first syllable), off the coast of Sicily, in order to escape the refugee camp. It is clear from Rossellini's letter that Bergman had quickly become bound up with his entire idea of the film: "I tried to imagine the life of the Latvian girl, so tall, so fair, in this island of fire and ashes, amidst the fishermen, small and swarthy, amongst the women with the glowing eyes, pale and deformed by childbirth, with no means to communicate with these people" (pp. 8–9). Her husband "lives beside her and loves her with a kind of savage fury . . . just like an animal not knowing how to struggle for life and accepting placidly to live in the deepest misery." Once she realizes she is pregnant, the woman tries to escape the harsh, uncomprehending life of the island by climbing over the volcano. Rossellini's letter continues:

> Frantic with despair, unable to withstand it any longer, she yet entertains an ultimate hope of a miracle that will save her—not realizing that a profound change is already operating within herself. Suddenly the woman understands the value of the eternal truth which rules human lives; she understands the mighty power of her who possesses nothing, this extraordinary strength which procures complete freedom. In reality she becomes another St. Francis. An intense feeling of joy springs out from her heart, an immense joy of living (p. 9).

What is perhaps most noteworthy in this treatment is Rossellini's obvious desire to represent women as real people with real difficulties and, like men, people who have to struggle with moral choices. As such, his project must have seemed enormously appealing to an actress who had probably reached her creative limit in Hollywood. As a popular magazine article of the time sympathetically, and correctly, suggested, she seemed to be looking for new challenges, and her two most recent pictures, *Joan of Arc* and *Arch of Triumph* had failed at the box office. It is also clear that she wanted to do something more serious than these Hollywood vehicles had ever allowed her to do. As for Rossellini, after staying for several weeks in early 1949 at the Lindstrom house in California, he was, according to Sergio Amidei,

> in a strange state of tension because what he was really interested in was capturing Ingrid not so much to make a film, and certainly not to make money, but for love, because he was completely in love. . . . There was also a little vanity involved. You have to realize what Italy was like in 1948, and what Bergman and Hollywood represented. What Bergman represented to a good-looking young Roman guy![3]

Originally, the film was to have been bankrolled by Sam Goldwyn, who had been pestering Bergman for years to make a picture with him. She had suggested Rossellini, and Goldwyn at first reacted favorably. A press conference was called, and Goldwyn proceeded to tell the reporters what the picture was going to be like. Unfortunately, his description did not at all accord with Rossellini's idea of things; Goldwyn then decided that he had better see more of Rossellini's work and arranged a screening of *Germany, Year Zero*. When the lights came back on at the end, there was only an embarrassed silence; everyone had obviously hated it. A few days later, Goldwyn called Bergman to tell her he could not produce the picture after all because Rossellini did not know anything about budgets and schedules (pp. 197–98).

The next financing possibility was Howard Hughes, who had also been after Bergman for some time and, according to the actress, with more in mind than just making a film. One day he called to tell her that he had just bought RKO so that she could do a film with him, and so when she was casting about for financing for *Stromboli,* she thought of Hughes. Even though he was totally uninterested in Rossellini's idea for the film, he agreed, thinking only of Bergman's *next* picture, which she would make in Hollywood for him.

Ingrid had been joyously greeted on her arrival in Italy, a country that had become thoroughly sick of its American liberators. In the words of Liana Ferri, who served as Rossellini's initial interpreter with Bergman, the symbolic value of Rossellini's "victory" was enormous. "Every woman in Rome was in love, it seemed, with an American soldier. . . . Then he had captured Ingrid. This great actress was in Italy to make a picture and she was in love with our Roberto Rossellini! 'Bravo, Roberto, bravo!' She had left that cold Nordic husband of hers. Now she would find the true meaning of life and love" (p. 208).

Rossellini, Bergman, and the rest of the sixty-five people in the crew sailed off on the four-hour boat trip to the forbidding island on April 4, 1949. The male leads, Mario Vitale (the husband, Antonio) and Mario Sponza (the lighthouse keeper from whom Karin seeks help), were played by fishermen the director had found in Salerno on the drive down the coast with Bergman. The priest who tries to help her accept her new life was an old classmate of Rossellini's, who the studio, at odds with the director concerning his improvisatory methods, had sent to provide a script. The house chosen for Karin and Antonio was so decrepit that it had to be shored up with wood, but because there was no wood on the island, an old boat had to be taken apart to provide it. Because of the appalling heat and dust, Rossellini was forced to shoot scenes over and over, contrary to his normal practice. Bergman had to become her own hairdresser, and do without make-up (or indoor plumbing). Nor was there a double for the difficult sequences—for instance, when she had to walk on jagged rocks through the water. Even more grueling was the incredible final scene, in which Bergman had to climb up the side of the active volcano—her hands, feet, and eyes actually burning—while violently gasping for breath. Hardly the treatment a Hollywood actress was accustomed to, and Bergman's persistence attests to her professionalism and, of course, her devotion to Rossellini. The conditions were, in fact, so bad that one of the director's assistants was overcome by the volcano's fumes and suffered a fatal heart attack.

Probably most difficult for Bergman was Rossellini's relaxed method of making films, without benefit of a prewritten script. She was appalled by his habit of writing out lines of script for the next day's shooting on a matchbox. Nor had she ever worked with nonprofessionals before, and she was amazed by Rossellini's system of yanking string tied to their toes as a signal for when they were to come in with their bits of dialogue. "I didn't have a string on my toe, so I didn't know when I was supposed to speak. And *this* was realistic film-making! The dialogue was never ready, or there never was any dialogue. I thought I was going crazy!" (p. 231). At times she simply blew up at Rossellini, totally frustrated. A great deal of expense was also incurred waiting for the right weather and for the volcano to cooperate in the filming of the scene that takes place at the edge of the crater. As to the actual eruption itself, Rossellini later told an interviewer that the volcano fortuitously started erupting one day while they were filming. "I always have confidence that these things will work out," he said.[4]

But all of these difficulties were smoothed over by the simple fact that Rossellini and Bergman had gloriously, if unwisely, fallen in love. The whole thing was messy from the first: paparazzi had followed them everywhere along their automobile trip down the Italian coast; a *Life* photographer caught them, in an unguarded moment in Amalfi, holding hands. At the end of March, Bergman wrote her husband telling him that she wanted to stay with Rossellini. The first official reaction to the brewing scandal came from Joseph I. Breen, head of the Production Code Administration. In a letter to Bergman, he mentioned the "expressions of profound shock" he had encountered everywhere regarding her apparent plans to abandon husband and daughter to take up with Rossellini, given that she was the *"first* lady of the screen." He also warned her that "such stories will not only *not* react favorably to your picture, but may very well *destroy your career as a motion picture artist.* They may result in the American public becoming so thoroughly enraged that your pictures will be ignored, and your box-office value ruined." He then urged her to issue a denial immediately to stamp out "these reports that constitute a major scandal and may well result in *complete disaster personally"* (pp. 235–36; emphasis in original). Walter Wanger, the producer of *Saint Joan,* which had just been released, sent her a nasty cable that concluded, "Do not fool yourself by thinking that what you are doing is of such courageous proportions or so artistic as to excuse what ordinary people believe" (p. 237).

Friends like Irene Selznick soon began offering support, however, and things became a little easier. Ernest Hemingway wrote, "If you love Roberto truly give him our love and tell him he better be a damned good boy for you or Mister Papa will kill him some morning when he has a morning free" (p. 241). But Ingrid continued to suffer guilt at leaving her family. The situation became even more difficult and melodramatic when Petter showed up in Sicily to "talk things over," and the possessive Rossellini threw a fit.

In the meantime, RKO was becoming increasingly preoccupied by the fact that the filming had gone over schedule by a month and, more importantly, over its $600,000 budget. Rossellini was given an ultimatum in the middle of July that if the picture was not completed in a week it would be abandoned. Bergman and Rossellini replied, detailing the tremendous hardships they had had to endure, and were given a short extension. Finally, in early August the shooting was finished.

Then trouble began in earnest. First, the world found out that Bergman was pregnant with Rossellini's child and the paparazzi began their twenty-four-hour stakeouts in the hopes of getting pictures. The baby, Robertino, was finally born on February 2, 1950, and to avoid the photographers, mother and child escaped from the hospital some days later in the middle of the night. Even the Congress of the United States became obsessed by the love affair. On March 15, 1950,

Senator Edwin C. Johnson of Colorado introduced a punitive bill in the Senate to license "actresses, producers and films by a division of the Department of Commerce." He assumed that the entire scandal had been manufactured to boost box-office receipts and denounced the "disgusting publicity campaign . . . the nauseating commercial opportunism . . . the vile and unspeakable Rossellini who sets an all-time low in shameless exploitation and disregard for good public morals" (p. 273). On the floor of the United States Senate, he complained: "When Rossellini the love pirate returned to Rome smirking over his conquest, it was not Mrs. Lindstrom's scalp which hung from the conquering hero's belt; it was her very soul. Now Mrs. Petter Lindstrom, and what is left of her has brought two children into the world—one has no mother; the other is illegitimate" (p. 274). Significantly, he added that Bergman had once been his own favorite actress, and suggested that now she must either be suffering from schizophrenia or was under hypnotic influence, since "her unnatural attitude toward her own little girl surely indicates a mental abnormality." He concluded that "under our law no alien guilty of turpitude can set foot on American soil again. Mrs. Petter Lindstrom had deliberately exiled herself from a country which was so good to her" (p. 274).

Problems with RKO continued to build. The original idea was to make two versions of the film—one Italian and one English—and the Italian version technically belonged to the "Berit Company," which had been set up by Bergman and Rossellini. The stock of this company was to have been held in escrow, as protection for RKO, but Rossellini never turned over the stock, and RKO became increasingly concerned about its million-dollar investment as shooting proceeded. Finally, RKO seized the negatives of both versions, but was unable to send them out of the country without Berit's authorization. At this point, Harold Lewis, RKO's production chief, hid the negatives in Rome; when Rossellini returned from Stromboli and discovered the seizure, he refused to turn over the negatives from the final week's shooting. The compromise that was finally reached was that Rossellini was to surrender the film and put Berit's stock in escrow, and RKO would return the negatives of the Italian version and allow him to edit it in Rome. The final Italian version would then be sent to Hollywood to serve as a guide for editing the English version.

What happened, however, was that RKO edited the English-language version exactly as the studio wanted to, and the result was so different from the director's original conception that he disowned it. Making things worse, the film's release in the United States was accompanied by lurid posters with which, according to Hollywood producer Dore Schary, Howard Hughes meant to capitalize on the scandal. Schary characterizes the poster's volcano "as a rather obvious phallic symbol"; Eric Johnston of the Motion Picture Producers Association even threatened Hughes with expulsion if he did not withdraw the posters immediately.[5]

The problem in properly evaluating this film is that the version seen in the United States—probably the only version that will ever be seen—is precisely the one disowned by Rossellini. Hence, most analyses have been skewed from the very beginning by not having the proper text to work with. The English version is actually some twenty minuts shorter than its Italian counterpart, presumably in order to "streamline" the plot. I will therefore want to consider the longer version in some detail, so as to begin to set the record straight. Most important, however, is the fact that the ending was drastically changed by the studio, though it must be said immediately that even Rossellini's ending is problematic in its religious emphasis and will not be to every viewer's taste. Nevertheless, I think a case can be made for the rightness of this ending, at least in terms of the dynamic that the film itself establishes. No such case can be made for RKO's version, however, and the utter unbelievability of its ending has long kept viewers from a proper appreciation of the film.

The primary differences between the two versions in the beginning and middle of the film are clear-cut. In the beginning of the Italian version, the credits play out against a background of clouds, perhaps clouds of smoke from the volcano. In the English version, however, they run against a map of the Mediterranean, with the camera dollying ever closer to the island of Stromboli as the credits continue. The point of all this is to set the events geographically, a typical Rossellini maneuver, and thus one suspects that here, at least, his plans for the English version were being heeded. Even more important than the map, however, is the footage of island life that immediately follows the credits. In the Italian version, the action begins in the refugee camp; in the English version, however, a crisp voice-over (the principal difference between the two versions) outlines the island's physical characteristics, how the people earn their living, and their ongoing, complicated relationship with that representative of death in their midst, the volcano. Only then does the voice-over of the English version move us to the displaced-person's camp, once the island's documentary reality has been set. Thus, the beginning, at least, of the version Rossellini felt compelled to disown is very close in spirit to his own practice.

The next great disparity is that many of the details of Karin's troublesome adaptation to island life are cut in RKO's version. For one thing, all the "useless" transition scenes are removed, such as the couple leaving the camp, catching the train, sailing on the big boat, transferring to the small boat, and so on. What remains, however, is melodramatically heightened. The young lighthouse keeper to whom Karin will later appeal, for example, is on the same boat, but in Rossellini's version, his possible importance to later events is only visually hinted at by a simple insert of him sitting on the floor of the boat. In the English version, however, the threat he represents is made clear by a strong dose of theme music. This version also rhetorically cuts to a much closer shot of the volcano's seething crater when they first arrive—a shot that is visually and narratively unmotivated—while the volcano's fearsomeness is further underlined by its rumbling on the sound track.

The most important changes, however (excluding the changes in the film's ending, which will be discussed later), come after the couple have had a violent quarrel. Karin has accused Antonio of not understanding that they are from different classes, telling him coldly that he will need much more money to take care of a woman like her. At the close of her outburst, she begins crying. In the English version, surprisingly, much of her crying is retained, far beyond the usual limits for such a scene. In Rossellini's version, however, the crying goes on even longer, and leads imperceptibly to several other narratively unfocused scenes that establish the creative *temps mort* we last saw in the finale of *Germany, Year Zero,* and that hearken back to similar moments in Rossellini's pre–*Open City* trilogy. Here, the crying scene is dragged out so long that Karin seems to go through several different stages of grief, filling us with tension because the rules of conventional filmmaking are deliberately being flouted. She hears a baby crying, puts money in a purse, hides the purse, and, still whimpering, goes outside, where the sequence finally ends. It is here, in fact, that Rossellini's long-take technique, characteristic of nearly all his subsequent films, assumes its definitive shape.

The sequences that immediately follow have also been removed from the English version, presumably because nothing "happens" in them and the narrative is not overtly advanced. First, we are shown an extreme long shot from a completely vertical bird's-eye view, looking down on the town, which turns its poor houses and narrow alleyways into a highly stylized maze. Karin runs around frantically, like the laboratory mice in the later *Fear,* shouting, "I want to get out!" The film then cuts to other, similar vertical shots that continue the maze pattern for quite some time, nicely spatializing Karin's mental and physical situation. Meanwhile, the baby is still crying and Karin continues her search for this other form of human life on the island. She then finds a small boy and tries to speak to him in English and pidgin Italian: "Say something to me!" she begs him. "Talk! Talk!" (Again, the Rossellinian urge for communication.) Frustrated at his refusal, she walks disconsolately past bare trees, harsh rocks, and various cacti that serve as a *Waste Land*–like index to the islanders' spirit and her own increasing desperation, a motif that looks forward, again, to the films of Antonioni. Most importantly—and most technically daring for 1949— she leans over the rocks, the cactus behind her, and begins chewing a piece of grass and stroking her cheeks with it in what becomes an extremely long take. Karin's ability to find pleasure on this godforsaken island, we realize, is reduced to the simple sensuality of a blade of grass on her face. The very length of the shot, and its "purposelessness," has allowed us to know her in a way utterly different from the more obvious techniques of conventional film narrative.

When this part of the scene is over, the camera follows Karin back to her pitiful house, and there we find some old men who have begun fixing things up on her husband's orders. She begins talking to them, and it turns out that they have all returned from America because they are old and they want to be buried on the island when they die. One of them, the most ancient, adds a nice comic touch when he says that he is going back to Brooklyn in about ten years. This scene is also significant because it continues the theme of the desperate emigration long associated with the island, which finally becomes an obsession with Karin. Even more importantly, perhaps, the old men cheer her up. We realize that Karin, like people in real life, may shift moods drastically, even if this shifting appears "inconsistent" in classic realistic acting and narrative terms. Again, none of the scenes described above remains in the RKO version of the film.

Apart from the differences, though, the two versions obviously share a great deal of common ground, and it is on this that we should focus. For the most part, the film works in terms of paired oppositions, the principal being, of course, that of Karin, the tall, fair, cold, somewhat awkward northerner, and Antonio, the short, swarthy, warm-blooded southerner, at home in his environment. Rossellini was fond of saying that the real division in the world was not between East and West, but between North and South, and this theme will reappear in the later Bergman films, most notably and most richly in *Voyage to Italy*. Here the contrast is always visually before us, given the physical characteristics of these two actors; Vitale, in fact, seems to have been chosen for the part precisely because his physiognomy contrasts so sharply with Bergman's.

Karin and Antonio's differences are stated immediately, accompanied by an overt use of symbols. Thus, when we first see them together in the camp, they are kept apart by barbed wire, which serves to suggest both the psychological and emotional separation that will continue to plague them, as well as the pain and violence they will inflict on each other. When they laughingly try to talk—in another appearance of Rossellini's obsessive language theme—they can barely make themselves understood, and in frustration Karin at one point says, "I don't understand!" He wants to marry her, he says, a proposition Karin welcomes as a way of escaping the hated camp. She says to him, "What if I'm different?" thus putting into play one of the film's key terms. Antonio responds by saying, "I know women and if you're different, I'll . . ." meanwhile laughing and making a hitting gesture that prefigures the sexual violence to come.

Some critics have felt that one of the flaws of the film is Bergman's "excessive prominence," to quote Pierre Leprohon. A variant of this theme—still the orthodox Hollywood version of the Rossellini-Bergman collaboration—is that Rossellini ruined both of their careers because he did not know how to use her properly. It is just as easy to claim, however, that Rossellini knew *exactly* what he was doing, for he clearly means to play her in counterpoint against type. As Karin, Bergman is complexly amoral, and the ambivalence of this role proved to be one more insuperable difficulty for those already outraged by the difference between her on-screen Hollywood roles (Joan of Arc and the nun in *The Bells of St. Mary's,* for example) and her "scandalous" real life as Rossellini's lover.

From the very beginning, Bergman smashes stereotypes; cold and calculating, Karin first does everything possible to get a visa to go to Argentina. The cutting itself nicely suggests causality, for after she tells her fellow "inmates" of her obsession with getting out of the camp, the film cuts to the scene of the hearing of the visa board. When her application is denied, we cut to her wedding, implying that this legal ceremony is merely an alternate version of the one that failed. Karin is distracted during the wedding mass and could not care less. Not coincidentally, one of the very first people she meets on her arrival on the island is the local priest, and it is here that many of the film's oppositions are first articulated. He tells her that she *will* be happy here, this is her home now. She must, in short, give up whatever individuality she retains to live by the group's rules. We sympathize with her plight, but her expedient view of the wedding, and the priest's kindly and warm manner, contrasting with her rather uncivil responses, make us feel that she is not being fair, that she has not given the island and its inhabitants a chance. And thus is initiated one of the most complex and important dynamics in the whole film. What makes *Stromboli* unique is precisely this refusal to completely favor either Karin or Antonio in their struggle, but rather to continue to insist, contrary to Celestino's view in *La macchina ammazzacattivi* and most conventional cinema practice, on the complexity, the mass of grays, that mark all human relationships, and that must also mark our moral judgments of others, including characters in a film. This refusal to take sides is the source of Rossellini's famous "distance" in the Bergman-era films, but it must be remembered that the distancing results primarily from the deliberate alternating of audience emotional response, rather than any supposed "coldness" on the director's part. This emotional alternation will be a major feature in the other Bergman films as well, and it is this that gives them their power. In fact, one of the major weaknesses of *Fear,* their last collaboration, is the breakdown of this dynamic, for in that film, despite Rossellini's apparent intentions, almost all the audience's sympathy is vested in the female character.

Karin asks Antonio why he kissed the priest's hand, and his response seems utterly foreign to this deracinated woman, this prime specimen of the spiritual decay of the postwar European world: "It's the custom," he says simply. They come to the broken-down shack in which he means to establish their family and he tells her grandly, "This is our home." Plunging forward, as always, he manifests his comfortableness and full insertion in this environment (cheerfully breaking down the door on the way), and in the process allows the camera to isolate her and reveal her increasing anxiety. Inside the crumbling house, Karin is further isolated against its grays and blacks, her apprehension in counterpoint to Antonio's obvious happiness. The scene then dissolves to a shot of him walking behind her toward the sea, the site of her outer limitation (and also the obvious place of escape that is denied her), and the impression we have of him is as a hulking ape. He speaks hopefully of the land on the island on which crops can be grown, and when he cannot remember the English word, he picks up a handful to show her. (Throughout the scene, his feet are symbolically bare, in contact with the land, while hers remain shod.) Just as he embraces her and says, "I'm so happy," the music builds to a climax and she violently pushes him away. She screams that she wants to go far away from the island, and Antonio reverts to the only set of values that he knows. "This is my home and you are my wife," he says firmly. "You stay here because I want to." For him, of course, words like *wife* and *home* have fixed, uncomplicated meanings.

Our own emotional position at this point is unclear. On the one hand, Antonio is clearly falling back on a model of male supremacy that we find unpalatable (and probably would have in 1949 as well). But we also appreciate his genuine love for Karin and for the earth, natural things, and his homeland. She, on the other hand, though clearly put upon, is absolutely uncompromising in her haughty demands. Rossellini will hold us in this complex emotional limbo throughout the film.

His purposeful ambivalence toward these characters was apparently there from the beginning. Regarding Antonio, he told Bergman in the long letter in which he initially outlined the story of the film:

I am quite sure you will find many parts of the story quite rugged, and that your personality will be hurt and offended by some reactions of the personage. You mustn't think that I approve of the behavior of HIM. I deplore the wild and brutal jealousy of the islander, I consider it a remainder of an elementary and old-fashioned mentality. I describe it because it is part of the ambience, like the prickly pears, the pines and the goats (p. 196).

So far so good. But then Rossellini betrays an admiration at another level for Antonio, and its *Wuthering Heights* brand of romanticism does not obscure a strong whiff of sadism: "But I can't deny in the deepness of my soul there is a secret envy for those who can love so passionately, so wildly, as to forget any tenderness, any pity for their beloved ones. They are guided only by a deep desire of possession of the body and soul of the woman they love. Civilization has smoothed the strength of feelings" (p. 196).

A split second after Antonio's assertion of the male prerogative, we understand the wide, unbridgeable emotional gap that separates them. The camera, echoing their feelings, cuts quickly to an extreme long shot that pins them in their forlorn isolation against the harshness of rock and sea. Karin walks away, leaving Antonio standing there. The camera begins suddenly to move in the opposite direction, panning up the hill past the pitiful town to the top of the volcano, that theophallic symbol of the ordering power of authority. This shot is followed by a cut to the bubbling crater, an obvious analogue to their own upset feelings, and then to their bedroom, where they sleep in different beds. In a short and wordless scene of great subtlety, we sense that Karin, who lies awake, is wrestling with ambivalent feelings. But she does not go to Antonio.

Our emotional division regarding the characters continues through the following scenes. Karin seems selfish and unfeeling when she tells Antonio that he is not good enough for her, that he will need much more money to keep a woman like her. In insisting that *she* is not an animal, she implies that he is, and an important motif is begun. Another scene casts Karin's fragile flesh against the forbidding backdrop of craggy rocks, and when she cries out to the priest that "this island drives me mad," and that she desperately wants to leave "the black rocks, the desolation, the terror," the emotional balance shifts once again in her favor. The priest, like Antonio, is hardly equipped to deal with a sophisticated women like Karin, and, falling back on his training, counsels patience while they save enough money to leave. But in the meantime, he tells her, she should make a "good home for her husband." And, in some easily missed lines, a new motif is articulated that is meant to prepare the way for, and make more believable, Karin's recognition of God at the end of the film. The priest says, "God will be merciful." She replies at the very last moment of the scene, "With me, God has never been merciful."

The next scene is principally documentary in tone, as we learn how the men make their livelihood fishing. Antonio is successful and returns with a pocketful of money and, developing the animal motif, a large fish for dinner. On one level, which will be elaborated later, the fish reminds us of Karin's status as victim. At another level it seems to be an alienating presence in the middle of the table, a challenge, and as such it signals the intrusion of nature, of the basic facts of life and death—Antonio's realm—into Karin's attempts to order her existence. It is this very dichotomy that will be so brilliantly worked out in *Voyage to Italy*. Here, an extraordinarily long take, like the earlier one of her crying, focuses almost clinically on Karin's reactions to the fish's presence.

Momentarily reconciled to her situation, she decides to decorate the house. In the process, however, she inadvertently activates the second phase of her difficulties, for the local women strongly disapprove. (In the Italian version, which includes more details of this scene, she paints a Matisse-like fresco on the wall, has a man cut off the legs of the chairs to make them low, and brings in a cactus.) Worst of all, she removes Antonio's pictures of his family and his favorite saints. His aunt tells her she is not "modest." This clash with local customs continues when she goes to the home of a "bad woman" (who happens to own a sewing machine) to have a skirt altered. She and the woman joke harmlessly with some of the local rowdies who have gathered below the window, and Antonio, returning from his day's work, happily joins the fun. When he discovers to his embarrassment who is behind the curtain, he yanks Karin out of the house and in the process has to undergo a painful-to-watch male showdown ritual in order to pass. Later in the film, Karin, in a provocative outfit, is sunning herself in a scene that recalls the sunbathing American beauty of *La macchina ammazzacattivi*. She plays innocently with the children among the rocks, but we are also conscious that she is showing quite a bit of leg. The lighthouse guard, who we first glimpsed on the boat crossing to the island, and who Karin had discovered in the "bad woman's" house recovering from malaria, rows up at this point and shows her how to catch an octopus using a barrel. She falls in the water, he helps her up—her clothes clinging to her body—and they exchange a subtle, but meaningful, look. Then a sudden, chilling cut reveals a long line of black-clad women watching the whole performance with great relish from above. (In the English version, the powerful reticence of this scene is vitiated by the reductive voice over that tells us how tongues will wag over this "simple, thoughtless act.") What follows is a brilliant sequence of Antonio on his way home; bawdy songs and imprecations calling him *cornuto* (cuckold) echo from quickly-closed windows along his way. When he finally reaches home, he fulfills the promise of violence we have expected from him all along and, without a single word, beats Karin savagely. The next morning, all of the old family and religious pictures have been returned to their original locations.

The struggle between the man and the woman is intimately tied up with the larger question, What is the proper balance between the needs of the individual self, especially one who is "different," and the needs of the group, as embodied in their life-regulating social customs? Part of the excellence of the film is its refusal to come down on one side or the other of this difficult question, like its refusal to make us identify exclusively with either Karin or Antonio. As Robin Wood has pointed out, in spite of the fact that almost everything we see is from Karin's point of view, "our sense of the alien-ness of the primitive community seen through Karin's eyes is everywhere counterpointed by our sense of the integrity of Stromboli's culture and its functional involvement with nature, against Karin's sophisticated needs and moral confusion."[6] Some critics have, for their own reasons, not wanted to credit this rich ambivalence, but have preferred to attack Rossellini for portraying Karin as unambiguously at fault. The editors of the British Film Institute dossier on Rossellini, for example, insist that "the logic of the film itself leaves little doubt that Karin is the 'trouble,' not the priest-ridden village where wife-beating appears to be part of the 'simple' life close to the 'authentic' values of human existence."[7] Borde and Bouissy, earlier anti-Rossellini polemicists, lump together all the Bergman-era films and egregiously maintain that they are all about "the redemption of the unworthy woman," all concerned with effacing "the sin of having a wet and hairy sexual organ." They move quickly to a global indictment:

> In summary, Rossellini specializes in an antiwoman cinema, or more exactly, the film of the familial settling of accounts. It's the old reactionary theme: ever since Eve listened to the serpent, she's been an idiot or a whore. The married man has a double function as redeemer. In accomplishing his conjugal duty, he transforms her into a mother. In torturing her for a good cause, he transforms her into a moral being.[8]

Sex *is* complexly present in *Stromboli,* but it is rarely expressed in any of the conventional ways. Indeed, Karin is a sexual creature who openly uses her sexuality to gain advantage in an unequal struggle. Yet Rossellini refuses to essentialize—at least in this instance, on the subject of woman—taking instead an *individual* woman's problems seriously and making them the focus of his cinematic effort. His essentializing move is rather to make her stand for suffering humanity.

The first important "sexual" scene is Karin's private meeting with the priest, at his home, which occurs the day after Antonio has discovered her in the "bad woman's" house. She goes to the priest in desperation, searching for someone who will understand her. She tells him that she is unhappy and thinks she's going mad, but the priest says that Antonio is unhappy too. (Her inner turmoil is visually signaled by the fact that, under her black sweater, she is wearing a dress with a bizarre, jagged-edge pattern.) She begs the priest for money that has been entrusted to him by emigrants for upkeep of the cemetery, making a convincing case in favor of supporting life rather than death—but we quickly realize that she is only thinking about herself and does not care in the slightest about the island's traditions. During her confession, she moves closer and closer to the priest, consciously or unconsciously, and tells him, "You are the only man here who can understand me." The point, of course, is that he is not a "man," but a priest, with a clearly circumscribed spiritual role to play, and it is this that she does not understand. As Karin gets closer, his discomfort increases. He denies that he is the only one who can comfort her. She moves even closer, and when his housekeeper enters with a liqueur, they guiltily jump apart. Throughout this part of their encounter, the shots are very tight (mostly over-the-shoulder), the kind of shots often associated with love scenes. After twice resisting Karin's continuing advances, the priest finally tells her that he can talk to her only in confession, and that she must leave. We cut to a one-shot as her pleading face is suddenly flushed with hatred. She screams that he is "just like all the rest."

This must have been a rather raw scene in 1949, but there is more than just a sexual drama going on here. One of the main problems causing most spectators to see the religiousness of the film's ending as unprepared for and un-

Victims: Karin (Ingrid Bergman) tries to protect a rabbit from her husband (Mario Vitale) in *Stromboli* (1949).

motivated is that it is easy to take the priest in this scene, as Karin does, as just another person she is talking to about her problems, rather than as the representative of God that he and his villagers take him to be. In the film's terms, in other words, he is a spiritual figure who is trying to lead her to a more unselfish life, one that has a place for God. Thus, during their encounter she overtly puts matters in moral terms when she tells him, "I've sinned, I've been lost. I've chased illusions, adventures, as though an evil force were behind me." Confessing that she was a collaborator during the war, dating Nazi officers, she says, "I realize now how wrong I've been. I want to make something of my life. But this is too much—I can't go from one extreme to another." Finally, when the priest rejects her entreaties, she shouts, "Your God won't help!" The very power of this scene's sexuality, in other words, can cause the spectator to miss the spiritual drama unfolding at the same time.

Another important moment follows, a moment extending the animal-sexual motif that will reach its peak in the famous tuna-fishing sequence. Karin has come off badly in the scene with the priest, in spite of our initial sympathy with her plight, but again Rossellini turns the emotional tables. She finds Antonio in front of their home on her return from the priest, and he shows her an animal she has never seen before. She asks what kind of an animal it is, and is told that it is a ferret for hunting and killing rabbits. He proceeds to give her a gruesome display of how quickly and violently the ferret is able to dispatch the rabbit he releases. All of Karin's frustration built up during the scene with the priest now pours out as she pounds Antonio wildly and calls him a "stupid, savage beast," but he only laughs at her inability to do any physical or psychological damage to him. The real source of her frustration, however, is that she sees *herself* as an animal, the defenseless rabbit being attacked. In the Italian version, Rossellini makes the point even more strongly as we cut back to the animals' death struggle; in a series of horrifying shots, including some close-ups, the ferret destroys the still wildly kicking rabbit and drags it away.

What follows is the interlude with the lighthouse keeper, mentioned earlier, the gossip of cuckoldry, and Antonio's savage beating of Karen to reclaim her as his property. He takes her on a "public relations" tour of the village—to the cemetery, to the church—where, with all the eyes of the villagers on them, he publicly reasserts his mastery over her. Her defeated, distracted presence in the church, far from any real religious devotion, suggests again, as we saw in several earlier films, the basic inability of organized religion to fulfill spiritual needs.

In spite of—or because of—her humiliation, this brutal treatment seems to have the desired effect, and a rapprochement of sorts begins to develop, leading to another emotional climax in the magnificent tuna-fishing sequence that was incorrectly identified by Claude Mauriac in his influential *L'Amour du cinéma* (to Rossellini's anger) as having been filmed by another director. In the very beginning of the sequence, Karin inappropriately has herself rowed out to the scene of the tuna fishing, again asserting her difference, for no village woman would ever think of intruding onto this male territory. With some of the very few pleasant words she ever says to Antonio in the entire course of the film, she tells him, "I want to be with you. I'll go if you want; I don't want to embarrass you in front of the other men." The coarse and simple Antonio, in love but clearly in over his head with this sophisticated woman, affectionately tells her it is all right for her to stay: (The warmth of this moment, of course, is greatly vitiated by the knowledge that it presumably *results* from her beating.)

The pace quickens as the nets are brought in closer and closer, and the sea begins to churn as the still-unseen fish try desperately to escape. The voice-over of the English version casts the scene in an overtly documentary mode, linking the annual reappearance of the tuna in the same place with the workings of a "higher power." The entire sequence is a brilliant textbook illustration, reminiscent of the Po episode of *Paisan,* of how to build emotion through rhythm, expectation, and suspended fulfillment. But the abstract beauty quickly turns into the more concrete reality of killing as the huge fish are speared one after the other and heaved inside the boat. As the violence mounts, the intercuts of Karen's shocked reaction come more quickly, resulting in an even more profound version of the revulsion she experienced in the scene with the ferret and rabbit. Again, however, she is not horrified just by the violence, but also because she sees an analogue of her own situation in that of the tuna. Were she merely reacting to the violence, we might be justified in considering her hopelessly alienated from the "true," "natural," life of the village. Instead, we understand that, like the tuna, she is a helpless victim whose selfhood is being extinguished by forces beyond her control. There is also an obvious sexual subtext operating in this sequence, and, as with the ferret scene, one that is clearly sadistic. Jean-

Claude Bonnet has suggestively described one of these elements: "The stranger who faints at the sight of enormous harpooned and bloody fish is sprinkled by the rough slap of a tuna's tail. 'It was horrible,' she cries in the next scene during the eruption, when we find out that she is pregnant."9 The question that remains open, as usual, is where is Rossellini in all of this? Is he sympathizing with woman as social and sexual victim, or heaping more pain on her, trying to "redeem" her?

After the violence—sexual and otherwise—of the "day of the slaughter of the tuna fish," as the voice-over identifies it, we move to the obviously phallic expression of the volcano in *its* fullest moment of violence. From a shot of the volcano, we cut to a shot of Karin trying to light a fire in her oven, and almost as though she has begun some natural chain of events with her innocent act, the volcano begins to grumble in its loud bass voice. Again, the rhythm of the editing is perfect, and the beautifully composed shots move quickly before our eyes. United in the face of the overwhelming danger of an infinitely more powerful and more basic nature, Karin and the villagers momentarily put aside their superficial struggle as everyone moves out to sea on the fishing boats in order to escape the volcano's fury. The people in the water now become a kind of floating village, and we realize again that the village is indeed its people, not the houses or the earth on which they stand. They have taken their spiritual values with them, and gain solace in the monotonous repetition of the Catholic litany of the saints, offered as an incantation to propitiate the pagan god of the volcano. We learn that Karin is pregnant, and in the peace of the scene we think that a longer-range truce might be possible through the intermediary of the child, who will be both hers and the village's, in a way, a living merger of the self and the group. Significantly, she is no longer seen in isolated one-shots, but is now part of the larger whole. Her "different" culture, however, keeps her from joining in the recitation of the litany.

And, indeed, such a truce is not to be. The conditions of her existence on the island are simply not bearable; whether this is her fault or not is finally beside the point. Rossellini means to describe an existential condition rather than assign blame: this is simply the way things are, and now that a child is coming, her situation becomes all the more urgent. When she decides to leave the island, and will not be turned from her resolve, Antonio literalizes the film's continuing animal imagery by boarding up the doors and windows of the house, turning her into a caged beast. Once again, she must use her "feminine wiles" to escape her husband's ignorant brutality, and, like so many women before her, she is forced to turn to another man for her liberation, considering the physical threat against her. She plays up to the lighthouse keeper, luring him into a cave on the beach; this is obviously *her* place, the place of Circe and Calypso, of the vagina and the womb (It's peaceful here," she says), as opposed to the masculine power and patriarchal authority that reign everywhere else on the island and are embodied in the volcano. She tells him in blatantly manipulative tones, which make it difficult for us to side with her in spite of the pain she has suffered, that her husband "beat her like a beast." We also realize, however, that she *must* be manipulative, as this is the only weapon that remains to her. Refusing to wait a minute longer, she decides to escape by ascending the forbidding volcano, a gesture laden with symbolic import. For Rossellini, as we have seen, the volcano represents the awesome power of nature that must somehow be engaged and submitted to in order to behold the power, majesty, and beauty of God. It is equally possible, of course, to see the volcano as the very embodiment of the patriarchal order of things, which Karen challenges, an order that must break the spirit of the independent, threatening female to its will.

As Karin ascends the volcano, she symbolically loses, one by one, all of her ephemeral appurtenances—her suitcase, her purse, and the money she has taken from Antonio to finance her escape. Powerful in the world of men, this money is worthless in the more basic world of nature. Smoke from the volcano billows around her, suggesting the fires of hell or purgatory, intimating that, from the director's perspective, she must be shriven of her pride to be able to come through, both physically and morally, to the other side. For Rossellini, what is important is the decisive, traumatic moment—the moment when the forces of the universe and the inner soul come into delicate balance and, as in a Wordsworthian vision, one is allowed a glimpse into the spiritual heart of things. At one point Karin is uncertainly poised halfway between the world of men and the world of God (Rossellini clearly distinguishes them) and significantly looks up to the crater and then back to the village. Bathed in a magnificent light that makes her radiant against the blackness of the lava, she decides to continue upward, repeating Nanni's gesture in *The Miracle,* moving ever closer to the rarified atmosphere of the spiritual, away from the earthly. Too many critics have seen her choice as merely one of going on with her individual life or resigning herself to the constricted life of the village, but clearly this is only its secondary manifestation. Rather, the film poses her choice as between continuing to be a selfish individualist or realizing the existence of something higher that transcends and enfolds within it mere social questions of the individual versus the group.

The religious resonance of the ending also becomes clear, for the horrible ascent up the fearful volcano is Karin's dark night of the soul. As the dangerous smoke and fumes surround and choke her, she is offered a literal vision of hell. Throughout this sequence, in close-up after close-up, her wedding ring is greatly in evidence, a constant reminder of the social ties that are calling her back to the village; these ties also pale into insignificance in the face of the primordial power of the volcano. Sobbing wildly, she cries out, "I'll finish it, but I haven't the courage; I'm afraid!" She also cries out the name of God twice, but as an expletive, a neutral verbalization of her frustration and exhaustion (again, like Nanni's *"Dio, Dio"* at the end of *The Miracle*). The image then fades to a more peaceful moment sometime later. The stars are out. The film cuts again a few seconds later to morning and, as Karin wakes up, she blocks the sun with her hand. Again she says, "Oh God!" twice, but now the expletive has been transformed into an act of homage to the magnificent stillness all around her. She touches her abdomen, recalling her child for us, and, looking around, cries, "What mystery! What beauty!" in a way that, to this viewer at least, seems utterly convincing. Through her ghastly trial she now seems to have arrived at a better understanding of her place in the world. Then the film cuts to a shot of birds wheeling in the sky (presumably symbolic of Karin's spiritual rebirth), a shot that has been prepared for with similar shots of birds flying around in the peace following the volcano's eruption.

It is at this point that the English and Italian versions of the film distinctly divide, and if its finale is to be condemned, it should be Rossellini's rather than RKO's. For some, of course, the very religiosity of the ending, in either version, is cause enough to dismiss the entire film. Those who *have* been able to accept its spiritual dimension have for the most part, however, objected to Karin's apparent decision to return to the village at the very last moment, totally sub-jugating her own sense of self to the will of others. In the English version, her return is clear-cut and unambiguous, even praised; in the Italian version, how-ever, the ending is more characteristically ambivalent, and Rossellini refuses to provide a satisfying closure.

In the RKO version, the obtrusive voice-over comes straight out and tells us exactly what to think: "Out of her terror and her suffering, Karin had found a great need for God. And she knew now that only in her return to the village could she hope for peace."[10] While the "uplifting" musical theme soars, the camera cuts between her smiling, beatific face and the village, ending on a slight zoom on the village, within the context of the extreme long shot. Even apart from the obvious sexist wish fulfillment of this ending, it is clearly the forced, explicit naming of the religious theme in this way that has made the final scene so unpalatable to American viewers.

In Rossellini's version, the voice-over is, as throughout the film, completely absent. After Karen cries, "What mystery! What beauty!" the film cuts to a long shot of the mountain. The camera then pans up the mountain, empha-sizing its active participation in Karen's religious conversion, and then pans back down to find her. In a full shot, she stands on a small hillock, looking down at the village. The film cuts to the village in long shot and we hear her say offscreen, "No, I can't go back!" Cut back to her. She sits down. Cut to a tight head-and-shoulders shot. "They are horrible. It was all horrible, she says. Cut back to an extreme long shot of the village, pasted on the very edge of the vast sea, another brute power of nature. "They don't know what they're doing," she says offscreen, in one of the Christological references Rossellini is fond of, which would link Karin even more closely to that earlier female Christ-victim figure, Nanni. The difference between the two women becomes immensely clear in the next line, however, for Karin is an intelligent being in full command of her rational faculties: "I'm even worse," she says. Cut to an extreme close-up on her face, as she looks away, disgusted both by the village and by herself. She begins crying, quickly turns her head back, and says, "I'll save him." Cut to a full shot in which she holds her abdomen and says, "My innocent child!" Cut to a close-up as she shouts, "God, my God! Help me! Give me the strength, the understanding, and the courage!" She buries her head, sobbing, then cries more softly, "God, God." Cut to birds flying overhead as the camera pans across the sky. Offscreen, we hear her saying, "My God! Oh merciful God!" (or perhaps "Almighty God!") as the birds continue to fly past. In this version, the film ends with a shot of the billowing smoke of the volcano.

Clearly, what is important for Rossellini is the individual's growth from selfish ego toward a transcendent spirituality. It is much less important here than in the English version whether or not Karin returns to the village. It is equally possible, of course, to read this ending as the submission of the independent female to the patriarchal authority; but the patriarch here is God, not her husband Antonio or his male-dominated society. In the mid-sixties, Adriano Aprà and Maurizio Ponzi asked Rossellini in an interview if Karin is leaving or returning to the village at the end. He replied:

> I don't know. That would be the beginning of another film. The only hope for Karin is to have a human attitude toward something, at least once. The greatest monster has some humanity in him. . . . There is a turning point in every human experience in life—which isn't the end of the experience or of the man, but a turning point. My finales are turning points. Then it begins again—but as for what it is that begins, I don't know. I'll tell that another time, if it has to be told. If things haven't happened there's no point in going on and getting involved in another story.[11]

In a 1959 interview he put it even more directly: "A woman has undergone the trials of the war; she comes out of it bruised and hardened, no longer knowing what a human feeling it. The important thing was to find out if this woman could still cry and the film stops there, when the first tears begin to flow."[12]

Critical orthodoxy on the ending of *Stromboli*, even in its Italian version, is negative. Most have felt that the ending is simply too abrupt and unprepared for; even the Catholic phenomenologist Henri Agel is lukewarm about it. Nevertheless, I think an argument can be made that various elements of the film (for example, the early scenes with the priest, the fact that the full title of the Italian version is *Stromboli, Land of God,* and so on), which are perhaps more subtle than the harsh male-female, individual-group clash that occupies the surface, contribute to the rightness, in its own terms, of the film's spiritual resolution. Rossellini has pointed out with some justice that anyone properly attentive to the epigraph from Isaiah in the opening credits would be able to understand how appropriate the ending really is: "I have hearkened to those who have asked nothing of me. I have let myself be found by those who were not looking for me" (Isa. 65:1). Robin Wood is right, I think, to find Karin's conversion "meticulously prepared for," though never specific. Though Wood's essentialist language is somewhat troublesome, he is on the right track when he says, "More than with any other director the essential meaning has to be read behind and between the images, in the implications of the film's movement which rise to the surface only in rare privileged moments whose significance is never overtly explained and which draw their intensity as much from the accumulations of context as from anything present in the image."[13]

Beyond its ending, an even grander chorus of voices has condemned this entire film and, indeed, the entire series of Bergman-Rossellini collaborations. Some, like Mida, have found fault with Bergman, who forced Rossellini to betray his "real interest" in *coralità,* making him altogether too "intellectual." Others—and this is still the dominant opinion in Hollywood—refuse to concede that Rossellini was up to something altogether different (whether it was successful or not is another question) and blame him for "ruining" Bergman's career. However, another, more recent view—one that I share—considers these films with Bergman as among Rossellini's greatest, and, in spite of their faults, among the most significant films made since World War II. Andrew Sarris, for example, has said that "Rossellini's sublime films with Ingrid Bergman were years ahead of their time, and are not fully appreciated even today in America."[14] Nor, he might have added, anywhere else. Bruno Torri, in his *Cinema italiano: Dalla realtà alle metafore*, has perhaps come the closest to accounting for the brilliance of these films, and his remarks provide an important clue to understanding why the young style-conscious critics of *Cahiers du cinéma* would become their first champions:

> They undoubtedly represent the most advanced that Italian cinema was able to produce in those years beyond the paths already travelled. . . . His is a cinema of questions, not answers; and therefore, also under this profile, the heuristic function ("socratic," as has been justly noted) which his films develop brings with it a final step toward the full autonomy of film style, a decisive freeing from the "banal" (and from cultural parasitism) and finally, what counts the most, a major attempt to make the spectator more responsible, since he is now called on not so much to consent or dissent on more or less univocal messages, to pronounce on attitudes and propositions ideologically already known, as to take up on his own behalf the thread of a discourse specifically cinematographic in a concrete and open time, just as any reality is concrete and open.[15]

For better or worse, then, *Stromboli* and the other Bergman-era films are "pure" Rossellini. The director himself once insisted that *Stromboli* was important to him, and whoever did not like it had no reason to like any of his other films either.[16]

13

Francesco, Giullare di Dio
(1950)

At the very height of the scandal, while Bergman and Rossellini were being accused of the most heinous crimes against morality and human decency, Rossellini was busy making the most overtly religious film of his life. Later films like *Augustine of Hippo, Acts of the Apostles,* and *The Messiah* are, as we shall see, ultimately more concerned with history than theology or the spiritual life. *Francesco, giullare di Dio* (Francis, God's Jester) to give it its full title, is delicately poised between the two. Thus, it clearly fits into the religious search and questioning of "crisis-era" films like *The Miracle, Stromboli,* and *Europa '51,* its modern-day "sequel," which immediately followed. At the same time, however, *Francesco* signals the beginning of Rossellini's interest in the depiction of history per se. (It is also possible, of course, to see *Open City, Paisan,* and *Germany, Year Zero* as "historical films" that depict the recent past.)

This new interest in history is obvious throughout the film, but especially in the beginning of the American version (which, unlike *Stromboli,* Rossellini seems to have been responsible for).[1] There, we are historically situated through paintings and frescoes to give us the proper context to understand what we are about to see. In this, it is similar to the American version of the opening of *Stromboli* and, of course, the map and voice-over that move us through *Paisan.*[2] In other words, a strong didactic interest reigns in this film, as in most of Rossellini's films; this impulse is more overt in the later television work, but it is present from the first. Here the frescoes function to create an otherness in time, a past place that the film will consciously seek to represent, to signify, without attempting to recreate the historical period illusionistically. The difference may seem slight, but is in fact crucial and is the strategy that makes many of the later historical films more epistemologically sophisticated than they seem at first glance. The frescoes, which Rossellini's camera pans while the voice-over explains the historical events they represent, complexly negotiate the distance between the filmic representation of the past and the past itself. They *represent* the past for us, yet they, in fact, also *are* the past because they were made then, but continue to exist in our day.

This strategy is characteristic of the whole film, and not just the opening of the American version, for Rossellini has not chosen to represent the historical Saint Francis, but quite clearly, as the opening credits tell us, to base the film on the *prior representation* of Francis and his followers in the *Fioretti* (*Little Flowers*), first written right after Francis' death. This can, of course, be regarded as an attempt to get closer to the "truth" or "essence" of Saint Francis; but it also is a subtle admission that we cannot really get back to the past, as *Ding an sich,* but only represent it in ways that will always be more or less "distorted" by previous interpretations of it. As a version of the *Fioretti,* a genuine piece of writing from the past that continues to exist into the present, the film is both more authentic and yet further removed from real historical events themselves. In the Italian version, this process of mediation is even more deliberately foregrounded, as intertitles taken directly from chapter headings of the *Fioretti* are flashed on the screen before each new vignette. As we shall see, this general strategy of temporal doubling continues through the later historical films, when Rossellini insists on words and more words drawn from actual historical documents. In a sense, it is really the words, which exist in two times, that make these films "historical."

Rossellini has recounted in several interviews how *Francesco* came to be made. During the filming of *Paisan,* the director found himself with three German prisoners who were cooperating with the filming, if rather uneasily, and who finally took refuge in a monastery, where they knew they would be safe. When Rossellini and Fellini went to fetch them, they discovered the lovely shelter that became the setting for the monastery sequence of *Paisan.* From that day on, both men were intrigued with the idea of using these monks to make a film on Saint Francis himself, a film that would go back to the roots of the innocent naïveté and generosity (even if mistaken) that marks the monastery episode of the earlier film.[3] According to Brunello Rondi, who was associated with the film in its early stages, shooting began with a twenty-eight-page treatment (including only seventy-one lines of dialogue!) that had been worked up by Rossellini and Fellini alone. Fellini told his biographer Solmi that he had personally suggested the humorous scene with the tyrant Nicolaio; nevertheless, the film has always been regarded by those involved as Rossellini's creation. This fact must be insisted upon because of the common rhetorical tactic, used by an older generation of Communist critics to discredit Rossellini's films during this period, of suggesting that the film's "mysticism" and religiosity were the fault of the even more intensely disapproved-of Fellini, who had turned his back on anything even remotely resembling social realism. The screenplay, such as it was, and the rest of the dialogue were written later, during the actual shooting, as was Rossellini's wont, by the director, Rondi, and Father Alberto Maisano, who was in charge of the novices. Rondi has attested that no one else was involved (in spite of the fact that the credits say that two priests, Felix Morlion and Antonio Lisandrini, also participated in the screenplay), and that at no time was there any church interference with Rossellini and Fellini's original idea. This testimony is important because some have accused Rossellini of making Catholic propaganda in this film; Rondi contends that, on the contrary, ecclesiastical authorities were displeased with the film because of its too-human portrayal of the saint.[4]

As the credits proudly state (hearkening back at least eight years to *La nave bianca*), "The actors were taken from real-life," with the exception of Aldo Fabrizi (as in *Open City*), in the role of the tyrant Nicolaio. Rossellini preferred working with nonprofessionals, but he never insisted that a real fisherman had to play a fisherman, a real farmer a farmer. Here, however, the coincidence is exact, and the friars are all played by real Franciscans.

When the film appeared, critical reaction was mixed, and it failed miserably at the box office. Interestingly enough, many neorealist critics who had sadly shaken their heads during the period of Rossellini's "crisis" warmly welcomed the film as a return to his "true" theme and mode, *coralità*, and in fact, an *overcoming* of the director's proclivity toward mysticism. Marxist critics, on the other hand, with Pio Baldelli leading the charge, attacked it as being little more than propaganda for the Church and, since 1950 was a papal holy year, Rossellini's attempt to get back in the Vatican's good graces.

The extensive polemic surrounding this film has revolved chiefly around the question of its historical veracity to the times, the Franciscans, and the saint himself. The debate is marked, on both sides, by appallingly simplistic notions concerning what it would mean to be historically true to a past epoch, and how one would go about finding a neutral ground from which one could portray the past "in its own terms," or even better, "objectively." Thus, the argument centers around claims of Rossellini's success or failure in this area, rather than the very possibility of presenting history objectively. It seems clearer today that the film offers itself, through the intermediary of the *Fioretti*, rather as a reading of history, of history as a text that cannot be grasped in a direct and unmediated form. At this point, at least, Rossellini seems to realize that all interpretations must be subjectively based, like all depictions of "reality," whether they are of an earlier era, or, as we shall see in *India*, of an alien culture.

But Rossellini would have refused to make the next step, toward either the utter unknowability of history or a radical relativism. In the later historical films, in fact, where more is at stake, he even wants to elide the subjective element altogether in favor of an "unbiased" presentation of facts. Rossellini also subscribes to an idea of history composed in grand outlines of major turning points, shifts in consciousness—a view of history that is itself, of course, only another interpretation. Thus, in *Francesco* he is not trying to portray merely a specific saint and his way of being in the world—though he is doing that as well—but also, as in his later historical films, what he takes to be a turning point in world history. Similarly, the title's emphasis on the person of Saint Francis is itself belied, for from the very beginning of the film—when for the longest time Rossellini refuses to single out Francis—great pains are taken to decenter the saint, to see him as a member of a group and as part of an era. (Some critics have complained that Brother Ginepro, the foolish monk around whom many of the unconnected episodes revolve, is accorded too much importance in the film, at the expense of Francis, but it is clear that this is a crucial and conscious tactic.) Rossellini's later historical films will repeat this contradictory double stress on the individual and his time: films like *Augustine of Hippo, Pascal, Socrates,* and so on all point, even in their titles, to a "great man" theory of history, but since the individual figures serve in the films chiefly as organizing devices for the presentation of the characteristics of an age, the theory is at the same time undone.

Of earlier critics, Mida seems closest to a proper sense of Rossellini's historical relativism. For him, the interpretation of Francis is rather "loose" and poetic, but he prefers this to a cold recital of facts: Rossellini "is faithful to history, but it is a faithfulness that must be understood through the fantasy of an artist, who takes everything from the legend which inspires and moves him."[5] Later critics like Jose Guarner have rightly insisted that the historical recreation has been whittled down to a recreation of ideas; and Giorgio Tinazzi has pointed out, the principal idea here is "Franciscanism as a way of existence."[6] In other words, Rossellini's interest in the depiction of history primarily for its informational value is not nearly as developed as it will be later in the films made for television. Here, he remains a captive of the religious impulse of films like *The Miracle* and *Stromboli*[7] (remember that Saint Francis was also mentioned in Rossellini's first letter to Bergman), and *Francesco* serves retrospectively as a *grounding* for the relentless spiritual striving of these earlier films.[8]

But if religious values are privileged over the "facts," Rossellini nevertheless had a didactic purpose in mind in making this film. As in the other films of this period, he is concerned with the despair and cynicism facing postwar Europe, and unashamedly offers Saint Francis and his philosophy as answers, as a way back to an essential wholeness. Just as the turn to God at the end of *Stromboli* may embarrass us nowadays with its overt religiosity, so too the "message" of *Francesco* is militantly old-fashioned, as Rossellini told students at the Centro sperimentale di cinematografia in the early sixties:

> It was important for me then to affirm everything that stood against slyness and cunning. In other words, I believed then and still believe that simplicity is a very powerful weapon. . . . The innocent one will always defeat the evil one; I am absolutely convinced of this, and in our own era we have a vivid example in Ghandhism. . . . Then, if we want to go back to the historical moment, we must remember that these were cruel and violent centuries, and yet in those centuries of violence appeared Saint Francis of Assisi and Saint Catherine of Siena.[9]

Marcel Oms may claim that one does not vanquish tyrants by nonviolence, as Brother Ginepro does in the *Fioretti* and the film, but Rossellini clearly feels otherwise. Revolutionary after his own fashion, the director believes, with Shelley, that the individual must first be changed before society can be changed. Naturally, this can seem to be the kind of phony "revolution" always fostered by the bourgeoisie, who speak of spiritual values rather than material ones because their material lives are relatively comfortable. In any case, it obviously took courage for Rossellini to offer such transparently "retrograde" values to a modern audience, and in many ways the radicalism of this film lies in its fearless exposure of the director's vulnerable idealism. As we shall see, this courage is even more evident in his next film, *Europa '51*, which carries the same message as *Francesco* but removes it from the comfortable safety of the distant past to the startling present of its title.

In formal terms, *Francesco* is a film whose thoroughgoing unconventionality makes the polemics surrounding its historical veracity almost irrelevant. For one thing, there is really no plot in the film, and scarcely more characterization. It revels in the partial, the hint, the barely glimpsed, shunning the fully "narrativized" or the straightforwardly presented. Aside from Brother Ginepro's violent encounter with the tyrant Nicolaio and his men, we get little more than humorous misunderstandings about needing a pig's foot to make soup (Ginepro "convinces" a still-living pig to donate its foot), Saint Francis telling the birds to be quiet so that he can pray, and the loving, simple preparations for the visit of Saint Clair. Again, as we have seen in other Rossellini films, the sketch, the vignette, and the illuminating anecdote are favored over a doggedly linear exposition. The individual scenes from the *Fioretti* chosen for "dramatization" do not seem inevitable, nor do they really cohere (as some have complained), but, then again, they were never meant to. Rather, an atmosphere is created and a minimalist structural system of opposites elaborated in a denuded and thoroughly unrealistic setting. As part of this strategy, the process of symbolization is foregrounded throughout in the constant references to the purgative emblems of fire and rain. The monks' full-throated Gregorian chant, which links many of the vignettes, also contributes to the purposeful lack of realism, for it was obviously recorded by a large choir singing in a church. Similarly, gestures and other movements of bodies and heads are greatly slowed down, further stylizing the film in the direction of greater simplicity. What is at stake, once again, is an *idea* rather than an illusionistic reconstruction.

History, or better, historiography, on the other hand, is linear, fully elaborated, logical, supremely rational. There are beginnings and endings and—at least to judge by the work of most historians—clear-cut narratives, with the rising action, falling action, and climax all properly arranged, according to the neat codes of realism, no matter what violence may be done to the actual fabric of lived experience. In other words, in the depiction of the "divine madness" that afflicted Saint Francis and his followers, it was important to Rossellini in 1950 to avoid the rigors of a supposedly objective historiography because its logical linearity would itself have been inimical to the Franciscans' crazy world of faith. As Henri Agel has reminded us, these early Franciscans, thought eccentric, were simply disaffected with the power of rationality that we hold so dear. In this regard he compares Rossellini's film to Dreyer's *Ordet*: in both, "Faith blows up all the logical mechanisms."[10] Elsewhere, Agel says of *Francesco* that it demonstrates "a perfect disaffection of the soul vis-à-vis the mental processes of a civilized adult."[11] Thus, an "accurate" historical recreation will be one more logical mechanism that Rossellini must blow up if the film's form is to reflect its subject matter.

One very obvious casualty will thus be the rigorous logic of narrative itself. Strictly speaking, narrative is continually defeated in this film (at least in its largest sense, for "narrative" per se can never be finally defeated, since even a single shot can be "narrativized" at some minimal level), in favor of the incomplete, the aleatory, and the suggestive poetic anecdote that is, narratively, a dead end. Here the tableau, the anecdote, and the image exist more easily in a stylized world of symbolic values than would a strongly plotted film full of "realistic" action. Henri Agel describes this technique as Rossellini's "aesthetic of insignificance," an aesthetic we have seen as early as *La nave bianca* and *L'uomo dalla croce*—where it manifested itself as a documentation of reality for its own sake—as well as in the long takes of later films. In many ways this aesthetic of insignificance, of "banality," as Agel calls it elsewhere, is directly related to the famous long-take sequence invented by Cesare Zavattini for De Sica's *Umberto D.*, made two years later, in which we spend several minutes watching a maid clean up the kitchen in the early morning, while nothing "happens." Both point toward the indirect, meandering antinarrativity of Antonioni's films of the late fifties and early sixties. As Brunello Rondi has nicely put it: "The sequences of *Francesco* do not have an irresistible rhythmic movement which leads them toward certain conclusions sensed from the beginning. They seem rather to wander weightlessly, to appear on the surface in the purest gestures, making up an order which is abstract, but intensely revealing; they are, precisely, 'atonal.' "[12]

One of the most interesting things about the film is that it seems to occupy the same kind of ambivalent, complicated medieval space, simultaneously realistic and stylized, that is the hallmark of the *Divine Comedy* (which Ingmar Bergman was also to capture a few years after *Francesco* in *The Seventh Seal*). Rossellini has, of course, paid lip service to the ordinary demands of historical verisimilitude trying to get the costumes right, for example—but, even more important, the film is imbued with the rough greatness of neorealism that allows us to feel the monks' scratchy tunics and the drenching rain. Yet, at the same time, *Francesco* flaunts its visual stylization. This is especially true in Rossellini's use of the art of the period as a kind of model or template to teach us how to watch the film; he seems very consciously to have shot the film with the stylized, severe simplicity of medieval art. For example, in the longer European version of the initial sequence, Francis lies down in the mud so that the friars can walk on him: the arrangement of bodies and the overall composition of the frame are clearly taken from Giotto's depiction of Saint Francis' death in a famous fresco. Throughout, we see the monks in almost total isolation from any "real" world, functioning, like medieval art, symbolically, as an emblematic community of the possible. Giorgio Tinazzi has pointed out that even the shots are continually flattened to eliminate perspective, thus putting man and nature on the same level.[13] I would merely add that another, perhaps more important, effect of this flattening is to suggest the two-dimensionality of the highly symbolic space of medieval art before the conquest of Renaissance "realistic" perspective, which entails an entirely different worldview. As a matter of fact, Rossellini's entire technical, emotional, and thematic trajectory can be summed up, if reductively, in this movement from the medieval to the Renaissance, not

The flattened perspective of the medieval world: the monks of *Francesco, giullare di Dio* (1950) walk in the rain.

only in terms of their visual aspects, specifically their art, but in terms of their distinct ways of looking at the world. At this period of his life, he is concerned with the mystical, the personal, the religious, and the emotional—in short, the medieval. Later, beginning tentatively with *India,* Rossellini will move toward the factual, the rational, and the privileging of scientific knowledge, a movement that reaches its zenith, as we shall see, in the Renaissance figure Leon Battista Alberti of *The Age of the Medici.*

Linear, temporal narrativity and worldly logic, then, are being refused by means of an aesthetic of symbolic space, discontinuity, and fragmentation. Thus, when Pio Baldelli complains that "within each scene, the studied elaboration of individual details does not create a unified architecture, but rather multiple articulations of isolated parts,"[14] we may very well object that this is precisely what Rossellini was after. But, just as we saw in *Paisan,* what is discontinuous at one level in a Rossellini film usually becomes essentialized and thus made continuous on a higher plane of abstraction. In the earlier film, Rossellini's aesthetic of difference and fragmentation, in other words, was ultimately aimed at describing a unity or essence of "human nature." Here, in addition to the film's antinarrativity and overt stylization, Rossellini decenters Saint Francis as the main focus, as we saw, but only in order to recenter the film in "the spirit of Franciscanism" itself. The decision not to individualize the friars is also clearly part of this essentializing strategy. Hence, unlike in conventional cinema, Rossellini does dally with the "inessential," but always does so to reach a grander essence at the end.

The essence of Franciscanism that Rossellini is striving for is elaborated structurally in visual and spatial terms. The pictorial flattening discussed above creates a kind of minimalist *paysage moralisé* out of the monks' simple community, a stylized, antirealistic locus of genuine Christian kindness and joy that operates principally in symbolic terms. Against this quiet, spatially uncomplicated place, Rossellini sets the tyrant Nicolaio's camp, one of the few times in the film that we venture beyond the enclosed, protected world of the religious community. Here in the camp is the discontinuous world: noisy, rude, violent, marked by continual frenzied movement to and fro, it stands in vivid contrast to the simplicity that has occupied the screen up to this point, and the spectator is visually and aurally overwhelmed. The frame is crammed with trees, tents, and rough, shouting warriors, all of this clashing violently with the open, loose framing of the bare territory of the brothers. When Ginepro is brought before Nicolaio, the structural contrast is continued in Ginepro's simple robe and the tyrant's enormous, comic suit of armor that can be put on or taken off only by an entire retinue of followers operating an elaborate pulley system. The values of simplicity and the "essential" are clearly favored over the complex and the superfluous.

Most important here is the choice of Aldo Fabrizi, the only professional actor

The discontinuous world versus pure spirit: the tyrant Nicolaio (Aldo Fabrizi) bullies Brother Ginepro in *Francesco*.

in the film, to play the part of Nicolaio. Most critics have seen his histrionic acting as the film's chief fault, but it may be one of its virtues. His acting— overacting, really—is precisely what is necessary to augment the structural opposition between the brothers' simplicity and Nicolaio's worldliness: in other words, the familiar opposition of nature and culture. His performance is purposely foregrounded, made self-reflexive, as is Magnani's in *Una voce umana*, and thus serves, itself, as part of the film's meaning. By this means, the structural opposition is carried to a kind of metalevel as well, beyond the level of the story to its mode of telling.

But the world's discontinuities are finally not to be as easily mastered as the tyrant Nicolaio, and the essence cannot forever be maintained. For one thing, an essence, paradoxically, as we saw in the chapter on *Open City*, can be represented only by means of the inessential, imperfect signifiers that present themselves to the senses. The final scene of the film, when the brothers must disperse to bring their (essential) message to all parts of the world, demonstrates the inevitable gap that all representation entails, even, or especially, the representation of that which is eternal. Francis has them spin around and around until they get dizzy and fall to the ground (a wonderfully apt metaphor for their way of being in the world and in this film); whichever way they fall is the direction in which they are to proceed to begin their preaching. Rossellini wisely decided to hold the camera immobile at this point, for the camera itself becomes the locus of their unity and the symbol of the wholeness of an unmeditated vision, and we are treated to an understated, but intensely emotional, shot of the brothers walking off in different directions. Most of the action in this shot occurs in the foreground, and the landscape is visually present throughout, beckoning the friars and thus challenging the unity that is, in fact, about to be broken up. The director could have ended the film with a moment of narrative, spatial, and emotional unity, of course; it is as though he and the logic of the film itself were driven to reveal the gap in representation. The film seems deliberately to skirt the edge of the abyss because it knows that everything can be made right again in some final moment of transcendence. But can it? One after another, the friars turn around for just one more look, as they get further and further away. Those at the far left and right disappear, then Francis and another friar walk toward and past the camera, out of the shot. Finally, only three small figures remain in sight, far away in the background. Dispersal and discontinuity seem to reign. At this point, however, Rossellini reveals his last, most powerful, stroke, a double gesture that attempts to master both the visual and aural track and unify them in a "transcendent" moment.

For, as the monks separate visually, their singing gradually grows louder, holding them together in spite of everything. The singing, of course, is a repetition of the Word and the continuity of the Franciscan message, and the fact that what they are singing is the Te Deum, points nicely toward the source of any possible transcendence. Thus, the aural track is enlisted against the dispersion of the visuals. Even the discontinuity implied in the visuals is mastered by a new unity, however, as Rossellini tilts up at the last moment to a shot of the moving clouds in the sky, a shot that he will repeat at the end of *The*

Messiah a quarter of a century later, toward a vision of final, divine transcendence that unifies and reconciles all earthly difference.

But the difference inherent in the sign itself, the interval that always exists between the signifier and the signified, will forever have the last word. For one thing, we can project some future point (soon) when the singing must stop and the aural unity will disintegrate. More important, though, the very image that Rossellini offers us of a fixed, unified point of "grounding"—heaven above—is in fact not a single place at all (though this is the signified we are meant to understand here). Instead, it can only be seen (otherwise the screen would be utterly blank and thus signify, literally, nothing) because of the many discrete, discontinuous clouds that paradoxically constitute it and body it forth, without which it would, literally, not exist.[15]

Rossellini's desire for an essence, in other words, will always be defeated in advance by his need to represent that essence. This is not to say that there is no continuity, no unity, no essence; merely that these "entities" can only be achieved or, better, constructed by means of their opposites.

14

Europa '51
(1952)

Rossellini's next film, *Europa '51*, his second with Bergman, has been seen only rarely in the United States or elsewhere since its initial release in 1952. It is not a film that reveals its depths on a first viewing, and, in that regard, is similar to Rossellini's Bergman-era masterpiece *Voyage to Italy*. It does, however, have its excellent moments. The placidity of *Francesco* is now absent, for here the director returns to the moral discontinuities of the postwar era. *Francesco's* themes are still in evidence, however, now transposed to the modern world, and if the saint's "perfect joy" eludes Irene, the heroine of *Europa '51*, her "madness" is clearly a contemporary variety of the strange behavior of those marginalized figures of the Middle Ages. Bergman, in fact, reported that Rossellini told her, immediately after making *Francesco*, "I am going to make a story about St. Francis and she's going to be a woman and it's going to be you."[1]

The plot concerns a young society woman who is more devoted to giving parties than to her young son. Early in the film, he attempts suicide—recalling the earlier child suicide of *Germany, Year Zero*—and, after a short period when he seems to improve, dies suddenly of a blood clot. Irene, enormously upset by her son's death, casts aside her former life and, on the advice of Andrea, a cousin who is a Communist journalist, begins devoting herself to the poor. She becomes so intensely involved in her charity work that she is finally committed to an insane asylum, for in her quest for a truly moral life in the service of others, she is judged to be abnormal by all the representatives of society, including her rich husband, the psychiatrist, and even the priest and the Communist cousin.

Again, the characteristic Rossellinian refusal to be judgmental is in evidence. So, for example, while we realize that Irene and her husband have been remiss in not paying more attention to their son, it is difficult to estimate just how much blame we can attach to them. It is always possible that the child is hypersensitive and would have attempted suicide in any case: we simply don't know. Similarly, at the end, though most evidence leads us to suppose that Irene is not really insane, at the same time her behavior is truly "abnormal," that is, not like other people's behavior. What other definition of mental illness do we finally have? Some of the dialogue also perversely goes counter to the rest of the information we are receiving. Thus, when Irene is asked by the priest at the end if she has performed all of her eccentric good deeds out of love, she says no, it was out of hatred for herself and what she was. The line carries just enough manic charge to suggest that perhaps she is mentally unbalanced after all. Despite these ambiguities, however, the characteristic and central ambivalence of the other Bergman films, the man-woman relationship, is here not as sharply etched. Rather, it is Irene's moral struggle that occupies center stage, and the marital relationship is barely portrayed at all. George, her husband, is firmly on the side of the establishment, but is in no sense involved personally with her in an emotional or sexual struggle, as are Bergman's other "husbands."

Other influences besides *Francesco* were involved in the choice of subject, including Simone Weil, the French social philosopher, mystic, and Resistance fighter who died of starvation in England during the war after renouncing food in solidarity with her countrymen still under the Nazi yoke. One of the most brilliant sequences of the film, when Irene goes to work in a factory one day to fill in for one of her poor friends, seems to have been inspired by Weil's account of the year she spent in the mid-thirties working in an automobile factory, a book published much later in English as *The Need for Roots*. Since one of the principal areas of disagreement concerning this film has centered on its depiction of Irene's experience in the factory, I want to return to it later.[2]

In formal terms the film is more linear and conventionally "dramatic" than *Francesco,* probably due to the exigencies of the star system, but it nevertheless remains highly elliptical and the implausible plot development is halting at best. As with the earlier film, these features can be seen as formal manifestations of the shared thematic emphasis on the nonlinear and the irrational. The early scenes laconically portray the domestic life of the Girard family, with little or no time wasted on establishing narrative suspense or on the development of subsidiary characters. Jose Guarner has characterized the film as merely a "statement of the facts," and maintains that the conflict is sketched in Irene's face (close-ups of which obsessively punctuate the film at regular intervals), which he sees giving the film its coherence, similar to Falconetti's face in Dreyer's *La Passion de Jeanne d'Arc*.[3] Maurizio Ponzi, unconsciously suggesting the complex interplay between the stylized and "real" that we considered earlier in *Una voce umana,* has in fact called it a "documentary on a face."[4]

Europa '51 can perhaps be best understood as a *film à thèse*. Rossellini has discussed his intentions in this film in virtually the same terms that he had used earlier concerning *La macchina ammazzacattivi*. The remarks are important enough to quote in full:

In each of us there's the jester side and its opposite; there is the tendency towards concreteness and the tendency towards fantasy. Today there is a tendency to suppress the second quite brutally. The world is more and more divided in two, between those who want to kill fantasy and those who want to save it, those who want to die and those who want to live. This is the problem I confront in *Europa '51*. There is a danger of forgetting the second tendency, the tendency towards fantasy, and killing every feeling of humanity left in us, creating robot man, who must think in only one way, the concrete way. In *Europa '51* this inhuman threat is openly and violently denounced. I wanted to state my own opinion quite frankly, in my own interest and in my children's. That was the aim of this latest film.[5]

Rossellini made this statement in the early fifties (note the hint of cold war rhetoric), and his next mention of the film, some twenty years later, is disparaging. By the seventies, of course, his view of the relative merits of the "concrete" and the "fantastic" was quite different, and his emphasis had shifted dramatically to science as the most productive link between the rational mind and the facticity of the world. But, in *Europa '51*, rationality is still the enemy because it is associated with the antihuman and the mechanical, those forces that seek to reduce the complexity of the world and human beings to a formula. Whether that formula is scientific, religious, legal, or political makes no difference at all.[6]

Just as we have seen in the films following *Open City*, Rossellini is operating a complex, dynamic relationship between what might be called the realistic and the expressionist in *Europa '51*. In the earlier films, this dynamic took the form of an implied critique, by means of various self-reflexive gestures, of realist aesthetics. Here, what is being questioned is film's ability to penetrate into the "heart" of a character it chooses to study. Still committed to the "documentary of the individual," which came to the fore wih *Germany, Year Zero*, Rossellini seems increasingly dubious about the efficacy of film to penetrate much beyond the surface of raw human phenomena. On one level, then, the film seems to say that it can finally be little more than a "documentary of the face" after all. Irene's character has been interpreted by critics in so many different ways that the final unknowability of the other can even be seen as one of the film's principal themes. Near the end, when she is being "scientifically" tested for mental illness, the flickering tachistoscope that is foisted on her, so closely resembling a film projector, suggests a homology between science and the cinema in the futility of their mutual attempts to penetrate to a sure knowledge of any human being.

Perhaps the film's most obvious theme arises as early as its title: *Europa '51*. At first glance, this seems to attest strongly to Rossellini's close attention to "reality." He is not just telling any old story, in other words, but a story that is expressly marked by a specific time and place. Paradoxically, however, Rossellini's title, by its *very specificity* names a general essence: this is a story not simply about a woman named Irene whose son commits suicide, but one that is meant to be emblematic for an entire continent and an entire historical period—the film's "now." Of course, any character can be seen in essentializing terms as "representing" an age; the difference here is that this fact is so firmly insisted upon that virtually no other possibility remains. Though *Europa '51* avoids being a film about people in general or "human nature," because it is a film about people at a very specific historical juncture, it clearly presumes to tell us about "all people" in this time and place.[7]

Other themes reappear, including the one that defines so much of Rosselini's career, the war. Except for the background of the camp from which Karin, in *Stromboli*, wants so desperately to escape, however, this is its first reappearance since *Germany, Year Zero*. But Rossellini does not go back to the bombed-out cities, as he was urged to do by his well-meaning supporters who wanted him to return to his "authentic self." Instead, the war functions as a moral horizon that has redefined the human condition; the subject is no longer the killing of the body that so occupied the first two films of the postwar trilogy, but rather the spiritual killing so painfully present in *Germany, Year Zero*. Now the spiritual decay, the director suggests, has spread beyond the destitute inhabitants of Berlin to encompass the middle class as well.

Nor is there any relief available through the *coralità* that redeemed the horrors of *Open City* and *Paisan*. A possibility is briefly offered early on, when we encounter Irene playing the charming hostess for her society parties. We understand soon enough, however, that this is a false *coralità*, an inauthentic subgroup (unlike that of the Franciscans) that will turn on Irene the moment she asserts, like so many other Rossellini women, her difference. Irene's difference from the group cannot be tolerated, however unthreatening it may appear to us, and a character at the end of the film overtly recalls the men to their duty to "protect society" from the likes of her. Society defends itself by marginalizing these threats, categorizing them as mad or "abnormal." Nanni, Karin, Francesco, and now Irene: the differences among them more a matter of degree than of kind. The *coralità* of earlier films is thus bitterly reversed, and that which had earlier fostered the individual now kills.

Like other films of this period, *Europa '51*, to the dismay of those critics who would make of Rossellini the supreme realist, quickly announces its stylized, expressionist mode. It opens with a car cruising through wet, visually rich streets, an opening that will be repeated and reach its expressionist peak in *Fear*. In an early scene the boy complains to his mother that his teacher "gets too close"—another reference to *Germany, Year Zero* meant, as in the earlier film, to stand for a more global sense of corruption that affects society at all levels. During this discussion to which the mother barely attends, the camera focuses on the boy and his obvious lack of affect, while she speaks offscreen. In conventional terms, it is rather early in the film to separate voice and body in this way, but here it serves nicely as a visual-aural manifestation of the disjunction between them. The boy casually pretends to strangle himself with his mother's necklace (recalling a similar gesture in *Una voce umana*), and the necklace, as a synecdoche for her socializing, operates efficiently as a causal analysis of his later suicide attempt. (After his death, his picture turns up in several scenes, always between the actors, suggesting the ongoing accusatory force of his moral presence.)[8]

An active, expressionist camera is present from the first. Constant dollies, here filling the role later taken up by the development of the Pancinor zoom lens, seem to offer instant intimacy with the characters, but since this intimacy is always blocked—at least at this point in the film—the spectator's attempt to grasp the purposely two-dimensional characters is continually frustrated. The camera also catches the immediacy of the boy's suicide attempt. The camera is absent when it happens, which is appropriate considering the difficulty of film-ing a convincing suicide attempt, but also because the absence of the camera marks the absence of any concern, parental or otherwise, toward the boy. In-stead, the camera chillingly replicates his quick, fatal movement up over the railing and down the circular stairwell. (In addition, Rossellini explicitly men-tions in a later interview the importance of the jagged rhythm that has the boy attempt suicide, seem to recover, and then, when least expected, die.)

The absolute horror of the suicide provokes a traumatic moment in the life of the protagonist.[9] Rossellini's aesthetic of the existential moment has been clearly in evidence before (the suicide at the end of *Germany, Year Zero* and the revelations of transcendent meaning at the end of *Stromboli*) and will be again at the end of *Voyage to Italy*. Here the difference is that the traumatic moment comes near the beginning of the film, and instead of the narrative being *resolved* in these epiphanic, transcendent terms—to which one is able only to assent in the other films, since they are instantly over—the rest of *Europa '51* is, uniquely, a working out of the consequences of that moment. *Europa '51* also stages a moment of realization at the end, but this epiphany more closely resembles those of *Paisan,* where the realization of the moment's meaning occurs princi-pally within the spectator, rather than the three separate groups of characters depicted (the insensitive rich, Irene's family; the uncomprehending poor, Irene's adopted family; and Irene, now reduced more to suffering victim than active naysayer to society's corrupt values).

Strangely, it is not until sometime after the suicide attempt, when Irene is seen in the car with her Communist cousin, Andrea, that we actually learn that the boy died of a blood clot.[10] Before this, the spectator is unsure of what has happened—characteristically, Rossellini is in no hurry to elucidate things—and it seems at first as though he has attempted suicide again, this time successfully. Andrea takes Irene to Michelangelo's Campidoglio in Rome, which contained, at the time the film was made, an original classical statue of Marcus Aurelius that visually and ironically opposes the profound values of antiquity to those of the present day, in the manner of Godard's film *Contempt*. For the Com-munist, however, the point is to place Irene's problems in the context of present, rather than past, history, to combat her overwhelming sense of individual guilt. He tells her, as a good materialist, that she must begin to pay attention to "things as they are." When she insists that it is either her fault or society's, he replies, in what must be the most unconvincing line in the entire film, "Blame this postwar society." Later, of course, Irene will reject the Communist answer along with all the others, and a lively debate has arisen concerning the portrait of the Communist that this film offers. At this point, however, the Communist is regarded in a clearly favorable light; if his answer is not the correct one, finally, because it is as overly programmatic and "rational" as the others, he nevertheless serves the important function of moral catalyst for Irene, allowing her to see the world in a new light. When he mentions the injustice of a little boy who is dying

The ubiquitous Rossellini automobile: Irene (Bergman) with her Communist cousin (Ettore Giannini), in *Europa '51* (1952).

because his family does not have enough money to pay for his expensive drugs, Irene is motivated enough to transcend her narcissistic suffering and begin moving beyond the concerns of self toward the service of others.

Another important nexus of the film's themes comes up in Irene's encounter with "Passerotto" ("Little Sparrow"), a down-to-earth representative of the working class played by Giulietta Masina. (Her dubbing into English has unfortunately turned her into an Italian Shelley Winters, but as Robin Wood has pointed out, the dubbing problem in the Bergman-era films simply must be overlooked by the viewer who does not want to get mired in the ultimately superficial.) With her brood of fatherless children, she stands in clear opposition to Irene: as a woman who is presumably more closely in contact with the realities of life, she represents the vibrancy of the life force itself, in contrast to Irene's sterility. It must be insisted, however, that no one-to-one, simplistic equation is made between having children and natural happiness—it is Masina's vitality in general that Rossellini seems to approve of. It has also been argued by some Marxist critics that aligning Passerotto with the "life force" in this way is also a form of *popolismo,* the not uniquely Italian error of idealizing the working classes. Rossellini gets around this charge, however, by thoroughly demystifying the poor and downtrodden people portrayed in the film. Thus, when Irene manages to find Passerotto a job in a factory, Passerotto decides that a date with her boyfriend is more important than showing up on what was to be her first day at work. Irene is persuaded to fill in for her—setting the stage for the most powerful scene in the film—but Passerotto's refusal to give up the immediate gratification of meeting her boyfriend for a middle-class notion of getting ahead is significant, and gives evidence of a sophisticated sense of class value systems. Rossellini's clearly favorable portrayal of Passerotto in all other ways works nicely against our own bourgeois offense at her lack of interest in the factory job, and renders her character as complex and many-sided, and as finally irresolvable, as any other in the film. This act of demystication is repeated later when Irene helps a prostitute who, instead of being eternally grateful, turns out to be quite grumpy and thankless.

When Passerotto asks Irene to fill in for her at the factory, Irene says that she would have no idea what to do there. Passerotto replies, with incontrovertible logic, "Neither would I." Unable to respond, Irene goes to the factory. Suddenly, the whole texture of the film changes: the rather stylized realism that has prevailed turns into the harsh graininess of the documentary sections of *La macchina ammazzacattivi*. We see Irene entering the factory with obviously real workers, who assert their reality, and thus clash with the codes of realism, by defiantly looking straight into the camera, momentarily destroying the fabric of the film's illusionism.[11]

The sequence shot inside the factory is immensely powerful. It recalls at once the expressionist scenes of the underworld of industrial life in Lang's *Metropolis* and Rossellini's own footage in *La nave bianca*, in which the mechanical bowels of the ship are shown simply for the sake of their dynamic, demonic interest. Irene and the other human figures are lost in extreme long shots that dwarf and isolate them. Huge, whirling machines reduce her to a nonentity, she who has been so selfish and egocentric, while the overpowering noise assaults her senses. A close shot brings her face up to us, and we see her eyes bob violently up and down, trying to keep track of the workings of the machine she has been assigned to. Rossellini's editing takes an Eisensteinian turn here, as it had ten years earlier, becoming faster and faster, upsetting us, but managing to convey at the same time the thrill of the machine's inherent vitality as it spits out its product. Quick cuts between a close-up of Irene's face and the pounding of the metal press link the two emotionally for us; she is clearly on the edge of breaking down. The film then cuts suddenly to a scene of "polite society" to emphasize the contrast.

George, Irene's husband, reacts to her quest in a typically patriarchal way, assuming that the only reason for a "woman of her class" to be involved in such foolishness is another man. The Communist Andrea, by earlier making an amorous advance to Irene, has put himself into this same system of values, which the film clearly insists is *beside the point*. Neither man is able to understand that Irene's values occupy a different register. Having earlier spurned Andrea's advances, she now turns down his Communist philosophy as well, and this has not endeared the film to Communist critics. It is certainly true that Andrea's Marxism is not very sophisticated, offering as it does a picture of an earthly paradise that will be realized when the revolution is victorious. But, not surprisingly in a film by the director who made *The Miracle, Stromboli,* and

Francesco, Irene insists that "the problem is much deeper than that, it's spiritual." She wants God to help her in her search "for the spiritual path." She needs the possibility of a life where there is also a place for her dead son, as she says, not just an earthly paradise for the living. She articulates a philosophy of love that is clearly Franciscan in inspiration.

What has particularly bothered Marxist critics is that her experience in the factory leads Irene to reject not only the promise of an earthly utopia, but also the very worth of work itself. When Andrea suggests that work ennobles, Irene insists that it is horrible. Naturally, this condemnation is troublesome, coming from a rich bourgeoise after one day spent getting her hands dirty. Yet, Rossellini and Irene are clearly talking about the alienating assault on the mind and body that most labor in an advanced moment of the industrial age has become, and no serious Marxist would want to argue that factory work as presently constituted in capitalist countries is anything but deadening.

If Irene rejects politics, however, the Church is not the answer either. We remember that it failed Edmund, Nanni, and Karin, and it fails Irene as well. As the chiaroscuro of the visuals becomes more pronounced in the final section of the film, indicating her deepening spiritual and psychological crisis, Irene heads for a church. As in the earlier films, the whole scene is handled without a single word of dialogue: she walks up the stairs, goes in, looks uncomprehendingly at the priests, the baroque altar, and some old ladies dressed in black, and goes back out the door. The Church is clearly the place of the dead, and only the dead; while it supplies the spiritual element missing in communism, it is unable to minister to the living.

Irene next encounters the ungrateful prostitute who is dying of tuberculosis. In a lovely series of visuals, Irene goes out into the night in search of a doctor for the woman, and a long shot appropriately emphasizes her new isolation. For by helping a prostitute, she is performing an act of charity that not even any honest working-class person would perform, thereby implicating them as well in the general critique of modern society. Her situation has become analogous to that of Eliot Rosewater in Kurt Vonnegut's novel *God Bless, You, Mr. Rosewater* (1965): she wants to help people simply because they need help, irrespective of all other factors, and thus she is thought insane. Since the vast majority of us have already succumbed to what Vonnegut calls "Samaritrophia," we need to call these people crazy. Irene gets so caught up in the prostitute's problems that we become uncomfortable, especially when she cries for her as though she has known her all her life. Isn't she overdoing it? Or is she simply being a good Christian? Again, Rossellini refuses to clarify the complex issue. As the prostitute dies, the camera briefly catches what looks like a picture of Saint Francis on the table next to her bed.

When Irene next becomes involved—rather quickly, and thus completely unrealistically—this time in the getaway of a young bank robber from the neighborhood, she tries to get him to give himself up voluntarily, but will not turn him in herself. At this point, she has finally crossed beyond what society will legally permit; the policeman to whom she attempts to explain the situation refuses to consider anything beyond the sheer letter of the law, in all its glorious abstraction from the exigencies of the moment. Her case is handled by three men—whereas most of her group of supporters and friends are women—and all of officialdom, including her family, want to attribute her craziness to the death of her son, in order, obviously, to explain and thus domesticate the irrationality of her behavior. Her husband treats her like a child and worries about all the publicity as he pilots his obscene Cadillac through the narrow streets of Rome.

The hospital they take Irene to is white and sterile, and Rossellini succeeds in conveying, as Hitchcock does in *The Wrong Man,* a visceral sense of what it would be like to be locked up against one's will. She is stuck in a room with no door handles on the inside, and the family sneaks off without a word of explanation. She does get sympathy from the hospital maid, across class lines, and appropriately again, from a woman. Against all odds, Irene manages to remain calm, even when she is brought into the "lounge" area, where the camera works out a stylized waltz that brings us violently up against one madwoman after another. The suggestion is that this is a subjective shot from Irene's point of view, but it carries a third-person feel as well, and thus does not naturalize and domesticate the madness we see before us by attributing the perception to Irene. The testing she next undergoes is as dehumanizing and psychologically violent as her day in the factory.

Rossellini's critique of organized religion is continued with the visit of the hospital's chaplain; the light that streams through the cell's windows and onto its sterile walls conjures up the church we saw earlier. The priest, just like the other males—judge, policeman, husband, and Communist—misunderstands as well because he cannot think beyond the hidebound rules he lives by to the human reality that the rules were originally meant to address. Irene offers a radical spirituality, not really much different from the radicality of Christ's teaching, but which organized religion has been at some pains ever since to tame: she tells the priest she wants to love all people as the sinners they are, instead of trying to change them. Looking more and more like Saint Joan, she insists that if this is done, a great spiritual force will take over and grow.

The psychiatrist next goes to work on her, grilling her about the "force" inside her. "Are you dominated by the great spiritual power of the saints?" he asks. "No," she replies, rejecting the connection with Saint Joan, "then I'd be crazy." "Then it's love?" "No, it's hate for all the things I was before, hatred for myself." Her words make sense, but isn't self-hatred also pathological? The men who consult to decide her fate cast their decision, as might be expected, in thoroughly linear, either-or terms: is she insane or is she a missionary? There is no other choice possible for them: society must be defended, they say. The priest questions her regarding her plans, and she confounds them again by saying she does not want to go home because she is sure that she would inevitably fall back into her old ways. She wants to devote herself to the people who need her, she says, not her husband, for her love is wider than that. "When you're bound to nothing," she says, in the film's most direct statement of Franciscanism, "you're bound to everybody."

The decision is made: she is to be committed. She looks saintly in her spare, sterile room; she has finally become Saint Francis, with all the ambivalence that attaches to him. She looks out through her bars and, in an economical and resonant image, we see her insensitive family moving away from her and the

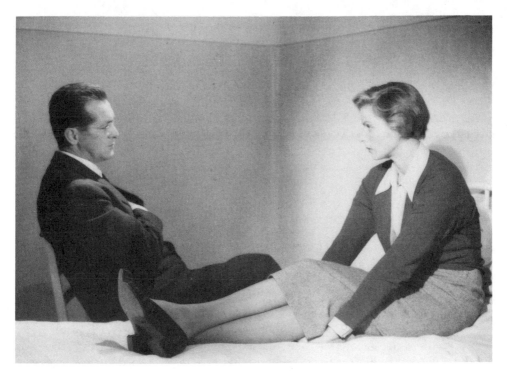

Irene being interviewed by a psychiatrist in the asylum in *Europa '51*.

asylum in their Cadillac, while her loyal followers, the poor folks led by Passcrotto, move toward her, chanting their love and admiration. It is a perfect moment of synthesis, as the poor proclaim her sainthood. The last, quite moving shot shows Irene's ravaged face, through the bars of her cell. From her eyes come what Eric Rohmer has called "the most beautiful tears ever shed on a screen."[12]

Even at the very end, and beyond, we still do not know how to take her. Irene is obviously the innocent victim of society's insistence on conformity—Rossellini's idea of the film's theme at the time[13]—but her extreme devotion to the poor does seem "abnormal" as well. More importantly, questions have been raised concerning the film's politics (Rossellini naturally maintaining no political views were expressed). Some have attacked the director for once again cloaking his suffering heroine in the obnoxious robes of religion and mysticism. Guido Aristarco has even attempted to turn the director's accusation on himself, by claiming that his denunciation of conformity and moral deafness is similar to those who "knowing themselves to be guilty, accuse others of the same fault."[14] Gianni Aiello has also brought up the vulnerable point of Irene's subjective motivation, insisting that her desire for solitude "stems only from personal motives, and has no objective justification. Thus the 'ideological' weakness of Rossellini takes shape."[15] Even a supporter like Gianni Rondolino has suggested that the problem with the film is that its depiction of society's problems is too closely wrapped up with that of Irene's own problems.[16]

By the 1970s, however, many younger critics and students, with the experience of 1968 behind them, were able to see the film's politics in a new light. Baldelli's seminar, to which I have referred earlier, is instructive in this regard. Some of the students still expressed strongly negative views of the film (even in Rossellini's presence), but others regarded it more favorably. It is easier for us to see now that, given the choice between the rigid dogmatism of the Communist party of the early 1950s, and the rigid dogmatism of the Church, Rossellini was trying to strike out into new territory, a territory that would exceed the limitations of binary thinking. As one of Baldelli's students rightly suggested, the film can in some ways be seen as a long, complex (and unresolved) meditation on the relation of political practice to the political theory offered by the leftist in the film.

Another debate on Rossellini, also held in the early 1970s, the transcripts of which have been collected by Gianni Menon in a book entitled *Dibattito su Rossellini,* shows signs of the same change in critical and political perspective. Enzo Ungari, for example, stresses the fact that *Europa '51* is, in spite of appearances, very political in its anticipation of the late-sixties revolt against orthodoxies of all stripes. He sees Irene's story, perhaps somewhat improbably, as the refusal of false consciousness, for to be really political for others, one must free oneself from all ideological schematism, and this is precisely what Irene does. Others in the debate felt that it would be a useful film to show on television because it would reach the masses, and serve as a "toned-down" mediator between the official cinema and more overtly leftist filmmaking. Maurizio Ponzi has elsewhere taken a similar position, maintaining that "at the ideological level, it is a subversive film, the revolution made film, because it doesn't judge, it doesn't insist, while at the same time it follows a story which protests in every frame."[17]

Perhaps the final word on this film and its openness to interpretation should be left to the eloquent Adriano Aprà. During the debate transcribed in Menon's book, he declared:

> Rossellini is a terrorist, like Irene in *Europa '51:* he puts you face to face with your personal responsibilities. You are either with me or against me. No compromises are permitted, no "we'll see later": you have to take a position, immediately. This evening many have rejected not the film, but a position, opposing an alleged rationality to a presumed irrationality. In so doing, they have rejected the possibility of a whole man and the necessity of error.
>
> Instead, it is necessary to make mistakes because making mistakes is life. Death does not make mistakes, it doesn't discuss or choose; all the dead are equal, they don't bother us, because corpses don't have eyes to look at us. Rossellini's films look at us straight in the eye. When a man looks at you in the eye, you either turn and run or you go toward him and by this action fulfill yourself.
>
> The majority of Italian cinema is a cinema of the dead, and "realistic" in the sense that it shows us how we are, it puts us at peace with ourselves, it conciliates, it does not show us what we are not and how we could become that. It's a cinema of peace, of pacification, while that of Rossellini is a cinema of war, of guerilla action, of revolution.[18]

15

Dov'è la Libertà?
(1952-54)

Immediately after finishing *Europa '51*, Rossellini began work on *Dov'è la libertà?* (Where Is Freedom?), conceived, uncharacteristically, as a vehicle for the popular Italian comic Totò. Filming proceeded fitfully, with serious interruptions: the trial scene, for example, which serves as the framing "present moment" from which the story proper is told in flashback, was shot a year after the rest of the film, during the summer of 1953. (Jose Guarner mentions in passing that this frame scene was filmed by another director, without naming him, but I have been unable to find any corroboration for this claim.) Further interruptions caused the editing to be put off until 1954, when the film was finally released. It has managed to go almost totally unnoticed in the intervening years, and even Rossellini, in all his many interviews, seems to have mentioned it only once. Critics as well, for various reasons, have either passed over the film with a single descriptive line or omitted it altogether.

This is a shame, for *Dov'è la libertà?* has its own unique place in Rossellini's oeuvre. Like *Europa '51*, it articulates an attack on modern society and offers a dark vision of the perfidy of the human race, but now the key has shifted to humor. The humor is bitterly won, however, and the film's vision, for all its "comedy," is even bleaker than that of *Europa '51*. *Dov'è la libertà?* also shares the loneliness and alienation of its predecessor at the level of decor, lighting and mise-en-scène, but at least here the *coralità* offered by a subgroup ultimately allows its protagonist, as in *Francesco* and unlike Irene in *Europa '51*, to escape the isolation of the self.

The story begins with the release from prison of a warm and decent Roman barber named Salvatore (played by Totò) who has served a sentence of more

Rossellini on the set of *Dov'è la libertà?* (1952–54) with Totò and Nyta Dover.

than twenty years for having cut the throat of his best friend, after discovering that he was having an affair with his wife. The world has changed a great deal since Salvatore was last in it, and he has difficulty coping with the constant stream of trickery and viciousness that he encounters. In fact, the entire tale is told in first-person flashback at his trial for "breach of a public building": he has been caught trying to sneak back *into* prison when his inhumane treatment by society convinces him that he was better off in jail. Salvatore recounts his adventures with a nonstop ballroom dancing contest in which his kind heart costs him all his money; an old prison "friend" who tricks him into passing a counterfeit bill; the shady landlady who puts him out in the street when he begins to notice her daughter; and his wife's family, scheming and vicious behind their Felliniesque exuberance. When he discovers that his new girlfriend has become pregnant by another man, he finally gives up and tries to reenter the prison. He is caught, put on trial, and, when the judge decides to fine him rather than incarcerate him, he is crushed. At the end of the film, he calculatingly bites his lawyer's ear—the lawyer who has tried his best to get him off, despite Salvatore's wishes—and we last see him convicted of assault, but happily reinserted into prison life.

The film is Totò's from the start, as the cute little cartoon of him peering out from behind bars makes clear in the credits. For the critic Massimo Mida, the encounter of the comic and the director was a disaster, for it did not give Totò a chance to find a newer and less schematic character, nor did it succeed as slick entertainment.[1] Pierre Kast, on the other hand, in an improbable access of enthusiasm, exclaimed in *Cahiers du cinéma* in 1956, when French support for the mistreated Rossellini was at its peak, that the film "stupified me with its cruelty and bitterness. It's a parable of the purest Swiftian type, unpitying and almost intolerable. For my taste, Rossellini's best film, and one of the few that I completely love."[2] A more balanced view might be that, while the film is ulti-mately rather unsuccessful, it nonetheless contains hints of the explosive mixture of Rossellinian textures and motifs that we saw in *La macchina ammazzacattivi*, a film with which it is closely related. While its comedy may "spoil" its serious side (and vice versa), it is also this uneasy mélange that makes it an interesting, if modest, moment in the Rossellini canon.

The director's single extant comment on this film makes its connection with his previous work explicit:

> Q: [*La macchina ammazzacattivi*] and *Dov'è la libertà?* both have a tone of fantasy which is unusual in your films. Do they represent a tendency or are they just isolated cases?
>
> A: They are experiments. *La macchina ammazzacattivi* is an isolated ex-periment, but *Dov'è la libertà?* which is like it in some ways, is much more a side-product of *Europa '51*: it's related to it because it's an attempt to inves-tigate the same situation. Then there's the extraordinary character of Totò. The film as it stands today is very much hacked about, it was much more cruel. The softening up was done by the producers and it makes it more light-weight. But they're not very important films, just experiments.[3]

The explicit connection with *Europa '51* establishes an interesting filiation: *Dov'è la libertà?* is a "side product" of *Europa '51*, which was a modernized "remake" of *Francesco,* which itself grew out of the monastery sequence of *Paisan,* whose subject had been conceived during the shooting of *Open City.* Perhaps more revealing is the link with *La machina ammazzacattivi:* it is mis-leading for the interviewers to suggest that both films "have a tone of fantasy," for the earlier film indulges in the supernatural as part of its plot, while nothing happens in the later film that is, strictly speaking, fantastic. The operative irony—that a man seeking freedom would want to return to jail—may be un-realistic in terms of everyday experience, but is not, for all that, otherworldly. The similarity of tone between these two films seems to stem rather from the stylization that they both self-consciously stage, which is further underlined by a provocative admixture of traditional neorealist realism, even if most critics have found them both disappointing mélanges that just do not work.

Dov'è la libertà? fairly shouts its "madeness," and instead of pretending to open a window on reality, it goes directly toward an essence, this time a moral one. Its narrative technique also works against naive realism, for the entire film is told in flashback, a technique that has not been seen since the Rome episode of *Paisan* and, with the exception of *Giovanna d'Arco al rogo,* will never be seen again in Rossellini's entire career. Since the flashback technique inherently fore-grounds the manufactured, constructed nature of what we are seeing—it is very self-consciously a story told by someone, who obviously has an interest in the telling—we can perhaps understand why it was condemned by Roy Armes as being "untrue" to neorealism. Once the myth of natural vision is given up, however, the flashback, given its subjective base, can be seen as problematizing and tugging against the insistent "reality" and apparent objectivity of the cinematic image. The audience's sense of a subjectively motivated story can lead, in turn, to an awareness of a more inclusive subjectivity at work—that of the director himself.

But the film's self-consciousness does not end with its narrative technique. From beginning to end, for one thing, it is particularly talky and quite theatrical in its staging. The sets are artificial—properly, if not purposely, so, I would argue—and the lighting is intensely expressionistic, in several outdoor scenes (clearly filmed on a set) exceeding even the even the most stylized Hollywood *films noirs* in this respect. The music, by Renzo Rossellini, is jarringly jazzy, much like the music of that equally nervous urban film of alienation made ten years later, *Anima nera*. It seems not to "fit" at all and, thus, is one more element serving to break the placid surface of verisimilitude. The cinematography follows the practice of that earlier comedian, Chaplin: extremely long-held shots by an utterly immobile camera, planted in what often seems to be the fifth row, are completely subservient to the gestures and play of the comedian. Early in the film, for example, we are treated to an exceptionally long scene in the prison barbershop, which is run by Salvatore. One of the prisoners is singing passionately of his desire to return home in a song called *"Casa mia"* (an idealized equation of freedom and the outside that will shortly be turned on its head). Salvatore has stopped shaving his client in order to listen to the singing, and the camera—as well as the singer and the other actors—remains absolutely motionless for what seems an enormously long time, certainly long enough that the viewer becomes aware that he or she is watching a performance. (Just as editing in a conventional film must remain "invisible" to give an effect of total illusion, the complete absence of editing for an extended period works in exactly the opposite way.) The scene remains a frozen tableau until the moment Salvatore puts his arm around the young man in a gesture of solidarity that is both humorous and emotionally convincing at the same time.

Furthermore, the film contains no dollies, and the backgrounds are only minimally sketched in so as not to distract attention from the protagonist's comic routine. Though a very few close-ups are used to excellent effect, the basic cinematographic unit here is the medium shot, which always favors performance. The wipe, the antithesis of invisible editing, is used frequently to make the transition from one scene to another, as it was in *La macchina ammazzacattivi*, and as it will be in one of Rossellini's most "artificial" films, the short he made on Ingrid Bergman in *Siamo donne*. A laugh track operates similarly to punctuate Totò's jokes in the courtroom, but, contrary to conventional practice, Rossellini never cuts to the laughing courtroom faces to "naturalize" and explain the laugh track. The effect of all these formal devices, once again, is to highlight the whole scene's theatricality and deny any possible claim to be directly representing reality. What is interesting about this film, however, as with *La macchina ammazzacattivi*, is that in the midst of all this artificiality, a jarring note of reality is introduced in the person of the dancing contestants that Salvatore meets just a short time after leaving prison. As the director proudly states in the opening credits, the people playing these dancers are the *real* dancing marathon champions themselves—Ines Targas, and Fred and Aronne. The knowledge we have that these people are not actors performing according to naturalistic conventions, but real people trying to "be" rather than to "act" (or rather, more complexly, being and acting at the same time) sets up a dynamic with the stylized elements that, instead of working against them, emphasizes them all the more.

In terms of its content, the film could not be more straightforward in its rather simple ironies. Contrasted with the ugliness of Salvatore's "family-in-law," the prisoners are seen to enjoy an intricate and mutually supportive social structure. If society as a whole is bad, the film tells us, the Italian myth of the family—especially if you are an outsider—is just as mistaken, and through their shabby treatment of Salvatore, despite their surface protestations of love, we learn that there is no *coralità* to be found here either. Rossellini's attack on the family is as vicious, and as funny, as anything in Fellini, but it is unrelieved by Fellini's tender indulgence. In fact, Salvatore is the film's only truly moral character, bent on righting wrongs and foolishly trying to protect all those who turn out to be more than capable of protecting themselves. One critic has condemned Salvatore for being just as petit bourgeois as the others in the film, but if so, it is clear that he has Rossellini's approval, and that Salvatore's values, if sometimes sexist and old-fashioned by modern standards, are clearly the best that the bourgeoisie has to offer.

When the perfidy of his pregnant girlfriend and the family (who, we discover, have stolen a Jewish friend's property while he and his family were interned in Auschwitz) become too great for Salvatore to bear, he realizes that "life outside is like being in a prison" and decides that he wants the freedom of jail. He conceives the idea of stealing the warden's hat and overcoat and, by disguising himself, sneaks back into prison. The longish "suspense" sequence of Salvatore's return is completely conventional and does not show Rossellini at his best, but the irony of the reversal provides some passing interest. Salvatore is discovered, and the penultimate scene puts us back into the present time in the frame tale of the trial. The prosecutor—that stalwart representative and protector of society, like the men who torment Irene in *Europa '51*—gets it precisely all wrong in his closing speech when he attacks Salvatore for being an immoral criminal. But, irony of ironies, the judge decides to be lenient, only fining Salvatore instead of sending him to prison, and Salvatore sinks.

The very end of this scene provides a satisfying emotional joining of the audience to Salvatore. Throughout, dramatic irony has operated against him; time and time again, we see how he is being used or cheated long before he does. At the end, however, as Salvatore asks his lawyer a series of questions about the penalties concerning physical attack, his plan slowly dawns on us. When he does attack the lawyer so that he will be sent back to prison, his knowledge is for once ahead of ours, and the dramatic irony is finally at the expense of one of his exploiters. The last short scene, without voices, shows him happily reinserted into the social fabric of prison life. We also realize, however, that the only reason Salvatore would want to return to prison is that Rossellini's idea of prison is precisely that, an *idea*, a site for a limp thematics of freedom, with absolutely no relation to real prison life as it has ever existed anywhere on earth. The film is thus also thoroughly stylized at its very broadest level.

As an exploration of an idea, however, it falls far short, even granting that its main purpose is comedy; the real problem of freedom is barely taken up, as Rossellini's pervasive bitterness of the moment short-circuits any sustained inquiry that might move beyond the two-dimensional irony that eventually wears thin. At this time, Rossellini's view of freedom is rather simplistic, as can be seen in this general remark made on the subject in the 1954 *Cahiers du cinéma* interview: "When people talk about freedom, the first thing they add is 'freedom, sure, but within certain limits.' No, they even refuse abstract freedom because it's a dream that is too beautiful. And that's why I find in Christianity such an immense power: there, I think, freedom is absolute, really absolute."[4]

The problem of freedom will be taken up again ten years later in *Vanina Vanini*, where in spite of the film's histrionic trappings, freedom is viewed in a complex relationship with sexuality and history. The real question that *Dov'è la libertà?* raises is political. Are people so malevolent that the only possible "freedom" is the regimentation of a prison? This does not seem to be an idea that could have brought comfort—or even laughter—to an Italy a bare ten years away from fascism.

The Italian critics Franca Faldini and Goffredo Fofi, in their book on Totò, put the film into what is perhaps its most revealing context. For them, it is true that the film does not "work" because it was too rigid a format for Rossellini, and too somber for Totò:

> And yet this film has, in our view, its own curious place in the history of neorealism, as its precise opposite. Like that extraordinary and almost involuntary masterpiece, [Visconti's] *Bellissima, Dov'è la libertà?* is an almost cynical film, a glance thrown back on the conventions of populism in order to step back from it almost disgusted, with the difference however that in *Bellissima* neorealism debates with and attacks itself, redeeming in an almost Gramscian manner the most serious popular values from the vision that the film itself presents of them. While *Dov'è la libertà?* goes still further, and saves almost nothing. . . . It's a profoundly reactionary apology, but heavy with an interesting thematic exasperation which goes decidedly against the grain of the rosy panorama of the neorealism of that time.[5]

16

Voyage to Italy (1953)

In no country in the world is death so domestic and affable as it is there, between Vesuvius and the sea.
                                                                    —Italian saying

Viaggio in Italia (Voyage to Italy), Rossellini's third film with Ingrid Bergman, is thought by many to be his finest, and, in fact, one of the greatest films ever made; thirty years after its premiere, it regularly makes the top-ten listing of *Cahiers du cinéma*. The film does not release its riches on a first viewing, however, and many knowledgeable film critics have been and continue to be reluctant to share the French enthusiasm for the film. Repeated screenings gradually begin to reveal its many subtleties and its links with Rossellini's previous films. Chief among the latter is the complex theme of marital conflict and its relation to environment, which was initiated in *Stromboli*. Rossellini has said: "I consider *Viaggio* to be very important in my work. It was a film which rested on something very subtle, the variations in a couple's relationship under the influence of a third person: the exterior world surrounding them."[1]

The film also may have been important to Rossellini as disguised autobiography. Pierre Leprohon has nicely described this aspect of the Bergman-Rossellini collaboration:

> For the man whose mission is to express passion and human sentiments, the woman in his life becomes, quite literally, his interpreter. It is her look, her voice, her gestures, her appeal that allow him to express himself. It is as if he married her a second time, by imparting to her his dreams, thoughts, and aspirations, since she, receiving them, makes them her own and communicates them to others. There is every reason to think that Ingrid Bergman made, as Rossellini's interpreter, a great contribution to his work, not only by her acting, but by her presence, by her aura.[2]

This much is certainly true; Robin Wood, however, finds almost exact analogues between the situations of characters in these films and Bergman's personal life.

Thus, *Stromboli* depicts her as the displaced person, *Europa '51* dramatizes her guilt over leaving her child, and *Voyage to Italy,* along with the final collaboration, *Fear,* concerns the breakdown of their marriage. While provocative, Wood's list finally seems too conjectural and, worse, too reductive, to be of any real use. Nevertheless, his description of the autobiographical dynamic in *Voyage to Italy* is suggestive. For him, Katherine Joyce is also Ingrid, the Swede in Italy, uncertain about her future: "The poignance of the sequences in question arises out of the fusion of the two, the projection of the tension and uncertainty they have in common. It is a fusion—closely connected with Rossellini's very personal but immensely influential blending of fiction and documentary—possible only in the cinema."[3] Wood's description of the tension in *Voyage to Italy* is clearly related to that interplay between realism and reality that we have been tracing in Rossellini's other films, especially to the ontological dynamic Anna Magnani enacts in *Una voce umana.*

Rossellini's original plan was to adapt Colette's novel *Duo* (1934), which concerns a "happily married" couple whose marriage falls apart because the husband insists on upholding traditional views of marriage rather than responding to the specific sexual and emotional needs of his wife. When the wife refuses to apologize or feel guilty for an old love affair that the husband has discovered, he begins to moralize obsessively, finally losing control and taking his own life. In its concentration on the dynamic shifts of power within a sexual relationship, the novel is obviously related to the film, and its choice by the director tends to lend credence to Wood's autobiographical thesis. The focus of the novel, however, is very intensely on the couple, with no attention paid to their environment, and it is here that the film most strikingly departs from Colette's fiction.

Looking for an international male star to play opposite Bergman, Rossellini settled on the superficially suave and controlled George Sanders who, since his death, has been revealed as the desperate and deeply unhappy man he always was. By the time Sanders arrived, however, Rossellini had discovered that the rights to Colette's novel had already been sold. To keep Sanders interested, he immediately set out to draft another screenplay, or rather, treatment, that was to retain some elements of Colette's novel. Rossellini was not in the habit of discussing his plans with his actors, however, and Bergman confessed in her autobiography, "I was quite bewildered too, but I thought Roberto is Roberto; he might do another magnificent *Open City.* After all, we're going to Naples and he'll be inspired there."[4] Like most Italian film critics, Bergman, too, was waiting for Rossellini to stop all the "foolishness" and return to the scene of his earlier successes. This passage and others from her autobiography suggest that Bergman, like the vast majority of contemporary Italian critics, was ignorant of what her husband was really up to and, in fact, suffered a great deal during the making of these films, sublimating her own strong sense of professionalism to her continuing conviction of Rossellini's genius. As the cowriter of her autobiography explains: "Even Ingrid began to have doubts after the first two weeks shooting which consisted of her staring at ancient statues in the Naples Museum while an equally ancient guide bumbled on about the glories of Greece and Rome."[5] The voice of Hollywood and its obsession with the new and young echoes clearly in this obtuse description of one of the most thematically complicated and emotionally fraught scenes of the film.

Sanders, trained to have the same expectations of standard Hollywood operating procedures as Bergman, became increasingly upset over Rossellini's penchant for assuring a spontaneous performance by withholding dialogue until the day before shooting. Each night found him talking by telephone to his psychiatrist back in Hollywood, and Rossellini finally sent for Sanders' wife, Zsa-Zsa Gabor, to try to cheer him up. More than once he simply broke down in tears, unable to continue for the frustration. At one point during the shooting, Sanders decided to go public with his anxiety, telling Riccardo Redi, a writer for the Italian journal *Cinema,* that when he complained about the lack of a finished script, "Rossellini decreed that I was an impossible man. People talk about neo-realism . . . it's a joke. The real reason that Rossellini films in the streets is that studio sets cost money. I've seen some misers before, but I've never met anyone who could equal him. . . . I've heard that the film will be called *Vino nuovo,* and that's a perfect title, for new wine is always bad."[6]

Finally, Rossellini put a fatherly arm around Sanders' shoulder and said, "What are you getting so depressed about, at the worst you'll have made one more bad film—nothing worse than that can happen. . . . We've all made good films and bad films. So we'll make another bad one."[7] Robin Wood has suggested, in his interview with Bergman, that "George Sanders does look terribly unhappy all the way through" and that "it's a rather serious blot on the film."[8] Viewed another way, however, Sanders' unhappiness and lack of ease can be said to put an edge on his interpretation of the character that actually works quite well within the context of the film's unconventional narrative technique. Nor was Rossellini himself unaware of this effect. In the Aprà and Ponzi interview, he implied that Sanders' problems were simply more grist for his mill: "To be frank . . . you have to make them work for you. . . . Don't you think he was obvious for the part? It was his bad moods rather than his own personality that suited the character in the film."[9]

Rossellini's refusal to do things in the Hollywood manner extended, as usual, to his storytelling as well, and *Voyage to Italy* represents the perfecting of unconventional narrative, affective, and thematic strategies already present in his work from the very first. Thus, all the film's dramatic moments are consistently undercut. Nor is there much plot to speak of—a marriage is breaking up under the strains of a trip to Italy, and we watch; little else happens. Apparently superficial detail, however—the smallest, most fleeting facial expression, for example—assumes enormous proportions, as it does in the work of Dreyer, Mizoguchi, and Bresson. Episodic rather than linear in its development, the film emphasizes rhythm, suggestion, and nuance. Longueurs and *temps mort* are left in the finished film, rather than being edited out through a snappy montage that presumably would have moved things along better. (But what things? The minimal plot? Here, the surface of life *is* its depths.) It is a film composed of elements as tiny as barely perceivable emotional textures, and as immense as the meaning of life and death.

The other names by which the film was known when originally released display its distributors' complete misunderstanding: *The Divorcée of Naples, The Greatest Love, Love Is the Strongest.* In England, of course, it is still known as *The Lonely Woman,* a title that stresses only one side of the film's emotional dynamics and, like the mistranslation of De Sica's plural *Ladri di biciclette* into the singular *Bicycle Thief,* denies the thematic point of the film. Initial critical reaction was also swift and predictable. G. C. Castello, writing in the influential *Cinema,* rose to new heights of righteous indignation in the campaign against the director: "By this time, we've given up on Rossellini. But what is beginning to get annoying is that he has managed not only to ruin himself, but he's also ruining the woman who would, not unworthily, have succeeded Greta Garbo one day."[10]

This same critic objects that the film does not give enough information, especially psychological information about the characters. He wants, he says, to know *why* their marriage is going bad. What Castello misses is that the film offers their situation as an existential given, purposely denying us a previous "psychological case history" (an essential component of the code of realism) that would reduce the characters' rich, impenetrable presence, so much like that of people we meet in everyday life. The brilliance of *Voyage to Italy* is precisely its refusal to specify a "why," for that would be to recuperate human complexity and ambiguity into the graspable, the knowable; an illegitimate domestication, like most films, of the troubling inconsistencies of life.

Fortunately, critical opinion has changed over the years. Even by 1965, when the Italian journal *Filmcritica* conducted a poll of twelve of its collaborators on "The Ten Best Italian Films From *Ossessione* to the Present," nine mentioned *Voyage to Italy*.[11] This is also the film that crystallized the support of the nascent French New Wave around Rossellini's work at a time when his fortunes with Italian critics were at their nadir. Of the early French responses to the film, perhaps that of Eric Rohmer, written in 1955, is the most provocative. For Rohmer, Rossellini is playing with our built-in, automatic film responses without actually trying to break them. He makes us look for some significance *behind* the characters' actions: "The ancient link between the sign and the idea is broken, and a new one arises which disconcerts us." According to the French critic, this aesthetic manifests itself in a wholly new style; Rohmer openly admits that his mind wandered at times during the screening, but insists this is unimportant. At this point, however, Rohmer moves from an almost protostructuralist position to his more characteristic religious essentialism: "In this film in which everything seems to be merely accessory, everything, even the wildest wanderings of our minds, is part of the essential." For Rohmer, the third character of the film, as in Murnau's *Sunrise,* is God. In this way, the critic is once again able to recuperate the fragmented and the aleatory as their inverse, that is, expressions of the wholeness and unity of being.[12]

In *Voyage to Italy* Rossellini's use of *temps mort* reaches a new level of complexity and suggestiveness, but develops clearly from the experiments undertaken in the uncut Italian version of *Stromboli.* In the much-remarked opening scene, for example, when we first see the Joyces driving along the highway toward Naples, the boredom is palpable. The car's engine hums soporifically, a train speeds in the opposite direction; immediately following the credits we have cut quickly to a train whistle that suddenly rends the image. Jose Guarner has described this sequence well: "This rather long-held image of reality . . . give[s] a curious feeling of continuance, as if the film had begun a lot earlier. We are not present at the opening of a story, merely coming in on something that was already going on, as we do in real life. *Viaggio in Italia* is also a film about time and duration."[13]

Seven years after the film was first released, Pierre Marcabru wrote in *Arts* that in this film the characters exist for themselves, not for the cinema, and thus proclaim a new cinema of immobility: "In the immobile and the insignificant is the very power of life."[14] Similarly, Leprohon explains why this kind of film is preferable to

> those which rivet us to our seats with suspense or the more elementary emotions. "Spectator involvement" is really a shoddy aim, and for its victim a second-rate satisfaction. The greatest literature sets up a resonance extending far beyond the immediate illusion that it creates; and the best films are those that have us *accompany* the characters as their friends rather than step into their shoes.[15]

Detail is built slowly, as when the couple is taken on a tour of the Neapolitan villa they have inherited from their uncle Homer. At first the time spent on the tour seems wasted. It is only later, as we shall see, when the stability and presence of the house are implicitly contrasted with the forever-moving automobile with which the Joyces surround themselves, that we realize the significance of this *temps mort* that almost any other director would have summarized with a series of quick cuts. It is also clear that Rossellini knew just what he was doing. In the interview with Pio Baldelli and his students in 1971, he referred obliquely to this sequence, linking it in an unexpected and not entirely clear way to his later films:

> If I don't live in the context of things, of everything, I can't arrive at those key points. . . . I've moved into the didactic phase in a very . . . it was continually showing signs of itself, for finally it was a need of mine that I hadn't identified very well. But do you remember, for example, *Viaggio in Italia?* Well, I had to do that long walk inside the house, seeing things, which everybody scolded me for. . . . Now, if this weren't there, if this milieu weren't there, how would you get to everything else? You wouldn't. If she [mistakenly "he" in the interview] hadn't gone through all those rooms, she wouldn't have gotten to the museum; if she hadn't gone to the museum, she wouldn't have gotten to the discovery of the bodies, she wouldn't have gotten to . . . she can't get there, because she could only have gotten there in that way, by means of . . . the improbable" [ellipses in original].[16]

Little is explained in this film. For example, when Katherine goes out for her first drive alone in Naples, reactions to what she sees play across her face, but only occasionally, when it is thematically pertinent, does the director actually show us in a countershot what she is looking at. Again, he is breaking one of the cardinal rules of "good" filmmaking, but the effect is to enhance the sense of waiting and the ever-fluttering possibility of a sudden outbreak of the unexpected. In any case, her reaction is more important than what she reacts to. At the same time, however, Rossellini's documentary interest, as in earlier films, is strong, and he also wants to show the "reality" of Naples itself. He knows, however, that this "reality" is not available except through the consciousness of the characters, who thus mimic the director's own mediation. Bazin has described this dynamic well, because it fits so neatly into a phenomenological paradigm of the intentionality of consciousness. For him, the reality of Naples, as presented in the film, is incomplete, yet whole at the same time: "It is a Naples as filtered through the consciousness of the heroine. If the landscape is bare and confined, it is because the consciousness of an ordinary bourgeoise itself suffers from great spiritual poverty. Nevertheless, the Naples of the film is not false. . . . It is rather a mental landscape at once as objective as a straight photograph and as subjective as pure personal consciousness."[17]

This play of the objective and the subjective also reappears at the level of character identification: As Leprohon has told us, we accompany the figures rather than "become" them, and, as in *Stromboli*, Rossellini refuses to allow us the luxury of facile moral judgments in favor of one character over another. Most critics have assumed that Katherine is the aggrieved party, the clear victim of Alex's callous devotion to work and making money, but this may be because what are considered typically "male" faults of cruelty and violence are expressed in more obviously obnoxious ways. Bergman's traditional association with "good-girl" parts may also be a factor here. Most important, of course, is the fact that the narrative unrolls, basically, from Katherine's point of view. Yet, somehow Rossellini successfully mounts a subtle balancing act in which now one has the moral and emotional power advantage, now the other. The closely related communication theme is also stated in a couple of obvious scenes of mutual miscomprehension, but it moves beyond *Stromboli* in that now words are used as weapons, or to *prevent* communication. As Leo Braudy has aptly put it: "*Voyage in Italy* contains some of the most abrasive scenes between a man and a woman that have ever been filmed. But it is an abrasion of boredoms, spawned by the inconsequential, space-filling dialogue that will be echoed in Antonioni's *L'Avventura*."[18]

At the first party they attend, Katherine is jealous over the attention Alex is paying to some of their young female acquaintances. At a later party given by Uncle Homer's aristocratic friends, Alex resents the obvious good time Katherine seems to be having, surrounded by admiring Italian men. During an early dinner scene, they seem on the verge of achieving reconciliation, and a chance word, an ungenerously interpreted phrase, sets them going at one another again. (Alex has suggested, in what seems to be good faith, that they try to enjoy themselves on their vacation, but Katherine responds with a curt, "If we don't enjoy ourselves it will be your fault.") Near the very end of the film, our sympathies perhaps begin to move more strongly toward Katherine as she assaults Alex's coldness again and again, only to be rebuffed. (Though it is a testimony to the film's unconventional handling of emotional dynamics that some critics have taken it for granted that it is *Katherine* who is being most difficult by the end.) When they do finally have their problematic rapprochement during the epiphanic finale—which will be discussed later—Alex's fear that Katherine will "take advantage" of him if he says he loves her makes it clear, in retrospect, that

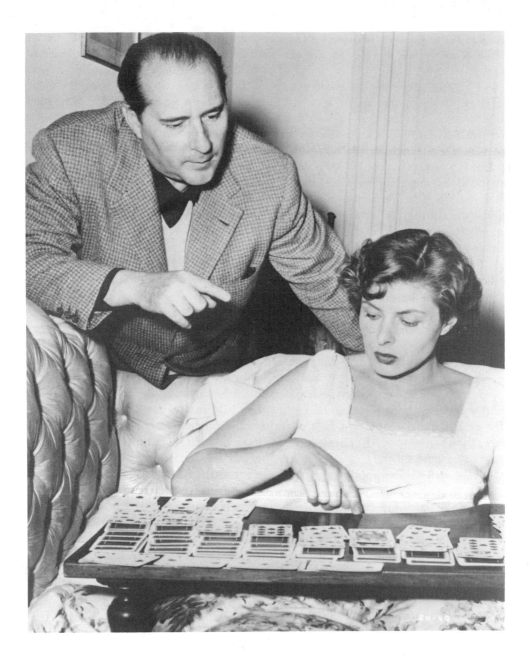

The director coaches his wife for the solitaire scene in *Voyage to Italy* (1953).

he has been resistant because he fears becoming vulnerable. In this case, we believe Katherine is sincere, for we can see her expression, but Alex has been refusing to look at her.

The most perfectly balanced sequence, however, a marvel of suggestion, occurs at Alex's return from Capri. Katherine has been waiting up for him, playing solitaire, hoping that he would return that evening. But when she hears his car pull up, she must immediately turn out the light and pretend to be asleep so that she will not in any way put herself at an emotional disadvantage. What follows is a subtle, but riveting, series of intercuts on her immobile face in the shadows as she registers and absorbs every sound he makes, her eyes darting everywhere. The petty noises—his gargling, for example—seem abnormally loud and penetrating, at least partly because they have been foregrounded by the nearly static visual track. An elaborate choreography follows of lights being turned on and off, as each fears giving an inch.[19]

Far more is at stake between Katherine and Alex, however, than their own emotional problems. For they also represent opposing sets of abstractions, neither of which we are meant to view favorably. (This, of course, is another reason why Rossellini does little or nothing to sketch in their past lives for us, or to define them in terms of personal idiosyncrasy.) Neither is a complete human being; they are parts of a whole, and thus the distortions of humanity decried by Nietzsche's Zarathustra. Alex clearly stands for a soulless materialism that, as we have seen in *Europa '51* and other films, was for Rossellini the chief evil of postwar European society. Alex is constantly thinking of his business affairs and worrying about the time he is wasting while in Italy, a country he views as the epitome of laziness and lack of industry. Katherine, however, represents an equally untenable spiritualism that is reflected in her idealization of her romantic poet friend Charles Lewington. He served in the British army near Naples and had written her about the city. As Alex nastily points out to Katherine, her visit to Italy has become a kind of spiritual pilgrimage to reevoke Charles' presence in the locations he had written about. As the couple sits in the hot Neapolitan sun, she intones from Charles' poetry: "Temple of the spirit, no longer bodies, but ascetic images, compared to which mere thought seems flesh, heavy, dim." Alex, his jealousy aroused like that of Gabriel Conroy in James Joyce's story "The Dead," from which Rossellini has borrowed,[20] says that he learned from Lewington that a man's cough can tell you more than the way he speaks.

> KATHERINE: What did Charles' cough tell you?
> ALEX: That he was a fool.
> KATHERINE (getting angry): He was not a fool! He was a poet!
> ALEX: What's the difference?[21]

As the film progresses, we realize that Katherine, at least, is learning from her contact with the Italian environment that is so foreign to both of them. She gradually becomes less romantically caught up in her poet's otherworldliness, for the forceful realities of her Neapolitan experiences begin to call her to the world. After being exposed to those things that Charles had written about—especially the powerful rawness of the statuary in the Naples museum—she begins to realize that his aestheticism was a projection of his own personality rather than a description of Italy. She admits to Alex, "Poor Charles, he had a way all his own of seeing things." This progression on her part also serves to bring us closer to her (there is no equivalent learning by her husband), but her recognition and overcoming of an excessive, crippling spirituality is only part of the process.

It is more than hinted that Katherine's problems are also sexual in nature; the penchant for spiritualizing her relationship with Charles is an obvious function of her presumed frigidity. But if we can fault Rossellini for having recourse to this sexist stereotype, it must also be said that this subject is implied rather than overtly thematized. Thus, when Katherine goes to the museum early in the film, she is overwhelmed; her guide's homely, banal chatter only serves to counterpoint the raw violence of these startling nude marble figures. They serve the additional function of representing a presumably more healthy and innocent past civilization, as when Irene and the Communist Andrea visit the Campidoglio in *Europa '51*, a motif that Godard borrowed in *Contempt*. (To point up his various borrowings, Godard has his characters at one point watch *Voyage to Italy*.) Her encounter with the statues is turned into a series of profound, almost physical, confrontations with them, and the obviously foregrounded movements of the camera—all fast crane shots that whirl as they move closer, worthy of the most choreographed moments in Ophüls—bring her into a forced proximity with the statues that is clearly threatening. As Michael Shedlin has correctly pointed out, most of the crane shots in the museum include Katherine and the statues in the same shot, as opposed to all the previous point-of-view shots that have kept her visually, and thus psychologically, dissociated from what she is seeing and experiencing.[22] Deeply moved by this encounter with the overtly physical, sexual presence of the past, she later confesses to Alex, "What struck me was the complete lack of modesty with which everything is expressed. There was absolutely no attempt—" At this point she is interrupted by a knock at the door, and the subject is never brought up again. Later, when she is touring the ancient site of the Cumaean Sybil, the old and presumably harmless guide demonstrates to her how marauders of the past would have tied up a "beautiful woman" like her. She huffs away, muttering, "All men are alike," and the bewildered reaction of the guide indicates that at least in Italian, male terms, her response was not appropriate. The last hint of the sexual theme comes at the end of the film when Katherine is trying to identify aloud the source of the animosity between her and Alex. She suggests that "perhaps the mistake in our marriage was not having a child," and Alex responds that she did not want one, and now he thinks that she was right, because it would only have made their impending divorce more painful.

If sexual frigidity is only suggested in the film, however, the Joyces' childlessness is more overtly linked with the poverty of their lives, but as symptom rather than cause. Superficial interpretations of the film have complained that because Katherine is constantly seeing pregnant women in her outings and because their friend Natalia is praying for a child, what Rossellini, in effect, is suggesting is that the couple's problems would be solved if only Katherine surrendered herself to her proper biological role (or fate). It is rather more complicated than that, finally, but to understand how, we have to probe more deeply into the dynamics of conflict in the film.

What rules *Voyage to Italy* is environment. Like Thomas Hardy's fictional Wessex, it becomes a powerful third character in the film, and its name is Italy. Most baldly stated, the film is about Katherine and Alex's confrontation with this otherness so utterly opposed to everything they know and understand. Where Alex is materialistic and superrational and Katherine is, initially, at any rate, overly aesthetic and otherworldly, Italy is sensual and earthbound. It might be argued, of course, that Rossellini is merely glorifying and idealizing his native land: if all those cold foreigners could only experience the warmth and carefree joy of Italy (and have lots of babies), their problems would be solved. What is important to understand, however, is the precise way in which a Mediterranean system of values is being touted over the coldness the northerners bring with them.

In many ways, the film could be included in the genre of "road films," given the massive, continual presence of their car (which I want to explore in more detail in a moment) and the theme of a hostile environment that makes one reassess one's most deeply held values and convictions. When on the road, you are vulnerable, and so are the Joyces. The undeniable presence of Italy, both physical and psychological, constantly forces itself into their consciousness, in spite of their desire to conduct their business as quickly as possible and escape back to England. They wrestle with their pasta, they do not know enough to take a siesta (and do not ask), they expect everyone to know English. After they eat, all the "garlic and onions" give Alex a thirst that he can not quench. He complains about the driving, about the rampant laziness; at the party given by Uncle Homer's aristocratic friends, the Joyces learn about "dolce far niente" (how sweet it is to do nothing), a concept totally alien to their Protestant souls. Uncle Homer, unlike the Joyces, was fully inserted into Italian life, and his friends miss him deeply. An even more important foil to the deadness and vicious advantage-seeking of the Joyces is the couple with whom they have most contact, Tony Burton (a fellow Englishman) and his Italian wife, Natalia. Here, North and South (which, as we saw in *Stromboli*, Rossellini always felt was the true division of the world, rather than East and West) are happily joined. Both husband and wife speak the other's language, and their relationship appears rewarding. They seem to embody that harmony of body, mind, and spirit that the film locates in classical civilization and continues to offer as a cure for present-day ills.

"Italy," the enemy, constantly intrudes upon the Joyces, in countless details, in nearly every frame. The Neapolitan singing that accompanies the opening credits is heard again and again, acting as the symbolic, but palpable, presence of Italy, occupying a sound track that constantly presses against a visual track concerned chiefly with the British couple. While they sit out on the roof of the villa drinking wine instead of taking a siesta like everyone else (with Katherine "shielding" herself from the Italian sun by wearing dark glasses), we see the symbolically suggestive Vesuvius volvano in deep focus in the background of the same shot.[23] Italy also intrudes in the form of sleep, about which much is made in the film. Both Katherine and Alex exclaim at different moments, "How well one sleeps here! Natalia tells Katherine at another moment that she should let Alex sleep because "sleep is always good for one." The laziness of Italy, anathema to the businesslike Joyces, has begun insidiously to affect them as well.

Probably the most important symbolic motif that furthers this conflict between Italy and the Joyces is their car, so obviously and continuously present. With its prominently displayed British license plates, it represents that combination of mind-set and ideology known as England, which naturally they bring with them to Italy. It is where we initially see them, in this little bit of England pushing through a foreign land, and we understand seconds later that the very first shots we see have been taken through the car's windshield and side window, suggesting the inevitable construction of reality through one's own particular culture. The car comfortably envelops them and protects them, initially at least, from the influence of this strange country. Appropriately, it offers a cold and mechanical contrast to everything organic and living that we see throughout the film (in the very beginning, for example, they force their way through a lazy herd of sheep). Later, it sticks out blatantly among the ruins of Pompeii.

This thematic use of the automobile also explains, in retrospect, the earlier, lengthy tour of Uncle Homer's villa, for the villa functions as the symbolically static opposite of the Joyce's car, as an overt manifestation of Uncle Homer's organic participation in Italian life. Similarly, at various points throughout the film, a slow (often panning) establishing shot on the stolid villa, which begins a scene, reminds us subtly of its symbolic role, opposing the ceaseless, frenetic movement of the automobile. When Katherine makes her trips into Naples, she can only grumble about how selfish and unfeeling Alex is, for as long as she is in the car, she is enveloped in her own miserable, little existence and its multiple blind spots. But, like Alex and Katherine themselves, the automobile is not impervious to Italy's influence, and the environment continues to assault Katherine through the windshield. Yet it is only when she actually gets out of the car—at the "little Vesuvio," the museum, the Cumaean Sybil, at Pompeii, and at the end of the film—that she becomes truly affected by what she experiences. Similarly, when Alex improbably has the car after his return from Capri, he picks up a prostitute. Until this point, he has remained rather shielded, unlike Katherine, but when the woman invades his physical and psychological territory by entering the car, she brings with her the messiness of life in the tragic story she recounts.

But what exactly does this continual presence of Italy stand for? Clearly it is not to be taken as the fulfillment of some tourist-brochure writer's fantasies about sun and fun. It does, of course represent a greater openness to sensuality and emotion, and a greater connection with what we might call the fecundity of life, but it stands just as closely to death. Italy is seen in this film as a place where one is more consciously aware of life *and* death: because life is contingent, and death holds final sway, life itself, as Heidegger claimed, is enhanced in value and intensity by an awareness of death. What the Joyces need is not to have babies (or not *only* to have babies), but to be snapped out of the abstraction their lives have become, linked as they are only with the conventional, decentered signs of money and the other intangibles that modern life substitutes for directly lived experience. Thus, while it is true that in one of her drives through Naples, Katherine is overwhelmed by the number of babies and

pregnant women she sees, her first experience of the city stresses a funeral carriage and numerous black-edged announcements of local deaths. In Naples, as
the epigraph to this chapter suggests, one is even closer to death than in the
rest of Italy, and Rossellini delighted in telling interviewers, when discussing
this film, how Neapolitan black marketeers spend the first big money they make
one elaborately decorated coffins rather than on food and clothing. Natalia takes
Katherine to visit the catacombs; the English woman is shaken by this place
drenched with mortality and overflowing with skulls, and cannot understand
why anyone would adopt a dead person to "take care of." Poor Alex cannot
pick up a prostitute without her instantly beginning to tell him of a friend's
recent suicide and her own temptations in that direction. In the interview with
Aprà and Ponzi, Rossellini insisted:

> [Katherine] is always quoting a so-called poet who describes Italy as a country
> of death—imagine, Italy a country of death! Death doesn't exist here, be-
> cause—it's so much a living thing that they put garlands on the heads of dead
> men. There is a different meaning to things here. To them death has an
> archeological meaning, to us it is a living reality. It's a different kind of
> civilisation.[24]

The death theme reaches its dramatic climax—a "climax" that is characteristically understated—in the magnificent scene that takes place at Pompeii.
Seconds after Katherine and Alex's most bitter argument, which has ended in
a decision to get a divorce, their host Tony comes to collect them and insists
that they go with him to the digs. The archaeologists have come upon a hollow
in the ground, which usually indicates a place where people were caught and
instantly killed in the great eruption of Vesuvius in A.D. 79. Their emotions
rubbed raw, the Joyces beg off the visit, but Tony insists that it is the chance
of a lifetime and that they *must* come with him. Unable to refuse, the distraught
couple accompanies Tony to the site, where the workers are to pour fresh plaster
of Paris down into the hollow through small holes they have drilled. As the
rather bizarre musical theme picks up (a theme we have already heard during
Katherine's other wanderings through history and the strange spots of Naples)
and then modulates into a tense, tragic, bitter melody, dirt is scraped off the
hardened plaster. One by one, body parts are revealed. The parts begin to form
themselves into a man and a woman; death has caught them making love, or
at least wrapped tightly in each other's arms. Suddenly, the museum, the catacombs, and the Cumaean Sybil all come together in one startling image: the
physicality and rawness of the ancient world, the ubiquity of death in life, and
love, however inadequate and flawed, as the only possible solution. At the sight,
Katherine breaks down sobbing and rushes away, and Alex moves to help her.
Rossellini offers no overt explanation for her reaction. Alex makes the standard
excuses to the men on Katherine's behalf, and they prepare to leave. To get
back to the protection of their car, they have to traverse what remains of the
Roman town, and the effect on us is similar to what Katherine has experienced
in the museum. In long shot, we see them move across the barren ruins, once
full of life and now so full of death. The tragic musical theme intensifies, and

Love, death, and Italy: the Joyces (Bergman and George Sanders) amid the ruins of Pompeii in *Voyage to Italy*.

the effect is truly moving. Finally, the emotional encounter seems to have had a positive effect on both of them. Alex ventures: "You know, I understand how you feel. I was pretty moved myself. But you must try to pull yourself together." Hopeful, she responds, "Oh, did it effect you the same way? . . . I've seen so many strange things today that I didn't have the time to tell you about. . . . There are many things I didn't tell you." She begins to apologize for their earlier argument, but Alex, perhaps assuming that she is only trying to trap him, rebuffs her: "Why? Our situation is quite clear. We've made our decision. You don't have to make any excuses." She hardens herself, and when Alex taunts her once again about her dead poet, she shouts, "Oh, stop it! Must you continue to harp on it? I'm sick and tired of your sarcasm. We've decided to get a divorce and that settles it!" They continue picking their way through the ruins, and suddenly the musical theme turns black. At this point, Katherine stops and utters the most convincing, devastating line of the entire film: "Life is so short!" The realization of death's ubiquity has completely overwhelmed her, given the "many strange things" she has been seeing all day, but there seems no way out of their endless bickering and advantage seeking. Alex replies ambiguously, "That's why one should make the most of it." The camera follows them for a long time in an utterly desolate long shot, until they reach their car.

Immediately after, we hear the joyful bounce of parade music and cut to Katherine and Alex, once again safely ensconced in the automobile, as they fight their way out of Naples. This is the final scene, the most controversial of the film. As we initially located them moving toward the city in the car, we now see them moving away. The circle seems to be complete, and while the constant presence of Italy has forced them to confront the emptiness of their married life together, it has yet to effect any internal changes, at least that we can see. But one does not go through such intense emotional encounters and emerge unchanged. Subtle influences are working on them without their knowledge.

They have wandered into the middle of a huge religious process in honor of San Gennaro, from whom Neapolitans virtually demand a miracle each year during his festival, as Rossellini told Truffaut and Rohmer in 1954. Horns blow and confusion reigns as the couple picks over the remains of their marriage. Katherine, who has been more deeply affected, seems to seek a reconciliation, but Alex, suspicious, continues to reject her advances. When he says it is lucky they have no children because "it would make the divorce even more painful," she jumps on this: "Painful? Is it going to be painful for you?" "Well, more complicated" is his cold response. They continue to push their huge British car through the crowd (and the claustrophobic visual effect is enhanced by the complete avoidance of long shots), cold steel against human flesh and religious emotion, and ultimately they are forced to halt. The car is eaten up by the wave of humanity, by Italy, the way water rushes over a seemingly immovable obstacle and carries it away. Attention shifts to the parade, which we watch for a while, until Alex, still seemingly unaffected by his Italian experience, says: "How can they believe in that? They're like a bunch of children!" She replies softly: "Children are happy." Then she suddenly blurts out, "Alex, I don't want you to hate me. I don't want it to finish in this way." And Alex replies with lines that make his resistance more understandable and that again right the emotional balance between them: "Oh, Katherine, what are you driving at? What game are you trying to play? You've never understood me, you've never even tried. And now this nonsense. What is it you want? "Nothing," she spits out at him. "I despise you."

Then the significant moment: they decide to get out of their car, away from the protection of their lifeless culture. Instantly the crowd begins shouting, "*Miracolo! Miracolo!*"; and though we cannot actually see anything—perhaps appropriate for a modern-day "miracle"—the immense crowd rushes forward, taking Katherine along with them. The shot is visually brilliant: the crowd moving powerfully ahead, away from us, Katherine pulled with them, fighting the emotional wave of the Italians, but turned back toward us and Alex, screaming wildly for help.[25] For once the sheer violent press of life forces them out of the sealed intellectual realm they have wanted to keep to, and into the swirling world of the emotions. Katherine needs Alex, suddenly, on a brute existential level that is apparently new to them. Alex rescues her, and the film cuts to a closer shot of them—the northern giants surrounded by the Neapolitan pygmies—as they clasp each other in their arms (like the Pompeian lovers):

KATHERINE: Oh, I don't want to lose you. (*They embrace*)

ALEX: Katherine, what's wrong with us? Why do we torture one another?

KATHERINE: When you say things that hurt me, I try to hurt you back, don't you see, but I can't any longer, because I love you.

ALEX: Perhaps we get hurt too easily.

KATHERINE: Tell me that you love me.

ALEX: Well, if I do, will you promise not to take advantage of me?

KATHERINE: Oh, yes, but I want to hear you say it.

ALEX: All right, I love you.

The camera at last pans away from them, resting a long time on the anonymous faces in the crowd, transfixed by the miracle they have just seen; it finally moves to an enigmatic one-shot of a single member of the band. As we, too, struggle to reconcile ourselves to the miracle we have just witnessed, the film ends.

The familiar Rossellini pattern is there: the sudden, cathartic, epiphanic moment of grace when all is righted (or in some films, where the point of tragedy is stated), a technique that goes back at least to *Open City* and the quick, ironic epiphanies of *Paisan*. The scene most closely resembles the "miraculous" ending of *Stromboli*, of course; there we saw the giving over of self to God through a primitive religious emotion, and here the giving of self to another person through the catalyst of the religious emotion of others. But if critics have been unconvinced by the ending of the earlier film, they have been even more vociferously disappointed by the ending of *Voyage to Italy*. What does it mean? Can we believe it? What has happened to alter the emotional pattern of years? Most critics have refused to accept the couple's reconciliation at face value and have seen it as either completely unconvincing or at best a momentary rapprochement that will shortly break down (Truffaut's view at the time). Rossellini himself had a complex opinion concerning the ending, which makes it seem even denser than that of *Stromboli*. He told Aprà and Ponzi:

> What the finale shows is sudden, total isolation. . . . Unfortunately it's not as if every act of our lives is based on reason. I think everyone acts under the impulse of the emotions as much as under the impulse of intelligence. There's always an element of chance in life—this is just what gives life its beauty and fascination. There's no point in trying to theorise it all. It struck me that the only way a *rapprochement* could come about was through the couple finding themselves complete strangers to everyone else. You feel a terrible stranger in every way when you find yourself alone in a sea of people of a different height. It's as if you were naked. It's logical that someone who finds himself naked should try to cover himself up.
>
> Q: So is it a false happy ending?
>
> A: It is a very bitter film basically. The couple take refuge in each other in the same way as people cover themselves when they're seen naked, grabbing a towel, drawing closer to the person with them, and covering themselves any old how. This is the meaning the finale was meant to have.[26]

But this does not mean that their gesture is any less genuine for being instinctive; in fact, it seems more so, and it is significant that Rossellini does not explicitly agree that it is "a false happy ending." We might also say that the very unbelievability of the ending is itself thematic, as we saw with aspects of

Francesco, because it is *not* logical—that function of almighty reason that Rossellini, whose views changed drastically in the fifteen years between film and interview, now wants to credit above all. (Note that at this point he says that "unfortunately" not everything in life is based on reason.)

However one might want to read the ending, it was not the only thing in the film that displeased its initial reviewers, and like the other two major Bergman collaborations, it was a failure both critically and financially. The French, however, who, along with the Americans, had discovered *Open City* for Italian critics, were immediately more sensitive to its subtleties. The Eighth International Session of Film awarded it a prize as best film of the season; significantly, the judges were Jean Cocteau, Abel Gance, and Jean Renoir. Also, the group of young cinephiles who had begun to form around the journal *Cahiers du cinéma* thought the film immensely powerful. For them, it perfectly embodied their desire for a personal style of filmmaking that was beginning to be known as *la politique des auteurs.* They also saw that its narrative and technical unconventionality pointed toward new possibilities beyond Hollywood.[27] Jean-Luc Godard, still five years from the making of his first feature, enthused:

> In the history of cinema, there are five or six films that one wants to write about simply by saying "It's the most beautiful film ever made." Because there's no greater praise. Why should one speak any further of *Taboo,* of *Viaggio in Italia,* and of *The Golden Coach?* Like a starfish which opens and closes, these films can offer and hide the secret of a world of which they are at the same time the sole depository and the fascinating reflection.[28]

In the April 1955 issue of *Cahiers du cinéma,* Jacques Rivette said this of the film: "And there we are . . . cowering in the dark, holding our breath, our glance suspended on the screen which grants us such privileges: to spy on our neighbor with the most shocking indiscretion, to violate with impunity the physical intimacy of human beings, subjected without knowing it to our passionate watching; and, at the same time, the immediate rape of the soul.[29] Above all, these critics were struck by the film's novelty. In the same article, Rivette said, "It seems impossible to me to see *Viaggio in Italia* without experiencing, like a whip, the fact that this film opens a breech that the entire cinema must pass through under pain of death." Patrice Hovald expressed the phenomenological sense of direct, originary meaning most forcefully, calling it "the first film of a cinema which has not yet been created, because it seems like the first film which does not exist as a function of the others, but which, taking its own meaning from itself, thus finds its unique dignity."[30]

But even if one is unable to share the rhetoric of complete originality articulated by the film's early French supporters, it is still possible to see in it a remarkable shift in filmmaking practice. In its "free style," in Gianni Rondolino's words, one can glimpse the films of Antonioni and Godard and all the others that were to come in the sixties.

> The mixture of genres, or the coexistence in a single work of narrative, dramatic, lyric, documentary, and essayistic elements, involves a kind of aesthetic "disharmony" . . . which opens the work beyond a more or less rigid structure. Then, this very placement of narrative and dramatic elements in the

finished structure of the film, with its frequent stylistic jumps, its unusual alternations, its formal carelessness, demands a lack of cohesion among its parts which favor the freedom of observation and the personal choice of the spectator. Finally and above all, the images and the dialogue are offered as "proposals" and not as "solutions."[31]

And in this new freedom of observation, it seems that Rossellini has finally fulfilled the hopes of André Bazin, not just on the level of the image or sequence, beyond which the French critic seemed unable to theorize, but on the more inclusive level of the film itself.

17

Three Sketches: "L'Invidia," "Ingrid Bergman," and "Napoli '43" (1951–54)

Along with feature-length films, Rossellini was also making sketches in the early fifties—fifteen- or twenty-minute "short stories" that formed parts of longer films. At the time, the episode film made by four, five, or six different directors was enjoying a great vogue (Rossellini was also involved in one called *Rogopag* as late as 1962), but, mercifully perhaps, no longer seems to be very popular. Presumably, the idea was that with more stars and more big-name directors, box-office appeal would be heightened, but few directors took the genre very seriously.

Nor, unfortunately, did the public. Consequently, all three of the sketch films that Rossellini participated in during the early fifties are either difficult to locate or have disappeared altogether. I have only been able to see the "Ingrid Bergman" sketch, from *Siamo donne* (We, the Women, 1952). This sketch, regarded by everybody (including its star and its director) "more or less as a joke," actually contains, for all its brevity and lack of seriousness, important thematic resonances that make it worth discussing. First, however, an attempt should be made, via the few critics who *have* seen the other two sketches, to outline their subjects and their place in Rossellini's overall canon.

Exact chronology differs in the major Rossellini filmographies, but most seem to agree that all three shorts were made between *Francesco* (1950) and *Giovanna d'Arco al rogo* (1954), in the following order: "L'invidia" ("Envy," part of *I sette peccati capitali* or *Les Sept Péchés capitaux* [The Seven Deadly Sins] filmed in October 1951); "Ingrid Bergman," which, according to her autobiography, was shot in the summer of 1952, and therefore between *Dov'è la libertà?* and *Voyage to Italy;* and finally, "Napoli '43," filmed in late 1953 after

Voyage to Italy and before *Giovanna,* as part of the film *Amori di mezzo secolo* (Mid-Century Loves).

The first, "L'invidia," was loosely based on Colette's short novel "La Chatte" (The Cat), which perhaps explains Rossellini's subsequent interest in doing a film with Bergman and Sanders based on her novel *Duo.* In "La Chatte," a young woman, jealous of the affection her artist husband lavishes on his cat, kills it by throwing it out the window. An early reviewer for *Cahiers du cinéma* found the entire film banal and clichéd, complained about the poor dubbing of the two Italian sketches into French, and otherwise said nothing about Rossellini's piece.[1] (This film appeared just prior to *Cahiers'* "rediscovery" of Rossellini.) Massimo Mida continued to express his disgust with the Rossellini of the "crisis" years, calling "L'invidia" "nothing more than an intellectual game without purpose, a piece of useless tinsel which clashes with his masterpieces."[2] In Verdone's somewhat more favorable view, the episode is a "subtle psychological conflict, though somewhat stretched," but he also felt that its "psychological mechanism" was not "perfectly regulated."[3]

Looking back a few years *after* their rediscovery of the director, however, the French came to think very highly of the sketch. Godard, for one, put it at the same level as "Ingrid Bergman," claiming that both sketches are the best things in their respective films: "Because Rossellini didn't try to provoke an artificial suspense by following the threads of an equally artificial plot; he contented himself with merely 'showing' a feeling without trying to analyze it, because if he would have done that, he would have filmed *Europa '51* or *Fear.*"[4] The ebullient Patrice Hovald went so far as to proclaim it an "absolute masterpiece" and a "modern classic of art." For him, it clearly takes its place with "the other five 'mediocre films' of Rossellini's which are going to change the face of cinema." Hovald found it especially interesting because, like the Bergman films, it takes as its subject "woman, one member of the couple; femininity and its behavior; her fundamental opposition to man; the beginning of misunderstanding; her guilt—and carries to its peak the genius of style. We are on that infallible track which leads, from masterpiece to masterpiece, to *India.*"[5] In the absence of the film itself, we can only guess whether this negative essentializing of woman is Hovald's or Rossellini's.

The third of these three sketches, "Napoli '43"—most conveniently considered at this point—is one that no critic, with the exception of Jose Guarner, has mentioned even in passing. According to the "Documentazione" of Aprà and Ponzi, all the episodes of *Amori di mezzo secolo* were scripted by the same four writers (Oreste Biancoli, Giuseppe Mangione, Vinicio Marinucci, and Rodolfo Sonego), which makes it different from most sketch films popular at the time, though not unique. Here Rossellini was teamed with successful, if second-level, directors like Glauco Pellegrini, Mario Chiari, and, especially, Pietro Germi and Antonio Pietrangelo, but again, the film failed. One contemporary review that appeared in *Rassegna del film* said that Rossellini's bittersweet treatment of a young soldier and a debutant actress falling in love at first sight in a Naples bomb shelter (only to be killed by a bomb at the end) was not all that bad. The reviewer had especially kind words for the "real-life" portrayal of the old men who sell coffee and candy in the shelter, but felt that the main characters were not seen in any depth, the plot lacked dramatic development, and the ending was hurried and unconvincing.[6] These judgments can be taken at face value, of course, but, interestingly, the enumerated "faults" are exactly those that most contemporary reviewers found in *Voyage to Italy* and the other Bergman films.

Given the paucity of critical accounts of this sketch, then, we must turn to Guarner as our sole source of information. For him, its chief interest lies in the combination of the realistic portrayal of Naples under a bombing attack and the fantasy of the story itself, a combination that, though he does not say it, links it directly to earlier films like *La macchina ammazzacattivi* and *Dov'è la libertà?* in their unsteady, but fascinating, mixture of stylization and the real. Guarner sees the story as part of the tradition of courtly love, offering us "a quiet variation on several well-loved themes, a bitter-sweet, rather distant evocation—in a way, his *Les Visiteurs du soir*."[7] The sketch is also Rossellini's first return to the heroic days of the war, the subject of his greatest successes, and anticipates his largely cynical "comeback," some five years later, with war films like *Generale della Rovere* and *Era notte a Roma*.

The most theoretically interesting of these sketches is the one the director did of his wife for *Siamo donne* in 1952. Like most of the other Rossellini films of this period, it has had an especially negative critical reception, when it has been considered at all. Borde and Bouissy complained, not without reason, that in it Bergman "makes a fool of herself,"[8] and Mida called it "a rather insignificant fragment of no interest or importance."[9] John Minchinton, writing in *Films and Filming* at the time the film appeared, was equally critical, specifically branding Bergman's "an embarrassing performance." A few sentences further on, however, we realize that something has caught his attention, for he notes that the final effect is rather interesting because "in showing the actress as a person, [it] reveals the actress as an actress."[10] In other words, though the film is virtually worthless if looked at in conventional terms, it is redeemed by the continuing problematization of the relation between realism and reality that we have seen at work in so many other Rossellini films.

Bergman has said, "The whole thing was made more or less as a joke. It was considered to be made for charity."[11] Rossellini has seconded her opinion, calling it "just a piece of fun. It was almost all improvised. It's not something that really happened, but it's true to life."[12] The other segments of *Siamo donne,* directed by Alfredo Guarini (who seems to have been responsible for the overall project), Gianni Franciolini, Luigi Zampa, and Luchino Visconti, are, in fact, much more narratively conventional than Rossellini's. These segments, which feature Alida Valli, Isa Miranda, and, interestingly for the film's inner emotional dynamics, Anna Magnani, are rather lighthearted (with the exception of Zampa's), but nevertheless "well made," tightly scripted and relatively clear-cut and unproblematic in execution. Rossellini's, on the other hand, is the only segment in which the illusion is broken, and the actress/person speaks directly to the audience, through the camera, as "herself" (a construct more complicated than it looks). Not only does Bergman's direct address to us destroy any possibility of our giving ourselves innocently to the fiction, but the actress also comments directly upon the story "within," which concerns a neighbor's chicken who eats Bergman's roses and against whom Bergman sets her dog. In effect, then, the film provides its own narrator, who comments directly upon the tale she is about to tell, calling it a "ridiculous story" and putting herself in a complex position both in and out of the narrative. (But *which* narrative?) The first-person form has commonly been accommodated in the cinema, of course, but principally as disembodied sound in voice-over (as with Magnani in Visconti's segment); here the voice becomes visualized, as it were, the direct presence of the actress. And while the inner story is played straight (that is without illusion-breaking asides to the camera), it is a fictional story ("It's not something that really happened") about the real person named Ingrid Bergman, played, naturally, by Bergman herself. It also attempts, in its own small way, to name an essence: "But it's true to life." The inner story also contains another woman, an actress, who, unlike Bergman, plays the neighbor according to the conventionalized system of character representation, rather than as herself. The illusion of the inner story, however, is itself broken by a wipe back to the narrator's "present" situation, the Rossellinis' summer home, the same location of the inner tale, and from which that inner tale is being created or repeated. In the outer tale, then, the home is real, while in the inner tale, the same home is a fictional set.

So the "joke" is a bit more complicated than it seems. Its complexity relates clearly to Rossellini's earlier film *Una voce umana*, which, as we saw, the director described as a "documentary about Anna Magnani." Both films manage to problematize the difference between actress and role, inevitably raising questions concerning the boundaries between such dualities. Can either term exist alone? Again, too, reality and realism clash and merge, merge and clash, both ending up hopelessly confused. All of the actresses in the different episodes of *Siamo donne*, in fact, are reenacting supposedly "true-life" happenings from their own lives. The stories are populated by actors, both professional ones playing specific characters not themselves and nonprofessional ones playing themselves rather than the real people of the original incident in the actress's real life. The situation grows more complex when one realizes that, though the stories present themselves as being invented by the actresses, the real inventors are the directors working at some metalevel above them. What Rossellini has done in his own sketch is to up the stakes further by foregrounding the story's narration as well, thus creating still another level that, even in as slight a tale as this, can suddenly reveal the abyss of representation. It may also be significant that the subject and "script" of Rossellini's sketch are credited to the foremost theoretician of neorealism, Cesare Zavattini, the man responsible for the famous lived-time sequence of the maid in De Sica's *Umberto D*.

The almost palpable sense of sadism in this sketch must also be mentioned, at least in passing. Bergman is so dreadfully uncomfortable throughout, especially in the narrating frame tale and when she gives chase to the chicken, that the unconscious point of the story seems precisely to make her look silly. Where is Rossellini here? The one large gap that is felt throughout is, in fact, Rossellini (as real person): we see their real villa, we see the real Bergman as herself, we see their real son Robertino as himself, but no Roberto. But just as he was "present," though unseen, in *Una voce umana,* he is here as well inscribed in the mode of the film rather than the visual or aural track per se: all, both inner and outer tales, is presumably evolving from his point of view, and his physical absence from the family underlines this fact even more. He is "creating" Ingrid Bergman in the same way that he has created Karin and Irene and Katherine. It is an act of creation with implications, both personal and theoretical, that extend far beyond this little "joke" of a sketch.

18

Giovanna d'Arco al Rogo (1954)

Around this time Rossellini turned, at least partly from financial necessity, to directing theater and opera. His first effort was Verdi's *Otello,* produced by the Teatro San Carlo in Naples, and it gained him the most acclaim he had had in years. Pasquale di Costanza, the director of the opera company, then asked Rossellini if he would like to do something with Bergman in it, and proposed Paul Claudel and Arthur Honegger's oratorio *Jeanne au bûcher* (Joan at the Stake), which had originally premiered at Orleans, France on May 6, 1939. Bergman knew the oratorio, as she had been given the recording of it during the production of the Hollywood version of Saint Joan. Rossellini had the records sent to him and began to imagine what he might turn the oratorio into.

His first innovation was a system of rear projection of photographs by means of which the setting could be instantly changed from a church to a landscape. The biggest problem facing the director, however, was that in the original, Joan remains motionless, tied to her stake throughout the entire performance, while dancers and a chorus interpret her memories of childhood and the events leading up to her trial. Characteristically, Rossellini waited until just before rehearsals were scheduled to plan his staging. Bergman tells us in her autobiography that "fortunately for me, Roberto took hardly any notice of Paul Claudel's stage instructions":

> And he got what I thought was a brilliant idea. The curtain rises, and another girl, a small child, is tied to the stake at the back, and she is Saint Joan. The flames rise and she is dying; then, out of the darkness I rise up on an elevator to my first position. I'm dressed all in black, only my face showing. That face represents my mind, the mind that can look back at my life and my ex-

Bergman as Joan of Arc at the stake in *Giovanna d'Arco al rogo* (1954).

periences. There are big gangways sloping up here and there, and on one of them I meet Brother Dominique who tells me of what I am accused. Then the gangways are lowered to the floor and I'm free to run around.[1]

The reception of Rossellini's version of the oratorio in Naples, and later at La Scala in Milan, was excellent, and he seemed genuinely pleased with his new métier where "I have accumulated nothing, no past, and everything is new."[2] When the production moved to the Paris Opera House, however, a serious problem arose in the person of Paul Claudel. He had heard of the changes Rossellini had "inflicted" on his oratorio, and even though all the performances were completely sold out, he withdrew his approval at the last minute. Bergman and Rossellini went to see Claudel, who lectured them on the purpose of the oratorio, and how important it was that Joan remain fixed throughout; nevertheless, he was prevailed upon to attend a dress rehearsal before rendering his verdict. At the end of the performance, Joan's final lines echoed through the nearly empty theater: "It is joy that is strong. It is love that is stronger. It is God that is strongest of all." As everyone in the cast waited tensely, Claudel rose slowly and said aloud, "And Ingrid is even stronger." And thus permission was granted to go ahead. Successful engagements followed in London, Barcelona, and Stockholm, though in Sweden, to which Bergman had not returned in sixteen years, a vicious attack was unleashed against her in the media.

It was next decided to put the oratorio on film, though it is not immediately clear why. Bergman told Robin Wood that it was filmed "more or less to have as a souvenir for ourselves," but this seems hard to believe given what it cost to produce this full-length film in color (Rossellini's first), a cost that was never to be recouped. Perhaps Rossellini felt this was his chance to redeem himself, and given his deliberate inattention to Claudel's original design, his remark to a Parisian interviewer at the time of the film's release must strike us as disingenuous (and political): "Since Claudel did the scenario, and not me, I hope that this film marks the reconciliation of the critics with my work. I am a simple man, and I don't want to be a man who's all alone."[3] In any case, the director was pleased with it, and he told Truffaut and Rohmer, interviewing him in 1954 for *Cahiers du cinéma*, "It's a very strange film; I know that it will be said that my involution has become so extreme that I've gone underground. But it is not at all a filmed play, but a film, and I would even say that it's neorealistic, in the sense that I always sought."[4]

Like his other films of this period, it struck the most sensitive (or most enthusiastic) commentators as evidence of a new order of filmmaking. Truffaut, in a contemporary review in *Arts,* employed another version of the rhetoric that had been applied so generously to *Voyage to Italy* a year earlier:

> As it's necessary, to appreciate Claudel, to take his words literally, exactly for what they're worth, it's necessary, to like Roberto Rossellini's film, to rediscover the innocence of a spectator seeing the film for the first time. Twenty years of allusive and elliptical cinema, and several thousand films which only exist *in terms* of each other make a film as elementary as *Jeanne au bûcher* look like a dangerous and abstract avant-garde enterprise.[5]

Theater Arts magazine at this same time quoted Bergman in a revealing moment of wish fulfillment, the understandable product of many years of coping with Rossellini's unorthodox methods:

> I think Roberto has made as great a break with standard technique and style with *Joan* as he did with *Open City*. He has changed his way of working, too. For the first time, I think, he carefully planned every step of every shot in great detail. The story and dialogue were there and could not be tampered with. The result was that all his creative energy and talent were concentrated on invention and direction.[6]

Unfortunately, the film fared no better than his other films of the period in finding an audience. The minister of education in France decided to distribute it throughout the country (an interesting foreshadowing of the mass-audience, didactic direction in which Rossellini would move for the first time four years later with *India*), but these plans fell through. In fact, the film was never released in France at all, nor anywhere else outside of Italy, and its run there, from September 1954 to August 1955, gained a pitiful 18.5 million lire, barely a quarter of the amount earned by the unsuccessful *Voyage to Italy*.[7] The film did find a few supporters, but most commentators were negative. Alessandro Ferraù, for example, writing in the February 1955 issue of *Bollettino dello spettacolo*, gloated: "The film is a big fiasco. . . . What surprises us is that a production company and a distributor even agreed to produce and distribute such a film. It's impossible to guess at what motivated Rossellini's direction . . . but it is undoubtedly harmful, considering the inevitable financial consequences, that such films should be made.[8]

The net effect of this initial hostility and lack of distribution is that all but one of the copies of the film have disappeared. For many years, it was occasionally seen on the art-house circuit in Europe, but no longer. Even as far back as 1958, Patrice Hovald complained about not being part of the "very small number of people who've been at rare, more or less private, projections of the film."[9] As recently as ten or twelve years ago, Baldelli, Rondolino, and Guarner were reporting a copy at the Centro sperimentale di cinematografia, but this copy also seems to have disappeared in the interim, and the authorities there have no record of it. The director of the Cineteca nazionale in Turin told me in 1984 that the only extant print of the film is in their collection, but that it is in such bad condition that it has been screened only once in the last seven or eight years. Since I have been unable to see the film, therefore, the following comments will necessarily be secondhand.

In many ways *Giovanna d'Arco al rogo* can be seen as a bridge between those films of the late forties and early fifties that purported to be "documentaries of the individual," and the films of the sixties and seventies that use an individual character to anchor the depiction of a specific historical period. Rondolino, for example, links it directly to the later historical figures whose "substantially static nature" becomes "the center around which turn the story, the facts, and the minor characters." He goes on to say:

> Joan of Arc is continually surrounded by slow, almost imperceptible movements of the camera, so that the character who is emblematic of a certain hu-

man condition also becomes a symbol of an anthropocentric vision of the world and of history, which, in different ways and in different accents, has already appeared in Rossellini's films. But the stylistic experimentation—the long takes, the slow and frayed editing, the tonal and coloristic relations between the background and the characters, the dramatic and symbolic use of the set design—also becomes a kind of technical essay, an original attempt to solve diverse and often complicated problems of expression.[10]

Guarner's discussion of the film, despite his minority view that it has "no close connection with [Rossellini's] film work or his usual preoccupations," is suggestive. Since the whole film is seen in flashback, as Joan mounts to heaven with Brother Domenico, Guarner suggests that everything in it is thus seen through Joan's point of view; later, he stresses the circles the camera makes around her, especially the "high-angle shot of people forming a ring around Joan" and gingerly offers the "tentative interpretation" that we are seeing Joan through the viewpoint of God and that "the whole film is only the point of view on a point of view."[11] He does not follow up on the implications of this doubled infolding, but it seems related to the self-reflexivity at work in the portraits of Bergman in *Siamo donne* and of Magnani in *Una voce umana*.[12]

Probably the most detailed account of the film appeared in the fall of 1962 in a special issue on the subject "Joan of Arc on the Screen" in the French journal *Études cinématographiques*. Included in the issue were two opposing articles on Rossellini's version. In one article, a more or less conventional Catholic critic objects to the film, and in the other, a critic associated with *Cahiers du cinéma* replies in vaguely phenomenological terms. It may be useful to summarize them briefly here in order to understand better the critical context for Rossellini's films of this period, something that is always more important on the Continent, of course, than in the Anglo-American world of filmmaking.

In the first article Michel Estève argues that the film is "a scarcely convincing work, in large part mistaken," because in it Rossellini continually opts for the "marvelous" rather than the truly "supernatural." Estève maintains that the oratorio itself was one of Claudel's weaker efforts, and that Rossellini has gone even further in the mistaken direction of the "Christian marvelous," away from "reality." Rossellini's techniques and "gimmicks" do not give us the "authentic supernatural," which is "neither the illusory nor the ordinary. On the contrary, it claims that it is inseparable from the natural and that it conforms to it, but the natural seen under a certain light which one is not used to seeing." Despite its subject, Rossellini does not in this film give us any sense of "the other dimension" of the universe, which is inaccessible to reason but can truly affect our lives, as do Bresson's *Diary of a Country Priest* and Dreyer's Joan of Arc film. What Rossellini's film lacks is "this union of the supernatural and the everyday, this weight of reality," as well as any sense of transcendence.[13]

The response was written by the director's ardent supporter Claude Beylie. For him, this version is "the most eloquent of all the versions of Joan on the screen, the most ethereal, but which also attaches itself at the same time to the most intimate fibers of the flesh." Beylie asks if "I dare say that we are, with Rossellini, no longer on the level of the flesh, nor of the spirit, nor of the soul, but in a sort of fourth dimension which brings them all together in a vertiginous maelstrom that I will call *the serenity of the abyss?"* He sees Joan as directly in line with Rossellini's other suffering heroines; here, too, the camera follows her with cold ferocity. (Beylie's formulation once again raises the significant question of the director's ambivalent depictions of woman as victim, especially since this time she is even burned at the stake.) According to the critic, *"Giovanna d'Arco al rogo* is really an act of pure contemplation, where the cinematic spectacle is reduced to its simplest expression, its most *primitive,* in the sense that one says of certain rocks that they are primitive." All that Estève has called banal Beylie sees as "meant to symbolize the mediocrity of earthly instincts" and Estève has missed all that is eternal about her: "Everything happens in reality as if Rossellini had tried to demystify the traditional marvelous by an overabundance of realism, obtaining a marvelous of the second degree, deeper than the first, whose equivalent I am unaware of in the entire history of the seventh art . . . a kind of unseen interior marvelous, in which reality has been totally recreated by dream, and vice-versa."[14]

There is a hint in Beylie's remarks of that dynamic relation between realism and expressionism, documentary and fantasy, that we have been tracing in Rossellini's films. What is more interesting about the above encounter, however, is how firmly both positions, though concerned primarily with the film's spiritual dimension, are anchored in a discourse of realism. To speak of Rossellini, at least until recently, is always to speak in these terms.

19

Fear
(1954–55)

La paura (*Fear;* also known by the German title *Angst*), the final collaboration between Bergman and Rossellini, is a clear falling off from their earlier films. For one thing, it is much more thoroughly "dramatized," in the conventional sense, and by the time it was released (in two versions, one doctored by the distributor), Rossellini's loss of energy and interest was apparent to everyone, especially his producers. He was not to make another film for three years.

Sergio Amidei, one of the principal collaborators on the screenplay, and a long-time Rossellini associate, has called it

> a very bad film. One of those famous lost opportunities. . . . But by this point Rossellini had gotten tied up in that complex of things, wives, children. . . . He hadn't changed, and he still had that extraordinary capacity to seduce you, but he had a lot of weight on his shoulders that he had to resolve. . . . There was the problem of survival, but a sense that he really didn't like this kind of cinema was also unconsciously growing inside him. It didn't interest him any longer, he did it against his will: let's tell the truth. The idea of the kind of cinema that he has done in the last few years, cinema that is more informational, was beginning to develop deep inside him.[1]

The strain of repeated failure also began showing up in Rossellini's family life as well, for it was obvious to everyone that Bergman's continuing loyalty to him was hurting her career. But she was chafing at the same time:

> I remember that *Angst* (*Fear*) was quite difficult because we had the children with us, and we were doing two language versions, one German, one English, and I suppose my emotions were showing through a bit. I always felt a little

resentful that Roberto wouldn't let me work with any other director. There were all these wonderful Italian directors: Zeffirelli, Fellini, Visconti, De Sica; all wanted to work with me and I wanted to work with them; and they were furious with Roberto that he wouldn't let me work for them . . . but in Roberto's terms, I was his property.

Roberto couldn't work with actresses except Anna Magnani. Maybe that was because they were the same stock, a good mix. We weren't a good mix. The world hated the Rossellini version of me, so nothing worked. And he was stuck with me. What did he want with an international star? Nothing. He didn't know what to write for me. And of course, by this time we both knew it. It was something we did not talk about. But the silences between us grew longer—the silences when I didn't dare to say anything because I would hurt his feelings. Roberto would take whatever I said, and, unhappy as he was, would make a scene about it. He liked to fight. And besides the traumas of our artistic life, our increasing debts worried me enormously.[2]

Angelo Solmi, in an article in *Oggi,* seems to have been speaking for the majority of Italian critics when he said: "The abyss into which Bergman and Rossellini have plunged can be measured by *Fear.* This is not because this film is any worse than their other recent motion pictures together, but because half a dozen tries with negative results prove the inability of the couple to create anything acceptable to the public or the critics."[3] Yet it *was* worse than their other films together, much worse. Nor have the film's fortunes improved very much since the dramatic shift in recent critical opinion in favor of the Bergman-era films.

Yet, somehow the film's aesthetic failures make it even more interesting from other points of view. For one thing, it is the most expressionist of all the films of this period—perhaps because of the German setting, as with *Germany, Year Zero*—and for another, it directly thematizes, consciously or unconsciously, various autobiographical details between husband and wife. It is also a kind of gathering-up of Rossellinian motifs and concerns that Jose Guarner has nicely summarized:

> It could well be called *Viaggio in Germania* or *Germania, anno sette,* or even *Europa '54,* so completely does it confirm the constancy of the director's thought and inspiration. *La paura* is a cool, northern film, almost Dreyer-like in contrast to the sensual warmth and erupting vitality of *Viaggio in Italia.* Significantly, it marked the end both professionally and maritally of Rossellini's partnership with Ingrid Bergman.[4]

The story itself, adapted from a novella of the same name by Stefan Zweig, is a suffocatingly banal bourgeois melodrama. It concerns Irene, a married woman with two children, who has taken a lover and feels guilty disguising this from her husband. While her husband was a prisoner of war, she had begun running their factory, and she continues to do so while he acts as chief scientist. Her crisis is precipitated by the fact that her lover's former girlfriend is blackmailing her, insisting on more onerous payments each time. Finally, her demands become too great and Irene simply gives up, saying she will go to the police. The blackmailer, frightened, admits that it was Irene's husband who asked her to do it, so that by gradually increasing the pressure on her, she would confess all to him and then be forgiven. Irene is thoroughly demoralized by the knowledge of her husband's "experiment" on her, exactly like his experiments with rats and guinea pigs in the laboratory, and resolves to kill herself. Just as she is about to take the poison they have been using on the lab animals, her husband stops her and they unite in a tearful embrace, forgiving each other and pledging their love.

This melodramatic plot is partially redeemed by the extensive use of expressionist elements that give the film a weighty sort of existential sullenness. Even the opening credits have a vertiginous Hitchcockian spiral whirling behind them to the accompaniment of a Renzo Rossellini musical score reminiscent of the tense scores of *Germany, Year Zero*, and *Una voce umana*. The first shots, part of a brilliantly photographed night scene, show a car making its way through rain-covered streets; obviously affected by *film noir* conventions, these images seem somehow sharper and more deeply etched than most films of the time. The very first image, actually, is a tilt shot that moves vertically down a darkened church tower until it reaches the ground, where it picks up the car. In this film of relentless horizontals and incessant leveling, such a strong vertical shot downward from the steeple seems to tell us right from the beginning that any form of transcendence will be utterly denied. Throughout the film we will be subjected to a purely human, almost material, level of event, idea, and emotion; the search for salvation that occupies many of Rossellini's other films will become an irrelevancy, almost an atavistic embarrassment amid the studied banality of *Fear*. As we follow the car's progress, a mood of existential anonymity envelops us as well, for until the end of the sequence, we do not have the slightest idea who is driving the car, or where, or why. The images are thus aestheticized when we expect exposition, and Rossellini refuses to diminish their intensity by the concession of a close-up of a human being to whom we can begin relating. This opening sequence alone almost rescues the film, in advance, from the vacuity of its plot and characters, and gives a indication of its ongoing visual richness.

As in *Germany, Year Zero* and the other Bergman pictures, the camera relentlessly tracks the protagonist throughout the film; she cannot seem to shake its incessant focus. When she leaves the kitchen after having asked her maid for a loan (to pay the blackmailer), the camera remains with the group of servants for a long moment, but, exercising great restraint, the director has them say nothing. A less austere film would certainly call for a comment here, an aside in her absence, to make sure we understood that this was strange behavior. Rossellini does not even allow the servants to nod to one another, or make the slightest gesture. Similarly, the director permits the *temps mort* of getting in and out of cars, for example, to stand in order, once again, to fashion a sense of lived reality despite this film's decidedly increased narrative and dramatic conventionality. In addition, as in *Germany, Year Zero*, emotional pressure is signified by pounding bass drums that jump out from the musical score, and the same pattern of light and dark emerges to form a symbolic landscape of the protagonist's interior state. The mise-en-scène is as stark and spare as the earlier film's, and both films are overtly concerned with a sense of instinctual guilt that appealed to Rossellini as evidence of the existence of a natural moral code. Thus, though Edmund has been told by Nazi philosophy that his father should be done away with because he is useless, and though Irene presumably believes it is exciting and adventurous to have a lover (at least she does in the novella; in the film her motives remain unexplained), both "instinctively" recoil at the touch of a loved one they are about to betray.[5]

One particular set of contrasting shots that Rossellini uses well is connected with automobiles, and is similar to the kind of dynamic we have seen in earlier Bergman-era films. One type of shot, in the cramped interior of a Volkswagen, is intensely claustrophobic; Irene and Martin argue in this crowded space, and later Martin plots, in the same location, with the blackmailer. The other type is the precise opposite of the first: here the camera is mounted directly on the front bumper or hood and makes us feel as though we are hurtling blindly through space, out on a limb, with no reference points beyond the flashes of reality whizzing past. The feeling of danger is strong in this kind of shot, but it is more than counterbalanced by an accompanying sensation of freedom. Its most vivid use comes when Martin and Irene are traveling through the forest to visit their children in the country. We sense the refreshment of body and spirit that the sight of the trees and the country road brings the couple, but the fact that the camera seems to be cut off from all support is simultaneously dismaying. Nor do we know just exactly *what* it is that we are so heartily plunging into. (A similar shot occurs at the beginning of *Voyage to Italy*, with the same mixed sensations of freedom and dread.) This queer combination of the superficially "happy" and the foreboding comes up again, a few minutes later, in the brilliant, if painful, fishing scene in which the family seems to be so fully unified and loving. The moment is marked by a dark undercurrent in the music, and the fish that we watch writhing on the hook as Martin pulls it in reminds us of the various symbolic fish of *Stromboli* and signals the presence of a similar animal-victim sexual motif in *Fear*.

This symphony of expressionist effects reaches a crescendo in the final fifteen minutes of the film. Irene meets her blackmailing tormentress in a bar—with its full complement of violent light-and-shadow effects—and, reaching her psychological limit, just like the guinea pig in her husband's laboratory, decides to give up. Rossellini's camera is active in pointing up truths and drawing conclusions here, for in the deep-focus shot that extends from the two women out into the *film noir* area of the street illuminated by a solitary light, we understand clearly, this time visually, that the real source of Irene's torment is her husband. At one point, in a bold, stylized composition, Martin exactly occupies the space between the two women, neatly completing the emotional equation.

Irene rushes out of the café, gets into her car, and, in an almost exact replication of the opening shots of the car prowling through the streets (suggesting more than anything else an animal trapped in a maze), returns to the factory. There the emotion is uncharacteristically heaped on as she makes a farewell suicide call to her children. While she is seated at her desk, the camera dollies in toward her, ever so slowly, enveloping her in a movement that is accompanied by a slight circling motion of entrapment, like the sequence of Edmund's walk toward suicide. (The shot also looks forward to Rossellini's later use of the slow zoom inward as investigative tool.) Again, as with Edmund, the director

Guinea pig: Bergman, as Irene, in the laboratory with her scientist husband (Mathias Wieman) in *Fear* (1954).

encourages his protagonist to indulge in random motions like absently playing with the telephone—motions that a more conventional director might have found distracting to the principal emotional focus of the scene.

In the final sequence Rossellini lets out all the expressionist stops. Irene opens the door leading to the laboratory, and the intense backlighting throws her enormous, grotesquely distorted shadow from one end of the ceiling to the other. She stumbles from one lab table to the next, toward her final destiny, as one set of lights after another is illuminated. Sobbing, heavily shadowed, she walks by all the cages, obviously empathizing with the trapped animals. One shot even shows her in extreme close-up *through* a cage, thus putting her visually inside it. She accidentally breaks a beaker, and the sound of the shattering glass causes a temporary emotional release in her and the audience. As she desperately searches for the curare that will release her from the psychological torment her husband has inflicted on her, as well as from what Rossellini sees as her own "instinctual" guilt, she is "rescued" at the last moment by the sound of her husband's voice calling her name. In an exquisite, if brief, moment of acting, Bergman/Irene seems unsure of how to respond to his pleas, but when he asks for forgiveness she embraces him and admits to simply being unable to confess her transgression to him. As she tells him that she loves him, her face is in full light, and the sudden transformation that occurs at the end of *Voyage to Italy* and *Stromboli* (in a different key) reigns once again, though now even less convincingly. She tells him breathlessly, "I couldn't take it any more, I love you."

This time, however, the ending is problematic for technical reasons as well. Various Rossellini critics have, in fact, reported quite different endings, and, given Rossellini's notorious lack of concern for the integrity of his films once he had finished with them, we shall probably never have anything resembling a definitive version. Guarner states flatly, "In *La paura*, the Wagners have no reconciliation (although it may be that the producer who renamed it *Non credo più all'amore* [I No Longer Believe in Love] for commercial distribution, also changed the order of the scenes to give a different impression, which in no way emerges from Rossellini's version), nor does the wife rush into her husband's arms imploring forgiveness."[6]

Aprà and Berengo-Gardin quote Mida to the effect that "Rossellini has also made a second version of this film, which contains some retouching and a different ending," and themselves add:

> To be precise, the retouching consists in the addition of Irene's voice-over which comments on several silent scenes, and the changing of the ending to several shots taken from one of the central scenes of the film, accompanied, once again, by Irene's voice offscreen.
> The film appeared in theaters in June of 1955 with the title *La paura* but, given its lack of success, it was withdrawn and rereleased later in the second version, but with the same results.[7]

This explanation makes matters even more confused, of course, because it associates Rossellini with the *changes* of the "original" version of the film. When the director himself was questioned about the repetition of the earlier scene at the end of the film (the version Aprà and Berengo-Gardin seem to ascribe to Rossellini), he said: "No, you see, these manipulations are done all the time: the distributors said . . . 'Look at this imbecile: he has Ingrid Bergman and he's not making a commercial film!' So the producer got his hands on *La paura* and made a commercial film out of it." When pressed as to the definitive ending, however, Rossellini could only answer: "Oh, I don't remember, I don't remember. It seems to me that it ended with those mouse cages . . . something like that. But I don't remember."[8] The version that repeats earlier family sequences at the end of the film and that incorporates Irene's voice-over seems, therefore, not to be the version that Rossellini would have preferred. However, it is still impossible to say whether he meant the couple to be reunited in the end (as in the version extant in the United States, which ends in the laboratory and contains no flashbacks and no voice-over) or to remain apart, as in the version Guarner describes.

Another potentially fruitful line of inquiry concerning *Fear* is the relation of the film version to Zweig's original novella, *Die Angst*. Some obvious changes stem from the different nature of the two media: thus, Rossellini adds the brooding shots of the car making its way through the anonymous city and he exteriorizes interior states through the use of music and visual images. He also shortens the exposition, primarily, in this case, to eliminate all information pertaining to Irene's lover's past and the history of their affair. In addition, the dreams that Zweig occasionally makes use of are left out of the film entirely, though their trace remains in Rossellini's expressionist treatment of the subject matter. Finally, Rossellini has also decided to locate the children in the country, so as to thematize the city-country dichotomy, while at the same time getting the children out of the way in order to streamline and focus the encounters between husband and wife.

Much more significant, however, are the alterations that give us direct evidence of Rossellini's continuing preoccupations and motifs. For example, everything connected with animals in this film was invented by Rossellini, and he explicitly mentioned this motif in an interview when describing "the doctor who treats his wife just like the guinea pigs he does experiments on."[9] Rossellini has also changed the husband's occupation from lawyer to scientist, apparently so that the animal parallels might be made more overt, but also to allow him to enhance the film visually by including equipment and apparatus, the tools of science that would fascinate him the rest of his life.

In Zweig's version we are presented with a rather insipid, morally flabby Irene who has little to do with the more interesting character played by Bergman. In the film, Irene's individual history is greatly diminished, perhaps so that she might more easily become a symbolic integer in the manner of the Irene of *Europe '51*. Similarly, Zweig's interest in the class difference between the leisured protagonist and her vulgar blackmailer disappears, as one might expect, in Rossellini's essentialized world, to be replaced by a greater subtlety in the apportionment of guilt. In Zweig, the woman carries most of the blame, but in Rossellini, consistent with the earlier Bergman films, the husband and wife seem meant to be regarded as equally at fault. Despite the director's intentions, however, the husband's sadistic need for a confession causes audience sympathy to remain firmly with Irene throughout the film.

By far Rossellini's most important changes concern his complicated and uneasy examination of sex and gender roles. Even if one is by training and inclination rather skeptical about autobiographical exegesis, it seems clear that the director is dramatizing his own insecurity and domestic troubles in this film. For example, all of the business about Irene taking over the factory and making it work while Martin was a prisoner of war was added by Rossellini. The fact that *she* continually drives the car, even when her husband is present, also seems significant, especially when she taunts him at one point for urging her to slow down with the words "Why, are you afraid?" Later, when she is harassed at the opera by the blackmailer, she asks Martin to take her home, but the next shot shows her at the wheel. (The autobiographical reference is perhaps even more direct in view of Rossellini's lifelong penchant for driving fast cars.) In another scene Martin tries to talk Irene into taking some time off from the factory, because "you've done even more than your share and it's time you slowed down. . . . I don't like to see you work, you could very easily enjoy a comfortable life like so many other women do in your position." When she accuses him of a lack of faith in her abilities, he answers, "It's simply that I don't want you to kill yourself working." These moments seem to point to a sharp gender role reversal that bothers Rossellini and that may be related to his continued failure to make a commercially successful film with Bergman. In this light, the film's formal links with the tradition of American *film noir* become even more significant, especially since these films, with their dangerous femmes fatales, have increasingly come to be seen as a manifestation of postwar male anxiety concerning women's successful assumption of male roles during the war years.

Even more overt are Rossellini's changes regarding the story's central thematic scene, when the daughter is accused of stealing something from the son, and both Zweig and Rossellini consciously underline the comparison between the daughter's refusal to confess and her mother's similar refusal. (Rossellini, however, leaves the already obvious parallel verbally unstated, whereas Zweig's less subtle narrator asks rhetorically, "Was he speaking about his wife or his daughter?") In Zweig's version the sibling disagreement is over a rocking horse, given to the brother, that his sister has broken and hidden. Rossellini takes this already sexually suggestive object and increases the stakes by changing it to a toy rifle. Earlier in the film, in fact, the rifle is stressed when Irene and Martin discuss what presents they should bring the children, and Martin says, "Bobby wants an air rifle, but the trouble is that Frieda wants one too. I believe it will be better if we buy her a doll." The guilt-ridden, distracted Irene can only meekly answer, "Yes."

When they get to the country, the little girl is upset at not having gotten a gun too, and her father replies, "No, little girls shouldn't play with rifles, little girls mustn't shoot." Angry with being stuck with a "silly old doll," Frieda hides her brother's rifle, a gesture laden with obvious psychoanalytic overtones. Furthermore, since the scene occurs right after the discussion about Irene working, quoted above, and since the mother-daughter guilt parallel is about to become overt, it seems possible to think of this symbolic "gun play" in terms of the husband and wife as well.

It is unclear what these changes add up to, and once again it is difficult to know just where to place Rossellini in all of this. Is he merely chronicling Martin's torture of Irene, or revelling in it? The compilers of the "Chronicle" included in the British Film Institute's dossier on Rossellini are, for once, more sanguine about this emphasis and more favorably disposed toward the director than the details warrant. They say, for example, that the film

> can be seen as a critical return upon Rossellini's way of looking, examining the "reverse" side of the "innocent" looking implied in all the films usually hailed as Rossellini's masterpieces. By inscribing the problem of the male's look at a woman at the core of the text, Rossellini simultaneously makes the previously "unproblematic" misogyny of his work available for critical scrutiny.

They also approvingly quote Jill Forbes' review of the film in *Monthly Film Bulletin* (no. 566) to the effect that "*La paura* addresses the issues of domestic politics with a fundamentally liberal understanding of the female condition which makes it extraordinary in its time—and indeed in ours."[10]

It seems equally plausible, however, to maintain that Rossellini's misogyny is "available for critical scrutiny" in this film because his increasing frustration and hostility has simply led him toward a more overt violence against woman. Given the explicit changes from Zweig's novella, in fact, Rossellini seems to be suggesting that, in the terms of the global critique we encountered in *Europa '51,* one of the things terribly wrong with present-day society is precisely the confusion of gender roles caused by the war. This confusion is one more manifestation of the general collapse of values that Martha, the old housekeeper, complains about too bitterly to Irene during the same momentous visit to the children. She is speaking of the Wagners' country home, of course, but, given the fact that the home is the proper purview of the female, and the locus of traditional values, the implication of her words extends far beyond that: "The devil is at work in this house, no order, no sense of duty. Have you had a look at the grounds? Nobody bothers to take care of them, or even to mow the lawn. The whole place is a terrible mess."

What, then, can we say about Rossellini's treatment of women, especially in those films he made with Bergman? Like the Japanese director Mizoguchi, although Rossellini sympathizes deeply and genuinely with his women as victims, in depicting their victimization he seems almost to enjoy punishing them. Which comes first, the sympathy or the punishment, and which causes which? Ultimately it is impossible to tell, and the matter must be left oscillating between these two poles, opposites that clearly constitute each other. But if Rossellini made Bergman "ugly" in these films, as some have said, he also made her a person. The saving feature, in other words, is that these women portrayed by Bergman and, earlier, by Magnani are always the central focus of their stories, always complex characters faced with difficult moral problems. They are more than the equals of their ineffectual lovers and stupid husbands. Of precious few male directors working in the late forties and early fifties can as much be said.

IV

India and
the "Commercial" Period

20

India
(1958)

By the mid-fifties Rossellini's career had reached rock bottom. His films with Ingrid Bergman had not only failed at the box office, but had failed critically as well. True, the French were calling them the heralds of a new age of film-making, but the people with the money were not listening. As we saw in the last chapter, Bergman, too, was growing dissatisfied with being Rossellini's "property." Nor was he insensitive to their problems, as he explained many years later:

> That was a very particular moment in my life, because I was married to a great, great actress. The point was that I risked too much and we were hated, I don't know why. Our films were not at all successful and we had big problems as we had three children. She was aware of the problems and she thought it would be wise to return to the industry just in order to save the material means of our life. I appreciated that thought very much, I believed it was wise. Unfortunately I was absolutely unwise myself and I did not want to be the husband of a great star. So very peacefully, very quietly and with a very full understanding and tremendous human compassion we decided to break. It was very hard, because we loved each other and we had three children. It was very, very painful.[1]

Now at his personal and professional nadir, Rossellini traveled to Africa, South America, and finally, in June of 1956, to Jamaica, where he was to make "The Sea Wife" with Richard Burton and Joan Collins. On his arrival in Jamaica, however, he discovered that the producers had changed the script he had written, presumably to avoid censorship problems; Rossellini immediately abandoned the project. (It was subsequently filmed by Bob McNaughton and released in 1957.)

Then the idea of going to India occurred to him. As he told reporters in Paris:

> The producers don't want to give me any more work because what I'm saying doesn't interest them any more. That's why I accepted the offer made by the Indian cinema. I have been given carte blanche: in India I'll be able to study the atmosphere, analyze the major problems, make the most of the magic, fakirist and philosophic tradition, juxtaposing it with contemporary voices which are rising and becoming important. It will be, in short, the great Indian civilization, in all its grandness, its past and future which will take me by the hand and trace the subject which has not in any way been imposed on me. It will be difficult to be a neorealist in such a fabulous atmosphere, but I will certainly find many similarities with things I have already treated while developing Italian themes.[2]

It must be remembered that these remarks were made for the benefit of the press and seem intended to pander to their perhaps less-nuanced sense of things—in film journals, for example, Rossellini had been denying for years that he was a neorealist. Nevertheless, the remarks offer an interesting summary of his thoughts as he was about to depart for India. He had always been fascinated by foreign cultures, but by this time he was becoming especially interested in what was beginning to be called the third world. Here he could closely examine a single traditional culture, but, more importantly in view of his later overwhelming interest in science and modern technology, he could try to depict a vibrant test case, an actual battlefield between tradition and technology. He was also immensely drawn to Ghandi, who had once stayed in his home in Rome for a few days, and he told Victoria Schultz in *Film Culture* that "Ghandi was the only completely wise human being in our time of history."[3] He was also impressed by Nehru, Ghandi's successor, and spoke of him as "an extraordinary man" and "a saint." Jean Herman, Rossellini's young French assistant, makes it quite clear in the article he wrote for *Cahiers du cinéma* during the filming that the final product was to be a kind of social analysis of India, and certainly not merely the personal impressions of an auteur: "This will be the objective summing-up of ten years of freedom, of ten years of work, and of all the snares and traps that lie in wait for India today."[4]

Rossellini told a reporter for the *New York Sunday News* that this new film was to be "a takeoff on one of my earlier films, *Paisan,* which made money in the United States,"[5] and, in fact, the films are similar in their episodic structure and method of filmmaking. In India, as in postwar Italy, Rossellini went from one end of the country to the other, filming interesting sights, on the lookout for promising material. As Herman tells us, the director came to India with the rough outline of an idea in his head, but, as always, he allowed the specifics of the events, people, and places he encountered to determine the final product, making him add, delete, and change continuously.[6] Another aspect of his filmmaking practice here that is important for his later career is the fact that the project originally took the form of short documentary films for Italian and French television, from which he would then cull the best material for release as a commercial film. At this point, however, Rossellini still sees television principally as a means to an end, a kind of dry run (and source of necessary funds) for what he *really* wanted to do.

A further similarity with his earlier, pre-Bergman practice, is his insistence on the incorporation of "real life" into his film. As in films as chronologically far apart as *La nave bianca* and *Francesco,* he tells us proudly in the titles of *India* (the film is also widely known as *India '58*) that "the actors, all nonprofessional, were chosen in the very locations in which the action takes place." To some extent the result is again, paradoxically, to destabilize the codes of realism, preventing our acquiescence in the illusion and always keeping before us the sense that what we are seeing has been *made.* He also returned to his previously standard practice of observing someone he might choose to be in the film in order to memorize his "natural" actions, then, when he became stiff and artificial in front of the camera, Rossellini would "build him up again, teach him to act the way he was before you began teaching him to act."[7] He was so taken by the successful adaptation of his old methods to a new subject matter that he told the French journal *Cinéma 59* that his future plans extended to South America, especially Brazil and Mexico. His remarks clearly foreshadow the great didactic project to come:

> I will send teams of young people into each country, and they'll do an initial scouting. They will include a writer, a photographer, a sound man, and a filmmaker, who will be the head of the team. And this is how I'll proceed: I'll make an index for each country, and I'll study, along with my collaborators, their problems, food, agriculture, animal raising, languages, environment, etc. As you see, the task of a geographer and ethnographer. But it won't remain merely scientific, and will give each spectator the possibility of discovery. The art will only be the end point of this preliminary work. My job will be to make a work which will be a poetic synthesis for each country. . . .
>
> I have tried to use this method abroad, but I could also use it in Europe. I've returned from India with a new way of looking at things. Wouldn't it be interesting to make ethnographic films on Paris or Rome? For example, a wedding ceremony. . . . Well, we need to rediscover the rites on which our society rests, with the fresh outlook of an explorer who is describing the customs of the so-called primitive tribes.[8]

The relation of this film to the rest of Rossellini's oeuvre is complex. Before it come the intensely introspective, expressionist fiction films made with Bergman, which seem to make only the slightest nod of acknowledgment toward external, surface reality. Immediately after it come the films of the only really blatant, self-consciously commercial period in his life, beginning with *General della Rovere* (1959) and ending with *Anima nera* and "*Illibatezza*" (both 1962). Yet Jean Herman is correct, I think, in regarding *India* as a "synthesis of the Rossellini oeuvre" that merges the exteriority of *Paisan* with the interiority of *Voyage to Italy.*[9] *India* itself, as Rossellini pointed out, is an amalgam of these two realities:

> The Indian view of man seems to me to be quite perfect and rational. It's wrong to say that it is a mystical conception of life, and it's wrong to say that it isn't. The truth of the matter is this: in India, thought attempts to achieve

complete rationality, and so man is seen as he is, biologically and scientifically. Mysticism is also a part of man. In an emotive sense mysticism is perhaps the highest expression of man. . . . All Indian thought, which seems so mystical, is indeed mystical, but it's also profoundly rational. We ought to remember that the mathematical figure nought was invented in India, and the nought is both the most rational and the most metaphysical thing there is.[10]

In this remark Rossellini is clearly trying to reinscribe the fantasy (here, mysticism) of *La macchina ammazzacattivi* and *Dov'è la libertà?* into a wider, now more inclusive, realist aesthetic. Instead of being opposed, fantasy will now become a subset not of realism, exactly, but of rationalism. This latter term, which in some ways will help Rossellini elide the contradictions of realism, will soon come to be paramount in his remaining films.

Rossellini's understanding of India is accomplished in four individual episodes, each with its own main "character," "story," and location, the whole bounded on both ends by a factual frame that, especially at the beginning, provides the information necessary to put the individual episodes in an overall context. (In itself, the episodic, fragmented nature of the film implies that our understanding can be only partial and fragmented.) An interesting, active dynamic is immediately set up between the frame sequence, which is marked by fast cutting, zooms, and quick camera movements—obviously appropriate to its concentration on the city life in Bombay—and the inner sequences of life in the villages, which are generally much slower, comprised primarily of long takes, medium shots, pans, and minimal cutting. Appropriately, the physical movement which the film celebrates is registered in two different ways, depending on location. In the opening urban sequence it is conveyed through the artificial excitement of montage. Where movement exists in more natural settings, however—for example the flight of birds and the scurrying of monkeys through the forest—it is also highlighted, but significantly, by following it through pans.

Our own movement, from the frame to the interior stories and back again, is itself thematic. The voice-over tells us in a dramatically heightened, pulsating way at the very beginning of the film that "the first thing that astonishes you [in Bombay] is the crowd: tens, hundreds, thousands, tens of thousands, hundreds of thousands, perhaps a million people who come together like the incessant current of a river." Rossellini seems to be suggesting that, while first impressions are important, they must be seen through, in order to come to any understanding of the reality of the country. Yet, at the very end of the film, after the four internal, personalized stories have been told, we are put back in the same place, back into the middle of the city that we have not seen since the beginning, back into the fast cutting and zooming on the mass of swarming humanity, while the voice-over murmurs, as though mesmerized, one last phrase: "And still, the crowds, the immense crowds." We wonder if we, as outsiders, are forever condemned to be prisoners of our first impressions, which of course are always a product of our own culture, the culture we thought we left behind.

The dynamic between the framing sequence and the internal sequences also underlines the presence of the filmmaker in the whole process. In the opening sequence of *India,* a thoroughly un-Rossellinian style of editing assails the viewer: the cutting is even faster, and more self-conscious, than it was in the early *La nave bianca,* so indebted to Eisenstein. While the voice-over bombards us with facts, the very presence of the massive statistics, despite their "objectivity," paradoxically seems to underline the fact that they were compiled and put together by *someone,* and thus from a particular point of view. At the same time, the visuals jump along quickly, often cutting in perfect unison with the verbal sound track (for example, in the exciting series of quick cuts that accompanies a string of rhyming verbs), further underlining the presence of a mediating mind. In the inner sequences, on the other hand, there are moments of quick cutting when the narrative demands it, but the sequences are primarily composed of long-take shots by an absolutely immobile camera. Here we see simple acts, like the ritual bath of a young engineer, or the attachment of a log to a chain, then the chain to an elephant—acts often long and drawn-out, unquestionably real—that are accomplished in a single take. (Also, of course, the lack of cutting is appropriate to the subject—in this case the elephants, the effect of whose ponderous, immense bobbing would be totally lost if the sequence were fragmented into a jazzy montage.) Though these inner sequences sometimes seem to offer themselves as privileged, direct glimpses of a "true" reality, the fictionalization of the episodes, as well as the return of the frame tale at the end, work against this.

The manner of presenting the inner tales and their information is complicated as well, for once they have been factually and contextually launched by a third-person voice-over, all, in one way or another, are told from a first-person point of view. Thus, each episode seems to be balanced between the desire to convey a certain amount of abstract information and the related, but different, desire to put this information in a human context. Though one might object that the individualizing of the portraits takes away from the typicality of the film as a documentary, it is clear that seeing things from a single individual's point of view, and, even more importantly, hearing "his" words (in Italian, of course) concerning that reality is what makes the film so memorable. The language used by each principal character is so utterly direct and spare that it carries the charge of a poem by William Carlos Williams. The old man of the third episode, for example, tells us in a stately, measured tone (with enormous pauses between most of the sentences and accompanied by a perfect correlation between the words and pictures):

> I am eighty years old. I have always lived here but the forest is still rich, appealing and full of secrets. Especially at night when it resounds with the fantastic love songs of the tigers. The jungle is the temple in which their rites of love are celebrated. When I awake at the rays of the sun, there is an explosion of joy which surrounds me. My wife and I do not need to exchange many words. Our gestures and looks are enough to express our unchangeable, daily solidarity. It has been a long time, after all, that our mutual duties have been shared between us. What else is there to say?

The entire film, in other words, has been subjectivized, and on several levels at once. The filmmaker has, for his part, made an attempt at objectivity, at getting beyond the Western self: Claude Baurdet, a reporter for *France Observateur,* wrote at the time, "The director insisted that he needed an intermediary with a true understanding of the lives of the Indian peasants, in addition to cinematic knowledge, in order to complete his project."[11] Rossellini also knew, however, and freely admitted, that everything that we see in the film, no matter how objectively obtained, has been filtered through his own (Western) consciousness. He told Godard in a famous interview for *Arts* (which Rossellini later claimed Godard had made up) not that the audience should learn the truth of India, but that they "should leave the theater with the same impression that I had while I was in India."[12] As a reporter for the *New York Times* pointed out, the film is successful precisely because Rossellini was so forthright about his *own* romantic notions concerning India, and he quotes the director to the effect that his ideas about the country were "gathered from books and newspapers . . . [and] are a rather stewy mixture of Ghandism, passive resistance, Jawaharlal Nehru, land distribution, the five-year plan, and spiritualism."[13] Even more important in this regard is the self-consciousness apparent in the title of the television series itself: in Italy, where it was broadcast between January and March 1958 in ten episodes of eighteen to twenty-nine minutes each, it was called "L'India vista da Rossellini" (India Seen by Rossellini), and in France, where it was shown between January and August of the following year, it was called "J'ai fait un beau voyage" ("I Had a Fine Trip"); in both cases, the mediation of the filmmaker's consciousness is clearly signaled.[14]

In important ways, then, this entire film stands opposed to the prevailing film fashion of the time, cinéma vérité. Rossellini felt, for one thing, that this kind of "direct cinema" could never achieve anything more than an undigested depiction of a not necessarily significant surface reality. He told the editors of *Cahiers du cinéma* in a 1963 interview that, unlike the *cinéma vériste* who forgets that the camera is only a tool, the real artist is one

> with a precise position, his own artistic dream, a personal emotion, who gets an emotion from an object and tries to reproduce it at any cost, who tries, even if he has to deform the original object, to communicate to someone else perhaps less sensitive, less subtle, his own emotion. You can see how the author enters into all this, how his choice is determined, how his style becomes the essential element of expression.

He spoke of being upset, bored, and angry at the screening of his friend Jean Rouch's *La Punition,* and when asked how his own film differs from cinéma vérité, he responded: "There is an enormous difference. *India* is a choice. It's the attempt to be as honest as possible, but with a very precise judgment. Or, at least, if there's no judgment, with a very precise *love*. Not indifference, in any case. I can feel myself attracted by things, or repulsed by them. But I can never say: I'm not taking sides. It's impossible!"[15] As we shall see, Rossellini forgets the impossibility of not taking sides when his subjects become historical figures. Here in *India,* however, he understands the problem full well, and as Bruno Torri has explained, the film was clearly meant to be "a harmonious and life-giving account of the interaction between what was observed and the point of view of the observer."[16]

Another site of the film's self-awareness is its fascination with *rhythm* of all sorts, visual, verbal, musical, and thematic, which Rondolino attributes to Rossellini's recent experience with opera and especially with the oratorio *Giovanna d'Arco al rogo.* A marvelous correlation exists between the visuals and the sound track (both its verbal and its musical components) that seems unique in Rossellini's films, and this rhythm provides the pleasure inherent in all forms of rhyming, repetition, and fulfilled expectations. The musical score itself stands out, but for once in a Rossellini film, not because it is annoying; composed almost solely of various forms of native Indian music, it seems utterly organic to what we are seeing. The score is augmented and complemented by sounds that come from the location—thus, the bells worn by the elephants insist on the immensity of these animals' presence in the sound track as well. (Herman tells us that the bells are put on the elephants because the animals are so quiet moving through the jungle that a human could easily be hurt without some advance warning.)

The voice-over commentary (anathema to cinéma vérité) also reminds us that the film was made from a particular point of view, but once the basic information is presented in the opening sequence, it becomes less obvious. Rossellini had, in fact, told the reporter for the *New York Times* in 1957 that the images were more important than understanding the dialogue, for "a healthy picture did not need more than a little bit of explanation here and there." However, those few who have been lucky enough to see the only copy available in the United States—an unsubtitled black-and-white print owned by the Pacific Film Archives at the University of California at Berkeley—know how important the Italian voice-over actually is to a basic comprehension of what is going on. It would be more accurate to say that, once the basics of the narrative line of each episode are grasped through the commentary, the images supply a resonance of their own that transcends the merely verbal.

India's emphasis upon the image is accompanied by a greatly enhanced sense of pleasure in composition that we last saw in some of the stylized sequences of *Fear.* Throughout his life Rossellini maintained that he was completely uninterested in "pretty pictures," and that, in fact, he always avoided them, but the evidence of *India*, at least, belies this claim. Many images are obviously meant to be experienced aesthetically rather than merely as neutral carriers of information. The best example is perhaps the astounding shot of the young engineer who takes his ritual bath in the artificial lake created by the dam he has helped to construct; the confluence of ancient tradition and modern technology is obviously the point of the shot, but our pleasure goes beyond this realization. The camera holds absolutely steady for what seems like minutes, creating a frame that is split in two by an unbroken horizon line, above which lies the untroubled sky, below the water, below that the land. The young man walks out into the water after shedding part of his clothes, bathes, then walks back onto the shore, picking up his clothes and walking out of the shot before there is a cut or a single movement of the camera. Examples such as this could be multiplied many times.

Let us now turn to a closer examination of the individual episodes of the film. The old themes are still present: for example, the concern with problems of communication and the attendant respect for diverse cultures are in evidence right from the opening title which, in an attempt to avoid a reductive Western "orientalism," shows the name of the film (and the name of the country) in Ital-

The elephant-bathing sequence from *India* (1958).

ian and English, in Urdu, and with the words, *Matri Bhumi* (Mother Earth), occupying the third position. Many conversations not absolutely crucial either narratively or informationally are presented at various times in three of the official
native languages of India. The animal motif, so closely connected in his earlier
films with the woman-as-victim theme, also reappears, but now it represents
the relation between man and nature. In the terms of the perhaps too-neat
formulation he gave Godard, "I wanted to show [in *Fear*] what there is of the
animal in intelligence, and in *India '58*, I showed what there is of intelligence
in the behavior of an animal."[17]

The first fully developed episode, which takes place in the jungle of Karapur
and centers on the relation between the professional elephant drivers and their
elephants, is a visual delight. We learn that "the elephant is India's bulldozer,"
and chuckle to see the elephants knock trees down and then carry them away.
The narration switches to the first-person point of view of one of the drivers,
who tells us how much elephants have to be fed, and, in a superb sequence, we
witness the care that has to be taken every day to give the elephants their baths
when it becomes too hot to work any longer. The elephants loll and roll over in
the water, as languorous as immense cats. When a company of puppet play-
ers arrives in the village, the young man becomes interested in the owner's
daughter, and from this moment on, the elephants (who are also "falling in

love") and the two young people are overtly compared in order to point up the harmony between man and nature that Rossellini finds in India. The young man goes to the schoolteacher for a formal letter to his father, asking him to speak to the girl's father in order to arrange their marriage. This scene and the one following (of the schoolteacher acting as mediator between the two fathers) are recorded entirely in the Indian language of the region, with no specific explanation provided in Italian. By the end of the episode, the young man tells us that the pregnant elephant must go away from the male halfway through her pregnancy, in the company of another female elephant who will minister to her needs, and because the demands of his work do not allow him to accompany his pregnant wife to her mother's, she, too, must be accompanied by another female.

The second episode, like the rest, begins with specific information that later will be put in more personal, individualized terms. Here the emphasis is on water. We start at the Himalayas, India's principal source of water, and learn about reincarnation, the sacredness of the Ganges, and the holy city of Benares along the way. The central focus of the episode, however, is the immense dam built at Hirakud, largely by grueling human labor. Our protagonist is a young engineer who has been working on the dam for seven years but who must now leave because his job is finished. He and his wife, we learn later, were originally refugees from East Bengal, due to the division of Pakistan, and since their child was born at Hirakud, they have come to look upon it as home. The husband seems sad but reconciled to the prospect of moving, but the wife complains throughout, refusing to understand, and at one point after a farewell party, an argument breaks out that ends with him pushing her violently to the floor.

The emphasis throughout is on the engineer's consciousness, and it is clear that this episode of the film, though visually magnificent, depends heavily on its verbal component to be understood. The young man makes one more trip back to the dam, where thousands upon thousands of unskilled workers—mostly women—carry rocks and dirt atop their heads, basket by basket, in their seemingly Sisyphean task. We learn from the engineer's voice-over narration that some 435,000 people work at the job site, and 175 died building the dam. But, "Before with the floods, if we had to build a monument to the dead, it would have taken a list as long as the dam itself to inscribe the names of all of them."

The chief theme of this sequence is the advent of technology into a traditional culture. Rossellini clearly believes in technology—and this belief will increase dramatically as the years go by—but at this point he is still concerned about its misuse. As Jean Herman tells us at the end of his article:

> Rossellini came here with his head stuffed with questions. He was afraid of the dangers represented by the [West's] too-clean-hygiene, the button-you-press-which-solves-all-your-problems, the books-on-how-to-teach-five-year-olds-in-five-days, the pills-which-save-you-from-eating.[18]

The director is clearly fascinated by the conflict raging in the mind of this young engineer between the desirability of modern technology and the demands of the traditional culture. In one powerful sequence the man is wandering amid the giant spools of electric cable and immense electrical transformers, and, in a voice made to reverberate like an echo chamber, he thinks: "Electricity. Magic.

The old man and his wife eat breakfast in a scene from *India*.

Everything can be explained. All it takes is to think. There is no magic. There are no more miracles. Knowledge. Mystery. No more mystery. Knowledge. Hirakud." In the next sequence, however, we are pulled in the opposite direction as he observes a ritual burning of a body on a funeral pyre and thinks aloud that, while death is difficult for those who have been left behind, it must be very good to be able to dissolve completely into nature. A satisfying synthesis is achieved in the shot described earlier, when the young man takes his ritual bath in the artificial lake that has been created by the dam. The family leaves the next day with the cart carrying the few pieces of their furniture; stretched out behind them is the overwhelming presence of the dam. The episode ends with a resonant, self-consciously composed shot of a file of workers moving off to the right, who are rhymed visually by different-colored stones in the curb in front of them; the camera pans right, away from the couple, to "discover" the workers, then remains immobile as they file out of the frame, one by one.

In the third episode we move to the land where the rice grows. Our protagonist here is an old man who we see in his daily rituals: making obeisance to the sun when he rises, having breakfast with his wife, giving advice to his sons. We see vaguely "documentary" material that serves to advance the narrative not a whit, like a woman breast-feeding her infant, and the old man's wife packing the sides of their hut with mud, reminiscent of similarly "aimless" sequences as far back as *La nave bianca*. The old man tells us, in a soft-spoken, simple prose that is thoroughly convincing:

> The only thing that is left in me is the need for contemplation and for that there is only one place on earth that can satisfy me: the jungle. I love my cows. They are beautiful and strong animals. I always bring them with me. . . .
> When I am alone in the jungle I feel strongly the presence of nature and it seems to me that little by little I become part of it.

He says that, even though he knows that the tiger he hears will not hurt him, still he is afraid.

Then one day his jungle peace is destroyed by the presence of three trucks full of men looking for iron; the old man has often heard of this substance, but believes it is a myth. And here Rossellini shows us the less pleasing side of technology. The noise of the motors causes all the animals to become upset (monkeys and vultures are juxtaposed in the editing in a clear foreshadowing of the next episode); in the commotion, the tiger is attacked by the porcupine, and, as the old man knows too well, only a wounded tiger is ever dangerous. The tiger finally does attack a man, as the old man feared; the cycle is complete when the prospectors decide to go on a tiger hunt for this dangerous animal. The old man asks, "Why kill? Isn't the world big enough for everybody?" In the last sequence of the episode, he sets a fire to convince the tiger to seek refuge in another part of the jungle, away from the hunters.

In the final segment Rossellini moves completely into the world of the animals by making one his protagonist. Again, a problem is posed and a piece of information supplied; this time it is the inverse of the water of the second episode—the devastating effects of drought. The camera tilts down from the "sky of steel" to reveal a man and his trained female monkey wandering through the parched desert. The man collapses and, as he slowly dies, the monkey tries vainly to protect him from the vultures that are gathering to attack. The sequence becomes a veritable feast of camera "trickery," with rhythmic pans, faked shadows, and suggestive editing all used to exacerbate the sense of danger. The sequence continues much longer than one might normally expect of a wordless event like this, and the effect is to make us even more aware of the elaborate rhythmic choreography of camera, physical shapes, light and shadow. In a chilling image, vultures bounce along the ground, their enormously long wings fully outstretched, but seemingly more in order to frighten than to propel them into the air. The monkey finally gives up her quixotic act of protecting her dead master and breaks loose from the chain that holds her, as the editing becomes faster and faster and the vultures close in—again, all through the suggestivity of the cutting rather than through any actual proximity between the monkey's master and the vultures about to attack.

This sequence is followed by a quick cut to the fair toward which the man had been traveling when he collapsed. Characteristically, we are not told that this cut signifies the continuation of the monkey's narrative; we do not see her or hear her, in fact, until the location and the environment of the fair have been fully placed before us. Only after many shots of the various performers does the monkey come into the frame, and we are left with the impression, as always, that the individual story is not important in itself, but only as a vehicle for presenting whatever reality has been found and/or constructed in the encounter between the filmmaker and the country. Then the film cuts suddenly to furious cart-and-oxen races, which apparently are part of the fair but, again, are narratively unmotivated and remain unexplained by the laconic voice-over.

The monkey has come to the fair out of training or instinct and, lacking a master, pitifully goes through her paces, doing what "she is used to doing, picking up coins that she does not understand the use of." She is unable to provide for herself because she has lost her connection with nature, and, at the same time, wild monkeys threaten her because she is deeply tainted with the smell of man. We see unhappy shots of her sleeping on the temple steps like a bum, forlorn and hungry, while her more natural relatives send up a howl at her presence. Finally, she is rescued by a new owner, and the last image we see of her is in her "new life" as a performer on a miniature trapeze. The voice-over gives only the barest information and is painfully reticent and noncommittal about how we are to read this image of her swinging back and forth above the awed crowd. Again characteristically, Rossellini refuses to move to a simplistic closure regarding this final example of the relationship between man and animal. Most viewers will find the image degrading, I think, and while we may have been intended to take this training as one more example of the wonder of man's skills, the monkey seems to represent a message counter to that which has gone before. Man and animal, and by extension all of nature, are in close harmony in India, but the two realms *are* distinct, finally, and must remain so. The monkey is awkwardly suspended between the world of men and the world of animals, and not comfortable or even able to take care of herself in either one. The monkey's split between nature and culture is, however, emblematic of the human condition, Rossellini seems to imply, especially in terms of advancing technology. In fact, in the 1959 *Cahiers du cinéma* interview he said, cryptically, that the monkey's division is "exactly the story of all of us. It's the battle that we're engaged in." The episode ends immediately after this shot, with a close-up on the human faces that file past the camera on their way out of the small circus tent. We then go back suddenly to the final short piece of the framing sequence, which completes the decisive return to human beings. For Rossellini the humanist, it is good that men and animals can be in such a harmonious relationship, finally, because it is good for men.

The film was first presented at the 1959 Cannes festival, out of competition, and was well received; its commercial release in Italy did not come until June 1960, however, and by April 1961, the film had grossed only 15 million lire—another box-office failure. This time, at least, the general critical reaction was favorable. The French appreciated the film, of course, especially Godard:

> *India* goes against all standard cinema: the image is only the complement of the idea which provokes it. *India* is a film of an absolute logic, more socratic than Socrates. Each image is beautiful, not because it is beautiful in itself, like a shot from *Que Viva Mexico,* but because it's the splendor of the true, and because Rossellini takes off from the truth. He has already departed from the place most others won't even reach for another twenty years. *India* gathers

together the entire world cinema, like the theories of Reimann and Planck gather up geometry and classical physics. In a forthcoming issue, I will show why *India* is the creation of the world.[19]

Even Rossellini's most bitter Italian critics, those who had pilloried him during the Bergman era, welcomed him back to the fold, anxious to "forgive" him. In Mida's words, "with a wipe of the sponge, he has wiped out all the earlier mistakes, all the uncertainties of an obvious decadence."[20] More recent critics, like Baldelli, however, have mounted a serious attack:

> The eye isn't enough when an exact politico-cultural preparation and a complete immersion in the circumstances are lacking. Rossellini shortens and at the same time confuses the historical distances from the moment he begins to see India as a gigantic example of his usual themes: a boundless South crawling with "paisans" and the fabulous presence of antique temples, a remote past which is always equal to itself, a perpetual seat of equilibrium between nature and history.

He complains that Rossellini shows the irresistible, harmonious onward march of technology that in actuality proceeds at the expense of the masses. He faults Rossellini's devotion to the passive nonviolence of Gandhism, the whole film becoming, for Baldelli, little more than a transference of the ideals of Saint Francis to the Indian masses. Finally, he objects to the film's neglect of topics like starvation, the caste system, religious superstition, and the inability of the masses to read.[21]

Of course, Baldelli is right. Seeing the film, however, is a profound and moving experience that perhaps covers up, but also redeems all its shortcomings at the same time. Of the films of Rossellini's that are not available for public viewing, this is perhaps the greatest loss, not only for the proper understanding of Rossellini's career, but for the proper understanding of the potential of cinema itself. Andrew Sarris has called it "one of the prodigious achievements of this century,"[22] and he is only overstating by a little.

Before concluding this chapter, it may be useful to describe in more detail the major shift that was taking place in Rossellini's thinking at the time, which is signaled by the new emphases, especially on technology, apparent in *India*. The principal text will be his interview with Fereydoun Hoveyda and Jacques Rivette published in the April 1959 issue of *Cahiers du cinéma*. It is here that the director first spells out his increasing interest in the powers of human reason, an interest that will remain submerged in the more blatantly commercial films that immediately follow, but will soon after become nearly obsessive.

In the interview he professes first of all to be amazed that modern abstract art could have become the "official art," given that it is the least intelligible. The reason for this, he believes, is that man is being forgotten, that he is becoming just a cog in a gigantic wheel. This situation must be seen in historical terms, however, as part of an eternal alternation between long periods of slavery and all too brief moments of freedom. But today things are worse because now we are held by a "slavery of ideas." The cinema, television, radio, through their sensationalism, all bear part of the responsibility for this sorry state of affairs. Instead of pandering to the worst in man, we must try to understand him and his world. Most of all, we must avoid the smiling, false optimism that leads us to alcohol, tranquilizers, and the psychiatrist to avoid every possible anxiety in the world.

Rossellini says, furthermore, that we must begin to reestablish the rapport among various nationalities that existed immediately after World War II, and the cinema has a significant role to play in this attempt, as does the newer medium of television. He speaks approvingly of his own television series on India, for "there I could not only show the image, but speak and explain certain things." At this point in his career, however, it is still the cinema that is paramount, and, in light of his later didactic films, for the somewhat surprising reason that it can be more emotional, finally, than the more factual material prepared for television: "Perhaps my television broadcasts will help people to understand my film. The film is less technical, less documentary, less explanatory, but because it tries to penetrate the country through the emotions rather than statistics, it allows us to penetrate it better. That's what I think is important and what I want to do in the future."[23]

Rossellini's concerns have not yet been broadened, or made more subtle, and they are obviously marked by their fifties' origin. Yet, here in embryo, we can detect the founding beliefs of the final fifteen years of his cinematic practice. In 1959, though, they were little more than beliefs. Ironically, Rossellini will next, for virtually the first time in his career, begin to make cinema the old-fashioned, conventional way—though not, certainly, what he had begun calling the cinema of "holdups and sex." His goal of freeing himself forever from the demands of the commercial cinema of sensation will finally be fulfilled, but only after five more years of struggle.

21

General della Rovere
(1959)

As we have seen, Rossellini's own voyage to India had an enormous impact on his artistic sensibility and his view of what the cinema had to become. However, *India* was a box-office failure as well, and, in fact, represented one of the lowest financial points of his career. His situation in 1958 was thus an awkward one: he had yet to find the alternative financing of television that he would successfully exploit for the last fifteen years of his life, yet he no longer had the lure of Ingrid Bergman to insure a steady stream of prospective investors, ever hopeful for a hit.

There had always been offers to do films that were more overtly "commercial," though little documentation exists to tell us just what these projects were. The actor Vittorio Caprioli recounts how one night he and the producer Morris Ergas were having dinner with Rossellini and Sergio Amidei when Caprioli mentioned that Diego Fabbri had just finished writing *La bugiarda* for him and that Ergas should produce it. The eager Rossellini immediately suggested that he direct the picture, but Ergas said no. Amidei then mentioned a sketch by Indro Montanelli he had recently seen in the Milanese newspaper *Corriere della Sera;* Ergas and Rossellini expressed interest, and the film was on its way.[1]

Montanelli's sketch, followed closely in the film, tells the story of a petty thief and gambler who is forced by the Germans to masquerade as General della Rovere, an important Italian military leader and Resistance figure who has been secretly killed by the Germans while attempting a clandestine landing. Bertone, the gambler, is put in prison in order to discover the identity of the leader of the Resistance, for while the Germans know that they have him in the same jail, they do not know which prisoner he is. Bertone becomes so absorbed by the role he is playing that at the end of the film he willingly goes before the firing squad with his "fellow" partisans rather than reveal the identity of their leader.

The screenplay was written principally by Amidei, Diego Fabbri, and Montanelli,[2] but it is unclear how closely it was followed by Rossellini. Just after the film was completed, the director was claiming rather grandly:

> I don't need traditional methods to make a film. For me, the inspiration comes on the set. My work on the scenario of *General della Rovere* consisted in tracing out the general lines of my story and of imagining, very close up, the personality of my character. I have no preconceived notions before I begin filming, and it's the first shot of a film which determines the entire work. It is then that I really feel the rhythm that I must give it, which leads me to imagine the thousand things which are the essence of my film. I want to arrive at the film location with a new feeling.[3]

Five years later he bluntly insisted, that "The only thing that really existed of the film was the screenplay which I read quickly and then put aside during the shooting. Many people, including the producer, have taken credit for the organization of that film, but this is the real story."[4]

It is ironic that Rossellini should have been so intent on claiming authorship of a film that he so obviously disliked, both during production and later. It was not the last film he was to make out of sheer necessity, but it was the first. Even the rather forced humor of the Totò vehicle *Dov'è la libertà?* had been closer to his heart. Years later, in fact, he named *General della Rovere* as one of the two films (the other being *Anima nera*) that he was actually ashamed of having made, because "it's an artificially constructed film, a professional film, and I never make professional films, rather what you might call experimental films."[5] In another interview conducted at the same time, he explained why he undertook the project in the first place, relating his motives to the new discoveries he had made about himself in India:

> I had decided to change [my methods of filmmaking] completely. And so I said to myself: "In order to change and to put my new ideas into operation, I'll need at least six months, or a year," and so I tried to find something by which I could save my life. Well, there were a lot of people who were very happy that I had finally given in, that I had obeyed, that I was following the rules (though I wasn't). Instead, it took some five or six years to get started in a serious way, and that was a bad surprise.[6]

Even during he shooting he was uneasy. He told the interviewer for *Arts* magazine, "I would reproach my film for being too well constructed, for relying on the continuing development of the story." His enormous ambivalence shows, as he continues: "I'm afraid that my film is going to be a big success and, in spite of everything, I hope it will be. Was it perhaps a tactical error for me to have made it? I don't really know yet, because I'm still too much in it. I have been trying to imagine the pros and the cons, the dangers for the continuation of my research and the possibilities that it holds out to me. Let's wait and see.[7]

It is clear now that *General della Rovere* was not his kind of film, despite the superficial similarities to past successes that made some critics ecstatic that Rossellini had seen the light. Even Massimo Mida, who heralded the film as opening up a renaissance in Italian cinema through its return to the past, and who saw in it the end of Rossellini's period of "involution," nevertheless realized that the director was unenthusiastic and that the final product was little more than a tired rehash of his earlier triumphs. Mida admits that *General della Rovere* "was not the film that Rossellini would have wanted to direct and was not, at that moment, his ideal film," and quotes instead a significant array of "projects closer to his heart": Brasilia, The Dialogues of Plato, The Death of Socrates, Tales From Merovingian Times, Bread in the World.[8] These titles indicate clearly where Rossellini wanted to be, and where, after a few more years of frustration, he would be.

Of all his films, it is only *General della Rovere* that can and must be judged by the conventional standards of the "well-made" film.[9] It is immediately likable in a way that many of his other films are not, but it contains barely a hint of the depth or resonance of a film like *Voyage to Italy,* say, and ultimately registers as little more than a bravura piece of acting. Rossellini had been able to prevent Bergman from "acting" through the sheer force of his will over her, but De Sica, an immensely successful star by this point (and as a director perhaps even more prestigious than Rossellini), could not be so easily restrained. Nor is it certain that Rossellini even tried to control him; having already accepted the idea and the script, he perhaps may have given in on this point as well. For Rossellini, "saving his life" took the form of reassuring producers that he could make a conventional film if he wanted to, making it clear in the process that the other films, however "poorly made" they seem on the surface, were, for better or worse, like that on purpose. In fact, *General della Rovere* contains more than a few excellent passages of conventional filmmaking that can stand with anything produced by the most "professional" of Hollywood directors.

One very significant aspect of the film is its return to the war and the Resistance, the scene of Rossellini's earlier victories. Strangely enough, it was one of the first Italian films to go back to that period, and in the wake of its financial success, a host of others quickly followed. At the time, Rossellini told a reporter for the *New York Herald Tribune* that he had returned to this subject because he felt "that it is necessary to re-introduce the great feelings that moved men when they were confronted face to face with final decisions."[10] In addition, there was now a whole new generation who needed to have these anti-Fascist values inculcated in them, young people who had had no direct experience of fascism. Unfortunately, these values have not been reinvigorated in the film and seem less than fresh. Rossellini's earlier theme of *coralità* reappears, but when mixed with his more recent emphasis on the individual, the result is a dynamic of leader and followers, which is closer than ever to the superficial psychologizing of the standard Hollywood product.

If *General della Rovere* marks a return to the content of the earlier films, in formal terms it is a return to the dramatic and narrative conventionality of *Open City,* not to the dedramatized distanciation of *Paisan.* Thus, the film's plot, narrative thrust, and suspense have all been greatly intensified. In this film, things definitely *happen.* Lots of things. Nor are the dramatic moments undercut, as usual in Rossellini's films, but are lingered upon and played for all they are worth. Similarly, our relationship with the protagonist is now completely changed, and Rossellini's typical distance separating the spectator from the character, a distance that seemed to foster a morally preferable sympathy rather than a manipulative and emotionally constricting identification, now disappears. Some contemporary critics praised the increased psychological subtlety of the film's characters, and it is true that we get more time to come to "know them as people." The method of accomplishing this, however, is that of the banal film that relies on the transparent, "telling" detail to "reveal" characters, as when the German officer straightens his tie before receiving della Rovere's real wife at the prison. The "richness" of the psychological portraits is, in fact, based on an amassing of clichés. Other critics applauded the director's newfound sense of humor, but, again, it is a humor that is totally predictable and painlessly digestible, accompanied by little wit and less irony.

Rossellini went even further to make his new backers happy. According to *Variety*, the entire film was shot in thirty-one days for a mere $300,000.[11] Rossellini later said that, even though he had been given twelve weeks for the shooting, he began July 3 and took the finished, edited film to the Venice film festival on August 24![12] And the reward for his capitulation? *General della Rovere* was awarded the Golden Lion (along with Mario Monicelli's *La grande guerra*) at the festival, and in its initial release grossed over 650 million lire, more than forty times the box-office receipts of *Voyage to Italy*.

Professional, "accomplished," a well-made, if rather straightforward, adventure story of the Resistance. But is it? As one might expect from a film by Rossellini, all is not what it appears on the surface: "They thought I had given in, that I had obeyed, that I had followed the rules (which I hadn't.)" In spite of the work's apparent seamlessness and conventionality, in other words, there remain recalcitrant elements that refuse to fit. These elements have proven particularly frustrating for critics bent on finding organic unity, especially since they occur in a work that seems so utterly direct and obvious. First, there is the film's blatant artificiality, especially in terms of its lighting and its sets. The lighting, for example, is cast in the stylized *film noir* mode of a movie like *Fear*, rather than the serviceable, "natural" flatness of *Open City*. Furthermore, Rossellini is now shooting in a studio, and the familiar rubble has been manufactured by his crew. The sets are not obviously artificial, of course; they are, simply, just not real. Of a piece with the slickness of the rest of the production, they are in fact "well done," and one critic even complimented Rossellini on doing a better job at capturing the "true" Milan on a Roman studio set than any other director had been able to do in the real city.

Again, there is a strange dynamic at work. For, intercut within the scenes shot in the studio (often by means of a wipe, an ostensibly more "artificial" means of transition that is used much more frequently in this film than in his previous films), we are shown real footage, or at least "real" in the sense of taking place in a real, preexistent location: marching soldiers, bombing raids, the landing of the true General della Rovere via a submarine and a raft (a sequence shot by the director's son, Renzo), and the truck on the road. Events depicted in this "real" footage happen with the quickness that in *Paisan* added powerfully to the sense of seeing a real event happen before our eyes. There are

A "well-made film": Vittorio De Sica peers out from his jail cell in *General della Rovere* (1959).

also moments early in the film where presumably "real" people, that is, non-actors seemingly unaware of the camera's presence, are standing around watching wrecking crews knock down actual bombed-out buildings, in a De Chirico–like reprise of early scenes from *Germany, Year Zero*. All of this contrasts continuously with the blatant unreality (because so tidy and *managed*) of the studio locations, especially the unconvincing bombing raid on the prison.[13] The result, once more, is an extension of that revelatory dialectic, in muted form, that we saw at work earlier between the conventions of cinematic realism and the depiction of reality itself. Here, however, the film's code of realism is not threatened or invigorated by any perception of the potentially dangerous incursion of this reality. Hence, the clash of the footage shot on the set and those few bits shot on location is more reminiscent of the comic self-reflexivity of *La macchina ammazzacattivi* than of the exciting, unstable mixtures of *Paisan*. At the same time, the dominance of the code of realism in this film affirms the utter impossibility of a true return to the earlier films, no matter how devoutly wished by the director's supporters, at least in anything other than an ironic or self-aware mode.[14]

Yet even this minor disjuncture between realism and reality operates thematically in *General della Rovere*. One scene, for example, when a group of partisans still at liberty meets specifically to discuss whether or not the man in prison is the true della Rovere, is shot using rear projection, with actual snowy streets and a bombed-out church serving as background to their meeting. Since the rear projection is rather unsteady, however, the artificiality of the scene is foregrounded, thus raising the same question of appearance and reality that is at the center of the partisans' discussion. Furthermore, what *General della Rovere* openly problematizes is the nature of the self and the reality of identity, and thus serves in an indirect way to extend patterns we have seen operating in *Una voce umana* and the "Ingrid Bergman" segment of *Siamo donne*. Just as Magnani's status as actress was foregrounded in *Una voce umana*, so, too, what we are not allowed to forget here is Vittorio De Sica as actor, playing a role. De Sica, the well-known actor and director, is playing a down-on-his-luck con man named Bertone. Bertone, for increased credibility with the families of the interned men he is trying to help (while helping himself financially) masquerades as a certain Colonel Grimaldi. When he is arrested by the Nazis and made to work for them (significantly, the Nazis want him to discover the identity of a Resistance leader), De Sica/Bertone/Grimaldi steps into his greatest role, that of General della Rovere, which he assumes so completely that he dies. Again, the *abîme* of representation and the self opens up at our feet as the continuity and certainty of self-identity seem to be threatened. Which is the real man?[15]

These complications reach their peak in the final scene. It would seem that the one thing that can ground this endless play of selves, of appearance and reality, is death. But, in fact, death does not resolve or explain the ongoing displacement, but only halts it, in the most purely functional and banal manner. At the end we are still utterly in the dark concerning Bertone's motives. Some critics have seen his decision to die with the partisans as a decision to end his own rhetoric and the falsity that has defined him since the beginning. It seems equally plausible, however, to view his death as the apotheosis of self-deluding rhetoric, his final histrionic moment, since in terms of the logic of the narrative, he could have told the German officer that he had not been able to discover the true identity of the sought-after leader of the Resistance.

Perhaps most annoyingly to recent Italian commentators, the film is politically ambiguous as well. As in *Open City*, the Italian Fascists are barely portrayed at all; they parade by in the first few seconds of the film singing their marching song *"Camice nere,"* but this seems to serve more as a historical marker than anything else. Thus, Italians are again seen only as victims, as when Bertone first encounters the German officer and struggles to find the most ingratiating answers to his questions, rather than the perpetrators they also were. In addition, while generally pleased that Rossellini has softened or even subverted Montanelli's consistent glorification of militaristic and nationalistic values (for example, when Rossellini has Bertone's final courageous resolution spring from the resolve of the others rather than himself), many leftist critics have felt that too many traces of these values remain in the dramatic structure of the film. And it is difficult to disagree. For one thing, the politically progressive figures in the film are portrayed as weak, in need of a strong leader to calm them, like children, during the bombing attacks. Clearly from an aristocratic class, della Rovere is "born to lead," and when he shouts, "Long live Italy!" and "Long live the king!" he unequivocally aligns himself with the military caste. Bertone's change of heart, furthermore, is clearly an ahistorical moral decision rather than one based on a greater understanding of the ideas and ideals of the Resistance, and is related to a certain conflation of religion and the fatherland espoused by Montanelli and his followers. Thus, for Guido Aristarco, perhaps the foremost Communist film theorist in Italy, the film fails because it does not put Bertone's change of heart in a sociohistorical context: if Bertone's idea of the *patria* were examined critically, Aristarco insists, we might have a better idea why there was such a rush to reestablish the traditional pre-Fascist state after the war.[16] Bertone says he does it out of "duty," but duty is a nonspecific value that can be felt as much by a Fascist as by an anti-Fascist. The ultimate Marxist complaint, then, is that the Fascist past is seen by modern audiences as merely "a moment of human wickedness," in Lino Miccichè's phrase, that all right-thinking men joined to combat: "A prisoner of his Montanellian character, the director made of him a symbol of an anti-Fascist vision which oscillated continually between a vague humanism of the feelings and a cunning and nebulous ethic of 'duty,' almost as if the struggle against fascism had been a question of abstract moral debate rather than a concrete political choice."[17]

This is closely related to the complaint that a new generation of Marxist critics has lodged, not unconvincingly, against *Open City* and *Paisan*. Unfortunately, it seems to be the only real link between *General della Rovere* and the successes of the past, now fifteen years distant.

22

Era Notte a Roma
(1960)

Era notte a Roma (It Was Night in Rome) has most often been seen as a companion piece to *General della Rovere* since it, too, looks back to the war years and the Resistance for its subject matter. The films, in fact, do share common themes, attitudes, and formal techniques, but are finally quite different than their chronological proximity would suggest.

Era notte a Roma tells the story of three escaped Allied prisoners—a British captain, an American lieutenant, and a Russian sergeant—who are reluctantly hidden by Esperia, a beautiful black marketeer, while they are in Nazi-occupied Rome seeking to rejoin their lines. (The period is thus the same months of severe deprivation portrayed in *Open City*, but now seen through the eyes of three outsiders.) The Fascist Tarcisio, a crippled, "spoiled" priest, spies for the Germans; when he tracks down the Allied soldiers' hideout in Esperia's attic, the Russian sergeant and Esperia's boyfriend Renato, a working-class Roman Communist, are killed. Pemberton, the British officer, is subsequently hidden by an aristocratic Roman family and later in a monastery with other escaped Allied prisoners disguised as priests. While trying to help Esperia, he is forced to kill Tarcisio, who wants Esperia to go north with him when the Germans abandon Rome. After their night of suffering ends with the coming of dawn and the American liberation of the city, Pemberton and Esperia are, at the end of the film, too psychologically exhausted and overwhelmed by events to celebrate.[1]

Era notte a Roma is a curious film, not easily domesticated and understood, because it straddles an aesthetic fence. On the one hand, the film is clearly related to the conventional "good" filmmaking that we saw in full operation in

The Resistance revisited: The Russian sergeant (Serge Bondarchuk), the British major (Leo Genn), the Italian Communist (Renato Salvatori), and the black marketeer Esperia (Giovanna Ralli) in *Era notte a Roma* (1960).

General della Rovere. It has a strong plot, dramatic emotion is heightened whenever possible rather than undercut, the music is scored for a full orchestra, and the lighting is professional if unexciting. Yet conventional narrative expectations are not always fulfilled. Thus, when Bradley, the American, decides late in the film to try to get back to the American lines at Anzio on his own, this potentially exciting interlude is casually reported to Pemberton as though it were an offstage death in Greek tragedy. The spots of "dead time" are also less thoroughly pruned here than in *General della Rovere.* The film seems, in other words, to occupy some uncomfortable position between two aesthetics and often threatens to fulfill neither. The problem for criticism arises when one tries to judge: looked at from the perspective of *General della Rovere,* it might be said that these moments when "nothing happens" are boring and that the entire film needs to be cut drastically in order to enhance dramatic interest. But if judged from the perspective of *Voyage to Italy,* say, we can regard Rossellini's longueurs as *temps morts* that refuse the shortcuts of conventional film grammar and thus begin to move from a smooth realism toward the disjunctive real.

In many ways *Era notte a Roma* is excellent as a "straight" film, and its depiction of immobility and stasis, the claims of Christian brotherhood, and the desire of all good men to live in peace is convincing and often moving. One scene, in particular—the touching Christmas dinner in the attic—is especially memorable. The film likewise seems to be a fair portrayal of a particular historical moment: "Jane Scrivener" reports in *Inside Rome With the Germans*, her detailed diary of the occupation of the city, that it was quite common for Jews, patriots, and escaped prisoners of war to hide in extraterritorial Vatican convents and elsewhere, as Pemberton does, and her diary entry of January 8, 1944, estimates that more than four hundred escaped British prisoners were being hidden in Rome at that time.[2] Other aspects of the film, however, are much less conventional, especially its presentation of character. Thus, the American is "unconvincing" by any normal acting standards, but like "Joe from Jersey" in *Paisan*, he thereby challenges the film's prevailing realism with the tonic power of the apparently more real. The Englishman delivers his lines so slowly and artificially (in a manner that looks forward to the ponderous, yet effective, deliberation of *La Prise de pouvoir par Louis XIV*) that we are continuously prevented from identifying with him emotionally. The Russian remains a mystery to us because he speaks only Russian throughout. In effect, Rossellini refuses to let us get to "know" these men. Similarly, years of indoctrination by Hollywood-style filmmaking lead us to expect that when Esperia and Pemberton get back together again at the end, after her boyfriend Renato's death, some love interest will develop between them. In fact, a ghastly publicity photo reproduced in Renzo Renzi's book on the film shows Leo Genn (Pemberton) and Giovanna Ralli (Esperia) enormously uncomfortable in each other's arms, trying to look amorous. Nothing could be further from the spirit of the film, however, and, defeating conventional expectations, nothing of the sort ever arises. For Rossellini, the depiction of the historical situation is more important than any banal love story. Even more powerfully, most viewers must surely be struck by how hard Pemberton takes Tarcisio's death at the end of the film. The moment is even further underlined by the uncomfortable silence and a restless, wandering camera. In most conventional films, of course, only women are allowed to be horrified after they have killed someone, and it comes as something of a shock to realize just how deeply disturbed Pemberton is. Paradoxically, our shock first registers in terms of a lack of belief, for Pemberton's is an emotion that somehow does not "fit," and thus a sense of "real-life" emotion once again breaks the illusionistic web of realism. What is perhaps most interesting is that, while we see these characters as somehow closer to the real, it is also true that they are stock types. The Russian is impetuous and emotional,[3] the American is practical but whiny, and the Englishman, replete with pipe, is the very embodiment of propriety and good sense. Though many critics have objected to this kind of national stereotyping, our double, contradictory sense of them as types and as unknowable, unpredictable individuals, "real people," actually makes them even more forceful as characters in a film.

This tension between realism and the real is also seen in Rossellini's typical opposition of fiction and documentary, and during the course of the film we see archival footage of the Allied landing at Anzio, the Americans arriving in Rome at the end of the film and, of course, the Germans leaving. Most important is the footage at the very beginning. We learn of the hundreds of Allied soldiers, especially pilots, who were rescued by ordinary Italians at great risk to their own safety. A voice comes on, speaking American English, with the clear purpose of putting things in context for the film we are about to see, but surprisingly, this neutral, objective, unidentifiable voice suddenly moves into the first person and says, "I'd like to make a statement."[4] Here, perhaps, Rossellini is rehearsing the lesson of *India:* the only truth is a subjective one, and must always be based in the vagaries of the individual perceiver. In this case, the perception is thematically and formally made relative through its presentation by this unnamed American officer. (During the filming, the director told a reporter for the *New York Times* that the film would be "an eyewitness testimony . . . as seen by three hiding soldiers.") The voice functions both specifically, as an eyewitness, somebody who asserts and fills the "I" category of grammar, thus motivating the narrative, and generally since, unnamed, it is meant to stand for the entire group of Allied prisoners.[5] And then, brilliantly, Rossellini removes even the grounding of the subjective consciousness, for the speech ends by lavishly praising the "Christian charity" that was everywhere evident and that was the source of these good deeds, and insisting that no one *ever* acted out of selfish motives. At this moment the film cuts to the three "nuns," in a humorous visual ironization of the voice-over's remarks; we soon see what sharp dealers they are, and how little interested in accepting responsibility for the prisoners, doing so only when it appears they will profit financially.

Another major theme that reappears is that of communication. The languages come at the audience in an alarming and confusing barrage as the characters struggle to understand one another. Early in the film, for example, a comic scene has Pemberton say to Esperia in his faulty Italian, "I want you" instead of "I want tea." The communication theme is also broadened to include the relativity of culture. Thus, when Ivan is ashamed at having chased a live turkey out into the street, thus risking his friends' lives, he wants to leave the attic where they are hiding so that the others will be safe. He warmly embraces them one by one, but since he is speaking only Russian, they have no inkling of his intentions. He then abruptly sits down (which, we learn later, is part of the Russian ritual of leave-taking). Even more moving is the moment during the Christmas dinner in the attic when Ivan, trying to express how much his friends mean to him, begins with a few words of broken Italian, gives up, and speaks passionately in his native language. Neither we nor the others have the faintest idea what he is saying, but the experience is intensely emotional nonetheless. Heavily stressed in terms of the Pancinor zoom technique (which I will discuss in more detail later in this chapter), the moment obviously represents to Rossellini the dream of a full, feeling communication unmediated by the imperfections and false boundaries of diverse human languages. As such, it can be seen as obliquely related to the neorealist dream of the direct presentation of the essence of reality on the screen. This language-subverting outburst works so well, however, precisely because it occurs in the context of, and is defined against, all the other conventional linguistic signification generated in the film.

Other typical Rossellinian themes, such as concealment, imprisonment, and waiting, are continued in *Era notte a Roma,* but are less narrowly focused on a single strong personality like De Sica's in *General della Rovere.* Here the narrative is carried by a number of people—which some critics have claimed gives it a certain undesirable diffuseness, but which also relates it to the decentered *coralità* of *Francesco*. Yet Rossellini had already gone too far in his exploration of the individual to be able to reimmerse himself in a simple anonymous group with a mind and will and spirit of its own, and in many ways the film is less choral than simply about a loose collection of individuals who remain individuals.

The theme of appearance versus reality of *General della Rovere,* especially located around the construction of self and identity, is here, too. Thus, the attic in which most of the action takes place is reached only through a fake cupboard, and the film is preoccupied with disguise and role-playing. Esperia and her fellow black marketeers are first introduced to us as innocent nuns on a foraging expedition among the farms in the Cerveteri region, where they agree to accept the escaped prisoners in exchange for olive oil and some very good prosciutto. This disguise (kept from the spectator as well) leads, back in Esperia's apartment in Rome, to some pleasant comic business when she begins to disrobe in front of the soldiers. Similarly, Pemberton's last disguise is as a priest.

The particular form of these disguises also points up a specific and important connection between *Era notte a Roma* and *Open City,* the association of Catholicism and the largely Communist Resistance. Priests like Don Valerio, for example, risk death by hiding Pemberton and the other soldiers in their monastery. Their religious charity, clearly an ongoing value of exceptional importance to the director, hearkens back to the innocent monks of the monastery sequence of *Paisan* and to the "perfect joy" of *Francesco*. Most important, it is they who show *coralità* when, in the second half of the film, the camera zooms slowly back from them at the refectory table (after the news of the German massacre of more than three hundred civilians at the Fosse Ardeatine) from an individual shot to a powerful group shot that suggests a modern recreation of the communality and brotherhood of the Last Supper, the scene represented in the fresco behind them.

Opposed to their goodness stands the corruption represented by Tarcisio, who is short, crippled, and—perhaps worst of all for Rossellini—a spoiled priest.[6] Like the lesbian Ingrid and the sadist Bergmann in *Open City,* and Enning, the homosexual teacher of *Germany, Year Zero,* Tarcisio functions emblematically throughout the film. This is true even when he is dead; at the very end, as the approaching dawn brings the American liberators, his lifeless foot sticking out of the door clearly signifies the death of a decadent fascism as well. Even more impressive is the scene in which Tarcisio, having tracked the escaped pilot to the monastery, is able to separate the real priests from those merely masquerading as priests by forcing them to complete a Latin prayer (and thus perverting its purpose). Don Valerio and his fellow priests foil Tarcisio's plan and effect a beautiful, literally choral statement of brotherhood at the same time by beginning to recite the prayer *in unison*. Tarcisio is shown in a one-shot, appropriately, completely frustrated.

Perhaps the film's closest connection with *Open City* is the motif of Rome itself. In the earlier film, it will be remembered, the Germans could come in contact with the city only through second-level representations like maps and photographs. In *Era notte a Roma,* as well, the outsider Pemberton can look out upon Rome only through the window of his attic prison, as through a frame. Again, the visual shorthand for this motif becomes the dome of Saint Peter's, which is made much of throughout. It is, in fact, as though the director meant to enfold the whole of *Open City* within the later film, providing it with a significant intertextual resonance that also, of course, is meant to help legitimatize it.

As a marker and reification of history, Rome represents the possibility of a future beyond and without the Nazis, because it so clearly stands for the power and vastness of the past, before the German occupation. The cripple removes all doubt about his depravity when, at the end of the film, he says he longs for all of Rome to be destroyed when the Germans leave. The Latin language operates in similar terms: though Tarcisio temporarily controls the language and uses it for corrupt purposes, the real priests, as we saw, move quickly to reinstitute its historical and spiritual claim. The link with the past is asserted in other places as well: just as in *Europa '51* and *Voyage to Italy,* classical sculpture—which in this film is packed for safekeeping, significantly, in the underground head-quarters of the Resistance—states the ongoing presence of a potentially fruitful, if temporarily mislaid, tradition and further legitimatizes the anti-Fascist struggle. (Nor is it an accident that, when we first meet the three escaped soldiers, they are hiding in an ancient Etruscan tomb.) In addition, the unexplained presence of the religious statuary that crowds Esperia's attic and the continuous appearance of bells and churches (as well as the dome of Saint Peter's and the Latin language itself) are clear indications of the central place of the Catholic church in this tradition.

Rossellini's original impetus in making this particular film seems to have been didactic, for he told Renzi that he was concerned about the younger generation's ignorance of fascism. What worried him was the story he had heard about an Italian high school student who, when asked who Mussolini was, guessed that he was a neorealist film director. Yet one would be hard pressed to claim that *Era notte a Roma* is a historical film in the manner of the films of the last period of the director's career. Nor can it be compared with films like *Francesco* or even *Europa '51;* history is taken up here, yes, but the commercial demands for high drama and a strong plot line based on character, however unconventional that character might be, seem finally to work against any truly didactic purpose, at least as Rossellini would later define it.

In terms of technique and mise-en-scène, however, *Era notte a Roma* is clearly the prototype of the films to come. For one thing, the space before the camera, which the camera creates, now becomes fuller, thicker, more volumetric. To accomplish this, Rossellini returns to the large objects, especially tables, that he had used sporadically to organize and give form to this three-dimensional space. In addition, camera and character have been articulated together on a more equal psychological footing; now that the central female object (or victim) of the camera's gaze is gone, the camera is less obsessively stalking its prey. The sense of pursuit of the earlier films was largely an effect of their emotional distanciation coupled with the tracking camera, physically moving its way through space, and the particularly pressing psychological resonance that can accompany such movement. Here even the tracking shots are different. Thus, during three distinct sequences (in the palazzo of the aristocratic family, at the Vatican, and in the monastery, when the disguised Allied soldiers read about the partisans' attack on the Nazis in the Via Rasella), the camera moves lyrically through space—with moments of stasis alternating with flowing pans—but always in tandem with the choreography of the characters, actively discovering new pieces of narrative and thematic information.

At the opposite pole from the Magnani and Bergman—era tracking shot is the most important new technique of all, the Pancinor zoom device, invented and operated by the director himself, which will completely alter his future filmmaking practice.[7] On one level, of course, the smooth optical mobility of the zoom lens promotes an even greater sense of mastery and command of space than does the tracking shot. It also gives the impression that it does not want to miss a single gesture or expression. Nevertheless, in this and in subsequent films, the zoom seems cooperative rather than threatening. Perhaps this is because Rossellini's use of the zoom is always slow and restrained, and because its intrusion on the character is optical rather than palpably physical, as with the tracking shot. It comes to seem more a benign recording device, a simple technological feature of the medium, rather than itself part of the forces oppressing the protagonist.

The device was first used in *General della Rovere,* as we have seen, but only twice. In *Era notte a Roma*—despite Renzi's reports of constant breakdowns of the device and the fact that the movement of the lens is not always as smooth as it will be in later films—it comes fully into its own, complementing the new sense of space that has been created. The first major benefit is that it allows Rossellini to reframe without having to cut. This does not mean that there are no cuts in the film; in fact, there are many, and they are handled much more conventionally—carefully cutting on head movements and other action—than in any previous film.[8] Nevertheless, when the director begins a take in medium or long shot and then wants to move in closer to pick up a character's expression, he is able to do so with the zoom, without having to cut to a closer shot. The principal result is to enhance greatly the possibilities of the *plan-séquence* always so dear to Rossellini and his supporter Bazin; now the only constraint on the length of the take is the amount of film stock that can be held in the magazine at one time. Perhaps the greatest practical benefit, however, one rarely acknowledged by critics, was financial, for the optical "editing in the camera" accomplished during the shooting of the film saved a great deal of postproduction time and expense. It is no exaggeration to say that the later historical films could never have been made without the economies afforded by the use of the zoom.

Aesthetically, the zoom gave Rossellini additional expressive possibilities. He told Renzi, "The Pancinor is like a camera in a vacuum, like holding a camera in your hand. The director, in the course of the scene, can put the accents wherever he wants."[9] One good example of how the Pancinor works occurs during Ivan's impassioned Christmas speech in Russian that was discussed earlier. As he begins speaking, the camera is in medium shot and then, very slowly, almost imperceptibly, zooms in for maximum emotional effect. (Later the zoom will also be utilized as a rather more distanced probing or investigative device, not unlike the earlier tracking shots—though without their psychological pressure—but in this film its effect is primarily the conventional one of heightening emotion.) As Ivan gives up and begins speaking Russian, the camera zooms back out, just as slowly, as though his very being were expanding through love to encompass the others in the room as the lens movement ends as a group shot. (The other magnificent use of the Pancinor in this film occurs in the Last Supper sequence in the monastery, described earlier.)

These are only the moments that stand out. Ultimately more significant is the general sense of space that is created within the frame when zooms more frequently replace cuts. Simply put, the zoom seems to make the space more whole and, at the same time, more plastic. Because the optical eye can so effortlessly traverse it, this space seems as infinitely expandable and collapsible as a giant accordion. In a way, space comes to seem more malleable, more vulnerable to artistic manipulation; it is less rigidly and uninvitingly simply *there* as a flat represention, a picture of only two dimensions that lacks depth. With the zoom, space can be entered, pierced, penetrated—but omnisciently, almost magically, without the gross physicality of the tracking movement. Thus, it would seem to approach even closer the neorealist dream of the unmediated presentation of the essence of reality. What is particularly interesting, however, is that, paradoxically, the zoom always insists on calling attention to itself as an effect of technique. This new cinematic device will not ever let us forget that it is precisely that, a cinematic device.

23

Viva l'Italia!
(1960)

Successful among the public and the widest range of Italian opinion-molders for the first time since *Paisan*, Rossellini was next commissioned by the Italian government to make a film on Giuseppe Garibaldi. The film—*Viva l'Italia!*—was to be part of the celebration of the centenary of the Italian hero's exploits with "the Thousand" in liberating the south of Italy from the Bourbons, the first step in unifying all of Italy. Rossellini was now back in the good graces of those who mattered, and the film premiered at the Teatro dell'Opera, with the president of the republic in attendance. Once released, the film was moderately successful at the box office, earning over 43 million lire in its initial run and, by the time Aprà and Berengo-Gardin gathered their data in April 1961, it had earned a total of nearly 165 million lire.[1]

This cinematic complicity with the ruling elite has seemed suspect to many, both at the time and since. The editors of the British Film Institute dossier on the director, echoing anti-Rossellini criticism in Italy, have described it as "in many ways a remake of the fascist propaganda film *1860* made by [Alessandro] Blasetti in 1933."[2] It is true that Rossellini's film is unarguably "patriotic" in the most blatant ways, even beginning and ending with the Italian tricolor waving proudly to the militant strains of the national anthem. Nor is it critical in any serious sense, aside from rehearsing the standard revisionist view of the risorgimento as the "betrayed revolution." Yet Rossellini's version is of a vastly lower key than Blasetti's. Guarner has recognized this as well and offers an exemplary contrast between the two. The earlier film, he says, shows Garibaldi

> walking among his men declaiming his famous speech "Qui si fa l'Italia o si muore!" [Here we make Italy or we die!] Transformed into a mythical figure,

Humanizing a hero: Garibaldi (Renzo Ricci) directs his officers in *Viva l'Italia!* (1960).

he remains invisible, as his progress is suggested by subjective camera-move-
ments. It is entirely faithful to a heroic tradition in the cinema and is not
lacking in strength. The aim is obviously to dramatise historical fact and to
add the desired emphasis to the events shown [In Rossellini's film the]
scene is treated quite differently. Giuseppe Garibaldi eats bread and cheese,
asks for salt and then in a lengthy, static shot, explains that the slope of the
land offers tactical advantages against General Landi's army, calmly concluding "Qui si fa l'Italia o si muore!" as a quiet acceptance of fact.[3]

This dedramatization of historical events is clearly related to the fictional dedramatization of Rossellini's earlier films, and is directly linked to his simultaneous attempt to demystify the Garibaldi legend.

Rossellini made a great deal out of this "humanizing" of Garibaldi, and, in
the interview with Pio Baldelli and his students ten years after the film was released, was still complaining about the insults he had received because he had
dared to present Garibaldi as less than utterly heroic. It is true that the demysti-
fication of national heroes, which paralleled the rise in world literature of the
fictional antihero, was rather novel for 1960, and it is also true that conserva-
tives were scandalized by this "desecration." Yet Rossellini is avoiding the real
issue, for his insistence on showing Garibaldi warts and all finally ends up erect-
ing, as we shall see, a different, but equally heroic, monolith in its place. Nevertheless, this "new" myth is hardly one that would have been pleasing to Fascist

propaganda, and thus the comparison with Blasetti's Garibaldi is misleading at best.

Viva l'Italia! occupies a peculiar and obviously transitional place within Rossellini's oeuvre. Many critics have unproblematically placed in among the director's history films, but while this placement is correct according to a certain classic Hollywood idea of history, the film differs significantly from those of Rossellini's final creative period. In fact, it shares a great deal with the "commercialism" of his two previous films and the two films that follow. Despite the dedramatization of historical events, dramatic emotion is often, though not consistently, played up, and a love interest is provided (in a brief and frivolous scene when the Thousand cross the Strait of Messina from Sicily) by the beautiful and totally implausible Rosa, played by Giovanna Ralli (Esperia of *Era notte a Roma*). Furthermore, battle scenes, hand-to-hand combat, and intense moments replete with firing squads occupy the screen almost from the very start. In fact, the battle scenes are enormously well done, the long shots of clashing armies reminiscent of the best of Griffith's *Birth of a Nation,* and among the most powerful ever filmed. (These sequences make it clear, once again, that if Rossellini had chosen to, he could have been quite successful as a conventional filmmaker.) Despite its insistence on a "plain" Garibaldi, the film luxuriates in spectacle instead of thematizing and problematizing it, as *La Prise de pouvoir par Louis XIV* would six years later. Perhaps the most basic difference from the later films is that Rossellini is here playing to popular tastes, retelling an already thoroughly known story rather than trying to inform his audience about something new.

Formally, short, sketchlike scenes—a longtime Rossellini technical staple usually in the service of narrative unconventionality—function perfectly in tandem with the uncharacteristically quick cutting, in places, to keep the level of dramatic excitement high. For example, early in the film conventional cutting on the various moving parts of a printing press expresses the hurly-burly of the moment and also allows Rossellini to indulge his penchant for showing how mechanical objects, especially from an earlier period, work. (In addition, the very presence of the antique press itself, as we have seen in the other protohistory films, helps to bridge the gap between past reality and present representation, because it is part of both.) Immediately after, the details of the historical moment are conveyed to us in the most classic narrative fashion, with a montage of newspaper headlines outlining Garibaldi's progress. The sound track contains many songs from the period (during one especially effective scene, the opposing forces even compete against each other's singing), as well as a full complement of Hollywood-style historical epic music. The acting is relaxed, appropriate to the desire to depict a "real-life" Garibaldi, yet traditional at the same time: gestures, expression, timing, and delivery are much more conventional than in the later history films. In other words, what have somewhat sloppily been called the Brechtian elements of Rossellini's later aesthetic are severely understated or even absent in *Viva l'Italia!*

The film is thus clearly *à mi-chemin* between the conventional techniques of the fiction film and the more rigorous demands of the didactic films to come. Sometimes the two impulses even seem at war with one another. For example, in the scene that shows the Bourbon general staff planning its next encounter with Garibaldi, the officers are "acting" for all they are worth, something that Rossellini never would have allowed in the Bergman-era films. Yet the camera itself, in a kind of understated, emotionally neutral counterpoint, remains stationary, merely records, and refuses to participate in the elaboration of spectator involvement. The camera, in fact, seems to become the locus of the elements of the film that resist total capitulation to the conventional and the commercial. In addition to preferring the stasis of the *plan-séquence,* for example, the camera almost always opts for the static two-shot, never giving in to emotion-heightening close-ups or standard shots of action and reaction.

The zoom, though by now a fixed part of Rossellini's technique, is used quite sparingly in *Viva l'Italia!,* compared with both *Vanina Vanini,* Rossellini's next film, and *Era notte a Roma,* and the constant use of the zoom in those films to reframe and tighten is missing here. When the zoom *is* used, it seems disguised; thus, standard Rossellini camera movements back through a crowd listening to a speech or watching some spectacle are here so subtle that it is even difficult to tell definitively, especially in interiors, whether they are zooms or simple dollies. The zoom is sometimes used thematically, as well—for example, to suggest the oneness of men and their landscape. Even in scenes of the troops resting, the perspectival flattening of the long zoom lens seems to inscribe the men ever more totally into the surrounding hills and valleys. Before one important battle, the camera lyrically plays over various "domestic" scenes in Garibaldi's camp. Then, in the same shot, it picks up the enemy on a distant ridge, and, in an extremely subtle zoom that is almost completely masked by an accompanying pan, moves in closer, thus suggesting the coming physical encounter by first enacting it visually and spatially. Similarly, Garibaldi's deep connection with the people is demonstrated by the zoom lens. When Naples has fallen, for example, the camera shows us a huge, celebrating crowd from behind; then, as Garibaldi's words are heard, the camera seems to seek him out, the zoom finally finding him in the midst of giving a speech from a balcony. Since the long shot of the crowd and the final tight shot on Garibaldi are both part of the same *plan-séquence,* the equation between him and the people is forcefully made.

The extremely lengthy long shots of the battle scenes also serve a distancing or objectifying function. One marvelous shot, for example, shows Garibaldi's men charging up the hill against the king's troops, accompanied by a slight zoom for clarification, all in one continuous take as the battle rages. In spite of the distance, the effect is more dramatic than ever, as though we were witnessing the drama of history itself, the drama of men's collective struggles—a resurgence, perhaps, of *coralità*—rather than the merely individual. A Hollywood war movie would want to "humanize" the battle by seeing it in terms of a few soldiers. Here, all we can identify is the flag moving up and down the hill, according to the fortunes of the battle: it comes to stand metonymically for the men, and is somehow more emotionally affecting than a closer shot would have been.[4]

In spite of this distancing, however, *Viva l'Italia!* is still far from the rigor of the later history films, and its historical approach is actually more closely aligned with a film of ten years earlier, *Francesco,* in which a similar intention to get to the "real man" was paramount. The primary difference between the two films is that Rossellini is now more interested in event and situation, and their interaction with character, than in spiritual truth. Thus, the most famous battles of the Sicilian and southern penisular campaign are reenacted in excruciatingly exact (and fascinating) historical detail, as Rossellini insisted he had gotten everything from contemporary historical sources.[5] But if Rossellini's attempts was to portray Garibaldi, like Saint Francis, in all his raw humanity, and thereby to demystify him, the force of a century of hagiography consistently elevates the man above all other men. Thus, Garibaldi shows his nobility by pointing out to his staff that the wounded enemy troops are Italians, too, "just like us." He visits the enemy and tells them how well they have fought. When they try to kiss him, he insists that he is only a man, and then kisses *them*. He says, *"Siamo uomini uguali"* (we are all equal men), clearly speaking for the director, but the adoring response of the wounded soldiers in fact denies his statement. Earlier in the film, he has been shown single-handedly stopping a panicky retreat of his inexperienced men. They see him as godlike and, thus, despite all the homely and affecting business about peeling oranges, rheumatism, and pince-nez reading glasses, made so much of in the film, we must see him the same way, divinely transformed through the intensity of his troops' devotion.

Throughout the film Rossellini walks a formal tightrope. Thus, with the famous, obligatory words (naturally much less of a problem for a non-Italian audience) *"Qui si fa l'Italia o si muore"*: the actor Ricci utters them dramatically enough, but to an audience of one. In this way the director achieves the anti-rhetorical mode he wants, yet still slightly underlines the significance of the moment by means of the second or two of hesitation by Garibaldi's companion, who has been clearly impressed by the words. (As with so many other elements of the film, Rossellini is in a transitional phase here; most of the famous phrases of the later history films, especially Christ's words of *The Messiah,* arguably the best-known words of all, will be uttered with such a lack of emphasis and drama that they are almost lost.) Similarly, the legendary meetings between Garibaldi and Mazzini, for example, or between Garibaldi and King Emanuel II manage to be both low-key and yet subtly dramatic at the same time. The best example comes at the end, when, for political reasons, the king has come to put Garibaldi's troops in reserve. The people are shouting for the hero of the revolution as much as for this "foreign" king, but Garibaldi submits to his fate. One lovely, severely understated long shot of him standing in front of a peasant's shack, victorious in battle but defeated in peace, quietly and efficiently shows the extent of his disappointment.

Another effect of Rossellini's attempt to desanctify Garibaldi, again as in *Francesco,* is an occasional welcome decentering of the hero. Thus, in one scene in which the director seems to move toward a wider perspective on the historical events themselves, we are treated to a magnificent moment of the abdication of the Bourbon king Francis II and his departure from his residence in Naples. There is obviously no need to treat the king and queen as villains (and to turn us against them), at least not one hundred years later, and their nobility and gentle grace are allowed to speak well for them. The camera shoots through the long, magnificent halls in extreme long shot and in long take as the characters move diagonally, in exquisite compositions, down the monumental staircase and across the screen. The maids sob, and we realize again the historical truth that every victory is a defeat for *someone* who is innocent (in this case, the maids) and that history is always more complicated than simple narratives of good triumphing over evil.

But if Rossellini avoids painting Garibaldi's Bourbon adversaries in a negative light, the same cannot be said for his political adversaries, most especially Count Cavour. Popular myth has it that this Machiavellian prime minister of the house of Savoy blatantly manipulated Garibaldi for his own ends. In some ways, this is quite literally true; more recent views, however, tend to see Garibaldi and Cavour as necessary, complementary opposites, the two poles of the dialectic that enabled the final unification of Italy to occur. Cavour is nowhere, and yet everywhere, in Rossellini's film. He is the clear villain of the piece, and some have felt, not without justice, that the director would have done better to treat the situation more dialectically himself, as a struggle between the wish and the reality of politics, rather than between conniving villains and innocent heroes. Mario Verdone has not implausibly suggested that Rossellini gave in to the anti-Cavour view of Italian history because he saw him, in quite personal terms, as the enemy of all that the director stood for: "generosity, enthusiasm, adventure, and most of all, improvisation."[6] (It is clear, in any case, that Rossellini identified strongly with Garibaldi, as he would later identify with Socrates, Leon Battista Alberti, and Jesus Christ.)

One of the more interesting views concerning Cavour's absence in the film has come from Colin MacCabe, writing in *Screen*. Working from a Lacanian-Althusserian model that describes how films "construct" the viewers who watch them, MacCabe accuses Rossellini of allowing the viewing subject to be constituted in terms of the dominant discourse of the screen itself. Assuming that the best film is the one that reveals its constructed nature, MacCabe chides the director for not presenting the camera directly. Eliding the camera, in effect, makes what is offered in the film "in some sense beyond argument." MacCabe is right here, of course, but surely he is expecting too much of Rossellini, who, in spite of his technical innovations was, ideologically speaking, always thoroughly unselfconscious. He also forgets Rossellini's lifelong, if inconsistent, placement in the economics of mainstream cinema. Besides, such a blatant self-reflexivity surely would not have been possible in a film commissioned by the Italian government. Yet MacCabe's remarks are valuable nonetheless, since they help us understand the film's epistemological strategies, and deserve to be quoted at length.

> In *Viva l'Italia!* the glaring omission of the film is the absence of Cavour. It is wrong to attack this omission on purely political grounds for it is an inevitable result of a certain lack of questioning of the camera itself. Garibaldi can be contrasted with Francisco II of Naples because their different conceptions of the world are so specifically tied to different historical eras that the camera can cope with their contradiction within an historical perspective. Here is the way the world is now—there is the way the world was then. But to introduce Cavour would involve a simultaneous contradiction—a class contradiction. At this point the camera itself, as a neutral agent, would become impossible. For it would have to offer two present contradictory articulations of the world and thus reveal its own presence. This cannot happen within a Rossel-

lini film where if we are continually aware of our presence in the cinema (particularly in his historical films)—that presence itself is not questioned in any way. We are not allowed any particular position to read the film but we are allowed the position of a reader—an unproblematic viewer—an eternally human nature working on the material provided by the camera.[7]

This is not the whole story, as we shall see when the history films proper are taken up, but it is clearly one important perspective on Rossellini's filmmaking practice.

Perhaps the most problematic aspect of this film lies in its attempt to depict historical truth or historical reality, however these terms might be defined. This is a crucial question, of course, and it became an important feature of the polemics surrounding the films made during the last period of Rossellini's career. Is this the way the events really happened? Can we ever reproduce historical reality? One of Baldelli's students insisted in the interview with the director that a recital of facts is not enough, that they must be motivated, must be interpreted. Rossellini replied, "I don't want to teach anything. I only want to look. I'm only a worker, a go-between, and that's it. Why do I have to interpret?" When pressed a few minutes later by another student he responded testily:

> Look, you're always saying the same thing: that you have to be critical and that being critical, you have to accept a certain point of view, and accepting this point of view, you absolutely have to convey it to others. But why do I have to do this digestive work? Those who watch the film should do it. If we had a plate of pasta in front of us, everybody would want to eat it. They wouldn't wait for me to eat it and digest it so that, avoiding the exertion, they could then eat it. It would be disgusting, no?[8]

As these remarks indicate, Rossellini's view of the possibility of conveying *historical* reality is at odds with his clear awareness, in the earlier films, of the impossibility of depicting anything other than a subjectively based present reality. His reluctance to admit a subjective bias to the portrayal of history may, in fact, have a simple explanation: an audience might easily accept present-day Italy, Germany, or India as "seen by Rossellini," but since history is commonly considered as something more or less fixed, the overt relativization implied in "Rossellini's view" of Garibaldi, Socrates, Descartes, and so on, would be unacceptable. As we saw in *Francesco,* however, Rossellini is perhaps more sophisticated on this subject than his detractors have thought, for he is not really attempting to represent historical reality as such, but the historical artifacts that continue to exist in the films' present. Thus, one could make the claim that in *Viva l'Italia!* Rossellini is faithfully recreating and representing the historical *documents* of the period, which are already a representation, of course, but obviously more immediately available than the period itself. Similarly, Gianni Menon has pointed out an interesting feature of the film's dialogue that escaped the ear of this nonnative speaker of Italian. One of Garibaldi's officers, major Bandi (played by Franco Interlenghi), since he is the author of the memoirs on which the film is most directly based, speaks throughout in a nineteenth-century form of written Italian, while the others speak more or less modern

Italian.[9] The implications of this strategy are overwhelming to consider, and a larger discussion of this issue will have to be postponed until later.

No matter how one charts the complexities of historical representation, however, there is a certain sense in which the film fails as "education for the masses" because it never really goes beyond the level of popular myth. For Pio Baldelli, who has been most eloquent on this point, the film could have been useful had it provided a real analysis of poverty at the time (including why peasant participation in Garibaldi's expedition was discouraged by his staff) or had it depicted the clash of northerners and southerners, thus making it a *Paisan 1860*, "the facts seen from the point of view of the people."[10] Alternatively the film could have explained the social and economic reasons for the expedition, the international circumstances surrounding it, and the various *political* forces represented by Garibaldi, Cavour, and Mazzini. In Baldelli's view, and it is clear that Rossellini would have agreed with him, especially in the later period, historical films should stop portraying history merely as encounters of specific famous individuals.[11] When the film was released, a related dispute developed in the left-wing newspaper *Il Paese* as Rossellini conducted a guerrilla war of letters with some of his screenwriters. They had wanted to draw the political parallels with *contemporary* life more firmly; in Rossellini's view, this would have violated the film's validity as history.[12]

In spite of its problematic relation to history and politics, however, the film is important in Rossellini's increasingly irregular "development." He is obviously trying to follow up on some of the lessons learned in the making of *India*, moving toward reliance on reason, on intellectual analysis, yet he is still trapped in the exigencies of conventional filmmaking, and will continue to be for at least two more films. But he is clearly on his way.

24

Vanina Vanini
(1961)

Once again, Rossellini was unable to extend his string of successes, and his next venture, *Vanina Vanini* (1961), was another box-office disaster. What is especially interesting about this film, though, is the particular way it has been treated by the critics; in the twenty-five years since its initial release, it has been praised and reviled in equally strong terms. It seems to have been, and to be, a matter not of simply liking the film or disliking it, but of elevating it into a masterpiece or consigning it to the realm of the unspeakable. Furthermore, even the mundane particularities of production have been rife with controversy, and both the director and the principal screenwriters have disowned the picture, though for completely different reasons.

The basic story, characters, and even much of the dialogue are taken from a story of the same name by Stendhal, part of his *Chroniques italiennes* (1829). Set in early nineteenth-century Rome, it concerns a young princess named Vanina Vanini whose father, Asdrubale Vanini, is an important member of the papal court. A revolutionary named Pietro Missirilli, bent on overthrowing the Pope's temporal power in the name of a free Italy, has been captured while in Rome to assassinate a papal spy who has infiltrated the *carbonari*, as the members of his sect are called. Pietro escapes but is wounded in the process, and because Prince Asdrubale's mistress, who met Missirilli on the coach to Rome, may be compromised if he is discovered, the prince takes him to his own palace to recuperate. There he is discovered by Vanina, and they fall passionately in love. As the weeks pass, their love becomes physically and emotionally all-consuming, but both are troubled—she by religious scruples, he by his apparent seduction away from his revolutionary cause. In a desperate attempt to keep Pietro, she betrays his group to the papal authorities. Since Pietro is the only one who has not been captured, however, he turns himself in to avoid the suspicion of betrayal. In prison, Vanina reveals to him what she has done; he utterly rejects her, beating her with the very chains that bind him. At the end of the film, they seem to achieve a peace of sorts—he by climbing the gallows, she by fleeing to the solace of a convent.

Unfortunately, the version of the film currently in circulation is, in important ways, not Rossellini's. Jean-André Fieschi has called it "a mutilated masterpiece, like the Victory of Samothrace," and Rossellini himself has told a sad story of checking during postproduction with the color lab responsible for putting the film together. When he informed the lab personnel that they had mistakenly put the opening credits on the *fourth* reel rather than the first, they replied that they were only doing what they had been told.[1]

The villain of the piece is the producer Morris Ergas, whose list of misdeeds is long. First, he forced the film's star, Sandra Milo, allegedly his mistress at the time, on a reluctant Rossellini. Years later the director defended his acquiescence in this imposition by maintaining that for him the important thing was to get the film done. Trying his best to salvage the character, Rossellini then dubbed Milo's voice, which he found "breathy" and hard to understand, with the voice of another actress, Andreina Pagnani. (Given the American obsession with authenticity and "naturalness," this might seem to be the kind of thing that would be done to Rossellini rather than by him, but in fact, the practice was not at all uncommon in Italian cinema of the period, especially after the heyday of neorealism. Since all voices are "dubbed" in a studio after the actual filming itself, it is obviously only a short step to dubbing with a different voice to achieve the strongest performance possible.) But even here Rossellini was frustrated, because Ergas had Milo do her own dubbing, once again behind the director's back, ostensibly to make her eligible for the best actress award at the Venice film festival, since by the rules, actresses whose voices had been dubbed by others were not eligible. Pio Baldelli also reports (without giving a source) that a scene was added during the sixth reel as well—without Rossellini's knowledge—to give Milo more play.[2]

Other changes were even more serious. Thus, the role of the Countess Vitelleschi, Prince Vanini's mistress (played by Martine Carol) seems, in the extant version, inconsistent and poorly developed; according to Rossellini, it was her part that suffered the most from Ergas' behind-the-scenes editing. Baldelli claims, for example, that a full fifteen minutes was cut from her opening carriage scene with Pietro Missirilli, footage that Rossellini had included to sketch in the history and mores of the period but that apparently was cut because it did not contain any "action." Fieschi, writing in *Cahiers du cinéma,* says that an early scene in which Pietro is chased across the top of the *castello* of San Nicola was also cut, a decision that, given the producer's apparent commercial priorities, seems baffling.[3]

The opening of the film at the Venice film festival, which Rossellini tried to prevent, was an utter disaster. Italian critics loathed it. Gian Maria Guglielmino, for example, writing in the *Gazzetta del Popolo,* called it "a really bad film: decidedly, incredibly, bad." For him, the battle of words between the producer and

History and sex: Vanina Vanini (Sandra Milo) begs the forgiveness of her lover Pietro (Laurent Terzieff) in *Vanina Vanini* (1961).

the director was a mere smoke screen, for it was obvious that both of them were trying to shirk the responsibility for this horrible film. He also insisted that, even with the missing footage, the film could not have been redeemed.[4] The film's ill luck did not stop at Venice, either, for according to Fieschi, it was badly distributed in France, was poorly dubbed, and was not even released in a subtitled version (which is true for only the most commercial of film releases in that country).[5] It was not shown in the United States until the distribution rights were purchased by Corinth Films in 1979.

Rossellini also ran into trouble on his left flank, as it were, for the two principal screenwriters (as listed in the credits), Antonello Trombadori and Franco Solinas, disclaimed responsibility for the final version of the film. A few cynical commentators have suggested that they, too, were merely trying to abandon a sinking ship, but on the surface, at least, their response seems more ideologically motivated. Both were members of the Communist party, and they seem to have been responsible for whatever remains in the final script of contemporary political criticism.[6] They were particularly bothered, as might be expected, by Rossellini's changes concerning religion. Thus, they objected to the director's addition of Vanina's sexually troubled confessor and the placement of the priest "at the center of the film" (an exaggeration), giving "the story an ideological orientation which is foreign to us." Similarly, they complained about Rossellini's major departures from his source material in portraying Vanina as tormented by her religious convictions and in ending the film with her entering a convent.[7]

One of their more interesting complaints is that Rossellini changed the scene of the meeting of the *carbonari* from the "dramatic" mode, to one stressing it as "ritual." For us this indicates that even in this mutilated, operatic, enormously melodramatic and sentimentalized film, Rossellini's informational, antinarrative impulse is still alive. Thus, we are given a full treatment of the freemason's meeting (which is not described in Stendhal), not because it advances the narrative line (it does not), but because it is, again, something factual of the period that seems worth knowing for its own sake. Also evident is Rossellini's continual fascination with his native city: the film is marked with many shots of its towers, a papal parade, and the ever-present, overarching symbol of the city, the dome of Saint Peter's. Further, in his desire to evoke a specific time and place, he has freely availed himself of the work of the early-nineteenth-century Roman dialect poet Giuseppe Gioachino Belli for various anecdotes concerning the social life of the city, and has obviously gone back to Piranesi for many of his opening visual images. In fact, while the main story lines have been taken from Stendhal's story "Vanina Vanini," Rossellini has also borrowed liberally from the French writer's other works set in the same location, such as *Les Promenades dans Rome, Napoli Roma Firenze,* and, especially for the colloquy at the ball between the homosexual and the German ambassador, the essay *De l'Amour.* Guarner reports that one of the early titles the director considered was the kind of inclusive, documentary-flavored one that was in fact the singular form of the one chosen by Stendhal, *Chronique italienne.* Like Stendhal, in other words, but even more strongly, Rossellini wanted to portray a place and an age, not just tell a story.[8] However, if we can trust the director's complaints in this regard, most of the Rossellini documentation ended up on the cutting-room floor, for it is, as usual, precisely this kind of "slow" material, not directly related to the advancement of the narrative, that can seem expendable to a more commercial mind. Nevertheless, some of Rossellini's "digressions" have remained—notably, the colloquy on love and the Freemason ceremony, referred to above—moments that, as J. Hoberman has approvingly pointed out in the *Village Voice,* "account for the film's unconventional narrative flow—alternately elliptical and expansive."[9]

It is clear that the desire to approach the past and dramatize its ideas ("I made the film as a work of historical research," Rossellini said in 1972) is here just as strong as it was in *Viva l'Italia!,* but the film's simultaneous status as romantic costume drama works against the fulfillment of that desire. History is seen only in terms of its effects on specific individuals, and their overheated passions obscure Rossellini's historical investigation, which is centered on the Church's role as temporal ruler. Again, the director has sidestepped questions of representation by not attempting to recreate history itself; *Vanina Vanini* does not pretend to be an accurate portrayal of Rome in the 1820s, but offers itself rather as an adaptation of Stendhal's fictional rendering of that period. Appropriately, then, a great deal of the film's dialogue is taken verbatim from Stendhal's story.

As costume drama, the film is also intensely self-aware, in the manner of Visconti's *Senso,* with which it is often compared. Both films stress their operatic mode, primarily through mannered acting, overblown musical scores, and non-naturalistic lighting and sets (especially in night scenes). Early in *Vanina Vanini,* for example, we find Pietro looking for his confederate in Rome while trying to avoid the police. He ducks into a brothel, and as he runs quickly through its rooms, the colors change blatantly, and inexplicably, from yellow to green to red to blue. Similarly, Rossellini's refusal of banal over-the-shoulder and reaction shots in favor of the two-shot inevitably makes the entire film seem staged.[10] Perhaps most obvious in this regard is the use of the Pancinor, Rossellini's director-controlled zoom mechanism, for it is in this film that the device reaches its apotheosis of lyric expressivity. The nervous zoom so constantly reframes, moving dramatically from long exterior shots to intimate two-shots without cutting, that the spectator can hardly fail to notice the movement itself. Space becomes amorphous, and the least bit of looseness in the frame is relentlessly suppressed. These movements are also often gracefully choreographed with crane shots, somehow perfectly appropriate in a film in which the morality of the waltz is discussed. (This combination of camera and zoom movement, which we saw the hesitant beginnings of in the second half of *Era notte a Roma,* is also used to discover various groups discussing politics at the papal court; this movement will become a standard expository device in Rossellini's later didactic films.) The zoom can also sometimes carry an emotional charge, as when Vanina declares her love for Pietro and the camera zooms in as though to pin and trap him, foreshadowing what the emotional effect of this love affair will be. At other times, such as the proclamation scene, when harsh punishments are announced for antipapal activities, the zoom becomes aligned with the government forces as the agent of an implacably active search as it restlessly scans the crowd.

Color is also important to a film as melodramatic and as stylized as this, and the Eastmancolor of the prints in circulation in the United States is almost as bright and fresh as the best Technicolor prints of older films. The overall effect in many of the scenes suggests the warmth of an old master oil painting. The colors become especially effective in the scenes in Vanina's room before she falls in love, with their soft combination of light pastels, beige, and off-white. The strongly stated colors of the rest of the film are also clearly meant to be taken in a structural or symbolic sense, in general working expressionistically to suggest emotional states and basic oppositions, as when Vanina, all in black, stands between the two cardinals, all in red, as she pleads for Pietro's pardon.[11]

Despite the commercialism of the film, the code of realism is again subverted by Rossellini's refusal to underline traditional dramatic "high points." Thus, the action is so leveled that the murders are very quickly done, with no emotional buildup at all, like the shootings in *Paisan*. Similarly, Vanina's decision to inform on Pietro's coconspirators is taken in a moment and merges imperceptibly with the putting on of her gloves. The dedramatization of these moments is particularly striking in the context of the film's self-consciously emotional content. In this way, it matches Stendhal's presentation of the same subject matter, for the *mode* of his presentation is, as well, severely understated. Jean-André Fieschi is right, in this regard, to insist that "the visual violence of the film, the sudden character of the most important acts, is an exact equivalent of the sharp, abrupt, inexorable side of [Stendhal's] short story."[12]

Even more complicated is our relation to the characters. Once again, Rossellini offers us an examination of male-female relations, and again, as in the Bergman-era films, we are kept from siding with either the man or the woman. The ambivalent misogynism of the earlier films also reappears. The religious torment that Vanina undergoes (in a sense, simply an extended, more violent version of what Karin experiences at the very end of *Stromboli*) was Rossellini's invention; not a trace of it exists in Stendhal's text. In other words, Rossellini again chooses to inflict emotional punishment on his female lead, but this punishment also functions, once again, to make Vanina a real character of equal weight with the male protagonist, and as Hoberman claims, Vanina's "romantic Catholicism is taken as seriously as Pietro's revolutionary ardor."[13] In Stendhal's version, Vanina is selfish and vain, in a very uncomplicated way, and once Pietro rejects her, she simply goes off and marries the most eligible bachelor of the papal court, who has been pursuing her from the beginning.[14] Thus, if Rossellini punishes the woman, he at least takes her seriously as an ethical being whose moral conflicts are as significant as any man's. There is also a level, as we saw with Carmela and Harriet in *Paisan,* on which Rossellini appreciates the primitiveness of her emotions.[15] And in his portrayal of Prince Asdrubale (played by Paolo Stoppa, the Bixio of *Viva l'Italia!*), who speaks to his mistress in exactly the same childish terms he uses with his daughter, the director clearly suggests that this society's treatment of women as playthings is one more sign of its corruption.[16]

The parity of the male and female figures is also made clear in sexual terms: both are equally complicitous and equally obsessed. Rossellini is masterful at suggesting the deeply sexual without having to show the least bit of explicit lovemaking. Other filmmakers, for all the steaminess of their character's physical encounters, often seem unable to capture the easy slide of sex toward obsession, the deepest threat to individual consciousness. Rossellini's characters insist upon their dying "love" for one another, but we sense that what is really at stake is sex. They initially find a freedom of sorts in their total abandonment to the flesh, but it soon enough becomes their prison; when Pietro beats Vanina at the end of the film for betraying his friends, it is ironic that only when his chains have finally become physically manifest does he become free. (It is also significant that this final meeting takes place in the chapel of the prison. There, the lovers are surrounded by objects of devotion, one last palpable sign of the Church's pressure, in different modes, on both of them.)

Earlier, when Pietro wants to leave because he feels guilty for abandoning his fellows, Vanina begs him to stay by saying that if she were a peasant girl, he would pay her, so he should pay her with three days of his time. In this, she reminds us of the prostitutes encountered early in the film by Pietro and the man he will kill—the joining of sex and money clearly manifesting the fleshly corruption that pervades papal Rome, which will come to a head in the ball scene and in Pietro and Vanina's destructive love. Pietro's internal conflict is also represented visually: when he is plotting against the pope, he stands boldly upright, but when he accompanies Vanina back to her bedroom in the castle, he cravenly slinks through the courtyard, obviously afraid. The mise-en-scène and the camera work create the same effect: the interior scenes, so oppressively claustrophobic, provide an exact equivalent for the spectator of the character's inner states, and our own restlessness matches theirs. After one enormously long scene in the bedroom, for example, we and Pietro are longing for the freedom of the outside; but Pietro decides to stay, there is a cut, and—we are still in the bedroom, just as Pietro is. At another point, the lovers seem utterly sick of one another's presence, and only their obsession keeps them together for "one more night" so that Vanina can inform on Pietro's friends. The deed done, Rossellini brilliantly conveys, through *temps mort,* their emotional lassitude and the fact that they have totally worn each other out. Their problem is the very opposite of Katherine and Alexander, the emotionless British couple of *Voyage to Italy,* for their overinvestment in the life of the flesh makes them just as unhappy as the Joyces' overinvestment in the opposite direction.

Rossellini continues his exploration of sexual obsession in the figure of the priest who is Vanina's confessor. He is obviously physically attracted to Vanina, but having renounced the pleasures of the flesh, he must struggle mightily to control himself. Rossellini has invented an extraordinary scene between him and Vanina in which raw sex is in the air, though its expression is disguised by the priest's invocation of renunciation and self-control. In this way, it is reminiscent of the masterful scene between the priest and Karin in *Stromboli,* though there, of course, it was the woman who was the sexual predator. The scene in *Vanina Vanini* is also marked by an exceptionally nervous and jerky use of the zoom, which calls attention to itself and seems perfectly appropriate to the scene's emotional charge. (Another scene cut by the producer before release, mentioned by Fieschi, apparently showed the priest flagellating himself before a statue of the Virgin.) Later, when the priest has been captured by the *carbonari,* he feverishly maintains that his mission in life is to free people from the flesh.

In a quick but eloquent gesture, his captor exclaims, *"Bella libertà!"* ("Some freedom!"). The film seems to suggest that one must find the proper balance between the flesh and the spirit, between Pietro and Vanina, on the one hand, and Katherine and Alex Joyce, on the other: a classical ideal that accords perfectly with Rossellini's increasing interest in the "whole person" in whom reason reigns. As Dante wanted us to learn from Paolo and Francesca, sexuality without the restraint of reason is debilitating and leads inevitably to the loss of individual freedom.

The priest serves a synecdochic function as well, for the entire society seems built on the repression or disguised expression of sexuality. He also serves Rossellini more directly as a diversionary displacement, for, in Stendhal's story, it is instead the cardinal, the principal candidate to become pope, whose nephew Vanina ends up marrying, who has "the taste . . . for beautiful women" (p. 333). In the film Vanina goes to beg forgiveness for her lover, and is met by two cardinals; in the story she never says that it is her lover she wants to free, and the encounter takes place alone with the cardinal in his bedroom. This whole scene in the story is actually quite strangely overdetermined, and flaunts an erotic resonance that nearly destroys the literal level.[17] None of this, of course, remains in the film, and it is obvious that one of the reasons for inventing Vanina's chaplain was to allow Rossellini the possibility of maintaining Stendhal's link between sexuality and the Church without offending the Vatican.

The two are also linked in Vanina's moral struggle: her sexual guilt is treated seriously and in no way, in 1961, considered old-fashioned. Nor does Rossellini think the issue can be rationally explained away as merely an example of the sexual repression inherent in Catholic moral teaching. Vanina's oscillation between guilt and sensual relapse is, in fact, scarcely less convincing than Stephen's in Joyce's *Portrait of the Artist as a Young Man.* The spiritual striving that has marked many of Rossellini's films is simply seen here in its most institutional form. What counts for him here and elsewhere, however, is not the Catholic church per se, but the claims of the spiritual and the moral realm on our consciousness. Thus, Vanina's flight to the convent at the end of the film is only another version of the religious crisis endings of *Stromboli, Voyage to Italy,* and *The Miracle,* none of which are specifically Catholic. (The last film, in fact, clearly suggested the failure of organized religion to answer human spiritual needs.) Similarly, Vanina's impassioned speech to the cardinal in favor of love over religious objections links her with the misunderstood Irene of *Europa '51;* both insist that they are merely taking the Church's teaching about love seriously. The Church as institution is, once again, in conflict with the Church as repository of moral truth.

On another level, however—and this is where the film is perhaps most interesting—the Catholic church *is* important, for it is, after all, the dominant institution at the particular time and place that the film treats. What Rossellini manages to catch so well in *Vanina Vanini,* which is perhaps really understandable only to another Italian, is the peculiar position of the Church in Italian history as supreme in both the spiritual *and* the temporal worlds. Thus, if Stendhal focuses on the Church as a social and historical entity, with hardly a nod to its function as spiritual presence, we can see that Rossellini's addition of this dimension constitutes, in a sense, a legitimate "Italianizing" of the French writer's material.

The film ends as both characters "close" their lives—Pietro on a scaffold, Vanina in a convent. At the end of each short sequence, first Pietro and then Vanina boldly look out of the frame in identical, childlike gestures. Breaking the realistic frame of the story, they seem to be sharing one last farewell, or perhaps, like Tristan and Isolde, uniting beyond the confines of the social and physical world, where their love has been impossible. They attempt to transcend the limits of the narrative that has held them captive by breaking the bounds of cinema itself. In a very short while, Rossellini will attempt the same desperate gesture.

25

Anima Nera
(1962)

Quite active during this frustrating period, Rossellini valiantly tried everything to free himself from commercial cinema. In 1961 he produced a compilation documentary known simply as *Benito Mussolini* in Italy (and in the English-speaking world as *Blood on the Balcony*). Its director is listed as Pasquale Prunas, but its accent on raw information over analysis reveals Rossellini's presence; in any case, the film is straightforward and unexceptional. At the same time, he put his name to another documentary for television entitled "*Torino nei cent'anni*," which through the use of stills and newsreel footage documents Turin's place in the history of the last one hundred years. (Despite the fact that Aprà and Berengo-Gardin list this film in their "Documentazione," I have been unable to locate it. The director's son Renzo suggested to me that his father would sometimes allow the use of his name as a favor, and he doubted whether *anybody* had ever seen this film.)[1] Rossellini also directed the original stage version of Beniamino Joppolo's *I carabinieri* at this time, and, most important, is listed as a coscreenwriter of Godard's film version of the play. It is unclear just how much Rossellini actually had to do with this film, however, and it will not be discussed here.

His principal occupation during this period was a rather unfortunate feature film called *Anima nera* (Black Soul). In a career full of low points, it is nevertheless possible to mark this, Rossellini's last full-length commercial film, as the absolute nadir of his creative life. Ten years after it was made, Rossellini himself called it an "awful film," and claimed that it was one of only two films he was actually ashamed of having made. Based rather closely on an indifferent play of the same name by Giuseppe Patroni Griffi, it stars Vittorio Gassman (an-

Rossellini's nadir: Adriano (Vittorio Gassman) pays off a friend in *Anima nera* (1962).

other sign of its atypicality) as Adriano, a used-car dealer and small-time hustler approaching middle age, who marries Marcella (Annette Stroyberg), the twenty-year-old offspring of a proper bourgeois family. After their marriage, Marcella is visited by the aristocratic sister of one of Adriano's friends. The friend has recently been killed in a car accident and has left the family villa to Adriano; his sister strongly implies to Marcella that Adriano accomplished this by manipulating and tricking the brother, a homosexual. Outraged and hurt, Marcella leaves home, and in revenge, Adriano looks up his old girlfriend Mimosa, who is now a prostitute. We later learn that the homosexual brother left the villa to Adriano precisely in order to incense his despised sister. A final dramatic encounter takes place between Mimosa, who has spent the night with Adriano, and Marcella, who has not gone back to her parents as Adriano had thought. Adriano's wife finally "rescues" him from the clutches of his dissolute past, and the film ends with her insistence that he give up the villa for moral reasons and the outline of her plans for their "normal, banal" life together.

To say that Rossellini's heart was not in this picture would be a vast understatement. Anxious to move on to the grand didactic project he had been dreaming of since *India*, he marked time by taking on projects that he could make with the "normal ingredients," as he said later, "which is very easy to do." Unfortunately, this formula led to boredom and, thus, "Some small stuff was being produced, but really small stuff. It was the position that was dishonest, the way that I was approaching things that was dishonest."[2] The result was a film, made in twenty-seven days, that is awkwardly marked by a uncharacteristic desire to be "up-to-date." At its worst moments it becomes an unconscious parody of the alienated jazziness of the slightly earlier films of Antonioni's trilogy and Fellini's *La dolce vita*. For once the master imitates, and badly, his students.

Even Rossellini's most enthusiastic admirers have disliked this film, which has, unsurprisingly, never been released in the United States. Giuseppe Ferrara has called it "an almost complete surrender to commercialism."[3] Guarner says that it is "stuck at the level of a weepie" and that

> it is real torture to see the director of *Paisà* and *Viaggio in Italia* resorting to supposedly modern movie components right down to strip-tease and sports cars. After the extreme economy and the almost miraculous spontaneity of his previous work, this is just a film. For the first time in his career, Rossellini is visibly working at Cinema. . . . *Anima nera* is a film of extraordinary sadness, because it shows Rossellini no longer believing in the cinema.[4]

I think it is now possible to see, however, that *Anima nera* has perhaps been treated a little too harshly. It has its moments. (And the final shot, which I want to discuss more fully below, is one of the most powerful of Rossellini's career.) For one thing, the film's visual style is not without interest: the strong blacks and whites of the exteriors are enhanced by the vibrant white backgrounds of the interiors, against which the characters become more sharply etched. The resultant visual harshness destroys any soft lines and thus accords well with the film's theme of alienation. In addition, while Rossellini has gone through the motions of "opening up" the play with the mandatory exterior scenes (as opposed to his wise refusal to dilute the claustrophobia of Cocteau's *La Voix humaine*), the majority of shots are boringly static. Unlike the brooding long takes that deepen the vision of so many of his other films, here the camera simply shoots straight ahead, for the most part, in standard two-shots that suggest little more than a play being recorded on film. Yet even the very flatness of the camera work seems appropriate, and if the actual experience of sitting through the film is visually unexciting, in retrospect one can understand that, perversely, it all fits. There is also a scene with Adriano and Mimosa that takes place on a deserted beach at night in which the completely unconvincing set takes on a ghostly suggestivity. Interestingly, the set was not a studio reconstruction, but was done entirely with mirrors. The director confessed to Baldelli and his students that he was pleased in a way that they thought it had been done in a studio: "Well, that consoles me. It was all done with mirrors, becaused I was obsessed with them at the time, trying to free myself. I was trying to use anything I could, even this form of prostitution."[5]

Another noteworthy feature of *Anima nera* is that, while Fellini's and Antonioni's films are clearly being recycled—especially in the frenetic, jazzy score that scrapes the nerves, the blank walls of alienating urban architecture, and the tired striptease of the nightclub scene (which the stripper plays directly to the camera, thus implicating the male viewer the way he is implicated by the young girl's direct gaze at the end of *La dolce vita*)—Rossellini's film is in some ways even closer, in its cultural critique, to Godard's work during this period. For example, it opens with a collage of still photographs of traffic scenes in Rome, displaying the cacophonic juxtaposition of the old and the new, over which the credits are superimposed while the jazz score blares. The first thing we hear in the story itself is the visceral, ripping sound of cars and trucks screaming through the night at high speed, a kind of perverse mirror image of the opening of *Voyage to Italy*. High beams flick off and on in a disturbing, surreal vision that suggests giant, atavistic beasts prowling an ancient earth. Trapped in their car and in their banal conversation, Adriano and Marcella are completely unaware of the historically rich monuments of Pisa, now transformed to tourist "sights," passing over them unnoticed, reflected on the windshield (a motif that is clearly related to Rossellini's, and Godard's, ironic use of classical sculpture in several earlier films). When they stop along the way to eat at a restaurant, a long take pins them in the lower right-hand corner of the frame, and we see as much of the annoying, alienating bustle of the restaurant as we do of them.

As in Godard's work of the early sixties, traffic is everywhere in this movie, from beginning to end. Televisions announce musical themes from the state-controlled news programs. Jackhammers rip up streets, and new apartment buildings, one uglier than the next, sprout up almost before our eyes. In this way, Rossellini mounts a full-scale assault on the spectators' nerves that goes beyond the harsh visuals of Antonioni, whose relatively empty sound track generally works in counterpoint, encouraging contemplation. The similiarity with Godard continues when Adriano's former girlfriend Mimosa is seen on the balcony in a very long take doing "nothing," thus anticipating the protagonists of *Une femme mariée* and *Deux ou trois choses que je sais d'elle*. What they all see is the wasteland of the bourgeois dream of the good life. Similarly, appliances reign supreme over people, and Marcella can think only of the latest domestic conveniences that will fill their apartment. Visual artifacts in the frame comment as well, as they do in Godard, and as the characters leave the thoroughly depressing nightclub scene, they pass a De Chirico reproduction that underlines the emptiness of what the characters take to be modern life.

Money is the film's obsessive topic of conversation, and it pervades every relationship. Again, Rossellini is examining the couple—but now both the man and the woman are so thoroughly drenched in the false values of modern civilization that the director seems barely able to stand either one of them. Marcella is seen as a pretty-faced, but empty-headed, product of a sterile bourgeois culture. Adriano, it is true, has more animal vitality than anyone else in the film and occupies a strategic emotional position as the central point of view, but he is finally no more sympathetic than the superficial Marcella. He has had to claw his way up from the poorest classes, he tells Mimosa, through deeds that would scandalize his middle-class wife. In spite of his problems, however, we are unable to feel sorry for him.

Nevertheless, in some small ways the film does favor the compromised, but full-blooded, figures of Adriano and Mimosa, especially in its haunting final scene, which is not part of the original play. Having successfully gotten rid of Mimosa, her only rival for Adriano's affections, Marcella undertakes to reform him. She wants him to give up his claim to the villa, in the name of morality, even though we have since found out that he did not trick his homosexual friend into giving it to him. It will be "good" for him, she says. But Adriano, exhausted from the continuous effort merely to survive, can barely understand what she is talking about. It is here, in this final scene, that the film begins to take on some weight. The final shot begins tight on Marcella's face as she goes on and on about living more "simple," more "normal" lives, being just two "banal persons." The camera zooms or dollies back (probably zooms; it is difficult to tell in the interiors), to reveal a large empty space to Marcella's right (screen left) that isolates her and suggests spatially the emptiness of her bourgeois aspirations. The ever-widening shot finally includes Adriano, barely listening, as he peers out through the window, away from her, his face pushed up against the glass. He looks utterly devastated at his realization of the price he will have to pay for respectability. The two characters are divided compositionally by the frame of the French window that intrudes between them. Construction noises from outside combine with the resurging harsh jazz score to drown out her words, further underlining their total superfluity. The camera then begins moving back in, closer on Adriano's horror-stricken face, as Marcella, still talking, is gradually cut out of the frame. The sound track becomes rich with symbolic sound: a baby cries throughout this final movement of the camera, and the ripping noise of truck traffic that occupied the very beginning of the film now nastily reasserts itself. At the end of the shot, the camera is tight on Adriano's face. His hand is stretched out on the glass in front of him, almost as if in protection, as he moves his eyes desperately to and fro, shaking his head yes to words we can no longer hear. At this point, the film ends.

In spite of the power of this last sequence, however, nothing in the rest of the film attempts to build any sustained sympathy for Adriano. Furthermore, his treatment of all the women in the film (his wife, Mimosa, and a business associate he has strung along for her interest-free financial support of his used-car dealership), as in Patroni Griffi's play, is brutish. Rossellini has also added a particularly unpleasant scene in which Adriano physically forces Mimosa to leave her female dinner partner at a restaurant to go and commiserate with him over his problems. If in *Stromboli* we are continuously prevented from identifying moral or emotional right exclusively with either the man or the woman, here we are unable to identify with either because we cannot decide which one is less dislikable.

Part of the problem comes from the source material, Patroni Griffi's play, for the playwright seems to have even less sympathy for his characters than Rossellini does. He gives each of them annoying, petty tics (Adriano always stops to comb his hair, for example, every time he passes a shiny surface), which make their words seem even more selfish and reprehensible. These tics are wisely omitted in Rossellini's version. More important, almost all the unconvincing, sleazy sexual innuendo comes from the play. Adriano, we learn, was a deserter during the war who was rescued from execution by the Nazis by an S.S. officer with "a pair of gold glasses." He says: "Oh, I'm the kind who always knows what he's doing, but everything happens to me as if I were some kind of lost soul. . . . You know I don't like to talk about myself, or else I'd have to admit that if I'm alive I owe it to the love of a German. . . . They killed him on the Via Rasella with the others: the night before he had let me escape."[6]

In the film, unsurprisingly, the word *love* is omitted from this speech, and the line goes: "If I'm alive, I owe it to a German." The homosexual implication is still present, of course, but less overtly. Alessandra, the sister of Adriano's more recent homosexual friend, we also discover, is a lesbian who was attracted in the past to Mimosa. The motif of homosexuality is used in both the play and the film in a manner unfortunately little advanced from *Open City* and *Germany, Year Zero:* it is the marker or sign of corruption, a locus of evil. Then it signified Nazi corruption, now the corruption of a materialistic society.

Aside from some minor scene additions and a somewhat different chronology of events, there are other intriguing differences between the play and the film version. Patroni Griffi's play is somewhat stylized, for one thing, in that action on two different sets sometimes occurs at the same time. In the film, Rossellini must necessarily make the action more linear and logical, befitting the exigencies of the commercial cinema. Other changes, probably originally motivated by the necessity of more exterior shots for the film adaptation, also attempt to add an extra "metaphysical" resonance decidedly alien to the play. Thus, during the scene on the beach, Adriano helps some people whose car has become stuck in the mud. Later, as he and Mimosa are returning from the beach, they pass the wreckage of an automobile in which everybody has clearly been killed. It is the car of the people he had helped earlier. We watch, horrified, as a policeman vainly tries to cover a body with sheets of newspaper that keep blowing away; the very futility of his gesture adds to the poignancy of the moment. We recognize again, as in the climax of *Voyage to Italy,* the brevity and uncertainty of life. If the sentiment in *Anima nera* is only a weak reflection of the film of ten years earlier, it does have the distinction of being subtly underplayed, offered in a few seconds, and casually tossed away.

Anima nera is far from worthless. It seems more a case of opportunities missed through laziness and lack of interest. This is what has bothered most critics of this film, I think: Rossellini is no longer taking the trouble to hide his disgust with the whole process of commercial filmmaking. He is only going through the motions.

26

"Illibatezza"
(1962)

Anima nera was to be Rossellini's last full-length commercial film and, as we have seen, his lack of interest and deep cynicism are everywhere apparent in it. There was to be one more small effort in this direction, the short sketch "Illibatezza" (Chastity), the opening segment in the group film called *Rogopag* (1962). Though the sketch unfortunately shares the somewhat whining pop-psychological themes of *Anima nera*, it manages to transcend them at the same time. For one thing, it is mercifully cast in the tones of comedy, and thus, as in the earlier *Dov'è la libertà?*, the themes are simultaneously offered and made fun of. In fact, despite the creative difficulties of this period, "Illibatezza" represented almost the perfect situation for Rossellini: it *is* commercial filmmaking, of course, but because the other segments of the film could carry the burdens of the box office, Rossellini was free to indulge himself, to experiment, and even to comment self-reflexively on the whole filmmaking process. In this way, the sketch hearkens back to that other "playful," yet significant, piece of ten years earlier, the "Ingrid Bergman" sequence of *Siamo donne*. Rossellini would have insisted, of course, that both sketches were totally frivolous. Yet it is perhaps through this willed frivolity that certain ongoing aesthetic and epistemological themes can more easily surface.

The film's title, *Rogopag*, derives from the initials of the four directors involved: Rossellini, Godard, Pasolini, and Ugo Gregoretti. (Pasolini's segment, "La ricotta," caused the film to be banned initially; it was rereleased a short time later under the title *Laviamoci il cervello* [Let's Wash Our Brains].) The extent of Rossellini's disaffection with the cinema can be gauged by the film's opening title: "Four stories by four writers who confine themselves to recounting the gay beginning of the end of the world." Nothing, of course, could have been further than this silly, "sophisticated" tone from what Rossellini was saying in interviews at the time. Godard's episode, "The New World," is a bizarre, rather cryptic science-fiction piece set in a Paris over which an atomic explosion has just taken place. Gregoretti's sketch, "The Scratching Chicken," easily the funniest of the four, satirizes the effect of subliminal advertising in a grossly consumerist society. Pasolini's important, openly blasphemous episode features Orson Welles as a stand-in for himself—Welles even reads from Pasolini's book *Mamma Roma*—a director who is trying to film a crucifixion scene. In true Pasolini fashion, boys go off into the woods with one another, but a serious social point is made as well, through an offbeat humor that suddenly turns into bitter parody.

Rossellini's sequence is, on the surface, the least interesting of the four. It tells the story of Anna Maria, a beautiful, yet sweet and innocent, flight attendant for Alitalia who films all of her travels for her boyfriend back home in Italy. During a flight to Bangkok, a dumpy, middle-aged American salesman (named Joe, of course) falls in love with her and, after they land, follows her everywhere. Anna Maria calls her boyfriend to ask what to do, and he in turn consults a psychiatrist friend who says she must feign a complete role change, becoming a vamp, so that the American will lose interest. Totally frustrated by Anna Maria's new personality, the American is left only with the films *he* had earlier taken of the young woman while she was still in her "virginal" state. As the segment ends, he is wildly and unsuccessfully trying to grasp and hold on to her film image, which plays across his chest.

The pop-psychological tone that relates "Illibatezza" to *Anima nera* is overtly (and, one hopes, comically) stated in an opening quotation from the psychologist Albert Adler: "The man of today is frequently bothered by an indefinite anxiety and in his daily troubles, the unconscious suggests to him the refuge which protected and nourished him: the maternal womb. For this alienated man, even love becomes a search for a protective womb." (In fact, three of the four sequences of this film concern the unconscious in one way or another, and reflect the influence of the first truly extensive, mass popularization of Freud's ideas.) But the main object of ridicule in "Illibatezza" is the American, a figure who had become the Ugly American, once the initial benefits of the Marshall Plan had worn off. Their material needs satisfied by the famous "economic miracle" for the first time since the war, Italians could finally begin to see at what cost prosperity had been bought. The Ugly American of this film reads a *Playboy* article on big-busted women (reflecting an ongoing comic view of the American male as maternally fixated), denigrates local tradition and complains that the Asians are backward, studies *How to Win Friends and Influence People,* and explains with gusto the Miss Rheingold Contest to Anna Maria. For him, Miss Rheingold is the very image of the perfect, maternal woman, and soon enough these fantasies have been displaced onto the flight attendant.

The American tries his best to seduce Anna Maria, clumsily following her around various tourist sights of Bangkok, putting Dale Carnegie's rules into practice, but all to no avail. He has gotten himself into the eternal double bind of the maternally obsessed male: a truly pure girl next door is certainly not go-

Rosanna Schiaffino in a self-reflexive moment of "Illibatezza," an episode of *Rogopag* (1962).

ing to be interested in cheating on her boyfriend. He does not give up easily, however, and in fact assails her with a surprising amount of emotional violence by begging, crying, cajoling, and finally, stealing her scarf. In a particularly annoying scene, he even descends to the level of physical assault, but when Anna Maria successfully resists, he turns back into the crying little boy she has to mother. The psychiatrist's strategy of changing her image finally works (Joe calls her a whore), but the Italian boyfriend is upset as well by her new personality.

A far more important theme of "Illibatezza," though also more clumsily ambiguous, concerns the cinematic representation of reality. Anna Maria tells Joe, "I photograph everything I do, my friends, all I see, so that [my boyfriend] can see my life when I'm far away." The effect of all this filming, of course, is that she never has the primary experience itself; we know that what we call experience is itself always a representation, but it is a representation that cannot be gotten beyond and thus in a way becomes basic. Anna Maria, however, concentrates solely on the second-level representation created by the lens of her movie camera. This theme also correlates with the pervasive American values being held up to scorn: Joe, as a specialist in advertising, is also a specialist in image-making (in both senses), and seeks profits by consciously manipulating reality.

As in *La macchina ammazzacattivi*, image making is foregrounded in the film itself, especially in the sightseeing sequences in Bangkok. Anna Maria's camera films the important sights, which are simultaneously filmed, along with Anna Maria, by the director's camera, but these "sights" are only present by means of an obviously phony rear projection. Rossellini also constructs a temple setting whose statues and other huge objects are clearly made from giant photographic enlargements. The representations of representations pile up, to the third and fourth levels, and any hope of getting back to "real" reality is lost. But was there any hope of attaining it in the first place? What is important is that this slippage is inherent in the filmmaking process itself, and thus Rossellini includes himself in the general critique. It is this that Mario Verdone misses in his criticism of "Illibatezza" when he says, "Rossellini seems to want to believe in gimmicks from now on—which certainly wasn't the case at the time of *Open City*—and he is even capable, after the experiments of *Vanina Vanini* (remember the scenes in the Piazza del Popolo), to reconstitute his Siam in Rome."[1] Rossellini's point seems rather to be that filming is impossible *without* gimmicks and tricks, at least in the realistic commercial cinema as it is presently constituted. In the long run, then, it does not matter if Siam is reconstituted in Rome, for it would be a reconstitution even on the spot. In this minor sketch, I think, can be seen a summation of Rossellini's twenty-year-old dissatisfaction with the naive realist aesthetic of the neorealist movement.

When Anna Maria films Joe, she chides him for posing instead of acting natural. The psychiatrist agrees with Anna Maria's boyfriend that Joe is a sex maniac who, instead of contenting himself with the filmed representation, wants to get his hands on the real original. But where is this "original"? By this point in the sketch, vamp and virgin, copy and original, representation and reality are thoroughly jumbled. Joe can only project her image on his wall and futilely try to grasp the reality that is said to stand behind all representation. The paradox of representation, however, is that it always pushes further away precisely that which it attempts to re-present, and Joe finds this out the hard way.

V

The Grand Historical Project

27

Introduction to the History Films

"Illibatezza" closes a certain chapter in Rossellini's career; apart from the last two films he ever made, *Anno uno* and *The Messiah*—which, though intended for theatrical release and shot in a wide-screen format, do not differ essentially from the previous decade's work for television—he was never to return to the commercial cinema. His always minimal interest in telling a "good story" is now gone completely, and his first priority becomes the production of information to aid human beings in becoming more rational, an impulse already at work as early as *India*.

Rossellini will now expunge whatever remains in him of the mystical and the spiritual in favor of the reconstruction of history. In the facilely symbolic terms mentioned earlier, it could be said that he once and for all leaves the Franciscan Middle Ages for the world of the Renaissance where, in theory at least, reason is king. It is therefore no coincidence that one of the major achievements of this period is the three-part series on the Age of the Medici. Even the historical films concerning other eras are informed by a cool Renaissance rationality that assumes a discoverable order in the universe, a cosmos in which all is inevitably centered on human beings and their ability to make sense of things and, in so doing, to master their world.

Unfortunately, it will not be possible to provide close readings of all the didactic films, principally because of their sheer massiveness: *L'età del ferro* is five hours long, *La lotta dell'uomo per la sua sopravvivenza*, twelve, *Acts of the Apostles*, six, and so on. In the face of this immense output, one can only hope to sketch out a general project and a particular way of seeing history and humankind. Another factor is that after *Acts of the Apostles* (1969) Rossellini's style or technique, his way of organizing his material, does not substantially change. There is some experimentation in the beginning—*L'età del ferro,* for example, is part documentary and part fiction film, set both in the past and in the present—but with the universally admired *La Prise de pouvoir par Louis XIV* (1966), Rossellini seems to have settled definitively on the format of the "great man" who is examined as a representative of his age, usually an age in which, according to the director, some profound change occurred in the history of human consciousness. The purpose of the present chapter, therefore, will be to discuss what these films have in common; differences will be left for later.

What also becomes important in this period are the director's writings, which include a great many articles, two books, and an enormous number of interviews (which were, for Rossellini, another form of writing, another way to get his message across). In the 1962 interview with the editors of *Cahiers du cinéma,* Rossellini, at the lowest point in his creative life, seems to have considered giving up film altogether since it "is incapable of establishing general ideas and discussing them because it is too expensive." He is convinced, at this moment at least, that "the book is still the basis of everything." Since he has nothing left to say with film, he will begin writing essays, no matter how difficult it is, as a way to engage "the world, in order to be able to study it, to understand it."[1] A short time later, of course, Rossellini will find the perfect medium—the didactic, essayistic film made for television—and his interest in the cinema will be reawakened. But it will be a cinema of an altogether different sort.

One of the earliest statements of his changing ideas comes in a 1959 open letter to the new minister of culture, Signor Tupini. In it Rossellini poses the basic question: "Will the cinema be considered on the level of art and culture or as a means of squalid escapism and the infantilizing of the public on the same level as television, for which the government is seriously responsible?" (This clear-cut placement of film, art, and culture on one side and an "infantilizing" television on the other will soon be modified.)[2] In his first real essay, "Un nuovo corso per il cinema italiano" (A New Direction for Italian Cinema; 1961), Rossellini attacks education for having sold out to specialization, forgetting the whole person. Culture has become a "pseudoculture" that does not represent the expression of an individual artist but is "manipulated by technicians to placate in different ways the anxiety of the masses," who are crushed by "the insistence on orthodoxy, obedience, and blind faith in the elite." These products of the pseudoculture are addressed simultaneously to children and adults, Rossellini complains, with the result that the former grow up too fast and the latter are kept in a state of childish conformity in which they want to be "maternally protected" by strong leaders.

Is there a way out of this mass conditioning? Rossellini suggests that, because half the world is illiterate and people learn best through audiovisual means, the mass media must become vehicles for the spread of "ideas and information which will allow man to begin to understand the complex world to which he belongs." Human beings are naturally curious and if offered mental stimulation will accept it gladly. Why do we not "feel a profound emotional impulse contemplating the conquests that man has achieved in the last two centuries?" he asks.

We need to spread among the masses the true essence of the great discoveries and of modern technology. . . . Doing this, we will help the large masses find themselves in the new world. . . . In order to rediscover man we must be humble, we must see him as he is and not as we would like him to be according to predetermined ideologies, and this, it seems to me, was one of the merits of the neorealist cinema.[3]

In another open letter, this time addressed to Senator Renzo Helfer, the undersecretary for the arts, Rossellini inveighs against the "false problems" of sexuality, loneliness, and juvenile delinquency.[4] But, as he maintains in the important *Cahiers du cinéma* interview in 1962, "education" is not the answer either: "I reject education. Education includes the idea of leading, directing, conditioning, whereas we must search for truth in an infinitely freer way. The important thing is to inform, to instruct, but it's not important to educate."[5] What lies behind this seemingly frivolous distinction between education and instruction is Rossellini's firm, and apparently untroubled, view that pure information, pure knowledge, can be conveyed neutrally. And where is information most pure? In science, of course, and thus his future project will be "to try to see with new eyes the world in which we live, to try to discover how it is organized scientifically. To see it. Not emotionally, not through intuition, but in its totality and with the greatest exactitude possible. What our civilization has given us is the possibility of conducting a scientific investigation, of examining things deeply in scientific terms, in other words, in such a way that errors, theoretically, can be avoided if the investigation is properly conducted. Today we have the means for working in this way, and it is here that we must begin to take up a new discourse" (p. 10).[6]

He compares his work to that of the *encyclopédistes* of the eighteenth century, but when asked if it "will have as its goal the destruction of the present capitalist world" (a question that surely must have been asked tongue in cheek), Rossellini responds that he does not know what the outcome of his work will be, but that he certainly does not want to "play at being a revolutionary" (p. 12). In any case, his work will be easier than that of the *encyclopédistes,* he says, for we now live in an age in which science is universally respected, and "a scientific world must logically produce scientific solutions" (p. 12).

What is especially interesting is that, at the time of this 1962 *Cahiers du cinéma* interview, Rossellini's creative fortunes were at their lowest point and, as we have seen, he had begun to distrust cinema itself. It has failed to become the art of our century, it has in fact been one of the chief causes of our present sad state, but even more fundamentally, its very nature seems to have kept it from dealing adequately with general ideas. He maintains that, as it stands now, the cinema only allows for small variations within a basically standardized product. Nevertheless, if the cinema is not useful for reopening the great debate, it still will have its function as documentation:

Film should be a means like any other, perhaps more valuable than any other, of writing history and of keeping the traces of societies which are about to disappear. Since, more than any other means of transcribing reality that we currently possess, today we have the *image* which shows us people as they are, with what they do and say. The protagonists of History are photographed with their voices, and it is important to know, not only what they say, but also how they say it. Now, the means which film possesses have sometimes been used for propaganda, but have never been used scientifically (pp. 13–14).

It is significant that, in the context of the "scientific" (or historical) film, Rossellini once again seems able to believe in the power of cinema to "show us people as they are." Increasingly, in other words, his earlier misgivings about the realist aesthetic seem to become displaced onto *fiction* films alone.

By 1963 Rossellini's ambivalent feelings concerning the visual image are completely gone. Geography and science can be much better taught through audiovisual means, he now decides; "The image can remove abstraction, analysis, and dogmatism from material which is primarily literary in content." Now he believes that words should be left to experts and specialists. Outlining what becomes essentially his own program, he says that with film we can finally understand history not as a series of dates and battles, but socially, politically, and economically. Above all, "Certain characters, psychologically reexamined, can become, through their human qualities, models of action." Seeing is now so highly privileged for him that it becomes the equivalent of understanding: "It is not a matter of giving up the pedagogical virtues of the scholastic tradition, but of giving them a new style, which is the style of those who are able to see, and therefore to understand."[7] In remarks made on a 1972 panel examining the state of Italian television, which were published in a book called *Informazione democrazia*, Rossellini moves even further toward a concept of pure, direct vision, to which he will later devote an entire book:

Images, with their naked purity, directly demonstrative, can show us the road to take in order to orient ourselves with the greatest possible knowledge. . . . All of our intelligence, as we know, expresses itself thanks to the eyes. Language, this human conquest which has justly been divinized (it is said that God is the Word), is the ensemble of the phonetic images by means of which, not being able to fix and save the images, we have catalogued all of our observations, the great majority of which are visual. [Language] has allowed us to express our intelligence by discerning, classifying, and connecting. Today, finally, we have the images; we have television, we have the RAI.[8]

What is noteworthy here is Rossellini's choice of words: "naked purity," "directly demonstrative." This is nostalgia for a pure, whole presence—with a vengeance. In this scheme, pictures speak directly, naturally, without mediation, and language was invented as an afterthought, little more than a poor filing system even if divinized, merely to be able to catalog and fix permanently what our eyes have already taught us. Again, what Derrida has called the logic of the supplement is at work here, for this impure language that Rossellini describes, this language that represents a falling away from the plenitude of the visual image, is paradoxically the only way, structurally and historically, in which that pure vision vouchsafed to us could be preserved or even expressed. Now that the RAI (*Radio-televisione italiana*) has restored the image to us, however, meaning will once again be direct, unproblematic, safe from the play of difference. What the director wants to forget is that, since this image is always a representation itself, it must employ prior conventions of representation to be understood: in short, images speak a language too.

In a 1963 essay Rossellini expresses the familiar romantic desire to "reexamine everything from the beginning," without asking whether such a return to a moment of pure origin is ever possible. Neorealism is looked back upon fondly as an example of this "starting from zero," completely free from "false intellectualism." We must examine everything in its "origins" and, like a schoolteacher, "try to tell the story of the great events of nature and history in the simplest and most linear fashion." Rossellini fails to see that linearity itself is already an interpretation of history. He insists that "we have to begin the discourse from the very beginning, from the first letter of the alphabet." But can we have a "first" letter without already having all the others, too? Over and over, Rossellini expresses a need to go back to "data that is impossible to confute,"[9] presumably to find—or construct—a ground that will not give way.

What we need now, the director tells us, is a cinema that is "didactic, also in the Brechtian sense."[10] The entire structure of filmmaking must be remade in the light of this new function, and all fancy technique must be forsworn in the interest of making films as cheaply as possible. What is especially annoying to Rossellini is the refusal of modern art to deal with contemporary industrial and technological reality. In 1965 he outlined to Aprà and Ponzi "the overwhelming victory of man over nature":

> But tell me who has been moved by it, what artists have dwelt on this amazing fact, which is at least equal to the discovery of fire, in fact greater. . . . Above all you have to take the reins of this civilization and be able to drive it towards ends that have to be thought out quite clearly and precisely. But instead, strangely enough, as science and technology advance—and I mean science and technology in the highest sense, the sense of knowledge which is human in its very fibre—art abandons itself to daydreams in the most irrational way imaginable. You build a rational world and the whole of art takes off into fantasy.[11]

Above all, as Rossellini tells Cahiers du cinéma in another interview in 1963, this new reality must be regarded from a "moral position," a phrase that recalls his earliest formulation of neorealism. And whence comes this moral position? From love and tenderness, which is lacking in most forms of modern art such as the nouveau roman and contemporary painting, which only make man even more infantile with their constant complaining:

> Today, you know you are in the avant-garde if you are complaining. But complaining is not criticizing, which is already a moral position. From the moment you discover that someone can drown if he falls in the water, and then you throw people in the water every day to see this abominable and terrible thing, that is, that the people you throw in the water can drown, I find that absolutely ignoble. But if, when I've realized that the people who've fallen in the water are drowning, I begin to learn how to swim so that I can jump in the water and save them, that's something different. And that's what caused me to give up making films, as I told you last year.[12]

He no longer cares about "making art"; rather, he wishes to become "useful." He explicitly rejects the role of artist in favor of that of craftsman.

For Rossellini, the art of our century has shamefully neglected to confront its great (and obvious) subject. How much have we tried to understand science from a moral point of view, "in order to penetrate it, to participate in it, and to find in it all the sources of emotion necessary to create an art?" In an earlier era, artists were directly involved in the development of man's consciousness. Men like Leon Battista Alberti (the Renaissance figure who appears in several of the films to come) saw no conflict between art and science, and insisted upon the importance of mathematical perspective and anatomy to architecture and painting. These artists "were able to plunge into a scientific reality, appropriate it, rethink it and bring it up to the rank of a superior art." Nor does Rossellini mean that all art must become figurative and literal again, for understanding can be expressed abstractly as well, and the true artist "can, with a single, pure, bare, abstract line give you the emotion that comes from his knowledge."

And how will Rossellini himself contribute to the elaboration of his ideas?

> The next film I make . . . but I don't want to call it a film, because it must not be of the cinema. Let's say "I'll put on film" the history of iron. Does that seem ridiculous to you? A guy who begins to do the history of iron, that's ridiculous. But I want to offer myself not as an artist, but as a pedagogue. And there will be so many extraordinary things, which will give you such a quantity of emotions, that, while I won't be an artist, I'm sure that I will lead someone to art.[13]

As we have already seen, Rossellini's pedagogical project raises many epistemological and historical questions that, more often than not, he refused to consider as seriously as he should have. His charm and unshakable certainty about what he was doing led most of his many interviewers, unfortunately, to be lenient with him, retreating in the face of what sometimes even becomes dogmatic assertion. But the questions remain, and they are not all of a theoretical order.

The first, rather minor, problem is to ascertain just who is the "author" of these films. *L'età del ferro* and *La lotta dell'uomo per la sua sopravvivenza*, after all, were directed—at least according to the credits—by Rossellini's son Renzo, who had been working with him as an assistant on the set since *General della Rovere*.[14] Rossellini was fond of shocking interviewers by telling them that the famous solitary banquet scene in *Louis XIV* was actually filmed by Renzo while the elder Rossellini was visiting his daughter Isabella in the hospital. (One strategy here, of course, was to demystify the idea of the creative artist in favor of the skilled craftsman.) Elsewhere, when questioned closely concerning the particulars of *L'età del ferro*, he replied, "Look, I did very little. My son Renzo did it all, he's the director. I only thought the idea up."[15] But then he goes on to explain in great detail what were, in effect, *his* artistic choices. The simple truth is that no matter what he might have said to the contrary, these are his films. He conceived, researched, wrote, and produced them. Renzo had, in fact, so totally absorbed his father's methods by this point that he was in effect simply able to substitute for him without missing an artistic beat; nor did he make any measurable personal impact on these films himself. As Rossellini had been saying as early as the postwar period, most of the actual shooting bored him terrifically; now, with a grown-up son, he had found the perfect solution to the tedium of day-to-day filmmaking.[16]

The plan for the filming of *L'età del ferro,* for example, was for the father to write a screenplay of sorts in blocks of three or four days, which Renzo would then shoot while Rossellini *père* stayed at home working on the next section of script. As Renzo explained to me in 1979, however, the situation was not a happy one for him:

> It was a perfect collaboration but it had its limits. I had to copy his manner of filming exactly. I had to conform my filming to his style, which was not mine. And because there was such a difference in age between us, naturally our visions were different. I would have wanted to develop the spontaneity of the takes, because for one thing I had a lot more enthusiasm for the medium. Instead I had to be very cold and distant. And the tiniest details could seem to him like giving in to the worst kind of formalism. To give you an example from *L'età del ferro:* At one point, the metalworker looks into the German truck to see what is inside. He pedals on a little further, then looks again and sees something. Well, the fact that I shot the sequence this way became such a big deal! My father said it was out of Buster Keaton, something from the thirties American film, a "double-take"! After all, he said, when somebody looks, he looks, and that's it. How terrible. This tiny little detail of the fiction, interpretive if you will, was for him absolutely unbearable. I enjoyed telling stories, therefore coloring them a bit, to add elements of fantasy to the story, to work with the actors, to be more what he always deprecatingly called a *"cinematografaro."* I wanted to use all the different means available to cinema, which seems natural in someone who loved the cinema so much. He thought all of this was "formalism." And so most of our arguments stemmed from this basic conflict, a conflict of form. I felt frustrated that I couldn't give it all that I wanted to. Instead, I had to copy perfectly his style [*calligrafia*]. This kind of thing made me eventually decide not to work with him any more, though I did shoot about twenty percent of *Louis XIV* and a lot, more than sixty percent, of the *Acts of the Apostles.*

Even these, then, must be considered his father's films.

Another, more complicated question about this new work for television concerns the formal relation between it and Rossellini's previous work destined for theatrical release. Now that he had denounced commercial filmmaking, it seemed important to him to insist that there was absolutely no difference in the two media. It is a commonplace in film theory that the spectator's psychological relationship to the larger-than-life theater screen is quite different from his or her relationship to the tiny screen that is looked *at* and can be walked around. The quintessential medium of the close-up, television generally foregoes the extreme long shot because it is simply too difficult to decipher. In an interview that appeared in *Filmcritica* in August 1968, however, Rossellini insisted on focusing solely on the economic differences between television and film, preferring television because it allowed more experimentation. When questioned about the formal or technical differences between the two media, he fell back on a fatuous analogy that the ideas of an essay will be the same whether it is published in a paperback or a deluxe edition: "The important thing is to say it. I've never had these aestheticizing worries; I'm completely devoid of prejudices from this point of view." Rossellini's other views on the subject are impressionistic and hardly provable, but are provocative nonetheless. Thus, further along in the interview, he claims that television is probably a better medium than theatrical film because spectators view the latter with "mass psychology," while, with television, "the (critical) spirit of the individual is more accentuated."[17] In the early seventies, Rossellini was again pushed on this point when an interviewer insisted that the "reading time" of each medium was different, and since the television screen was smaller, it was read more quickly. Rossellini responded:

> I think it's slower. That is, the image that you get in the cinema is so powerful that it just jumps on you: therefore you more or less get it all in one impression. That of the television, which is much smaller and more reduced, must be analyzed in order to get an impression. So the process is different, and the time of reading television is longer than that for the cinema. But I don't pay any attention to it anyway.[18]

One last minor question concerning Rossellini's didactic project—and one that inevitably leads to subjective considerations—is that of audience interest. Rossellini clearly meant to address these films to a mass audience of nonintellectuals, and it must be asked whether they have ever been successful in that regard. Except for *L'età del ferro*, which, as we shall see, makes its own kind of concessions in the quest for a popular audience, most average audiences, one suspects, would find these films so lacking in action, either physical or emotional, as to be virtually unwatchable. Even intellectuals supposedly inured to this kind of thing have found Rossellini's television films trying, and while some avantgarde critics have called them the harbingers of a totally new and revolutionary cinema practice, others, like the redoubtable Richard Roud, who greatly admires the hardly action-filled work of Straub and Huillet, has said, "I find Rosselini's historical works something of a bore."[19] Obviously, this is a question that can only be answered individually.

Without a doubt the most important problem connected with the history films, however, as we have already seen, is Rossellini's apparently complete faith in his ability to present "pure information" about history, science, and technology. He never seems to have fully understood (or to have wanted to understand) that information is always and inevitably constructed from a given point of view. James Roy MacBean, in his discussion of *Louis XIV*, thinks that Rossellini's claim to be involved in "pure research" is "possibly disingenuous": "In denying any political intentions, he speaks of the need to 'demystify history' and to 'get at simple facts'; but it hardly seems possible that he is unaware of the essentially political nature of the act of demystifying history."[20] Goffredo Fofi has summarized the situation well in saying that "what is important to him is the research but not the method of the research, and his presumed lack of ideology is the most mystified and conditioned form of ideology which exists.[21] Again, Rossellini is acting as Barthes' bourgeois man who finds the world natural, but confused;

clear away the unnecessary confusion, and a direct perspective on the facts will be possible. He seems to have given up his earlier view that reality could be represented only subjectively, now insisting on the possibility of accurately representing the past. But since history is commonly taken as something fixed and "finished," unlike present reality, perhaps he had no other choice: admitting that our view of the past is always constructed, the product of a point of view, would simply have been too radical a step and would have undermined the entire project. Furthermore, as we shall see in later chapters, this epistemological certainty about history is crucial to Rossellini's project and has wide implications concerning the relation of capitalism, visual perspective, Renaissance humanism, and a great many other matters.

Perhaps Rossellini's most straightforward statement of his philosophy was made during a 1966 interview with *Cahiers du cinéma.*

> CAHIERS: Do you believe in using ideologies as working hypotheses? For example, Marxism as a method of historical knowledge?
> ROSSELLINI: No. You have to know things outside of all ideologies. Every ideology is a prism.
> CAHIERS: Do you believe that one can see without one of these prisms?
> ROSSELLINI: Yes, I believe so. If I didn't think so, I wouldn't have made my life so difficult.[22]

Another interviewer, some ten years later, was more persistent, and the exchange is worth quoting at length. When Rossellini told him that the plan of *The Age of the Medici* (1973) was to show the interrelation of humanism and mercantilism, Jacques Grant leapt forward:

> That's what I mean when I say that your films take sides. Which also makes me believe that it's a stylistic matter. In the sense that you choose, from the lives of the characters which you put on the screen, very few events. For Louis XIV, you choose only those events which go in the direction of the taking of power by the bourgeoisie. The choices you make are obviously not innocent.
> ROSSELLINI: What you just said is not taking sides. It's looking attentively at the givens. Taking sides means demonstrating a thesis.
> GRANT: You say that because at this moment you only want to reason on the level of ideas. Taking sides means in reality choosing among the working of events. Let me ask my question in a different way: What is historical truth?
> ROSSELLINI: It's the things which happened and which had led to certain effects.
> GRANT: Therefore you choose your characters in terms of the important effects which they have had.
> ROSSELLINI: Obviously.
> GRANT: Which means that the careful realism you show in the historical films has a different meaning than the careful realism of your earlier films. Because in the earlier films, you showed a reality simply at the moment that it was happening, whereas in your historical films the reality shown serves to validate the effects. The choice of your objects becomes directly functional.
> ROSSELLINI: You're wrong. They have the same role as in my other films. It is simply that they are less recognizable. It was the everyday of that given epoch.[23]

Despite the contradictions in Rossellini's position, however, it should be said in his defense that, as we have seen in the earlier "protohistorical" films like *Francesco* and *Viva l'Italia!*, the films themselves skirt the issue of historical accuracy by being adaptations of artifacts of the period (works of art, literary and historical documents) that exist in both the past and the present, rather than claiming to recreate the period itself. Furthermore, while it is true that these television films present the historical *facts* upon which they are based as natural and given, rather than the product of a certain perspective, they do not claim the same status for their *representation* of these facts. Anybody who has watched them will agree that one hardly identifies with the characters or becomes "caught up" in their plots. Nor could one claim that these cold, distanced films that reject personal drama and emotion nevertheless "place" the subject-spectator in exactly the same way that a classic Hollywood film does. To refuse to make distinctions here would make subject-positioning theories so general as to be useless. The evidence provided by the films themselves must also be taken in account. Thus, as we shall see, the heady and unstable mixture of *L'età del ferro* (part documentary, part lecture, part fiction film, part anthology), makes the film willy-nilly self-reflexive. The resulting lack of illusionism itself calls into question the natural stance implied in the "objective" compilation of facts, no matter what the director's overt intentions.[24]

The force of Rossellini's didactic project is vitiated by the obvious political and ideological problems surrounding it, but it is also important to understand the ways in which these films are successful. Above all, it is easy to forget, in an era like the present when most great Italian directors also work for television, how courageous Rossellini was to turn from the much more prestigious cinema to the mass media. (Pierre Leprohon, for example, sniffed at the time that "the medium to which he has turned is infinitely less subtle than the one he has deserted," without offering any specific examples.)[25] Rossellini's television films must also be examined in the context of the huge number of Italian "historical" films of the fifties and sixties. Typical of this period was the series of pictures based on the exploits of ancient figures like Ulysses and Hercules (who even unite, in one film, to fight the Philistines). Leprohon has said of these films, "Anachronisms and other errors become gags; and historical truth—if such a thing is even possible—becomes the least of the concerns of directors for whom character and plot are merely pretexts for unbridled fantasy."[26] In this light, the contradictions inherent in Rossellini's representation of history may seem less blameworthy.

At the very least, it is clear that these films often brilliantly depart from previous cinema practice, including Rossellini's own. One thing that sharply distinguishes them from conventional cinema, especially beginning with *Louis XIV*, is the reappearance of Rossellini's penchant for dedramatization, which now reaches its zenith. In these films, characters boldly foreground their words, paradoxically, by delivering them in a flattened, often completely uninflected way. Physical movement is also minimal, and the consequently static nature of most visual compositions tends to focus attention, like the words, on the ideas and historical forces at work. And Rossellini is resolutely uninterested in his figures' emotional or psychological lives; all potentially emotional encounters are leveled, and there is little or no probing into an individual historical figure's character to discover the nature of his personal motivations.[27]

Claude Goretta's *Les Chemins de l'exil,* an excellent film on the life of Jean-Jacques Rousseau (which Rossellini had once contemplated making) is instructive in this regard. The advertising that accompanied this film upon its release in 1978 proclaimed that it was in "the great tradition of Rossellini's historical films," and to a certain extent, especially in comparison with most historical films, it is. For one thing, importance is laudably given to the development of Rousseau's ideas as well as to the contours of his life. The pace is slow and delightfully contemplative. But here the similarities end: the actor playing Rousseau situates himself clearly in the classic acting tradition, with abundant emotional expression, and Goretta has included many conventional character tics meant to "humanize" Rousseau. This is not wrong in itself, of course, but it is not Rossellini. Similarly, Goretta is quite obviously intent on the production of beautiful compositions and, much more than Rossellini, often allows themes to develop through the stylistic and iconographic content of the images themselves. Likewise, lighting is often extremely dramatic, and color is used extensively to heighten mood and emotion. Goretta's camera is itself so fluid and mobile that Rossellini surely would have considered it obtrusive. In spite of Goretta's increased commitment to Rousseau's ideas, in short, a great deal of emphasis is placed on Rousseau's personality as well, very much in the tradition of the Hollywood biography film. Yet while the audience is more involved emotionally in this film than it would be in a Rossellini film, it still manages to come away from it with a fairly comprehensive view of Rousseau as thinker and historically important figure.

Rossellini's increased emphasis on dedramatization and his refusal to create characters who would be convincing according to conventional codes of realism parallel his lack of interest in making viewers lose themselves in the diegetic space, making them feel that they are really there. Rather, a consistent yet unobtrusive, low-grade alienation effect pervades these films. Rossellini's mise-en-scène and his reconstructed sets attempt to be suggestive of a given historical period without actually trying to recreate it. In this way, the sets differ drastically, say, from Griffith's painstaking "historical facsimiles" in *The Birth of a Nation.* Nor is Rossellini's space crowded with the hustle and bustle of the DeMillean "cast of thousands." Instead, virtually all elements of the set are there for a specific reason: to convey an idea of the past era, or rather, to convey that particular era's ruling idea or ideas. The sets of *Augustine of Hippo,* for example, resemble line drawings rather than sumptuous historical paintings, since this bare-bones symbolic sketching, as opposed to realistic illusionism, fits perfectly with the general characteristics of early Christian art. In this way, as we shall see, many of these films attempt to recreate their eras in terms of the received visual images that have come down to us via the art of the period, enabling Rossellini once again to be complexly in the past and the present at the same time and also to suggest, self-reflexively, the source of our visual knowledge of the past.

Typically (except in *Louis XIV,* where sumptuous display is precisely the point), Rossellini contents himself with the minimal representation—usually basic costumes and bare settings, chosen with a brilliant eye—which further fore-grounds the idea that is being spoken. The reality Rossellini wants, despite his later insistence on the "directness" of the visual image, is, after all, in the words, both because they are "authentic," since they are taken from available historical sources whenever possible, and because what he wants to convey, finally, are ideas, which, whether he likes it or not, are in the words. Hence he is never tempted by a Belasco-like obsession for actual period detail. What he is looking for in all these films, once again, just as with his humans twenty years earlier, is always an *essence*.[28]

Having now considered in some depth the overall strengths and weaknesses of Rossellini's grand historical project, it is time that we move on to a discussion of the specific films themselves.

28

L'Età del Ferro
(1964)

At the time of *India,* as we saw, Rossellini was not really very interested in the medium of television, and the episodes broadcast were little more than outtakes from the later theatrical version. By 1964, however, when Rossellini had begun to take television more seriously, he had learned many things. One of them was that the commentary should add something to the images rather than try to replicate them verbally, as it had in the television series on India. In *L'età del ferro* (The Iron Age), therefore, the director appears on-screen, acting overtly as teacher and serving as a guarantor of the images, as it were, rather than as their competitor.

His goal in this five-part series is nothing less than a comprehensive overview of the entire Iron Age from the time of the Etruscans to the present day. Most of the early segments are devoted to the progressive refinement of iron implements and weapons, as we move from the earliest inhabitants of the Italian peninsula through the Roman era, the Middle Ages, the Renaissance, the eighteenth century, and the Industrial Revolution, finally coming to rest at an iron factory at Piombino during World War II. In the fourth episode, Rossellini boldly and imaginatively transforms his documentary into a fictionalized account of one metalworker's dealings with the Nazis and the Resistance. The final segment examines the present reality and the future promise of our technological society.

Bursting with what is for the most part recently acquired knowledge, the new teacher wants to teach us everything, all at one go. He will learn, as all teachers must, the virtues of pacing and selection. In fact, in the years to come, he will go back over much of this same material to expand and deepen his and our understanding of it. The series is also clearly transitional, for many of its dramatic strategies are little changed from the string of commercial films that began with *General della Rovere* in 1959, and bear little relation to the rigorous films to come. Rossellini is clearly grasping for the large popular audience that had eluded him since the glorious days of *Open City*, for now he has a mission. In the pursuit of this audience, he is not above resorting to the fast cutting he used as far back as *La nave bianca* (1941). The battle scenes, for example, are exciting in the best conventional sense. The very first scene, in fact, opens with a thrilling boar hunt shot principally in a flurry of close-ups; the scene becomes increasingly frenetic and, when the dogs hang onto the wild boar for all they are worth, very convincing. Yet even here Rossellini seems, as in the films to come, less interested in dramatic verisimilitude, and the characters' dialogue is often openly, even painfully, expository. The fast cutting and high drama of the chase and battle scenes, in other words, are always thematically subordinate to explanation and demonstration, clearly the order of the day.

This atypical desire to entertain through spectacle also accounts for the astonishing inclusion of scenes from earlier films (including *Paisan* and Abel Gance's *Austerlitz*). As he explained to his Spanish interviewers in the early seventies:

> It's very important to make the film spectacular because above all you must entertain people. These are films which should be of use not just to intellectuals but to everybody—if they were not it would be pointless to make them. They have to be spectacular and that means spending a lot of money, which you can't do for TV. These are cultural programmes and so they come furtherest down in the television budget. If you try to fight to change this you don't get any films made, and the important thing is to make films. So we took some sections of other films and re-used them in a different context, and in this way we got the spectacular effect for much less.[1]

In many ways, this is a desperate Rossellini speaking here. He is anxious to be successful in the new medium, obviously his last chance. To continue working—and what is life without work?—he knows he will need to be financially successful, or rather, financially inoffensive, spending as little as possible, continuing to amaze backers by how cheaply he can work.

The most important aesthetic effect of this borrowing, beyond pragmatism and economic exigency, is to establish a kind of conscious, fruitful intertextuality. In order to fill the five hours of time, Rossellini borrows freely from *Austerlitz* for the Napoleonic scenes, from *Paisan* for the immediate postwar scenes, and from *Scipione l'Africano, Luciano Serra, pilota* (upon which he had worked), other fiction films, and a certain amount of raw documentary footage. For one thing, this strategy marks a new variety of an old proclivity of the director's— the conscious working against the Hollywood-style slick seamlessness and "professionalism" that David Thomson has so masterfully dissected in his book *Overexposures*. Individual images now become secondary to Rossellini's larger project of discovering truth: "If you make a film in a very finished way, it may have a certain intellectualistic value, but that's all. What I am trying to do is to search for truth, to get as near to truth as possible. And truth itself is often slipshod and out of focus."[2]

What results from this mélange of documentary footage, older fiction film, on-screen directorial comment, and newly filmed "documentary" and fictional sequences is an intensely self-aware film. If Rossellini is seeking truth, he knows it does not come naturally. A revealing exchange in the Aprà and Ponzi interview is worth quoting in this regard:

> Q: What's the relation of this kind of montage to what you talked about in your interview with Bazin?
> A: It's not montage in that sense. There are some things I need to have which it would take months and months of work to make—I can find the same thing on the market, so I take it and use it in my own way—by putting my own ideas into it, not in words but in pictures.
> Q: Don't you think that even before montage the pictures have a meaning that montage can't completely destroy?
> A: They don't. You have to give them it. The pictures in themselves are nothing more than shadows.[3]

What is so fascinating in this exchange is that it is Rossellini who comes across as the avant-garde film theorist, articulating what is essentially a poststructuralist theory of meaning, and one especially close to some of Eisenstein's formulations concerning the relation of individual shots to the montage that, in a sense, constructs their meaning *after* the fact. For Rossellini—here, at least—these bits and pieces of earlier films are floating signifiers, in other words, unattached to any fixed, "natural" signified, and hence able to be shaped through montage (which Marie-Claire Ropars-Wuilleumier has linked with Derridean *écriture*) into whatever meaning the filmmaker desires.[4] This is a long way from both neorealist orthodoxy and Rossellini's later notion of the "essential image."

In effect, Rossellini rearranges his unattached signifiers into a new genre, the film essay. "You have to use everything that can make a point firmly and with precision. . . . So I jump from film taken from the archives to re-constructed scenes."[5] These "pieces made for something else" are used as sentences, even as words, in the construction of his new discourse. But the fact that these visual signifiers have not been (and could never be) completely emptied of their original signifieds is made clear in an unintentionally comic moment in the last episode. As the film is touting the productivity of Italian industry, we see many shots of busy factories filled with happy, productive workers. If the viewer looks closely at the empty cartons, however, it becomes clear that what Rossellini is using is stock footage of a General Electric plant in the United States.

The first conceptual high point of the series comes with the introduction of Leon Battista Alberti, the fifteenth-century Florentine architect, scientist, and humanist who, as one of Rossellini's most direct stand-ins, will appear again ten years later, greatly elaborated, in the second and third episodes of *The Age of the Medici* (1973). Alberti is the perfect manifestation of all that Rossellini has been preaching because, for Alberti, "painting *is* science." Machines, quickly being developed by advancing technology, fascinate Alberti as much as they do Rossellini, whose camera enthusiastically follows their intricate movements, just as entranced as it was twenty years earlier with the powerful engines of *La nave bianca*.

In the first two episodes we also witness the beginning of the industrial production of weapons and learn about the bronze casting of cannons (as a little boy urinates on the metal in order to temper it); throughout, the emphasis is on the cannon's simultaneous utility and beauty. The screen is filled with wonderful machines, most of them employed in the manufacture of weapons of destruction, but nowhere does Rossellini bewail the fact that all this progress and creativity is in the service of death. We see the humorous side of it all—men fitted for armor as though they were at the tailor's (a hammer is used instead of a needle and thread), and the fighting of two men so overladen with metal (reminiscent of the tyrant of *Francesco*) that they both collapse at the end from overexertion. We also witness what the film calls the "heroic struggle" to invent new ways to make more gunpowder, better rifles, uniform cannonballs—but with never a word of misgiving from the director.

It is at the end of the second episode that the most politically troublesome aspects of the series appear. For Rossellini, the Industrial Revolution and its aftermath seem to have been an unalloyed blessing. He now wants to demystify our notion of progress (a completely positive term for him), which, he contends, seems so miraculous only when its causes are unknown. Thus, he appears near the end of this episode to explain the causes of the Industrial Revolution, the invention of the steam engine, and the incredible development of machinery and production. Paradoxically, however, the massive onslaught of overwhelming statistics serves only to remystify the fantastic, blinding inevitability of everything subsumed in the word *progress*. Nor in this entire paean is there a single word about the exploited workers who were largely responsible for this outburst of creativity, or about the horrible slum conditions created in England and elsewhere in its wake. At the very beginning of the third episode, Rossellini does introduce the notion of class (appearing completely neutral toward it) and presents a few quick moments of documentary footage of strikes; then, suddenly, we are back into more war footage, and that is all we hear of the workers' struggle.

The remainder of the third episode takes us dizzyingly through World War I, Versailles, the rise of fascism, dirigibles, cars driving up the Campidoglio in Rome, coal mining, the manufacture of nylon, Hitler, the Japanese, and the Ethiopian war, following which Ethiopian sand is used to make machines that, in turn, are used to make spaghetti! At the end Rossellini summarizes the specific events leading to World War II, and the combination of shots, images, and facts presents a remarkably clear overview of the war itself. The accent throughout is purposely on guns and cannons in order to underline the historical and thematic connection with earlier episodes.

The fourth episode concerns itself largely with the fictional story of a metalworker named Montagnani, who, like many Italians, was caught in the middle by General Badoglio's surrender to the Allies on September 8, 1943, while the northern half of the country was still occupied by the Nazis. When the Germans attempt to dismantle the factory at Piombino, Montagnani altruistically sets off on a bicycle to find out where they are taking the raw material. His travels lead him to Florence, as he follows first the truck and then the train that the Germans plan to use to transport the material to Germany. Coming at this point in the series, his story serves the function of an anecdote in an essay, told

for illustrative purposes. Montagnani is meant to be seen as a representative figure, yet he is also sharply etched in historical terms. As we journey with him,
we also get a sense of the everyday lives of people simply trying to get along
in the face of a great historical upheaval: we meet Fascists, common villagers,
escaped British prisoners, and partisan train workers.[6]

Rossellini has included this fictional piece to make thematic connections with
earlier episodes, for Montagnani is seen primarily as a man intensely devoted to
his work and, therefore, to what will become of his factory. He takes pride in
his labor, the pride of an artisan (linking him overtly to the craftsmen we have
seen through the three thousand years depicted in the other episodes)—and is
in no sense an alienated worker, resentful of management or private property.
In this series, at least, Rossellini seems almost incapable of imagining this latter
possibility. Instead, he offers an image of a harmonious relationship between
management and labor based on a presumed commonality of interest, craftsmanship, and progress, a harmony barely conceivable in the context of real labor
history. In this sense, the spirit of the film recalls the wished-for unity of Catholic and Communist at the end of *Open City*.

On one level the series attempts to create a picture of humanity deeply influenced by its history, environment, and, above all, the technology it has created
along the way. (It is especially interesting that all of this is conceived in terms
of a *metal:* Rossellini is right to complain that technology has been overlooked.)
But his essentialist bias is still as strong as ever. For one thing, Montagnani
is overtly offered as an Everyman figure who links our present-day world to the
world of the past. Despite the superficial differences of modern civilization, Montagnani's view of his work, especially, is very little changed from the Etruscan
craftsmen portrayed, in the first episode, at the dawn of the Iron Age. The
many spatial and historical connections the film makes are also important for
Rossellini's essentialist theme. Much is made, for example, of the fact that the
government established the ILVA company in 1898 in order to exploit the min-
eral resources of the island of Elba, discontinued since Etruscan times, and
that Piombino, the location of Montagnani's factory, is the ancient Etruscan
city of Populonia, the site of the earliest iron works. Once again, Rossellini's insistence on carefully placing humans in history, in a given era and location, leads
to a transcendent humanist view that is ultimately ahistorical.[7]

The history he recounts here, as in most of the didactic films, also has a
strong teleological cast to it. In the final episode the war has ended, the Germans
have been defeated, and people everywhere are looking to rebuild their lives;
this larger theme is represented synecdochically in the quest of the factory at
Piombino to begin production again. The factory manager piously intones,
"Our duty is to give work," and the representative of the common man, Montagnani, is here reintroduced. He marvels at all the tremendous activity of re-
building that he sees around him, his wonder replicating that of the engineer
of the second episode of *India* who wanders about the site of the Hirakud dam
he has just helped to build. When the workers pour molten iron into its form,
we are visually reminded of the earlier episodes, and the message is clear that
what we are watching are merely different historical moments of a single human
enterprise whose final contours are preordained. At this point the film begins

The modern factory in *L'età del ferro* (1964).

praising the Italian economic *miracolo* to the accompaniment of stirring music, and Rossellini plunges into an orgiastic celebration of industrial productivity. Montage, presumably reflecting the masculine aggressivity of heavy industry, now takes over completely.[8]

Consumption is linked with progress, and, perhaps unsurprisingly for 1964, both are touted without a single word of doubt. The voice-over (which appears for the first time) warms to its task and begins shouting "Machines! Machines!" as it launches into a poetic outburst on the complexity of the equipment used to manufacture the refrigerators we see pouring off the assembly line.[9] Nothing could be more indicative of the shift from what Rossellini had begun calling the "morbid and complaining" films of the Bergman era to the new era of science and human possibility than the change in the portrayal of industrial machinery. In a climactic scene in *Europa '51*, it will be remembered, machinery was regarded as threatening and dehumanizing; now Rossellini seems to have become so enamored of the machines' impersonal beauty that he has completely forgotten the reality of the human beings operating them. As Pio Baldelli has pointed out: "As usual, the director exalts the geometry of the factory buildings, the rational cleanliness of the tools and the products, the mechanical perfection of the gears, but he does not bother himself about the fact that behind the naked and rational walls men are working."[10]

Rossellini's reply to this objection, of course, would be that if men once began to understand the modern world they would no longer be alienated from it, and thus an innate hostility between man and machine cannot be assumed. What the director would have a more difficult time answering is Baldelli's complaint that the series shows

> nothing concerning the cultural currents that feed a sort of business ideology which would like to model the perfect citizen of tomorrow and especially the patient worker of today, transforming him into an anonymous completer of tasks. "Democracy and well-being are the same," the instructor teaches. "The two decades of the Fascists were terrible, but look at the two decades of the Christian Democrats instead."[11]

As the final episode continues, the pace quickens. The voice-over, now almost feverish, shouts: "Motors! Life—always faster! Ve-lo-ci-ty!!!!" Even the words and phrases are broken up into sharp syllables that match the fast cuts on the image track. (One sight of this sequence alone would be enough to bury forever the simplistic notion of Rossellini as the man of the long take.) In fact, the fragmentation of voice and image, increasing continually in speed, *is* enormously exciting. The bizarre music also seems to fit perfectly as the voice-over applauds the uniformity that has permitted the economic miracle: "Few models! Thousands of cars!" Unfortunately, what seems to be elided here is that this uniformity has also spelled the end of the craftsmanship that linked Montagnani with the Etruscans. More importantly, Rossellini forgets that this very boom, founded upon uniformity, stepped-up production and consumption, and an uncritical faith in material progress, is exactly what his earlier films condemned as the cause of the selfish emptiness of figures like Irene of *Europa '51*.

The pace continues faster and faster, now bringing in "Skyscrapers, bridges, freeways, ve-lo-ci-ty! Ships!" (Shots of engine rooms make the parallel with *La nave bianca* nearly exact.) "Jet planes! Two hundred seventy meters in one second!" (The second is counted aloud.) "Atomic energy!" And, then, "Space!" This is the final link that is meant to tie all the episodes together: the steel of the spacecraft takes us back into space, whence, as the first episode explained, the earliest peoples thought all metal had come. The series closes with a view of the harmony and world brotherhood that will result from all this amazing economic progress, making conflict obsolete and unnecessary: "We work! Everybody together! Everybody equal! Ex-enemies!" The pictures, music, and voice-over have combined to move the viewer profoundly with the possibilities before us. What excitement![12] Then the viewer recalls the succeeding twenty years since the series was made, and the naïveté and willful forgetfulness of its vision become apparent.

In spite of its flaws, however, it is clear that Rossellini's amalgam of fact and fiction, documentary and previous film is boldly new. At this point his historical project must have looked very promising indeed. He was fully installed in his new medium, after all, and ideas for projects were constantly occurring to him. Even at this early date, however, it soon became obvious that the commitment of the RAI was halfhearted at best, and the series was aired on five successive Fridays between February 19 and March 19, 1965, at 9:15 in the evening. As

Sergio Trasatti has pointed out, despite appearances, this was a quite unfavorable time slot, since it was up against "Weekly Appointment With the Theater," and whoever chose to watch *L'età del ferro* would have had to skip *Julius Caesar, Antony and Cleopatra,* and *Sabrina.* Naturally, *L'età del ferro* did poorly, gathering fewer than a third as many viewers as the other channel. Nor, unfortunately, was this treatment unique, for with it began a sad pattern that would help to make the historical films, Rossellini's last chance, a failure as well. As Trasatti reports: "*L'età del ferro* is one of the few important programs of the RAI which was never reshown, like almost all the work Rossellini did for television. The only exception is *La Prise de pouvoir par Louis XIV,* which was transmitted for the second time, in a celebrative key, the day following the director's death."[13]

29

La Lotta dell'Uomo
per la Sua Sopravvivenza
(1964-70)

Given the fact that the series was not aired until 1970 and 1971, most Rossellini filmographies quite properly list *La lotta dell'uomo per la sua sopravvivenza* (Man's Struggle for Survival) after *La Prise de pouvoir par Louis XIV* (1966) and even after *Atti degli apostoli* (Acts of the Apostles, 1969). Yet, *La lotta* is actually much closer in plan, scope, and technique to *L'età del ferro* of 1964, and was, in fact, conceived at the same time. Many critics have been bothered by the apparent inconsistencies involved here. Why would Rossellini return to the marathon view of history after the success of the much smaller-scale *Louis XIV*? It is useful, therefore, to know that *Louis XIV* was initially thought of as a kind of interim project while the work on *La lotta* was at a standstill. (This, too, can be misleading, however, for evidence from later interviews shows that Rossellini probably would have preferred to alternate between large-scale and small-scale projects.) In 1979 Rossellini's son Renzo, who is listed as "director" of the series, explained the chronology to me in the following way:

> *Acts of the Apostles* and *La lotta* are very closely linked, because practically speaking, we made *Acts* to be able to finish making *La lotta*. We were filming the [earlier series] in Egypt when the 1967 Arab-Israeli war broke out. We were able to get out in time, but we had to leave all of our equipment behind. We had no idea how we were going to be able to finish the series, which we had originally begun in 1964. *Louis XIV* was just a slight interruption. We had spent a total of three years filming *La lotta,* and were a million and a half *dollars* in debt for quite a few years because of it, so when we went to Tunisia to shoot *Acts of the Apostles*, we shot the end of *La lotta*, which was the part that we had had to leave in Egypt, at the same time.

An early irrigation system in *La lotta dell'uomo* (1964–70).

La lotta, in any case, is surely unique in the history of the cinema; never before had a major film director conceived and executed a project on such a grand scale. The entire series runs a staggering twelve hours (Guarner reports that each of the twelve episodes was originally ninety minutes long and was later edited!) and even outdoes the ambitious *L'età del ferro* by surveying the entire history of humanity, beginning with the appearance of the first true men and women. Along the way, nearly every important historical era is represented in this exciting, if inconsistent, series. According to Rossellini, human beings stepped from their prehuman state when they first began to probe the mysteries of life and death, ultimately coming to revere the burial sites of their forebears. From there developed the use of the mind for survival and, for Rossellini, a concomitant belief in the supernatural. The earliest episodes of *La lotta* thus center around the agricultural revolution and the matriarchy Rossellini believes was a natural consequence of the relation of women to fertility and the cycles of the moon. From there we move to astronomy and the discovery of the solar year, the Bronze Age, the first machines, the rise of Egyptian, Greek, and Roman civilization, the barbarian invasions, the advent of Islam, the Middle Ages (including the preservation of ancient learning and the founding of the great universities), the Renaissance, the beginning of science and technology, the invention of electricity, the telegraph, radio, right up to the present era of space travel itself. Along the way, a surprising number of dramatizations show us such figures as Hippocrates, Christopher Columbus, Benjamin Franklin, and Gutenberg, all engaged in the struggle to advance human welfare. It is a breathtaking enterprise, perhaps one that could have been undertaken only by a man with the self-confidence and audacity of Roberto Rossellini.

A project of this sort would have to be gargantuan in terms of its support as well. Sergio Trasatti reports that the entire series cost over 800 million lire (well over a million dollars), with the RAI contributing 120 million lire and the French, Romanian, and Egyptian television networks financially involved as well. Certain of the medieval sequences, for example, were enormously costly, especially for a television production: the Crusades alone, according to Trasatti, required some eleven thousand extras. Since one of the prime reasons that Rossellini moved to television in the first place was financial, the expenditure of such huge sums presents something of an anomaly. In fact, Rossellini's production company was so strapped by the series' cost that he had to forgo accompanying his new television film *Socrates* to its premier at the 1970 Venice film festival. Instead, he went off to Latin America where he managed to interest several countries in showing the series on their networks.[1]

Rossellini later said that he wanted *La lotta* to provide "a sort of spinal cord to which I would attach the other productions."[2] Elsewhere, he described it as

> a history of new ideas, of the difficulty of getting them accepted and the pain-fulness of accepting them. The whole of human history is a debate between the small handful of revolutionaries who make the future, and the conserva-tives, who are all those who feel nostalgia for the past and refuse to move for-ward. The film gives an outline of history—I think it's useful as a start, be-cause school study programmes have degenerated so and don't meet modern needs. It gives me a kind of core around which I shall take certain key mo-ments in history and study them in greater depth.[3]

As such, the new series was conceived as a complement to *L'età del ferro* and another fully planned series on the Industrial Revolution, which was never filmed.[4] Later in the same interview Rossellini outlined the specific relation of *La lotta* to *L'età del ferro*:

> It's a matter of looking at history from different angles. *La lotta* is much more concerned with ideas, which are always related to technology as well. The agricultural revolution was a great advance for mankind, the first great revo-lution carried out by man, because from then on man was not so completely at the mercy of nature and began to use it to strengthen himself. He no longer feared nature and gradually embarked on the decisive conquest of it. *L'età del ferro* is more concerned with the development of technology. The tech-nology of iron brought advancement, and changed men's way of looking at things.[5]

In terms of technique, *La lotta* is clearly a more confident step beyond the uncertain mixture of *L'età del ferro*. The earlier series' bricolage of dramatized scenes (both factual and fictional), documentary stock footage, and sequences from older films was a fascinating experiment whose enthusiasm compensated for its failures. With *La lotta*, however, the rough, if exciting, hodgepodge disappears, and virtually all of the material, with the exception of the NASA stock footage of space travel, is presented in a dramatized narrative form, of either famous events or representative fictional details meant to convey the spirit of an age. The result is a slicker product, certainly, but I am not sure that Guarner is right to herald the abandonment of "archive material" as a definite advance in technique.[6]

Similarly, there seems to be much more attention being paid here to such formalist concerns, normally disdained by Rossellini, as composition and an aestheticized mise-en-scène. The color is also handled magnificently in the film—clearly a lesson learned from *Louis XIV,* with subtle pastels of green and brown and yellow, say, predominating in the episodes on early Egyptian civilization. Mario Nascimbene's music works well, moving, finally, beyond the limitations of Rossellini's brother's conventional Hollywood scoring. The Pancinor zoom orchestrates the choreography of every scene, and Rossellini is not afraid to shoot an entire lengthy sequence in one or two long takes. Onlookers explain to each other (and to us, of course) what is happening in each scene, as, for example, when the engineer describes the plan of the pyramids to the pharaoh. Individual frames sometimes even suggest the predominant art form of the period, though this device, which becomes increasingly important in the films focused on individual figures, is here naturally much more diffuse. The matte and mirror shots are also more convincing in *La lotta,* especially compared with the later films that were hampered by tiny budgets. (This would seem to indicate once again that any talk of Rossellini deliberately making the matte shots obvious simply misunderstands the director's own sense of professionalism.) Also, as we saw in *L'età del ferro,* Rossellini continually makes cross-references throughout the course of the series to remind us of the central motifs: thus, the burial and religious customs of many different civilizations are depicted, as well as the passing of power from one generation to the next, the use of water and machines, changing views of medicine, the advance of technology, and how ordinary things of the world like bread, glass, and paper come to be made.

Given the sheer size of the series, and the fact that the chances of it ever being seen in the United States (or elsewhere, for that matter) are quite small, I will have to limit myself to discussing in detail only one of the episodes. Since a polemic has developed most violently around the notion of matriarchy articulated in the opening episode, it will perhaps be best to concentrate our attention there.

The opening credits attempt to put what we are about to see, the earliest struggles of primitive humans, in the context of the present and the future so that we might marvel at how far we have come. Following obviously from the euphoria of the last episode of *L'età del ferro,* the credits are jazzy and hyped, and as we hear black Americans singing, we watch shots of New York skyscrapers and rockets blasting off into space. (For Rossellini, America is the principal locus of the energy of the new technology, and it is no accident that in the early seventies he was to work happily for a time at Rice University's Media Center with Houston's many scientists.) After the credits, the director himself comes on to emphasize how short a time humans have been in the ascendancy on the planet, an idea that has become by now something of a cliché, and that intelligence has always been their greatest weapon. The first sequence, the Ice Age, opens with shots of snowy woods. A cold wind blows on the sound track and the voice-over (not Rossellini) explains, over the sound of a single violin note, what we are seeing, but without ever overexplaining. (Often the voice-over is completely silent, wisely letting the visual track speak for itself.) Cave dwellers appear, and we learn that humans have already survived four ice ages and that the sheer brutality of nature has made them move into the mutual protection provided by communal living. The discovery of fire and cooking follows quickly, along with hunting and animal keeping. The breasts of the actresses playing the cave women are exposed (something difficult to imagine on American television in the sixties), and this fact, along with the superb costumes and the lack of makeup for the women (another benefit of using nonprofessionals) makes these scenes seem less awkward than the standard depictions of prehistory. Human beings begin to gain the upper hand over their animal foes when, through the use of their intelligence, they disguise themselves as animals. A short night scene then shows us the benefits of an increased security: one of the men, because he has become more reflective about the mystery of the world, begins to draw on the walls of the cave, and art is born.

The next scenes of the first episode show the end of the Ice Age, men and women beginning to eat roots and berries, washing clothes, abandoning caves for shacks, and learning to make bread by milling grain with a stone. An entire set is constructed merely to show this last activity, a sequence that occupies no more than a few moments of footage; obviously, Rossellini's preference for television because of its economies did not prevent him, on occasion, from thinking big. No dialogue inflates the scene depicting the establishment of agriculture, and the sound track is occupied only with strange, but understated, electronic music that contrasts favorably with the exuberant, blaring score of *L'età del ferro*.

As in all of the history films to come, much time is spent on the supposedly insignificant details of everyday life: food preparation, work, and daily chores. Rossellini's intellectual proximity to the French *annalistes* school, which was beginning to flourish at this time, thus also becomes clear. Similar to his use of *temps mort* in the earlier fiction films, the accent in the history films will be on downplaying the "grand events" in order to concentrate on ordinary life. This is the essence of Rossellini's historical method: the selection of revealing, though seemingly minor, details that are meant to represent, synecdochically, the consciousness of an age. The director himself provides an example in several interviews: a vizir who runs a gold mine far from any water source finds that his workers and animals are dying so fast that the mine is not productive. He goes to the pharaoh, who was considered the equivalent to a god, and asks for a miracle. The pharaoh logically declares that the vizir should take ten thousand men and dig a canal from the Nile to the mine; to us simply logical, but the vizir is astonished and calls the idea a "miracle." Rossellini's comment is that "through a thing like that you can discover the proportions of a civilization much more than any other sort of thing."[7]

The principal purpose of deemphasizing the grand events is, once again, to establish an essence of human nature. Rossellini would later explain:

In general, books of history tell us about the main events. History was also written to glorify power. But the real history is to discover man, the simple man whose life was never written. The research made in the last years is great in this sense, now you can find out a lot. History is the history of human beings who are like us, only chronologically at another moment in time. We have some knowledge and what we do now [sic]? That is the continued struggle of man.[8]

Thus, the director dedramatizes history partly for Brechtian purposes, so that the spectator may watch intelligently and understand the issues rather than being involved emotionally with the character. But more importantly, this is how one arrives at the human essence. True, we must be scrupulous about historical specificity, but we will inevitably find that "history is the history of human beings who are like us."

The focus of the first episode now turns toward the establishment of the matriarchy: since man's role in reproduction is unknown at this point, the fertility of the woman, the source of all life to an agricultural people, becomes exalted. A lovely sequence, enhanced by a perfectly executed zoom shot, shows the queen giving herself over to the power of the water so that she may become fecund. The role of the male changes when his part in reproduction becomes better understood, but the prestige still belongs to the woman: the consort must wear artificial breasts when he gives orders, and later he is ritually slaughtered so that his blood may fertilize the soil. Once astronomy begins in earnest, however, and solar time is privileged over lunar time (the latter associated with women), the male's ascendancy begins. As Rossellini later described it: "At the moment when the Hellenes, who had their own gods and were not agricultural people but shepherds, came from the East to the Mediterranean area, it became a patriarchal society. All Greek mythology is an explanation of what happened during that change from a matriarchal to a patriarchal society."[9] The first episode of the series ends at this point.

The utterly sweeping nature of Rossellini's generalization about the establishment of the patriarchy is indicative of his overall approach to history in this omnibus series. With the conviction of the autodidact, he is able to state categorically the single cause of an enormously complicated system of beliefs and cultural practices. On the other hand, it is true that the cautious steps of the scholar would be out of place when it comes to making a television series on the history of the world. In any case, for Rossellini the message was clear: given all that we humans have accomplished in the infinitesimal time we have occupied the planet since it first came into being, we must not give in to the naysayers and complainers who preach alienation. Instead, we should feel hopeful that we can and will solve the problems that confront us today. What Rossellini has perhaps forgotten in his enormous optimism in human potential, however, is that the movement of technology has developed a life and trajectory of its own, which human beings no longer seem to control. It could also be objected that the vast majority of new technological developments, as Paul Goodman pointed out years ago, have come about to rectify the problems caused by previous applications of technology.

More serious is the problem of authenticity. Even the most intense Italian supporter of Rossellini's television films, Sergio Trasatti, cannot help finding the undertaking so vast that a greater selectivity than usual is at work, with the result that the "objective and neutral" Rossellini is actually interposing himself more than ever. In Trasatti's words, it is "not an accident that *La lotta* seems to be the most opinionated of all these films." Nor can Rossellini's historical representations be legitimatized by the claim that he is relying solely on the testimony of authentic sources. As Trasatti points out, "In this film, more than any other, one notes here and there an obvious embarrassment concerning the lack of sources, the difficulty of verification, the complexity of the cultural relations among different facts and problems."[10]

In a sense, then, it is in this series that the inherent contradictions of Rossellini's method are most visible. It is not, of course, that the questions concerning the possibility of objectivity and authenticity do not arise elsewhere as well, but in better-documented periods it is easier for the director to deny his own mediation by appealing to the historical record. Here, on the other hand, when one is depicting the very beginning of civilization and societal life, one may have recourse to "the latest scientific knowledge," but the tactic is transparent. (He will have exactly the opposite problem portraying the too-well-known recent history of Italy in *Anno uno*.) Rossellini is offering an interpretation of events, in other words, an interpretation based on very sparse information indeed.

Thus, he is also vulnerable to disagreements with his depiction of humanity's origins. The Communist party organ *L'Unità* attacked the series, not surprisingly, for its "mystical vision of history and therefore, of man,"[11] and others have maintained that Rossellini's view of history in this series is at best simplistic. The theory of matriarchal society itself, based as it obviously is in religion, has come in for special attack by another writer for *L'Unità*, who applies to Rossellini Engels' answer to Bachofen, the first thinker to offer the matriarchal hypothesis: "It seems that for him religion represents the decisive lever of history."[12] In his book on Rossellini, Pio Baldelli has mounted a telling attack on this series, especially its depiction of the matriarchy. Baldelli complains that Rossellini neglects the division of labor and the "systems of kinship, the social and functional origin of systems of succession—through the maternal or the paternal line—the reasons for their evolution—by means of the incest taboo and successive exclusions of links between blood relatives—their relationship with changes in the economy: from collective property to private property."[13]

Unfortunately, Baldelli insists that Rossellini's problem is that he has failed to supply "the correct information," and thus the critic unwittingly demonstrates his own dogmatism. Nevertheless, in its main outlines, Baldelli's critique makes an important point; while Rossellini is right to simplify history in order to have the maximum effect on his mass audience, this is legitimate only if he shows himself to be "truly master of history, having digested it through study, long research, and consultations." For Baldelli this is precisely what is lacking, and in his refusal of analysis Rossellini "remains a prisoner of myth, beliefs, ritual, magic, and legends." It is clear, in any case, that a strong teleological sense of history is at work in the series, and Rossellini's depiction of the medieval era, for example, follows the conventional scenario of the horrid Middle Ages leading inexorably to the wonders of the Renaissance. As Baldelli astutely points out, this depiction is based on "the (among other things, Eurocentric) selection conducted after the fact by bourgeois culture which recognizes as a cultural manifestation only what prepared the terrain of its birth and rejects whatever bears witness to a possible, different dimension of man."

Baldelli's comments are, for the most part, cogent and convincing. Nevertheless, while one would certainly have appreciated a true rethinking of history in this series, it must not be forgotten that Rossellini's project represents one of the very few times since the beginning of television that *any* coherent vision of history has been presented to viewers. Furthermore, the sheer massiveness of the undertaking is impressive. The history of the world in twelve hours: clearly a labor of love. Unfortunately, once again, it was a love that was not facilitated by the powers that be of the French and Italian television networks. In Italy, the first episode was shown at 9:15 P.M. on channel 1, on August 7, 1970, traditionally a time (immediately before one of the biggest Italian holidays of the year) of little television watching. The next five episodes continued throughout the vacation month of August and the first part of September against very popular competition. To make matters worse, only the first six episodes were shown during the summer of 1970, and the interested viewer had to wait over a year, until the fall of 1971, to see the last six episodes, which began on September 4 (with a further delay of two weeks between the third episode of September 25 and the fourth episode, shown on October 3). In competition with the series on Saturday night were two of the most popular television variety shows of the period, "Ciao Rita" and "Canzonissima"—for most viewers what Trasatti calls "the central appointment of the week." Rossellini's average audience for an episode was 1.3 million viewers (out of 10 million subscribers), and only 400,000 when opposite "Canzonissima," which was watched by over 26 million people at the same time.[14] Nor may we point a finger solely at the benighted Italians: Claude Beylie angrily noted in *Écran* that the series was shown in France at 6:00 P.M. during the slowest part of the summer, and then only in black and white.[15]

30

La Prise de Pouvoir par Louis XIV (1966)

Originally conceived as an interim project, as we have seen, *La Prise de pouvoir par Louis XIV* (The Rise to Power of Louis XIV, 1966) has since become Rossellini's most widely appreciated didactic film, often ranked with *Paisan* and *Voyage to Italy* as one of the greatest films of his career. This is all the more amazing when one realizes that the entire shooting was completed in some twenty-three or twenty four days, working five hours a day. Postproduction, thanks to Rossellini's reliance on the zoom lens for in-camera editing, took only another few days, and the entire project was completed for about 100 million lire, or approximately $130,000.[1] Nonprofessional actors were used, reducing expense and avoiding the clunky phoniness that results when implausibly beautiful stars impersonate historical figures, but the film's sets and costumes, given the tiny budget, are surprisingly sophisticated. Money was also saved through Rossellini's standard, elaborate system of matte and mirror shots, enabling him to include, for example, a thoroughly "believable" scene of the building of Versailles.

In this film Rossellini turns for the first time to what was to become the standard formula for all of the historical-didactic films to come: focusing upon a single individual—always male—not so much for his own importance, but for his "representativeness." The grand sweep of *L'età del ferro* and *La lotta*, now that the main outlines of history have been sketched in, gives way to the more intense examination of historically specific periods.[2] (Again, though, Rossellini's insistence on the historical specifics of a given period must be seen in the context of his view of a basic, unchanging human nature.) What seems especially ironic is the fact that this first attempt is perhaps the most perfect. This may be because the intensely pictorial and "spectacular" film focuses expressly on Louis' seizure of power, which he accomplishes precisely through the mounting of spectacle; thus the medium itself is implicated thematically. Here the very idea of the film lies, for once, in its articulation of gesture and image, not in its words, as with virtually all the other didactic films.

Louis XIV opens with a static, painterly long shot of peasants at a dock across the river from a castle. This painterliness will continue throughout the film, and some interior scenes, especially, look forward to Stanley Kubrick's *Barry Lyndon*. In an important article on *Louis XIV,* the late Martin Walsh plausibly suggests Vermeer and Rembrandt.[3] He also convincingly maintains that the film's painterliness reduces its "degree of 'naive' realism" and suggests "the point of origin for our contemporary revisualization of a seventeenth century milieu."[4] Again, we can see that the film does not seek to represent the age directly, but rather to represent its prior representations.

In addition, the opening scene is important because, as James Roy MacBean has pointed out, it is the only scene that has been completely invented and because the peasants are virtually excluded from the rest of the film.[5] What they say is also significant, for they speak disparagingly of the English king who has just been beheaded, and briefly complain about the prerogatives of wealth and authority. Nevertheless, MacBean's insistence that this scene examines "the economic foundations and ideological overtones which enlist the common masses within the socioeconomic system of the French monarchy"[6] is a vast overstatement. Moreover, everything else in this film goes in the opposite direction, toward an ambiguous glorification of the king's accession to power through the manipulation of spectacle, and the peasant viewpoint is never heard again. It is clear that this scene was meant to serve as a kind of earthy counter to everything that follows, but during the next ninety minutes its exemplary force is completely overwhelmed.

In the following scene, doctors attend the dying Prime Minister Mazarin, the rather corrupt cardinal who has been the chief tutor of the young playboy King Louis XIV. Interestingly, the doctors see reality in terms of metaphor, rather than literally. When they debate whether or not to bleed Mazarin once more, one of them reasons that "the more bad water you take from the well, the purer it is; the more a mother feeds her baby, the more milk she has." Metaphors are important to Louis as well, and he delights in calling himself the "Sun King," from whom everything shall flow. This relation of the metaphoric to the literal nicely replicates the relation of appearance to reality, the film's central theme.

Finally, we are introduced to the king, but only after a long-take sequence showing his serving girl's morning chores. The ceremony of the levee, or king's rising, follows, the king mumbles through his prayers, and an obliging courtier explains to a fellow observer that the queen's handclapping signifies that the king has accomplished "his conjugal duty." The king goes to see the nearly moribund Mazarin, who, in a neat foreshadowing of Louis' later strategy to take control, spends a great deal of time applying makeup to look better for his sovereign. The king next asserts that he will take over the actual governance of the kingdom, but no one, including his mother, believes him until he refuses to let her attend council meetings. His chief assistant in this task will be Colbert,

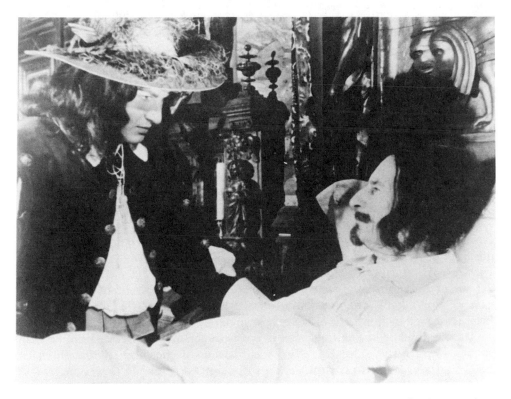

The king (Jean-Marie Patte) attends the dying Mazarin (Silvagni) in *La Prise de pouvoir par Louis XIV* (1966).

the son of a merchant and a palpable symbol of the rising middle class, who has great plans for the industrialization of France.

What follows is one of the more brilliant moments of the film, a Renoirean hunting sequence in which the camera follows a stag being chased by dogs at incredible speed. The scene ends when the king takes his mistress into the woods. His absence is filled by the plotting of Fouquet, his *surintendant* of finances, who refuses to take Louis seriously. Fouquet finally goes too far in attempting to bribe the king's mistress, and, in an elaborately staged arrest purposely undertaken for maximum theatrical effect in Fouquet's home base of Nantes, Louis removes him from the stage. The entire arrest is shot from a very high angle, exactly copying Louis' subjective point of view on the events; he and the camera seem to become complicitous in the elaboration of the double spectacle of politics and filmmaking. What Louis has realized, he says, is the truth of Fouquet's words: "Minds are governed more by appearances than by the deep nature of things."

From this moment on in the film, all interest centers on Louis' struggle to subjugate the nobles through the pleasures and burdens of spectacle. He purposely sets out to create a new, garishly elaborate style of dress, orders the nobles to live in his castle so they are completely in thrall to his disposition, and builds

Versailles on a deliberatively excessive scale. The culmination of this strategy comes when the king turns himself into a secular icon in a stunning scene in which he reveals his elaborate new dress, and the visual power of his presence coalesces perfectly with the power of film itself to create spectacle. A courtier who has not been able to keep up with the new fashions is made to feel utterly beyond the pale of civilization.

Perhaps the film's greatest moment of spectacle, however, is the famous banquet scene. Situated behind the ever-present spatially controlling table, the king eats alone, course after elaborate course, with his brother and other notables in attendance, serving, tasting the wine, unlocking "the king's meat," to which everyone in the kitchen has bowed on its way upstairs. Another dimension is added to the film's self-reflexivity in the kitchen as we follow the chef, who stands on a platform, directing every step of yet one more spectacle. When the king is served his wine, in another baroque ritual, the viewer also realizes the truth of Baldelli's observation that what we are watching is the "holy mass of absolute power." These shots continue for a long time, until we are as surfeited with the opulent display as the king himself must secretly be. He calls for music, a man of the court approaches the camera to execute his wishes, and, as the camera moves backward, we realize for the first time that this entire scene has been witnessed by hundreds of fawning courtiers—an audience, like us.

As the director has pointed out, it was actually his son Renzo who shot this sequence, since the elder Rossellini was visiting his hospitalized daughter Isabella in Italy. What Rossellini perhaps did not know about this scene was described to me by Renzo in 1979:

> I used a little trick in that scene that I never dared confess to my father. Since I had to move back from the table, gradually discovering the crowd watching the king eat, I had to use a little dolly moving backward because I had to raise up to see their heads. This little dolly is something that he would absolutely never have used, because he thought it was totally vulgar. So I had to do the whole thing secretly, taking advantage of the fact that he wasn't in France at the time. The production director, who swore never to say a word about it, helped me to sneak the dolly onto the set. And my father never found out.

Though it is indeed possible Rossellini *père* never found out—he rarely reviewed his films—it is hard to imagine that in the editing process, at least, this very obvious dolly (the courtier walks so far forward, toward the receding camera, that the king finally disappears from the frame, an impossibility in a zoom shot) would have escaped his sharp eye. Perhaps the father was more indulgent than the son imagined.

In the final scene the king is promenading in his garden, his retinue trailing behind him. The music on the sound track, used sparingly and delicately throughout the film, now begins a melancholy plaint, and suddenly we become aware of the immense loneliness of power. The king is reading from a little book, which he takes inside with him, as his courtiers make way. Once inside he is, for the first time in the film, completely alone. He begins stripping himself of his gaudy finery, the coat, the grotesque wig, the bright sashes; there is no music and no camera movement until, finally, he goes to the closet and puts on a coat of the plainest style. (During this sequence everyone else remains outside, presumably continuing the spectacle.) He sits down, and a deep sense of isolation seems to overtake him as he begins to read aloud maxims of the seventeenth-century moralist François de la Rochefoucauld. The second one is the enigmatic *"Ni le soleil ni la mort se peuvent regarder fixement"* (Neither the sun nor death can be looked at directly). Becoming pensive, the king closes the book as the camera zooms in. He repeats the maxim aloud. The music recommences, he picks up the book once more, and the film ends.

Many of the elements of Rossellini's technique that we have been tracing since the very beginning of his career reappear in *Louis XIV,* perhaps in their most fully realized form. The film is shot almost totally in *plans-séquences* made possible by the alternately static and dynamic Pancinor zoom lens, which moves easily from a close-up to a two-shot to a medium shot, all in the same take. (Even when a rare intercut reaction shot breaks the long take, it is clear that the basic shot was originally filmed without a pause, and therefore could have been even longer that it appears in the final version.) Nor is there any plot to speak of, as the above summary indicates, but rather seven or eight nearly self-contained episodes. If there is a single recurring dramatic element (beyond that of the idea of gaining power) that causes a kind of "suspense," pulling the viewer from episode to episode, it is manifested in the character of Fouquet, who refuses to believe that the king is serious about ruling directly, who tries to bribe the king's mistress, and whose brilliantly choreographed arrest constitutes whatever climax this film can be said to have. Similarly, Rossellini's penchant for dedramatization here reaches its zenith: the *idea* of the events, their historical significance, is what is dramatic and exciting, since the characters' dialogue, especially that of the king, is delivered in a rapid, clipped monotone that is utterly unconvincing in the normal sense of the word.[7] We are thus led to understand a historical process rather than to take sides with a character with whom we identify emotionally. This dynamic works especially well here because the film is not really about Louis XIV at all, but rather, as the proper translation of its title indicates, his *taking* of power. Thus, the interest revolves around a historical mechanism, a dynamic series of staged events aimed at a specific outcome, rather than around the fate of the character himself. In fact, the events portrayed in this film probably occupy fewer than ten pages of Philippe Erlanger's four-hundred-page biography of Louis, upon which the film was based. But these events, for Rossellini, are the most significant, for they constitute the first signs of the formation of the modern state and the rise of the bourgeoisie.

Even more radical is Rossellini's use of *temps mort,* for long moments are devoted to the supposedly "irrelevant" details of everyday life. Probably the most famous example of this is the long take of the king's servant, who, upon waking, opens shutters, takes out the king's clothes, folds her own pallet, all with such a natural, unhurried air that the famous *tranche de vie* kitchen scene of the maid in De Sica and Zavattini's *Umberto D.* (1952) comes to mind. The scene in Rossellini's film also correlates well with Louis' deadpan delivery, which Rossellini sees as being more authentic, and which serves to put events that are, after all, merely retrospectively significant, on the same dramatic footing as the obviously mundane.[8] This technique also creates, especially in the beginning of the film, a great proliferation of details that compete for our attention. The king, who has not yet established himself as the sole source of power, is thus little more than another object, another piece of visual information. As he gradually gains in control, however, he seems to take over the very screen itself. By the end of the film, we see him alone: his conquest of power and, concurrently, of the cinematic space, is complete.

All of this can perhaps make Rossellini seem very Brechtian after all, but a great deal more has been claimed in this direction than is warranted. Because Rossellini, like Brecht, wants us to think about what we are seeing, and because the main action of the film, Louis' creation of spectacle to achieve his ends, so clearly parallels the director's own mise-en-scène, one can easily overstate, as does John Hughes, Rossellini's "critique of spectacle": "Such a critique is essential to the film's central purpose, which might be described as an attempt to discover a correlative in the cinema for what Brechtianism meant to the theater."[9] But Rossellini's self-reflexivity is never as total as Brecht's, and there is no real attempt to destroy illusionistic representation or to place it radically in question; instead, there is a kind of bemused pointing to it, for, at a basic level, Rossellini's commitment to illusionism is firm. In Brecht, as in Godard (who Hughes identifies too closely with Rossellini), spectacle and representation are revealed as constructions, which, like all human knowledge, are mediated and derive always from a particular point of view. Rossellini's ultimate project in the history films, on the other hand, is in some ways the very opposite of this: drama is eliminated, along with plot and emotional identification with the character, precisely to convince the viewer that what he is seeing is "pure," objective, historical truth, uncontaminated by the demands of the code of realism, unmediated and direct. The way this works in *Louis XIV* has been summed up by Martin Walsh:

> Even while purporting to offer an intelligent examination of "spectacle," the film itself remains spectacular to a disturbing degree. The film may, as I have suggested, critique spectacle, yet (as James Leahy pointed out to me) LOUIS XIV remains "a process movie," the thrill of "how's he going to do it" shaping our fascination. Rossellini's *work* in the production of meaning is masked. Louis' manipulations hold stage-center throughout, and the result is that the viewer is "fixed in position" in his seat—victim of Louis' image, with no possibility for escape.[10]

This is a forceful and cogent critique, but it is by no means clear how a film that demonstrates Louis' fostering of spectacle can itself avoid being spectacular. The film's very power, in fact, seems to derive precisely from its hegemonic gesture, which seems to enlist the camera itself in Louis' project. In any case, Walsh is right to suggest that Rossellini's historical work is finally in the mainstream of "bourgeois art," whose main characteristic, according to many recent theorists, is the way it places the subject-spectator in a certain preestablished relationship with the text, thereby "constructing" this spectator as well. Just as Louis wants to fix each of *his* subjects in a specific, controllable place, so, too, Walsh insists, "Rossellini's viewer is firmly chained in his/her situation as viewer and asked to accede uncritically to what Rossellini presents rather than actively engage in the production of meaning."[11]

Unlike in *L'età del ferro* and *La lotta,* Rossellini has not been charged with any "distortion" of history in this film, largely because its raw material has been drawn from Erlanger's prestigious biography. It is difficult to estimate the extent of Erlanger's contribution to the film (the credits list him as coscreenwriter), but Pio Baldelli goes too far when, seemingly anxious to belittle even Rossellini's triumphs, he insists that the success of *Louis XIV* is due entirely to the fact that French television had forced an "iron-clad" screenplay, by Erlanger, on the director. In point of fact, there is evidence that Erlanger's role was even smaller than the screenwriting he is credited with in the film.[12]

Whoever was responsible for the screenplay, it is undoubtedly true that most of the material came from Erlanger's biography, as well as most of the historical analysis. But the film contains a great deal less of the latter than some critics have claimed. For James Roy MacBean, the core of the film is its portrayal of the working relationship that develops between the king, who actually wants to return to a feudal society in which all power emanates from him, and his prime minister, Colbert, the draper's son who becomes the master draftsman of the transformation of the French nation into a modern bourgeois state. This may indeed be a correct analysis of the historical forces at work in seventeenth-century France; in no way, however, can a spectator arrive at this analysis from an untutored viewing of the film itself, as MacBean seems to suggest. The thoughtful spectator will, of course, be thinking about the French revolution that will take place 130 years later, which will demonstrate conclusively that Louis' successors were unable to follow his example,[13] but more historical aware-ness than this is hard to imagine. Nor does the film do anything to promote such a wider historical view. Naturally, the de-emphasis on character psychology opens up a wider space for the representation of "history" itself, but the space that is opened is that of the contemporary historical moment alone. The events portrayed are seen teleologically in terms of the desired result, the taking of power, but to understand the significance of these events, we must already know what the film itself does not tell us, namely that Louis was the first European sovereign in two hundred years to actually seek total control. Similarly, it is impossible to argue from the evidence of the film alone, as MacBean does, that Rossellini means to show that Louis' reign "is by no means a healthy, fruitful flowering of the French monarchy. Rather, it is simply the last flowering—dazzling in its sickly hues—of a dying plant artificially kept alive in a hothouse."[14] MacBean's larger claim, that this film is Marxist in method if not in name, since it "is exemplary in bringing to the movie screen, for once, the depiction of class struggle as the motor of history," seems vastly overstated. One can perhaps infer an operative notion of class warfare here, but the film's images and words almost exclusively concern the attempt of one aristocrat to wrest power from the others.

In a sense, Mario Verdone is closer to a proper understanding of the film's strategies when he stresses its anecdotal quality, finding a link with Prosper

Mérimée's "The Night of Saint Bartholomew," which he quotes: "I love the anecdote in history and among anecdotes I prefer those where I seem to find a true representation of the customs and characters of an epoch."[15] What neither Mérimée nor Rossellini ever ask, however, is precisely how one verifies this synecdochically produced historical truth. The result is another version of the hermeneutic circle: how does one know if one has a true representation, unless the true essence of an epoch is already known in advance? And where does such essential knowledge come from, if not precisely from prior anecdotes? In an important statement made in 1974, Rossellini insisted:

> An historical event is an historical event. It has the same value as a tree or a butterfly or a mushroom. I don't choose the tree. I must get the tree which is there. There is not a choice of the tree. Not at all. I'm totally refusing all sort of aesthetic preconceived ideas, totally, totally, totally. That's the point. When you want to talk about something, you must know the thing. That's the point. When you know the thing well, you can say what is essential. When you don't know it well, you are lost in the middle of a lot of things which are impressive. I try to express the things which I think are essential. I refuse to accomplish any creative act.[16]

What is faulty here, of course, is the assumption that a tree and a historical event have the same ontological status, and that therefore they can be recognized, known, and described in equally unproblematic terms. But Rossellini needs this kind of simplification, again, to portray his search for the essence of an age as a neutral operation. This, in turn, always leads back to a grander transhistorical essentialist view of human beings. As he told the interviewer for *Film Culture:* "Man has not changed a great deal, it is the conditions that have changed."[17]

Louis XIV was first aired by the French ORTF on October 8, 1966, with an estimated audience of 20 million viewers, Rossellini's most massive audience to that point and ever since. It went on to enjoy a seven-week billing at La Pagode in Paris, three weeks at a second theater, and five weeks at a third.[18] The film was first shown on Italian television the following year, on April 23, 1967, and, as mentioned earlier, was not shown again until the day after Rossellini's death ten years later, in an egregiously delayed act of homage. In its initial Italian broadcast, it was in competition with a popular musical show, which got 7 million viewers; nevertheless, it managed to attract 6.3 million viewers of its own. As Trasatti reports, however, "the index of enjoyment" was low, barely fifty-five. Perhaps the most depressing thing is that this spectacular film about spectacle was shown on French and Italian television before either had been equipped for color broadcasting. Three years later, the film was released in Italy in commercial theaters.

When the film was first shown in the United States, at the New York Film Festival in 1967, it was greeted unfavorably, and thus Rossellini was unable to get the theater or television distribution he had been hoping for. When it was finally released in 1970, however, the same critics who, according to Paul Schrader, had called it a "mounting bore" now labeled it "surely a masterpiece."[19] The

New Yorker, Newsweek, and the *New Republic* were all favorably disposed toward the picture, and it even outgrossed Truffaut's *The Wild Child.* Schrader is right to be angry about the initial American reception of *Louis XIV.* Yet, if recognition came late, at least it finally came. More disturbing is the fact that it was the last that Rossellini would ever receive.

31

Acts of the Apostles
(1969)

After the success of the relatively small-scale *Louis XIV*, Rossellini returned to the multipart series of grander scope, this time undertaking a nearly six-hour adaptation of *Atti degli apostoli (Acts of the Apostles)*, the book of the New Testament that outlines the first faltering steps of the Church to establish itself in the absence of Christ. It is precisely this absence that comes to define the entire series, and thus even though the biblical account begins with Christ's Ascension into heaven, Rossellini appropriately omits it altogether. Faithful to its biblical source, the film traces the early activities of the apostles; the first conversions and baptisms; disputes over variant interpretations of Christ's words; and Paul's preaching to the Jews, the Greeks, and the Romans. Rossellini's admiration for Paul is clear throughout, and in spite of the initial impression of a dispersed focus, this film takes its place among the other studies of individual figures: "In the case of Paul, I am trying to communicate to the public the sense of immense grandness that the man had. Paul traveled in the opposite direction on the roads trod by the Roman armies and a religious movement without equal arises from the footprints of this obscure wayfarer, this small and mediocre Judean, this Tarsan upholsterer."[1]

The great value of this series is that in it Rossellini approaches the early days of Christianity as *history*, at least as he understood the word, rather than as fulfillment of the foretold. Apart from a general, probably inescapable, teleological thrust (after all, Christianity won), neither the apostles in the film nor the audience have the comfort of knowing that these original Christians will always make the right choice. Significantly, Rossellini eliminates almost all the various miracles performed by Peter and Paul, which, in the Biblical account, establish their spiritual authority.[2] In Rossellini's version they have nothing but their faith to rely on. Their own foibles and frailties are characteristically highlighted, because for Rossellini they are, like Saint Francis, always men before they are saints.

The television series consists of five episodes (the version in theatrical release is simply the first two episodes put together), and was shot by Rossellini and his son in the brilliant whiteness of the southeast corner of Tunisia, using Tunisian actors for all the roles except those of the most important apostles.[3] Principal filming took place in a location between Sousse and Kairouan because of its still-standing ancient architecture, and because one side faced the desert (whose sandstorms and scorpions plagued the filming), while the other was dotted with lagunas filled with photogenic flamingos. The magnificent authenticity of the houses, streets, and even the walls of Jerusalem are a result of this choice of location, and, with the aid of mirrors that substituted Jewish architectural features for the Islamic upper parts of various buildings, the great mosque of Kairouan easily became the temple of Jerusalem. The scenes of imperial Rome were filmed at Ostia antica, the restored Roman city located between present-day Rome and the sea, whereas for the scenes at the end of the series, Rossellini uncharacteristically reconstructed the Porta Capena of Rome.[4] The music of Rossellini's television films now also reaches its definitive form in Mario Nascimbene's brilliant score; here he uses a provocative electronic mixture of instruments such as ancient Jewish shofars and Indian sitars and tamburas.

The *Acts of the Apostles* was chosen not for any overtly religious reasons, as Rossellini's most serious attackers have insisted, but because he saw the advent of Christianity, reasonably enough, as an important turning point in the history of humankind. Baldelli criticizes the director for making the apostles' speeches seem "inspired," as though continuously guided from heaven; this is, of course, the way the apostles saw the matter, but Rossellini refuses to give outside, independent verification of supernatural intervention. And though Baldelli attacks the gap between the apostles' actions as real men and their inspired talk, it seems clear that it is precisely this fundamentally ambiguous space that the film seeks to inhabit and explore.[5]

Rossellini's overtly expressed reasons for making this film also reveal his own particular idiosyncratic view of things. He told interviewers that he made the film "because I think the arrival of Christianity was an important turning point changing man's relationship to nature and thereby putting him in a position to act. The result was Western civilization. This happened in the specific historical context of Greece, Rome, and Jerusalem. *Acts of the Apostles* is about Jerusalem. For Greece, I've chosen Socrates."[6] Elsewhere in this interview Rossellini insists, "Even more than being in harmony with nature, man must be conscious of it, and also dominate it." Thus, the thesis of *Acts of the Apostles*, for Rossellini at least, turns out to be only marginally related to a spiritual change in humans' minds, and much more closely linked to a historical shift in the human view of nature. Rossellini also outlined in a letter the position this series occupies: "We show the change in ethics in our history when the Hebrew idea of nature—a gift of God which man must use to distinguish himself from the ani-

Saint Stephen, the first Christian martyr, in *Acts of the Apostles* (1968).

mals—spreads, thanks to Christianity, through the Greek-Roman pagan world, which had regarded nature as something inviolable which men, through rite and ritual, tried to render benign."[7] His most direct statement, however, comes in the 1975 interview with *Écran*. "Before the apostles," he says, "nature was something untouchable for the pagan world. For the Christian religion, it became a gift of God to man, from which he was supposed to profit as best he could. The apostles' entire effort was to propagate this idea. It is a very profound change of ethics which they accomplished. And we've profited a little too much from it!"[8] What this view becomes in later centuries, simply put, is the Protestant ethic. In spite of being in the middle of the Bible, in other words, it turns out that we are not very far from *L'età del ferro* after all. The true historical importance of Christianity, Rossellini seems to be saying, is that it allowed the development of the scientific method, which brought in its wake manufacturing, technology, and capitalism. As we shall see, this view will dominate all the films to come.

Rossellini's other major theme concerns the law and its relative status in the Jewish and Christian communities. Throughout, the director stresses the clash of differing conceptions of the law, just as he will some six years later when he comes to make his final film, *The Messiah*. (This theme also relates to the theme of man's changing relation to nature, for it is principally through law that this relation is formalized and determined for succeeding generations.) Saul insists early on, before his conversion to Christianity, that Stephen must be stoned because he has broken the law; and Saul more than once explicitly imputes authority to himself because he is a man of the law and thus knows whereof he speaks. His request to hunt down the Christians provides a good summary of the way Rossellini sees Jewish law (since the speech is invented):

> But I too am a doctor of the law. Also of me it will be said: he defended the honor of the Temple, he preserved the purity of the law. . . . When the Messiah comes—this is the promise—Israel will rule the earth. We live in this waiting. This is the reason for the law which we gave ourselves. The holiest law and therefore, inviolable law. . . . This is why we must be ruthless.

Later, after his conversion, Saul, now Paul, provides the perfect complementary statement, also invented, from the Christian point of view:

> But today I tell you: the promise made by God to Abraham was that the Messiah would come. . . . And so that our people would faithfully wait the day of his coming, we were given the law in which we are enclosed, protected, as if we were prisoners. . . . This law, for centuries, has guided our people in their waiting for the Messiah. But now the Messiah has come! And it is not through the observance of the letter of the law but through faith in Him that we will be saved![9]

For Rossellini the essence of Judaism—and thus the essence of this period of human history and consciousness—is its relation to a law thought of as coming directly from God. In this, he aligns himself with an ancient theme whose most recent version is articulated in Matthew Arnold's *Culture and Anarchy*.[10]

As "accurate" representation of history, *Acts of the Apostles* is another of the historical films that creates its own hedge, since it makes no specific, overt claim to recreate the actual historical past, and can be seen simply as an adaptation of this particular book of the Bible. Edoardo Bruno finds it a wonderful history film because ancient daily life is so "accurately" rendered, while Goffredo Fofi finds it a bad history film because it does not show the reasons for events or the historic choices open to the apostles.[11] Bruno also attempts to co-opt the Marxist argument by claiming:

> Rossellini makes use of a text (Luke's) to discover a reality successively, and then to cancel it according to a method of dialectical observation, which is part of "critical Marxism." In this sense the objective dimension makes the represented stories, the human relationships, and the conflicts between tradition and politics both believable and unbelievable at the same time. And the more it exalts the ambiguity of the signs, the more, after all, it reduces the margin of imposed judgment, and it creates the premises for a free reexamination of the facts.[12]

Bruno's argument is finally not very convincing, however, and he does admit that occasionally the signs become less ambiguous and move back toward a "theological transcendentalism," against the grain of the rest of the film.

Another aspect of the question of adaptation is that, while very little is invented expressly for the film that is not in the Bible, and conversely, very little has been left out, the film version is necessarily quite different from its source in terms of its mode of presentation. The Bible, of course, is long on words and short on character, location, atmosphere, gesture, and drama, all of which must be added. Even the *Fioretti* of Saint Francis, for example, told stories that could be directly adapted for the screen, whereas the biblical *Acts of the Apostles* is little more than a dry record of what was said and, only minimally, what was done. In other words, for this film Rossellini must paradoxically *add* dramatic elements not found in his source to achieve his characteristic dedramatized look.[13] Similarly, Rossellini's Peter and Paul have a specific individuality, which, though still minimal by Hollywood standards, greatly exceeds the information provided by the biblical account.

Nevertheless, Rossellini's usual downplaying of the "great events" of history, putting them on the dramatic level of the most mundane, still predominates, and the blinding of Saul and the stoning of Stephen, the first martyr, are given barely more emphasis than the homeliest details of everyday life. In fact, the latter often have even more time devoted to them than the former; when gifts are brought to the community, for example, we see, all in one take, each gift laboriously recorded on clay tablets and then watch as the tablets are baked. It is, of course, the Pancinor zoom that allows these leveling long takes, a technique to which Rossellini is by this point firmly and unalterably committed. Peter Lloyd has maintained, interestingly, that the zoom is the "stylistic key to the movie," because it suggests context and thus relates the human to the spiritual. Thus, when Matthias is made an apostle, the camera zooms out to put the human in a spiritual context. With Peter, the camera at times zooms in to emphasize the human and the mortal and, at other times, zooms out for the spiritual context, resulting in a dialectical style that suggests both action and limitation, unified through a single image.[14] It is unclear, however, why a wider angle should necessarily imply the spiritual; it is all too easy to become categorical in this regard, and more dogmatic than Rossellini himself ever would have been. Also, Rossellini uses this specific zoom movement in all of the historical films from this point on; sometimes it works dialectically, but more often it is used simply for variety and even, very conventionally, to focus the viewer's attention. At this moment in his life, Rossellini is above all a pragmatist; he has a message that he wants to promulgate, and whatever will conduct him most directly to the realization of that goal is what is right. Thus, for the food riot that occurs in the third episode, the director does not rely on the zoom and long take at all, but returns instead to a more appropriate montage, with a great deal of fast cutting, unconcerned about compromising his artistic "purity."

As with all serious films, however, Rossellini's technical means are directly related to the themes he is trying to portray. Thus, the conflict between the old law and the new, mentioned above, is also symbolized structurally and visually in terms of the great attention paid to alternative forms of worship. The Jews, for example, are consistently seen in terms of sacrifice and obedience to an unchanging law, and much of this comes to reside in the obvious, but profound, symbol of fire. Conversely, the Christians are portrayed largely in communal terms, and it is this aspect of their worship that is emphasized; again, these values come together in their partiality for water, seen principally, of course, in the sacrament of baptism. Peter Lloyd has seen this opposition working in more formal terms as well, pointing out the contrast between the rectangle of the Christians' communal area and the rectangle of the Sanhedrin's sacrificial altar.

The latter is shot mostly at ground level, while the former is usually done in long shot, in panning movements, or from a high angle to stress the wholeness of community life.[15] For Lloyd this is evidence for the "essential dualism" of the film, yet in the rest of the five-part series (it is clear from his article that Lloyd is speaking only of the two-episode version in theatrical release), Christianity is seen principally as a *vehicle* by which essentially Hebraic ideas are spread across the known world, rather than as a superior religion.

The treatment of this series by the RAI was better than usual. By broadcasting it on successive Sunday evenings, traditionally the time slot of the most popular shows, the bureaucrats were taking a big gamble. It paid off, for the "enjoyment ratings" (an average of seventy-four) were the highest that any Rossellini television show was ever to have, and an average of 8.6 million homes watched each episode, Rossellini for once beating the popular competition. Trasatti insists that a great change in the sophistication of the television public since *L'età del ferro* was responsible for the increased success, but it seems more plausible to credit the religious nature of the subject in this still (officially, at least) Catholic country. Unfortunately, however, the top executives at the RAI were replaced just at this moment, and the new officials declared that the production of *Acts of the Apostles* was "crude and clumsy."[16] Thoroughly upset, Rossellini resigned from the directorship of the Centro sperimentale di cinematografia, the leading Italian film school, declaring that he would now have to go abroad to continue his filmmaking and thus could no longer work with students.

32

Socrates
(1970)

Around this time Rossellini also undertook a documentary on Sicily for American television. The film was mentioned in American trade newspapers as early as July 1967 and was broadcast on NBC in 1968 as "Roberto Rossellini's Sicily." In its final form, it is a one-hour film that tries to rescue the "idea of an island" (its title in Italian when it was broadcast in Italy on February 3, 1970) from the myths that have overtaken it.

Rossellini's sense of what he was trying to accomplish in this film (largely assembled by his son Renzo) was quite clear from the start. As he pointed out in an interview, he was more interested in putting the island in its proper historical perspective, which meant seeing it as a land that had been repeatedly invaded by countless races and cultures.

> Sicily has on average had a new master every 117 years. . . . To have an idea of the tragedy of Sicilian history, you only have to know that not a single plant on the island today is a native one; everything was imported. . . . Sicily has been devoured—and so of course the Sicilian people have developed a tendency towards secrecy as a form of defence. Women are always the first victims of invaders, and this is the origin of the distorted view of women Sicilians have. . . . My film was a kind of defence of Sicily.[1]

Not everyone, of course, will find Rossellini's "sociological" explanation of Sicilian sexism convincing.

Despite the fact that it has been called by some a glimpse into the "very soul of the Sicilians," and despite the director's good intentions in documenting this encounter between him and the island, the film is quite disappointing. One senses throughout that Rossellini is trying to say something different; in fact, he ends up reinforcing clichés, such as "every Sicilian sees himself as a hero" and "Sicilians are also shrewd." Rossellini's account of relations between the sexes is particularly offensive, and at one point he suggests that Sicilian men are intent on seducing foreign women as a way of "getting even" for all the foreign conquests they have had to endure. Further, because the director tries to cover too much ground in a short time—art, architecture, social customs, agriculture, politics, geography, history, work, and so on—the film's transitions are often jarring and little real information is conveyed in a coherent fashion.

Infinitely more important was Rossellini's next major didactic project, *Socrates*. According to Marcella Mariani, Rossellini's sister, the film was shot in Spain because of the availability of so many different facial types and because the director refused to shoot in a Greece then under military dictatorship.[2] A very few interior scenes were shot in the Samuel Bronston studios in Madrid, where such films as *El Cid, 55 Days in Peking*, and *King of Kings* had been made. The great majority of the location shooting, however, took place in a little town called Patones Arriba, about fifty miles from Madrid, whose open town square allowed perfectly for the reconstruction of the Athenian agora. Trasatti says that problems with the RAI continued, and at one point Rossellini actually stopped production until the network replaced its representative on the set. At the time, *Variety* reported that the director was upset with the RAI because it had taken nine months of negotiations to arrive at a final contract and budget for the film. Furthermore, of the total cost of 240 million lire ($380,000), the RAI had contributed only 81 million to get all the Italian rights *plus* four percent of foreign sales (excluding France), while the French network had put up 48 million lire for the French broadcasting rights alone.[3]

Rossellini had wanted to make a film on Socrates since the postwar days. Perhaps his deepest intellectual identification was with the Greek philosopher, and he laughingly agreed that they were alike in never having made any money from their professions. But he also acknowledged their common insistence on doing what interested them and what they judged useful: "Certainly Socrates is a character I feel very close to. Certainly the choice also came from a sympathetic affinity: that's inevitable, no? If I tried to resist this kind of attraction then I'd be acting like an intellectual, and I don't want to: I present myself with my guts in my hands, as I am."[4] It is clear that in his desire to go his own way despite all obstacles, his commitment to the power of reason, his belief that knowledge is the highest good that humans can attain (notwithstanding the apparent anti-intellectualism of the above remark), Rossellini is very close indeed to the spirit of Socrates.

It is also no accident that Rossellini should be interested in Socrates in a more philosophical sense as well, for it is with Socrates that the history of Western philosophy can be said to begin. He is the source of logocentrism, as we know it, the source of many of our most fundamental beliefs concerning reason, logic, language, and truth. It is these essentialist concepts, of course, that ground the Western humanism that is so crucial to Rossellini's project, and thus it is fitting that he make a film in which they are glorified. Rossellini saw Socrates as representing "the invitation to rationality, to good conscience, to responsibility"

The triumph of reason: Socrates (Jean Sylvère) addresses his fellow Athenians in *Socrates* (1970).

in the terrible atmosphere created by the fall of Athens to the Spartans. The philosopher asked, "What are good, evil, justice, truth, art, and what is man. . . . And Socrates died because he gave witness to the truth."[5] It is perhaps no coincidence that, during an interview conducted on the very set of this film, Rossellini also developed perhaps his most limpid statement of essentialism: "I make historical films, and I try to reconstruct civilizations, customs, and cultures, convinced that, at bottom, man does not change, but only the historical context. The human 'given' is permanent, while the cultural 'given' varies."[6]

Most of what we have come to expect from a Rossellini historical film reappears in *Socrates*. Thus, static medium shots prevail, the acting is flat, and there is little narrative building, at least until the last third of the film. In addition, a great deal of attention is paid to the everyday particularities of Greek life that have since become exotic: Socrates pays for something with a coin taken from his mouth, and the crowd applauds at various times by snapping its fingers. We also learn of the Greek respect for laws, their religious customs, the importance this civilization placed in democracy, how its rulers and judges were chosen, and so on. The city of Athens itself becomes a signifying entity in the same way Rome and Jerusalem do in other Rossellini films. The film opens, in fact, with the destruction of the walls of Athens, as the victorious Spartans look up in amazement at the acropolis, the jewel of the civilization they have just defeated. As usual, we are at an important turning point in Western civilization, a point of transition, and nobody knows what will happen next. The matte shots of the Parthenon and other Greek buildings are not very good (though they are more convincing on the small screen), but it seems clear this was not by design:

> *Socrates* was made with a processing system that we have developed. I did it in Spain with a Spanish cameraman, who was not at all used to those kinds of things, so the result is not very satisfactory, but I don't mind. I had a lot of the same kind of processing shots in *Louis XIV*, the building of Versailles and, in the beginning, the Louvre palace. But there I had a cameraman who was more capable than the other one.[7]

The inexperience of the Spanish cameraman also may have contributed to the more awkward use of the zoom in this film, as compared with the earlier *Louis XIV*. The lens movement is not always smoothly accomplished and sometimes starts and stops in a disconcerting manner, a far cry from the total fluidity that will be achieved in *Augustine of Hippo*. Yet it is also true that, in other places, the zoom is quite smooth indeed: when Socrates is being taunted by the satiric scene from Aristophanes, for example, the zoom-in on the philosopher is effectively intercut three or four times with shots of the comedian, while the zoom itself keeps moving.

Once again, the film is an *adaptation* of documents from the past—Plato's dialogues—rather than an attempt to portray history directly. Naturally, a good deal of liberty is taken in mixing material from different dialogues, and Guarner has made the obvious and correct point that this method is perfectly appropriate, given that Plato himself was not recording verbatim, but rather seeking to present a summarized view of Socrates' life and thought.[8] The period covered in the film is five years, from 404 B.C., when the Spartans tear down the walls of Athens, to 399 B.C., when Socrates drinks the fatal hemlock. Rossellini is careful, as usual, to put what we are about to see in its proper historical context, and thus the second shot is of the empty agora, held quite some time in order to permit us to situate ourselves. The camera finally picks up a man walking toward us and then begins following him through the streets, creating a bit of narrative suspense (where is he going?) and conveying documentary information at the same time. We are next treated to not one but *two* successive introductory banquet scenes in which the historical groundwork is rather cumbersomely laid while, at the same time, giving us a picture of upper-middle-class Greek life of the period. The minutiae of Athenian history quickly overwhelms the viewer, unfortunately, leading one to conclude that it might have been more useful to present the historical exposition throughout the course of the film, as it was needed.

The figure of Socrates himself emerges out of this context only after the exposition scenes, in the same delayed manner of Louis XIV, and in a thoroughly unheroic way: he is being beaten by a gang of Athenians who disapprove of his teachings. Again, as we have seen since the Garibaldi of *Viva l'Italia!*, Rossellini's portrait is of an ordinary man who also happens to be a genius, and who lived a banal, daily life like everyone else. In a typically quick and discreet bit of "humanizing," Rossellini has Socrates try to buy an octopus with too little money, and as the vendor is about to complain, Crito makes a sign behind the philosopher's back that he, Crito, will pay the rest later. Rossellini also makes an attempt at various points during the film to account for the fact that so many Athenians disliked Socrates—by including the satire from Aristophanes, for example—but in the context of the film's overwhelmingly positive view of the philosopher, we cannot help but see these objections as ill-humored and even laughable.

Furthermore, Rossellini is careful to foreground what might be called the "Christlike" elements of Socrates, both thematically and visually, for the philosopher and the crucified Jew are regarded as being engaged in the same quest for the truth. Hence, scenes of Socrates imbibing from a chalice with his disciples (who are called that throughout the film) are strongly reminiscent of Christian iconography, especially his drinking of the hemlock at the end, with its clear suggestion of sacrifice for others. (The iconography of Socrates' death scene is also a direct copy of Giotto's version of the death of Saint Francis of Assisi.) This Christological emphasis is strengthened by various remarks of Socrates concerning, for example, what it means to be a "good shepherd." It should be pointed out that this strategy did not originate with Rossellini, of course, and is visually suggested at least as early as David's painting *The Death of Socrates* (1787), which contains precisely twelve disciples.

The rest of the film follows the philosopher through several dialectical encounters with Athenians who scurry off when they realize he has gotten the logical better of them, the accusation by Miletus against him for having corrupted youth and substituted new gods (significantly, it is the latter charge that Rossellini focuses upon), the trial, and the final scene of his death, surrounded by his followers in a cave. It is with the trial and the long scene in the cave that Rossellini finally gives in to a palpable narrative drive as well as emotional interest, something that he consistently frustrates through the rest of the film. (When Socrates is first told that there is an accusation against him, for example, he goes to investigate, but just before he looks at the posted notice, he falls into a lengthy, abstract debate about the meaning of *pietà*.) The drama of emotions, at least until the very end of the film, is always subordinated to the drama of ideas.[9]

Socrates is, overall, uneven. Frankly, it is also boring in a way that most of the other historical films manage to avoid. First, there is the awkward, static attempt to convey too much historical information at one time. In *Acts of the Apostles*, the same expository technique is used, but it is, of course, information that, for the most part, we already know. More important, this is the first time that Rossellini attempts to convey the essence of a philosopher, an attempt that is unleavened, unlike in *Pascal* and *Augustine of Hippo*, with information of a more biographical nature. The problem of too much language is further exacerbated by the use of subtitles, so that, for a non-Italian-speaking audience, watching the film comes perilously close to reading a book; if there was ever a film for which dubbing was justified, it is this one. When Socrates is engaged in a dialogue, however, the language takes on a life and drama of its own, creating a bit of intellectual suspense as the audience waits to see how he will trap his interlocutor in the fine net of his logic.

Certain parts of the film are simply uninteresting, and so slow that one becomes aware that often the zoom is desperately trying to create a visual diversion, moving in and out for no good reason. One is never at ease with the flat, visually dead long takes of *Socrates* as one is with the pregnant long takes of the rest of Rossellini's career. (Significantly, this film contains many more close-ups than most of the other historical films, in an effort to provide visual variety and to emphasize what is being said.) Yet there are other "slow" moments in this film that function beautifully. The best example occurs near the end, when Socrates is walking back and forth to get the hemlock working in his legs. The scene seems to go on forever, yet it is so "human" (as opposed to a more conventional version, where the poison would work right away so as to avoid any possible dead time), that we are riveted. In fact, the entire last third of the film is laden with an enormous and moving sense of dignity, partly as a result of its slowness, that clearly redeems its earlier indirection and awkwardness. Though Trasatti and others cavil about whether the ending is too "emotional" compared with the other films (they excuse it by putting Rossellini in some mythical tug-of-war between spectacle and emotional distancing), it seems to serve no purpose to be more aesthetically "pure" than this very rigorous director himself felt it necessary to be.

Much more damaging is the lack of historical explanation where we do need it—for example, concerning the motivation of Socrates' accusers and the reason he had to die. This is, in fact, the principal weakness of the film. The trial and death of Socrates have always been clouded in mystery, of course, and if Rossellini had offered an analysis and an answer, they would have had to been based on little more than his own guesswork and intuition. Yet that is, in effect, what he does, though somewhat more covertly, for he attributes the philosopher's death solely to the fact that he "gave witness to the truth." Trasatti, a Catholic, agrees, because he also wants to see Socrates as a precursor of Christ, and he is impatient with the leftist critics who complain about the missing explanations. If they would only see the whole thing in a Christian light, everything would become obvious: "The motives behind Socrates' death, in Rossellini's vision, become extremely clear if the matter of the trial and the hemlock are looked at as a sort of 'Via Crucis.' "[10]

These leftist critics, of course, see things differently. Thus, Paolo Bertetto, writing in *Sipario,* complains that Rossellini erases all of Socrates' radicality and the confrontation of ideas by putting them in terms of a conflict between good and evil. The film thus becomes "a consoling gratification on the eternal battle between the supreme principles, according to the reading of a naturalistic narrative, fictionalized and preconstituted."[11] Baldelli, in the last two pages of his book on Rossellini, excoriates the film and sees in it everything that he dislikes about the director. For him, presenting the standard view of history like this can only serve the ideology of the state. Simply to offer Socrates as a model for today, out of his context of slavery and the disenfranchisement of women, aligns Rossellini with "the ruling conformity." What we learn from Socrates, the critic complains, is that parliamentary democracy is best, that the soul goes to heaven after death (the true liberation), and that one should not involve oneself in politics because it is too dirty. Socrates tells his followers to obey the law above all and serve the state with humility. Baldelli's basic question, a powerful one, concerns Socrates' refusal to claim knowledge:

> Knowing that you do not know, in order to further the autonomy of the individual: but knowing for what purpose, when you abstain from intervening on the most fundamental levels of existence? Certainly, it serves to discourage the presumption of possessing knowledge through heredity or dogma. But if knowledge, slowly gathered through great effort, does not augment the drive to change reality, it equals the inertia of wise contemplation which must proclaim that nothing *certain* exists if not the humility of tolerance. Which is exactly the reactionary ideology of a neutral science beyond the political fray, with the scientist or the philosopher who paternalistically lavishes truth and culture on his pupils.[12]

First shown at the Venice film festival in 1970, *Socrates* was awarded a prize out of competition. According to Trasatti, the film was not admitted into the normal competition because, at that point, producers and the major studios were very alarmed about the intrusion of RAI television into the making of films.[13] (Fellini's *The Clowns* and Bertolucci's *The Spider's Stratagem,* both financed by the television network, were also presented at the same festival.) The RAI was unable to capitalize on the favorable publicity the film had generated, however, for, inexplicably, it decided not to broadcast *Socrates* until the following year. Even worse, the two-hour film was split in half, completely destroying the logic of its internal rhythm; the first half was shown on Thursday, June 17, 1971, and the second on Sunday, June 20. As usual, it was put up against a very popular show and on the first night registered only 5 million viewers, while its competition garnered 16 million. On Sunday night the ratings rose to 7.5 million viewers. More importantly, however, and perhaps shocking to the RAI, the "index of enjoyment" was seventy for part one and seventy-five for part two, quite respectable figures.

33

Blaise Pascal
(1972)

During the early seventies Rossellini began to hit his stride. More active than at any time since the immediate postwar period, the excitement of his grand project of providing information manifested itself in a host of new ideas for films. It is unclear how serious he was about all of them, for, as he himself freely admitted more than once, he enjoyed researching new subjects more than actually making films out of them. From various sources—newspapers, interviews, and the like—the following astounding list of projects can be drawn up: the multipart series to document science[1] and another on the Industrial Revolution; a ten-part series to be entitled "Stories of Prejudice"; a film on the life of Saint Catherine of Siena; another on Catherine de' Medici (to star Anna Magnani!); a documentary on the research of some scientists at Rice University (where Rossellini began working after he left the Centro sperimentale di cinematografia), apparently in addition to the series on science; an epic project on the American Revolution, in time for the bicentennial celebration, to be coordinated and funded in part by the American Film Institute;[2] another epic on the Thirty Years' War; and biographies of Caligula, Pascal, Descartes, Alberti, Thomas More, Diderot, Daguerre, and Marco Polo. All of the above projects, however, with the exception of the biographies of Pascal, Descartes, and Alberti (the last of which became part of *The Age of the Medici* series) were to be abandoned, most of them in the planning stages.

Of the unfinished projects, perhaps *Caligula* had gone the farthest. In the early seventies Rossellini spoke expansively of it in several interviews, and in 1972 Baldelli published the entire script in his book on the director.[3] According to Rossellini the film on Caligula was meant to complement his previous studies of the Judeo-Christian and Greek traditions by attempting to "discover what was the Roman empire." Interestingly, Rossellini's interpretation of Caligula's famously bizarre behavior is somewhat bizarre itself, and departs more strongly from the available historical record than any of his other history films. The director considered Caligula a republican, like his father Germanicus; his vicious behavior was thus actually meant to provoke a reaction, by showing "in front of the eyes of the Romans that the empire was really a horrible thing. That is what he tried to achieve, but it didn't succeed."[4] Characteristically, again, Rossellini's other aim was to show the "real Rome" of fetid tenements: "In films you have seen something magnificent, everything in marble. There were only a few things like that, the rest was a fierce fight of very aggressive people."

The project that did get made into a film is one of the most memorable of the didactic period, the life of the seventeenth-century French philosophe, Blaise Pascal.[5] In this film Rossellini addresses what was perhaps the primary tension of his artistic life, that between reason and science on the one hand and spirituality on the other. Pascal—with whom Rossellini, once again, identifies very strongly—is a key figure in the attempt to resolve this classic dichotomy, for it is he who argues against Descartes' excessive reliance on rationalism, both because it fails to pay attention to the real data of the world and because it threatens to eliminate the divine mystery of the absolutely unknowable. The film effects the perfect Rossellinian synthesis by privileging human reason (especially vis-à-vis the superstition exemplified by Pascal's servant Jacques) while at the same time insisting upon its limits. As he told the RAI publicity service:

> Pascal is an opportunity to represent the question of the relation and conflict between science and religion. A problem which is not yet resolved or cleared. Pascal is at the beginning of the development of modern scientific thought, of the experimental method of mathematics. Pascal, who wears himself out in scientific research and Christian perfection practice, expresses better than anyone two essential aspects of his century: the scientific anxiety and religious piety.[6]

At the same time, the film attempts to synthesize science and art, another important theme during this period. For example, the director writes a short, vintage Rossellini speech for Blaise's father, Etienne, in which he explains to his daughter why she, the poet, should also appreciate the calculating machine Blaise has invented: "Poets love things which demand finesse and fantasy while the mathematicians reason rigorously: starting from a definition, deducing from principles, they then construct useful machines. What is necessary is to be both delicate and exact, together, if you want to be human."[7] (Another aspect of this theme is Pascal's portrayal as a latter-day version of Leonardo da Vinci, the quintessential "Renaissance man," when he invents a bus system for Paris.)

What is unique about this film is the important role played in it by Pascal's personality. The director had added slight humanizing touches to *Socrates* and *Acts of the Apostles,* but in neither is the main figure so delicately probed as in *Pascal.* This is perhaps why it seems more accessible to general audiences: on the one hand, the viewer is not overwhelmed with specific historical information unrelated to the principal figure, but more importantly, Pascal's "existential" strug-

The triumph of science: Pascal (Pierre Arditi) explains his experiments concerning the vacuum in *Blaise Pascal* (1972).

gle with the meaning of God and his own life, reminiscent of Karin's in *Stromboli,* are closer, perhaps, to our own anxious struggles. In spite of Rossellini's claim to the publicity service that "I only wanted to speak of Pascal, I only wanted to enunciate the facts, to tell them the way they happened, without fakery or emotional participation," there is simply a great deal more emotion in this film than in almost any other film of the period. This effect is enhanced by the unusually expressive electronic music that creates aurally the void of infinity that obsesses Pascal. At the end of the film, when Pascal is dying, it blends with an eerie, presumably godlike breathing heard on the sound track, as though the cosmos itself were pulling Pascal up from the earth. At the moment of his death, the music and breathing stop abruptly. The film ends abruptly at this point as well, like *Socrates,* for in this film about words and ideas, there is nothing more to say, or at least no further physical possibility of saying it.

Likewise, the struggle between science and religion is seen specifically in terms of Pascal's personality. As he becomes more and more successful mounting his scientific experiments, inventing the first calculating machine, proving the existence of the vacuum, and so on, we see his pride and selfishness increase, followed by religious doubts. It is no accident that his scientific reasoning has been brought to bear on the question of the vacuum (a debate that occupies a great deal of the film), for the question also has religious implications. Theologians had argued that the vacuum does not exist because it cannot be experienced, and God could not have created a "nothing." For Pascal, this kind of reasoning is merely indicative of the inadequacy of our minds in confronting the infinity that is God. Yet it is the very certainty of his reason that keeps him from God. His crisis comes to a head in the following exchange with his Jansenist sister Jacqueline near the end of the film:

> BLAISE: Listen: the vacuum is an image of infinity and if I search for the vacuum in nature, and I can demonstrate it, I will be able to discover what it corresponds to, by analogy, in the heart of man. When I have stripped bare the vacuum of my vanity, when my conscience is no longer taken by so many vain thoughts and desires, God, whom I have searched for through reason and whom, because of this, I do not know. . . . Can you know someone or love them, only through the reason? God, perhaps, will look lovingly on the place I will make for him inside of me, a place which will not have the size, finite and miserable, of my reason, but that of the infinity of the vacuum. Let God show himself! And I will know him.
>
> JACQUELINE: But there are other paths to know God. Wait for him silently and he will show himself to you. No, not like the educated, but like the most humble. Read the Gospels, and they will teach you all that you need to learn of Him.
>
> BLAISE: Yes, but nature contains the sign of God in itself! And I believe that love is not love, if it is not illuminated by the clarity of knowledge. And the only knowledge that man needs is to recognize that an infinity of things exist which surpass the reason. Reason is a very small thing when it is not aware of this (pp. 199–200).

Pascal seems, at this point at least, to be speaking for Rossellini, as though the director were retreating slightly from his claims regarding the all-powerful faculty of human reason. There will always be something greater; yet it is precisely this something greater that is reflected in the mind, as Alberti will argue in *The Age of the Medici,* and this is why we must continue to use and develop what God has given us. Earlier, Pascal makes a speech that clearly links him with Socrates and with the director's own oft-stated views:

> God remains beyond our reach, hidden from our mediocre capacities of reasoning. . . . Science has two extreme points, which touch each other. The first is pure natural ignorance. The other is that which the great spirits reach, who, once they realize how much man has to learn, realize they know nothing. Those who are in the middle, who have gone beyond natural ignorance, but who have not been able to reach the other—the wise man's ignorance—have only a smattering of science and pretend to be the learned ones. These are the people who create confusion and judge everything poorly (p. 196).

The film's form is that with which we have become familiar in the didactic films. The Pancinor zoom is used to excellent effect,[8] but this time a different sense of space and a much stronger feeling of depth are created as well. This is due mostly to an intense, dynamic chiaroscuro effect, as characters are continually seen emerging from deep, dark recesses, usually hallways, into the full light, a movement that visually echoes the thematic play between the ambiguous light of reason and the welcoming darkness of the unknowable. *Socrates* was bathed throughout in a strong, even light, appropriate to its philosophical certainty, but here, reason is doubted. Long passages of dialogue of scholastic disputation are included, and it is an open question as to just how much of this any audience can understand the first time through (or even the second). Nevertheless, Rossellini is, of course, right to insist that the audience must do its share of the work; even more convincing is his view that the point is not to explain everything definitively, once and for all, but to make the audience *curious*. He told Philip Strick: "If you try (as I do) to present something educational then talk is unavoidable. . . . We must get used to receiving a little more information. I'm aware of the danger of filming long sections of dialogue, but I am quite stubborn. I insist on them. . . . I want to arouse curiosity in the audience." He goes on to cite proudly the results of a RAI survey, which determined that, although fewer than one percent of all Italians had ever heard of Pascal prior to the broadcast of Rossellini's film, six months later a follow-up survey indicated that forty-five percent of the population had heard of him, and sales of books on him had increased dramatically during the same period.[9]

This insistence on the presentation of undiluted philosophical dialogue also, of course, works against the emotion, mentioned earlier, that is developed in other scenes. Furthermore, the emotion that is presented is watched rather than actively participated in. We see Pascal's feelings and sufferings, we even see them manfested in various aspects of the mise-en-scène, but, as in the Bergman-era films, we are not especially encouraged to identify with them ourselves. Thus, even in the scene that opens with a very conventional, uncharacteristic close-up on Pascal's bearded, ravaged face, we are almost immediately distanced from his suffering in an uncanny way that is difficult to describe. In the scene in the chapel, the camera circles Pascal while simultaneously zooming in on him to a very tight shot, coldly reenacting the emotional pressure he feels. (Conversely, in the only scene in which we see Pascal out in society, Rossellini never allows a close-up, or even a one-shot, and the camera remains remote, dryly focusing on the communal context.)

At many other moments in the film, Rossellini's technique characteristically overturns normal dramatic expectations. Thus, at the very beginning, attention is properly focused on Pascal's father, as Blaise is only seventeen years old. Like Louis XIV, Blaise must win his right to the screen, as it were, even if this frustrates our desire to see more of the famous protagonist. It is as though he must first become famous *through* the events of the film. Again, at the end of the witch trial, we rather expect Blaise to jump up and set everybody straight, because after all, he is a "genius." He does nothing of the sort. When he debates Descartes, the older philosopher does not say, "You're right! I'll completely change my philosophical views," as the conventional emotional logic of the scene might require. Instead, he more plausibly tells Pascal that his remarks were brilliant and that he will think about what the young philosopher has said.

Besides the increased interest, however distanced, in what might be called psychological realism, the other thing that is new is that Rossellini is attempting to reconstruct a life and an age without limiting himself to the adaptation of contemporary historical accounts. Naturally, much of Pascal's thought and dialogue comes from the *Pensées* and other lesser-known works, but the events of his life themselves, and their interpretation, are drawn from recent biographies rather than from documents contemporary with Pascal. Rossellini even goes so far as to invent a meeting between Pascal and Descartes that never took place (though they were in contact by letter).[10] In fact, this film is closer to the standard Hollywood "bio pic" than virtually anything else Rossellini was ever to do. Usually Rossellini chooses a decisive moment to analyze a specific turning point in history. In *Pascal,* however, we actually follow the whole of the subject's adult life, from the age of seventeen, when his father becomes the tax collector at Rouen, to 1662, when he dies at age thirty-nine. The film is thus overtly structured around Pascal's biography, and it clearly wants to understand this person just as much or more than this particular moment in the history of Western civilization. In fact, nearly everything significant in Pascal's life is included: his precocious successes at mathematical reasoning, his scientific experiments following upon the work of Torricelli in Italy, his movement out into society once his sister goes into the convent, and, especially, his conversion to Jansenism, the "fundamentalist" reformation of Catholicism, which gave fuel to his religious anguish and led him, despite papal censure and religious persecution, to do polemical battle with the Jesuits. Characteristically, though, the one episode from Pascal's life that Rossellini does not include is his close escape from death in a carriage accident that, according to legend, caused him to understand, for the first time on an emotional level, his own mortality. This episode obviously would have been highly cinematic, and it is difficult to imagine another director's film on Pascal not including it; for Rossellini, however, its spectacularity would have detracted from the film's emphasis on ideas.[11]

Despite the increased emphasis on biography, however, Rossellini also wants once again to give us a feeling for the age, especially through the everyday details of mundane living. Hence, one scene begins with the rising of Pierre Seguier, chancellor of France—reminiscent of the levee of Louis XIV—and we are treated to a host of homely details that seem completely unrelated to the principal thrust of the narrative. It is only a few minutes later, when Father Mersenne, Pascal's mentor, arrives with Pascal's new calculator, that we understand that the scene has a narrative purpose as well. Interestingly, though, whenever Rossellini does want to represent the "essence" of an era, it is always in terms of its intellectual configurations, which, in this film as in *Louis XIV,* means medical science. The inadequacies of seventeenth-century medical practice also serve as a foil for Pascal's insistence on the experimental method. One whole scene, for example, is devoted to the setting of his father's broken leg, including an explanation of the chewed herbs that are placed against the leg as cure. We also see how medical "testimony" is used in the witchcraft trial, as certain "points of insensitivity" on the woman's body are said to indicate clearly that she is in thrall to Satan. Another scene takes place in the apothecary's shop, as we watch him mix "newborn puppies and a half kilo of crushed worms" to make a paste for the younger Pascal's aching legs. At the end of the film, when Pascal is dying, Rossellini sets up a neat opposition between the old-style doctors who speak of humors and the like, and the new-style doctor, made fun of by the others, who actually bothers to take Pascal's pulse to determine his condition. The final joke is that both are wrong: the pulse taker pronounces Pascal fit and healthy moments before he dies.

Rossellini's luck with the RAI was somewhat better with *Pascal*. For one thing, the decision to split the film into two parts was less damaging than it had been for *Socrates* since, with some stretching, it is possible to think of the first half as "scientific" and the second half as "religious." More importantly, the broadcast had greater impact since the two episodes were shown on consecutive days, according to Trasatti, beginning Tuesday, May 16, 1972, at 9:00 P.M. on channel 1, against rather weak competition for a change.[12] The total number of spectators for the two nights was, in fact, the highest Rossellini was ever to have—16.1 million—though the "enjoyment index" was a rather low fifty-nine for the first episode, climbing to sixty-four for the second.

34

Augustine of Hippo
(1972)

Following work on *Pascal,* Rossellini traveled to South America in hopes of marketing his previous work for television. While in Chile, he filmed a discussion lasting some forty minutes between himself and Salvador Allende, then the freely elected Socialist president of Chile, soon to be overthrown in a CIA-backed military coup. The film was eventually shown on Italian television the evening of the coup, September 15, 1973, when it was too late for anything but grim irony.

The camera largely concentrates on President Allende, and the director's great admiration for him is obvious: Rossellini tells him immediately, "I have an immense sympathy for your ideals."[1] In the interview Allende traces his personal history, the history of his movement, and the goals of Chile's peaceful revolution, and Rossellini is clearly pleased by the fact that Allende seemed to be accomplishing his goals democratically, without repression. At one point Rossellini even summarizes: "You are trying to bring about a revolution fully respecting the laws of the land and those democratic rules that so many other revolutionary movements despise" (p. 16). Rossellini carefully draws from the Chilean president an in-depth analysis of Latin America's long-term economic problems, including a forthright, illuminating explanation that the real purpose of the Monroe Doctrine is to protect North American interests. Later he seems to align Allende with his own ongoing project: "You have been absolutely clear and have opened up horizons that are completely new to the present-day manner of thinking" (p. 17), and the accent throughout the interview is on the use of the media, on "educating public opinion." The film ends with Allende's very Rossellinian view of the future of humanity:

> [We] hope with all our hearts that the man of the 21st century will be a man
> with a different conception of the universe, with a just sense of values, a man
> who does not think and act basically in terms of money, a man who is fortu-
> nate enough to realize that there are wider dimensions to concentrate his in-
> telligence on, that intelligence that is his great creative strength. I have faith
> in man, but as a real human being with the accent on humanitarian quali-
> ties—a man who lives in a world where we are all brothers, not merely indi-
> viduals seeking to live by exploiting others (p. 19).

Seen today, in the context of Allende's murder a short time after the filming, the
interview is intensely moving.

Rossellini's next full-length film concerns the life of Saint Augustine, the fifth-
century theologian and one of the "fathers of the Church." Turning decisively
away from the personality probing of *Pascal,* Rossellini chooses to focus on the
last part of the saint's life (hence the title *Agostino d'Ippona* [*Augustine of
Hippo*]), characteristically omitting Augustine's early, licentious life so lovingly
detailed in the *Confessions.* One can scarcely imagine any other filmmaker voluntarily giving up such rich material to film what is, essentially, the life of a small-
town, premedieval bishop. Nor does Rossellini focus on Augustine's career as
theologian and philosopher. What seems to interest him much more is the collapse of the Roman empire and its effect on human consciousness. As usual, Rossellini places himself at a turning point in Western civilization, a moment that
might be situated roughly midway between classical Rome and the Middle Ages.
We learn the ways in which reality has come to be defined in terms of the empire; what confronts humankind in its stead is nothing but the black unknow-
ableness of the future. The very beginning of the film assails us with images of
ruins, barely a stone left upon a stone; bandits roam the land, and civilization,
as it has been known to this point, seems dead. The citizens of Rome, stunned,
seek to put the blame on the Christians, but Augustine offers decisive arguments
that the empire fell of its own internal corruption and makes clear that the only
hope for the future, in fact, lies with the Church. The sacrifices made by the
first Christians, as well as their strong sense of community, loom large in *Augustine of Hippo,* constituting a (retrospectively) "unified" tradition to live up to.
As we move further and further away from the direct and divine presence, however, toward the confusion of difference, truth is obscured and heresies spring up
like noxious weeds. Now we have only the written word to rely upon—a reliance
that had been denounced by Socrates—and the "guarantee" of living speech is
forever gone. Difference also inevitably threatens unity, and thus what is crucial
for Augustine (and, in a sense, for the director as well) is that the heretical Donatists he battles throughout the film "want to destroy the unity of the Church of
Christ."[2] The chief, unwitting irony of the film is that Augustine is finally able
to establish spiritual truth only by invoking the temporal authority of what remains of Roman law and government to suppress the Donatists.

If the film's sketchy portrait of the Donatist heretics is hardly appealing (considering that they mostly seem to enjoy beating up other Christians), Augustine's pagan opposition is more so, and we are made to sympathize with their
worry about the future. One of their principal objections to Christianity is its

focus on the spiritual and the otherworldly to the exclusion of the sensual and the here and now. In an efficient scene two pagans visit the studio of a "modern" artist. When they accuse the artist of "losing the sense of beauty" he replies that his sculptures "must not speak to the senses, but to the spirit." Volusiano, one of the pagans, replies that "the senses cannot be separated from the spirit. On the contrary, it is the senses which express the spirit. And in them lives beauty, strength . . . while your sculpture seems to belong to a world that is not ours" (p. 255). In a later scene Volusiano convincingly points out that the Christians "say that they love their neighbor, but then they teach that one should hate his beauty, his joy, his pleasure. There is no need for [the Christians]. Rome has always proven faithful to man and his virtues. Have we ever dared to say that the nature of man is spoiled, sick, and wounded, as if by a mysterious sin? The Christians teach this! It is right to persecute them, accusing them of misanthropy!" (p. 267).

Volusiano also points out that, while Rome always respected different religions, the intolerant Christians are forever fighting each other over obscure points of doctrine. In all of these remarks, Rossellini is obviously trying to make the best case for the other side, and in the process he gives the spectator the sense that at least there *was* another side, and that no advances are made without losses. Nevertheless, these few scenes constitute a small part of the film when compared with the overwhelming teleology and historic inevitability of the rest of it. In fact, Augustine, earlier in the film, has already answered Volusiano's objections by claiming that "Christians do not denounce the arts, letters, music . . . nor do they deny history. They say only that by means of it, man must always see better inside himself the light and the word of God which was made flesh and came among us" (p. 256).

Another theme that accords well with the concerns of *Acts of the Apostles* and, as we shall see, with *The Messiah*, Rossellini's last film, is the question of law. As in the earlier film, the uniqueness of Christianity is seen to lie in its different attitude toward this subject. So when Augustine is asked to preside over a civil case, he insists that justice is more important than mere legality. (The dramatic potential of this Solomon-like situation is abruptly deflated when it ends with one of the litigants deciding to go to the civil court after all—in effect, completely canceling the scene—because he does not agree with Augustine's verdict.) In another scene a Roman magistrate who is also a Christian wants to keep his private morality of turning the other cheek separate from his public and legal duty to be harsh. He wants to know, "How could the State survive if those who served it acted as Christians? If judges repaid the evil of thieves with good? If the generals gave the sackers of one Roman province another province?" Augustine convinces him that the law is "one" and that a Christian cannot make this kind of division: "The law of love does not make you weak, but strong, yet without wickedness and violence, and it would also make the State and the empire strong. . . . Morality is one, as God is one, as the conscience is one" (p. 273).

As usual, the film is also concerned with recreating the actuality of contemporary life: hence, we learn of various interesting customs of the early church, the relation of Church and State, and work and rituals of daily living.[3] Early in the film, for example, we cut to a giant pit in which fabric is being dyed, and the brilliant colors (of Christianity?) offer an overwhelming counterpoint to the bleak Roman ruins in the background. Again, the accent is on how things were done, even at the expense of the already minimal narrative and the characters who are kept in long shot, and who are thus seen only in relation to the pit. Technical strategies are also repeated and refined in this film, as, for example, when the camera appears to seek out the reluctant Augustine after Valerius, the Bishop of Hippo, names him as his successor. (It does seem too much, however, to identify the camera in this scene with destiny, as some critics have.) The thematic play between light and dark found in *Pascal* continues here as well, as when Augustine departs for his new diocese, and a long-take shot of a narrow, but brightly lit, street nicely focuses our attention. Augustine walks away from us and from his home and everything that is known, and once he has disappeared, a young boy runs the entire length of the alley, in the same direction, as if to further underline its vanishing point. Then the film cuts suddenly to a dark street from which Augustine emerges toward the unknown future that awaits him.

What is most striking in the film, however, is its overwhelming emphasis on the simple and the direct. The highly emotional music of *Pascal* is here greatly restrained, and because most of the film was shot in the Roman and Greek ruins of Pompeii, Paestum, and Herculaneum,[4] with their inherent understatement, the film achieves a new visual spareness as well. Furthermore, in his composition, color, and general mise-en-scène, Rossellini is once again, as in *Francesco,* consciously emulating the art of the period, which in this case, of course, consists of spare, abstract, highly stylized mosaics and frescoes. (Many scenes, in fact, are shot with these as background, making the kind of overt connections to visual art that will continue with the Renaissance tapestries and canvases of *The Age of the Medici,* Rossellini's next film.) The visual simplicity and directness correlate perfectly with Augustine's—and Rossellini's—insistence on truth and unity and the possibility of achieving them. The Catholic Trasatti, significantly, is overjoyed to report that this is "one of the least distanced" of the director's films and that in it "religious inspiration reaches its peak, and the thousand doubts typical of Rossellini's poetic world assume the contours of certainty."[5]

This new simplicity has its source, perhaps, in Rossellini's ever more dogged attempt to find an essential form to match his ongoing essentialist themes. Thus, following a screening of this film, he told the audience, "I have just discovered the great possibilities of the image. We all use it, but we don't know how to use it as an essential style that can attain everything."[6] In a talk at New York University in 1973, he elaborated this new idea of the "essential image":

All knowledge begins with the eyes, although the freshness of our earliest perceptions is soon clouded. Language and ideas are always preceded by our perceptual structuring of existence. My primary aim is to recapture the tremendous innocence of the original glance, the very first image that appeared to our eyes. I am always searching for what I call the "essential image." Such an image may be considered to be a truly materialist one, for it places itself beyond the reach of conceptual or verbal expectations. With the exception of Godard and a few others, this materialist type of cinema is an unexplored territory. Most films are made up of what I call "illustrations." The "essential

The "essential image," doubled: Saint Augustine (Dary Berkany) as bishop in *Augustine of Hippo* (1972).

> image" is totally opposed to the "illustration," which is an image that is determined by various conscious and unconscious preconceptions. Even at 66, I am still excited by the mystery of the "essential image."[7]

This new emphasis is immensely important, especially given Rossellini's lifelong denigration of the image and self-conscious composition. Furthermore, in view of the incredible preponderance of words in these historical films, these remarks (and many others like them) are clearly intended as a defensive maneuver to disarm critics of the films' "talkiness." Mostly, though, Rossellini seems to be indulging in the old neorealist dream—which he had earlier seemed to doubt—of an unmediated view onto the essence of reality, this time by means of an image that would come before language and therefore before difference. What he does not want to see is that *all* meaning is constituted differentially, not only the meaning associated with verbal language, and thus can only be understood in terms of what it is opposed to in a preexistent structure or system. And this includes perception as well: as soon as we begin to make out objects, we are applying our previous (unconscious) knowledge of perceptual and cultural codes—which are also languages—to create meaning. Rossellini's phrase "perceptual structuring" seems to grant this, but its idealist bias is clear when he equates it with "the tremendous innocence of the original glance." By definition, "the very first image that appeared to our eyes" would be incomprehensible if we had no context in which to place it, no way of understanding it in terms of an already existent system. (Thus Rossellini's invocation of Godard and his claim that the essential image is "a truly materialist one" are not to be taken seriously.) The familiar nostalgia Rossellini expresses for lost origins, for a pristine Wordsworthian moment of innocence before the "freshness of our earliest perceptions is . . . clouded" is not unlike Augustine's religious impulse toward a prelapsarian unity, a oneness, a fullness of being, which he locates in the Church.[8]

35

The Age of the Medici
(1972)

The year 1972 was the *annus mirabilis* of the last stage of Rossellini's career, for during this year he managed to complete *Pascal, Augustine of Hippo,* and the three-part series entitled *L'età di Cosimo de' Medici (The Age of the Medici).* This nearly four-and-one-half hour series, one of Rossellini's last major accomplishments, was originally conceived as two separate films on the fifteenth-century Florentine figures Cosimo de' Medici and Leon Battista Alberti. Putting the two biographical projects together proved to be a brilliant idea, for it is in fact this very joining—of politics and commerce with art and learning—that emerges as the principal theme of the series. The result is a superbly detailed examination of the rise of humanism in the context of quattrocento Florence.[1]

The overall arrangement of the series is kept simple, and early on, Rossellini sketches in the political conflicts that will structure the first two episodes. Rinaldo degli Albizi, the representative of the Florentine nobility, emerges as the Medicis' greatest enemy, and by the end of the first episode, he succeeds in having Cosimo exiled from Florence as a threat to the republic. The second episode concerns Cosimo's cunning manipulations, including bribery and threats, to return. From this point on, the political and economic context having been explained, the focus shifts toward Alberti and an examination of the philosophical and artistic underpinning of Renaissance humanism.

Rossellini again places himself strategically between two epochs, in this case the waning Middle Ages and the barely emerging Renaissance.[2] The latter period is equated with such other great moments of civilization as fifth-century Athens and the establishment of Christianity, and occupies a special place for the director as the source of the humanism that has underwritten the subsequent history of Western civilization. As he wrote in his book *Utopia, autopsia 10¹⁰:*

[Humanism is] the attempt to allow the human spirit to reach its full potential, in complete freedom of activity, beyond every constriction, putting the accent on the worth and dignity of man which express themselves in the capacity to understand, imagine, and invent. This attitude became concrete in the fifteenth century and reached back to the sources of the wisdom of classical antiquity, enriching them with study, meditation, and research. Its ideal was the *complete man*—or the most complete possible—capable of expressing the "known" and the "to be known" and also human "feeling." The Renaissance is the result of this rebirth of man, finally capable of thinking, experimenting, researching, and expressing himself.

These notions are little more than commonplaces, of course, but Rossellini goes on to make explicit the connection with the rest of his historical project, explaining how this humanism is related to science and the industrial revolution:

It is a period which is also the beginning of the development of "technique," understood in a new way, and which will become the foundation for that industrial revolution which will emerge three centuries later. But it is also the moment which creates so many new curiosities which will find their fulfillment with the development of the experimental method (Bacon, Galileo) and which will systematize the philosophical criteria used for the identification of the laws of Nature. This method leads to the Science of the nineteenth and twentieth centuries.[3]

The film opens with the funeral of Cosimo's father, Giovanni di Bicci de' Medici, with the attendant transference of money and power to the son. The point is made very quickly, in overheard conversations concerning the deceased, that it is possible to be rich and good at the same time (perhaps like being artistic and scientific?), though Rossellini leaves a final judgment on Giovanni di Bicci open, as we hear both positive and negative things said about him. On the surface, at least, this is Rossellini's technique throughout the series— to let us make up our own minds about things—but some naive critics have maintained that, in fact, Rossellini has no preestablished point to make and allows the viewer "total" freedom. This is nonsense, of course, for if we are allowed to make our own judgments in individual scenes, the overall course of events—like those surrounding the establishment of Christianity in *Acts of the Apostles*—flows past us as naturally as a river, as though the Renaissance and all that it brought with it were simply meant to be.

No sooner is the funeral scene over than we are launched on a grand survey of Florentine history, economics, politics, manufacturing, crafts, and art. As in *Acts of the Apostles,* we initially see everything through the eyes of a visiting foreigner, in this case a British merchant named Wadding. He is in town to buy goods, and the wonders of Florence are explained to him in loving detail. The city itself is emphasized as an entity from the beginning, even more strongly than are Jerusalem in *Acts* and Athens in *Socrates,* and we are treated early on to a matte shot of Florence from afar that underlines the city's status as another "character" in the film. This shot usually evokes laughter in the audience, but it is clearly not meant to be realistically convincing, as it is taken from a highly stylized, colored woodcut of the period. Again, Rossellini means to give us a visual summation of Florence as an *idea* rather than convince us that we are really there.

On their way to the city, Wadding and his guide encounter an old man who bewails the changes that have taken place, especially the increasing importance of the city over the country and the shift from a barter economy to one based on money: "Today all life has become money, money and usury. We are walking directly toward madness. It is the end of the world." Rossellini makes no attempt to account for this harangue in conventional dramatic terms, and it is clear that the old man is there simply for the sake of what he has to say. Structurally, he occupies the same place taken up later by the woman who argues with Alberti about the painter Masaccio's "blasphemy" of showing God in human terms and the man who denounces Pascal in the earlier film for slighting the ancients. Such commentary is meant to provide us a fresh sense of how various controversies looked to its participants, and may even foster the illusion of directorial neutrality. Given the subsequent course of Western history, however, we are finally unable to do anything but smile patronizingly on such "stupidities," and Rossellini knows it.

Information pours out to the English merchant. We hear of the tortuous rationalizations of the Florentines to allow usury (which at this time meant lending money with *any* demand of interest), even though it is expressly forbidden by Church law. When Wadding responds, "This clearly demonstrates that with a little subtlety and hypocrisy, one can elude the law," his Florentine guide merely laughs. (Throughout, Rossellini wisely allows mild aspersions to be cast on Florence—the Florentines often do it themselves—for he knows the city's exuberance and imagination will always redeem its sins.) We learn of different types of wool, the history of the plague years, and the Florentine guilds' ruthless protection of trade secrets. The sample of silk that Wadding has brought with him, in fact, turns out to be a fake; the guild meets, determines who the turncoat must be, and, with incredible economy, in the following scene we see the man killed and his house in Avignon set afire. Various papal intrigues are explained to us next, as well as the reasons for the war the Albizi have fomented against the neighboring city of Lucca. We are shown how coins are manufactured, how the government works, and how taxes are levied and collected; and we see Cosimo hiring professional troublemakers to win the people over to his side against the Albizi.

Perhaps the most significant moment of the early part of the series, which prepares the way for the last half's emphasis on humanism, comes when Wadding is taken to see Masaccio's luminous new frescoes in the Brancacci Chapel.[4] Wadding is amazed that so much money and effort are spent on such "beautiful, but useless" things, but this medieval man is even more overwhelmed by the naturalism of Masaccio's figures of Adam and Eve:

> I do not know what to say. I understand little of such things. Yet these works astonish me. I believe that such things do not exist in England. . . . So they allow these sensual images to appear in churches here? These things confuse me. True, these bodies are human, but they deny that which is spiritual in man. [There is a pause in the actor's delivery between each sentence.][5]

Rossellini wisely keeps Wadding's guide from replying, since the rest of the series constitutes the only proper response. The brilliance of the Renaissance, we come to understand, is precisely its synthesis of the pagan cult of beauty and the antisensual Christian values that were at odds in *Augustine of Hippo*. In the largest sense, what will be achieved is the reunification of the body and the soul.

This typical Rossellinian theme of unity is expressed in other guises as well. Thus, one of the major events of the film is the Florentine council during which the Church hierarchy seeks to unify the eastern and western churches, just as Augustine and the apostles struggled to put down heresy to preserve the early Church's unity. When Cosimo is applauded for facilitating this grand reconciliation, he is told: "We owe to you the unification of the Holy Roman church with the Greek Orthodox church. And also the unification of the inheritance of Athens and Rome" (p. 357). Everything of value in Western history thus has a stake in this question of unity, of oneness. Even the doctrinal agreement arrived at by the churchmen is that the Holy Spirit comes from the Father and the Son, "as from a single principle, and this truth of the faith must be believed and accepted by all Christians" (p. 358). The economic and social manifestation of this unity is found in the new ascendancy of Florence, which, as Alberti says a few moments later, "has become the center of Europe" (p. 359).

The desire for unity relates similarly to the other principal themes of the film. According with Rossellini's lifelong insistence on the necessity for the unity of the whole person, here the emphasis is on that remarkable Florentine blend of the ostensibly conflicting impulses of art, humanism, and commerce. Without actually analyzing it, Rossellini himself pointed to this conjunction in a 1975 interview: "The Medici are finally the grand joining of humanism and mercantilism, the great dream of the bourgeoisie which came to the surface with the economic organization which we know—banks, letters of credit, etc. These two things, which seem to have nothing to do with one another, manifested themselves at the same historical moment."[6] For Rossellini the rise of the bourgeoisie is seen as an almost unmitigated blessing, as it was in *L'età del ferro*, for it brings with it science and technology, with their "labor-saving" machines, as well as a new view of the place of human beings in the cosmos. Thus, it is no accident that Alberti is also portrayed, like Pascal, as a Leonardesque Renaissance man who is capable not only of art and architecture, but also of designing fortresses, weapons, the gadgets that spur his research into perspective, and, above all, the machinery that "works in place of the hands." We see this conjuncture most clearly when he shows off his new inventions to the infamous tyrant Sigismondo Malatesta (who was not only excommunicated, but in a unique ceremony actually "canonized to hell"). Alberti has been invited to Rimini to design what has since been known as the Tempio Malatestiana because of its reliance on classical models to solve contemporary architectural problems. This is not the end of his services, however, for he also invents a new cannon for Sigismondo, designs a fortress for him, explains how to defeat an enemy by using intelligence rather than force, and suggests how to lay out a city in such a way that internal dissent can be easily quelled. (Though after outlining the plans, he demurs: "However, this would be no ideal city—it is a tyrant's city, very different from that of a king or a republic" [p. 365]). It is difficult to locate Rossellini in all of this, but in spite of the film's overwhelmingly favorable portrait of Alberti, it is impossible to miss the connections here among religion, humanism, industry, war, and repression. Ambiguity reigns as well in an earlier sequence of the same scene: the machine-filled room that Alberti proudly shows off to Sigismondo is also noisy, crowded, and grim, as though unconsciously pointing toward the horrors—graphically depicted in *Europa '51*—that accompanied the wonders of the machine age which Alberti helped to inaugurate.

The theme of time is also relevant here, and in the second episode Brunelleschi shows Cosimo the clock he has invented, telling him, "I have always enjoyed experimenting with machines, and I think that a machine to measure time will be very useful in the future, don't you agree?" (p. 332). Very useful indeed, for it was precisely the measurement of time that permitted the organization of industrial labor, removed from the natural temporal rhythms of the seasons and the sun. Time is also an aspect of what is perhaps the film's most explicit linking of learning and commerce, in a scene in which Alberti convinces his brother that he is making a mistake by not charging interest on an installment contract with some foreign merchants. The merchants are outraged at first, but Alberti explains that time is a gift of God's like any other, and is therefore meant to be exploited by man. So, if they want to pay in installments, they will have to pay extra. Alberti then moves naturally to show them the latest of his magic perspective boxes (Brunelleschi has also shown a perspective box to Cosimo in the scene mentioned above); the box amazes them, and the whole comes together: "Our compliments and our respects to your great knowledge, as well as to your abilities as a merchant!" (p. 350).

The film continually celebrates the unique character of the Florentine mercantile community. As one character exclaims: "Florence is rich in florins and in generous men, and so there is work for all its artists. Its expanding business and commerce have elevated artisans of the simplest mechanical arts to the finer arts" (p. 354). And the grandest patron of all is Cosimo de' Medici, who emerges, in typical Rossellini fashion, as a fascinating and contradictory character. One of the film's great strengths, in fact, is that we are never quite sure how to take Cosimo. We are clearly meant to admire him, yet he is also shown as a man who will manipulate people and events to get his way, bribe officials, pay the debts of his friends to keep them loyal, hire troublemakers, and even try to get more deductions on his income tax than he knows he is rightfully due. He and his men scheme continually, and though they regard the arrival of the pope in Florence as properly moral and uplifting, they are gleeful that it will also be good for business.

One of the most powerfully ambiguous scenes in this regard is the one in which Cosimo goes to speak to the archbishop of Florence. We are aware throughout that Cosimo is committed above all to the law, but perhaps because it usually works in his favor. The specific conflict that surfaces in this scene is between morality, on the one hand, and civil law and duty, on the other, an issue that was also raised in *Augustine*. Cosimo insists that the law must be upheld (and, thus, those who exiled him must be executed) "because, as you know, cities cannot be governed with Our Fathers" (p. 355). The bishop replies that the most grievous injustices can be committed in the name of the law, and demands to know what Cosimo is planning to do with the prisoners his men have taken. Saying nothing, Cosimo throws himself abruptly at the feet of the archbishop, a gesture reminiscent of the moment in which Louis XIV insincerely begs his mother to forgive him for removing her from his council. The film then cuts instantly, in a tidy, wordless cause-and-effect equation, to a man being executed in a dark prison and then back to a tight shot on Cosimo's face that begins the next scene.

Throughout the film Rossellini is careful to sprinkle in negative views of Cosimo, but overall, the whole is orchestrated, even visually, to make us identify strongly with him and his cause—though, as in earlier Rossellini films, from a distance and not emotionally. One of the film's most powerful scenes comes when Cosimo returns to Florence from exile, and heroically insists on going into town alone and unarmed, where he is greeted by throngs of cheering citizens. He is continually associated with light, while the scenes of recruitment for his enemies' armies, for example, take place in dark basements. He is also explicitly shown to be a lover of the arts and learning, and when he spends a great deal of money to buy some rare books, he is overtly contrasted with the boorish German princes and merchants who have sold them merely to make a profit.

But if Rossellini is favorably disposed toward Cosimo, in spite of his faults, his true identification in this film—on a level with his sympathy for Socrates— is with Leon Battista Alberti, of whom he is nearly worshipful. Alberti first appears near the beginning of the second episode, and irregularly after that, almost in alternating scenes. (He does not really "take over" once and for all, splitting the film in two, as some critics have maintained.) Through him, we are introduced to all of the humanist topics of the day: the debate concerning the use of Latin rather than the vernacular (as might be expected, Alberti opts for the historically validated decision using the vernacular because of its greater accessibility), the competition between Brunelleschi and Ghiberti for the commission to build the cupola on top of the already-constructed dome of the Florence Cathedral, and so on. We visit Donatello's studio with him, where he marvels at the sculptor's bronze David, and wince when he is attacked for theorizing about architecture without being a practicing architect. We hear his theories about perspective, his plan for rescuing classical Rome from the ruins. We are made to understand the brilliance of his claim that much knowledge will come from the ancients, whose buildings and writings have lain untouched and buried for centuries. (For all his reverence for the ancients, however, by the end of the film Alberti is claiming, with Rossellini's support, that the men of Florence are their equals.) Overtly becoming the director's spokesman, he in fact implicitly criticizes the ancients by insisting again and again on the truth of Donatello's dictum that "it is necessary to study nature to understand what is true." When Alberti defends the human dimension of Masaccio's *Trinità* in the third episode, he is merely repeating what Rossellini has said many times in interviews:

But Christ came to us as a man. No doubt religious faith has its just value, but the artist must start from his own reality, a human reality. Masaccio rightly gave man his exact dimensions and he did well to give Christ so human a body. What is important to me in this painting is that art and knowledge are interwoven. There can be no fine art today unless it is as well fine science (pp. 346–47).

Similarly, the very opening scene of the third episode shows Alberti laboriously measuring a boy's head with calipers because he believes it is impossible to draw, paint, or sculpt without "assiduous study." Yet in spite of his insistence on looking at the world and on attending to its disparate empirical particulars, Alberti's purpose, like Rossellini's, is always to chart "essences." Thus, Alberti measures the boy's head to discover "the universal model of reality, one that exists in nature itself. The various parts which compose a body, all related by fixed proportions and symmetry. To discover the mathematical and geometric rules governing these relationships means to grasp the very essence of the archetype, the universal model on which nature builds" (p. 345). What is different in *The Age of the Medici* is that this thought of essences does not consistently or exclusively lead, as it does in other films, in a religious direction. In fact, Rossellini insists on the more conventional (and increasingly disputed) view of the Renaissance as human-centered, and God, whenever mentioned, seems little more than an afterthought. Even in Alberti's lengthy defense of Masaccio's work, God is barely spoken of except as a good subject for the painting.

Nevertheless, there are two seemingly important, if somewhat ambiguous, religious moments in the film that bear further examination. The first comes near the end of the second episode, and takes place in a church. The scene has not been prepared for, and a straight cut takes us to a medium shot of a priest preaching. His first words are: "Men of our time and our city are truly reputed to be the masters and creators of everything. They seek knowledge in the writings of pagans, and they forget that life and reason are fruits of the spirit which Christ our Lord has given us" (p. 334). The camera then pans the faithful, among whom are an expressionless Cosimo and Alberti, and in the same shot, a rather awkward panning and zooming movement closely details a medieval fresco that graphically illustrates the torments of the damned, while the preacher goes on at length about the beauty of the soul, salvation, and faith. Focused again on the preacher, the camera pulls back to split the screen exactly between him and a fresco of the Crucifixion, a subject that has not been mentioned thus far in the film. Though the preacher is in effect directly countering the spirit of everything else in the series, Rossellini sympathetically accompanies his words with the voices of a choir. There is no other comment, and we must puzzle out the apparent contradiction ourselves. Here Rossellini nicely succeeds, for once, in the attempt to present the material in a dialectical fashion, without prejudgment. (In fact, throughout the film—and it is more in evidence here than in any other film of the didactic period—several different characters, in a technique reminiscent of what Bakhtin called Dostoevsky's "dialogic imagination," offer widely divergent opinions in a given scene, and we are left to divine the "point" on our own.)

The other scene is more complicated. It takes place in the studio of the great

Alberti (Virginio Gazzolo, on the right) discusses the nature of the universe with the philosopher Cardinal Nicholas of Cusa (Ugo Cardea) and the mathematician Toscanelli (Bruno Catteneo) in *The Age of the Medici* (1972).

mathematician Toscanelli, immediately following Alberti's defense of Masaccio's *Trinità,* and includes Alberti, Toscanelli, and the noted scientist and philosopher Cardinal Nicholas of Cusa. We learn of Toscanelli's work with ancient Arabic mathematical texts, by means of which he has correctly calculated the circumference of the earth, made maps, and predicted the return of a comet. Nicholas, who confesses to being stupefied by these calculations, launches into a mystical speech, accompanied by emotionally heightened music on the sound track, in which all this apparent diversity of the world, once again, is unified:

> The universe is a pluralistic unity. It is difficult for us to understand, but, *though the universe is composed of a thousand parts, they are brought back to unity by God who lives in them.* And in this unity, opposites coincide. Heat and cold, light and shadow, high and low: we think of these as contradictions but they coexist in the universe and are rational, for in the universe, as in God, opposites are harmonious, at one and the same time containing the reason for their own being and for their opposites. Truth is in the one which is absolute, singular, and infinite. But human knowledge is relative, multiple, limited. It is only an approximation and every science is merely a conjecture. God and the universe are unknowable; the only remaining path is that of the unknowing sage [the theme of *Socrates* and *Pascal*]

and his constant organic study of conjecture. Only in God can one realize the summit of knowledge, for his infinite simplicity contains within itself the multiplicity of things [my emphasis]. (pp. 347–48).

The potentially dangerous deconstructive thought that opposites "at one and the same time" contain "the reason for their own being and for their opposites," a notion that seems to open an endless oscillation that could threaten the self-sufficiency of pure presence—in other words, the self-presence of entities or concepts that can come *first* and can stand alone—is here defused by anchoring it in a God who reconciles opposites and who is the source, center, and end point of the truth that is "one." The obvious plurality and difference of experience is thus nicely recuperated in a deity as the Derridean "transcendental signified," which can ground, or better, halt, the endless chain of signifiers and the difference and discontinuity that characterize the world. Nicholas' strategy is, in fact, not very different from the one undertaken by Bazin when he speaks of the "essence of reality."

This centering, unifying operation has its specifically visual side as well. In the very next scene Alberti is espousing his views of perspective and insists that painters will have to became geometricians if they are to paint properly. "Should human knowledge ever uncover all truth we would know that man and his world are at one predetermined harmony and rational plan." It is linear perspective, based on mathematics, that manifests this harmony, and again, the connection with commerce is not far behind. The art historian Samuel Edgerton, in his book *The Renaissance Re-Discovery of Linear Perspective,* suggests that in fifteenth-century Florence, mathematics had become the lingua franca that united businessmen, artists, humanists, and shopkeepers. It is to this fact that he attributes the ready acceptance of this new style of painting based on perspective. Men of commerce appreciated it because it rested "on tidy principles of mathematical order that they applied to their bank ledgers."[7] In the Middle Ages, of course, reality had been regarded as something chaotic and multiple (even if subsumed in the unity of God). With the birth of Renaissance perspective, however, reality began to be seen as though through a window—as something one looks *at* "objectively,"[8] rather than something one is *in* subjectively—in other words, a field available to the investigation of the single eye, and more or less stable and fixed. The film theorist Stephen Heath has examined the epistemological implications of this new system in some detail. He first quotes Pierre Francastel: "In the fifteenth century, the human societies of Western Europe organized, in the material and intellectual senses of the term, a space completely different from that of the preceding generations; with their technical superiority, they progressively imposed that space over the planet." Heath then continues:

> For five centuries men and women exist at ease in that space; the Quattrocento system provides a practical representation of the world which in time appears so natural as to offer its real representation, the immediate translation of reality itself. The conception of the Quattrocento system is that of a scenographic space, space set out as spectacle for the eye of the spectator. Eye and knowledge come together; subject, object, and the distance of the steady observation that allows the one to master the other; the scene with its strength of geometry and optics.

From here it is an easy step to the photographic camera, which also "fixes" the world, and then to the film camera, which presents "a world . . . conceived outside of process and practice, empirical scene of the confirmed and central master-spectator, serenely 'present' in tranquil rectilinearity."[9] It might also be added, in conjunction with Rossellini's vision of Western history, that this system of objectifying, of placing reality "out there," yet directly approachable through the conflation of eye/I and knowledge, leads inevitably as well to empirical science, technology, and the Industrial Revolution.

At times the link between filmmaking and Renaissance perspective theory is made even more explicit in the series as well, as, for example, when Alberti stands in directly for Rossellini not only by expressing his views, but by acting as a prototypical film director. Thus, when the merchants are amazed by Alberti's visual inventions, Alberti, like Rossellini a debunker, is quick to point out that there is nothing magical about them at all. He says that it is all just "a system of mirrors," nicely describing the visual aspect of Rossellini's historical reconstructions. When Alberti's friend replies, "It's almost a game!" Alberti becomes more serious, and the connection with Rossellini's own lifelong work is impossible to miss: "No, it is a means of discovering nature through images which measure our eyes' capacity to see and to be captured in illusion. To establish how best to guide one's hand when one would trace of nature, to capture its movements, its color" (pp. 350–51). The visual apparatus also allows both Alberti and the filmmaker to reach those continually sought essences through, or in spite of, the particularities of the image. In an insightful article on this film, Michael Silverman insists that both Alberti and Rossellini urge the viewer to forget the "materiality of the signifier," the materiality of what we are seeing and hearing:

> Rossellini and Alberti are both masters of the double image, but it is not a doubleness which promotes disharmony. The spiritual (whether it goes under the name of humanism or something else) is embodied corporeally and rigorously, even as it points elsewhere, to another center of power. For a director like Bresson the image is insufficient, it points to a breach; for Rossellini, inheritor of Alberti's teaching, the image is sufficient precisely because it legally denominates a spiritual system which sanctions the human eye even as it leads it toward a vanishing point.[10]

In some ways, though, Rossellini seems to be vaguely aware of the gap within this double image between signifier and signified, for the film's visual space is often played with. Thus, many of his scenes are composed in deep focus, where space is beautifully and complexly suggested, while others, usually when characters stand in front of a fresco or tapestry, are purposely and self-reflexively flattened.[11] Even the zoom is used ambiguously here, for while most critics think of it as a device that collapses space, in this film it often seems to have the feel of a dolly (mostly because characters and objects are arranged in circles, often with their backs toward the camera), and thus seems to be plunging through a real, three-dimensional field. The significance of this dynamic of illusionism and its unmasking remains unclear, however,[12] since the relation of the two-dimensional scenes to the three-dimensional does not seem to be determined thematically, but rather represents an unspecific problematizing of the question of space. Once again, as with the spectacularity of *La Prise de pouvoir par Louis XIV,* Rossellini seems to be pointing to a troublesome area without really bothering to explore it in depth.

As usual, Rossellini's treatment by the RAI was tantamount to an insult. The first episode was substituted for another program at the last minute and broadcast the day after Christmas in 1972, traditionally a time of little television viewing. In Sergio Trasatti's words:

> Here we were faced with Cosimo de' Medici, when we were expecting Mickey Mouse and Popeye. And what do we discover, in fact, but Popeye at the same time on the other channel. The first episode of *L'Età di Cosimo,* even if it was supposedly watched by ten million people, was drowned in an orgy of Max Linder sketches, cartoons, and acrobatic tricks from Billy Smart's circus. It would be interesting to have some statistics on the "enjoyment index" . . . but they are lacking. It is also strange that they are lacking for the next two episodes as well. For Popeye, however, the thermometer of enjoyment went all the way to 77, and the RAI was satisfied.[13]

36

Cartesius
(1974)

Rossellini's next film, variously known in Italy as *Cartesio* or *Cartesius*, depending on whether the Italian or Latin version of the name is used, concerns the seventeenth century French philosopher René Descartes. The film has never been released, nor, to my knowledge, ever shown, in the United States, and it is unlikely that it ever will. In making this two-and-one-half-hour film Rossellini seems to have wanted to determine, masochistically, just how far he could go, how much he could get away with, through the sheer force of his personality. Having somehow managed to convince the RAI to fund and air films on the unlikely figures of Socrates, Pascal, Saint Augustine, Leon Battista Alberti, and so on, he takes one more step, a film on the philosophy of Descartes. He joked to the American historian Peter Wood that he was planning it because someone had said that an interesting film could not be made on Descartes. His portrait of the philosopher is, as usual, distanced and intellectual, and his collaborators Luciano Scaffa and Marcella Mariani Rossellini understandably portray this refusal to accede to popular taste as a virtue:

> Rossellini was not even slightly tempted to give a psychological dimension to Descartes' "doubt." In several scenes, courageous for their toughness of style, he documents instead [Descartes'] genuinely methodological and coldly rational character, demonstrating once again his faith in the autonomous force of the intrinsic content of the information he wanted to convey to the public. . . . The film's rhythms, images, and its choice of texts minimize any gratuitous concession to spectacularity.[1]

Undoubtedly all true, but this time Rossellini may simply have gone too far. The film is so absolutely static and its drama so totally dominated by a welter of conflicting philosophical ideas impossible to comprehend on a first hearing, that watching it, frankly, is quite trying. It may have been for this reason that *Cartesius,* the last full-length television film that Rossellini was ever to make, was followed by a year of complete inactivity, the director's first since the mid-fifties.[2]

Nevertheless, the film is not without interest and its own delicate beauty. One of its strengths, for example, is its attempt to explain Descartes' philosophy in terms of the social, political, economic, and intellectual context of the time. The period seems to have had a special appeal to Rossellini, since it is virtually the same as that depicted in both *La Prise de pouvoir par Louis XIV* and *Pascal;* in addition, we know that one of his uncompleted projects was a film on the Thirty Years' War, also of this period. The attention to everyday detail of these earlier films is likewise repeated in *Cartesius.* For example, the scene in which Descartes is first awakened (he liked to sleep late and to work in bed) is strongly reminiscent of the apparent aimlessness of a similar scene in *Louis XIV;* at other times we see him ordering a trunk to be made or listening to his mistress and her friend discuss the price of tulip bulbs in otherwise purposeless scenes. A similar interest is shown in authentic scientific instruments (like the immense telescope that fascinates the philosopher) and in medical practices as an index of the scientific knowledge of the age, as, for example, when Descartes debates the new theories concerning the circulation of the blood, or when another character's doctor tells him that tea, the new import, is so good for the health that one should drink at least fifty cups a day. Nevertheless, Rossellini's typical emphasis on the everyday and the aleatory is less pronounced in *Cartesius,* as much more time and energy must necessarily be devoted to the explanation of Descartes' philosophy, no mean task.[3]

Descartes, as the founder of modern rationalism, is central to Rossellini's grand design of tracing Western intellectual history (and, as usual, the director assumes that intellectual history *is* history). The accent on Descartes coincides with the earlier focus on Pascal and Alberti: influenced profoundly by humanism's anthropocentricity, all three insisted upon observation of the real world and reliance upon human rational powers, rather than on blind acceptance of the wisdom of the ancients. More specifically, Descartes is crucial to an understanding of the origins of science and technology, Rossellini's principal project. As Barbara Ward Jackson and Rene Dubos have pointed out, Descartes' importance comes from the fact that his method allowed for "the reduction of fields of study to their ultimate components, the 'discrete objects' which make them up, irrespective of all the variables of changing situation and context."[4] This is, in effect, an operation analogous to the establishment of an "objective reality" through perspective, which was discussed in the previous chapter. Here, the multiplicity of reality, seen as field, is reduced to individuated *objects* that are unproblematically constituted, and thus open to scientific investigation as discrete entities "out there," by a single, unproblematic subject.

Yet there are differences as well. Alberti's utter confidence is somewhat attenuated in Descartes and Pascal, both of whom are troubled by religious doubts. However, while Pascal is tormented by an intensely personal religious anxiety that wastes his body and spirit, Descartes seems mostly bothered by the institu-

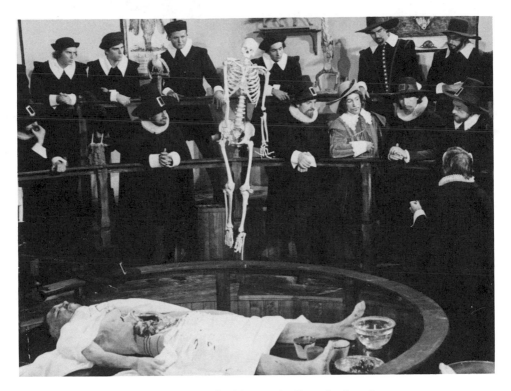

Descartes (Ugo Cardea) attends a medical lecture in *Cartesius* (1974).

tional forms of religion. In a telling scene, Descartes, after discovering that Galileo has been condemned for the heresy of relying on empirical evidence that the earth is not the center of the universe, prudently withdraws his own book, based on the same Copernican model, from the printer. More importantly, Descartes is not as committed to the empirical method as Pascal is because, as he points out several times, the information provided by the senses is often fallacious if it is not rigorously screened and controlled by reason. For Descartes, reason is exemplified principally in the exactness and clarity of mathematics, and for him the classic opposition throughout the film is between book learning (here meant as excessive loyalty to the teaching of the ancients) and the "evidence" provided by one's own ratiocination rather than by experiment.

As with the earlier films, the chief battle is represented as between the old and the new. One of the clearest moments of this confrontation comes when Descartes is being shown the marvels of a telescope by his friends Huygens and the astronomer Ciprus. Characteristically, Rossellini does not feel that it is necessary for his main character to occupy center stage at all times, and as this scene is Ciprus' show, he is the one whose lines carry the thematic weight:

CIPRUS: The telescope has revealed the movements of the heavens. As Bacon says, man is minister and interpreter of nature and he can understand it only by observing, through experience and intellect, its order. Man knows nothing more than this, nor can he.

HUYGENS: Nothing! Truly nothing!

CIPRUS: And it is ignorance of the causes which cuts us off from an understanding of the effects and which keeps us from acting on nature according to its own laws. . . . And thus which keeps us from subjecting it to our will. This too is an idea of Bacon's, because nature can only be defeated by obeying it. And when we do not know the causes, our explanations of natural phenomena come from our imagination, and God knows how fallacious that is! (p. 426)

The naysayer in this scene, like the nameless, functional characters we have seen in the other films, gives us a vivid sense of what the "new sciences" meant to those living at the time. What he is concerned about is the confusion that will be caused by discovering new planets in the universe.

This is all extremely imprudent! This is how people like you have ruined astrology and destroyed all its connections with medicine. They have added new heavenly bodies to the design of the sky without thinking of the consequences! They have broken the order of the zodiac, have overturned the known qualities of the fixed stars, the calculation of the months in the formation of the embryo, the influence and the ratios of the heavenly bodies in the course of the critical days, and other innumerable truths which depend on there being seven planets. (pp. 426–27)

Rossellini's principal emphasis, as might be expected, is on Descartes' search for a firm basis upon which to arrive at truth. The works of the ancients seem correct when studied within the walls of a library, the philosopher thinks, but less so when confronted with the multiplicity of existence. He goes off to join the Dutch army so that he will be exposed to the world: "I have decided," he tells a friend, "to reject every opinion, including my own, as if they were all false. And I have also decided that I will only accept, and only after examining them attentively with my reason, those opinions concerning which I have reached an absolute certainty" (p. 305). Watching the philosopher move restlessly from city to city and country to country throughout the film, we come to understand this movement as the physical counterpart of a ceaseless search for an intellectual place upon which to ground the working of his reason. Descartes finds his ground in the assumption of a stable, coherent self, a consciousness that is fully present to itself, that which thinks his thoughts. Nor does the film disappoint us in this regard, as we get to hear the philosopher say, "I think, therefore I am," plunging the Western world into the split between the subject and the object that has troubled philosophy ever since. What is especially ironic is that the real ground of Descartes' radical doubt, of course, is not in his consciousness at all, but in God, the transcendental signified who, the philosopher reasons, is too good to deceive our consciousness with false thoughts.

The personal element in this film is thoughtfully balanced. If it does not focus as intensely on the philosopher's life as did *Pascal*, clearly that is because Descartes' ideas were not as rooted in his own personality. Nevertheless, Rossellini does include most of the significant pieces of personal information known about the philosopher. For example, we see him explain his series of three dreams (another similarity to Pascal, who also had a vision) that show him the proper course his life and his work are to take. What is especially significant about these quasimystical scenes is the importance these rational men of science invest in occult signs. In fact, Descartes was apparently even more traditionally religious than Rossellini shows him to be, for immediately after his experience with the dreams, he made a long pilgrimage to Loreto, in Italy, an episode Rossellini omits.

Wisely, Rossellini chooses to humanize his portrait of Descartes, at least to an extent. Thus, we even hear the philosopher say something incorrect, in his debate over the circulation of the blood (he believes Harvey's theory, but insists that the heart works like a boiler rather than a pump). His domestic life, as well, is less than virtuous, and we detect a certain amount of selfishness in his dealings with his valet; when the servant dies, Descartes' principal concern is what he will do without him. The philosopher immediately takes up with his serving girl Helene, whom he makes pregnant. He wants to recognize the child, but never does so openly and, in fact, sends Helene off to have the baby so that he will not get into trouble. He rarely visits them, even after the birth of the child, and scene after scene shows him departing without them for some other place in pursuit of the life of the mind. What we do see of Helene, in fact, lightens the film considerably, for what is exemplified in her constant quoting of proverbs at the philosopher is an uneducated, but far more spirited and vital, version of the traditional scholarly orthodoxy with which Descartes must contend.

Near the end of the film we come to understand how important the child has become to Descartes. In a classic opposition, the child is beautiful to the philosopher because she is "a perfect machine of nature," whereas to Helene she is a "miracle," a formulation that Descartes explicitly rejects. When the child suddenly dies, at the very end, Descartes is immensely grieved: "Along with success, God has given me the greatest sorrows . . . Francine is dead, the light of my eyes, the reason I had come to live in this house with Helene. . . . I lived too short a time with Francine. . . . Science has kept me from living" (p. 448). Descartes ends the film by saying that from now on, "I will dwell only with myself, and live closed up inside myself, and perhaps, looking within, I will eventually, little by little, assuage the pain and confusion of these days." (At this point, Helene, ever the good domestic, having "understood his state of mind," as the stage directions tell us, "silently left the room, closing the door.") Interestingly, at the last minute Rossellini changed the final line of the original script from "I am certain of being a reality which thinks, and I know where this certainty comes from," to make it a question: "But where does this certainty come from?" (p. 448). This alteration is significant because it makes Descartes more Pascal-like (and more Rossellini-like): in spite of the immense development of human reason and its ever-increasing control of nature, something, some mystery, always lies beyond.

Cartesius was aired by the RAI on successive Wednesdays—February 20 and 27, 1974—opposite such films as Edward Dymytrk's *Warlock*, starring Richard Widmark, Henry Fonda, and Anthony Quinn. Trasatti rightly criticizes the RAI executives for their obsessive fear of "boring" the audience, since choosing to schedule popular fare like this against the Rossellini film virtually guaranteed that it would fail. In any case, the first episode of *Cartesius* was watched by 5.2 million spectators (against 17 million for a Diana Dors film), and 4.5 million watched the second (versus 18.8 million for *Warlock*). The "enjoyment index" for the two episodes of *Cartesius* was a respectable, if not overwhelming, sixty-four and sixty-one.

37

Anno Uno
(1974)

What Renzo Rossellini calls *un anno vuoto* (an empty year) followed the making of *Cartesius,* perhaps the most rigorous and methodologically uncompromising film of Rossellini's career. The reaction against it was so severe that the director lost even the tenuous connection he had maintained for ten years with the RAI-TV. According to his son, as soon as one film was finished, there had always been another one already in the preproduction phase. But not this time. Instead, he had to take what he could get: "The level of my father's prostitution coincided with financial need, and *Anno uno* came at the lowest point. After the films on Pascal and Descartes and the others, his reputation was at rock bottom; the public hated them, as well as the critics. At this point he was approached by the Christian Democrats, and he had to make this film out of economic necessity."[1]

The project was to make an "unbiased" film on the life of Alcide De Gasperi, the Christian Democrat politician who was the first prime minister of Italy following World War II, on the occasion of the twentieth anniversary of his death. Destined from the first for theatrical release, the film was produced by Rusconi Film, in the person of Edilio Rusconi, known for his right-wing views. According to *Variety,* the unknown Leandro Castellani was originally scheduled to direct the film, but Rusconi was finally persuaded by Amintore Fanfani, probably the most powerful man in the Christian Democrat party, to give the job to Rossellini.[2] What was especially annoying to leftists was that $1 million of the film's $1.3 million budget was guaranteed by the supposedly nonpartisan Italian state film distribution agency, Italnoleggio.

Many years earlier, in 1949, Rossellini had told an interviewer from the *New*

York Herald Tribune that, above all, he would not film the struggle going on between communism and democracy in his country: "There is a fight going on there between the two factions, it is true, but it is not dramatic." Strange words for Rossellini but, in any case, dramatic or not, financial exigency and the passage of time apparently convinced him of the wisdom of a return to this area of his former success (to which he had already unwillingly returned once before, in 1959–60, with *General della Rovere* and *Era notte a Roma*). The new film's working title was *Anni caldi* (Years of Tension—literally, The Hot Years), and the fact that it was changed to *Italia: Anno uno* (Italy: Year One)—subsequently shortened to *Anno uno*—indicates both a desire to give the project a more "constructive" tone and to allude to Rossellini's *Germany, Year Zero* of twenty-five years before, and thus retrospectively to take on the aura of the early films. *Variety* also reported that the film was to open with the final frames of *Paisan*, but, in spite of the fact that the film begins with the Resistance, this idea was dropped.

It should be mentioned at this point that Rossellini's vaunted "return to cinema," inaugurated by this film, was really no such thing at all. In fact, the director explicitly stated at the time, "My new film is exactly the same as the ones made for television,"[3] and the technique of *Anno uno* is virtually identical to that of the other history films. The long take employed in conjunction with the Pancinor zoom is the basic unit, as usual, and the editing remains unchanged, as does the method of conveying background information. Alcide De Gasperi is played in the usual severely understated fashion by Luigi Vannucchi who, in Philip Strick's apt formulation, "merges so self-effacingly with his environment as to become almost invisible in rooms occupied by more than two people."[4] Throughout, the color is characteristically rich and saturated, and Rossellini continues to organize his mise-en-scène around tables or semicircular groups of men, which establish an inner space through which the Pancinor zoom can move. (In one scene, located in a restaurant, the director overcomes the problem of cramped space by placing the group in front of a huge mirror, thus creating a similar sense of three-dimensionality.) In other scenes Rossellini uses his standard choreographic technique of walking groups, which provides exposition while simultaneously leading the camera to discover other groups on whom it lingers momentarily, before moving again. *Anno uno* also has the same editor, music composer, cinematographer, and screenwriters as Rossellini's previous film, *Cartesius*. Therefore, this film and the next, *The Messiah*, though not technically made for television, can be included under this rubric. It must also be said, however, that while technique remains unchanged, the intellectual ambitions of this film are much more modest than those of the earlier history films, and subtlety is not its strong suit. Early on, for example, there is a resonant image of Socialists and Christian Democrats driving around a statue of Garibaldi, the father of Italian unity—resulting in a subtle, almost subliminal, sense of wish fulfillment. The thematic effect of the shot is diminished, however, when the camera pans back toward the statue after the car has passed, and then zooms in. Passersby also make appropriate comments linking Italy's past and present, just in case anybody in the audience has missed the point.

Italian history of the period, unsurprisingly, is considered as being more or less synonymous with De Gasperi's aspirations and dreams for a united Italy; once again, Rossellini's concern for unity is paramount. The film opens with Resistance activities against the Nazis and Fascists in 1944, specifically the famous bombing in Rome's Via Rasella, which the Nazis answered by killing over three hundred Italians in the caves of the Fosse Ardeatine; this event epitomizes the horror of the German occupation, and has been alluded to in every Rossellini film set in that period. What follows are the immediate postwar manipulations of the various parties to tame the popular leader of the Resistance, Ferruccio Parri, and take political control themselves. Accompanying the depiction of these events are many external shots of Rome, which serve primarily as visual relief from the many unavoidably static internal scenes of discussion, but which also recall the importance of this particular city in Rossellini's career. The referendum of 1946, in which Italy passed from monarchy to republic, is followed by the decisive election of 1948, in which the Christian Democrats virtually take complete control of the government. Next comes the attempt on the life of the Communist leader Togliatti, which provokes vast protests all over Italy, but De Gasperi, through his alliances with minor parties (which has been the Christian Democrat strategy ever since), rides out this storm as well. In fact, we are made to feel quite sorry for the prime minister as he is booed by Communist crowds. Throughout, we see him working closely with the Americans, especially to keep the Communists out of government, but at the same we are led to understand that his own sympathies are principally liberal, even leftist. Thus, he works hard for European unity and shows great sympathy with the problems of the south.[5] His principal difficulties are shown to come from the right-wing of his party, which, in tandem with the Vatican, presses for an alliance with the neo-Fascists rather than allowing the Communists any power whatsoever. Perhaps his least sympathetic moment comes in 1953, when he attempts to push through Parliament what Italians called the *legge-truffa* (trick law), which would have given control of the government to the party with the greatest number of votes (even thirty percent, say), thus eliminating the need to form coalitions. His strategy fails, and a year later, the party shunts him aside in an emotional moment at their national convention in Naples. Quite uncharacteristically for Rossellini, the film turns rather sentimental at the end, as De Gasperi returns to his home town in the north, to die a few months later.

By this point in the director's life, despite the fact that his financial and critical failures far outweighed his successes, Rossellini's name carried immense prestige in Italy. He had been there at the beginning, after all, chronicling his country's rise from fascism and the destruction caused by the war. Thus, when the world premiere of *Anno uno* was held at the Teatro Fiamma in Rome on November 27, 1974, everybody who was anybody in Italian political life was present, causing editorialists to complain the following day about the stupidity of virtually the entire government gathering in one spot during this period of increasing terrorism. The president of the republic Leone came, as well as Prime Minister Mario Rumor and nearly all the heads of the various ministries. The leaders of all the major political parties were also crowded in together, including Fanfani of the Christian Democrats, Enrico Berlinguer of the Communists (who had to sit on the floor), and Giorgio La Malfa, the Republicans' chief.

No one came out of the screening happy, however, as Rossellini had once again managed to alienate everybody. Some of the negative reaction was of a piece with that occasioned by all of Rossellini's historical films: thus, the reviewer for *Variety* derided the "endless wordstream" that drowned out any visual interest the film might have, as well as the detached and expressionless acting (though he did admit that the original plan to star Gregory Peck in the lead role might have made things even worse). But the political reaction was even more severe. Giorgio La Malfa walked out during the intermission of the premiere, complaining of the film's "historical inaccuracies." Italian newspaper reviews, according to *Variety*, ranged from "bad to cruel," but the director's response was that *Open City* had also been panned when it was first shown, and ultimately the same success would come to *Anno uno*. (That success had not yet come five years later, for when I first saw the film in the summer of 1979, a violent shouting match erupted in the theater, with young people openly hissing De Gasperi's various pronouncements throughout the film.) No political party liked the portrait that Rossellini had painted, not even the Christian Democrats who had commissioned the film. Most upset, however, were the Communists, given the fact that the entire film is a chronicle of De Gasperi's success at installing the Christian Democrats in power and keeping the Communists definitively out (a situation that remains unchanged nearly forty years later). Rossellini was called a "servant of the regime," to which charge he responded angrily, "Only someone who delights in being servile could imagine somebody acting solely to make everybody happy."[6]

Rossellini's sister, one of the scriptwriters of the film, defends its anticommunism on the grounds that the Communists of the period were Stalinists, and had to be neutralized so as to prevent a totalitarian revolution. His son Renzo's interpretation is more complicated. According to him, if seen in its proper historical sequence (the director, in fact, insisted in his last years that his films should be seen in the chronological order of their *subjects*, not according to when they were made)—that is, after *Paisan* and before *Europa '51*—"this film would explain better than anything else why the little boy [of *Europa '51*] kills himself and why the mother ends up in the insane asylum. This film shows how the best hopes and aspirations for the postwar period were killed by the thousand manipulations of the politicians." Renzo even insists that, in spite of the fact that the film was virtually paid for by the Christian Democrats (who had placed a censor on the set whom Rossellini won over by letting him play with the equipment), it actually presents De Gasperi negatively. Or at least De Gasperi is seen using the hopes and support of the little people all over Italy as a form of currency in political exchange, taking his orders from Washington to put the Communists out of the majority, and so on. In *Stromboli* and other films, according to Renzo, we see the psychological and spiritual results of this kind of cynical manipulation. It is in this sense that, for Renzo Rossellini at least, *Anno uno* has "a tragic and emblematic value."[7]

This argument has its merits, but it cannot stand up to the experience of watching the film. For, throughout, De Gasperi is clearly seen in a quasiheroic light; rising above the petty politics in which lesser men are mired, he takes an only slightly less exalted place alongside Rossellini's other historical figures like

Socrates and Christ. Rossellini, as usual, insisted that he was merely presenting neutral, historical information without trying to interpret, telling Claude Beylie in 1975, "It's not a political film, it's a film about politics" (as if the two could be so neatly distinguished). He also gave a clear sign of his ongoing frustration: "Naturally, it was greeted in Italy with scorn. I was dragged in the mud once again. Since I refuse to serve the politics of the moment, there was a cabal against me."[8] To an Italian audience, he said:

This film on Italian life from 1944 to 1954 allows me to remain consistent with my principles and with that work of providing historical information that I began ten years ago on television. This film departs from the usual paths in which cinema has become fossilized. I was given the opportunity to make an educational work which would reduce the horizons of our ignorance. It seemed very useful to me to look carefully once again at what happened in those years when we were in the midst of complete ruin. We can still learn a lesson from it.[9]

Beyond the new urgency to relate the film's themes to the specific political situation of the mid-seventies, the words are calm, measured, almost Olympian: the reduction of the horizon of ignorance requires only close attention to the facts. We have already seen in the other historical films that such an "objective" presentation is always impossible. What is especially noteworthy about *Anno uno*, however, is that by taking on a more or less contemporary subject, the inconsistencies of Rossellini's historical method are plainly revealed. Though he is making the same kind of film, with the same assumptions, we are no longer dealing with historically sanctified figures like Socrates and Pascal, in whom viewers have little personal, emotional stake and about whom they have very little information before seeing the film. With De Gasperi, all this changes; not only does every Italian, depending on his or her political affiliation, have a version of what actually happened during the ten year period covered in the film, but many of its participants were still alive (and many of the men depicted in the film were sitting in the audience during its world premiere).

And the political battles over Rossellini, more or less dormant through the period of the historical films (once having objected fundamentally to Rossellini's method of studying history, what else was there for Marxist critics to say about each film as it appeared?), were reignited, first in the pages of the country's newspapers and then in somewhat more considered form in its film journals. Tullio Kezich, for example, an important leftist newspaper reviewer, called *Anno uno* a "pathetic attempt to contribute to the foundation of a Christian Democratic political culture."[10] The special problem for film journals, however, whether Catholic, modernist, or Communist, was that even within a journal opinions were mixed, and this much at least must be said for Rossellini's attempt to be neutral: there is barely a political position that one can take on this film that, looking at other evidence, cannot be easily reversed. Typical was the situation of the editors of the liberal Catholic journal *Rivista del cinematografo*, who, unable to decide what they thought of the film, ran two opposing articles, one strongly in favor, the other as much against. (Though these contrasting positions occurred in the context of a great and continuing admiration for Rossel-

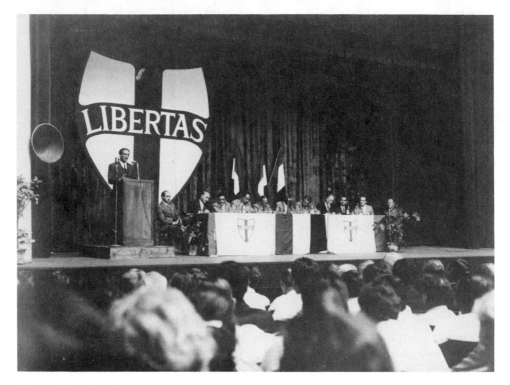

The problematic history of the present: Alcide De Gasperi (Luigi Vannucchi) speaks at a Christian Democrat party meeting in *Anno uno* (1974).

lini, whom the editors mention alongside De Gasperi as "two of the most important names in the last thirty years of Italian history.")[11] For the Communist *Cinema nuovo,* the film "unintentionally describes with crude realism the collapse of a myth, that is, the myth of Rossellini as eternal master and greatest author of neorealism." Furthermore, the film is seen as one more example of the current "fascination for fascism": "It celebrates the death of cinema and of conscience and of every progressive ideology." This critic also attacks the film for seeing history as the "product of the attitudes of political 'personalities.' "[12] He is right here, for while Rossellini clearly *wants* to make a film on De Gasperi's ideas, the figure himself cannot help but become valorized and even heroic in the process. After all, in a film that is more or less conventionally structured in narrative terms, ideas can be embodied only through personalities, and this embodiment can never be an innocent act. Thus, the American critic Tag Gallagher misses the point, I think, when he naively echoes Rossellini's view that this film should be considered a film on politics, rather than a political film: for him, Rossellini "holds up an idealized political theory and method as a *model* for his nation (and the world) today."[13] When "an idealized political theory" is put in the mouth of a specific politician, from a specific party, during a specific period, however, it always inevitably becomes something else.

Perhaps the most sophisticated attack on the film is the article by Sandro Zambetti published in *Cineforum*.[14] His initial complaint is that, since everything is seen from De Gasperi's perspective, much more information should have been provided to contextualize the events; newspaper headlines and small groups of politicians acting as De Gasperi's straight men are simply not enough. His principal criticism, however, is that Rossellini fails in his attempt to go beyond the standard methods of teaching history to the young, or the picture books published on important historical figures. As usual, Rossellini is presenting a specific point of view, in this case, "that of the De Gasperi centrism as democratic and secular choice, a firm rejection of fascism, but also a dignified resistance to any sort of religious collusion, a vigilant opposition to every attempt of the left to move the balance of power from the parliament to the streets, but also a noble opening to the social petitions of the country" (p. 22).

This is Rossellini's view of De Gasperi's politics, and it is also the historical view of itself that the Christian Democrat party has always fostered, even up to the present day—the middle road between the "two extremisms." Zambetti's telling critique is that this nonposition has served merely to fill a lack of any real Christian Democratic philosophy. The leading members of the party are right to insist that they are De Gasperi's heirs, since they have added nothing to his views; their continual urge to present themselves as the "party of the center" is meant to disguise what they have always been from the beginning, and continue to be: "the only right-wing politics possible in Italy, conservatism cloaked in moderation and with a touch of reformist cosmetics" (p. 23).

By making this film from their point of view, Zambetti continues, Rossellini is guilty of continuing to promote this image of the Christian Democrats:

> Next to the democratic De Gasperi, who refuses to exploit to its limits the absolute majority of the April 18 [, 1948,] election, preferring instead to rely on the collaboration with the other centrist parties, what is lacking is the De Gasperi of the "trick law." Or rather, he is there, but justified by the Jesuitical line of one of his party colleagues ("It's not a trick law: if the left would have won, they would have taken advantage of it too" as if the law had not been specifically written to exclude such a possibility). (p. 24)

We see the De Gasperi who wants to limit the power of the Vatican over the party, insisting on the party's laicism, but we do not see the De Gasperi who depended so heavily on the clergy's harangues from the pulpit to convince the people to give the Christian Democrats their overwhelming majority on April 18. We see the De Gasperi tortured by the problems of the south, but not the De Gasperi who does nothing about them. And so on.

According to Zambetti, the director resolves all of these problems by giving us a *good man*, over and over, a man weighed down by the incredible tasks that are continually thrust upon him. "At the center of the stage there is not a statesman and a politician, but a good man who, by chance, heads the government and guides a party." Rossellini shows the "suffering of power" that is part of the traditional baggage of the saintly figure:

> An anthology of virtues, in short, which we will not call into doubt, but of which it is necessary to say that it serves once more to displace the discourse

from the political level to the moral level, asking the spectator to become aware not so much of the political acts of the protagonist, but of the good intentions with which he has undertaken them and the principles which have inspired him, all the things which transform ten years of history which we should be concerned about into ten years of spiritual exercises. And which, above all, remove the politics of the Christian Democrats from debate, guaranteeing them in advance with the little flowers of De Gasperi. (p. 25)[15]

This time, then, history was simply too close. Its recalcitrant and disjunctive particulars had not yet been sufficiently forgotten or repressed, as they had been in all the other films of this period, to allow Rossellini to work his essentialist magic.

38

The Messiah
(1975)

Given his lifelong interest in the probably impossible task of uniting Marx and Jesus, politics and religion, it is fitting that Rossellini's last two major projects concerned biographies of Christ and Karl Marx. Only the first of these, *The Messiah,* was completed, however, and legal entanglements have kept it from general release for over a decade. This is unfortunate, for though *The Messiah* is not a flawless film, it is a great one. For one thing, since its subject is usually conceived of in apolitical terms, the inconsistencies of Rossellini's historical method are perhaps less bothersome than they are elsewhere.[1] Furthermore, the director's treatment of the all too familiar story is refreshingly astringent, and the typical strategies of dedramatized acting and antispectacular mise-en-scène here find their perfect subject. Rossellini's interest in the "essential image" also reaches its zenith, resulting in a new emphasis on visual beauty, and Mario Montuori's striking compositions and luminous color photography, coupled with the magnificent Tunisian locations, easily make this Rossellini's most beautifully photographed film.[2]

Different stories are told about how the film came to be made. In some of his interviews (which abound on this film), Rossellini gives the impression that he simply wanted to do a life of Christ and, not finding any backers, went ahead on his own. More likely is the story, reported in *Variety* and the *New York Daily News,* of one Father Peyton, an elderly Irish priest who had lived in the United States for many years. Well known for his evangelizing activities on radio and television in the late forties and early fifties, Father Peyton is the author of the famous slogan "The family that prays together stays together." According to the *Daily News* of October 14, 1975, Father Peyton wanted "not just another movie

on Christ, but one that would 'make people love Him,' " and for that he wanted
the best filmmaker he could find, "whatever the cost." He asked the advice of
"Hollywood Catholics like Mike Frankovich and Gene Kelly and made a special plea to his patroness, the Blessed Virgin. Within 48 hours, he was in the
home of Rossellini." (Another version has it that the Virgin appeared to Father
Peyton in his sleep and told him to get the "best filmmaker in the world: Roberto Rossellini.") The *Daily News* story continues: " 'I poured out my dream
to him,' Peyton recalls in his lilting Irish brogue. 'I said would you be interested? And indeed he was.' . . . It was Rossellini who suggested signing their
agreement while before Michelangelo's *Pieta* [*sic*] in St. Peter's Basilica."

Renzo, the director's son, however, has said it was Father Peyton who made
the suggestion about the signing, and they decided to humor him.

> Father Peyton read the terms of the contract out loud to the Virgin. All the
> Japanese tourists were wildly photographing this rather bizarre scene. Then
> Father Peyton got us all to kneel down—it was the first time for me in my
> adult life—and began praying the rosary. My father and I, terribly embar-
> rassed, mumbled our way through the responses, because we didn't know the
> correct ones. And thus the ten-page contract was signed in front of the
> Virgin.[3]

According to *Variety* (October 15, 1975), the $4.5 million budget, clearly the
biggest Rossellini ever had to work with in his entire life, was divided between
Family Theater, Father Peyton's group, and Orizzonte 2000, Rossellini's production company. Father Peyton retained the rights in North and South America
and wherever English is the principal language, but all other rights were ceded
to the director. The *Daily News* cheerfully reported that Father Peyton would
stick to the financial end of things, leaving the creative aspects "entirely to Rossellini." Peyton was predicting that the film would be "beautiful and heartrend-
ing," and, the article continued, "Rossellini has earned Peyton's undying respect, as an artist and a man: 'He's a friend of the Lord. He wants this to be the
crown of his life' " (p. 52).

Well, hardly undying, for once Father Peyton saw the completed film, the
clearly frivolous distinction between the "financial" and the "creative" disinte-
grated. It was judged to be poorly put together, too long, and too boring; apparently what was especially disappointing, despite the fact that Father Peyton had
told *Variety* that it was not to be a "religious film," was the lack of miracles and
the absence of God's voice at the appropriate moments. The De Rance Corporation of Milwaukee, Wisconsin, a Catholic distribution company associated with
Father Peyton, refused to allow the film to be shown anywhere in North or
South America. When critic Eric Sherman, on the selection board for the Los
Angeles-based Filmex festival, tried to screen Rossellini's version of the picture
in 1978, the De Rance Corporation got a restraining order, claiming that they
wanted to cut thirty minutes of the film, rearrange the scenes, and add a voice-
of-God narration. According to Sherman, they also persuaded Thomas McGowan,
one of the makers of *Born Free*, to sign an affidavit attesting that Rossellini's version would definitely be reviewed negatively and would therefore endanger

De Rance's $1.5 million investment in the film.[4] (McGowan told *Variety* [May 3, 1978] only that he had been hired to "perfect the English language version," the cost of which he estimated at another $100,000.) Suits and countersuits were filed, and the film, apart from scattered showings of the Rossellini family's print at college campuses and elsewhere, has yet to be released in the United States.

Many of the trademarks of Rossellini's historical period are in evidence, though the luxury of a larger budget results in a definite shift of technique. Among the typical emphases we find a desire to give us a "real-life" Christ, one who was familiar with work. (Rossellini even has him deliver one of his sermons while doing some carpentry.) In the interests of historical documentation, we are shown a perhaps overly graphic display of Jewish sacrificial slaughter. The handclapping game played by the little boys, which is actually Tunisian, feels authentic even if it is not. Similarly, we see fishermen casting nets, Mary making bread, and other constant emphases on the unspectacular events and activities of daily life. Much of this quotidian imagery derives almost directly from *Acts of the Apostles* (1969), as does the film's emphasis on community, and just as in that earlier film, the miraculous and the spectacular are indeed decidedly muted. For example, the scene of Christ walking on the water is omitted, as is the usually mandatory and highly emotional *via crucis,* Christ's carrying his cross to the site of his crucifixion on Golgotha. For Rossellini, including the latter scene would have been not only too dramatic, but also inessential when compared with Christ's words.

In an interview with the editors of *Filmcritica,* Rossellini elevated this antispectacular technique almost into a metaphysics, saying that he wanted

> a reconstruction of everyday life, of the most normal data, and then to set the event in this context. Everything then becomes extremely simple. . . . This data is the *reality* on which everything is based. All the parables, even though they have an abstract meaning, aren't really abstract in the least; they all refer to the small facts of everyday life, the facts that we have lost, that we no longer know.[5]

He goes on to link this concretization with the aesthetics of the zoom itself, which is able to "furnish a great quantity of contextual data." By means of what is perhaps a less than innocent subjectivist misreading of Marx, he even claims for the long take and zoom a special neutrality, beyond that of the regular shot, that it obviously cannot have:

> Marx once said a beautiful thing: "The concrete is the synthesis of many determinations." If you want to get to the concrete, you must present a quantity of determinations which everyone can synthesize according to his own personality, his own nature. The *plan-séquence* allows me to present all this data, without falling into the "privileged" point of view of the fixed shot (pp. 126–27).

Matching this typical dedramatized presentation of "facts" is Rossellini's portrayal of a Christ who is, unsurprisingly, a thinking Christ, a humanist Christ (Rossellini told one interviewer that he saw Christ as "the perfect man," rather than as God). Accordingly, the director accentuates Christ's loving, human side and pays little attention to the divine, especially as it might be revealed in miracles. A remark he made to the interviewer for *Écran* sums up his attitude perfectly: "Can you imagine, in order to think of Christ as a great man—or a great God, if you prefer—they had to add miracles! When actually the guy who said 'the Sabbath was made for man, and not man for the Sabbath' was making a political statement of fundamental importance."[6]

Rossellini's Christ is the logocentric Christ incarnate in the Word of the Gospels, and thus, again, the director does not attempt to "capture" the period itself, but rather to adapt the Gospels, the already clearly mediated contemporary report of that period. Rossellini, in fact, insisted on his fidelity to the Gospels, claiming to have "put Jesus' words in the foreground."[7] The viewer also comes to re-appreciate in this context Rossellini's inclusion of *temps mort:* when "nothing happens" on the screen, one is forced to attend, perhaps for the first time, to what the familiar words actually mean and what they might have meant within the social and religious context of the era. Rossellini's displacement of some of Christ's words to the apostles and disciples who surround him is further evidence that, as Claudio Sorgi has pointed out in an excellent essay, "the true protagonist of the entire film is the Word of Jesus, as the penetrating, clear, incontestable realization of the ancient word. A word that is received by the disciples, taken up, and amplified."[8] It should also be pointed out that Rossellini's insistence on the actual "real" words of the Bible whenever possible paradoxically almost *guarantees* the artificiality and stiffness—the lack of "realism"—that many have complained about in this film. The words of the Bible are written words, after all, and will never sound like actual speech. The result of this strict adherence to biblical language is a further self-reflexive distancing that accords well with the film's general strategy of dedramatization.

What also interests Rossellini about the Word is its relation to law, just as we saw in *Acts of the Apostles*. In fact, Christ sees his principal role, as did the apostles in the earlier film, as providing a reinterpretation of the law. Similarly, we are encouraged to understand Christ in terms of Jewish customs, and in one scene, Mary carefully rehearses these traditions for the child Jesus. The director especially stresses the tradition of messianism (as is evident in the film's title), exploring its sources by opening the film in 1050 B.C., far earlier than most conventional depictions. With the larger budget, the magnificent zoom now moves through an entire desert, onto a small nomadic tribe, situating it in its geographical and historical context (a thematically important shot whose effect would have been greatly decreased on a television screen; in spite of what Rossellini says in interviews, in other words, the increased financial backing is making the director think more "cinematically"). The dialogue that ensues explains the roots of messianism, the longing of a people for the "king who will bring justice." Throughout the film we are given much more information about Jewish history than is usual, and we come to share the Jews' burning desire to be free from Roman domination and their fear of being destroyed as a race. Though some have suggested that *The Messiah,* like *Acts of the Apostles,* is anti-Semitic in tone (which is, strictly speaking, unavoidable if one faithfully follows the New Testament), this is, in fact, the first film on the life of Jesus to treat seriously and in any real depth the Jewish tradition from which Christ sprang. Throughout, the Jews' motives are always seen as historically complex, and their rejection of Christ, at least from their point of view, completely justifiable.

Christ's life, furthermore, is placed firmly within this context. In the depiction of his early years, for example, he and his family are seen almost exclusively as members of a community; he is little more than another boy among many. Rossellini's penchant for radical understatement works perfectly in this regard, revitalizing tired views of overfamiliar events by purposely making them mundane. The Nativity happens in seconds, nearly in the dark, in an out-of-the-way corner. Like Louis XIV and Pascal, Christ must struggle to win his right to the center of the screen; even after screen has been conquered, however, the Beatitudes are delivered as quickly and in as unemphasized a fashion as Lincoln's Gettysburg Address. At the end, Auden's poem "Musée des Beaux-Arts" comes to mind, as the children continue to play and sing songs while a man named Jesus Christ, completely unnoticed by all but his family and friends, dies on the cross.

Similarly, the crowd scenes are decidedly un-deMillean, and no miracles are directly portrayed, though some are presented to us by ellipsis (for example, the enormous catch of fish and the later multiplication of the loaves and the fishes) and we hear of others. Thus Rossellini is not purposely *negating* a divine side of Christ (presumably verified by such miracles), as some Catholics critics have alleged, but is simply attempting to despectacularize his life. To viewers not accustomed to Rossellini's severely understated style, this minimalism can be disappointing. Nevertheless, the brilliance of the director's choices comes to be appreciated on subsequent viewings of the film. For one thing, Rossellini assumes and even plays against what the spectator already knows (and thus the dynamic here is much different than in the other historical films); the effect is not unlike some recent productions of Shakespeare's best-known plays. Familiar scenes like the Nativity and the Crucifixion actually become notations, almost signs of the idea of the events rather than a realistic representation of the events themselves. Yet their very minimalism makes them somehow even more resonant and iconographically powerful. The Sermon on the Mount is so utterly denuded that it even comes dangerously close to becoming a visual joke: Christ steps up on a minuscule hillock, hardly more than a bump, and delivers the Beatitudes in about thirty seconds. Yet it works. Similarly, the scene at the manger is desolate, and thus feels right, and the entire scene of the Last Supper is filmed in complete silence—no words and no music—and is perhaps the most powerful version of that event ever filmed. This minimalist mise-en-scène also becomes starkly symbolic at times, as when Christ, like Socrates, is associated with the blinding light of the exteriors, and the Pharisees who seek his downfall, with the darkness of the inside.

Rossellini's technique, as mentioned earlier, is also modified in this film due to the amelioration of the usual financial difficulties. Hence, *The Messiah* includes many more cuts, which increase postproduction costs; obviously thinking of Rossellini's use of the zoom in a solely aesthetic way can be misleading. As Renzo Rossellini insisted quite strongly to me, the zoom and the long take were used in the earlier historical films because they were infinitely faster and therefore infinitely cheaper. (In addition to the savings brought about by the long take in the editing process, lighting and camera setups had to be done only once for each scene, and thus a much smaller crew was required.) Of course, this does not mean that the zoom does not have any aesthetic effects, only that its use was often dictated by the most banal considerations.

The increased cutting and the greatly enlarged number of scenes (some eighty or ninety) also make *The Messiah* move much faster and thus seem less ponderous than some of the other history films, especially in terms of the long speeches. (Yet now a new problem arises, for the quick cuts sometimes sententiously underline what Christ says as unsubtly as if his words were accompanied by great blasts of Hollywood-style music.) Camera movement increases as well, and we are treated to many circular turns reminiscent of films like *Germany, Year Zero* and *Fear*. Now, however, the tight, claustrophobic circles of those earlier films expand to the wider circles of the apostles and Christ, which visually replicate their communal togetherness, and to the even larger circles that suggest the historical unity of an entire race. As in *Vanina Vanini*, Rossellini's lyrical camera movements in this film become positively Ophülsian.

The zoom, however, is by no means forgotten, and in fact is the principal means by which the film is organized spatially. Yet in this film—especially in extreme long shots, as in the shot at the very beginning of the film, mentioned earlier—the zoom now seems to flatten out perspective, to insist more strongly than ever on the two-dimensionality of the screen image. Most theorists consider this to be the usual effect of the zoom, but, as we have seen, Rossellini often counters this tendency by arranging groups and objects in semicircles that the zoom then penetrates optically, at least, to give an impression of depth and three-dimensionality. Here, however, because the vast majority of the shots are exteriors, and in enormous spaces, this effect of spatial penetration is lacking. The result of this flattening is to insist, in a stronger way than ever before, on the painterliness of Rossellini's compositions, and to suggest self-reflexively, once again, the sources of his iconography and even his choice of events to dramatize, since the visual traditions of Western art had long isolated certain "photogenic" events for treatment. A scene like Christ driving the money changers from the temple, for example, seems clearly based on late Renaissance prototypes, specifically Titian and Tintoretto.[9]

The most stunning iconographic aspect of the film, and one that has surely struck every viewer the film has ever had, is the depiction of Mary, *throughout* the film, as a very young woman, even an adolescent. Played by Mita Ungaro, a Roman woman who at the time of the filming was only seventeen years old, the youthful Mary blends quite easily into the narrative in the beginning of the film. By the time of Christ's death at age thirty-three, however, her youthfulness does not realistically work at all and is, in fact, quite jarring. At one point Rossellini overtly emphasizes the enigma he has created and provides its solution at the same time. This comes during what is perhaps the most visually powerful moment of the whole film: Christ has been taken down from the cross and laid on the lap of his mother, and together they form a superbly beautiful Pietà, a direct quotation of Michelangelo's famous work. The suffering, if exquisitely beautiful, Mary has the enormously long body of Christ draped across her, in a raw and courageously lengthy shot that comes close to being blatantly sexual. (Claudio Sorgi speaks of Michelangelo's marble having become flesh in Rossel-

Rossellini's *Pietà* in *The Messiah* (1975). (Pier Maria Rossi and Mita Ungaro.)

lini's film, and this effect is heightened by the slow zoom through or past this "icon" onto the watching men behind, perhaps the strongest effect of depth in the film.) The iconography also points to the source of Mary's youthful looks, for Michelangelo chose to make Mary as young as or younger than her son in his magnificent sculpture, and Rossellini is following the sculptor's icongraphic choice to the letter.[10] Another possible source for Rossellini's choice—and apparently Michelangelo's—is Dante, who in canto 33 of his *Paradiso* refers to Mary as *"Vergine madre, figlia del tuo figlio"* (Virgin mother, daughter of your son).[11]

The effect of Mary's youthfulness, in any case, is to disturb the surface realism of the film text and, like the minimalist mise-en-scène and the biblical language, to foreground its artificiality. The French critic Jacques Grant has even argued that Mary's youthfulness is a self-conscious Hollywood image, which Rossellini uses as "a moving counterpoint, upsetting and malicious, to the essence that he is looking for in the events,"[12] but this seems an idiosyncratic view. On the contrary, Mary is clearly at the heart of *The Messiah* and, as Mireille Latil Le Dantec has pointed out, all its feeling resides in her, for her physical and emotional trajectory is what organizes and leads us, by means of the camera that follows her, through the film.[13] She even seems to stand in for Christ during the missing *via crucis:* hearing of her son's being taken to Golgotha, she rushes off to be with him, falling twice in the process. One would be hard pressed to say if this was intentional or not on the director's part, but he did not reshoot the scene because of "mistakes."

One item that remains to be discussed is just how religious this film is. Many Catholic writers have claimed Rossellini for their own throughout his career, but in spite of his often overt religiosity, he has almost perversely refused to join their cause. The following exchange elicited by Jacques Grant at the end of 1975 is instructive in this regard:

> Q: So you began *The Messiah* at a historic moment of rupture, of confrontation?
> A: It's Jesus, the history of Jesus, that's all. I made *The Messiah* with a great deal of respect for everyone. What is great in Jesus's message is his faith in man. That is what is irreplaceable, even though I am a complete atheist.
> Q: People usually think just the opposite.
> A: Everyone is permitted to fool himself however he wants. If someone just wants to place me, he can always say that I am a Christian without knowing it. But one can also perhaps place oneself, and ask why one is interpreting incorrectly.[14]

In another interview Rossellini says, "I'm not religious at all. I'm the product of a society that is religious among other things, and I deal with religion as a reality."[15] But if Rossellini is uninterested in Christ as God, he is very taken, indeed, with his life and teachings. Thus, he says elsewhere of *The Messiah*, "I always thought that this would have to be the point of arrival. In my maniacal search for an abcedarium of wisdom I had to put down so many letters to reach, sooner or later, the highest point, the compendium of everything."[16]

This kind of sentiment was unfortunately not enough to endear the film to most religious people, however, who have generally not liked it because it is not "religious" (that is, dramatic and emotional) enough. On the other hand, political critics have opposed it because, as Lino Miccichè has somewhat unfairly insisted, it dehistoricizes Christ's message and thus "loses sight of its subversive value."[17] Once again, Rossellini occupies an awkward and hopeless position between two camps: in fact, he was unable to find a distributor for the film at first, even in Italy, and he complained bitterly about this fact in an article entitled "E reazionario parlare di Gesù?" (Is It Reactionary to Speak of Jesus?) published in the Communist-leaning daily *Paese Sera* on May 8, 1976. In the article he attacked the revolutionary Left, the conventional film industry, and those who wanted to be "cultural" but had old-fashioned ideas of what that meant: for him, this unlikely combination had insured the film's failure. Ultimately, Rossellini did find a distributor, but *The Messiah* has been seen by only a few, even on the Continent. It is to be hoped that this superb film, in many ways the climax of Rossellini's career, will be released in the English-speaking world one day—in the state in which he left it—by those whose religious vision seems so impoverished when compared with that of this self-styled atheist.

39

Final Projects
(1975–77)

The Messiah was to be Rossellini's last full-length film. He had for several years been planning a biography of Karl Marx, and at the time of his death, the finished screenplay was lying on his desk. Entitled *Lavorare per l'umanità* (Working for Humanity), the film was to have covered Marx's earliest adult years, from 1835 (when he was seventeen years old and about to go off to the University of Bonn) to the grand revolutionary year of 1848. What strikes one above all in this venture is the delightful bravado of a seventy-year-old director deliberately challenging his leftist detractors of nearly three decades. Not only does he take on *their* subject, but he goes further and insists that they had got it all wrong, and that present-day orthodox Marxism has nothing whatever to do with the real Karl Marx.

Not surprisingly, Rossellini's Marx is fashioned in his own image. In his introduction to the screenplay, which was published posthumously in a special issue of *Filmcritica*, the director, objecting to those who interpret the word *revolution* solely in terms of violence, stresses instead Marx's view that "the revolutionary struggle presupposes a self-aware proletariat which becomes a class with its own thought, its own group of intellectuals, its own 'values,' and its own 'cultural models' in order to oppose them to those of the bourgeoisie."[1] Rossellini also implicitly validates his own didactic project by quoting Marx's opinion that "ignorance has never been useful to anyone" (p. 364), as well as Marx's repudiation of Willich in 1850: "While we are saying to the workers: you must go through fifteen, twenty, fifty years of civil and international war not only to change the situation *but also to change yourselves and to make yourselves suitable for political power,* you are telling them: we must immediately achieve power, otherwise

349

we can go back to sleep" (p. 364; Rossellini's emphasis). Rossellini goes on to point out, correctly, that Marx was never simply "against" capitalism, seeing it rather as a necessary step in humankind's battle to overcome the forces of nature, and thus he was not "against" Rossellini's beloved Industrial Revolution, but merely aware of its negative aspects. He also told an interviewer for *Cinéaste*, in terms which will sound familiar by now, that Marx was "a very severe critic of all religious structures that served powers in government, but he considered atheism as another religion, as a prejudice. He was against any kind of prejudice, any kind of dogma. He said the important thing for man is exploration, and knowledge without dogma. That is why he was against atheism."[2]

Though he does not explicitly say so, in Rossellini's scheme of things, dialectical materialism unsurprisingly turns out to have a great deal in common with the thought of Socrates, Christ, Pascal, Alberti, Descartes, and the others, and the German political philosopher is quickly enlisted in the director's familiar exaltation of reason and "pure" knowledge. Marx and Christ are specifically joined, finally, by making Marx, like Socrates, another Christ, for all seek the same "essential truth." Despite Rossellini's obvious desire to appropriate Marx for his grand essentializing project, however, it is clear from dialogue included in his own screenplay that Marx's view of human essence was much more dynamic than his own. According to Marx:

> That "human nature" is the "complex of social relationships" is the most satisfying answer, because it includes the idea of becoming: man becomes, changes himself continuously with the changes in social relationships. . . . Is my thought clear to you? Human nature is not a "unity" given at the beginning. It is a "unity" possible at the end, it constitutes itself, do you understand? It constitutes itself in history, in the "practice" of man, in his combined practical and theoretical activity of changing the world (p. 412).

Rossellini's introduction to the script was accompanied by an article entitled "L'abbecedario di Rossellini," written by Silvia D'Amico Bendicò, Rossellini's friend and collaborator during his last years. In it she traces the difficulty she and the director had choosing a particular period of Marx's long and eventful life upon which to focus. She reports that first Rossellini had opted for the period of the Paris commune (1871), an unsatisfying choice for various reasons, and then, in March of 1975: "the obvious solution: Marx and Engels from 1835 to 1848; in a word: who were Marx and Engels, how did they become Marx and Engels, and why." She reports that in six months the treatment, a very detailed one hundred pages with all the essential dialogue, "all of it rigorously taken from the 'Works' and from the letters of the protagonists," was finished. It is this document that follows in the special issue of *Filmcritica*.

One is thankful to have it, certainly, but it is not Rossellini's. Bendicò, in fact, claims authorship of the script (with assistance by Rafael Guzman), yet at the same time maintains, "That which is published here is the part of the screenplay which Rossellini had already read and approved" (p. 363). That may be, but the script shows few traces of the director's hand. For one thing, never in his entire life had he worked from such a detailed script; such things were written to impress producers, perhaps, but were scarcely to be taken seriously during the actual shooting. More important, the published script contains little evidence of Rossellini's typical themes, techniques, or sensibility. Instead, endless pages are spent elaborating personal details presumably intended to humanize the characters—not an intrinsically bad thing to do, of course, but most un-Rossellinian. For example, a great deal of time is spent on Marx's relationship with his wife Jenny von Westphalen, including their growing love for one another (which is foisted upon us in the very first scene), the objections of her family, and so on. In fact, Jenny appears as much in the script as does Karl. From the very beginning, the script's emphasis is on psychologizing Marx, understanding him as a human being, and only a very few, uncharacteristically brief speeches are devoted to adumbrating his ideas. The philosopher's relationship with Engels is continually and almost exclusively shown in terms of Marx's initial crusty disapproval of the other's character and personality, which the charming Engels eventually overcomes through sheer effort. Other humanizing motifs concern Marx's anti-intellectual mother, his incessant cigar smoking, blood on his handkerchief from too much intellectual effort (à la Pascal), and his poor handwriting (commented upon three or four different times). Furthermore, while a great deal of conventional stage business is invented to make the scenes more "realistic,"[3] we see very little of Rossellini's usual accent on how the ordinary things of daily life were done, other than some passing interest shown in the printing press of Marx's newspaper *Die Rheinische Zeitung*. Perhaps worst of all is the heavy voice-over, which provides nearly all the exposition through a laborious explanation of the various visual bridges, a technique completely absent from the other historical films (with the exception of the more appropriate narrative voice-over, drawn from the Bible, of *The Messiah*).

Other projects in the planning stages at this time included "The History of Islam" (which was projected at some twenty episodes to be filmed by young directors); the series on science that had not yet been abandoned; a film on what Bendicò calls "the advent of the civilization of the image," concerning the early photographers Niepce and Daguerre; and a biography of Rousseau. To follow were series on the American Revolution, the conquistadors, and the history of food.[4] Unfortunately, there would be time to do only two short films, two projects that could not be further apart and whose opposition is perhaps emblematic of the themes of Rossellini's final period.

The first is a fifty-five-minute documentary of sorts, commissioned by the French Ministry of Foreign Affairs and shot by Nestor Almendros, on the futuristic Centre Georges Pompidou in Paris, known familiarly as Beaubourg. To construct this monument to high-tech, late-modernist culture, several old and colorful Parisian neighborhoods had been torn down, and one wonders what the authorities were thinking of when they entrusted this work, obviously meant to publicize Beauborg, to Rossellini. They may have been attracted to his pronouncements concerning the place of science and technology in modern life, or to his attempts to "educate" the masses, as the Centre Pompidou was meant to do. For Rossellini, however, Beaubourg represented not the forward-looking aspects of modern technological life, but everything in it that was confused, sterile, and inauthentic.

Naturally, Rossellini never overtly says, in the film, that he abhors its subject—for one thing, the film contains not a single word of explanation, and the sound track is composed entirely of aleatory sounds and voices picked up by hidden microphones. But his distaste is evident nevertheless. The film opens with a long, slow zoom back from the heart of the city, with typically urban noises filling the sound track. Finding Beaubourg in the distance, the camera nervously cuts several times to poor neighborhoods, each cut leading to a pan that rediscovers Beaubourg from a different angle. Next the film cuts to a static exterior shot of the building and then quickly inside, where the camera continually investigates and reveals—the first floor, the art gallery—as the voices of the people we see try to identify the various portraits that hang there. The camera pans the posters to identify what events are going on; there is a cut to crowds pressing against the door and then entering, as the lens zooms back to allow them space to enter. All the while the dynamic potpourri of street noises and voices on the sound track complements the restless movement of the camera. Throughout the film, in fact, the sound track is completely "natural" and stems from whatever we happen to be seeing (though, to be sure, Rossellini is carefully selecting what we see and what we hear). Long panning shots of the city from Beaubourg are followed by shots of Oldenburg's soft sculpture, as a child's voice articulates Rossellini's own often-expressed dislike of modern art by asking, "What's that good for?"

The camera is intent on showing us everything going on in the building, but always in terms of the people involved; in doing so, Rossellini seems to be trying to work against Beaubourg's sterile formalism by obsessively, and unsuccessfully, recalling it to a human scale. We move back to the art gallery and listen to the guide and the people trying to make sense of the paintings. (Typically, the camera will follow someone, then pan back to discover someone else, very casually, exactly as another spectator would see things.) The camera pans through the window to show us Sacre-Coeur. Finally, after many more minutes of apparently aimless wandering, there is a cut to the same extreme long shot that began the film, the one that shows Beaubourg placed exactly in the middle of the city. By now we understand how absolutely out of place it is, and how totally inappropriate to everything else in Paris, like Sacre-Coeur, that Rossellini sees as whole and organic. The final shot is a very slow zoom back out, a movement that does not end until the building is totally lost amid the city's haze.

In an interview Rossellini characteristically maintained that he was not interested in denouncing Beaubourg, but in merely showing it and letting it speak for itself, without his interference one way or the other: in fact, he says, the only trickery involved is that the remarks gathered by the hidden microphones were so totally negative that he had to make up positive ones so the film would be more balanced. His own view is less ambiguous, however:

> I personally believe that people confuse culture and refinement. Refinement, for me, has nothing to do with knowledge. But when people speak of "culture," they really mean refinement. But before being refined, we have to be thinking beings, people who understand what it means to be man. We learn to be accountants, doctors, journalists, filmmakers, but who teaches us the principal profession, the profession of being man? Beaubourg is a flagrant thing: it is the exposition of refinement at all costs.[5]

Opposing all this sterile modernity and "refinement" is the other project of his final year, the "Concerto per Michelangelo," a RAI-sponsored Eurovision broadcast of a concert performed in the Sistine Chapel. The program was broadcast in color on Holy Saturday evening, April 9, 1977, two months before Rossellini's death, and consists of a loving tour of Michelangelo's Vatican, including the *Pietà*, the iconic center of *The Messiah*, and the cupola of Saint Peter's, Rossellini's favorite signifier of "Rome" since *Open City*. The main focus, however, is on the Sistine Chapel, perhaps the highest artistic expression of the director's beloved Renaissance. The program takes the form of a biography of Michelangelo's Roman period, beginning with his first call to the city in 1508. The artist's task, the voice-over informs us, was "the representation of a humanity which had fallen from its state of original purity," a task that Rossellini replicates by returning us, his confused contemporaries, to the "purity" of the Renaissance. Complicated chronological and thematic links are made among the various subjects that Michelangelo dealt with, and thus we see the ever-youthful Virgin of the *Pietà* as the new Eve, who represents the sufferings of all humanity, and the *Last Judgment* and the *Pietà* are related by focusing on the angels holding the instruments of Christ's passion in the former. We then hear a concert of polyphonic sacred music sung by the choir, as the camera seeks out connections between the visual program in the chapel and the words of the music. The camera then moves outside of the chapel to focus on Michelangelo's turn away from painting and sculpture toward architecture. We are told by the voice-over:

> Obsessed by thoughts of death, tormented by his anxieties, Michelangelo sought peace and quiet, and aspired toward serenity. Painting and sculpture, with which he had wanted to translate into images the high mystic fervor achieved through his religiosity, no longer satisfied him. Architecture opened for him a new way toward a greater catharsis, offered him the possibility of definitively transforming the aesthetic discourse into an ethical and moral one.[6]

One can easily imagine these words applying as well to the entire trajectory of Rossellini's career, especially the movement from personal artistic expression to the mathematical grandeur and architectural simplicity of the great didactic project.

Next the film moves to the Cappella Paolina, the Vatican grotto (where the death theme continues in the many tombs we see), and the construction of the great dome of Saint Peter's. The camera cuts from the interior of the basilica to a beautiful panoramic shot of Rome itself. How very appropriate that Rossellini's career should end precisely where, practically speaking, it began—the city and the dome of Saint Peter's—like the final bittersweet, simultaneously hopeful and hopeless shot that ended *Open City* thirty-two years before. We return, finally, to the interior of Saint Peter's, the camera shooting down from the dome as the chorus of the alleluia rises to its climax. The film closes with a shot of Michelangelo's self-portrait in the *Last Judgment* (as the skin of Saint Bartholomew), and his words taken from a letter to Giorgio Vasari: "Nothing remains for me to do except to return to Florence ready to rest in death, whom I seek to become accustomed to so it won't treat me any worse than other old men."[7]

EPILOGUE

In May, a month after the broadcast of "Concerto per Michelangelo," Rossellini went to the Cannes film festival, where, to his great surprise, he had been asked to be president of the jury. True to form, he insisted that an informational panel on the financing of films be set up before he would consent. While at the festival, he fought hard that the Taviani brothers' *Padre padrone* be awarded the grand prize, not so much because he liked the film itself (though he did), but because it had originally been made for television. He wanted, to the very end, to break down the artificial barriers between cinema and television that he knew could only harm both. Returning exhausted from Cannes, he began working on an article for *Paese Sera*. In the article he spoke of his first contact with the "cinema" in fifteen years; he was excited that he had been able to see for himself what was going on in that world he had left behind. What he had discovered, however, was that the cinema of the auteur had been reduced to "navel gazing": "Many so-called auteurist films are pure exercises in a useless and schizophrenically personal aestheticism," he wrote. On the other hand, even worse were the purveyors of the entertainment products of sex and violence. What bothered him the most, though, were the complaints he heard concerning the "crisis" of the cinema. As he pointed out in the article, if television were included, one would quickly realize that there was no crisis at all, but that audiences were larger than ever: "Through an enormous error of vision, or of perspective, many take as a crisis that which in reality is a boom."[8] Now that *Padre padrone* had won, the first time ever for a film made outside the power group of the commercial cinema industry, he insisted, the problem would be distribution, the final way to block new ideas.

But the article was not to be finished. As he was about to leave his apartment to do some errands on the afternoon of June 3, 1977, Rossellini suffered a massive heart attack and died within minutes. He was seventy-one years old, but not yet done with life.

The ironies and tensions of his life and career continued after his death. In homage to his films on the Resistance, and especially since it was known that he was working on a film about Marx, the Communists claimed him for their own, displaying his body at the Communist Culture House, amid bouquets of bright red flowers. The family insisted on a Church funeral, however, given Rossellini's lifelong interest in religion, and the nation was treated to the unusual spectacle of Enrico Berlinguer, the head of the Communist party, attending Rossellini's funeral mass at Sant'Ignazio. Even more surprisingly, he sat next to Aldo Moro, the most powerful man in the Christian Democrat party, and the architect of the famous "historic compromise," which was designed to bring the Communists into the government for the first time in Italian history. Perhaps the wish of *Open City,* the union of priest and partisan, was about to be fulfilled after all. But it was not to be. Within the year, Moro was kidnapped and assassinated by members of the Red Brigades. Anxious to make a symbolic point, they left his body exactly halfway between the Roman headquarters of the Communist party and the Christian Democrat party, and the historic compromise was dead as well.

It is significant that Rossellini was claimed by both groups, for in truth he was of neither, this religious atheist and bourgeois revolutionary, preferring always to make his own highly individualistic way in the world. In his art or craft, as well, he was a victim of wrong expectations; from the commercial filmmaking establishment, who wanted him to be commercial, from the political and avant-garde, who wanted him to be those things. What is perhaps most tragic and most sublime about his wonderful, failed career, is, once again, that he was neither, or both, the supreme example of the modernist artist working in a commercial medium that clung desperately to the narrative and dramatic forms it had inherited from the nineteenth century. As such, Rossellini's career remains perhaps the perfect emblem of the frustrating contradictions and unique glories of cinematic art.

Notes

Preface

1. Andrew Sarris, "Rossellini Rediscovered," *Film Culture*, no. 32 (Spring 1964), 63.
2. Vincent Canby, *New York Times*, June 19, 1977, p. D7.
3. Robin Wood, "Rossellini," *Film Comment*, 10, no. 4 (July–August 1974), 6.

1. Early Film Projects

1. Interview with Marcella Rossellini Mariani, conducted in Rome in 1970.
2. Renzo Rossellini, *Addio al passato: Racconti ed altro* (Milan: Rizzoli, 1968).
3. Pio Baldelli, *Roberto Rossellini* (Rome: Edizione Samonà e Savelli, 1972), p. 253.
4. In a recent interview, Assia Noris maintained that she and Rossellini were actually married, with the consent of their families, in the Russian church that she attended. But for some reason—she could not say why—the civil ceremony never took place, her father came and "rescued" her from a San Remo hotel, and forty-eight hours later the marriage was annulled. According to Noris, the photographs of their "honeymoon" were never printed in the newspapers because Fascist censors considered the whole affair scandalous. In the same collection of interviews, Marcella De Marchis, usually considered Rossellini's first wife, and a lifelong collaborator on his films as well as the mother of his son Renzo, recounts how in May of 1936 she met Rossellini, who had been left by Assia Noris by that time for Mario Camerini, a popular director of comedy in the thirties. Marcella's family was very much against the marriage, especially since Rossellini's family had gone through all its money by this time, but Roberto worked his charm on them until they agreed. They were married that September, further upsetting her family when he refused to go through an elaborate religious ceremony. (See Franca Faldini and Goffredo Fofi, *L'avventurosa storia del cinema italiano raccontata dai suoi protagonisti (1935–1959)* [Milan: Feltrinelli, 1979], p. 12, for both interviews.)
   Newspaper accounts of Rossellini's early life as a "notorious playboy" flourished early

in 1950 with the outbreak of the scandal surrounding his love affair with Ingrid Bergman. These accounts are replete with juicy details of spurned lovers taking their lives, accusations against the morality of Rossellini's parents, and stories of Rossellini's days as a race-car driver before he "settled down." At this distance, however, it is impossible to separate the real from the sensational in these accounts. The interested reader is referred for further details to a two-part story that appeared in the *New York Post* on February 15 and 16, 1950.

5. Massimo Mida, *Roberto Rossellini* (Parma: Guanda, 1953), pp. 39–40.

6. "A Discussion of Neo-Realism: Rossellini Interviewed by Mario Verdone," *Screen,* 14, no. 4 (Winter 1973–74), 75. (Interview originally published in Italian in 1952. Here and elsewhere I have modified this translation.)

7. "A Panorama of History: Interview With Rossellini by Francisco Llinas and Miguel Marias," *Screen,* 14, no. 4 (Winter 1973–74), 96. (Interview originally published in Spanish in January 1970.)

8. Mario Verdone, *Roberto Rossellini* (Paris: Seghers, 1963), p. 19.

9. Faldini and Fofi, *L'avventurosa storia,* p. 48.

10. Ibid., pp. 26–27.

11. Francesco Savio, ed., *Cinecittà anni trenta: Parlano 116 protagonisti del secondo cinema italiano, 1930–1943* (Rome: Bulzoni Editore, 1979), vol. 1, p. 31. Quite another view is offered by Jose Guarner, the author of a small book on the director, who states quite simply, without citing any evidence, that "it seems very likely that Rossellini reshot most of the sequences directed by Alessandrini." (*Roberto Rossellini* [New York: Praeger, 1970], p. 6.) In Perilli's account, Alessandrini was filming on location in Africa while Rossellini was filming interiors in Rome, and Alessandrini was upset when he discovered that his film had been tampered with. (Savio, *Cinecittà anni trenta,* vol. 3, p. 924.)

12. Faldini and Fofi, *L'avventurosa storia,* p. 48.

13. Savio, *Cinecittà anni trenta,* vol. 3, p. 962.

14. Baldelli, *Roberto Rossellini,* p. 252. Rossellini goes on to say in this interview that everyone considered him crazy, but full of ideas. "So they used me, you know, like a drop of vinegar in a salad." He then tells the story of how he would ghostwrite scripts for a famous writer who paid him three thousand lire, one thousand in advance. When that money was gone, Rossellini would go to a little copying store in the tram station on Via Principe Amedeo, dictate the first half of the film, and then collect the second thousand lire. When that was gone as well, he would dictate the second half and be paid the final installment: "And with this kind of work I went ahead for a couple of years, not concerning myself with it in the slightest." (Incidentally, in this interview, the film is incorrectly referred to as *Un pilota ritorna,* but it is clear from the context that he is speaking of *Luciano Serra, pilota.*)

15. This organization was established in 1927 to provide instruction films, but eventually graduated to more overtly propagandistic films like *Il Duce,* which portrayed Mussolini in a favorable light.

16. Edward Tannenbaum, *The Fascist Experience: Italian Society and Culture, 1922–1945* (New York: Basic Books, 1972), p. 269.

17. Adriano Aprà and Patrizia Pistagnesi, *I favolosi anni trenta: Cinema italiano, 1929–1944* (Milan: Electa, 1979), p. 109.

18. Various histories of Italian postwar cinema have included the following as precursors of neorealism: early Neapolitan films such as *Assunta Spina* (1914) and *Sperduti nel buio* (1916); Griffith's *The Musketeers of Pig Alley* (1912); Renoir's *Toni* (1934); Blasetti's *Sole* (1929) and *1860* (1934); Camerini's *Rotaie* (1929); Ruttman's *Acciaio* (1933); nineteenth-century Italian verists, such as the novelist Giovanni Verga; American genre films; American fiction; futurism; the writer and painter Leo Longanesi; and so forth. Obvi-

ously, the question is an enormously complicated one, too large to be taken up here; hence I have concentrated upon *direct* influences on Rossellini, rather than considering the sources of neorealism in general. The interested reader is referred to two useful recent histories of the period in English (Peter Bondanella, *Italian Cinema: From Neorealism to the Present* [New York: Ungar, 1983], and Mira Liehm, *Passion and Defiance: Film in Italy From 1942 to the Present* [Berkeley: Univ. of California Press, 1984]). The definitive history of the roots of neorealism, however, is Gian Piero Brunetta's *Storia del cinema italiano 1895–1945* (Rome: Editori Riuniti, 1979).

19. Georges Sadoul, *Histoire générale du cinéma*. Volume 6: *L'Époque contemporaine: Le Cinéma pendant la guerre (1939–45)* (Paris: Éditions Denoël, 1954), p. 105.

20. *Film*, no. 34 (September 17, 1938), quoted in Tannenbaum, *The Fascist Experience*, p. 275.

21. Savio, *Cinecittà anni trenta*, volume 1, p. 32.

22. Tannenbaum, *The Fascist Experience*, pp. 275–76. His quotation is from Mino Argentieri's article in *Il cinema italiano dal fascismo all'antifascismo*, ed. Giorgio Tinazzi (Padua: Marsilio Editore, 1966), p. 70.

2. La Nave Bianca

1. Faldini and Fofi, *L'avventurosa storia*, p. 58. One difference between Rossellini and De Robertis that Bava does not mention is, that while the extent of the former's Fascist sympathies may be debated, most evidence indicates that he was neither more nor less Fascist than any other average apolitical citizen. De Robertis, on the other hand, was a firmly committed member of the party who joined Mussolini and the Nazis in the north of Italy when the Republic of Salò was formed in 1943, after the Duce had been jailed by the king and freed by the Nazis. De Robertis, in fact, maintained that his third feature-length film, *Uomini sul cielo*, was meant to demonstrate that "fighting exercised a beneficial effect on the minds of those who have not withdrawn from the supreme experience which life destines fatally to each man." (Quoted in Roy Armes, *Patterns of Realism* [South Brunswick and New York: A. S. Barnes, 1971], p. 42). It is utterly impossible to imagine Rossellini ever making a similar statement.

2. Savio, *Cinecittà anni trenta*, vol. 3, p. 968

3. Faldini and Fofi, *L'avventurosa storia*, p. 59.

4. "A Panorama of History," 96.

5. "Je profite des choses," interview with Jacques Grant in *Cinéma* [Paris], no. 206 (February 1976), 67.

6. Quoted in *Roberto Rossellini: Il cinema, la televisione, la storia, la critica*, ed. Edoardo Bruno. (Città di Sanremo, Assessorato per il turismo e le manifestazioni, 1980), p. 13.

7. Interview, *Cahiers du cinéma*, no. 37 (July 1954), 3–4.

8. "A Discussion of Neo-Realism," 72. (The word *corale* is misleadingly rendered as "human warmth" in the *Screen* translation.)

9. It should also be pointed out that the "rhetoric" of the love story is somewhat attenuated by the equally rhetorical, but excellent, musical score by Rossellini's brother, Renzo, which often substitutes for the less subtle dialogue. Similarly, one of the earliest critics of the film, Enrico Fulchignoni, writing in 1941, was impressed that at the high point of emotion at the end of the film, looks take the place of dialogue. (*Bianco e nero*, 5, no. 10 [October 1941], 4.)

10. In a generally negative article that appeared just after the director's death in 1977, Jacques Demeure mentions seeing the Fascist insignia on the nurse's blouse, next to the Red Cross. ("Un débutant méconnu: Roberto Rossellini," *Positif*, no. 198 [Octo-

ber 1977], 37.) It is difficult to contest a personal observation, but the print of the film that I saw at the Museum of Modern Art in New York showed only the Red Cross. Roy Armes, in *Patterns of Realism,* also says, "The film ends with a close-up of a red cross" (p. 44). It is easy to imagine that Rossellini might have wanted to cut certain compromising shots, but impossible to believe that he could go into a close-up showing two insignia and remove one of them. The source of Demeure's error seems to be an article written some twenty years earlier by Marcel Oms, the most vicious attack ever directed against Rossellini, in which he says, "The film, finally, ends on a camera movement which frames the Fascist insignia pinned to the blouse of the nurse." ("Rossellini: Du fascisme à la démocratie chrétienne," *Positif,* no. 28 [April 1958], 10.) No other critic has ever mentioned the Fascist insignia.

11. Maria-Antonietta Macciocchi, *Les Femmes et leurs maîtres* (Paris: Christian Bourgois Editeur, 1978), p. 81.

12. Maria-Antonietta Macciocchi, *La donna "nera"* (Milan: Feltrinelli, 1976), p. 156.

13. Pietro Bianchi, *L'occhio di vetro: Il cinema degli anni 1940–43* (Milan: Il Formichiere, 1978), p. 95. The article originally appeared October 31, 1941.

14. Adolfo Franci, "Diorama della Mostra di Venezia," *Primi piani* (October 1941).

3. Un Pilota Ritorna

1. Faldini and Fofi, *L'avventurosa storia,* p. 59.

2. Savio, *Cinecittà anni trenta,* vol. 2, p. 606.

3. Savio, *Cinecittà anni trenta,* vol. 3, pp. 963–64.

4. It is this latter version of the scriptwriting struggle that Marcella De Marchis, Rossellini's first wife, seems to support when she says that "Roberto always tore the cinematography of the regime to bits. . . . There was a big fight with Vittorio, because he wanted the security of a completed script, while Roberto was creating and improvising, and there were fierce discussions because he hadn't turned in a beautifully finished script. So Roberto then made me his accomplice: 'Ask Marcella. I worked all night, no? Tell them, Marcella!' And he told them the script was ready, but he had forgotten it at [the summer house]. Actually, we played cards all night with some hunting friends, and at dawn we went hunting. When *Un pilota ritorna* came out, there still wasn't a real script." (Faldini and Fofi, *L'avventurosa storia,* p. 59.)

5. Giuseppe De Santis, "Un pilota ritorna," *Cinema* [Rome], no. 140 (April 25, 1942), 227. Perhaps even more revelatory of the small world of Italian cinema is the fact that after writing negative reviews of *Un pilota ritorna* and *L'uomo dalla croce,* De Santis, later an important director in his own right (*Bitter Rice*), went on to screenwriting chores for Rossellini's next, never-completed film project, originally entitled *Scalo merci.*

6. R. M. DeAngelis, "Rossellini romanziere," *Cinema* [Rome], no. 29, n.s. (December 30, 1949), 356.

7. Aprà and Pistagnesi, *I favolosi anni trenta,* p. 109.

4. L'Uomo dalla Croce

1. Giuseppe De Santis, "L'uomo dalla croce," *Cinema* [Rome] no. 168 (June 25, 1943), 374.

2. Gianni Rondolino, *Rossellini* (Florence: La Nuova Italia, 1974), p. 48.

3. Baldelli, *Roberto Rossellini,* p. 19.

4. This oscillation between the authentic and the artificial is also manifested in the dialogue, for Rossellini has included many regional accents and dialect words in his soldiers' speech. One could praise his concern to reflect the actual composition of the army,

not allowing important regional differences to be dissolved in the false uniformity of standard speech. A harsher view, however, might regard this heterogeneity as forced and artificial, each soldier being made to mouth typical pronunciations and phrases that will instantly identify him for his fellow Italians. We see this, of course, in the war films of all countries, certainly in those of Britain and the United States, where each unit has its Scot or Brooklynite, Yorkshireman, or drawling Alabaman. One might also view this dialectal variation as in some way reflecting the Fascist ideology of the army as the great leveler, the transcendent, symbolic expression of the will of a country finally unifying itself to present for perhaps the first time in history a single face to the enemy.

In any case, as early as *Un pilota ritorna*, as we have seen, Rossellini is scrupulous about the languages his characters speak. This concern presents a problem in a country that has always abhorred subtitles, and thus large parts of *Open City* and *Era notte a Roma*, for example, go by in an untranslated German or English. At the time *L'uomo dalla croce* was made, Rossellini's interest in the authentic depiction of language was present, but unsure and confused. For example, when the priest is waiting with the wounded man, we hear Russian being spoken before we actually see the soldiers emerge from the dust and smoke (and, as in *Un pilota ritorna*, the images even carry Italian subtitles). In an earlier encounter between the Italian soldiers and the Russian peasants, each comically speaks his or her own language, and the Italian is able to get the eggs he wants only by means of an involved pantomime. Later, however, in the *izba*, Sergei and his girlfriend speak an unsubtitled Russian, while some of the peasants, presumably because their lines are more important to the plot or theme, improbably speak Italian to the priest.

5. One interesting quirk, which as far as I know occurs in no other Rossellini film, is a Kurosawa-like use of wipes to indicate a passage of time or a change in space. This technique is perhaps also appropriate to the heightened action of the war film, but its use is neither as convincing or as exciting as, for example, Kurosawa's in *The Seven Samurai*. At one point, Rossellini even moves from the outside of a tank to reveal its interior and its inhabitants by using an explosion wipe. The effect is one of artificially induced excitement that is thoroughly unconvincing.

6. Baldelli, *Roberto Rossellini*, p. 227

7. Interview, *Cahiers du cinéma* (1954), 4.

8. Strangely enough, the rest of her story does not add up to one powerful effect. This seems to be either the fault of sloppy writing or an attempt to reflect honestly the fact that real human beings and the stories of their lives usually do *not* add up. Thus, after a lonely childhood, the young woman went to the university, became active in a party organization for lack of anything better to do, but "all the romantic and bourgeois ideas that I had inherited from my mother choked me." After that, she married a brute and discovered that "a man can love a woman in many different ways," like drinking a glass of liquor or tearing meat from an animal. Hour by hour, this man robbed her of her spirit until Sergei came along, who wanted her just for herself. Clearly, the anti-Communist message is somewhat vitiated by casting Sergei, the commissar, in the role of a loving, caring savior of the girl, though he is gotten rid of rather quickly. Conversely, the theme of the purposeful destruction of another's spirit, always important to Rossellini, is weakened by becoming more narrowly political in the rest of the film.

9. Mino Argentieri, "Storia e spiritualismo nel Rossellini degli anni quaranta," *Cinema sessanta*, 14, no. 95 (January–February 1974), 33. Marxist critics have often wanted to see pre–*Open City* Rossellini as utterly Fascist, so that it would be easier to discredit the post-*Paisan* Rossellini of the "crisis." But apologists for the director are equally wrong when they try to get him off the hook, as when Massimo Mida calls *L'uomo dalla croce* the "least Rossellinian" of the early films because he found it embarrassing. Argentieri falls

into the same trap when he implies that the distasteful parts of the film were solely the work of Fascist screenwriter Asvero Gravelli, with whose basic idea "Rossellini identifies partially: for half of it, he believes in what he is doing and this part of the film, if not convincing, is not, at least, execrable; the other half is in the service of Minculpop and the film doesn't try to hide it, collapsing into ridiculousness" (p. 32).

10. Sadoul, *Histoire générale du cinéma*, p. 105n.

5. Desiderio—A Special Case

1. Other sources, including Adriano Aprà's extensive filmography in *Le Cinéma révélé: Roberto Rossellini*, ed. Alain Bergala (Paris: Les Éditions de l'Étoile, 1984), pp. 162–86, maintain that more than half of the footage in the extant version of the film was shot by Rossellini.

2. Savio, *Cinecittà anni trenta*, vol. 3, p. 966.

3. In another interview, Rossellini said he had begun filming on July 15 or 16. (Baldelli, *Roberto Rossellini*, p. 237.)

4. Faldini and Fofi, *L'avventurosa storia*, p. 70.

5. Giuseppe Ferrara, *Il nuovo cinema italiano* (Florence: Le Monnier, 1957), p. 83.

6. Faldini and Fofi, *L'avventurosa storia*, p. 48.

7. Rondolino, *Rossellini*, p. 50.

8. Raymond Borde and André Bouissy, *Le Néo-réalisme italien: Une expérience de cinéma social* (Lausanne: La Cinémathèque suisse, 1960), p. 26.

9. Nino Frank, *Cinema dell'arte* (Paris: Bonne, 1951), p. 151.

10. De Santis mentioned this in the context of an anecdote that also helps to explain Rossellini's unique position vis-à-vis the Fascist authorities: "We were writing the script of *Desiderio* and one evening . . . we were going home when we were stopped by a police patrol which demanded to see our papers. I didn't have a Fascist party card—but only because I had forgotten it at home in a drawer . . . and I could have gotten into trouble. Well, Rossellini, of whom Vittorio Mussolini and the Fascist Federation thought very highly, intervened, and everything was taken care of. (Faldini and Fofi, *L'avventurosa storia*, p. 69).

11. Ferrara, *Il nuovo cinema italiano*, pp. 45–46.

12. It is also easy to understand his relationship with Vittorio Mussolini in terms of personal friendship rather than politics; Rossellini's first wife, Marcella De Marchis, has stated that the two men never talked about the regime and neither she nor Roberto were ever enrolled in the Fascist party. (Faldini and Fofi, *L'avventurosa storia*, p. 59).

13. Faldini and Fofi, *L'avventurosa storia*, p. 69.

6. Open City

1. Faldini and Fofi, *L'avventurosa storia*, p. 90. An entertaining book by Ugo Pirro, *Celluloide* (Milan: Rizzoli, 1983) tells the story of the beginning of neorealism in enormous detail, including the filming of *Open City*. The problem is that the account is heavily fictionalized, with invented conversations and so on, and in the absence of a single note, source, or reference to an interview, the book cannot be taken as a definitive account of the period.

2. Faldini and Fofi, *L'avventurosa storia*, p. 94.

3. Fabrizi has given an utterly different, completely unconvincing version of the genesis of this film. According to him, the idea of the full-length film was his, and he suggested adding the story of the children and the woman killed by the Nazis; the enlarged plot was then given to Rossellini, who Fabrizi introduced to Fellini. (See Angelo

Solmi, *Federico Fellini* [London: Merlin Press, 1963], pp. 76–78, for a discussion of both accounts.)

4. Money posed a continual problem. De Sica tells an amusing story that gives a rather more realistic picture of how works of "genius" are made:

> It's not as if one day we were all sitting around a table on the Via Veneto, Rossellini, Visconti, I, and the others, and said, "Hey, let's start neorealism." We hardly even knew each other. One day I was told that Rossellini had started working on a film again: "A film on a priest," I was told, and that was it. Another day I saw him and Amidei sitting on the entrance steps of an apartment building in Via Bissolati. I asked them what they were doing. They shrugged their shoulders and said, "We're looking for some money. We don't have enough dough to finish the film." "What film?" "The story of a priest, you know, Don Morosini, the one that the Germans shot" (Faldini and Fofi, *L'avventurosa storia*, p. 90).

A small amount of money did come, eventually, from an unsteady stream of entrepreneurs and first-time producers, who contributed whatever small change they could and then went their way. Several years later Rossellini was to tell a reporter for *Variety* that it had cost 11 million lire ($19,000) to make the film, complaining that it should only have cost 6 million ($10,400) (*Variety*, November 3, 1948). Rossellini himself sold nearly everything he and his estranged wife owned to finance the filming (he ended up losing about $600), which was done in a makeshift studio in the Via degli Avignonesi small enough, according to Fellini, to be filled with the smoke from ten cigarettes. The only scenes shot in this "studio" were those in the Nazi headquarters (meant to replicate the infamous S.S. center on the Via Tasso), Don Pietro's room, and Marina's apartment. (During the filming of the sequence in Marina's apartment, the actress apparently went to open the door because the script required her to listen in on Manfredi, only to find that the door had been painted on). One other reason for making the film here was that they could tap into the electricity that the Allied forces were providing for the newspaper *Il Messagero*. Since the electricity came on only at night, it was then that the principle interior shooting was done. All the other scenes were shot on actual streets.

According to Omar Garrison in the *New York Post* (February 1, 1950), Rossellini had hidden a stolen camera in his apartment on the Piazza di Spagna and had secretly begun shooting sequences of the Germans changing the guard, one day accidentally finding himself filming the roundup of hostages. There is no other evidence, however, to suggest that Garrison's account is in any way correct. Similarly, the often-repeated story that Rossellini filmed the actual departure of the German troops from Rome is more a testimony to the convincing power of his mise-en-scène than to the truth. (In one interview, however, Rossellini does insist that filming began on January 19, 1944, that is, five months before the Germans left, but other testimony has it that this date actually marks the beginning of the preproduction planning of the film. It is true, nevertheless, that Rossellini was able to use real German prisoners of war in the film.) Another exaggeration is George Sadoul's statement, not supported by any elaboration or listing of sources, that the scenario for the film was "almost literally dictated" to Rossellini and Amidei by one of the heads of the Resistance. (*Histoire du cinéma mondial des origines à nos jours*, 9th ed. [Paris: Flammarion, 1972], p. 329).

The story of how the film finally found its way to the United States, with such great success, is fascinating. It seems that on the floor above the makeshift studio of the Via degli Avignonesi was a bordello, heavily frequented during the hours of shooting, unfortunately, and especially popular with the newly arrived American troops. A continuous stream of lust-minded young men would stumble into the filming area, drawn by the bright lights, thinking that they had found what they had been looking for. Fellini tells a wonderful story about how a drunken American sergeant named Rod Geiger stumbled in the studio one evening while looking for a girl, fell flat on his face, and commenced bleeding profusely from the nose. When he had recovered sufficiently to ask what was going on, he insisted that he was a big American film producer and wanted to buy the film. In fact, he did precisely that, finally paying twenty thousand dollars for the rights. He took the few copies to the United States, sold the rights to a real distributor, and the film went on to enjoy an enormous success at the World Theater in Manhattan, where it ran uninterrupted for over a year.

5. In later years Sergio Amidei, clearly the principle motivating force behind the initial screenplay, became somewhat bitter, as screenwriters are wont to do, because he was largely excluded from the encomia heaped upon the director. As he tells it—and independent evidence often supports him—many of the characters and the episodes of the film were taken directly from his own life. Much more politically committed than the rest of the production team, he had, in fact, once escaped the Germans by going over the rooftops of the surrounding apartment houses, just as Manfredi does in the beginning of the film. Cesar Negarville, an important Resistance leader on whom the character of Manfredi is said to have been principally based, actually had a room in Amidei's apartment, put there by Amidei's landlady, who appears in the opening shots of the film. Maria Michi, Amidei's girlfriend at the time, had also actually once called Amidei while a German raid was in progress, just as happens in the film. Amidei further maintained that the episode in which Pina is shot down by the Germans as she chases after her captured fiancé, Francesco, was taken from a real event that had occurred on the Piazza Adriana that he had learned about in *Unità*, the underground Communist newspaper. The actual iconography of Pina's moving, desperate gesture, though, interestingly enough, came from an altogether less elevated source. According to Amidei, Magnani was arguing furiously one day with her boyfriend of the moment: to save himself, he jumped on the back of a film production truck that was just then pulling away, and the company was treated to the sight of Magnani running after him, violently hurling the worst insults in his direction. It seemed such an effective piece of drama that Amidei wrote it into the script. (See Amidei's "*Open City* Revisited," *New York Times* [February 16, 1947, sec. 2, p. 5].) What Amidei neglects to mention is that, according to Patrizia Carrano, Magnani's biographer, he wanted to trip her with a wire to make the scene more convincing, but Rossellini refused. (*La Magnani: Il romanzo di una vita* [Milan: Rizzoli, 1982], p. 98.)

Many of the film's details were suggested by the real life of Father Giuseppe Morosini. "Jane Scrivener" tells us, for example, that he was betrayed to the gestapo, who found arms and a transmitter he had collected for the men he was hiding. The pope tried to save him, to no avail, but he was allowed to say mass on the morning of his execution. Her account of his last moments is very close to what happens in the film:

> Before being blindfolded he kissed his crucifix, blessed the platoon of soldiers who were to shoot him, and publicly forgave the man who had betrayed him. Possibly because the executioners were overcome by his quiet heroism, he was not killed by their volley, and fell to the ground, wounded but conscious. He begged for the Sacrament of Extreme Unction . . . , after which the commanding officer shot him at the base of the skull with a revolver (*Inside Rome With the Germans* [New York: Macmillan, 1945], p. 152).

Even Don Pietro's last lines—"It's not difficult to die, it's difficult to live"—are, according to Giuseppe Ferrara, who quotes from Salvatore Morosini's book on his brother Don Morosini, the real priest's final words (*Il nuovo cinema italiano*, p. 106. Ferrara also suggests that the Nazi Bergmann was a composite of Kappler, the head of the S.S. on the Via Tasso, and Dolman, the German commander of Rome during the occupation.)

6. Faldini and Fofi, *L'avventurosa storia*, p. 95. Another aspect of the film's "conventionality" is that characters often seem to be filling preconceived roles derived from the stage and vaudeville. Thus Rossellini uses a kind of character shorthand to fix a "type,"

as in his treatment of Don Pietro. He is presented as a buffoon right from the beginning—when he is hit with the soccer ball—and the effective, if somewhat cute, piece of comic business with the statue of San Rocco and the naked Venus seems instantly to fix him for us as a whimsical, and in many ways frightfully innocent, man, enhancing the incongruity of the fact that he is about to enter a clandestine printing shop. All of this is well done; the only point to be made is that this kind of character typing (Manfredi as the heroic partisan, Pina as the poor but honest *romana*, Marina as the corrupt prostitute) so dear to the nineteenth-century novel, the popular stage, and Hollywood melodrama, is something that Rossellini will for the most part avoid in his later work.

7. *The War Trilogy of Roberto Rossellini* (New York: Grossman, 1973), p. 126. (All further references to the script will be included in the body of the text.)

8. Magnani's account of her feelings about this scene are revealing:

> During the roundup, when I walked through the front door, suddenly I saw everything all over again, and I was taken back to the time when they took away the young men. Boys. Because these were real people standing against the walls. The Germans were real Germans from a P.O.W. camp. Suddenly, I wasn't me any more. I was the character. And Rossellini had prepared the street in an incredible way. Do you know the women were white when they heard the Nazis talking among themselves? This made me understand the anxiety I projected on the screen. Terrible. Who would have expected an emotion like that? That's how Rossellini worked. And, at least with me, let me say it again, the system worked (Faldini and Fofi, *L'avventurosa storia*, p. 95).

9. Leo Braudy, *Focus on Shoot the Piano Player* (Englewood Cliffs, N.J.: Prentice-Hall, 1972), p. 4; Jean Desternes, *Revue du cinéma*, no. 3 (December 1946), p. 65.

10. Baldelli, *Roberto Rossellini*, p. 227. Giuseppe Ferrara has somewhat impressionistically described another technical aspect of the film—its lighting—which, while certainly conventional, is nevertheless accomplished with consummate skill, especially given the home-movie myth that encumbers most discussion of this film. Though the lighting is described by Amidei as thoroughly unexciting, Ferrara notes the complex thematic ways in which Rossellini uses it. For example, much of the film takes place in cramped interiors, outer darkness, or deep shadows, since this is where, according to Ferrara, "the human struggle itself takes place." When we first see the "natural" figure of Pina early in the film, daylight enters the apartment to warm and highlight her features. The corrupt Marina, on the other hand, is seen only by means of harsh, bright, artificial lighting in one scene after another. In the gestapo headquarters of the Via Tasso, the light is dense and stagnant, symbolic of the sick and dying atmosphere it fills. At the film's most hopeless moment—not the final murders, of course, because they are in their own way speak of transcendence, but, rather, in the cell where Manfredi, the priest, and the Austrian deserter are kept—we can barely make out the figures or even the walls in the oppressive darkness. (Ferrara, *Il nuovo cinema italiano*, p. 111.)

11. Quoted in *Lo splendore del vero: Quarant'anni di cinema di Roberto Rossellini, 1936–1976*, ed. Giuliana Callegari and Nuccio Lodato (Pavia: Amministrazione provinciale, 1977), p. 42.

12. Armando Borrelli, *Neorealismo e marxismo* (Avellino: Edizioni di Cinemasud, 1966), pp. 81–84.

13. Mario Cannella, "Ideology and Aesthetic Hypotheses in the Criticism of Neo-Realism," *Screen*, 13, no. 4 (Winter 1973–74), 22–23.

14. Mino Argentieri, "Storia e spiritualismo," 37.

15. Baldelli, *Roberto Rossellini*, p. 49. Interestingly, the initial reaction of one of America's greatest film reviewers, James Agee, was surprisingly like that of Baldelli. Writing in the April 13, 1946, issue of the *Nation*, Agee said that, while he was not sure, he thought that the coalition between the Church and the party depicted in *Open City* was

not to be believed and that the Italians were "being sold something of a bill of goods." His worry, perfectly in character for the author of *Let Us Now Praise Famous Men,* was that the common people could very easily be sold out for the benefit of the two institutions, at the expense of their own freedom.

16. Others have discussed the sexual subtext of this film from alternative points of view, but with unconvincing results. Thus, the historian Pierre Sorlin, for example, comparing *Open City* with Vergano's *The Sun Rises Again,* finds a dark allegory of sexual punishment at work in the two films. Noting that a woman is also killed in Vergano's film, he insists:

> There is no narrative necessity for the two women to be shot. Look at them, lying on the ground: both are photographed from above, with the feet in foreground, the head in the background, the skirt tucked up, the thighs conspicuous. The shots were carefully arranged, and chance played no part in the exposure of two half-naked [sic!] women. In both films, Pina and Matelda were guilty of sexual transgression, Pina for being pregnant without being married, Matelda for having lovers. . . . The series of victims is well arranged, in ascending order: war-fighting-men have to die. Why is there a war? Because somewhere there is guilt. Offence: sex; punishment: the death of the "bad women."

(Pierre Sorlin, *The Film in History* [London: Oxford University Press, 1980], pp. 201–2; quoted in *BFI Dossier Number 8: Roberto Rossellini,* (London: BFI, 1981), p. 10.) The editors of the British Film Institute dossier further compound Sorlin's distortion in their simple-minded summary of the film from this point of view, when they insist, "In this set of equations underpinning the textual economy of *Rome Open City,* straight sex (heterosexuality) is punishable by death while homosexuality is associated with fascism. Under these circumstances, it appears almost logical that the only solution possible is catholicism and priesthood" (p. 10). Even were Sorlin's terms granted, of course, Pina is being punished for sex before marriage, thus the neat reductio ad absurdum equation the editors offer neglects the alternative of "wholesome" sexuality in marriage.

17. Ben Lawton makes an interesting, if not altogether convincing, case in this direction, seeing the crippled boy leader of the band, Romoletto, as "little Rome," and thus a founder of a new Rome, like Romulus. Only this time, he is crippled, both emotionally and physically ("Italian Neorealism: A Mirror Construction of Reality," *Film Criticism,* 3, no. 2 [Winter 1979], 14).

18. Carlo Lizzani, *Film d'oggi* (November 3, 1945). It is certainly true that Lizzani expressed reservations about what he regarded as the amateurishness of the scenes in the gestapo headquarters, but it is a serious distortion to try to make out his review as negative, as some have.

19. Alberto Moravia, *La nuova Europa* (September 30, 1945), 8.

20. Alessandro Blasetti, *Cinema italiano oggi* (Rome: Carlo Bestetti, 1950), p. 48.

21. Mario Gromo, *Film visti* (Rome: Edizioni Bianco e Nero, 1957), p. 7.

22. Desternes review, *Revue du cinéma,* 66. Henri Agel will later say of *Open City* that it is here, where reality shows itself bloody and torn, that "we discover the secret meaning of things." (*Le Cinéma a-t-il une âme?* [Paris: Éditions du Cerf, 1952], p. 50.)

23. Georges Sadoul, *Les Lettres françaises* (November 15, 1946). Making his own preference for realism very clear, he insists that he would give all of Cocteau's *La Belle et la bête* for the single shot of the floating dead partisan in the opening of the last episode of *Paisan.*

24. John McCarten, *New Yorker* (March 2, 1946), 81.

25. *Life* (March 4, 1946), 111.

26. James Agee, *Nation* (March 23, 1946), 354.

27. Jurij Lotman, *The Semiotics of Cinema* (Ann Arbor: University of Michigan Press, 1976), p. 67.

28. Lotman, p. 69. Georges Sadoul said something similar, using a different frame of reference, many years ago in connection with *Paisan:* "Rossellini's method excluded neither research nor elaboration. *Paisan* was the most expensive Italian film made in 1946. Its poverty was only apparent, and it would be ridiculous to explain the birth of neorealism by the hardships that reigned in the country at that time. The distrust of beautiful 'photography' was in fact a supreme refinement, the creation of a new style, soon to be imitated everywhere" (*Histoire du cinéma mondial,* p. 330).

29. Interview with Fereydoun Hoveyda and Jacques Rivette, *Cahiers du cinéma,* no. 94 (April 1959), 6.

30. André Bazin, *What Is Cinema?* (Berkeley: University of California Press, 1976), vol. 2, p. 27.

31. Ibid., p. 100.

32. Ibid.

33. Ibid., p. 60.

34. Quoted in Linda Nochlin, *Realism* (New York: Penguin, 1971), p. 14. This kind of essentialist language is not limited to phenomenologists or Hegelians, of course. Thus, Giuseppe Ferrara considers the Po sequence of *Paisan* the peak of neorealism because: "Flaherty, Murnau, and Renoir, even though they had understood man and nature, are here leapt over with a single jump, in a savage aggression on the object, a vital incision into things, detailed to the limits of the bearable, when every mythology is broken apart and reality reveals itself to our eyes, which then penetrate it to its roots" (Ferrara, *Il nuovo cinema italiano,* p. 138).

35. Maurice Merleau-Ponty, "What Is Phenomenology?" in *European Literary Theory and Practice,* ed. Vernon W. Gras (New York: Dell Publishing, 1973), p. 80.

36. Harold Brown, *Perception, Theory, and Commitment* (Chicago: Precedent Publishers, 1977), pp. 81–82.

37. Quoted in *Realism and the Cinema,* ed. Christopher Williams (London: Routledge & Kegan Paul, 1980), p. 177.

38. Lotman, p. 65.

39. Bazin, *What Is Cinema?,* vol. 2, p. 97.

40. Ibid., p. 101.

41. Jacques Derrida, *Of Grammatology* (Baltimore: Johns Hopkins University Press, 1976), p. 203.

42. Bazin, *What Is Cinema?* vol. 2, p. 27.

43. The overwhelming impression of reality in the film was such that Maria Michi reported being threatened with a knife because she collaborated with the Germans. In fact, one reads reports rather often of the same sort of basic confusion of realism and reality occurring in the minds of present-day, supposedly visually sophisticated, television viewers. One actress has even told the story of how she was watching herself on television one night. Her character was about to get out of the car, and an aggressor was waiting for her. Just at that moment the telephone rang; it was the actress's cousin, calling to warn her not to get out of the car.

44. Pio Baldelli commits himself so thoroughly to a realist Rossellini that he complains peevishly about "unrealistic" elements that have been noticed, as far as I can determine, by no one else. Thus, he objects to the fact that the children could not realistically have been present at the priest's execution, that the parents surely would not have let them out, that the soldiers surely would have seen the children or heard them whistling, and so on. (Baldelli, *Roberto Rossellini,* p. 38.)

7. Paisan

1. In Geiger, Rossellini seems to have found a somewhat coarser brand of himself, a talk-it-up salesman full of the grandest schemes, but lacking the director's genuine charm and culture. Fellini's account is worth quoting in full:

> "Who do you want?" Geiger said. "What do you mean, Gregory Peck? I'll bring them all here for nothing, they'll come with me." So a list of names was made— Gregory Peck, Lana Turner. He then goes off to America, and one day sends us a telegram: "Am arriving in Naples." So we went to Naples. A boat moors, and this character gets off. It was Geiger, who got off with six people and said: "These are the new American stars. Who cares about Gregory Peck and Lana Turner, these are the ones popular in America." We believed everything because we knew nothing. "This one here is better than Paul Robeson," and he presents a Negro to us. "This one here . . . who cares about Lana Turner?" Later, talking to these people who were rather intimidated and modest, we found out that one was a cafe waiter, another was a secretary, the black was a singer. . . . In other words, they were people he had just picked up and given a couple of bucks. (Faldini and Fofi, *L'avventurosa storia*, p. 108.)

Ian Johnson, in a short article in *Films and Filming* (12, no. 5 [February 1966], 40) reports that Gar Moore (Rome sequence), Dale Edwards (Po), Dots Johnson (Naples), and Harriet White (Florence) were those brought over by Geiger.

2. Massimo Mida, who served as an assistant director on the film, has reported that plans for the entire first sequence, which concerns the encounter of the newly arrived American forces with a Sicilian village and the young girl with whom one of them becomes involved, were seriously affected by the strong presence of the young Sicilian woman found near Naples and the American soldier chosen from among the American soldiers then stationed in the same city. In fact, Rossellini's efforts to "direct" Carmela, the Sicilian girl, proved difficult, as she had grown up in acute poverty in primitive conditions, and could barely read and write. According to Mida, she had a great deal of trouble mastering the lines and the movements, but the choice had been made, and Rossellini plunged ahead. Her astonishing presence on the screen obviously makes up for whatever difficulties she may have caused. After spending time with this "civilized" troupe, unfortunately, she was unable to go back to her former life, and it is with some embarrassment that Mida calls her "the first victim, therefore, of neorealism." (*Roberto Rossellini*, p. 36; see also Faldini and Fofi, *L'avventurosa storia*, p. 109).

Similarly, the Naples episode, which concerns the meeting of the black G.I. and the poverty-stricken shoeshine boy living by his wits, was developed only after the characters had been chosen. For the Florentine episode, former partisans were asked for "technical assistance," while the episode that takes place in the monastery was completely rewritten after Rossellini had come in contact with the real monks he was about to film. (Mida takes some pains to convince us that the fact that monks actually from the Amalfi coast were passed off in the film as being from the area around Bologna makes no difference. He is absolutely right. It is only the mythic aura and rhetoric of "realism" that makes him feel he has to argue the point in the first place.)

3. Quoted in Suzanne Budgen, *Fellini* (London: British Film Institute, 1966), p. 88.

4. Roy Armes suggests that the source for this episode is Curzio Malaparte's novel *The Skin,* which also concerns the "buying" of a black soldier long enough to get him drunk and steal his things (Armes, *Patterns of Realism*, p. 77).

5. Armes complains that this is the most contrived episode in the film because the flashback is a "remove from true neo-realist practice." (Ibid.) This is a good example of the kind of gratuitous rule making that afflicts many critics of Italian neorealism, more intent on establishing prescriptive categories and defending them than on describing

what they see. It is even more useless when this "rule" is applied retroactively to one of the very films most often thought as *establishing* neorealism.

6. It should be remembered, however, that the thematic connections among these episodes are always more suggestive than specific. Thus, I think that Ian Johnson, in the article in *Films and Filming,* is moving in an unprofitable direction when he says that the six episodes of the film correspond to the "Six Great Evils of War": "injustice, human misery, degradation, the universality of war's suffering, insensitivity through familiarity, and futility" (p. 42). Rossellini simply does not work in this overly programmatic way.

7. Interestingly, all of the English that American audiences hear—and it is a great deal—is also retained in the Italian version of the film; thus bereft of subtitles, since they are rare in Italy, Italian audiences are forced to reenact the struggles of their fellow Italians to understand their American "friends."

8. In his brilliant, if eccentric, essay on *Paisan,* Robert Warshow complains that the existential truth of this sequence is ruined by the failed communication between Joe and Carmela, which attempts "to draw vague populist sentiment out of a purely accidental limitation, as if there were some great truth still to be discovered in the fact that one person speaks English and another Italian, and yet both are human beings" (*The Immediate Experience,* 2d ed. [New York: Atheneum, 1971], p. 252). In this formulation, at least, his characterization of Rossellini's theme seems reductive, fashioned primarily to score rhetorical points.

9. Armes, *Patterns of Realism,* p. 78.

10. Warshow, *The Immediate Experience,* p. 259. Callisto Cosulich relates the interesting anecdote that in order to pass the *American* censorship then in effect, the film treatment that Rossellini and the others prepared for Admiral Stone showed each episode ending with a white cross in a military cemetery; they explained to him that "this means that the film is meant as a respectful and affectionate homage to the memory of those Americans who lost their lives for the liberation of Italy, and is meant to be a message to their country" ("*Cosi nacquero 'Paisa' e 'Roma, città aperta,'*" *Antologia di Cinema Nuovo 1952–58,* ed. Guido Aristarco [Rimini: Guaraldi Editore, 1975], p. 674). This anecdote suggests that the Italians were a little less servile to the Americans than other circumstances might indicate.

Baldelli reports that Amidei's original version of the last episode was meant to stoke Italian patriotic feelings by having the American officer parachute into the mountainous Val d'Aosta rather than the plains of the Po, where he was to meet big, strong partisans all taller than he. Apparently, there was difficulty finding snow, and when the company stopped in the Po delta, the story of Dale and Cigolani was invented on the spot and filmed (Baldelli, *Roberto Rossellini,* p. 60).

11. Roger Manvell, "Paisa, Rossellini, e la critica inglese," *Cinema* [Rome], no. 28 (December 15, 1949), p. 322. The quotation from McGregor is from the original English, in *Time and Tide,* rather than a retranslation of Manvell's Italian version.

Others have at the same time seen the film as anti-British, especially, as might be expected, the British. Manvell said in the above-cited article that, while British opinion of the aesthetic quality of the film was mostly favorable (with a handful of naysayers), the dismay about the film's anti-Britishness was general. The principal points of contention concern, first, the two British officers sightseeing from the hills of Florence with their binoculars while partisans are dying in the streets below, and second, the sarcastic remark by an American in the last episode, "These people aren't fighting for the British Empire. They're fighting for their lives."

12. Armando Borrelli, *Neorealismo e marxismo,* pp. 81, 85. Henri Agel has argued persuasively, from a phenomenological point of view, against an overly tragic and depressed reading of the final sequence, especially in terms of the last images that come

before us. Disagreeing with the common critical view of the ending as thoroughly down-beat, Agel instead makes the point that the ending must be read in the fuller context of Rossellini's other films. In support of his view, he quotes Gaston Bachelard's *L'Eau et les rêves,* in which the philosopher says that water is "the essential ontological metamorphosis between fire and earth." Water can also be seen as the source of fecundity—in other words, as the location of a possible physical and spiritual rebirth—and Rossellini in fact uses this association, according to Agel, in the opening sequence of the film he made four years later on the life of Saint Francis of Assisi in which the monks are bathed in a wonderfully insistent and life-giving rain. Thus, when the partisans are pushed into the water at the very end of *Paisan,* it can be seen as a birth and death at the same time. The voice-over announcing the Allied victory in the spring, in this reading, would not be the bitter and ironic counterpoint that most critics have seen in it, but rather a kind of cause-and-effect analysis. It is, in fact, the men's sacrifice, says Agel, that *causes* the liberation of Italy that the voice-over is announcing as about to take place in the future. (*Poétique du cinéma: Manifeste essentialiste* [Paris: Éditions du Signe, 1973], p. 81).

13. Freddy Buache, *Le Cinéma italien d'Antonioni à Rosi* (Yverdon, Switzerland: Le Thiele, 1969), pp. 24–25.

14. Roland Barthes, *Mythologies* (New York: Hill and Wang, 1972), pp. 138ff.

15. Warshow, p. 256.

16. Gian Luigi Rondi, *Cinema italiano oggi* (Rome: Carlo Bestetti, 1966), p. 39.

17. We should also distinguish here, perhaps, between "past documentary" and "present documentary." Something about the absolute raggedness of *all* the elements of the documentary footage (for example, of the Allies entering Rome) tells us this is a filmed record of something that actually happened and that it preexisted the filming itself. On the other hand, at least the Naples episode further complicates matters by inserting the fiction *into* the documentary, in a process that seems to be the opposite of the use of the past documentary. I am thinking specifically of one of the exterior shots of this episode in which the boy drags the drunken soldier across a piazza toward the puppet show. The sequence is filmed in a real location, with hundreds of obviously genuine Neapolitans peopling the shot who clearly have no idea what is going on, many of whom, in fact, are looking directly at the camera. In some sense that remains to be specified, this, too, is documentary footage.

18. A good example of what I mean here might be the elaborate overlapping of sounds that has become the trademark of Robert Altman's films. When this technique first appeared in his film *M*A*S*H,* audiences were bewildered by the fact that everybody was talking at once. We know of course that this is in fact the way groups of people talk in real life, but, with the exception of limited use by Orson Welles and a few others, it was new to the screen. Nevertheless audiences quickly became used to this expansion of the "realistic" toward the "real," or, better, the incorporation of this aspect of the latter into the former, and now it has become a staple of television shows that vaunt their realism, like "Hill Street Blues." Needless to say, the almost complete inscription of this "aspect of reality" into the code of the realistic has made it much less exciting and vibrant, and seeing it repeated, week after week, makes its conventionality totally transparent (along with the hand-held camera in front of which characters continually walk, "realistically" blocking our view.)

19. Warshow, pp. 252–53.

20. Warshow attributes the power of sequences like these to their lack of ideas:
The speed of the action combined with the neutrality of the camera tends to exclude the possibility of reflection and thus to divorce the events from all questions of opinion. The political and moral distinctions between the snipers and their captors do not appear (even the visual distinction is never very sharp), and the spec-

tator is given no opportunity to assent to the killing. Thus the scene derives its power precisely from the fact that it is not cushioned in ideas: events seem to develop according to their own laws and to take no account of how one might—or "should"—feel about them (pp. 253–54).

21. Similar to the unresolvability of the monastery sequence is a point of undecidability that Ben Lawton has noticed concerning the Naples episode. In his view, the puppet-show battle between the Moor and the Saracen (into which the drunken G.I. wades feetfirst to "help out" his fellow black man) offers us a key to how to read the whole film:

> The distinction between oppressor and oppressed is tenuous at best. Although present throughout the film, this concept is perhaps most perfectly synthesized in the G.I. in the second episode: Joe is Black (and as such oppressed), a member of the American occupation forces (and, as such, an oppressor), drunk (and, as such, oppressed), and an M.P. (and, as such, an oppressor). Which is he ultimately? (Lawton, "Italian Neorealism," p. 16)

22. Solmi, *Federico Fellini*, p. 80.

23. Faldini and Fofi, *L'avventurosa storia*, p. 110.

24. Ingrid Bergman, *My Story* (New York: Delacorte Press, 1980), pp. 3–4.

8. *Germany, Year Zero*

1. Roberto Rossellini, "Dix ans de cinéma," part 2, *Cahiers du cinéma*, no. 52 (November 1955), 5.

2. Ibid.

3. Ibid., p. 4.

4. Faldini and Fofi, *L'avventurosa storia*, p. 111.

5. Ibid. Quentin Reynolds, who was gathering material for his book *Leave It to the People*, wrote that Rossellini told him that the film would cost $115,000 to make, and the reason it was so expensive was because of all the location shooting in Germany. The "actors" were chosen, in Rossellini's normal fashion, from among those with little or no experience. Accompanied by an old friend who had been locked up in a Nazi jail for fifteen years, Rossellini found real British soldiers, assorted Nazi generals, exwrestling champions, and literature professors to round out the cast.

6. Faldini and Fofi, *L'avventurosa storia*, p. 112.

7. *The War Trilogy of Roberto Rossellini*, p. 374. All further references will be included in the text.

8. From the film: "EDMUND: Aren't you a teacher any more? ENNING: No. The authorities and I don't see eye-to-eye any more on—(*he caresses the whole length of the boy's arm up to his neck, then under the chin*)—educational policy" (p. 383).

9. Enzo Ungari's remarks are recorded in *Dibattito su Rossellini*, ed. Gianni Menon (Rome: Partisan, 1972), p. 31.

10. Quoted in R. M. DeAngelis, "Rossellini romanziere," 356.

11. The semiotician Colin MacCabe has also noted what he calls the film's "subversive subtext." In a provocative article entitled "Realism and the Cinema: Notes on Some Brechtian Theses" (*Screen*, 15, no. 2 [Summer 1974], 19–20), MacCabe articulates an analysis, based on Lacanian and Althusserian theories of subject positioning, of the "classic realist text," in which he equates the metalanguage of the nineteenth-century realist novel with the simple "narrative of events" found in the cinema. According to MacCabe, they are comparable because both envelop the subdiscourses found within them, explain and pass judgment on them, while pretending at the same time to be "objective," and, in fact, invisible. I think his comparison finally does not work because he too easily assumes that film's narrative of events and the "reality of the image" are

always taken by an audience at face value, unproblematically, to be "the ways things are," rather than constructed. But of course the image or narrated event *usually* offers itself as authoritative, and in so disguising its status as discourse it pretends to naturalness rather than revealing itself as a specific articulation. In the films of Rossellini, however, especially *Germany, Year Zero*, MacCabe finds a *continuing strategy* of subversion of the dominant discourse, in fact, a "systematic refusal" of it. This is his analysis:

> In *Germany, Year Zero* . . . we can locate a multitude of ways in which the reading subject finds himself without a position from which the film can be regarded. Firstly, and most importantly, the fact that the narrative is not privileged in any way with regard to the characters' discourses. Rather than the narrative providing us with knowledge—it provides us with various settings. Just as in Brecht the "fable" serves simply as a procedure to produce the various *gests,* so in Rossellini the story simply provides a framework for various scenes which then constitute the picture of Germany in year zero. . . . Indeed the narrative of *Germany, Year Zero* can be seen as a device to introduce the final *gest* of Edmund's suicide—and in this it closely resembles the first reel of Brecht's own *Kuhle Wampe* (p. 20).

The problem here is that MacCabe is utterly neglecting the active part the very well-developed—and heavily melodramatic—narrative plot line plays from beginning to end in this film. If any film's dominant discourse can be identified with its narrative of events, then surely this one can be as well. Furthermore, MacCabe's privileging of Edmund's suicide over all other elements of the text is really little more than a sophisticated version of an error of twenty years' standing made by critics who have taken too literally Rossellini's remark that the only part of the film he was interested in was the finale. MacCabe continues:

> Secondly, Rossellini's narrative introduces many elements which are not in any sense resolved and which deny the possibility of regarding the film as integrated through a dominant discourse. The Allied soldiers, the street kids, the landlord, the Teacher's house—all these provide elements which stretch outside the narrative of the film and deny its dominance (p. 20).

How are these elements "not resolved"? They are all features of Edmund's story that discharge their narrative function and then disappear, just as they would in any film. With the exception of the Allied soldiers, as I have mentioned above, these are characters and places that enable Edmund's preordained narrative to go forward, unconventionally, perhaps, but with no less speed and no more problematically than any other character or place in the film. MacCabe's final point is that "the characters themselves cannot be identified in any final way," and thus end up being only a complex sum of differences. Of course, it is possible to read *all* characters, in fiction or in film, as virtual sites of a play of differences (and contradictions) rather than as having fixed identities. The problem is that MacCabe makes the claim for *this* film as against the mass of others. He is, in fact, offering what amounts to too radical a reading of Rossellini's actually rather mild antinarrative strategies in this film. His view of Rossellini's *technique,* on the other hand, where he does find evidence of a standard "realist ideology," is more convincing, and even rather obvious:

> If the reading subject is not offered any certain mode of entry into what is presented on the screen, he is offered a certain mode of entry to the screen itself. For the facts presented by the camera, if they are not ordered in fixed and final fashion among themselves, *are* ordered in themselves. The camera, in Rossellini's films, is not articulated as part of the productive process of the film. What it shows is in some sense beyond argument and it is here that Rossellini's films show the traditional realist weakness of being unable to deal with contradiction (p. 20).

12. The phenomenologist priest Amédée Ayfre praised the scene, claiming that it was here that Rossellini introduced "phenomenological description" to the cinema, and through specifically cinematic rather than philosophical means. What he means by this

term is the attempt "to describe directly our experience such as it is, and without regard for the psychological genesis or causal explanation which the scientist, historian, or sociologist can furnish for it." For Ayfre, Rossellini's originality stems from the fact "that at no moment does the child give the impression of 'acting,' of being an actor. One can't say whether his acting was good or bad. . . . This child has simply lived, he has simply existed before us and the camera has surprised him in this existence" (pp. 7–8).

Ayfre, unlike Rossellini's Marxist critics, sees the problem as a matter of *rescuing* neorealism from analysis and simple naturalism. Thus *Germany, Year Zero* points to the solution because it shows "concrete human events in which is co-present the entire mystery of the Universe. In other words, the mystery of being is substituted for the clarity of construction" (Amédée Ayfre, "Phénoménologie et néo-réalisme," *Cahiers du cinéma,* no. 17 [November 1952], 10. See also Ayfre's book, *Le Cinéma et sa vérité* [Paris: Les Éditions du Cerf, 1969], pp. 141ff.)

13. "A Discussion of Neo-Realism," 73.

14. Oms, "Rossellini: Du fascisme à la démocratie chrétienne," 13.

15. Borde and Bouissy, *Le Néo-réalisme italien,* p. 37.

16. Faldini and Fofi, *L'avventurosa storia,* p. 112.

9. *Una Voce Umana*

1. Jean Cocteau, *La Voix humaine* (Paris: Librairie Stock, 1930), p. 11. Mario Verdone has suggested a possible origin for Cocteau's play in a piece Sacha Guitry did for the troops in 1915, an entire act of nothing but him and a telephone, called *Faisons un rêve.* (Mario Verdone, "L'amore," *Bianco e nero,* 9, no. 9 [November 1948], 76.)

2. Roberto Rossellini, "Dix ans de cinéma," part 1, *Cahiers du cinéma,* no. 50 (August–September 1955), 6–7.

3. Interestingly, Rossellini has omitted something from Cocteau's version that, in fact, would have turned us against the man even more (but that also would have made the woman appear more victimized). Presumably in the interests of streamlining and focusing the action, the director has removed the occasional comic moments when other callers on the party line break in to the lovers' conversation. Thus, at one point, Magnani's reply to a woman who has been listening in tells us that the woman has apparently castigated the man for his callousness. Magnani searches desperately to soothe his hurt feelings by saying, in lines obviously meant to drip with dramatic irony, that the other woman just does not know him and mistakenly thinks he is just like all other men.

10. *The Miracle*

1. There is some dispute concerning the ending of the film. In Fellini's original version, according to Angelo Solmi, "Nanni rings the bell of a little church to announce the event. These ignorant men understand and fall on their knees crying that it is a miracle" (*Federico Fellini,* p. 82). Rossellini wisely avoided this ending, and in so doing made it consistent with the absence of a visible, verified miracle at the end of either *Stromboli* or *Voyage to Italy.* Guarner, however, says that "for the Paris presentation of *L'Amore* in 1956, Rossellini removed the end of the film in which bells rang out in greeting as the peasants welcomed the birth of the new saviour. The film now ends with the mother's first words to her child 'mio santo figlio' " (*Roberto Rossellini,* p. 28). As far as I have been able to discover, however, the version shown in Britain and the United States has always had this latter ending.

2. The Italian critic Mario Verdone and various elements of the South American press later claimed that the story was plagiarized from a novel called *Fior di Santita* by

the South American writer Ramon Maria del Valle-Inclan (1869–1936). The parallels are in fact remarkable, but Fellini continued to insist that it was his own invention. (See Verdone, "L'amore," 76–77).

3. Quentin Reynolds, *Leave It to the People* (New York: Random House, 1949), p. 149.

4. Ferrara, *Il nuovo cinema italiano*, p. 247.

5. "A Discussion of Neo-Realism," 72.

6. Borde and Bouissy, *Le Néo-réalisme italien*, p. 106.

7. Quoted in Ferrara, p. 245ff.

8. Interview, *Cahiers du cinéma* (1954), 4.

9. Quoted in Lillian Gerard, "Withdraw the Picture! the Commissioner Ordered," *American Film* (June 1977), 31. Gerard, who was managing director of the Paris at the time, is the source of much of the information in this chapter on the film's American reception.

10. Quoted in Gilbert Seldes, "Pressures on Pictures," *Nation*, 172, no. 5 (February 10, 1951), 133.

11. Quoted in Lillian Gerard, " 'The Miracle' in Court," *American Film* (July–August 1977), 27.

12. Interview, *Cahiers du cinéma* (1954), 4–5.

13. Quoted in Gerard, " 'The Miracle,' " 26.

14. This motif is suggested in *The Miracle*, however, especially in Nanni's relationship with the ambivalent, perhaps "divine," goat at the end of the film (the cause and effect of whose minor "miracles" are always suggested cinematically rather than verified). It is the goat, in fact, that leads Nanni to her place of "natural" childbirth.

11. *La Macchina Ammazzacattivi*

1. Massimo Mida, *Roberto Rossellini*, p. 55.

2. Guarner, *Roberto Rossellini*, p. 38.

3. Mario Verdone suggests the story may have come from a Maupassant short story in which a printer sends to hell everyone he makes calling cards for (Verdone, *Roberto Rossellini*, p. 40).

4. "A Discussion of Neo-Realism," 76.

5. Peter Bondanella, "Neorealist Aesthetics and the Fantastic: 'The Machine to Kill Bad People' and 'Miracle in Milan,' " *Film Criticism*, 3, no. 2 (Winter 1979), 26–27.

6. Ibid., p. 26.

7. Interview, *Cahiers du cinéma* (1954), 1.

8. Guarner, *Roberto Rossellini*, p. 34.

9. Baldelli, *Roberto Rossellini*, p. 85. The judgment of Borde and Bouissy is more violent and less convincing: "In 1948, the Fascists were showing themselves again. Everywhere people began preaching pardon, national reconciliation, and the cessation of all weeding out of former Fascists. Rossellini brought to the enterprise a contribution whose modesty is only due to his own awkwardness (118th at the box-office during 1951–52)" (Borde and Bouissy, *Le Néo-réalisme italien*, p. 109).

12. *Stromboli*

1. Bergman, *My Story*, p. 1. All further references to this book will be included in the text proper. Any seemingly bizarre shifts of point of view in citations from this work are accounted for by the fact that it was written by the actress in conjunction with a professional writer, and it alternates from first to third person throughout.

2. Bergman relates a fascinating series of contretemps that nearly prevented the actress and the director from ever getting together. An Italian she met in America told her she could reach Rossellini by writing to Minerva Studios. Then, the studio head-quarters burnt down just after her letter arrived; sifting through the ashes, they found the letter, but when the studio tried to contact Rossellini, he kept hanging up, since he was in a dispute with them at the time. When the letter finally managed to get to him, he had to have his secretary translate it from English—and then asked her who Ingrid Bergman was. Once apprised of her international fame, he quickly responded with an urgent telegram on May 8, his birthday, that it was "absolutely true that I dreamed to make a film with you," and that a long letter would follow, detailing his plans.

3. Faldini and Fofi, *L'avventurosa storia*, pp. 201, 203. One of the complications attending Rossellini's new interest in Bergman was the status of his current lover and star, Anna Magnani. Many are the stories of plates of spaghetti being thrown, of Rossellini cowering under hotel beds when Magnani found out. More important for cinema history is that Magnani sought her revenge by making her *own* version of *Stromboli*, called *Vulcano*, a rather undistinguished American film directed by William Dieterle on a neighboring island. It is a grandly overheated tale of love and deceit, with Magnani not in the romantic lead, interestingly enough, but rather playing the worldly-wise older woman who is trying to make her beautiful younger sister understand that the cad (Rossano Brazzi) will not marry her, as he says, but wants her for the white slave trade. She finally gets her way by seducing Brazzi, in the process permanently alienating her sister.

Though the specific details of the plot are thus quite a bit different, the harsh, de-nuded atmosphere of *Vulcano* and the hostile reception Magnani receives from the women when she returns to the island are embarrassingly close to the infinitely more subtle *Stromboli*, at least in spirit. In addition, Dieterle seems to share Rossellini's inter-est in documenting the daily lives of his characters at work. The film also includes an-other Rossellini favorite—the religious procession—as well as an ascent to the volcano and its eruption. Probably the most outrageous similarity is the tuna-fishing sequence, the idea for which seems to have been taken directly from Rossellini's film. Some footage is almost identical in the two versions, but in Dieterle's there is no attempt to relate the sequence thematically to the rest of the film. Brazzi says that after the filming session each evening, Magnani would go out to the end of the island and shout curses in the direction of Stromboli. Unfortunately, Magnani was not to get her wish of upstaging "la Bergman," because critics were hostile, finally, to both pictures. The ultimate irony is recounted by Jone Tuzzi, who had been spying for Rossellini on Dieterle's set: "At the premier of *Vulcano*, which came out before *Stromboli*, Magnani was expecting that everybody would be talking about her. Instead, the next morning the papers were filled with enormous headlines announcing that Bergman had given birth. So they even ruined her premier!" (Faldini and Fofi, *L'avventurosa storia*, p. 204).

4. "A Panorama of History," 99.

5. Dore Schary, *Heyday* (Boston: Little, Brown, 1979), p. 271.

6. Robin Wood, "Rossellini," *Film Comment*, 10, no. 4 (July–August 1974), 11.

7. *BFI Dossier Number 8: Roberto Rossellini*, p. 13.

8. Borde and Bouissy, pp. 109–10. The moral truculence of this view is matched by the naïveté of its quaint opposite, expressed by Giuseppe Ferrara, that "the way traveled by Bergman obviously signifies the lacerations of the Catholic woman in the modern world" ("L'Opera di Roberto Rossellini," in *Rossellini, Antonioni, Buñuel* [Padua, Venice: Marsilio, 1973], p. 40).

9. Jean-Claude Bonnet, "Roberto Rossellini ou le parti pris des choses," *Cinéma-tographe*, no. 42 (January 1979), 22. Rossellini himself has said of the tuna sequence, "I

tried to reproduce that eternal waiting under the sun, and the horribly tragic moment in which man kills: death which arrives unexpectedly after an extraordinary wait, abandoned, urgent, *I would say almost loving*, under the sun's rays." (Quoted in Claude Mauriac, *L'Amour du cinéma* [Paris: Albin Michel, 1954], p. 128; my emphasis.)

10. All quotations are taken from tape recordings of the two versions' sound tracks.

11. Adriano Aprà and Maurizio Ponzi, "An Interview With Roberto Rossellini," *Screen,* 14, no. 4 (Winter 1973–74), 114. (Interview originally appeared in Italian in 1965.)

12. In *Cinema 59,* no. 36 (May 1959), 50. (Note the suggestion of sadism in the desire to make Karin cry.) Bergman has given yet another reading of the ending, a reading that may have been influenced by her own circumstances. She told Robin Wood that the film "ended only with this woman looking at the sky; there *was* no end, which the public objected to. Of course, she would realize that there was a duty that she had to go back and have the child and live with her husband; but at the same time you don't know it, you have to guess it" ("Ingrid Bergman on Rossellini," *Film Comment,* 10, no. 4 [July–August 1974], 13). Complicating matters further is a lightweight piece of publicity fluff that appeared before the filming actually began. At this time the film was known as "Dopo l'uragano" (After the Hurricane), and the article gives a plot summary, the ending of which I include for its curiosity value: Karin tries to escape with the lighthouse keeper (in this version a fisherman), but a storm drives the boat back to land, where the husband catches up with them. A chase scene up the volcano follows between Antonio and Karin; Karin gets near the crater and starts a rock slide to kill her husband, but he escapes. At this point, Karin, exhausted, collapses into tears and an invocation to God. "Finally, pacified, she returns to the village and, made humble, goes back to her home." ("Ingrid come Karin," *Cinema* [Rome], no. 11 [March 31, 1949], 335).

13. Wood, "Rossellini," 10.

14. Andrew Sarris, "Beyond the Fringe," *Film Culture* (Spring 1969), 30.

15. Bruno Torri, *Cinema italiano: Dalla realtà alle metafore* (Palermo: Palumbo, 1973), p. 45.

16. "Je ne suis pas le père du néo-réalisme," interview with Henri Hall, *Arts* (June 16, 1954).

13. *Francesco, Giullare di Dio*

1. While the Italian version of the film is in many ways different from the version released in the United States, the mood and themes have generally not been as disturbed in the translation process as they were in *Stromboli.* In the European version of *Francesco,* there are no frescoes to set the historical scene; rather, it opens directly with the famous long shot on the road of the monks being drenched by rain. A voice-over explains that they have been granted approval by the Pope to form a new order. In this version, the initial scene is also much longer than in the American version; abstruse medieval debates about the best way to preach and Rossellini's increasingly characteristic accent on *temps mort* give the Italian version a greater feeling of "authenticity," but since the entire film is so deeply marked by the aleatory and the fragmentary, unlike *Stromboli,* the American version has not been unduly harmed by the "streamlining."

The most important changes are the two scenes omitted from the American version. In the first, Francis is lying on the ground, crying. He hears bells, looks up, and encounters a leper who tries to avoid him. Francis forces himself on the leper, finally kissing him on both cheeks. The leper moves away, and Francis falls to the ground again, crying. No words are spoken throughout the entire scene. The other scene missing in the American version concerns Francis' search for *letizia,* or "perfect joy." Walking along, he complains to his companion that he can perform miracles, but he has not yet achieved perfect joy. They arrive at a well-appointed house and begin badgering its owner to "serve the Lord"; when they refuse to give up, he throws them down the stairs and violently beats them. Francis then tells his companion that he has now found perfect joy. Clearly, this complex scene, delicately poised between the comic and the spiritual, must have been omitted as being too offbeat.

In addition to these two major omissions, sequences presumably considered "unmotivated" or too grossly physical were omitted from other scenes that, in the main, have been preserved. Thus, in the final scene, the monks' visit to a small church has been cut, and in the long scene in the tryrant's camp, a sequence of a man trying to fill an entire cup with blood from his nose has been removed, as well as a sequence of Brother Juniper being dragged along the ground by a horse.

2. Also like *Stromboli, Francesco* opens with an epigraph. In this case, it is taken from Paul's first Epistle to the Corinthians (1:27–28): "But God hath chosen the foolish things of the world to confound the wise; and God hath chosen the weak things of the world to confound the things which are mighty; And base things of the world, and things which are despised, hath God chosen, yea, and things which are not, to bring to nought things that are." In this film the struggle toward God, which seems to erupt so suddenly at the end of *Stromboli,* has already been achieved, or, better, is continually in the process of being achieved.

3. Rossellini's manner of speaking about the monastery sheds light, I think, on his intentions in both films:

> I was very moved by their innocence. It was magnificent. A very wise old monk, Fra Rafael, who was a servant, not a real priest, said he was a poet. I asked him what kind of poetry he was doing. He said, 'I wrote a poem about a rose.' I asked him to tell it to me. He closed his eyes and lifted his face toward the sky and said 'Oh, Rose!' and that was the whole poem. How can you have a better poem than that? It was also a sign of tremendous humility. I became very close friends with a number of the Franciscans and I thought of making a film about Saint Francis.

(Victoria Schultz, "Interview with Roberto Rossellini, February 22–25, 1971 in Houston, Texas," *Film Culture,* no. 52 [Spring 1971], 12–13.)

4. Brunello Rondi, "Per un riesame del *Francesco* di Rossellini," *Rivista del cinema italiano,* 4, no. 1 (January–March 1955), 89.

5. Mida, *Roberto Rossellini,* p. 73.

6. Jose Guarner, *Roberto Rossellini,* p. 48; Giorgio Tinazzi, "Per un riesame di Rossellini," in Mario Verdone and Giorgio Tinazzi, *Roberto Rossellini* (Padua: Centro cinematografico degli studenti dell'università di Padova, 1960), p. 34.

7. The shift from *coralità* to an active questioning of the group, which we saw in operation in these two earlier films, continues in *Francesco.* Critics who welcomed it as a return to *coralità* forget that this quality is seen only in terms of the values of the tiny group of equally "crazy" people. In the terms of the larger social group, which is here barely seen, these religious figures are as marginal as Karin, Nanni, or Irene in *Europa '51.*

8. It can be argued, of course, that Rossellini always shows those who are striving, incomplete, imperfect creatures to be women, and the ones who have already attained peace, rest, and happiness to be men (the Franciscans). This depiction, however, seems to have been the result of a return to the historical beginnings of the search for joy and simplicity, rather than an argument for the spiritual superiority of men over women. Furthermore, the scene in which Saint Clair and a few nuns visit the friars clearly indicates that the women have reached the same spiritual level as the men.

This distinction is important in light of the extensive attack on Rossellini, on ostensibly feminist grounds, by the editors of the British Film Institute dossier on the director.

They rely on the scurrilous article by Marcel Oms, "Rossellini: Du fascisme à la démocratie chrétienne," for their "ammunition." Thus, they quote approvingly from the essay:

> Rossellini's misogyny had two possible conclusions: the first one was to destroy the
> woman, that is to say, to make a film of Honegger's and (above all) Claudel's ora-
> torio *Joan of Arc at the Stake*. The second way of despising woman was to ignore
> them. What could have been more logical in Rossellini's oeuvre than the filming of
> that monument to stupidity which is *Francis, God's Jester*. Never before have Chris-
> tianity and cretinism been so close to one another. . . . To the film's credit is its
> testimonial value. Because of its realism, *Francis* remains an objective and irrefutable
> document about those who are in need of wits. Also there remain a few images of
> masochism when Francis gets himself trampled on by his brothers or when Ginepro
> faces the tyrant. . . . Unfortunately, it is not by humiliating oneself in front of
> them that one brings down tyrants (ellipses in BFI citation, p. 14; Oms, pp. 15–16).

It is bad enough that as late as 1981 the editors choose to rely so heavily on Om's article,
which they call "violent but fair." The more egregious choice is to elide in their citation
from the article the few sentences in which Oms displays that he is perhaps talking about
his own problems more than about the film. This is the part in which he fantasizes about
how much better the film would have been if Saint Francis and Saint Clair "discovering
passion, would have shut themselves up in the little hut or would have made love in
front of the brothers. . . . Then Francis would have sung the praises of the flesh, and
given up preaching in order to live. . . . But I'm dreaming, because the film is far from
having this grandeur" (p. 15). Clearly, Oms is not the best source for a critical judgment
concerning this film.

9. "Un cinema diverso per un mondo che cambia," interview in *Bianco e nero*, 25,
no. 1 (January 1964), 14.

10. Henri Agel, *Poétique du cinéma*, p. 83.

11. Henri Agel, *Le Cinéma et le sacré* (Paris: Éditions du Cerf, 1961), pp. 76–77.

12. Brunello Rondi, *Filmcritica*, nos. 147–48 (July–August, 1974). Quoted in *Lo splendore del vero: Quarant'anni di cinema di Roberto Rossellini*, ed. Giuliana Callegari and
Nuccio Lodato, p. 73.

13. Tinazzi, "Per un riesame di Rossellini," p. 34.

14. Pio Baldelli, "Dibattito per 'Francesco' di Rossellini," *Rivista del cinema italiano*,
3, nos. 11–12 (November–December 1954), 60.

15. The forever "otherness" of God does not challenge the tenets of the metaphysics
of presence, as one might expect, but in fact enables it. As Jacques Derrida has said,

> The infinite alterity of the divine substance does not interpose itself as an element
> of mediation or opacity in the transparence of self-relationship and the purity of
> auto-affection. God is the name and the element of that which makes possible an
> absolutely pure and absolutely self-present self-knowledge. From Descartes to Hegel
> and in spite of all the differences that separate the different places and moments in
> the structure of that epoch, God's infinite understanding is the other name for the
> logos as self-presence (*Of Grammatology*, p. 98).

Francesco's need for the discontinuous, marked clouds to represent a continuous, un-
marked heaven recalls Shelley's poem "The Cloud" (1820), which ends with the following lines, told from the cloud's point of view:

> For after the rain, when with never a stain,
>   The pavilion of Heaven is bare,
> And the winds and sunbeams, with their convex gleams,
>   Build up the blue dome of Air—
> I silently laugh at my own cenotaph,
>   And out of the caverns of rain,
> Like a child from the womb, like a ghost from the tomb,
>   I arise, and unbuild it again.—

14. *Europa '51*

1. "Ingrid Bergman on Rossellini," p. 13.

2. Claude Mauriac has quoted a long passage from Weil, a passage whose source he does not identify, in his discussion of *Europa '51*. Its emotional texture is so close to that of the scene in the film that it seems useful to translate it here:

> My body and soul were in shreds. This contact with unhappiness had killed my youth. . . . I knew that there was a lot of unhappiness in the world, I was even obsessed by it; but I had never experienced it in such a prolonged way. Coming out of the factory, confused in everyone's eyes, including my own, with the anonymous masses, the unhappiness of the others went right into my flesh and into my soul. Nothing separated me from it, for I had actually forgotten my past and looked forward to no future, and I found it difficult to imagine the possibility of surviving these trials. What I had lived through had marked me in such a profound way that even today, when any human being, whoever he is, in whatever circumstances, speaks to me without brutality, I can't avoid the impression that there must be some mistake and that the mistake will soon disappear. In that place I received forever the mark of slavery, like the mark from the red-hot iron the Romans put on their most despised slave. Ever since, I have always thought of myself as a slave (*L'Amour du cinéma*, p. 115).

One further source that Rossellini has mentioned in one or two obscure interviews, without elaborating on it, is an early book of Herbert Marcuse's, presumably *Reason and Revolution* (1941). Rossellini said that while the film, of course, was not based on the book, it nevertheless made him think about things "differently."

3. Guarner, *Roberto Rossellini*, p. 51.

4. Maurizio Ponzi, "Due o tre cose su Roberto Rossellini," *Cinema e film,* 1, no. 2 (Spring 1967), 25.

5. "A Discussion of Neo-Realism," 76.

6. Two years after the interview with Mario Verdone quoted above, Rossellini was telling François Truffaut and Eric Rohmer the story of the scientist friend who was forced to rule on whether to send a woman to an insane asylum. The scientist told Rossellini that he had to "dissociate the human being from the scientist even in myself; science has its limits, it must calculate, see, measure, regulate itself according to that which it has conquered, that which it knows. You must completely forget everything that's beyond these limits." Rossellini's reponse to his story was, "In a century which is dominated by science—and we know that it's imperfect and has such atrocious limits—I don't know to what point it's right to trust in it. That's what the film's about" (Interview, *Cahiers du cinéma* [1954], 8). In the years to come, he will exactly reverse this early position.

7. The film also shares in the dynamic we have seen at work in the earlier films, where an artifact (such as a fresco) or the words themselves provide an ontological bridge between the present and the past because they are *of* the past (not merely a representation of it) and yet *in* the present as well. Here, in a complex way, we can think of this very film as being an equivalent artifact that, like all films, exists in both the past and the present and thus mediates between them.

8. Other objects also function as blatant visual symbols: the contrite mother's tears at the hospital clash with the luxuriance of her mink coat; later the same contrast is enacted in the family's Cadillac, particularly ostentatious and out of place in the crowded streets of Rome's teeming poor.

9. The scene in which Irene is told of the boy's death is very powerful. When she is nearly prostrate, the camera catches her face against a starkly white pillow, a composition that resonates for mysterious reasons. Her husband says that "life goes on," refusing by

that remark to take any blame for what has happened. (Earlier, the "competent" father says, "I've solved many problems," but confesses that the unhappiness of his son is one that he has not been able to "solve.")

10. This scene in the car is iconographically important, for it marks the beginning of an extensive use of this visual and spatial motif that becomes central in *Voyage to Italy* and in *Fear,* functioning far beyond its obvious utility as visual and narrative punctuation between other spatial locations.

11. This additional method of calling the "naturalness" of the cinematic representation into question through the interjection of the "real" into the "realistic" can also be considered in the light of Lacanian psychoanalysis. Just as Holbein's anamorphic death's head in his painting *The Ambassadors* calls into question the wholeness of vision by making it dependent on a particular point of view, so, too, throughout his career Rossellini allows shots of nonprofessional actors looking directly into the camera to stand, even though they blatantly challenge the film's illusionism.

12. Eric Rohmer, "Europa '51," *Cahiers du cinéma,* no. 25 (July 1953), 45.

13. "We are prisoners . . . of our desire to be in harmony with everything and everyone. Worshippers of the rule, we live in terror of one day becoming the exception." Because Irene becomes a nonconformist, says Rossellini, she is considered mad. "She doesn't recognize the fiction of honesty, like all the others? Then she's crazy! She doesn't accept the hypocrisy of charity beneficial to oneself, as the others accept it? Then she's crazy! . . . Crazy, everyone outside of political parties! Crazy, everyone outside of churches! Crazy, everyone outside the bounds of conformity!" (*Rassegna del film* [February 1, 1952], quoted in Borde and Bouissy, *Le Néo-réalisme italien,* p. 110).

14. Guido Aristarco, "Europa '51," *Cinema nuovo,* 1, no. 1 (December 15, 1952). Reprinted in *Antologia di Cinema Nuovo 1952–58,* p. 685.

15. Gianni Aiello, *Il cinema italiano negli ultimi vent'anni* (Cremona: Gianni Mangiarotti Editori, 1964), p. 32.

16. Rondolino, *Rossellini,* p. 81. André Bazin, in a little-known 1953 review of the film, defends it against the charge of reactionary politics and then, as might be expected, moves toward a phenomenological and spiritual reading of the film. In the process, he attempts to incorporate what I have been calling Rossellini's expressionism or stylization into a larger conception of "realism." His remarks are worth quoting in full:

> Rossellini doesn't have his actors *act,* he doesn't make them *express* this or that feeling; he only makes them *be* a certain way in front of the camera. In such a mise-en-scène, the placement of the characters, the way they walk, their movements and gestures are much more important than the feelings shown on their faces, and even more important than what they say. . . .
>
> That such a mise-en-scène requires a highly evolved stylization is obvious in *Europa '51.* This realism is completely the opposite of what is "taken on the spot": a strict and austere language, stripped sometimes to the point of asceticism. At this point, neorealism discovers classic abstraction and its generality. Whence this apparent paradox: the correct version of the film is not the one dubbed into Italian, but the English version, which has the maximum number of original voices. At the limit of this realism the exactitude of exterior social reality becomes unimportant. Roman street children can speak English without our thinking that it's unconvincing. Reality, by the tricks of style, renews itself through the conventions of art.

(André Bazin et al., *Cinéma 53 à travers le monde* [Paris: Éditions du Cerf, 1954], pp. 88–89).

17. Ponzi, "Due o tre cose," p. 25.

18. *Dibattito su Rossellini,* ed. Menon, p. 87.

15. *Dov'è la Libertà?*

1. Mida, *Roberto Rossellini*, p. 72.

2. Pierre Kast, *Cahiers du cinéma*, no. 56 (February 1956). Quoted in Patrice Hovald, *Le Néo-réalisme italien et ses créateurs* (Paris: Éditions du Cerf, 1959), p. 117.

3. "A Panorama of History," 99. It is difficult to know just how much to credit Rossellini's statement concerning the film's producers. As we have seen, he often claimed that his films had been changed against his will, yet he rarely bothered to go into detail concerning the changes.

4. Interview, *Cahiers du cinéma* (1954), 6.

5. Franca Faldini and Goffredo Fofi, *Totò: L'uomo e la maschera* (Milan: Feltrinelli, 1977), p. 110.

16. *Voyage to Italy*

1. Interview with J. Douchet, *Arts*, no. 739 (September 9, 1959), 6.

2. Pierre Leprohon, *The Italian Cinema* (New York: Praeger, 1972), pp. 132–33. His play on the French word *interprète*, which means both "interpreter" and "actor," is lost in the translation.

3. Wood, "Rossellini," 10.

4. Bergman, *My Story*, p. 307.

5. Ibid.

6. Riccardo Redi, "Buono o cattivo il vino nuovo?" in *Cinema*, no. 124 (1953), quoted in Adriano Aprà and G. P. Berengo-Gardin, "Documentazione su Rossellini," *Bianco e nero*, 25, no. 1 (January 1964), 34. The interested reader should also see Sanders' autobiography, *Memoirs of a Professional Cad* (New York: Putnam, 1960), for further negative impressions of the filming. Concerning the Bergman-Rossellini collaboration, Sanders' final analysis was, "Far from being devoured, Ingrid was eventually to emerge triumphant, and Roberto was destined to bite the dust of obscurity, having improvidently exhausted his marvelous talent for raising money." (Sanders, p. 125.)

7. Quoted in Aprà and Ponzi, "An Interview With Rossellini," pp. 120–21.

8. "Ingrid Bergman on Rossellini," 12.

9. Aprà and Ponzi, "An Interview with Rossellini," 121.

10. G. C. Castello, *Cinema*, nos. 146–47 (December 1954), 738. On the other hand, an exceptionally fine contemporary analysis of the film, written by the French critic Phillipe Collin, can be found in *Télé-Ciné*, no. 50 (July–August 1955), 2–10.

11. *Filmcritica*, nos. 156–57 (April–May 1965). Five also mentioned *Paisan*.

12. Eric Rohmer, "Voyage en Italie," *Cahiers du cinéma*, no. 47 (May 1955), 40.

13. Guarner, *Roberto Rossellini*, p. 57.

14. Pierre Marcabru, "Les Derniers Feux du néo-réalisme," *Arts* (June 21, 1961), 13.

15. Leprohon, *The Italian Cinema*, pp. 138–39.

16. Baldelli, *Roberto Rossellini*, pp. 222–23.

17. Bazin, *What Is Cinema?*, vol. 2, p. 98. Bergman also told Robin Wood in her interview with him ("Ingrid Bergman on Rossellini," 14):

> In *Voyage to Italy*, it was also to show Pompeii. He adored Pompeii. He knew everything about it. He was only looking for a story into which he could put Pompeii and the museums and Naples and all that Naples stands for, which he always was fascinated with, because the people in Naples are different from the people in Rome and Milan. He wanted to show all those grottoes with the relics and the bones and the museums and the laziness of all the statues.

18. Leo Braudy, "Rossellini: From 'Open City' to 'General della Rovere,'" in *Great*

Film Directors: A Critical Anthology, ed. Leo Braudy and Morris Dickstein (New York: Oxford University Press, 1978), p. 668.

19. It is perhaps not overreading to find the play of the lights more than visual choreography. They can also be seen as parallel to the sun, with its multiple opportunities for rapprochement, as we shall see (especially through its connection to the idea of "Italy"); when the lights are on, there is a chance the couple will begin to communicate, but for fear of exposing herself, Katherine each time extinguishes the light and plunges herself and their relationship back into the darkness.

20. This minor, if problematic, point of conscious intertextuality should be mentioned here—that is, the clear references that the film makes to Joyce's brilliant concluding story of *Dubliners.* The film's characters' last name is Joyce, of course, and the mention in the film of a romantic, rather tubercular, poet who courted Katherine just before she married Alex parallels Joyce's story. Even a few of Katherine's lines seem to have been lifted from "The Dead." Nevertheless, Rossellini has done little to develop these links.

Luciana Bohne has usefully explored this connection in "Rossellini's *Viaggio in Italia:* A Variation on a Theme By Joyce," *Film Criticism,* 3, no. 2 (Winter 1979), 43–52. Her reading of the film is refreshingly unconventional, especially in the way she interprets the final sequence, but her articulation of the film's themes with those of the story is vitiated by a univocal reading of Joyce's immensely ambiguous short story.

21. Lines quoted from the film are taken directly from the English sound track and from a transcription of the sound track of the Italian version published in *Filmcritica,* nos. 156–57 (April–May 1965). At times, the dialogue differs markedly in the two versions.

22. Michael Shedlin, "Love, Estrangement, and Coadunation in Rossellini's *Voyage to Italy,*" *Women and Film,* no. 2 (1972), 46.

23. Here the volcano seems to operate on two levels, suggesting both the male principle, as in *Stromboli,* and the "femaleness" of its crater, negated in the earlier film by the crater's violent, threatening activity.

24. Aprà and Ponzi, "An Interview with Roberto Rossellini," 113.

25. Jean Renoir quotes this shot, transposed to a comic vein, in the opening minutes of *Eléna et les hommes* (1956), the first film Bergman made with another director after the beginning of her collaboration with Rossellini.

26. Ibid., p. 112.

27. In more practical terms, Truffaut and his friends were helpful as well. The French distributor, who was also one of the coproducers, had, according to Rossellini, "completely changed" the film, including the title (to "The Divorcée of Naples"), and even the story line itself. Truffaut mounted a critical boycott of this version of the film, forcing the distributor to rerelease the original version of the film, with subtitles. It was from this contretemps that the friendship with the men who were to become the New Wave began. This relationship is immensely complicated, of course, and cannot be done justice in a note. Rossellini did coauthor the script of Godard's *Les Carabiniers* in the early sixties, but admitted that he had never seen the film. He also once mentioned a moment in 1956 when he approached a French producer with the script of Truffaut's *The 400 Blows,* Chabrol's first script, and "many ideas" of Godard's, requesting 200,000 francs and offering his own services as producer, but the project fell through. According to Rossellini, his own influence on the aesthetic side of the New Wave was slight:

> We're good friends, we see each other frequently, I sometimes act as their father, their mother, their nurse, in other words, when they have problems, even personal ones, they come to me: but we've never really discussed aesthetic problems. I think what they saw in my films was disdain for the traditional forms of cinema. I remember that there was a time when all the critics were accusing my films of being badly made, or accusing me of inattention or even distraction. Well this criticism, which

came from critics who were very tied up with the traditional forms, really riled these boys. So I think that their enthusiasm was not so much due to the artistic material as to the manner in which things were expressed and also to the mental attitude of liberty, the true and total freedom which means that you can't be tied to anything. ("Un cinema diverso per un mondo che cambia," 9.)

28. Quoted in Patrice Hovald, *Roberto Rossellini* (Brussels: Club du Livre du Cinéma, 1958), no page; no citation given.

29. Jacques Rivette, *Cahiers du cinéma*, no. 46 (April 1955), 19.

30. Patrice Hovald, *Le Néo-réalisme italien et ses créateurs*, p. 121. In his *Cahiers du cinéma* review, Eric Rohmer proclaimed more overtly the religious tendencies of this approach: for him, it is quite proper that the film ends with a miracle because "that's in the order of things, and this order, ultimately, is ascribable to miracle." There is no need to worry about the fallen condition of sacred art, either: "So what if the cinema takes over from the cathedrals!" (Quoted in Hovald, p. 121).

31. Rondolino, *Rossellini*, p. 84. For a more detailed formal analysis than the one presented in this chapter, the interested reader should see two exceptionally rigorous semiotic analyses of the film, based on the earliest work of Christian Metz. Both were published in *Cinema e film*, 1, no. 2 (Spring 1967). The first is by Gianfranco Albano, Paquito Del Bosco, and Luigi Faccini, "Materiali per un analisi in svolgimento su Rossellini." The second is by Adriano Aprà and Luigi Martelli, "Premesse sintagmatiche ad un'analisi di 'Viaggio in Italia.' "

17. Three Sketches

1. Jean-José Richer, review of *Les Sept Péchés capitaux*, *Cahiers du cinéma*, no. 13 (June 1952), 67. The other episodes of this largely French film, and their directors, are: Yves Allégret, "La Luxure" (Lust); Claude Autant-Lara, "L'Orgueil" (Pride); Carlo Rim, "La Gourmandise" (Gluttony); Eduardo de Filippo (a noted comedy writer, only recently deceased, who had done the screenplay for Rossellini's *La macchina ammazzacattivi*), "L'Avarice" (Greed) and "La Colère" (Anger); Jean Dreville, "La Paresse" (Sloth); and Georges Lacombe, who did the connecting sketch.

2. Mida, *Roberto Rossellini*, p. 77.

3. Verdone, *Roberto Rossellini*, pp. 47–48. Verdone also mentions that the sketch was shot in the Via Margutta, the painters' quarter of Rome, and that it used real art critics, dealers, and painters (including the male lead) to construct a "real-life tableau."

4. Jean-Luc Godard, *Cahiers du cinéma*, no. 92 (February 1959); quoted in Callegari and Lodato, *Lo splendore del vero*, p. 80.

5. Hovald, *Roberto Rossellini*, no page.

6. *Rassegna del film*, 3, no. 20 (January–May 1954). Another contemporary account of this film is by the cinematographer Tonino Delli Colli, who tells us of the incredible expense he had to go to to light the bomb shelter. Luckily, the producer Intascelli was "a crazy man who didn't worry about expenses." (Faldini and Fofi, *L'avventurosa storia*, p. 268).

7. Guarner, *Roberto Rossellini*, p. 67.

8. Borde and Bouissy, *Le Néo-réalisme italien*, p. 90.

9. Mida, *Roberto Rossellini*, p. 79.

10. John Minchinton review of *Siamo donne*, *Films and Filming*, 1, no. 3 (December 1954), 18.

11. "Ingrid Bergman on Rossellini," 14.

12. "A Panorama of History," 99.

18. Giovanna d'Arco al Rogo

1. Bergman, *My Story*, p. 310.
2. Quoted in Patrice Hovald, *Le Néo-réalisme italien*, p. 122.
3. "Je ne suis pas le père du néo-réalisme," 3.
4. Interview, *Cahiers du cinéma* (1954), 12. Twenty years later he was to tell interviewers that *Giovanna* was an experiment, and that he was mostly interested in the "technical side" of the film ("A Panorama of History," 100).
5. Quoted in Hovald, *Le Néo-réalisme italien*, p. 123.
6. "Joan at the Stake," *Theatre Arts*, 39 (May 1955), 31. In the same article, the magazine, presumably guessing, also said that when Rossellini came to film the oratorio, he changed everything except cast and costumes, just for a challenge.
7. Aprà and Berengo-Gardin, "Documentazione," 34.
8. Alessandro Ferraù, review in *Bollettino dello spettacolo* (February 1955), quoted in Aprà and Berengo-Gardin, "Documentazione," 35.
9. Patrice Hovald, *Roberto Rossellini*, no page.
10. Rondolino, *Rossellini*, pp. 85–86. Rossellini has, in fact, explained at great length the chemical and optical intricacies of the mirror technique he used to film *Giovanna*, a technique which became standard practice in both dramatic films like *Anima nera* and didactic films like *La Prise de pouvoir par Louis XIV*. (See the interview portion of Baldelli, *Roberto Rossellini*, pp. 202–3.)
11. Guarner, *Roberto Rossellini*, pp. 68–69.
12. Guarner mentions two other features of the film worth repeating: first, that Joan is here imagined as intensely human: "she is celebrated as a woman—you can even see her breasts through the tunic," as opposed to the sword-fighting youngster of Victor Fleming's earlier version with Bergman. The second point is an elaboration of Rondolino's concerning the film's circularity. Though he has spoken of it as a representation of God's point of view, as we saw, he also convincingly describes it as a literalization of the earthly prison that surrounds Joan, which she desperately tries to escape:

> The idea of the circle recurs at all levels in the film, in a) the dramatic construction, which ends where it began, b) the visuals, with all their circular forms, c) space, constantly closed in on itself, like a cyclorama which includes the whole set, and d) finally, the camera-movements characterised by pans and circular tracking shots which sooner or later are completed to close the circle. *Giovanna d'Arco al rogo*, though seeming static, is in fact an enormous slow gyration, gradually travelling round to reveal its start (Guarner, pp. 69–70).

13. Michel Estève, "Les Séductions de l'oratorio filmé ou le merveilleux contre le surnaturel," *Études cinématographiques*, nos. 18–19 (Fall 1962), pp. 65–71.
14. Claude Beylie, "Défense de *Jeanne au bûcher* ou la sérénité des abîmes," *Études cinématographiques*, nos. 18–19 (Fall 1962), pp. 72–78.

19. Fear

1. Faldini and Fofi, *L'avventurosa storia*, pp. 338–39. All ellipses except first are in the original.
2. Bergman, *My Story*, p. 326.
3. Quoted in Bergman, *My Story*, p. 327.
4. Guarner, *Roberto Rossellini*, p. 73. The point about their marital collapse is, of course, somewhat overstated, as their marriage did not end for some years, an end that did not seem irrevocable until Rossellini fell in love with another woman during the filming of *India*.
5. As Rossellini told an interviewer: "It's the instincts which interest me. If that's

what the critics call neorealism, I agree. And, in all my films, I have always tried to get closer to the instincts." (Quoted in Verdone, *Roberto Rossellini*, p. 95.)

6. Guarner, *Roberto Rossellini*, p. 73.

7. Aprà and Berengo-Gardin, "Documentazione," 35.

8. Baldelli, *Roberto Rossellini*, p. 242.

9. Quoted in Verdone, *Roberto Rossellini*, p. 95.

10. *BFI Dossier Number 8*, p. 18.

20. India

1. Interview, *Film Culture*, 24–25.

2. Cited in Aprà and Berengo-Gardin, "Documentazione," 35.

3. Interview, *Film Culture*, 25.

4. Jean Herman, "Rossellini tourne India 57," *Cahiers du cinéma*, no. 73 (July 1957), 3. Ironically, many of the social problems mentioned by Herman, such as the nearly impenetrable Indian bureaucracy, are never taken up by Rossellini in the film.

5. *New York Sunday News*, May 26, 1957, p. 86.

6. See also Jean Herman, "Rossellini: L'Anti-digest défakirisateur," in *Cinéma 57*, no. 21 (September–October 1957), 44–49. Mario Verdone, on the other hand, faults Rossellini for not really opening himself up to the country, and Ferdinand Hoveyda, a former editor of *Cahiers du cinéma*, even claims: "Leaving for India, Rossellini had taken the precaution of putting in his suitcase a scenario which he had written while still in Paris. But I don't think that this was a violation of his principles." He then goes on to specify the preparations that Rossellini had been going through since 1955: reading English-language Indian newspapers, novels, letters, books about religion and philosophy. When he finally got to India, according to Hoveyda, he shot over forty thousand feet of color footage. ("La Photo du mois," *Cahiers du cinéma*, no. 69 [March 1957], 35; cited in Aprà and Berengo-Gardin, "Documentazione," 36). Herman paints a daunting portrait of the hazardous conditions the company endured to make this film: ants everywhere, often no phones or electricity, cobras, pythons, wild elephants (one almost killed Aldo Tonti, Rossellini's cameraman), heat reaching 108 degrees Fahrenheit, and eternal mechanical problems with the equipment. At one point Rossellini found out that one of his close friends had been killed during an automobile race. Exhausted by driving the enormous distances between locations and upset about his friend's death, Rossellini told Herman: "It's just like the whales when they're in a big group and they throw themselves against the shore of an island and kill themselves. What pushes them to do it? I feel this whale so strongly in myself" (p. 8).

7. *New York Times*, February 10, 1957, II, 5.

8. Interview, *Cinéma 59*, 51–52.

9. Herman, "Rossellini tourne India 57," 8–9.

10. Translated in *Screen*, 14, no. 4 (Winter 1973–74), 119–20.

11. Cited in Aprà and Berengo-Gardin, "Documentazione," 35.

12. Reprinted in *Jean-Luc Godard par Jean-Luc Godard* (Paris: Pierre Belfond, 1968), pp. 238–39.

13. *New York Times*, February 10, 1957.

14. There is very little information available on the footage made specifically for television, though it is known that it was shot first on sixteen-millimeter film, while the footage for theatrical release was shot on thirty-five-millimeter stock later (with the sequence of the tiger and the old man blown up from sixteen-millimeter to thirty-five-millimeter). From all appearances, the final product assembled for television was very sloppily constructed and the episodes rarely hung together. The version shown on Italian

television was somewhat different from that shown on the French (see Aprà's filmography in *Le Cinéma révélé* for titles of all the episodes, for both countries) and was rather poorly greeted due to an unsympathetic journalist who acted as "anchorman," and who very clearly had no idea what he was talking about. Renzo, the director's son, told me that the format consisted of this journalist and Rossellini commenting extempore on what was being projected at the moment. The journalist was apparently a terrible embarrassment who affected astonishment at everything Rossellini said about the country: "You mean they really have steel pipe there? Come on, you're kidding," and so on.

15. Interview, *Cahiers du cinéma*, no. 145 (July 1963), 4–5. Later, he rhetorically asks his interviewers, "Do you seriously believe that there can be art without the intervention of personality?" And then, in a surprising outburst, showed how emotionally charged the entire issue was for him:

> I went to a showing and said to myself: Well, this is cinéma-vérité. There was a camera on the floor [identified in a footnote as belonging to the Maysles brothers], and everyone was worshipping it, even though it was just a camera. A camera is a camera. It's just an object. That doesn't excite me, and it drives me crazy that a camera can excite someone. It's unbelievably stupid! This camera, which was exciting the minds and genitals of the people present, was something which left me absolutely indifferent. If I can't get excited by a camera, I can't understand the people who can. There are also pederasts in the world, but because I'm not a pederast, I can't understand them. You don't have any idea how ridiculous that evening was (p. 6).

He recognizes clearly, however, that Rouch's position is simply the logical extension of his own refusal of preordained scripts and professional actors: "I was saying the same things, yes, but I was saying them without totally destroying everything" (p. 7).

16. Torri, *Cinema italiano*, pp. 62–63.

17. *Jean-Luc Godard par Jean-Luc Godard*, p. 238.

18. Herman, "Rossellini tourne India 57," 9.

19. Originally appeared in *Cahiers du cinéma*, no. 96 (June 1959); reprinted in *Jean-Luc Godard par Jean-Luc Godard*. It has also been reported to me by Daniel Toscan du Plantier, the former head of Gaumont and a close friend of Rossellini during the last two years of his life, that when the director heard that Godard had said that *India* was more real than life itself, Rossellini told him he was crazy.

20. Mida, *Roberto Rossellini*, pp. 8–9. Unfortunately, Rossellini was not to enjoy his critical triumph in tranquility. Before he went to India, it was clear that his marriage with Bergman was not going very well, given the various professional and personal strains it had to endure. While abroad, Rossellini became romantically involved with his chief assistant, Sonali Das Gupta, who became pregnant. Like Bergman eight years earlier, this woman was already married, and the husband, a well-known Indian producer and director, understandably put up a fuss. Rossellini was threatened with expulsion from the country at various points, and the seamy details of the love triangle were played out in the world's tabloids for all to savor. Once back in Europe, after an embarrassing series of denials, the marriage of Rossellini and Bergman was annulled, freeing Rossellini to marry Das Gupta, who had by that time managed to escape from India to a private hideaway in Europe.

21. Baldelli, *Roberto Rossellini*, p. 148.

22. Andrew Sarris, "Rossellini Rediscovered," 61.

23. Interview with Fereydoun Hoveyda and Jacques Rivette, *Cahiers du cinéma*, no. 94 (April 1959), 11.

21. *General della Rovere*

1. Faldini and Fofi, *L'avventurosa storia*, p. 398.

2. Amidei complained in the interview cited above that, after the screenplay had been completed, Montanelli used it as the basis of a novel published solely under his own name, with no credit given to his fellow screenwriters (Faldini and Fofi, *L'avventurosa storia*, p. 398).

3. Quoted in Verdone, *Roberto Rossellini*, pp. 106–7.

4. "Un cinema diverso per un mondo che cambia," 19.

5. "A Panorama of History," 93.

6. Interview in Baldelli, *Roberto Rossellini*, pp. 231–32.

7. Interview with J. Douchet, *Arts*, 6.

8. Mida, *Roberto Rossellini*, pp. 90–91.

9. This is essentially the way in which Stanley Kaufmann's appreciative article ("Take Two: General della Rovere," *American Film*, 4, no. 6 [April 1979], 54–56) reads it. He tells us how much he likes the film, how it gets better on every viewing, because it is "one of that elite group, the necessary films" (p. 56).

10. *New York Herald Tribune*, November 20, 1960, 11.

11. *Variety*, January 11, 1961, 7.

12. "Un cinema diverso per un mondo che cambia," 9. Renzo Rossellini, the director's son, has said that finishing the film in time for Venice was producer Morris Ergas' idea. To accomplish it, they shot film during the day, and edited and dubbed at night.

13. It is during this bombing scene that Rossellini uses his newly invented Pancinor zoom for the first time, zooming in and out rather awkwardly on the prison windows three times. It is used once more, after Bertone has been beaten by the Nazis. The use of the zoom was to have a profound effect on Rossellini's mise-en-scène and sense of created space, as well as on his shooting methods and postproduction work. However, since it is employed only a handful of times in this film, I will defer a full discussion of it until the next chapter, on *Era notte a Roma*, where the zoom was utilized throughout.

14. Another way of saying this, in the vocabulary of the realist Rossellini, lies in Gianni Rondolino's formulation:

> This time, lacking the references to everyday concrete reality the representation becomes opaque, not very meaningful, even mystifying. Because . . . the historic background remains precisely that, a background, an appearance rather than a reality, notwithstanding the precise references to this or that meaningful detail, to this or that chronological or naturalistic aspect. The characters are dropped into a social and ambient reality which is sufficiently well-defined, but this "definition" does not exceed the limits of the kind of lithograph which tries to look like an oil painting. It does not cut into the genuine critical relations between reality and fiction, document and fabulation (*Rossellini*, pp. 97–98).

15. Of the various critics of this film, only Leo Braudy has came close to an understanding of what is at stake here:

> The importance and novelty of *della Rovere* for Rossellini's career derives directly from its acceptance of artifice—role-playing, the assumption of disguise—as a way toward moral truth. . . . [This film] introduces the idea that role-playing and disguise can lead to a liberation and realization of the self. By stressing De Sica playing Bardone [sic] playing Grimaldi playing della Rovere, it brings together for the first time in Rossellini's films his double interest in the naturalness of his characters and the artifice of his actors and actresses, and looks forward to the elaborate exploration of role-playing and artifice that Rossellini will conduct in *The Rise of Louis XIV*.

Braudy is right to stress the film's fascination with role-playing and artifice, but as we have seen, Rossellini had already been experimenting with it for over ten years. And

Braudy prefers, quite plausibly, to read the fantastic and the artificial as a way to further and more solidly ground the self and reality. It seems also possible, however, to read these elements as part of a general *destabilizing* of any and all fixed notions of self and of reality ("Rossellini: From 'Open City' to 'General della Rovere,' " p. 673).

16. Guido Aristarco, *Cinema italiano 1960* (Milan: Il Saggitore, 1961), pp. 15–17.

17. Lino Miccichè, *Il cinema italiano degli anni '60* (Venice: Marsilio Editore, 1975), pp. 35–36.

22. *Era Notte a Roma*

1. Sergio Amidei, the principal screenwriter, has said that he first got the idea for the film as an answer to the insults of General Montgomery, who had claimed that most Italians turned in escaped Allied prisoners rather than run the risk of hiding them. (Quoted in Baldelli, *Roberto Rossellini*, p. 154.)

2. "Jane Scrivener," *Inside Rome With the Germans*, p. 85.

3. The Russian is a new character in Rossellini's gallery, or almost new for, in fact, we saw Russian in *L'uomo dalla croce* (1943). In the earlier film, the Russian is a cynical ideologue, a *senza Dio* (godless one) who Rossellini portrays as negatively as the corrupt Nazis of *Open City*. After this film, the Russian simply disappears for seventeen years, to be reborn as the amiable, warm sergeant played by Serge Bondarchuk, the Soviet director. (According to Renzo Renzi, he was the first Russian since World War II to participate in a film made in the West.) As everyone at the time and since has recognized, the sergeant is a clear nod by Rossellini toward hopes for the continuance of détente after so many years of cold war. (In fact, Rossellini and Giovanni Ralli were awarded prizes at the Czech film festival in Karlovy Vary that same year for their work on the film.) It is precisely on these grounds that leftist critics such as Adelio Ferrero have attacked the film as "abstractly pacifist and basically mystifying," and thus a stupid attempt to inject sixties ideas about détente back into the Resistance period (Adelio Ferrero and Guido Oldrini, *Da Roma città aperta alla ragazza di Bube* [Milan: Edizioni di "Cinema Nuovo," 1965], p. 68).

4. This voice-over does not appear in the screenplay published in the "Dal soggetto al film" series (*Era notte a Roma di Roberto Rossellini*, ed. Renzo Renzi [Bologna: Capelli, 1960]), but was present in versions of the film that I saw both in the United States and in Europe. In the four versions of the film I have seen, each had different scenes missing. The published screenplay has both gaps *and* additional scenes that I have seen in none of the film versions. The time usually given in Italian sources is 120 minutes; Guarner gives 120 minutes in his filmography, but in his text says it lasts 145 minutes. The versions I have seen have run between 120 and 140 minutes. In this situation, the fixing of a definitive version is obviously impossible.

In this connection, it should be pointed out—and marveled at—how much English (and Russian) is left in the version of this film shown in Italy. Since subtitles are quite rare in that country, this means, as we saw earlier with *Paisan*, that contemporary Italians must fight the barriers of language as valiantly as the film's characters. Aprà and Berengo-Gardin report in their "Documentazione" that the Italian version of the film has more Italian in it, and while this seems correct, many moments important in terms of both dramatic emotion and narrative understanding pass completely in English.

5. *New York Times*, December 19, 1959. The idea of the film as the Resistance and Rome *as seen from the point of view of foreigners* is often stressed in interviews given by various people connected with the film. Brunello Rondi says that they had initially considered calling the film "The Anniversary," since, as originally planned, it was a return fifteen years later for "the Englishman who tells the story in the first person." According

to Rondi, the whole film was to be understood as told by Pemberton, but Rossellini decided to remove the narrated beginning. In the finished film some narration remains, but the identity of the voice is confusing. Though the voice never identifies itself as one of the protagonists, Rondi clearly suggests that it is Pemberton's voice (*Era notte a Roma*, ed. Renzi, pp. 68–71). Similarly, Jean-André Fieschi automatically assumes that the voice is Pemberton's ("Dov'è Rossellini?" *Cahiers du cinéma*, no. 131 [May 1962], 21). The problem is that the voice is clearly *American,* a fact that nonnative speakers might miss, but which can probably be ascribed to simple carelessness on Rossellini's part.

In any case, in this film the shift to a subjectively based depiction of reality is problematic and only partial, refused even the ground of its own doubt, for during the footage of the Anzio landing, another voice "objectively" narrates the events, speaking perhaps as the "voice of history." The point seems to be that the largest outlines of the great movements of human beings can perhaps be objectively stated, but any closer examination, if it is to be carried out with sincerity, inevitably entails a subjective relativization of these events.

6. When asked about this character in 1970, Rossellini told his interviewers, "This was someone I knew in real life. I had to hide from him for months. He was crippled, and that gave me some insight into his psychology, which gave rise to the character in the film" ("A Panorama of History," 97). Rossellini's easy conflation of physical, psychological, and moral deformities leads one to think that these bits of stylized characterization were based more on prejudice and sloppy thinking than on aesthetic grounds.

7. In the Spanish interview, Rossellini describes his increasing use of the zoom as a reaction to the excessive motion of hand-held cameras. "My system has two interlocking motors, and one of them acts as a counterweight to stop the lens oscillating as it moves, so that you don't get a zoom effect. This gives me great mobility—for example, I can zoom from an angle of 25 degrees to one of 150 degrees, and this opens up enormous possibilities." He also speaks of how well the set must be organized in advance in order to take advantage of the zoom as it follows the characters in all of their movements. "I was tending to do this even before: in *Europa '51* there were many very difficult moving sequences, which had to be shot with the camera on a dolly following the actors around the whole time. In Hitchcock's films the moving shots are very important and he has to have special sets built that the actors can appear and disappear in, which is extremely complicated. But the travelling lens simplifies all this enormously" ("A Panorama of History," pp. 103–4).

8. This may be because Rossellini did not yet feel at ease with the zoom, nor had he yet worked out the proper relation between the zoom and the cut, and was thus falling back on the most conventional editing patterns he knew. John Belton, in an excellent article on the dynamics of the zoom, entitled "The Bionic Eye: Zoom Aesthetics" (*Cinéaste*, 11, no. 1, 20–27) refers to an article by Joseph V. Mascelli published in 1957 in *American Cinematographer,* in which Mascelli describes how to disguise the zoom as a tracking shot by using a lot of doorways for the lens to "move" past. Given the plethora of doorways in *Era notte a Roma*, Rossellini may also, at this point at least, have been trying to disguise his new technique.

9. *Era notte a Roma,* ed. Renzi, pp. 39–40.

23. *Viva l'Italia!*

1. Aprà and Berengo-Gardin, "Documentazione," 37.

2. *BFI Dossier Number 8,* 22.

3. Guarner, *Roberto Rossellini,* pp. 87–88.

4. Andrew Sarris has also developed an interesting formulation of the zoom in this

film in the dynamic terms in which I have been speaking of it. If he errs on the side of overschematization, and of an overly rigid view of the continuity of history and time, nevertheless his comments offer a provocative symmetry:

> It is as if a painter could establish a dynamic relationship between his painting and one of its internal details. Garibaldi's men fight on a hill. Long shot equals *then*. Zoom shot equals *now*. The two shots in tandem are no longer limited to an imitation of an event. What we are watching is our own aesthetic and ideological distance from the event ("Rossellini Rediscovered," 62).

A related statement by Sarris about the relation of camera position and "moral position" concerns the sequence which shows the girl running to the beach, as the Thousand are preparing to cross the Strait of Messina to reach the mainland. Sarris correctly points out that the camera follows the girl through the sleeping town very closely, but, just as she gets to the beach and the troops are about to land, the camera pulls back "to emphasize the vast lateral distance involved between a moral impulse and a moral decision." The girl is killed, but "the camera keeps its cosmic distance." History is thus also kept distant, according to Sarris, in Rossellini's refusal to give in to a cheapening close shot. The problem with this analysis is that it completely ignores the heavy (Hollywood-style) sexual coding of this scene.

5. All of his material, with one exception, came from the standard contemporary accounts by Abba, Bandi, Dumas *père*, and others. The exception was the climactic meeting between Garibaldi and Mazzini, at which no one else was present. For this dialogue, Rossellini went to letters Mazzini wrote shortly after the meeting.

6. Verdone, *Roberto Rossellini*, p. 71.

7. MacCabe, "Realism and the Cinema," 20–21.

8. Baldelli, *Roberto Rossellini*, pp. 248, 250–51.

9. *Dibattito su Rossellini*, ed. Menon, p. 104. In the 1964 interview in *Bianco e nero*, Rossellini explained, rather cryptically, that using an older form of Italian for the dialogue "could become a little boring because of its antiquated form and the words that have fallen out of use. The result is that the realism of the dialogue is no longer realistic in our day, but it remains realistic because it is historically exact. But it's not with this that I want to make a claim to realism" ("Un cinema diverso per un mondo che cambia," 18).

10. Baldelli, *Roberto Rossellini*, p. 159. Actually, Mino Argentieri reports that the project began with this title because of Rossellini's desire to make it a chronicle of everyday life between May and October of 1860—and also with a view toward an American market for the film, which never developed ("Lo stivale di Garibaldi," *La fiera del cinema*, 2, no. 10 [October 1960], 37–41). Argentieri, in fact, quotes Sergio Amidei as saying that both films are about the liberated placing too much hope in their liberators.

11. Baldelli, *Roberto Rossellini*, p. 159. Another of Rossellini's proclivities may, according to Baldelli, have distorted the historical record in a small way. Early on in the film we see "partisans" hiding and conspiring in a monastery, much as they do in *Era notte a Roma* and other films. Later, the rebels are blessed by priests, and we see shots of monks running with rifles in their hands to Garibaldi's assistance, thus making clear the director's continual attempt to link religion and resistance. Baldelli has rightly pointed out that the Church itself was a bitter opponent of Garibaldi's, famed for his intense anticlericalism (nothing of which appears in the film), and that if these monks and priests joined the rebels, as Rossellini would have us believe, they did so under pain of excommunication.

12. See *Il Paese* for January 28 and February 7, 10, and 21, 1961.

24. *Vanina Vanini*

1. Rossellini maintained in an interview some years ago that the only *authentic* version of the film was stored at the Cinémathèque française. This bit of information has been dutifully repeated by one Rossellini critic after another, but I was unable to locate the print at the Cinémathèque. In the absence of the definitive print against which to compare the released version, we will have to rely on Rossellini's testimony and the testimony of later critics (most of whom, however, simply repeat Rossellini; one gets the impression reading the criticism that *no one* has ever actually seen the "authentic" version).

2. Baldelli, *Roberto Rossellini*, p. 169.

3. Jean-André Fieschi, review of *Vanina Vanini, Cahiers du cinéma*, no. 135 (September 1962), 41. The mystery of the definitive text continues in the United States as well. The only version of the film extant in the United States is distributed by Corinth Films, which lists it at 113 minutes; the Italian version, however, even after the producer's cuts, is listed at 125 minutes.

What is especially interesting in this controversy is that, despite his machinations, producer Ergas had obviously come completely under the spell of Rossellini's charm, as witness a newspaper interview he gave at the opening of the Venice film festival:

> It is my belief that the public is not only interested in junk; people also like to think, in fact, and to enjoy films which show some sensitivity. Our job as producers . . . is also cultural: to disseminate classic texts, through the expressive medium of the cinema, making them live again in the images of a film. Thus was born *Vanina Vanini* (Quoted in Aprà and Berengo-Gardin, "Documentazione," 38).

4. Gian Maria Guglielmino's criticism was excerpted in the film monthly *Il nuovo spettatore cinematografico* (no. 24 [August–September 1961]), whose editor declared that Rossellini obviously did not know the first thing about making a film.

5. Fieschi, review of *Vanina Vanini*, 41.

6. For example, at one point Vanina suggests to her lover that they run away to America, and Pietro replies, "No, because only money counts over there." Another invented line of dialogue not in Stendhal, which looks forward to Visconti's *The Leopard*, has Pietro shout at Vanina: "Remember that your world is doomed to disappear. You're all dead, and you don't know it."

7. Quoted in Verdone, *Roberto Rossellini*, pp. 74–75. Among their other charges: Rossellini changed Pietro from being rigorous and prudent (presumably the model for revolutionary heroes) to being vain and impulsive; he added a sexual interest between Pietro and the countess Vitelleschi (only a hint of which remains in the extant version); and he made Prince Vanini more debonair, as opposed to their Vanini, who had been based on the famous Jewish banker Torlonia. They also wanted the film to end during the Roman carnival, overtly recalling the ending of Carné's *Les Enfants du paradis*. Baldelli also reprints a long letter on the subject sent him by Trombadori. (See Baldelli, *Roberto Rossellini*, pp. 299–300, n. 23.)

8. Some ten years later Rossellini told Baldelli and his students: "I pushed it further toward a chronicle of the times, to a chronicle traced by a craftsman rather than by an artist like Stendhal. I don't know if . . . that is, I departed from his own mode, which was pretty romantic, no?" (Ibid., p. 241).

9. J. Hoberman, "Viva l'Italia II," *Village Voice*, November 19, 1979.

10. Hoberman has also pointed out the predominance of fluid two-shots of the lovers in this film over the more conventional combination of close-ups and reverse-angle shots. Along with Rossellini's "Sirkian lighting," he rightly claims that this causes it to become "a supremely tactile film" (Ibid.).

11. However, I would reject the obsessively overschematized reading of the color symbolism in which Paul Mayersberg indulges in an article on this film in the British journal *Movie* (no. 6 [January 1963], 321–34). Mayersberg also insists on specific symbolic readings of clothing, wood, and fire, in addition to the colors. In one short scene, for example, we see at a great distance some cut trees that have been stacked and other trees that remain standing. Mayersberg's very precise delineation of the political "meaning" of this lumber seems completely arbitrary.

12. Fieschi, review of *Vanina Vanini*, 42.

13. Ibid.

14. Stendhal's ending is incredibly abrupt. Pietro beats Vanina with the chains, and then the story ends with the following two sentences: "Vanina resta anéantie. Elle revint à Rome; et le journal annonce qu'elle vient d'épouser le prince don Livio Savelli" (Vanina was utterly overcome. She returned to Rome, and the newspaper announced that she had just married Prince don Livio Savelli) (Stendhal, *Chroniques italiennes* [Paris: Gallimard, 1952], p. 338). Rossellini was also very aware of the difference between his portrayal of Vanina and Stendhal's: "Stendhal's character is so cynical—a Roman noblewoman who believes in absolutely nothing and satisfies specific instincts, so this is where there is a substantial change in the character" (Aprà and Ponzi, "An Interview With Roberto Rossellini," 119).

15. Adriano Aprà has maintained, provocatively if rather reductively, that the film is about the absolute separation of the male and female worlds, which of course are also totally dependent on one another. Pietro is the line and Vanina is the circle; Pietro is the day and Vanina is the night. Now, however, the creature of the day is enmeshed in this film of the night, and the various light changes in the whorehouse are meant to signal that he is a mediator in the dream world of the film. In Aprà's paradigm, the liberation of the people becomes paradise, Pietro purgatory, and Vanina hell; or, alternatively, revolution, democracy (Pietro) and fascism (Vanina), though she is a "rebellious daughter" of the Fascist Church. (*Dibattito su Rossellini*, ed. Menon, p. 110).

16. There is a hint that the relationship between the Prince and the Countess Vitelleschi was originally meant to serve as a foil for, or commentary on, the relationship between Vanina and Pietro, for early in the extant version of the film the countess turns him away by declaring, "We've already sinned enough," thereby introducing the theme of sexual guilt that will haunt the young lovers. If so, this material was edited out with the rest of the first three reels.

17. In the story Vanina goes to the cardinal dressed as a man (thus paralleling Pietro's early disguise in both the story and the film as a woman), is discovered behind the curtain, pulls a gun on the cardinal, and informs him that she has removed the bullets from his own gun. She is described as "ravishing" and promises the cardinal a kiss if he helps Pietro. The conversation then turns cute, considering that it began with her brandishing a pistol. Finally, "Notre marché est fait! s'écria Vanina, et la preuve, c'est qu'en voici la récompense dit-elle en l'embrassant. Le ministre prit la récompense" (p. 334).

25. *Anima Nera*

1. Renzo Rossellini's statement is obviously not meant to be taken seriously, however. Adriano Aprà, in his recent filmography in *Le cinéma révélé*, reports that the forty-six-minute film was broadcast on September 10, 1961, at 10:45 P.M. The credits say that it was "realized" by Federigo Valli and directed by Rossellini.

2. Baldelli, *Roberto Rossellini*, p. 232.

3. Giuseppe Ferrara, "L'Opera di Roberto Rossellini," in *Rossellini, Antonioni, Buñuel*, 42.

4. Guarner, *Roberto Rossellini*, p. 102.

5. Baldelli, *Roberto Rossellini*, p. 232. Mirrors have long been used in filmmaking, Rossellini explains, but only with an immobile camera. His contribution was to devise a way to use mirrors in conjunction with the Pancinor zoom, so that both the camera and the characters could move during a scene without botching the take. His explanation of the optics involved goes on for some three pages in Baldelli.

6. Giuseppe Patroni Griffi, "Anima nera," in *Teatro* (Milan: Garzanti, 1965), p. 142.

26. "Illibatezza"

1. Verdone, *Roberto Rossellini*, p. 81.

27. Introduction to the History Films

1. Interview, *Cahiers du cinéma*, no. 133 (July 1962), 6.

2. "Responsabilità del governo passati e presenti," *Cinema nuovo*, no. 141 (September–October 1959), 413.

3. Roberto Rossellini, "Un nuovo corso per il cinema italiano," *Cinema nuovo*, no. 152 (July–August 1961), 307, 311–13. This essay was originally written as part of a conference held in Milan the previous year concerning "The Audio-Visual Media and the Man of Scientific and Industrial Civilization."

4. "Censure et culture" (open letter to Renzo Helfer), *Cinéma 61*, no. 60 (October 1961), 26.

5. Interview, *Cahiers du cinéma* (1962), 5. Further references to this interview will be included in the text.

6. Later, in 1965, he adds in his newspaper article "Difendere la speranza che è dentro di noi" the startling opinion that "the State, especially, will intervene to spread truth and knowledge." He affects the grand tone in his 1966 "La ricerca di stile e di linguaggio e il rinnovamento del contenuto" (*Filmcritica*, no. 167 [May–June 1966], 265), ending this essay with one of his most passionate appeals:

> I, a free man without preconceived ideas, do not favor optimism, but rather the knowledge of things. I'm against the professional mourners of progress, I'm against complaining, moaning, pulling out your hair, and all those who are so used to doing it. I think it is beautiful and exalting to live in the grand current of history, to live therefore in the midst of progress, not in its wake but with an alert mind and a critical sense so that it can be governed and we can find our way with it.

Rossellini's interest in science links him to another major figure of the twentieth century, Sergei Eisenstein, who also wanted, in the words of Barthélemy Amengual, "to reconcile the paths of science and those of poetry, reason and myth, thought and emotion" (Barthélemy Amengual, *Que Viva Eisenstein!* [Lausanne, Switzerland: Éditions L'Age d'Homme, 1980], p. 585). Most of Eisenstein's films, of course, were filled with physical action, and thus differ sharply from Rossellini's. However, one relatively little-known (and astonishing) project of Eisenstein's, the filming of Marx's *Das Kapital*, was closer to the spirit of the Italian director. Perhaps the clearest statement of the similarity of the two men's ideas comes in this 1930 remark of Eisenstein's made first at the Sorbonne:

> The intellectual film is the only thing capable of overcoming the discord between the speech of logic and the speech of imagery. On the basis of the speech of kino-dialectic, intellectual cinematography will not be the cinematography of episodes,

not the cinematography of anecdotes. The intellectual kino will be the cinematography of concepts. It will be the direct expression of entire ideological systems and systems of concepts.

My new conception of the film is based on the idea that the intellectual and emotional processes which so far have been conceived of as existing independently of each other—art versus science—and form an antithesis heretofore never united, can be brought together to form a synthesis on the basis of cinedialectic, a process that only the cinema can achieve. The scientific formula can be given the emotional quality of a poem. I will attempt to film *Capital* so that the humble worker or peasant can understand it in the dialectical manner.

(Quoted in Marie Seton, *Sergei M. Eisenstein*. Revised edition [London: Dennis Dobson, 1978], p. 153. The lecture was originally published as "Les principes du nouveau cinéma russe," in *Revue du cinéma*, no. 9 [April 1930].)

However, while both directors want to aid their audiences to "think" better and presumably more critically, Rossellini believes that the process of thinking is itself unproblematic, and he sometimes seems to be saying that what is important is the sheer amount of information transmitted. For Eisenstein, however, the purpose of filming *Das Kapital* will be not to convey information, nor even to teach Marxist principles, but to aid the spectator in learning to *think dialectically*. Amengual explains that as part of this attempt

to liberate the spectator and not to subjugate him, to give him an instrument (dialectical materialism) and not to indoctrinate him, Eisenstein planned—an idea that was more Vertovian than Brechtian—to reveal his own game periodically and thus make his passive "subject" a partner who had been warned: "The mechanics of production must be made explicit. To conduct the spectator, by means of a chain of cinematic provocations, up to a specified emotional effect, and then furnish him a card saying 'Well, now we arrived at such and such a point' " (p. 588).

Except for certain complicated aspects of *Louis XIV*, which I will look at more closely later, Rossellini emphatically does not (intentionally) reveal himself or his game in these films.

7. "Cinema: Nuove prospettive di conoscenza," *Filmcritica*, nos. 135–36 (July–August 1963), 52.

8. *Informazione democrazia: La RAI TV in Italia*, ed. Beppe Lopez (Rome: Dedalo Libri, 1973), p. 59.

9. "Conversazione sulla cultura e sul cinema," reprinted in *R.R.: Roberto Rossellini*, ed. Edoardo Bruno (Rome: Bulzoni, 1979), pp. 29–31. (All of Rossellini's articles and interviews originally published in *Filmcritica* are reprinted in this useful volume.)

10. The relation between Brecht and Rossellini is complicated. For one thing, their attitudes concerning the place of emotion in representation are equally contradictory, for while both wanted to appeal to the spectator intellectually rather than emotionally, they also felt, like Eisenstein, that intellectual curiosity and the life of the mind could be emotionally fulfilling in their own right. The most important difference between them, however, is that, while Brecht was continually at pains to point out the constructed, made nature of the spectacle through the famous *Verfremdungseffekt*, the unrelenting destruction of illusionism, Rossellini's entire conscious aesthetic was built upon the necessity of illusionism. As we have seen throughout his career, Rossellini realized that it was impossible to portray reality directly, without mediation, and various experiments reveal that realization in subtle ways. Yet once in the realm of the overtly historical and "scientific," when the overriding project is to inform, Rossellini seems to want to forget the problematic nature of representation. The situation is complex, of course, for there is a way in which the long takes, the refusal to give in to Hollywood-style illusionism (which is paradoxically based on short takes), is in itself illusion-breaking. Nevertheless, his efforts in this direction are tentative and finally minor, at least com-

pared with Brecht's and those of his cinematic offspring Godard, and it is misleading to call Rossellini Brechtian, as many have.

One other important difference is the essentializing nature of Rossellini's films: as we have seen, all of Rossellini's vaunted placing of human beings in a specific time and place leads nevertheless and inevitably to the discovery of a timeless human nature. Nothing could be further from Brecht's project. This quotation from Brecht, in which he distances his own practice from that of conventional theater, can also serve to distinguish him from Rossellini:

> The bourgeois theatre emphasized the timelessness of its objects. Its representation of people is bound by the alleged "eternally human." Its story is arranged in such a way as to create "universal" situations that allow Man with a capital M to express himself: man of every period and every colour. All its incidents are just one enormous cue, and this cue is followed by the "eternal" response: the inevitable, usual, natural, purely human response.

(*Brecht on Theatre: The Development of an Aesthetic*, ed. and trans. by John Willet [New York: Hill and Wang, 1964], pp. 96–97. For a more detailed comparison of Brecht and Rossellini, see my "Just How Brechtian Is Rossellini?" in *Film Criticism*, 3, no. 2 [1979]. This article is also reprinted in the BFI dossier on Rossellini.)

11. Aprà and Ponzi, "An Interview With Rossellini," p. 122.

12. Interview, *Cahiers du cinéma*, no. 145 (July 1963), 8.

13. Ibid., 13.

14. Renzo Rossellini told me in 1979 that his father involved him in this film "to save me from something dangerous." Renzo had been working in France at the time and at age 17 had become involved as a "sympathizer" with the revolutionary FLN. (Interview with the author, Rome, June 1979.)

15. Aprà and Ponzi, "An Interview With Rossellini," p. 124.

16. Renzo Rossellini has said that this entire period, when his father was moving toward the history films, was the "most important intellectual experience of my life." In their interminable discussions about civilization and world history, which began the summer during which *General della Rovere* was filmed, Renzo admits that his father was the "free spirit" and he the dogmatic one, instead of the usual roles assigned in father-son debates. At the time, Renzo was committed to a Marxist and materialist perspective, while his father took the Rousseauist, humanist position of an admirer of the French Revolution. The result was a dialectic that, according to Renzo, was for him the "greatest university possible."

17. Interview, *Filmcritica*, no. 190 (August 1968), 351.

18. Baldelli, *Roberto Rossellini*, p. 225. Adriano Aprà sees the television-cinema relationship as part of an elaborate male-female dialectic working throughout Rossellini's career. In his model, the cinema is essentially feminine, and thus Rossellini's move to television is also a definitive move to the possibility of a cold, masculine examination. Using McLuhan's terminology, Aprà finds that neorealist films were too "hot." He also suggests that Rossellini found the cinematic situation of the darkroom and the projected light very manipulative, making the cinema a kind of maternal womb, as scathingly depicted in "Illibatezza," his last theatrical film. ("Rossellini oltre neorealismo," in *Il neorealismo cinematografico italiano*, ed. Lino Micciché [Venice: Marsilio Editore, 1975], p. 297.)

19. *Cinema: A Critical Dictionary*, ed. Richard Roud (New York: Viking, 1980), vol. 2, p. 900. Again, one person's meat seems to be another's poison: I have discussed these films with critics who have no difficulty with Antonioni's longueurs who find them excessively slow, and with nonspecialist audiences—interested almost totally, as Rossellini would have wanted, in their content—who have found them fascinating.

This question of "boredom" is obviously one of the main reasons that Rossellini's didactic films have never, with the exception of *Louis XIV*, been shown on American public television. Another problem, examined over ten years ago by the *New York Times* television critic, John J. O'Connor (April 30, 1972, II, 17) is that the dubbing is painfully obvious to Americans, though it does not seem to bother Europeans. Since these films rely so heavily on words, subtitled versions do make one feel as though one has been reading a book rather than seeing a film. Obviously, dubbing is preferable since there is no special concern with preserving a star's voice, and in dubbing virtually everything can be translated. O'Connor reported that in the future Rossellini planned to have his actors mouth English on the set so that the postproduction dubbing into English would seem more natural, thus enabling him to get American television contracts. (In fact, Rossellini did exactly that in the three-part *The Age of the Medici*, the definitive version of which is in English, and stories are told of minor characters mouthing words that had absolutely no meaning for them. It was all for naught, however, as one might have suspected, since this excellent and complex work has never been shown on American television either.)

20. James Roy MacBean, *Film and Revolution* (Bloomington and London: Indiana University Press, 1975), p. 210.

21. Goffredo Fofi, *Il cinema italiano: Servi e padroni* (Milan: Feltrinelli, 1971), p. 160.

22. Interview, *Cahiers du cinéma*, no. 183 (October 1966), 18–19.

23. *Cinéma* [Paris], no. 206 (February 1976), 70–71. The most straightforward recent version of Rossellini's position can be found in Paul Schrader's remark that "the facts of the past must be framed in such a manner to reveal *their*—not Rossellini's, not our—intrinsic truth." (Schrader, "The Rise of Louis XIV," *Cinema* [Beverly Hills], 6, no. 3 [Spring 1971], 4.)

24. Another theoretically provocative formulation of this view is that of Pascal Kané, writing in *Cahiers du cinéma*. For him the fascinating contradiction of history films is that a presumably unknown historical period must somehow be represented, and thus *recognizable* at the same time. The remainder that is always left over is what Kané calls "l'effet d'étrangeté." Comparing Rossellini's *Louis XIV* with Pasolini's *Thousand and One Nights*, Kané finds that, for Rossellini, the point is to locate an absolute historical truth and then to convey it:

> The strangeness of the representation, the resistance which history opposes to its own deciphering by the spectator, is therefore not the product of an insufficient reading, of a lack of knowledge concerning the context. The feeling of strangeness doesn't have any other source, it belongs in no case to a fact of narration, it is not (or at least shouldn't be) the support of any *jouissance*. It is only the effect of a "more than real" asked of a particular representation. The signifieds which are produced, among other didactic ones, will therefore be totally identified with the historical referent of the story.

Pasolini's film, on the other hand, offers the "absolute strangeness of practice and discourse, but also of bodies and places":

> It is a cinema fascinated by "the Other," pure *jouissance* of the heterogeneous, and absence of every foundation, of every historic, sexual, economic, and even architectural referent of the story. . . . History is no longer anything but a particular case of mythic discourse.
>
> To the omnipresence of the Rossellinian historic reference . . . and correlatively, to its eliding of the narration, of the "time of the enunciation," is here opposed an infinite distancing from all contexts, dissipated in the infinite difference of the narration, the only true reference. . . . With Rossellini, the signified will be identified exactly with the referent of the fiction (supposedly full) without ever constituting an autonomous production. With Pasolini, every discourse is only a discourse on the narration itself, the only tangible referent, the only foundation of meaning (the historic reference is emptied of every role).

(Pascal Kané, "Cinéma et histoire: L'Effet d'étrangeté," *Cahiers du cinéma*, nos. 254–55 [December 1974–January 1975], 78, 80–81.)

25. Leprohon, *The Italian Cinema*, p. 213.

26. Ibid., p. 176.

27. An interesting comparison can be made with the CBS television program of the 1950s entitled "You Are There." In at least one "dramatization"—the "Death of Socrates"—the two projects overlap. In the American television version, as might be expected, the overwhelming emphasis is on the highly dramatized clash of personalities, with little or no attempt to explain Socratic ideas.

28. He does not want to include anything deliberately anachronistic, of course (this kind of insistently illusion-breaking device never interested him), but this pursuit of the essential idea of an era explains why he was not concerned by the obvious artificiality of some of the matte shots in *Socrates* and other films. These sometimes totally unconvincing matte shots have disturbed many American critics. One practical matter that must be kept in mind, however, is that, while these films are usually seen on the giant screen, they were intended for television, where the matte shots would obviously be much less noticeable. John Dorr makes many of the same points I have made above concerning Rossellini's search for essence, but I think he goes too far in claiming that Rossellini *deliberately* zooms in on the artificial matte shot of the acropolis in *Socrates* in order to stress that this kind of historical illusionism is unimportant ("Roberto Rossellini 1974," *Take One*, 4, no. 3 [May 1974], 15).

A great deal has also been written concerning Rossellini's use of the zoom in these films. Dorr makes the point that its use enables the director to capture the "meaning" of an event in staging it, rather than later, as with most filmmakers, in the more analytic editing process. Dorr is clearly following Bazin here, but also, I think, follows him into error when he ontologically privileges the long take over montage (without, of course, using those terms): "His camera is free to move about the action without destroying its wholeness. . . . The scene retains its immediacy, its reality as event" (Ibid.). This notion of the wholeness of an event is intriguing, though it entails gestalt and phenomenological questions that cannot be gone into here. Nevertheless, since the camera can never take in the *whole* event all the time, an elaborate psychological proof would be necessary to demonstrate just how the inevitable fragmentation of an event produced by the *frame* at any given moment differs essentially from the fragmentation produced by montage. But it is also possible to talk about the use of the zoom in ways that go beyond Dorr's neo-Bazinian terms. Thus, Fred Camper, writing in the *Chicago Reader*, says that Rossellini's zoom lens' "multiple perspectives, its ability to change from close-up to long shot and back again, express the continual interdependence between individual and environment, between part and whole, throughout history" (November 3, 1978; quoted in Belton, "The Bionic Eye," p. 22). And Robin Wood has correctly pointed out the inherent distancing properties of the zoom that result from its obtrusiveness: "Its expressive strength lies in our awareness that our perceptions are being guided, our attention focussed. . . . Properly used, the zoom is itself a distancing device, subtly and persuasively reminding us of the presence of the director who is directing our perceptions as surely as he directs the actors" ("Rossellini," 8).

28. *L'Età del Ferro*

1. "A Panorama of History," 86.

2. Aprà and Ponzi, "An Interview With Rossellini," 125.

3. Ibid., 124–25.

4. The importance of Eisenstein's (and Rossellini's) theory is that it calls the Saus-

surean notion of the sign into question. For a further discussion of this complicated sub-ject see Marie-Claire Ropars-Wuilleumier, *Le texte divisé: Essai sur l'écriture filmique* (Paris: Presses Universitaires de France, 1981).

5. Aprà and Ponzi, "An Interview With Rossellini," 124.

6. The fictionality of this episode clashes productively with the rest of the series, which is composed of documentary footage or historical recreations, thus allowing a mild form of anti-illusionism at the same time. Near the end of the episode, the fiction is undercut again with further documentary footage concerning the taking of Monte Cas-sino, and the liberation of Rome and Florence (including footage from *Paisan*). The surprisingly dissonant music of this episode is also vastly different from the music of earlier Rossellini pictures and abets the anti-illusionistic effect. It also looks forward to Mario Nascimbene's electronic scores composed for the later historical films.

7. Throughout this period of his career, Rossellini will be attacked on these grounds from both the Left and the Right. Thus, if Marxists complain about his ahistorical hu-manism, religious critics have not appreciated it either. The Catholic Giuseppe Sala, for example, chides the director for his "faith in Man which is never cracked by an Augustinian anxiety or by a problematic doubt." Rossellini's "optimistic vision of progress and of human finalism" links him with Sartre and Moravia and their view of man as an end in himself. For Sala, this "ideological position" threatens the "sense of love and mystery" of his best films (*Desolazione e speranza nel cinema italiano d'oggi* [Rome: Salvatore Sciascia Editore, 2d ed., 1963], p. 56).

8. After a while the episode begins to resemble the thirty-minute documentaries made for American television by the National Association of Manufacturers, which, some thirty years ago, touted the latest advances of American industry every Saturday morning. (One small irony in the footage that Rossellini uses, in addition to the one mentioned earlier, is that all the machines are made by Mesta Machine Company, an American manufacturer, which inadvertently shows the extent of American economic influence in this grand "Italian" upswing.)

9. Concerning the refrigerators, Rossellini told Aprà and Ponzi ("An Interview With Rossellini," 126):

> It used to be the case that to show something grandiose you would show a cathedral, not a refrigerator. . . . It's true there is something absurd about the refrigerator: it's a luxury, it's superfluous, but it's also of practical importance. You have to be able to look at things without preconceived ideas to know what's right and what isn't. You have to be able to state things. This is exactly what I've tried to do in the fifth episode, bringing together a lot that can perhaps point to a clearer way forward.

10. Baldelli, *Roberto Rossellini*, p. 180.

11. Ibid., pp. 17–80.

12. Amazingly, Rossellini told Aprà and Ponzi that "the pictures in the fifth episode . . . are never grand or celebrative, they simply analyze the phenomenon" ("An Inter-view With Rossellini," 126).

13. Sergio Trasatti, *Rossellini e la televisione* (Rome: La Rassegna Editrice, 1978), p. 38.

29. La Lotta dell'Uomo per la Sua Sopravvivenza

1. Trasatti, *Rossellini et la televisione*, pp. 65–66.

2. Quoted from a private letter in Tag Gallagher's article "Roberto Rossellini and Historical Neo-Realism," in *Artforum*, 13 (Summer 1975), 44.

3. "Panorama of History," 83. A paradigmatic example of Rossellini's theme of the

movement of history and his use of dramatic irony concerning the future comes at the very end of the third episode, when the civilizations of the Egyptians and Greeks, as well as the beginnings of Christianity, have already been explained. Two Romans, talking in a mill, complain about the increasing use of machines: for them, this means that slaves will no longer be necessary and that, therefore, the world as they know it will come to an end. The episode then closes with the jazzy, vibrant black American music with which the first episode began, along with the shots of galaxies and rockets to put the necessarily shortsighted views of the two Romans in the context of later history.

4. Guarner reports that as of his writing in May 1970, Rossellini was reediting the last three episodes of *La lotta* to link up more clearly with this never-filmed series on the Industrial Revolution. It, too, was to be twelve hours long, an obviously important factor in its never coming to fruition (*Roberto Rossellini*, p. 120). After struggling for six years to finish *La lotta*, however, it is astounding that Rossellini could speak so optimistically at the time about the series he envisioned:

> It shows the beginning of a complete transformation of the world, and the origins of the modern world. It starts with short scenes from the Middle Ages, as you always have to have a definite starting point. The Middle Ages saw the establishment of a completely vertical kind of civilisation, with very strictly defined values, and a clearly established way of thought. We had to show the normal everyday life of the artisans, the guilds and the corporations. The film goes on from these brief scenes to the discovery of the technology which gave rise to the Industrial Revolution, and therefore to a related series of phenomena like colonisation, new forms of social organisation and the new political ideas ("A Panorama of History," 87).

After *this* series, Rossellini was also planning films on the French Encyclopedists, "the history of colonisation," and the history of Japan (Ibid.).

5. Ibid., p. 85.

6. Guarner, *Roberto Rossellini*, pp. 119–20.

7. Interview, *Film Culture*, 18.

8. Ibid., p. 9.

9. Ibid., pp. 8–9.

10. Trasatti, *Rossellini e la televisione*, pp. 68–69. It is probably no coincidence that Rossellini begins the second episode by insisting how much documentation actually exists concerning the Egyptian period. He maintains that nothing has been "invented"; the material has merely been put in the form of a screenplay.

11. September 12, 1970; quoted in Trasatti, *Rossellini e la televisione*, p. 68.

12. August 8, 1970; quoted in Trasatti, *Rossellini e la televisione*, p. 68.

13. Baldelli, *Roberto Rossellini*, p. 302, n. 29.

14. All statistics from Trasatti, *Rossellini e la televisione*, pp. 64–65 and 290–91.

15. Claude Beylie, review of *La lotta*, *Écran*, no. 29 (October 1974), 8–9.

30. *La Prise de Pouvoir par Louis XIV*

1. Reported in the *Chicago Sun-Times*, February, 21, 1971. According to Sergio Trasatti, this figure even included the cost of the color film stock that was used. He may be right, moreover, that it was precisely these extreme conditions, reminiscent of the hard but heady days of *Open City*, that accounted for the film's excellence.

2. As was pointed out in the previous chapter, the fact that *La lotta* was first shown four years after *Louis XIV* is mostly an accident of logistics. When asked near the end of his life whether there wasn't a contradiction between his immediate postwar avoidance of focusing on individuals and the television films, almost all of which concentrate on individual figures, Rossellini answered that the latter were not really about the individ-

uals but about "stages of conquest of knowledge" and are seen, generally, through the writings these figures have left (Interview, *Cinématographe*, no. 18 [April–May 1976], 26–27).

3. Martin Walsh, "Rome, Open City; The Rise to Power of Louis XIV: Re-Evaluating Rossellini," *Jump Cut*, no. 15 (1977), 13–15. Rossellini later told the interviewer for *Film Culture* that the film's gradual movement to a greater luminosity was "partially conscious and partially unconscious," but insisted, characteristically, that it was "very easy to do, you can turn on some more lights, that's all" (p. 15).

4. Walsh, "Re-Evaluating Rossellini," 14.

5. Rossellini has said that the only invented scene in the film is the one that comes later with the tailor, when Louis designs a new mode of dress for his court: "The dialogue with the tailor is invented in a sense because there was no such dialogue in the records, but the argument that Louis XIV uses in the scene is one he had used a thousand times before in other contexts" (Interview, *Film Culture*, 7). Obviously, Rossellini has simply forgotten the opening scene.

6. MacBean, *Film and Revolution*, p. 213.

7. Nevertheless, Martin Walsh is correct in pointing out that much of rest of the acting—for example, the deathbed scene of Mazarin in the beginning of the film—is quite conventionally dramatic. Similarly, when Rossellini was asked by the interviewers for the French journal *Cinéma* in 1975 if he said to Jean-Marie Patte: "You are in Louis XIV's skin, do this and that," he gave the surprisingly conventional and decidedly non-Brechtian response, "No, of course not! But he ended up by getting into the skin of Louis XIV. If you dress him like Louis XIV, if you plunge him into a Louis XIV ambience, he will become Louis XIV" ("Roberto Rossellini: Je profite des choses," *Cinéma* [Paris], no. 206 [February 1976], 66).

8. Related to this is a story told by Edoardo Bruno about the day Patte forgot the word he was supposed to say and spent so much time trying to remember it that the scene had to be completely reshot. When it came time to edit the film, Rossellini retained the original shot as a way, he said, of rendering "better the impression that the king was struggling to find the 'right' word" (*Filmcritica*, no. 172 [November 1966]).

9. John Hughes, "Recent Rossellini," *Film Comment* (July 1974), 17.

10. Walsh, "Re-Evaluating Rossellini," 14.

11. Ibid. A related, but different, question concerns Rossellini's attitude toward Louis, which is clearly ambivalent. On the one hand, he obviously admires his cleverness, but also indirectly compares him with Hitler, who, like Louis (according to Rossellini), was exalted by his subjects precisely when he was treating them most badly (Interview, *Film Culture*, 6). "What I love about the character is his absolute audacity: the scene with the tailor, for example. It's even insolent. But you sense at the same time his terrible timidity" (Interview, *Cahiers du cinéma* [1966], 19).

12. Baldelli's source for this information is an article entitled "Louis XIV la grande émission de Philippe Erlanger et Roberto Rossellini," which appeared in the French magazine *Télé Sept Jours* in October of 1966. As the magazine is a kind of French equivalent of *TV Guide*, I have been unable to locate it, even in France, in order to verify Baldelli's claim. In any case, it is impossible to believe that Rossellini would have so drastically changed his working methods merely to accommodate the producers at the ORTF. When asked by the interviewer for *Film Culture* a few years later how he wrote the script for this film, Rossellini gave his standard reply: "Well, when you have found the angle, you need a great deal of documents because I don't like to have a script and prewritten dialogue. I do the dialogue the last thing in the evening and I work with people who are used to working with me. I have my own ideas, I follow them and I choose

things that make it more clear" (p. 7). A more important piece of evidence comes up in a 1975 interview with Écran, at which Jean Gruault, listed in the credits as responsible for the "adaptation and dialogue" of Erlanger's "scenario," was also present. Rossellini explained to the interviewer how the film came about: "My basic idea was that Louis XIV had changed the world through a change of style, dress, and etiquette. Gruault got the documents together for me, with Philippe Erlanger as the history advisor, and, quite simply, we made the film from that" Écran 75, no. 34 [March 1975], 16). It is difficult to imagine Rossellini making such a statement in front of Gruault if it were true that the screenplay had been completely finished by Erlanger beforehand and that Rossellini had been forced to follow it to the letter.

13. Paul Schrader has maintained, "As the spectator's desire to clean out the cluttered frame, to overturn that basin of dead man's piss, grows, so does his comprehension of the unrestrained frenzy of the French Revolution. In Rossellini's film there is both the image of complete order and restraint and the suppressed rage for chaos" ("The Rise of Louis XIV," 5). This scenario of projective anachronism is clearly more Schrader's than Rossellini's or the film's.

14. MacBean, Film and Revolution, p. 225.

15. Mario Verdone, Il cinema neorealista: Da Rossellini a Pasolini (Rome: Celebes Editore, 1977), p. 56. Rossellini's use of anecdotes that do not seem strictly "necessary" to the plot has occasioned much of the debate over this film among American critics. The opening sally was MacBean's praise of Rossellini's "materialist mise-en-scène, in which things—the material objects of seventeenth-century France—are not mere props and backdrops for the drama, but share equal billing, as it were, with the human figures" (MacBean, Film and Revolution, p. 212). While it seems clear that MacBean is claiming too much conscious intentionality on Rossellini's part for this "Marxist technique," he has hit upon the director's long-standing proclivity for the mechanical, for objects and tools, for how things are made or done. As an example, he cites the scene early in the film in which a trio of doctors examines Mazarin's bodily fluids, smelling his sweat and his urine, and prescribes yet more bloodletting, while considering the administration of pills made of rhubarb and ground-up precious stones. Clearly, this sequence is only minimally narrative, for its principal purpose is to summarize the state of knowledge concerning the human body in the seventeenth century. Brian Henderson, in an article that attempts to resuscitate Bazin's reputation, argues on the contrary that in Louis XIV "there are no scenes included for historical background or period flavor; none is included as historical description of the seventeenth century, materialist or otherwise. Once a scene is included—its boundaries determined exactly by its pertinence to the seizure process—it may be realized with a multi-layered complexity that Bazin called 'synthesis'" ("Bazin Defended Against His Devotees," Film Quarterly, 32, no. 4 [Summer 1979], 35). The vague "multi-layered complexity" does little to account for the extranarrative density of this scene in which the doctors' collective ruminations are so heavily foregrounded. Henderson's argument becomes most specious when he tries to justify, as narrative, the inordinate attention paid to the rituals surrounding the king's levee because "they reveal how, when, and where the king receives the message 'Mazarin wants to see you when you rise'; and affect whether he will receive it in time" (p. 36). In order to make a polemical point in favor of Bazin, Henderson seriously misrepresents the dynamics of this film.

16. Quoted in Tag Gallagher, "Roberto Rossellini and Historical Neo-Realism," 44.

17. Interview, Film Culture, 6.

18. Baldelli, Roberto Rossellini, p. 302. Overall, some 38,000 tickets were sold in Parisian theaters, for a box office of the equivalent of around 50 million lire ($75,000).

19. Schrader, "The Rise of Louis XIV," 3.

31. Acts of the Apostles

1. Quoted in Trasatti, *Rossellini e la televisione,* p. 51.

2. Similarly, we hear thunder when the Holy Spirit visits the apostles at Pentecost, and we see the *results* of this visit when the apostles are understood by everyone in the crowd in his or her own language (and Peter explains what happened later), but Rossellini visually spares us the tongues of fire. He *does* include the first miracle accomplished by Peter, the healing of the crippled beggar, but it is done offhandedly and seems present primarily to allow Peter to give the important speech attributing his healing powers to God rather than to himself. Likewise, we later see Saul being struck blind by lightning, and we hear Christ's voice asking why Saul is persecuting him, but Lo result is perhaps the most discreet miracle ever portrayed in cinema history.

3. Peter, for example, was played by a French clown named Jacques Dumur. "Peter was a fisherman, so I knew that I needed a man who would be completely at ease with his own body and have certain, innocent is not the right word, kind of eyes. I found the clown and he is absolutely great. The important thing is to find a face, when you have the face you have a great part of the character and if he is not competent you must make him so" (Interview, *Film Culture,* 22).

4. All production information comes from Luciano Scaffa and Marcella Mariani Rossellini, *Roberto Rossellini* (Rome: Eri/Edizioni RAI, 1980), p. 20. This excellent book, put together by Rossellini's sister and a close collaborator, contains, along with a great deal of production information, the painfully reconstructed scripts, including camera movements, of five of Rossellini's television films and series: *Acts of the Apostles, Socrates, Blaise Pascal, Augustine of Hippo, The Age of the Medici,* and *Cartesius.*

5. Baldelli, *Roberto Rossellini,* p. 190. Peter Lloyd, writing in *Monogram,* has also pointed out that while the film is "humanist" rather than Christian, nevertheless Rossellini's mise-en-scène consistently defers to the sanctity of the environment, where Christ was ("Acts of the Apostles," *Monogram,* no. 2 [1971], 19).

6. "A Panorama of History," 83.

7. Quoted in Gallagher, "Roberto Rossellini and Historical Neo-Realism," 44.

8. Interview, in *Écran 75,* 17.

9. Scaffa and Rossellini, *Roberto Rossellini,* pp. 56, 84.

10. The principal conflict that rends the early Church, in fact, is whether or not Christianity is only for Jews or is to be offered to Gentiles as well. If the latter, must Gentiles who wish to become Christians also submit to Jewish laws and customs and be circumcised? Thus Peter, when he is called to the house of Cornelius, the Roman centurion, creates scandal because Jewish law forbids a Jew to enter the house of the uncircumcised. After his conversion, Paul is similarly accused, by the Jews he tries to convert, of blasphemy and sacrilege against the law. Near the end of the series, Paul is asked by his friends to make an appearance at the Jewish temple to prove that he still follows Jewish law, even though this puts him in great danger. When he is arrested by the Jewish authorities who want to execute him, he escapes by insisting on his legal rights as a Roman citizen.

Another argument occurs late in the series between two merchants, one of whom insists that the lending of money for profit violates Moses' law, the other replying that this is the only way he is able to save his business. The interest of the argument is that it anticipates one of the principal themes of the 1973 three-part series on the Medici.

11. Fofi, *Il cinema italiano,* p. 162.

12. Edoardo Bruno, *Filmcritica,* no. 196–97 (March–April 1969), quoted in *Lo splendore del vero,* p. 137.

13. For instance, speeches are usually cut to their core, and, unlike in the Bible, are presented as the result of an interplay between an apostle and the crowd he is addressing. A similar example concerns the first baptizing: the Bible laconically states that three thousand were baptized that day, whereas in the film it fittingly becomes an entire, joyous scene. Nor is Rossellini afraid to bring in material from other parts of the New Testament to fill in gaps in sermons and dramatic situations: thus, Paul's famous speech about the tinkling cymbals and the primacy of love is imported from 1 Cor. 13:1–11 into his confrontation with the Greeks. There are also moments included that serve to humanize, rather than individualize, the apostles, and that fit the texture of the film very well. Nor is Rossellini above an editorial interpretive comment: thus, where the Bible speaks merely of the apostles eating together communally, Rossellini in effect restages the first Eucharist—an interpretation in line with that of most theologians, but one that is not explicit in the Bible.

Only two major scenes have been added. One is a short scene in which two merchants on a trading caravan, Zaccaria and Bethel, almost come to blows over their differing interpretations of Mosaic law. The more important addition, which opens the series, features a Roman magistrate who has just arrived in Jerusalem, and a Greek scribe, a slave, who serves as his guide. Sensing the leisure of more than five hours of film ahead of him, Rossellini allows the Greek to outline the historical context in a very detailed fashion. They discuss the great temple, the status of slaves, the Hebraic Weltanschauung and attachment to law, how Herod the Great took power, the seven separate Jewish sects and the politics of each, as well as various customs like circumcision. The Greek also mentions the new Christian sect, and the two of them go to Golgotha, the site of the death of "this man called Christ" some fifty days earlier. By adding these two figures, Rossellini not only provides us with the necessary information to understand what we will see, but the *way* they talk about already extremely well-known matters helps also to defamiliarize them and make them new and, somehow, still in process.

Perhaps more important, however, are Rossellini's *omissions* from the biblical account. For one thing, his version is somewhat less anti-Semitic than the New Testament itself, which continually insists that the Jews hate Paul because they are envious over the large crowds of Gentiles attracted to him, whereas Rossellini implicitly blames their enmity on the clash of cultures and ideologies, and differing conceptions of the law and tradition. Second, almost all the minor miracles performed by Peter and Paul through the Acts are omitted, and the emphasis seems to be on avoiding the overspectacular, except when necessary to make some thematic point, but also on downplaying the element of divine intervention, placing the men before us as men. Thus, Rossellini omits the rescue of Peter by the angel from Herod's prison and the earthquake that frees Paul.

There is a sense, however, in which Rossellini has also unfairly "edited" the material to give us a more favorable picture of the apostles. Thus, he leaves out Paul's deliberate blinding of the false prophet and, even more importantly, Peter's anger at Ananias and Sapphira, who hold back part of the money they have received from selling their goods instead of handing it all over to the community. When Peter questions him, "Ananias hearing thse words fell down, and gave up the ghost: and great fear came on all them that heard these things." When Ananias' wife returns and Peter tells her what happened to her husband, "Then fell she down straightway at his feet, and yielded up the ghost" (Acts 5:5,10). Here we see the saint's (or God's) vengeful side, and the fear that accompanied the love in the making of the Christian community.

14. Lloyd, "Acts of the Apostles," 19.

15. This account of the fire-water opposition is much superior to that offered by Adriano Aprà, who, speaking at the debate transcribed and edited by Gianni Menon,

correctly points out that Rossellini refuses to show the sacrifice as a whole, but then claims too much by linking the fire of the Jews and the water of the Christians, respectively, to montage and long takes (*Dibattito su Rossellini*, pp. 129–30).

16. Trasatti, *Rossellini e la televisione*, pp. 59–60.

32. *Socrates*

1. "A Panorama of History," 102.

2. Socrates and his wife, Xanthippe, are played by French theater actors, which Trasatti claims is symptomatic of Rossellini's disillusionment with the Italian television network. Rossellini has said, however, that Jean Sylvère, who plays Socrates, "had those wonderful eyes and he is a nice man. I needed the eyes and I built the face of Socrates around them" (Interview, *Film Culture*, 20). Sylvère does indeed bear a striking resemblance to the standard Hellenistic representation of Socrates found on many surviving busts. It is unclear how this need for physical "fidelity" fits into Rossellini's approach to history, but it seems to be another way of approaching historical reality through past *ideas* and past representations of what "history" looked like.

3. *Variety*, May 27, 1970.

4. Quoted in Trasatti, *Rossellini e la televisione*, p. 75.

5. Quoted in Scaffa and Rossellini, *Roberto Rossellini*, pp. 131–32.

6. Quoted in Trasatti, *Rossellini et la televisione*, p. 77.

7. Interview, *Film Culture*, 15.

8. Guarner, who also acted as an assistant director of the film, has helpfully reviewed Rossellini's sources and reports that the director used the *Apology, Euthyphron, Crito,* and *Phaedo,* and bits and pieces from other dialogues. The exhortation on rhetoric is borrowed from the *Phaedrus,* for example, but here put in the dramatic context of Socrates trying to discourage his would-be defense attorney Lysias (Guarner, *Roberto Rossellini*, pp. 135–36). Rossellini also told *Film Culture* that the scene in which Socrates and Crito witness the sacrificing of a cock to Aesculapius was invented so that Socrates' well-known last line on his deathbed would make sense (p. 7).

Interestingly, Guarner complains that Socrates' wife, Xanthippe, known throughout history as a shrew, has been made too sympathetic in Rossellini's version. She seems quite shrewish enough to this viewer, however, for at several points she berates Socrates for his "foolishness" and for his refusal to take proper care of his family. If Rossellini allows her to be a little more sympathetic at the end, when Socrates is about to die, he should perhaps be applauded rather than chastised for departing from legend, especially since there is little factual evidence for one interpretation or the other.

9. Even at the end, Rossellini was apparently restraining himself. He told *Film Culture* that he purposely avoided close-ups in the final sequence because he did not want to become emotional. "The timing of the scene is all and it is chosen for clarity as I don't want to seduce" (pp. 4–5).

10. Trasatti, *Rossellini e la televisione*, p. 80.

11. Paolo Bertetto, *Sipario*, no. 294 (October 1970), reprinted in *Lo splendore del vero*, pp. 147–48.

12. Baldelli, *Roberto Rossellini*, p. 195.

13. Trasatti, *Rossellini e la televisione*, p. 81.

33. *Blaise Pascal*

1. His collaborator at Rice University, Dr. Clark Read, said concerning this series, "We are trying to examine science as an expression of humanism and the possibilities it

offers man in terms of a humanism" (Interview, *Film Culture*, 35). See this interview for an extensive discussion of the project. Robert J. Lawrence, an American who was connected with Rossellini's production company, Orizzonte 2000, was quoted in *Variety* as saying that the series on science would be almost totally visual and could be narrated in any language. According to Lawrence, preparation for the filming had been stalled "by the need to develop special equipment, such as cameras to film the universe and for microphotography to make possible magnification from 1 to 4,500 in a continuous zooming motion" (March 29, 1972, p. 50). Rossellini apparently planned to take his Pancinor technique even into the world known only to the microscope.

2. In discussing this project, Rossellini again showed his political naïveté (or disingenuousness) by describing the American Revolution as "a revolution which is totally different from all others. It was not a class taking over the power of another class, but was based only on ideas" (Interview, *Film Culture*, 28).

3. This screenplay should not be taken too seriously, however, as Rossellini rarely paid much attention to what had usually been written down only for the purpose of obtaining financial backing. In fact, he says in the interview portion of Baldelli's book that the script had been written by someone else (*Roberto Rossellini*, p. 235).

4. Interview, *Film Culture*, 11–12. In another interview Rossellini claims directly, "In my opinion Caligula, as the son of Germanicus, is a Republican" ("A Panorama of History," 84).

5. Most of this film about seventeenth-century France was shot, surprisingly, in a small town near Rome called Magliano Sabina, only a few hundred yards from the Autostrada del Sole, the main freeway running the length of the Italian peninsula. Some thirty of the forty-six scenes were filmed there, and most of the rest were shot at the Odescalchi Palazzo in Bassano Romano. The scenes of the monastery at Port Royal and of the witchcraft trial were filmed at the abbey at Fossanova. (The locations are so rich that Daryl Chin, writing in the *Soho Weekly News*, has even complained that the Italianate settings are too lush for the austerity of the subject ["Rossellini in the Past," June 2, 1977].) The script book edited by Luciano Scaffa and Marcella Rossellini, which is the source of this production information, also points out the great care taken to reproduce as authentically as possible Pascal's scientific equipment and the bus that he invented later in his life (p. 177). The principal actors, Pierre Arditi as Pascal and Rita Forzano as his sister Jacqueline, were theater actors with little cinematic exposure. The actress who had played Socrates' wife, Xanthippe, reappears in this film as an accused witch, and Christian De Sica, the son of the director, plays her prosecutor.

6. Quoted from an unpublished RAI publicity handout.

7. Scaffa and Rossellini, *Roberto Rossellini*, p. 191. All further references to this book will be found in the text.

8. As Andrea Ferendeles, who worked as an assistant director on the film, points out in a somewhat useful "diary" of the shooting, published in *Filmcritica* (no. 218 [September–October 1971], 354–61), the witchcraft trial, early on, is the only scene shot in individual cuts rather than with the long-take zoom "editing" (actually, there is at least one other—the debate with Descartes). She also makes the excellent point that the continuous movement of the actors is as much a part of the "zoom montage" effect as the movement of the lens and the camera.

9. "Rossellini in '76," *Sight & Sound*, 45, no. 2 (Spring 1976), 90.

10. When accused by Jacques Grant of taking Pascal's side over Descartes' in this debate, Rossellini responded with one of his most tortured attempts to maintain his doctrine of objectivity:

"No, no! I just don't like Descartes very much, that's all. I am simply reproducing a conflict that existed between them. Perhaps I was more impressed by one or the other, but I try to be as objective as possible, since, a priori, you can't be. Now, maybe it's you who is on Pascal's side rather than Descartes', and so if my film helped you to make up your mind, that means that it was useful for something! I only present the givens, I don't take sides" (*Cinéma* [Paris], no. 206 [February 1976], 63).

11. This reticence can also be noticed in the scene in which Pascal reads aloud what he has written concerning a mystical experience he has just had. As Louis Norman has pointed out, "Restaging the *recording* of the vision, instead of attempting to portray the vision itself, retains intact the sensory mystery of Pascal's experience while rendering the essence of its effect" ("Rossellini's Case Histories for Moral Education," *Film Quarterly*, 27, no. 4 [Summer 1974], 14).

12. Aprà, however, in the recent filmography published in *Le Cinéma révélé: Roberto Rossellini*, as well as Scaffa and Rossellini, claim the two episodes were shown a week apart.

34. *Augustine of Hippo*

1. The entire interview was transcribed and translated in *Take One*, 4, no. 3 (May 1974), from which these quotations are taken.

2. Scaffa and Rossellini, *Roberto Rossellini*, p. 245. All further page references to this script will be included in the text.

3. An important difference in this film, however, lies in its greater emphasis on the relation between the past and the present. Up to this point Rossellini has always avoided this kind of social commentary disguised as history (witness the controversies over *Viva l'Italia!* and *Vanina Vanini* when his collaborators wanted to make more obvious connections with modern problems). Here, however, he stresses the similarity between the sense of loss and confusion surrounding the collapse of the Roman empire and our own confusion in the twentieth century. The intention is laudable, perhaps, but it does not work very well in this film, where the connections seem forced and obvious, and end up being little more than annoying anachronisms. There is one particularly forceful scene, for example, that takes place in a barbershop patronized by transvestites; no doubt the scene is historically "accurate" (shooting was apparently held up for hours until it could be established exactly how the men of the period shaved), but we are also meant to take it as a demonstration of Augustine's contention that Rome is collapsing of its own corruption and loss of its former "manly" virtues. When the script describes young men and women who are dressed and made up "without being distinguished sexually," causing an old man to complain that one can no longer tell the men from the women, we are not sure whether Rossellini is teaching us history or criticizing present-day mores.

4. The other locations were the paleo-Christian basilica of Castle S. Elia, built by Saint Benedict on top of an ancient temple to Diana, and the church of Santa Costanza in Rome.

5. Trasatti, *Rossellini e la televisione*, p. 98.

6. Quoted in Trasatti, *Rossellini e la televisione*, p. 101.

7. *Village Voice*, May 10, 1973, 89.

8. *Augustine of Hippo* was aired, once again, in two one-hour parts, on successive Wednesdays, October 15 and November 1, 1972, at 9:30 P.M. on channel 1. The programmers at the RAI obviously had little confidence in the film, and they put it up against two American movies guaranteed to pull a much larger audience. *Augustine* was watched by 4.1 and 3.7 million spectators, respectively, while the American films garnered 15.8 and 14.3 million. The "enjoyment index" for Rossellini's film was a surprisingly high 69 and 65, but its competition received 75 and 79 (Trasatti, *Rossellini e la televisione*, p. 102).

35. *The Age of the Medici*

1. As usual, Rossellini used largely nonprofessional actors in most of the roles. The actor who played Cosimo, like Rossellini's Pascal and Socrates, was chosen for his resemblance to existing portraits, and his unhandsome, flat features remind one of the uninflected face of Louis XIV. The actor who played Alberti (Virginio Gazzolo) played Bishop Alipio, Augustine's colleague, in the director's previous film. Locations were chosen with great care, and many scenes were filmed in Florence and its hilltop neighbor, Fiesole, and in small villages like Gubbio and San Gimignano in Tuscany, which have largely kept their medieval aspect. Some scenes were filmed on location at the Medici palace at Careggi, outside Florence, which again served the purpose of ontologically bridging the past and the present.

Financing was even more precarious than usual because the French ORTF, which had originally agreed to act as cosponsor, dropped out. Interestingly, the film was shot in English, as Rossellini still entertained hopes of breaking into the American television market, and he was aware of American sensitivity to the lack of lip synchronization. The effect must have been rather comic, as many of the actors did not know a single word of English and thus often had no idea what they were saying. The voices were dubbed later, and thus the "original" version of this film, if that term has any meaning in the Italian industry, is in English. Unfortunately, the timing of the phrases in English is rather awkward, even beyond the slow, painfully measured cadences of standard Rossellinian dialogue. The mixture of British and American voices in the dubbing presents an additional unnecessary problem. As might be expected, the film has never been shown on American television.

2. The tension between the two eras is nicely thematized late in the film when the Byzantine hierarchy comes to Florence for the conference on reunifying the Church. The splendor of their apparel dazzles the men of the early Florentine Renaissance, and Ciriaco, Alberti's curial colleague, compares the color and decoration of these costumes to those in the early medieval mosaics at Ravenna. Alberti is proud, however, that the Florentines have surpassed this era.

3. Roberto Rossellini, *Utopia, autopsia 10¹⁰* (Rome: Armando, 1974), pp. 86–87.

4. Rossellini was apparently unable to film the actual frescoes, probably because of their fragility and the smallness of the chapel, and his reconstruction of them is a disappointment. The copy is second-rate, and the *Rendering of the Tribute Money* has been moved from the top row to the bottom row, presumably so that it could be more easily seen.

5. Scaffa and Rossellini, *Roberto Rossellini*, p. 296. All further references to this book will be found in the text.

6. Interview in *Cinéma* [Paris], no. 206 (February 1976), 70.

7. Samuel Edgerton, *The Renaissance Re-Discovery of Linear Perspective* (New York: Basic Books, 1975), p. 39. It must also be remembered, however, that these ideas were not completely new with the Renaissance. Thus, Michael Baxandall quotes Dante's view that "geometry is lily-white, unspotted by error and most certain, both in itself and in its handmaid, whose name is Perspective" (*Painting and Experience in Fifteenth-Century Italy* [New York: Oxford University Press, 1972], p. 124).

8. It should also be kept in mind that linear perspective was not consciously adopted by Renaissance artists because it was more "realistic" or "objective," but because it was another manifestation, like mathematics, of the perfection of God and the perfectability of man. As Edgerton puts it: Renaissance artists used perspective "because it gave their depicted scenes a sense of harmony with natural law, thereby underscoring man's moral responsibility within God's geometrically ordered universe" (p. 56).

9. Stephen Heath, *Questions of Cinema* (Bloomington: Indiana University Press, 1981), pp. 29–31. The quotation from Francastel comes from *Études de sociologie de l'art* (Paris: Denoël, 1970), pp. 136–37.

10. Michael Silverman, "Rossellini and Leon Battista Alberti: The Centering Power of Perspective," *Yale Italian Studies,* 1, no. 1 (Winter 1977), 141.

11. Another reason for this technique, of course, is that Rossellini is pointing to his visual sources, as we have seen him do in so many other films. Thus his incredibly static characters are often arranged in fixed compositions that suggest specific paintings and frescoes of the period. (One scene of Cosimo with his back to the camera, for example, recalls the back of the figure in Masaccio's *Rendering of the Tribute Money.*) At other times the characters stand in front of seemingly empty landscapes or cityscapes in paintings and frescoes, as though Rossellini were suggesting the historical and ontological provenance of these characters. Figures continually present themselves in the most stylized manner to the camera, thus making us more aware of the process of filmmaking and its relation to other forms of visual representation, especially in conjunction with the de-dramatized acting and the antidramatic plot.

12. The question of self-reflexivity is greatly complicated by the fact that this is one of the sloppiest films Rossellini ever made. Thus, the editing is sometimes careless, as for example when, after we watch a speaker from his side, the reverse shot includes his back, producing a disconcerting, almost jump-cut, effect. At other times the framing is inattentive, as when one character, totally obscured by a tree, speaks for a few seconds in the scene of the debate concerning Latin and the vernacular. Other awkward spots, clearly unintentional, foreground the film's artificiality, as for example when the tax man looks directly at the camera during his scene. At other moments, some of the actors can be clearly seen looking beyond their interlocutors at some out-of-camera-range cue cards. During the sermon in the church, the bodies are obviously rearranging themselves in front of the camera as it dollies back. Throughout the film, in fact, there is a great deal of distracting body movement that seems motivated only by the need for greater visual variety. The presumably unintentional self-reflexivity of these moments is augmented by others that seem more conscious. Thus, the camera at times seems to be intensely, almost perversely, static, and at other times, nervous, continually zooming in and out. In the scene of Cosimo's party, the effect is very stylized, as the camera stays absolutely still watching one group of speakers after another move in front of it to say what they have to say. (In many of the other films, the camera and zoom will themselves move to discover the different groups, but the effect, in any case, is to underline the artificiality of the whole process.) The acting, as well, is stiff and stylized, almost more than in any other of the didactic films, and there is even less concern than usual to convince the viewer that "you are there."

13. Trasatti, *Rossellini e la televisione,* p. 109.

36. *Cartesius*

1. Scaffa and Rossellini, *Roberto Rossellini,* p. 387. All further page references to this script will be included in the text.

2. The director himself rarely spoke of the film in interviews, probably because of its unavailability, and his only words on the subject are found in a *Paris-Match* article published some seven or eight years before the film was actually made. There he says that he first got the idea for it from reading Benedetto Croce's book on Giambattista Vico, a violently anti-Cartesian Neapolitan Jesuit, and this made him want to show "the prodigious period of disorder into which Descartes was born" ("Louis XIV à la loupe," interview in *Paris-Match* [October 8, 1966], pp. 96–98).

3. Formally, this film is of a piece with the others of the grand historical project: it uses electronic music to underline the moments of intellectual insight, and tables organize space, as do the characters with their backs to the camera in the foreground, creating a three-dimensional space into which the zoom can penetrate like a dolly. The sets and costumes are magnificent—one continues to wonder how Rossellini was able to achieve such rich production values on such a limited budget—and several scenes, such as the autopsy in the grand hall of the university and the scene in which the dead are carried off by men wearing grotesque bird masks, are radiant and memorable.

Interestingly, for a film with so many different locations in France and Holland, all of it was shot near Rome. The actor playing Descartes (Ugo Cardea) was, once again, chosen for his physical resemblance to contemporary portraits of the philosopher; Rossellini's sister told me, however, that Cardea was quite disappointing to the director, because he "didn't have it."

4. Cited in Trasatti, *Rossellini e la televisione*, p. 114. The quotation in the text, however, has been taken from the original English version (*Only One Earth* [New York: Norton, 1972], p. 14).

37. *Anno Uno*

1. Interview with the author, Rome, June 1979. Another film made by Rossellini around this time was a two-hour documentary called "The World Population." According to Adriano Aprà (cf. his filmography in *Le Cinéma révélé*), it was made for UNESCO, projected during a world conference on population held at Bucharest in 1974, and subsequently distributed throughout the world by the United Nations. Apart from these meager facts, however, little is known about this film.

2. *Variety*, March 6, 1974, 6.

3. Quoted in Trasatti, *Rossellini e la televisione*, p. 118.

4. "Rossellini in '76," 89.

5. At one point De Gasperi goes to an impoverished southern village called Matera, which, as the British critic Geoffrey Nowell-Smith has ironically noted, served perfectly as a location for the film in 1974, since conditions had not gotten the slightest bit better in the almost thirty years since De Gasperi's visit (*Monthly Film Bulletin*, no. 503, quoted in BFI dossier on Rossellini).

6. Quoted in Trasatti, *Rossellini e la televisione*, p. 120.

7. Interview with the author, 1979.

8. Claude Beylie, "Brève rencontre avec Roberto Rossellini," *Écran 75*, no. 34 (March 1975), 18.

9. Quoted in Trasatti, *Rossellini e la televisione*, p. 119.

10. Quoted in Beppe Cereda, "La sfida della coerenza e della novità," *Rivista del cinematografo*, 48, no. 1 (January 1975), 19.

11. Beppe Cereda's favorable article, "La sfida della coerenza e della novità," stresses Rossellini's attempt to establish a new relation with his audience and argues that, if the film were thought of as dramatized "discourse" rather than a drama with too many words in it, opinion would be much more favorably disposed toward it. For him, the film offers a denuded image, "a word reflected upon rather than participated in (read rather than said)" (p. 20). The negative article, "L'Educazione regressiva di Rossellini," by Aldo Bernardini, attacks the film for its exclusive focus on De Gasperi and the Christian Democrats, because this results in a "necessarily simplified, schematic, and partial vision, in which De Gasperi is presented as the 'deux ex machina' of the situation, the man of Providence who stands above parties, the enlightened politician who fights for the unity of the democratic parties, for a united Europe" (p. 23). Bernardini goes on to complain

that De Gasperi's words are given an absolute value, especially his famous aphorisms, which remove them from the flux of their historical context. Thus, in spite of the film's many fine moments, "It seems to be a regressive film, the fruit of a paternalistic and uni-directional educational choice on the part of the author" (p. 24).

12. R. Alemanno review, *Cinema nuovo*, no. 233 (January–February 1975), 50, 51. In the following issue, no. 234 (April 1975), an article by Vittorio Gorresio, which had origi-nally appeared in *La Stampa*, was reprinted. In it, Gorresio attacks Rossellini's portraits of all the individual characters of Italian politics, including Amendola, Nenni, and Fanfani, and the film's tendency to give all the wisdom to De Gasperi in this "group of fools" (p. 101).

13. Gallagher, "Roberto Rossellini and Historical Neo-Realism," 48.

14. Sandro Zambetti, "Operazione De Gasperi: Sullo schermo l'immagine istituzionale dell'azienda DC," *Cineforum*, no. 140 (January 1975), 17–28. All further page references to this article are included in the text.

15. Zambetti also quotes an interesting reply of Rossellini to Callisto Cosulich, a for-mer collaborator, which appeared during a debate in *Paese Sera*. Rossellini talks about bringing Catholics and Marxists together again (a theme that goes all the way back to *Open City*, of course). This could not happen in the past, however, because of all the mutual distrust.

> How can we get beyond the neurotic to the rational? As always, by knowing and accumulating data. In the film *Anno uno* it is clearly said that the beginning of reconstruction came about through the collaboration of all the political parties: Christian Democrats, Communists, Socialists, actionists, liberals, etc. The debate and the political struggle took place in a certain way, but the history of those years shows us that what people are afraid might come from the "historic compromise" today did not happen at all. Well?

Zambetti takes these remarks, perhaps unfairly, to mean that Rossellini is suggesting that the Communists should be brought in to help us out of our current mess, and if they go too far, we can always kick them out again, as we did before (p. 28).

38. *The Messiah*

1. Though Lino Miccichè is right to point out that to like *The Messiah* but not *Anno uno* is a contradiction because the "nonideological" method of both films is the same. (*Il cinema italiano degli anni '70* [Venice: Marsilio Editore, 1980], p. 246.)

2. Unfortunately, the first screening of the film for the Italian press, on October 25, 1975, was an audiovisual disaster, and most of the subsequent criticism of the film seems to have stemmed from this original screening. According to reports, the film appeared to be completely colorless, much too dark, and poorly photographed in general. The film must have been reprinted subsequently, for the copy I have seen (owned by the Rossellini family) is none of these things and is, in fact, visually superb.

3. Interview with the author.

4. "Save 'The Messiah,' " *Take One*, 6, no. 7 (1978), 2.

5. Interview, *Filmcritica*, nos. 264–65 (May–June 1976). Reprinted in *R.R.: Roberto Rossellini*, ed. Edoardo Bruno, p. 126.

6. Interview, *Écran 77*, no. 60 (July 15, 1977), 47.

7. Quoted in a short review of the film by Françoise Maupin in *La Revue du cinéma*, no. 305 (April 1976), 96.

8. Claudio Sorgi, "Il Messia," *Rivista del cinematografo* (December 1975), 543. Sorgi's article is invaluable as well because it carefully sorts out Rossellini's sources and his modi-fications of them. His conclusion is that "it is certain no film on the Gospels has ever re-flected such up-to-date lines of biblical research," especially since, according to Sorgi, *The*

Messiah follows the theory known as "Formgeschichtliche Methode," which holds that the Gospels were born as oral tradition between the time of Christ's death and their actual writing.

Sorgi believes that the principal source for the film is the Gospel of Mark, mainly because of its popularism and its accent on the mystery of messianism, but "the fundamental theory of the film derives from Matthew: Jesus seen as the realization of promises and the continuous correlation between what Jesus does and says and what was predicted of him" (p. 543). Among the many small shifts that Sorgi catalogs are the words instituting the Eucharist, which John does not report, and which Rossellini borrows from Paul's First Epistle to the Corinthians, chapter 11. The colloquy between John the Baptist and Herod concerning power, freedom, and poverty is invented; Sorgi suggests that it may have come from *Acts of the Martyrs,* a book written during the early Christian period. Other critics have thought it comes from a suggestion in Mark 6:20. Rossellini has also put Psalm 86 in Judas' mouth (as he remarked in an interview), and, as mentioned, redistributed some of Christ's speeches among other characters.

9. I am indebted to Gridley McKim-Smith for this suggestion.

10. Though Rossellini did maintain, unconvincingly, in one interview that he was only *later* told that Michelangelo's Mary was younger (interview in *Amis du film et de la télévision* [Brussels], no. 239 [April 1976], 14).

11. The art historian Charles DeTolnay, in *The Youth of Michelangelo* (Princeton: Princeton University Press, 1943), p. 92, tells us:

> This youthfulness [of the Madonna] is said to have been criticized by Michelangelo's contemporaries. Michelangelo is supposed to have defended himself with the argument that a pure woman preserves her youth longer and he wished to symbolize the chastity of the Madonna. Indeed, according to Neo-Platonism, the body is the image of the soul and participates in its inner qualities. The youthfulness of the Virgin in Michelangelo's *Pietà* thus expresses a moral as well as a physical beauty.

Frederick Hartt, in *Michelangelo's Three Pietàs* (New York: Abrams, 1976), points out that most Pietàs of the period showed Mary as middle-aged. Perugino had painted her as about the same age as Christ, but Michelangelo went even further.

12. Jacques Grant, *Cinema 76,* no. 208 (April 1976), 117.

13. Mireille Latil Le Dantec, "Le Messie," *Cinématographe,* no. 18 (April–May 1976), 38. I think Latil Le Dantec is also right to see in Mary an embodiment of Rossellini's aesthetic, for she is often seen to be looking at Christ from a hidden place.

14. Jacques Grant, *Cinema 76,* no. 206 (February 1976), 68.

15. "Rossellini in '76," 90.

16. Interview in *Avvenire* (October 26, 1975); quoted in Sorgi, "Il Messia," 541.

17. Miccichè, *Cinema italiano degli anni '70,* p. 248.

39. Final Projects

1. "Introduzione al 'Marx'," *Filmcritica,* nos. 289–90 (November–December 1978), 366. All further page references to this article appear in the text.

2. Interview with Giovanna Di Bernardo, "Roberto Rossellini Talks About Marx, Freud, and Jesus," *Cinéaste,* 8, no. 1 (1977), 33.

3. The comet that appears in the first scene of the screenplay, as the young Marx is about to go off to the university, is defended at great length by Rossellini in the *Écran* interview. His fear was that it would seem too spectacular, too grand a "portent" of things to come, but decided to include it anyway. Ironically, Rossellini told an interviewer that he would not include in his film the fact that Marx slept with his maid when his wife was sick because it was "so irrelevant": what counted were Marx's ideas. (*R.R.: Roberto Rossellini,* ed. Bruno, p. 131).

4. This list comes from Bendicò, "L'abbecedario di Rossellini," 362.

5. Interview, Écran 77, no. 60 (July 15, 1977), 46.

6. Quoted in Virgilio Fantuzzi, "L'ultimo Rossellini," Rivista del cinematografo, 50, nos. 7–8 (July–August 1977), 292.

7. Ibid.

8. The unfinished article is included in Trasatti, Rossellini e la televisione, pp. 219–23.

Filmography

DAPHNE. Short, 1936.

PRÉLUDE À L'APRÈS-MIDI D'UN FAUNE. Short, 1938.

FANTASIA SOTTOMARINA (A Fantasy of the Deep). Presented by Incom. *Music:* Edorado [*sic*] Miccuci. *Photography:* Rodolfo Lombardi. *Director:* Roberti [*sic*] Rossellini. Distributed by Esperia Films. Short, 1939.

IL TACCHINO PREPOTENTE (The Overbearing Turkey). *Photography:* Mario Bava. Short, 1939.

LA VISPA TERESA (The Lively Teresa). *Photography:* Mario Bava. Short, 1939.

IL RUSCELLO DI RIPASOTTILE (The Brook of Ripasottile). Short, 1941.

LA NAVE BIANCA (The White Ship). 1941. *Subject and supervision:* Francesco De Robertis. *Screenplay:* Francesco De Robertis and Roberto Rossellini. *Photography:* Emanuele Caracciolo. *Set design:* Amleto Bonetti. *Music:* Renzo Rossellini. *Editing:* Eraldo Da Roma. Produced by Scalera and the Centro Cinematografico del Ministero della Marina. With nonprofessional actors. 77 minutes.

UN PILOTA RITORNA (A Pilot Returns). 1942. *Subject:* Tito Silvio Mursino [Vittorio Mussolini]. *Screenplay:* Michelangelo Antonioni, Ugo Betti, Gherardo Gherardi, Rosario Leone, Massimo Mida, Margherita Maglione, Roberto Rossellini. *Photography:* Vincenzo Seratrice. *Music:* Renzo Rossellini. *Editing:* Eraldo Da Roma. Produced by ACI. With Massimo Girotti (Lieutenant Rossati, the pilot), Michela Belmonte (the girl), Gaetano Masier, Piero Lulli, Elvira Betrone, Piero Palmerini, Jole Tinta, Nino Brondello, and the officers and men of the Italian air force. 87 minutes.

L'UOMO DALLA CROCE (The Man of the Cross). 1943. *Subject:* Asvero Gravelli. *Screenplay:* Asvero Gravelli, Alberto Consiglio, G. D'Alicandro, Robert Rossellini. *Photography:* Guglielmo Lombardi. *Set design:* Gastone Medin. *Music:* Renzo Rossellini. Produced by

Continentalcine, Cines. With Alberto Tavazzi (the priest), Roswitha Schmidt (Irina), Aldo Capacci, Franco Castellani, Attilio Dottesio, Doris Hild, Zoia Weneda, Antonio Marietti. 88 minutes.

DESIDERIO (Desire). 1943–46. [Completed by Marcello Pagliero in 1946.] *Subject:* A. I. Benvenuti. *Screenplay:* Rosario Leone, Giuseppe De Santis, Roberto Rossellini, Diego Calcagno, Marcello Pagliero, Guglielmo Santangelo. *Photography:* Rodolfo Lombardi and Ugo Lombardi. *Music:* Renzo Rossellini. Produced by Sovrania, SAEIR. With Elli Parvo (Paola), Massimo Girotti (Nando), Carlo Ninchi (Giovanni), Lia Corelli, Francesco Grandjacquet (Riccardo), Roswitha Schmidt (Anna). 102 minutes.

ROMA, CITTÀ APERTA (Open City). 1945. *Subject:* Alberto Consiglio and Sergio Amidei. *Screenplay:* Sergio Amidei, Federico Fellini, Roberto Rossellini. *Photography:* Ubaldo Arata. *Music:* Renzo Rossellini. *Editing:* Eraldo Da Roma. Produced by Excelsa-Film. With Aldo Fabrizi (Don Pietro), Anna Magnani (Pina), Marcello Pagliero (Manfredi), Maria Michi (Marina), Harry Feist (Bergmann), Giovanna Galletti (Ingrid), Francesco Grandjacquet (Francesco), Carla Rovere (Lauretta, Pina's sister), Vito Annichiarico (Marcello, Pina's son), Nando Bruno (Agostino), Joop Van Hulzen (Hartmann), Akos Tolnay (the Austrian deserter), Alberto Tavazzi (a priest). 100 minutes.

PAISÀ (Paisan). 1946. *Subject:* Sergio Amidei, with the collaboration of Klaus Mann, Federico Fellini, Alfred Hayes, Marcello Pagliero, Roberto Rossellini, Vasco Pratolini. *Screenplay:* Sergio Amidei, Federico Fellini, Roberto Rossellini. *Photography:* Otello Martelli. *Music:* Renzo Rossellini. *Editing:* Eraldo Da Roma. Produced by Mario Conti and Rod E. Geiger for the OFI in collaboration with Foreign Film Production, Inc. With (first episode, Sicily) Carmela Sazio (Carmela), Robert Van Loon (Joe from Jersey); (second episode, Naples) Dots M. Johnson (black M.P.), Alfonsino (boy); (third episode, Rome) Gar Moore (Fred), Maria Michi (Francesca); (fourth episode, Florence) Harriet White (Harriet, the nurse), Renzo Avanzo (Massimo); (fifth episode, Romagna) Bill Tubbs (American priest) and Franciscan monks; (sixth episode, the Po) Dale Edmunds (Dale), Cigolani (the partisan). 124 minutes.

GERMANIA ANNO ZERO (Germany, Year Zero). 1947. *Subject:* Roberto Rossellini. *Screenplay:* Roberto Rossellini, Carlo Lizzani, Max Kolpet. *Photography:* Robert Juillard. *Set design:* Piero Filippone. *Music:* Renzo Rossellini. *Editing:* Eraldo Da Roma. Produced by Alfredo Guarini and Roberto Rossellini for Tevere Film, in collaboration with Salvo D'Angelo Production (Rome), Sadfi (Berlin), and UGC (Paris). With Edmund Moeschke (Edmund), Ernst Pittschau (his father), Franz Krüger (his brother), Ingetraud Hintze (his sister), Erich Gühne (his teacher). 78 minutes.

L'AMORE (Love). 1948.
    Part 1: UNA VOCE UMANA (The Human Voice). *Subject:* From the one-act play "La Voix humaine," by Jean Cocteau. *Screenplay:* Roberto Rossellini. *Photography:* Robert Juillard. *Set design:* Christian Bérard. *Music:* Renzo Rossellini. *Editing:* Eraldo Da Roma. Produced by Roberto Rossellini for Tevere Film. With Anna Magnani. 35 minutes.
    Part 2: IL MIRACOLO (The Miracle). *Subject:* Federico Fellini. *Screenplay:* Tullio Pinelli, Roberto Rossellini. *Photography:* Aldo Tonti. *Music:* Renzo Rossellini. *Editing:* Eraldo Da Roma. Produced by Roberto Rossellini for Tevere Film. With Anna Magnani (Nanni) and Federico Fellini ("Saint Joseph"). 43 minutes. [NOTE: This episode was originally released in the United States in 1950 by Joseph Burstyn, as part of an episode

film entitled *Ways of Love*. The other two parts were Marcel Pagnol's *Joffroi* and Jean Renoir's *A Day in the Country*.]

LA MACCHINA AMMAZZACATTIVI (The Machine to Kill Bad People). 1948–52. *Subject:* Eduardo De Filippo, Fabrizio Sarazani. *Screenplay:* Sergio Amidei, Giancarlo Vigorelli, Franco Brusati, Liana Ferri, Roberto Rossellini. *Photography:* Tino Santoni, Enrico Betti Berutto. *Music:* Renzo Rossellini. *Editing:* Jolanda Benvenuti. Produced by Universalia, Tevere Film. With Gennaro Pisano (Celestino, the photographer), Giovanni Amato (the mayor), Bill Tubbs and Helen Tubbs (American tourists), and the people of Majori, Amalfii, and Atrani. 83 minutes.

STROMBOLI, TERRA DI DIO (Stromboli, Land of God). 1949. *Subject:* Roberto Rossellini. *Screenplay:* Roberto Rossellini, Gian Paolo Callegari, Renzo Cesana, Art Cohn, Sergio Amidei. *Photography:* Otello Martelli. *Music:* Renzo Rossellini. *Editing:* Jolanda Benvenuti and Roland Gross (for the American version). Produced by Berit Film (Roberto Rossellini and Ingrid Bergman) and RKO. With Ingrid Bergman (Karin), Mario Vitale (Antonio, her husband), Renzo Cesana (the priest), Mario Sponza (the lighthouse keeper), and the people of Stromboli. 105 minutes (81 minutes in the American version).

FRANCESCO, GIULLARE DI DIO (Francis, God's Jester; The Flowers of Saint Francis). 1950. *Subject:* Roberto Rossellini, from *The Little Flowers of St. Francis* and *The Life of Brother Ginepro*. *Screenplay:* Roberto Rossellini, Federico Fellini, with the collaboration of Father Felix Morlion and Father Antonio Lisandrini. *Photography:* Otello Martelli. *Music:* Renzo Rossellini, and for the liturgical songs, Father Enrico Buondonno. *Editing:* Jolanda Benvenuti. Produced by Giuseppe Amato for Cineriz (Angelo Rizzoli). With Aldo Fabrizi (Nicolaio, the tyrant), Arabella Lemaitre (Saint Clair), and nonprofessional actors, including Brother Nazario Gerardi (Saint Francis). 75 minutes.

"L'Invidia" (Envy), fifth episode of I SETTE PECCATI CAPITALI (The Seven Deadly Sins). 1951. *Subject:* Roberto Rossellini, from the short novel "La Chatte," by Colette. *Screenplay:* Roberto Rossellini, Diego Fabbri, Liana Ferri, Turi Vasile. *Photography:* Enzo Serafin. *Set design:* Hugo Blaetter. *Music:* Yves Baudrier. Produced by Film Costellazione (Rome) and Franco-London Film (Paris). With Orfeo Tamburi (Orfeo), Andrée Debar (Camille), Nicola Ciarletta, Nino Franchina. 20 minutes. [NOTE: The directors of the other episodes were Yves Allégret, Claude Autant-Lara, Carlo Rim, Jean Dreville, Eduardo De Filippo, and Georges Lacombe.]

EUROPA '51. [Also known as The Greatest Love]. 1952. *Subject:* Roberto Rossellini. *Screenplay:* Sandro De Feo, Roberto Rossellini, Mario Pannunzio, Ivo Perilli, Diego Fabbri, Antonio Pietrangeli, Brunello Rondi. *Photography:* Aldo Tonti. *Set design:* Virgilio Marchi. *Music:* Renzo Rossellini. *Editing:* Jolanda Benvenuti. Produced by Carlo Ponti and Dino De Laurentiis. With Ingrid Bergman (Irene), Alexander Knox (George, her husband), Sandro Franchina (her son), Ettore Giannini (Andrea, the Communist), Giulietta Masina ("La Passerotto"), Teresa Pellati (Ines, the prostitute). 110 minutes. [NOTE: This film was awarded the International Prize "ex-aequo" at the Venice film festival in 1952, along with John Ford's *The Quiet Man* and Kenji Mizoguchi's *Life of Oharu*.]

DOV'È LA LIBERTÀ? (Where Is Freedom?). 1952–54. *Subject:* Roberto Rossellini. *Screenplay:* Roberto Rossellini, Vitaliano Brancati, Ennio Flaiano, Antonio Pietrangeli, Vincenzo Talarico. *Photography:* Aldo Tonti, Tonino Delli Colli. *Set design:* Virgilio Marchi. *Music:* Renzo Rossellini. *Editing:* Jolanda Benvenuti. Produced by Carlo Ponti, Dino De

Laurentiis/Golden Films. With Totò (Salvatore Lojacono), Nyta Dover, Vera Molnar, Leopoldo Trieste, Franca Faldini. 89 minutes.

VIAGGIO IN ITALIA (Voyage to Italy). 1953. *Subject and screenplay:* Roberto Rossellini, Vitaliano Brancati. *Photography:* Enzo Serafin. *Set design:* Piero Filippone. *Music:* Renzo Rossellini. *Editing:* Jolanda Benvenuti. Produced by Sveva, Junior, Italiafilm. With Ingrid Bergman (Katherine Joyce), George Sanders (Alexander Joyce), Leslie Daniels (Tony Burton) Natalia Ray (Natalia Burton), Marie Maubon (Maria), Anna Proclemer (the prostitute). 75 minutes.

"Ingrid Bergman," episode of SIAMO DONNE (We, the Women). 1952. *Subject and screenplay:* Cesare Zavattini (for all the episodes), with the collaboration of Luigi Chiarini for the Rossellini episode. *Photography:* Otello Martelli. *Music:* Alessandro Cicognini. *Editing:* Jolanda Benvenuti. Produced by Titanus and Film Costellazione. With Ingrid Bergman as herself, the Rossellini children, and Albamaria Setaccioli. 20 minutes. [Other episodes by Alfredo Guarini, Gianni Franciolini, Luigi Zampa, and Luchino Visconti.]

"Napoli '43," episode of AMORI DI MEZZO SECOLO (Mid-Century Loves). 1953. *Subject and screenplay:* Roberto Rossellini. *Photography:* Tonino Delli Colli (in Ferraniacolor). *Set design:* Mario Chiari. *Music:* Carlo Rustichelli. *Editing:* Jolanda Benvenuti, Dolores Tamburini. Produced by Carlo Infascelli for Excelsa, Roma Film. With Antonella Lualdi, Franco Pastoriano. 15 minutes. [Other episodes by Glauco Pellegrini, Pietro Germi, Mario Chiari, and Antonio Pietrangeli.]

GIOVANNA D'ARCO AL ROGO (Joan of Arc at the Stake). 1954. Subject from the dramatic oratorio by Paul Claudel, with music by Arthur Honegger. *Cinematic adaptation:* Roberto Rossellini. *Photography:* Gabor Pogany (in Gevacolor). *Set design:* Carlo Maria Cristini. *Music:* Arthur Honegger. *Editing:* Jolanda Benvenuti. Produced by Produzioni Cinematografiche Associate (Rome), Franco-London Film (Paris). With Ingrid Bergman (Joan of Arc), Tullio Carminati (Brother Domenico), Giacinto Prandelli (Porcus), Saturno Meletti, Augusto Romani. 76 minutes.

LA PAURA (Angst; Fear; also known as Non credo più all'amore [I No Longer Believe in Love]). 1954-55. *Subject:* From the novella by Stefan Zweig. *Screenplay:* Sergio Amidei, Franz Treuberg, Roberto Rossellini. *Photography:* Carlo Carlini. *Music:* Renzo Rossellini. *Editing:* Jolanda Benvenuti, Walter Boos. Produced by Ariston Film (Munich) and Aniene Film (Rome). With Ingrid Bergman (Irene Wagner), Mathias Wieman (her husband), Renate Manhardt (Johanna Schultze). 83 minutes.

INDIA ['58]. (Also known as India, Matri Bhumi [India, Mother Earth]). 1958. *Subject:* Roberto Rossellini. *Screenplay:* Roberto Rossellini, Sonali Senroy Das Gupta, Fereydoun Hoveyda. *Photography:* Aldo Tonti (in Gevacolor, Ferraniacolor, Kodachrome; surviving copy in the United States is in black and white). *Music:* Philippe Arthuys. *Editing:* Cesare Cavagna. Produced by Aniene Film (Rome), Union Générale Cinématographique (Paris), with the aid of Indian Films Development. Nonprofessional actors. Four episodes, 90 minutes. [NOTE: A four-hour, ten-episode, sixteen-millimeter version of this film was broadcast in 1959 on Italian television as "L'India vista da Rossellini" (Rossellini Looks at India) and on French television as "J'ai fait un beau voyage" (I Had a Fine Trip).]

IL GENERALE DELLA ROVERE (General della Rovere). 1959. Subject from the story by Indro Montanelli, adapted from a true story. *Screenplay:* Sergio Amidei, Diego Fabbri, Indro

Montanelli, Roberto Rossellini. *Photography:* Carlo Carlini. *Set design:* Piero Zuffi. *Music:* Renzo Rossellini. *Editing:* Cesare Cavagna. Produced by Morris Ergas for Zebra Film (Rome), Gaumont (Paris). With Vittorio De Sica (Bertone, alias Grimaldi), Hannes Messemer (Colonel Muller), Sandra Milo (Olga), Giovanna Ralli (Valeria). 130 minutes. [NOTE: This film won the Golden Lion at the Venice film festival in 1959, shared with Monicelli's *La grande guerra.*]

ERA NOTTE A ROMA (It Was Night in Rome). 1960. *Subject:* Sergio Amidei. *Screenplay:* Sergio Amidei, Diego Fabbri, Brunello Rondi, Roberto Rossellini. *Photography:* Carlo Carlini. *Set design:* Flavio Mogherini. *Music:* Renzo Rossellini. *Editing:* Roberto Cinquini. Produced by International Golden Star (Genoa), Film Dismage (Paris). With Leo Genn (Pemberton), Giovanna Ralli (Esperia), Serge Bondarchuk (the Russian sergeant), Peter Baldwin (Lieutenant Bradley), Renato Salvatori (Renato), Paolo Stoppa (Prince Antoniani), George Petrarca (Tarcisio), Hannes Messemer (Von Kleist). 120 minutes.

VIVA L'ITALIA! 1960. *Subject:* Sergio Amidei, Antonio Petrucci, Carlo Alianello, Luigi Chiarini. *Screenplay:* Sergio Amidei, Diego Fabbri, Antonio Petrucci, Roberto Rossellini, Antonello Trombadori. *Photography:* Luciano Trasatti (in Eastmancolor). *Set design:* Gepy Mariani. *Costumes:* Marcella De Marchis. *Music:* Renzo Rossellini. *Editing:* Roberto Cinquini. Produced by Cinematografica, Tempo Film, Galatea, Zebra Film. With Renzo Ricci (Garibaldi), Paolo Stoppa (Nino Bixio), Franco Interlenghi (Giuseppe Bandi), Giovanna Ralli (Rosa), Raimondo Croce (Francis II), Tina Louise (foreign journalist). 128 minutes.

VANINA VANINI. 1961. Subject taken from Stendhal's *Chroniques italiennes. Screenplay:* Roberto Rossellini, Antonello Trombadori, Franco Solinas, Monique Lange, Diego Fabbri, Jean Gruault. *Photography:* Luciano Trasatti (in Technicolor). *Set design:* Luigi Scaccianoce. *Costumes:* Danilo Donato. *Music:* Renzo Rossellini. *Editing:* Daniele Alabiso. Produced by Zebra Film (Morris Ergas), Orsay-Film (Paris). With Sandra Milo (Vanina), Laurent Terzieff (Pietro Missirilli), Martine Carol (Countess Vitelleschi), Paolo Stoppa (Prince Asdrubale Vanini), Leonardo Botta (Vanina's confessor), Nerio Bernardi (Cardinal Savelli). 125 minutes.

TORINO NEI CENTO ANNI (Turin Through the Last 100 Years). 1961. *Subject and screenplay:* Valentino Orsini. *Commentary written by:* Vittorio Gorresio. *Photography:* Leopoldo Piccinelli, Mario Vulpiani, Mario Volpi (sixteen-millimeter). Produced by RAI-TV. Television documentary, 46 minutes. [NOTE: Broadcast September 10, 1961, at 10:25 P.M.]

ANIMA NERA (Black Soul). 1962. *Subject:* From the play by Giuseppe Patroni Griffi. *Screenplay:* Roberto Rossellini, Alfio Valdarini. *Photography:* Luciano Trasatti. *Music:* Piero Piccioni. *Editing:* Daniele Alabiso. Produced by Documento Film (Rome), Le Louvre Film (Paris). With Vittorio Gassman (Adriano), Annette Stroyberg (Marcella), Nadja Tiller (Mimosa), Eleonora Rossi Drago (Alessandra), Yvonne Sanson (Olga), Giovanni Cocuzzoli (Sergio). 97 minutes.

"Illibatezza" (Chastity), episode of ROGOPAG. 1962. *Subject and screenplay:* Roberto Rossellini. *Photography:* Luciano Trasatti. *Set design:* Flavio Mogherini. *Music:* Carlo Rustichelli. *Editing:* Daniele Alabiso. Produced by Arco Film (Rome), Société Lyre Cinématographique (Paris). With Rosanna Schiaffino (Anna Maria), Bruce Balaban (Joe), Carlo Zappavigna (Anna Maria's fiancé). 33 minutes. [NOTE: Other episodes were directed by Jean-Luc Godard, Pier Paolo Pasolini, and Ugo Gregoretti.]

L'ETÀ DEL FERRO (The Iron Age). 1964. *Director:* Renzo Rossellini. *Subject, screenplay, and supervision:* Roberto Rossellini. *Photography:* Carlo Carlini. *Set design:* Gepy Mariani. *Costumes:* Marcella De Marchis. *Music:* Carmine Rizzo. *Editing:* Daniele Alabiso. Produced by 22 Dicembre and the Istituto Luce, for RAI-TV. With nonprofessional actors. Five episodes, approximately 50–60 minutes each. [NOTE: Broadcast on channel 2 of the RAI during February and March of 1965.]

LA LOTTA DELL'UOMO PER LA SUA SOPRAVVIVENZA (Man's Struggle for Survival). Begun 1964, completed in 1970. *Director:* Renzo Rossellini. *Subject, screenplay, and supervision:* Roberto Rossellini. *Photography:* Mario Fioretti. *Set design:* Gepy Mariani, Virgil Moise. *Costumes:* Marcella De Marchis. *Music:* Mario Nascimbene. *Editing:* Daniele Alabiso, Gabriele Alessandro, Alfredo Muschietti. Produced by Orizzonte 2000 (Roberto Rossellini), RAI, Logos Film (Paris), Romania Film (Bucharest), Copro Film (Cairo). With nonprofessional actors. Twelve episodes, approximately 50–60 minutes each. [NOTE: The first six episodes were broadcast on channel 1 of RAI in August and September of 1970, and the remaining six were broadcast on channel 2 in September and October of 1971. Titles of individual episodes: 1. Prima della storia, l'uomo (Before history, man); 2. La civiltà che nacque da un fiume (The civilization which rose from a river); 3: Dall'angoscia dei miti al Dio che è salvezza (From the anxiety of myths to the God who is salvation); 4: Un'arca nel diluvio: il monachesimo (An ark in the flood: monasticism); 5: Il medioevo, età di pietra e di ferro (The Middle Ages, age of stone and iron); 6: Verso la scienza, patria dell'uomo (Toward science, man's country); 7: In cerca delle Indie oltre l'oceano ignoto (In search of India beyond the unknown ocean); 8: Dall'età della magia all'età della scienza (From the age of magic to the age of science); 9: Lo spirito scientifico conquista il mondo (The scientific spirit conquers the world); 10: Questa nostra grandiosa civiltà della fretta (This great hurried civilization of ours); 11: Un'arte nuova in un mondo di macchine (A new art in a world of machines); 12: Nonostante tutto, ancora più lontano (In spite of everything, still further).]

LA PRISE DE POUVOIR PAR LOUIS XIV (The Rise to Power of Louis XIV). 1966. *Screenplay:* Philippe Erlanger [?]. *Adaptation and dialogue:* Jean Gruault. *Photography:* Georges Leclerc (in Eastmancolor). *Set design:* Maurice Valay. *Costumes:* Christiane Coste. *Editing:* Armand Ridel. Produced by the ORTF (French television). With Jean-Marie Patte (Louis XIV), Raymond Jourdan (Colbert), Silvagni (Mazarin), Katharina Renn (Anne of Austria), Dominique Vincent (Madame Du Plessis), Pierre Barrat (Fouquet). 102 minutes.

IDEA DI UN'ISOLA (Sicily: Idea of an Island; version shown on American television entitled "Roberto Rossellini's Sicily"). 1967. *Screenplay:* Roberto Rossellini. *Photography:* Mario Fioretti. *Music:* Mario Nascimbene. *Editing:* Maria Rosada. Produced by Orizzonte 2000. Documentary made for American television (NBC). 52 minutes. [NOTE: Broadcast in color on NBC in 1968, and later broadcast by channel 2 of RAI on February 3, 1970, in black and white.]

ATTI DEGLI APOSTOLI (Acts of the Apostles). 1969. Subject taken from the Acts of the Apostles in the New Testament. *Screenplay:* Jean-Dominique de La Rochefoucauld, Luciano Scaffa, Vittorio Bonicelli, Roberto Rossellini. *Photography:* Mario Fioretti (Eastmancolor). *Set design:* Gepy Mariani, Carmelo Patrono. *Costumes:* Marcella De Marchis. *Music:* Mario Nascimbene. *Editing:* Jolanda Benvenuti. Produced by Orizzonte 2000 for the RAI, the ORTF, TVE Madrid, Studio Hamburg. With Edoardo Torricella (Paul), Jacques Dumur (Peter), Renzo Rossi (Zacharia), Mohamed Kouka (John), Bradai Ridha (Matthew), Beppy Mannaiuolo (Phillip). Broadcast by the RAI in five episodes (each an hour or more) on consecutive Sundays in April and May, 1969.

SOCRATE (Socrates). 1970. *Screenplay:* Roberto Rossellini and Marcella Rossellini Mariani. *Dialogue:* Jean-Dominique de La Rochefoucauld. *Photography:* Jorge Herrero Martin (Eastmancolor). *Set design:* Giusto Puri Purini, Bernardo Ballester. *Costumes:* Marcella De Marchis. *Music:* Mario Nascimbene. *Editing:* Alfredo Muschietto. Produced by Orizzonte 2000 for the RAI, the ORTF, TVE Madrid. With Jean Sylvère (Socrates), Anne Caprile (Xanthippe), Ricardo Palacios (Critone), Beppy Mannaiuolo (Appollodorus). 120 minutes. [NOTE: Broadcast in two parts on channel 1 of the RAI on June 17 and 20, 1971.]

BLAISE PASCAL. 1972. *Screenplay:* Roberto Rossellini, Marcella Rossellini Mariani, Luciano Scaffa. *Dialogue:* Jean-Dominique de La Rochefoucauld. *Photography:* Mario Fioretti (Eastmancolor). *Set design:* Franco Velchi. *Costumes:* Marcella De Marchis. *Music:* Mario Nascimbene. *Editing:* Jolanda Benvenuti. Produced by Orizzonte 2000, RAI-TV, ORTF. With Pierre Arditi (Blaise Pascal), Rita Forzano (Jacqueline, his sister), Giuseppe Addobbati (Etienne, his father), Bruno Cattaneo (Jean Deschamps), Bernard Rigal (Seguier), Claude Baks (Descartes), Tullio Valli (Father Mersenne). 131 minutes. [NOTE: Broadcast in two parts on channel 1 of the RAI in May 1972.]

INTERVISTA CON SALVADOR ALLENDE (Interview With Salvador Allende). 1971. Directed by Emidio Grego. An interview between Roberto Rossellini and Allende, then president of Chile. Produced by Orizzonte 2000 and La San Diego Cinematografica. 36 minutes. [NOTE: First broadcast by the RAI on September 15, 1973, just after the right-wing coup that ousted Allende.]

AGOSTINO D'IPPONA (Augustine of Hippo). 1972. *Screenplay:* Roberto Rossellini, Marcella Rossellini Mariani, Luciano Scaffa. *Dialogue:* Jean-Dominique de La Rochefoucauld. *Photography:* Mario Fioretti (Eastmancolor). *Set design:* Franco Velchi. *Costumes:* Marcella De Marchis. *Music:* Mario Nascimbene. *Editing:* Jolanda Benvenuti. Produced by Orizzonte 2000, RAI-TV. With Dary Berkany (Augustine), Virginio Gazzolo (Alypius), Cesare Barbetti (Volusianus), Bruno Cattaneo (Maximus), Leonardo Fioravanti (Milesius), Beppy Mannaiuolo (Severus), Dannunzio Papini (Roman judge). 117 minutes. [NOTE: Broadcast in two parts on channel 1 of the RAI on October 25 and November 1, 1972.]

L'ETÀ DI COSIMO DE' MEDICI (The Age of the Medici). 1972. Titles of the three episodes: "L'Esilio di Cosimo" (Cosimo's Exile; also known as Cosimo de' Medici), "Il Potere di Cosimo" (The Power of Cosimo), and "Leon Battista Alberti." *Screenplay:* Roberto Rossellini, Marcella Rossellini Mariani, Luciano Scaffa. *Photography:* Mario Montuori (Eastmancolor). *Set design:* Franco Velchi. *Costumes:* Marcella De Marchis. *Music:* Manuel De Sica. *Editing:* Jolanda Benvenuti. Produced by Orizzonte 2000, RAI-TV. With Marcello Di Falco (Cosimo), Virginio Gazzolo (Alberti), Tom Felleghi (Rinaldo degli Albizi), Mario Erpichini (Totto Machiavelli), Adriano Migliano (Carlo degli Alberti), John Stacy (Ilarione de' Bardi), Sergio Nicolai (Francesco Soderini), Michel Bardinet (Ciriaco d'Arpaso), Mario Demo (Sigismondo Malatesta), Ugo Cardea (Niccolò Cusano), Lincoln Tate (Thomas Wadding), Marino Mase (Francesco Filelfo). 250 minutes. [NOTE: Broadcast in three parts on channel 1 of the RAI on December 26, 1972, and January 2 and 9, 1973.]

CARTESIUS (Cartesio; Descartes). 1974. *Screenplay:* Roberto Rossellini, Marcella Rossellini Mariani, Luciano Scaffa. *Photography:* Mario Montuori (Eastmancolor). *Set design:* Giuseppe Mangano. *Costumes:* Marcella De Marchis. *Music:* Mario Nascimbene. *Editing:* Jolanda Benvenuti. Produced by Orizzonte 2000, RAI-TV, ORTF. With Ugo Cardea (Descartes), Anne Pouchie (Elena), Claude Berthy (Guez de Balzac), Gabriele Banchero (Bretagne), John Stacy (Levasseur d'Etioles), Charles Borromel (Father Mersenne), Kenneth Belton (Beeckman), Renato Montalbano (Huygens), Vernon Dobtcheff (the astronomer Ciprus). 150 minutes. [NOTE: Broadcast in two parts on channel 1 of the RAI on February 20 and 27, 1974.]

ANNO UNO (Italy: Year One). 1974. *Screenplay:* Roberto Rossellini, Marcella Rossellini Mariani, Luciano Scaffa. *Photography:* Mario Montuori (Eastmancolor). *Set design:* Giuseppe Mangano. *Costumes:* Marcella De Marchis. *Music:* Mario Nascimbene. *Editing:* Jolanda Benvenuti. Produced by Rusconi Film. With Luigi Vannucchi (Alcide De Gasperi), Valeria Sabel (Francesca, his wife), Dominique Darel (Maria Romana De Gasperi), Rita Forzano (Lucia De Gasperi), Ennio Balbo (Nenni), Luciano Gaudenzio (Longo), Renato Montanari (Secchia), Paolo Bonacelli (Amendola), Francesco Di Federico (Saragat), Tino Bianchi (Togliatti). 115 minutes.

THE WORLD POPULATION. 1974. Documentary on the population explosion, produced by UNESCO for the United Nations. Approximately 120 minutes. [NOTE: According to Aprà's filmography in *Roberto Rossellini: Le Cinéma révélé*, the film was shown during a congress on world population held in Bucharest in 1974 and subsequently distributed by the United Nations throughout the world.]

IL MESSIA (The Messiah). 1975. *Screenplay:* Roberto Rossellini, Silvia D'Amico Bendicò. *Photography:* Mario Montuori (Eastmancolor). *Set design:* Giorgio Bertolini. *Costumes:* Marcella De Marchis. *Music:* Mario Nascimbene. *Editing:* Jolanda Benvenuti, Laurent Quaglio. Produced by Procinex, FR3 Télé-Film Production, Orizzonte 2000. With Pier Maria Rossi (Jesus), Mita Ungaro (Mary), Carlos de Carvalho (John the Baptist), Fausto di Bella (Saul), Vernon Dobtcheff (Samuel), Antonella Fasano (Mary Magdalen), Jean Martin (Pontius Pilate), Toni Ucci (Herod Antipas), Vittorio Caprioli (Herod the Great), Anita Bartolucci (the Samaritan woman), Cosetta Pichetti (Salome), Raouf Ben Amor (Judas), Luis Suarez (John), Hedi Zouglami (Peter), Renato Montalbano (Matthew). 145 minutes. [NOTE: Originally produced in Italian, French, and English versions.]

CONCERTO PER MICHELANGELO (Concert for Michelangelo). 1977. *Photography:* Mario Montuori (35-millimeter film and video). Filmed in the Sistine Chapel in the Vatican with the participation of the chorus of the Cappella Musicale Pontificia, directed by Maestro Domenico Bartolucci. Produced by the RAI. Approximately 60 minutes. [NOTE: Broadcast on channel 2 of the RAI on Holy Saturday, April 9, 1977.]

BEAUBOURG, CENTRE D'ART ET DE CULTURE GEORGES POMPIDOU. 1977. *Photography:* Nestor Almendros (Eastmancolor). *Editing:* Véritable Silve, Colette Le Tallec, Dominique Taysse. Produced by Création 9 Information-Film, Jacques Grandclaude. 57 minutes. [NOTE: The credits state that Rossellini finished the film on May 6, 1977, and had in mind to make some final changes but was prevented from doing so by his death on June 3, 1977.]

NOTE: More complete details can be found in Adriano Aprà's filmography published in *Roberto Rossellini: Le Cinéma révélé*, edited by Alain Bergala. Though Aprà's filmography is seriously marred by typographical and other errors, its massive scope clearly makes it the definitive Rossellini filmography, and it is the source of some of the information provided above.

Index